AWS®
Certified Data Engineer
Study Guide
Associate (DEA-C01) Exam

Syed Humair
Chenjerai Gumbo
Adam Gatt
Asif Abbasi
Lakshmi Nair

SYBEX®
A Wiley Brand

T0369857

Copyright © 2025 by John Wiley & Sons, Inc. All rights, including for text and data mining, AI training, and similar technologies, are reserved.

Published by John Wiley & Sons, Inc., Hoboken, New Jersey.

Published simultaneously in Canada and the United Kingdom.

ISBNs: 9781394286584 (paperback), 9781394286607 (ePDF), 9781394286591 (ePub)

No part of this publication may be reproduced, stored in a retrieval system, or transmitted in any form or by any means, electronic, mechanical, photocopying, recording, scanning, or otherwise, except as permitted under Section 107 or 108 of the 1976 United States Copyright Act, without either the prior written permission of the Publisher, or authorization through payment of the appropriate per-copy fee to the Copyright Clearance Center, Inc., 222 Rosewood Drive, Danvers, MA 01923, (978) 750-8400, fax (978) 750-4470, or on the web at www .copyright.com. Requests to the Publisher for permission should be addressed to the Permissions Department, John Wiley & Sons, Inc., 111 River Street, Hoboken, NJ 07030, (201) 748-6011, fax (201) 748-6008, or online at www.wiley.com/go/permission.

The manufacturer's authorized representative according to the EU General Product Safety Regulation is Wiley-VCH GmbH, Boschstr. 12, 69469 Weinheim, Germany, e-mail: Product_Safety@wiley.com.

Trademarks: WILEY, the Wiley logo, and Sybex are trademarks or registered trademarks of John Wiley & Sons, Inc. and/or its affiliates, in the United States and other countries, and may not be used without written permission. AWS is a trademark or registered trademark of Amazon Technologies, Inc. All other trademarks are the property of their respective owners. John Wiley & Sons, Inc. is not associated with any product or vendor mentioned in this book.

Limit of Liability/Disclaimer of Warranty: While the publisher and authors have used their best efforts in preparing this book, they make no representations or warranties with respect to the accuracy or completeness of the contents of this book and specifically disclaim any implied warranties of merchantability or fitness for a particular purpose. No warranty may be created or extended by sales representatives or written sales materials. The advice and strategies contained herein may not be suitable for your situation. You should consult with a professional where appropriate. Further, readers should be aware that websites listed in this work may have changed or disappeared between when this work was written and when it is read. Neither the publisher nor authors shall be liable for any loss of profit or any other commercial damages, including but not limited to special, incidental, consequential, or other damages.

For general information on our other products and services or for technical support, please contact our Customer Care Department within the United States at (800) 762-2974, outside the United States at (317) 572-3993 or fax (317) 572-4002. For product technical support, you can find answers to frequently asked questions or reach us via live chat at https://sybexsupport.wiley.com.

Wiley also publishes its books in a variety of electronic formats. Some content that appears in print may not be available in electronic formats. For more information about Wiley products, visit our web site at www.wiley.com.

Library of Congress Control Number: 2025930429

Cover image: © Jeremy Woodhouse/Getty Images
Cover design: Wiley

SKY10098287_021125

Acknowledgments

Collaborating on this Study Guide has been an incredible experience. We are immensely grateful to Amazon Web Services (AWS) for their certification program and, in particular, for developing the AWS Certified Data Engineer – Associate exam. This is an extremely important certification that will strengthen and empower professionals across the industry.

We want to thank the Wiley team, including Ken Brown, Satish Gowrishankar, Kelly Talbot, Saravanan Dakshinamurthy, and everyone at Wiley, for their assistance in creating, editing, and publishing this Study Guide. Your patience with us during the editing process was amazing. Thank you for your help and support during the process. We especially want to mention Kelly's effort to help us raise the bar for this Study Guide to help potential test takers.

We also appreciate the input, guidance, and insights of all our colleagues at Amazon and AWS in our professional lives and in our efforts to create this book.

We are especially thankful for the support and understanding of our families, friends, and colleagues as we devoted an inordinate amount of time to writing this book.

Last but not least, we would like to thank you, our readers, for pursuing the AWS Certified Data Engineer – Associate exam certification and for your devotion to helping the industry, clients, and people across the world maximize the power and potential of AWS.

— Syed Humair, Chenjerai Gumbo, Adam Gatt,
Asif Abbasi, and Lakshmi Nair

About the Authors

Syed Humair is a Senior Analytics Specialist Solutions Architect at Amazon Web Services (AWS), renowned for his expertise in data engineering, machine learning, and enterprise architecture. With nearly two decades of experience, his skill set encompasses data strategy, data warehousing, business intelligence, and data analytics, with a particular emphasis on cloud-based solutions. Humair's impact spans diverse industries, including retail, travel, telecommunications, healthcare, and financial services. In his role at AWS, Humair excels in guiding customers through the complexities of data analytics and AI, solidifying his status as a knowledgeable author and an invaluable asset in the field.

Chenjerai Gumbo is an AWS Solutions Architect Leader of Analytics and an Institute of Directors (IOD) Member. He is a technology leader with a keen interest in leadership, business models, data, and process improvement, with exposure to telecommunications (fixed and mobile), utility (electricity), and AWS cloud environments. As a leader, he is constantly pursuing an understanding of the synergy between business, people, and technology in order to help organizations transform their businesses. He holds an MBA from the University of Stellenbosch Business School.

Adam Gatt is a seasoned data architect with over 20 years of experience. He specializes in data warehousing, business intelligence, and big data. His career includes positions at Amazon Web Services (AWS) and Hewlett-Packard, as well as contributions to various industries such as mass media, cybersecurity, insurance, and telecommunications. Adam has built a reputation for translating complex technical ideas for non-technical audiences and delivering innovative solutions for business challenges. He is currently a Senior Redshift Solution Architect at AWS, helping customers build robust, scalable, and high-performance analytics solutions in the cloud.

Asif Abbasi is a Solutions Engineering and Architecture Leader and a Principal Solutions Architect at AWS, driving innovation across the EMEA region. His passion lies in leading technology teams and facilitating customer adoption of data, analytics, and AI/ML. As a published author in AWS data analytics, Generative AI, and Apache Spark, Asif empowers organizations to overcome complex business challenges through strategic implementation of analytics and AI ecosystems. With two decades of experience, Asif is dedicated to bridging the gap between business problems and technological solutions. Asif specializes in simplifying technology for CXOs, business and IT directors, and data scientists, ensuring seamless understanding and implementation.

Lakshmi Nair is a Senior Analytics Specialist Solutions Architect at AWS. She specializes in designing advanced analytics systems across industries and diverse geographies. She focuses on crafting cloud-based data platforms, enabling real-time streaming, big data processing, and robust data governance.

Contents at a Glance

Contents

Foreword

In the rapidly evolving landscape of cloud computing and data engineering, the AWS Certified Data Engineer – Associate certification has emerged as a must-have credential for data professionals seeking to demonstrate their expertise in designing, building, and managing data solutions on Amazon Web Services. This comprehensive exam preparation guide, crafted by a team of seasoned industry experts, delivers deep technical knowledge and practical insights to empower aspiring data engineers to excel in their certification journey and professional careers.

As someone who has witnessed the transformative power of data engineering firsthand, I understand the challenges practitioners face in navigating the comprehensive depth and breadth of AWS data services. The authors—Syed Humair, Chenjerai Gumbo, Adam Gatt, Asif Abbasi, and Lakshmi Nair—bring a wealth of real-world experience that transcends traditional textbook learning. Their approach combines rigorous technical depth with practical, hands-on guidance that reflects the complex realities of modern data engineering.

What sets this book apart is its holistic approach to exam preparation. Beyond simply teaching to the test, it provides a robust framework for understanding AWS data services, architectural patterns, and best practices. From data ingestion, storage, transformation, governance, security, and analytics, each chapter is designed to both prepare you for the exam and increase your technical competency.

The methodical breakdown of complex concepts, coupled with practical examples, sample exam questions, and strategic exam-taking tips, make this guide an indispensable resource. Whether you are a professional looking to validate your skills, a student entering the field, or a technologist seeking to expand your cloud data engineering capabilities, this book offers a clear and guided pathway to success.

I am confident this guide will not only help you pass the AWS Certified Data Engineer – Associate exam, but will also serve as a foundational reference for your continued professional development.

Imtiaz Sayed
Worldwide Tech Leader - AWS Data Analytics
Dec 09, 2024

Introduction

In today's data-driven world, the demand for skilled data engineers is at an all-time high. AWS offers some of the most powerful and widely used cloud solutions, making AWS data engineering skills essential for anyone looking to thrive in this field. By mastering AWS Certified Data Engineering, you can work with cutting-edge technologies for processing, storing, and analyzing vast amounts of data, whether in batch or real-time scenarios. This knowledge will not only enhance your career prospects but also prepare you to design efficient, scalable, and secure data solutions that meet the needs of modern organizations.

Even if you are already familiar with other data engineering platforms, AWS expertise will set you apart, as it is the leading provider of cloud services worldwide. Gaining a solid understanding of AWS data engineering practices will help you make informed decisions about how to implement robust data solutions and handle real-world challenges.

The AWS Certified Data Engineering Associate Certification

This certification validates your ability to work with data-related services on AWS, including data ingestion, transformation, storage, and visualization. The exam is designed to test your skills in building automated pipelines, managing data catalogs, ensuring data security, and implementing governance policies. As a certified associate, you demonstrate the knowledge needed to design and maintain reliable, efficient, and secure data workflows on the AWS platform.

The Purpose of This Book

This book is designed to help you pass the AWS Certified Data Engineering Associate exam. Covering all key exam topics, such as streaming and batch data ingestion, building automated data pipelines, transformation, and storage, this book provides detailed explanations, practical examples, and valuable insights. Each chapter aligns with core AWS services and concepts, ensuring you gain a comprehensive understanding of data engineering in the AWS ecosystem.

Beyond exam preparation, this book serves as a lasting reference guide. From setting up secure data pipelines to monitoring and troubleshooting operations, you will find the knowledge and skills needed for real-world scenarios. Whether you're an aspiring data engineer or a seasoned professional, this book will equip you with the tools to advance your career and excel in the ever-growing field of data engineering.

 Don't just study the questions and answers! The questions on the actual exam will be different from the practice questions included in this book. The exam is designed to test your knowledge of a concept or objective, so use this book to learn the objectives behind the questions.

The AWS Certified Data Engineer – Associate Exam

The AWS Certified Data Engineer – Associate exam is designed to validate the skills and expertise required to build, maintain, and optimize data processing systems on the AWS platform. It focuses on assessing the candidate's ability to manage data throughout its life-cycle, including ingestion, transformation, storage, and analysis. The exam is particularly relevant for professionals involved in creating robust, scalable, and secure data infrastructure, which is critical for data-driven decision-making and AI-powered solutions.

This certification covers a range of topics, including streaming and batch data ingestion, automated data pipeline construction, data transformation techniques, storage services, and database management. Security and governance, such as encryption, masking, and access controls, are also critical components. Additionally, the exam tests knowledge of advanced topics like data cataloging, monitoring, auditing, and troubleshooting data operations, ensuring candidates can maintain efficient systems. By earning this certification, professionals demonstrate their ability to work effectively in AWS's dynamic cloud environment, positioning themselves as key players in the data engineering landscape.

Why Become AWS Certified?

The field of data engineering is rapidly growing as organizations increasingly rely on data to drive decision-making and innovation. As we transition into a world dominated by AI and Generative AI technologies, the role of data engineers is becoming more critical than ever. These professionals are the backbone of systems that collect, transform, and manage data—tasks that are essential for deploying advanced AI models and driving innovation in industries ranging from healthcare to finance and beyond.

The AWS Certified Data Engineering – Associate exam is designed to validate the skills required to build and maintain data infrastructure on the AWS cloud platform, one of the leading platforms for scalable and secure data operations. The certification equips individuals with the expertise to design data pipelines, manage data storage, implement security protocols, and optimize data systems. This certification serves not only as a stepping stone for those entering the field but also as a benchmark for professionals looking to advance their careers in cloud-based data engineering.

According to industry analyses, the demand for data engineers is on a steep rise, with salaries reflecting the growing importance of this role. In 2024, the average salary for data engineers in the United States is estimated at $153,000 annually, with experienced professionals earning even higher. Data engineering is also increasingly intertwined with machine learning (ML) and AI. Nearly 30 percent of job postings now cite ML-related skills as critical for data engineers, highlighting the evolving role of these professionals in shaping AI systems. Furthermore, the expansion of remote work opportunities in this field is making data engineering an attractive and competitive career path globally.

As businesses race to integrate Generative AI and other emerging technologies, having a solid foundation in data engineering is essential. Building automated pipelines, ensuring data privacy, and maintaining robust infrastructure are key tasks that enable organizations to effectively implement and scale their AI strategies. This makes certified data engineers indispensable in today's job market and positions them as vital contributors to the technological advancements of the future.

The purpose of this book is to prepare you for the AWS Certified Data Engineering – Associate exam by covering all the essential topics, including:

Chapter 1: Streaming and Batch Data Ingestion

Chapter 2: Building Automated Data Pipelines

Chapter 3: Data Transformation

Chapter 4: Storage Services

Chapter 5: Databases and Data Warehouses on AWS

Chapter 6: Data Catalogs

Chapter 7: Visualizing Your Data

Chapter 8: Monitoring and Auditing Data

Chapter 9: Maintaining and Troubleshooting Data Operations

Chapter 10: Authentication and Authorization

Chapter 11: Data Encryption and Masking

Chapter 12: Data Privacy and Governance

Chapter 13: How to Take the Exam

Additionally, the book comes with a test bank that includes practice exams and flashcards to reinforce key concepts. These resources will not only help you pass the certification exam but will also serve as a comprehensive reference for practical data engineering tasks.

By mastering the material in this guide, you'll not only enhance your expertise in AWS's data services but also position yourself as a key player in the evolving landscape of data-driven innovation. As the demand for skilled data engineers continues to grow, this certification will provide you with the knowledge and credibility needed to excel in this exciting and dynamic field.

How to Become AWS Certified

The AWS Certified Data Engineering – Associate exam is available to anyone interested in validating their skills in building, maintaining, and optimizing data infrastructure on the AWS platform. This certification is accessible to everyone—you don't need to work for a particular company or meet specific prerequisites to qualify.

The exam is administered by AWS through authorized testing partners, including Pearson VUE and PSI. Candidates can choose to take the exam either online from the comfort of their homes or at a testing center near them. Upon passing, you'll receive an official certificate from AWS that verifies your expertise, as well as a digital badge to showcase your achievement on professional platforms like LinkedIn.

To register for the exam, visit the official AWS Certification portal at `https://aws .amazon.com/certification`. You'll need to create an AWS Certification account if you don't already have one. From there, select the AWS Certified Data Engineering – Associate exam, choose your preferred testing method (online or in-person), and follow the prompts to schedule your exam. During registration, you will be asked to provide details such as your name, contact information, and payment method to complete the process.

> Exam policies can change from time to time. We highly recommend that you check both the AWS and Pearson VUE sites for the most up-to-date information when you begin your preparation, when you register, and again a few days before your scheduled exam date.

Study Guide Features

This study guide uses several common elements to help you prepare. These include the following:

Summaries   The summary section of each chapter briefly explains the chapter, allowing you to easily understand what it covers.

Exam Essentials   The exam essentials focus on major exam topics and critical knowledge that you should take into the test. The exam essentials focus on the exam objectives provided by AWS.

Chapter Review Questions   A set of questions at the end of each chapter will help you assess your knowledge and if you are ready to take the exam based on your knowledge of that chapter's topics.

The review questions, assessment test, and other testing elements included in this book are not derived from the actual exam questions, so don't memorize the answers to these questions and assume that doing so will enable you to pass the exam. You should learn the underlying topic, as described in the text of the book. This will let you answer the questions provided in this book and pass the exam. Learning the underlying topic is also the approach that will serve you best in the workplace—the ultimate goal of a certification.

Interactive Online Learning Environment and TestBank

Studying the material in the *AWS Certified Data Engineer Study Guide: Associate (DEA-C01) Exam Study Guide* is an important part of preparing for the AWS Certified Data Engineer – Associate certification exam, but we provide additional tools to help you prepare. The online TestBank will help you understand the types of questions that will appear on the certification exam.

- The Practice Tests in the TestBank include all the questions in each chapter as well as the questions from the Assessment test. In addition, there are five practice exams with 50 questions each. You can use these tests to evaluate your understanding and identify areas that may require additional study.

- The Flashcards in the TestBank will push the limits of what you should know for the certification exam. There are 100 questions, which are provided in digital format. Each flashcard has one question and one correct answer.

To start using these to study for the AWS Certified Data Engineer – Associate exam, go to www.wiley.com/go/sybextestprep, and register your book to receive your unique PIN. Once you have the PIN, return to www.wiley.com/go/sybextestprep, find your book, and click Register or Log In and follow the link to register a new account or add this book to an existing account.

Like all exams, the AWS Certified Data Engineer – Associate certification from AWS is updated periodically and may eventually be retired or replaced. At some point after AWS is no longer offering this exam, the old editions of our books and online tools will be retired. If you have purchased this book after the exam was retired, or are attempting to register in the Sybex online learning environment after the exam was retired, please know that we make no guarantees that this exam's online Sybex tools will be available once the exam is no longer available.

AWS Certified Data Engineer – Associate Exam (DEA-C01) Objectives

AWS Certified Data Engineer Study Guide: Associate (DEA-C01) Exam Study Guide has been written to cover every AWS exam objective at a level appropriate to its exam weighting. The following table provides a breakdown of this book's exam coverage, showing you the weight of each section and the chapter where each objective or subobjective is covered:

Subject Area	% of Exam
Domain 1: Data Ingestion and Transformation	34%
Domain 2: Data Store Management	26%
Domain 3: Data Operations and Support	22%
Domain 4: Data Security and Governance	18%
Total	100%

Exam Objectives	Chapter
Domain 1: Data Ingestion and Transformation	
Task 1.1 Perform data ingestion	1
Task 1.2 Transform and process data	3
Task 1.3 Orchestrate data pipelines with AWS	2
Task 1.4 Apply programming concepts with AWS	2
Domain 2: Data Store Management	
Task 2.1 Choose a data store	4, 5
Task 2.2 Understand data cataloging systems	6
Task 2.3 Managing the lifecycle of data	4, 5
Task 2.4: Design data models and schema evolution	5
Domain 3: Data Operations and Support	
Task 3.1 Automate data processing by using AWS services	9
Task 3.2 Analyze data by using AWS services	7
Task 3.3 Maintain and monitor data pipelines with AWS	2, 8
Task 3.4 Ensure data quality	3, 6

Subject Area	% of Exam
Domain 4: Data Security and Governance	
4.1: Apply authentication mechanisms	10
4.2: Apply authorization mechanisms	10
4.3 Ensure data encryption and masking	11
4.4 Prepare logs for audit	8
4.5: Understanding data privacy and governance	12

How to Contact the Publisher

If you believe you have found a mistake in this book, please bring it to our attention. At John Wiley & Sons, we understand how important it is to provide our customers with accurate content, but even with our best efforts, an error may occur.

In order to submit your possible errata, please email it to our Customer Service Team at wileysupport@wiley.com with the subject line "Possible Book Errata Submission."

Assessment Test

1. For compliance reasons, a company needs to delete records from Amazon S3 data lake once it reaches its retention limit. Which solution will meet the requirement with the *least* amount of operational overhead?

    A. Copy the data from Amazon S3 to Amazon Redshift to delete the records.

    B. Configure the tables using Apache Hudi format and use Amazon Athena to delete the records.

    C. Configure the tables using Apache Iceberg format and use Amazon Redshift Spectrum to delete the records.

    D. Configure the tables using Apache Iceberg format and use Amazon Athena to delete the records.

2. You've been asked to recommend the right database solution for a customer with relational data who requires strong durability, high availability, and disaster recovery. Which overall solution will best suit their requirements?

    A. Amazon DocumentDB with additional replicas for enhanced read performance

    B. Amazon DynamoDB with its automatic replication across multiple availability zones

    C. Amazon RDS with a Multi-AZ DB instance deployment

    D. Amazon Neptune to optimize instances of highly connected data with additional read replicas for high availability

3. Which of the following services supports real-time processing through streaming capabilities?

    A. Only Amazon EMR

    B. Only AWS Glue

    C. Only Amazon Redshift

    D. All of the above

4. A financial services company stores its data in Amazon Redshift. A data engineer wants to run real-time queries on financial data to support a web-based trading application. The engineer would like to run the queries from within the tradition application. Which solution offers the *least* operational overhead?

    A. Unload the data to Amazon S3 and use S3 Select to run the queries.

    B. Configure and set up a JDBC connection to Amazon Redshift.

    C. Establish WebSocket connections to Amazon Redshift.

    D. Use the Amazon Redshift Data API.

    E. Unload the data to Amazon S3 and use Amazon Athena to run the queries.

5. A telecommunications company needs to implement a solution that prevents the accidental sharing of customer call records containing PII across AWS accounts while maintaining an audit trail of all access attempts. Which combination of services would best meet this requirement?

   A. AWS IAM policies with CloudWatch Logs

   B. Lake Formation with AWS CloudTrail and Macie

   C. S3 bucket policies with access logging

   D. AWS Backup with cross-account controls

6. An online retailer is developing a recommendation engine for its web store. The engine will provide personalized product recommendations to customers based on their past purchases and browsing history. The engine must efficiently navigate a highly connected dataset with low latency. This involves complex queries to identify products similar to those purchased by the customer and find products bought by other customers who have purchased the same item. Which solution best addresses this use case?

   A. Use Amazon RDS for PostgreSQL with the Apache AGE (graph database) extension.

   B. Use Amazon DocumentDB (with MongoDB compatibility) to efficiently handle semi-structured data.

   C. Use Amazon Neptune to efficiently transverse graph datasets.

   D. Use Amazon MemoryDB for Redis for ultra-fast query performance.

7. A company has moved its data transformation job to an Amazon EMR cluster with Apache Pig. The cluster uses on-demand instances to process large datasets. The output is critical to operations. It usually takes 1 hour to complete the job, and the company must ensure that the entire process adheres to the SLA of 2 hours. The company is looking for a solution that will provide cost reduction and negligibly impact availability. Which combination of solutions can be implemented to meet the requirements? (Choose two.)

   A. Add a task node that runs on Spot instance.

   B. Configure an EMR cluster that uses instance groups.

   C. Use Spot instance for all node types.

   D. Configure an EMR cluster that uses instance fleets.

   E. Assign Spot capacity for all node types and enable the switch to the on-demand instances option.

8. In Amazon Athena, what is the purpose of using partitions?

   A. To increase the maximum query complexity

   B. To reduce the amount of data scanned and lower query cost

   C. To enable real-time data analysis

   D. To create visualization directly in Athena

9. A customer is experiencing poor performance with a query on Redshift. The query joins two large tables on a single column key and aggregates the result. Each table has hundreds of millions of rows. What would be the best distribution style to use on each table?

    A. Use the ALL distribution style to create a copy of each table on every compute node.

    B. Use the EVEN distribution style to distribute rows round-robin to each compute node.

    C. Use the KEY distribution style and set the columns used in the join as distribution keys.

10. A data scientist is developing a REST API for internal applications. Currently, every API call made to the application is logged in JSON format to an HTTP endpoint. What is the recommended low-code approach to stream the JSON data into S3 in Parquet format?

    A. Set up a Kinesis Data Stream to ingest the data and use Amazon Data Firehose as a delivery stream. Once the data is ingested into S3, use AWS Glue job to convert the JSON data to Parquet format.

    B. Use Amazon Data Firehose as a delivery stream. Enable a record transformation that references a table stored in an Apache Hive metastore in EMR.

    C. Use Amazon Data Firehose as a delivery stream. Enable a record transformation that references a table stored in an AWS Glue data catalog defining the schema for your source records.

    D. Use Amazon EMR to process streaming data. Create a Spark job to convert the JSON to Parquet format using an Apache Hive metastore to determine the schema of the JSON data.

11. When using AWS Glue DataBrew, which of the following is *not* a built-in transformation?

    A. A. Handling missing values

    B. B. Standardizing date formats

    C. C. Training machine learning models

    D. D. Removing duplicate records

12. You are working as a data architect for a company that runs an online web store on Amazon DynamoDB with high throughput volumes. You want to send customers an email when their order status has changed to "Shipped." What would be the best approach to handle this requirement?

    A. Set up a DynamoDB Stream on the Orders table with a Lambda trigger that sends an email via the Amazon Simple Email Service (Amazon SES) when the order status has changed to "Shipped."

    B. Export the Orders table into S3 once an hour to maintain a complete history. Run an AWS Glue job to identify orders whose status has changed to "Shipped" and send an email via Amazon SES.

    C. Set up a nightly extract into Amazon Redshift using the COPY command. Run a Lambda function to check for any status changes to "Shipped" and send an email via Amazon SES.

13. A company using an on-premise Hadoop cluster for various batch processing jobs (Spark, TensorFlow, MXNet, Hive, and Presto) anticipates a data surge. They want to migrate to AWS for scalable and durable storage. However, they want to reuse their existing jobs. Which solution will meet these requirements *most* cost-effectively?

A. Migrate to Amazon EMR. Store the data in Amazon S3. Launch Transient EMR clusters when jobs need to run.

B. Migrate to Amazon EMR. Store all the data in HDFS. Add more core nodes on-demand.

C. Re-architect the solution with the serverless offering of AWS Glue.

D. Migrate to Amazon Redshift. Use Amazon Redshift RA3 instances for frequently used data and Amazon S3 for in-frequent data access and optimize the storage cost.

14. Which AWS service automatically detects and reports sensitive data stored in Amazon S3 and security issues with S3 buckets?

A. AWS Security Hub

B. Amazon Macie

C. Amazon EventBridge

D. Amazon Key Management Service (AWS KMS)

15. Your company has a website application running on Amazon RDS for MySQL and a data warehouse on Amazon Redshift. The analytics team has a requirement to show real-time information from the application on a dashboard, along with historical data from Redshift. What approach would you advise the team to use that would involve the *least* amount of effort?

A. Use the RDS MySQL native export functionality to unload data to S3 and load it in parallel into Redshift with the COPY command.

B. Implement Athena federated queries to query across the RDS MySQL database and Redshift.

C. Utilize a Redshift federated query to directly query the MySQL RDS database and combine the results with historical Redshift data in a database view.

D. Use the RDS MySQL native export functionality to unload data to S3 and query the data using Redshift Spectrum. Combine the data from the Spectrum query and historical data stored in Redshift in a database view.

16. In an oil and gas company, a data analyst needs to implement anomaly detection on the pressure sensor data stream collected by Kinesis Data Streams. While Lambda can trigger the valve actions, the focus is on cost-effective anomaly detection within the data stream. Which of the following solutions would be recommended?

A. Launch a Spark streaming application using Amazon EMR cluster and connect to Amazon Kinesis Data Streams. Use ML algorithm to identify the anomaly. Spark will send an alert to open the valve if an anomaly is discovered.

B. Use the RANDOM_CUT_FOREST function in the Amazon Managed Service for Apache Flink to detect the anomaly and send an alert to open the valve.

C. Use Amazon Data Firehose and choose Amazon S3 as data lake storage of the sensor's data. Create a Lambda function to schedule the query of Amazon Athena in S3 query. The Lambda function will send an alert to open the valve if the anomaly is discovered.

D. Provision an EC2 fleet with a KCL application to consume the stream and aggregate the data collected by the sensors to detect the anomaly.

17. Which of the following is *not* a primary purpose of the listed AWS services?

   A. Amazon EMR: Big data processing and analysis

   B. Amazon Redshift: Data warehousing and analytics

   C. AWS Glue: ETL and data integration

   D. Amazon MWAA: Real-time data processing

18. A large digital newspaper business is running a data warehouse on a provisioned Amazon Redshift cluster that is not encrypted. Its security department has mandated that the cluster be encrypted to meet regulation requirements with keys that can be rotated and have comprehensive logging. What is the easiest and fastest way to do this?

   A. Unload the data into S3, apply SSE-S3 encryption, and then load the data back into Redshift via the COPY command.

   B. Unload the data into S3, apply SSE-KMS encryption, and then load the data back into Redshift via the COPY command.

   C. Take a manual snapshot of the cluster, and then create a new cluster from the snapshot with encryption enabled.

   D. Enable encryption on the cluster with a KMS customer-managed key.

19. Which open table format is natively supported by AWS Glue Data Catalog for registering and managing table metadata, allowing for improved query performance and schema evolution?

   A. Apache Hudi

   B. Apache Iceberg

   C. Delta Lake

   D. All of the above

20. Which of the following is *not* a best practice for effective data visualization?

   A. Using consistent color schemes across related visualizations

   B. Including as much data as possible in a single visualization

   C. Providing clear titles and labels for axes and data points

   D. Tailoring the complexity of the visualization to the audience

21. A data engineer has custom Python scripts that perform common formatting logic, which is used by many Lambda functions. If there is any need to modify the Python scripts, the data engineer must manually update all the Lambda functions. Which solution will meet the requirement where the data engineer requires less manual intervention to update the Lambda functions?

   A. Package the common Python script into Lambda layers. Apply the Lambda layers to the Lambda functions.

   B. Assign aliases to the Lambda functions.

   C. Store a pointer to a custom Python script in environment variables in a shared S3 bucket.

   D. Combine multiple Lambda functions into one Lambda function.

22. A data analyst creates a table from a record set stored in Amazon S3. The data is then partitioned using `year=2024/month=12/day=06/` format. Although the partitioning was successful, no records were returned when the `SELECT*` query was executed. What could be the possible reason?

   A. The analyst did not run the `MSCK REPAIR TABLE` command after partitioning the data.

   B. The analyst did not run the `MSCK REPAIR TABLE` command before partitioning the data.

   C. The newly created table does not have read permissions.

   D. The S3 bucket where the sample data is stored does not have read permissions.

   E. The analyst needs to use the `CTAS` command `CREATE TABLE AS SELECT` while creating the table in Amazon Athena.

23. You are working for a global company with multiple AWS accounts. There is a requirement to perform cross-account encryption, where one account uses a KMS key from a different account to access an S3 bucket. What steps are required to configure encryption across these AWS account boundaries securely? (Choose two.)

   A. In the account that owns the key, enable S3 Server-Side Encryption with AWS Key Management Service Keys (SSE-KMS) and assign the KMS customer-managed key to the S3 bucket.

   B. In the account that owns the key, enable S3 Server-Side Encryption with AWS Key Management Service Keys (SSE-KMS) and assign the KMS customer-managed key to the S3 bucket. Grant access to the external account on the key's key policy in AWS KMS.

   C. In the external account, create an IAM policy with the required permissions on the key and attach the policy to users or roles who need access to the key.

   D. In the external account, enforce TLS for S3 access by specifying `aws:SecureTransport` on bucket policies.

24. A company is planning to migrate a legacy Hadoop cluster running on premises to AWS. The cluster must use the latest EMR release and include its custom scripts and workflows during the migration. The data engineer must re-use the existing Java application code on premises in the new EMR cluster. Which of these solutions is the recommended approach?

   A. Submit a `PIG` step in the EMR cluster and compile the Java program using the version of the cluster.

   B. Submit a `STREAMING` step in the EMR cluster and compile the Java program using the version of the cluster.

   C. Submit a `spark-submit` step in the EMR cluster and compile the Java program using the version of the cluster.

   D. Submit a `CUSTOM_JAR` step in the EMR cluster and compile the Java program using the version of the cluster.

25. Which AWS service is best suited for visualizing and analyzing the behavior of applications, identifying performance bottlenecks, and troubleshooting request failures?

   A. Amazon CloudWatch

   B. AWS CloudTrail

   C. AWS X-Ray

   D. Amazon EventBridge

26. A multinational bank processes customer data from European and Asian markets with strict requirements to keep regional customer data within its respective geographic boundaries. The bank needs to implement a solution that prevents accidental replication of EU customer data to Asia-Pacific regions. The solution should be automated and provide compliance reporting. Which approach would be most suitable?

   A. Use Amazon S3 bucket policies with manual region restriction checks.

   B. Implement AWS Config rules with AWS Organizations service control policies (SCPs).

   C. Configure AWS CloudWatch with custom metrics for data movement.

   D. Deploy AWS Backup with cross-region replication enabled.

27. A game retailer stores massive amounts of user purchase data (several TBs) in a 3-month window on a MySQL RDS instance. The retailer analyzes this recent data frequently. However, older historical data is needed for quarterly trend reports, requiring joins with the recent data. What is the most cost-effective and performant solution for this scenario?

   A. Use AWS Glue to perform the ETL and incrementally load an year's worth data into Amazon Redshift. Run regular queries against Redshift. Catalog the data in Amazon S3 and use Amazon Athena to join the historical and current data to generate the reports.

   B. Set up a multi-AZ RDS database and run automated snapshots on the standby instance. Configure Amazon Athena to run historical queries on the S3 bucket containing automated snapshots.

   C. Use RDS read replica to sync a year's worth of data. Export the older historical data into Amazon S3 for long-term storage. From the data in S3 and Amazon RDS, create a data catalog using AWS Glue and use Amazon Athena to join historical and current data to generate the reports.

   D. Schedule the export of your data from Amazon RDS to Amazon S3 every day. Load a year's worth of data in Amazon Redshift and use it for regular queries. Join the historical data and current data using Amazon Redshift Spectrum to generate the trend reports.

28. Which AWS service would you use to create a flow chart or diagram to visualize a data pipeline?

   A. Amazon QuickSight

   B. AWS Glue

   C. Amazon Managed Workflows for Apache Airflow (MWAA)

   D. AWS Step Functions

29. You work as a data analytics specialist for a retail company that uses Amazon EMR cluster to ingest and provide query capabilities for its massive amounts of shipments and delivery information. You need the metastore for your EMR cluster to be persistent. Which option gives you the best metastore option with the *least* amount of effort?

A. Save your metastore information in your Hive MySQL database on the master node file system.

B. Save your metastore information in an external metastore in Amazon Aurora.

C. Save your metastore information in an external metastore in AWS Glue Data Catalog.

D. Save your metastore information in an external metastore in Amazon DynamoDB tables.

30. A data engineer attempts to run an AWS Glue job to read the data from Amazon S3. However, after a few minutes, the job fails with an out-of-memory error. Which solution will resolve the error?

A. Increase the MaxRetries variable in the AWS Glue job definition.

B. Increase the timeout limit in the AWS Glue job definition.

C. Enable autoscaling.

D. Define predicate pushdowns in the AWS Glue job.

Answers to Assessment Test

1. **D.** Open table formats like Apache Hudi, Apache Iceberg, and Delta Lake tables are recommended to implement upserts and deletes on Amazon S3 data lakes. Redshift Spectrum with Apache Iceberg and Amazon Athena with Apache Hudi only supports read-only format. To cater to the least operational overhead, configuring the tables using Apache Iceberg and deleting the records using Amazon Athena is the recommended approach for this use case.

2. **C.** Amazon RDS is the correct service to use for relational data. RDS Multi-AZ DB instances ensure durability, high availability, and disaster recovery, with a standby instance created in a different AZ and synchronous replication from the primary instance to the standby.

3. **D.** All of the options are correct, as they all have the following real-time streaming capabilities: Amazon EMR (Spark streaming), AWS Glue (Glue streaming), and Amazon Redshift (streaming ingestion).

4. **D.** Using Amazon Redshift Data API, a customer can run individual queries from within your application or submit a batch of SQL queries within a transaction. There is no need to manage WebSocket or JDBC connections.

5. **B.** Lake Formation provides fine-grained access controls; CloudTrail maintains comprehensive audit logs; and Macie automatically identifies PII data. This solution enables preventive access controls and provides detailed access reporting. Answer A is incorrect because it lacks automated PII detection capabilities. Answer C is incorrect because basic bucket policies don't provide comprehensive protection. Answer D is incorrect because AWS Backup doesn't address data sharing controls.

6. **C.** Amazon Neptune is a high-performance graph database that is purpose-built for highly connected datasets. It can efficiently and quickly traverse data with large numbers of complex relationships.

7. **D, E.** There is no need to add a task node, as the current job takes less time than the SLA. Considering the cost reduction, the recommended approach would be to use an instance fleet configuration. You can specify target capacities for on-demand and Spot instances within each fleet. When the cluster launches, Amazon EMR provisions instances until the targets are fulfilled. When Amazon EC2 reclaims the Spot instance in a running cluster, EMR tries to replace the instance with the instance type that you specify.

8. **B.** Partitioning in Athena divides tables into parts based on column values, such as date, country, or category. This allows Athena to scan only the relevant partitions instead of the entire table, reducing the amount of data scanned and lowering query costs.

9. **C.** The KEY distribution style will collocate rows related by the join column on the same compute nodes. This allows Redshift to join rows on each compute node without having to move data around the nodes, which can be expensive.

10. **C.** Amazon Data Firehose is the easiest way to load the streaming data into S3. When you enable the record transformation, JSON data gets automatically converted to Parquet format.

Amazon Data Firehose references table definitions stored in AWS Glue. You can choose to select the Glue catalog table and specify the schema for your source records.

11. C. AWS Glue DataBrew provides many built-in transformations for data cleaning and preparation, including handling missing values, standardizing formats, and removing duplicates. However, training machine learning models is not a built-in transformation in DataBrew.

12. A. The DynamoDB Streams feature simplifies tracking and auditing data changes. Streams can be combined with Lambda functions to build near real-time applications triggered by changes to items in a table.

13. A. Storing the data in Amazon S3 is the most cost-effective and durable solution. Additionally, using transient clusters for batch jobs is recommended, as it automatically terminates once the last step runs. Amazon EMR also allows you to reuse the existing jobs developed with Hadoop frameworks on premises. Hence, the recommended option here will be to migrate to Amazon EMR and launch transient clusters with data stored in Amazon S3.

14. B. Amazon Macie provides automatic detection and visibility of sensitive data in Amazon S3, such as personally identifiable information (PII), and security issues with S3 buckets, such as public accessibility.

15. C. The Redshift federated query feature allows you to query external databases such as RDS MySQL directly in real time. The results can be combined in a single query or database view with historical data stored locally on Redshift.

16. B. Random Cut Forest (RCF) is an algorithm widely used for anomaly detection use cases. Amazon Managed Service for Apache Flink can be configured to run RCF on input streams with large throughput.

17. D. While Amazon MWAA (Managed Workflows for Apache Airflow) is used for orchestrating data pipelines, it's not primarily designed for real-time data processing. Its main purpose is workflow management and scheduling.

18. D. The easiest and fastest way is to enable encryption on the cluster. Redshift will encrypt the data files without having to create a snapshot or unload the data. A KMS customer-managed key provides in-depth logging and allows you to rotate keys.

19. D. AWS Glue Data Catalog natively supports Apache Iceberg, Apache Hudi, and Delta Lake table formats. These table formats allow for more efficient data access patterns, leading to faster query execution, and also adapt to changing data structures over time without breaking the existing queries.

20. B. While it's important to provide comprehensive information, including too much data in a single visualization can lead to clutter and confusion. Best practices for data visualization include keeping visualizations simple and focused, using consistent design elements, providing clear labels and context, and adjusting the complexity based on the audience's needs and expertise.

21. A. AWS Lambda layers (.zip file) allow you to package libraries, custom runtime, and other dependencies that can be reused across multiple Lambda functions.

22. A. In Amazon Athena, after creating a partitioned table, any new data partitions added to S3 remains unrecognized by Athena. The MSCK REPAIR TABLE command synchronizes the table's metadata with the actual data layout in S3.

23. B, C. To enable cross-account encryption, you need to grant access to the KMS key to the second account on the key's key policy, and then create an IAM policy in the second account with permissions on the key and assign it to users and roles.

24. D. A custom JAR runs a compiled Java program that you can upload to S3. You can compile the program against the version of Hadoop you want to launch, and then submit the CUSTOM_JAR step to your EMR cluster.

25. C. AWS X-Ray allows you to visualize and analyze the behavior of your applications, identify any performance bottlenecks, and troubleshoot request failures. It provides insights into your application's behavior over time, allowing you to observe patterns, which you can use to improve the performance of your applications.

26. B. SCPs provide preventive controls at the organization level, and AWS Config rules enable automated compliance monitoring. Option B provides automated enforcement and reporting, scales across multiple accounts and regions, and provides an audit trail for compliance purposes. Option A is incorrect because manual checks are not scalable and are prone to human error. Option C is incorrect because CloudWatch alone doesn't prevent unauthorized data movement. Option D is incorrect because this would enable cross-region replication, contradicting the requirement.

27. D. The requirement mentions an optimal and cost-effective solution. Using Amazon Redshift Spectrum, customers can easily query the data in Amazon S3. The older and historical data (cold layer) can be accessed by the users and can be joined with the latest data in the Amazon Redshift cluster. With Amazon Redshift Spectrum, you only pay for the resources you consume for the duration of your query. Only the frequently accessed current data (hot layer) will be stored in the Amazon Redshift table.

28. D. While AWS Glue can be used for ETL workflows, AWS Step Functions provides a visual workflow service that enables you to create and run a series of checkpointed and event-driven workflows that maintain the application state. It offers a visual interface to create flow charts representing your data pipelines or other workflows.

29. C. You can configure Hive to use the AWS Glue Data Catalog as its metastore. While using an Amazon Aurora database as your external metastore for your Hive is a valid option, it is not as simple to implement as Glue Data Catalog.

30. D. Predicate pushdown is an optimization technique that helps to retrieve selective data, thereby reducing the time and amount of the data being processed. The other options will not help solve the OOM errors.

Chapter

1

Streaming and Batch Data Ingestion

**THE AWS CERTIFIED DATA ENGINEER –
ASSOCIATE EXAM OBJECTIVES COVERED
IN THIS CHAPTER MAY INCLUDE, BUT ARE
NOT LIMITED TO, THE FOLLOWING:**

✓ **Domain 1: Data Ingestion and Transformation**

   ▪ Task 1.1 Perform data ingestion

The Evolution of Application Architectures and Data Stores

In order to understand batch and streaming data ingestion, we need to understand how data architectures have evolved over time and why the exam focuses on certain topics. To understand the evolution of data architecture, we should look at the applications that are typically the data source for the data engineering pipelines and understand how the application architectures have evolved (see Figure 1.1).

FIGURE 1.1   The evolution of application architectures

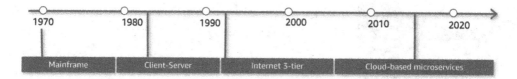

Application architectures have actually changed quite a bit in recent decades. Originally, companies used on-premises mainframes to handle their critical applications. These mainframes combined all aspects of an application—compute and storage—and ran for years without interruption.

Then, applications were split into pieces using a client-server architecture. The server responded to requests from various clients, which allowed for more distributed systems. The clients and servers could be on the same computer, but the separation allowed for more scalable systems when needed. Clients and servers could be split up so they would not compete for resources.

With the rise of the Internet, the three-tier architecture became prominent. Applications were split into groups by function: a presentation tier served as the user interface; an application tier handled the business logic and processing; and a data tier provided long-term, persistent storage. Again, this increased the scalability of applications because each tier could be scaled independently.

Each of these moves focused on splitting up your application to improve scaling and resiliency. The most recent architectural trend, which aligns well to cloud best practices, is to move to microservices. With microservices, you split your application into different services based on functionality. For example, rather than having one application that handles both your inventory data and order history data, you might split those into two separate services that are focused on their domain. This split allows the two services to scale independently and provides more agility between development teams.

Parallel to the evolution of application architecture is the evolution of how we store and access data. This evolution is worth a quick review to provide context to the tools and best practices that apply to modern data architectures (see Figure 1.2).

FIGURE 1.2   The evolution of data stores

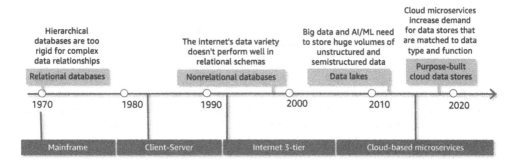

Relational databases replaced hierarchical databases, which had limited abilities to define relationships among data. Relational databases have been around since 1970 and continue to be the workhorse of many applications.

As the Internet era took off, organizations started to get more varied types of data, which they wanted to be able to analyze. This new variety of data was less structured and needed less rigid rules. This led to the development of nonrelational databases in the late 1990s.

With the growth of big data and artificial intelligence and machine learning (AI/ML) applications, organizations realized that they wanted to collect as much data as possible for potential use without the rigors of transforming it into a formal structure. Organizations wanted to simplify the collecting and querying of data in its most raw form. With a data lake, raw data could be loaded into the data store, where it could be held for a variety of use cases.

Cloud computing gave organizations the freedom to scale data stores up and down based on actual usage. Coupled with a move toward microservices, the flexibility of the cloud made it attractive to connect different application components to different databases, rather than relying on a single multipurpose one. Purpose-built data stores emerged to let developers optimize the storage that is connected to a component to match the data type and processing of that component. For example, developers might use a ledger database for financial transactions.

While data stores were evolving to handle different types of data, data architectures were also evolving to handle a continued increase in volume and velocity (see Figure 1.3).

FIGURE 1.3   The evolution of data architectures

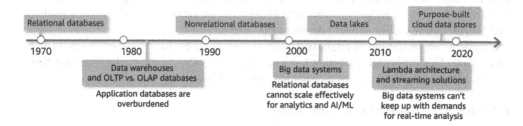

In the 1980s, data warehouses evolved as a way to separate operational reporting, which requires read-heavy querying across a full dataset, from the application's transactional database, which is focused on fast reads and writes in a much smaller set of records. Data warehouses are still relational databases, but they have been optimized for reporting and analytics. Online analytical processing (OLAP) databases are optimized for reporting, whereas online transaction processing (OLTP) databases are designed for transactions, such as creating an order or making an ATM withdrawal. The extract, transform, and load (ETL) process was introduced to extract data from OLTP databases, transform it, and then load it into the data warehouse.

As noted earlier, the rise of the Internet brought new data to be collected and analyzed. Even with a data warehouse dedicated to analysis, keeping up with the volume and velocity of incoming data created database bottlenecks. Administrators could scale vertically (i.e., increase the size and speed of the database), but there wasn't an easy way to scale horizontally (i.e., to distribute the load across multiple databases). Big data systems or frameworks addressed this shortcoming in the 2000s. Big data frameworks were designed to distribute data across multiple nodes and handle any failures automatically. These frameworks also allowed the big data systems to handle many ETL transformations, which helped to increase the speed with which analysis could be done.

Work was still mostly done by batching at some scheduled interval. Batch processing created a lag between the arrival of new data and its being included in analytics results. The continually increasing volume and velocity of new data meant that the time between batches created an increasingly large gap in the timeliness of data being processed. The volume and velocity also prevented more real-time analysis and decisions. As noted earlier, data has its greatest value when it can be analyzed as early as possible to when it was created. But as you also learned, the most valuable, predictive insights are more difficult to derive. To find a balance between value and complexity, Nathan Marz proposed the Lambda architecture—an approach that combines the use of batch processing with stream processing to support close-to-real-time insights. This approach has become a standard way to process big data.

So, which of these data stores or data architectures is the best one for your data pipeline? The reality is that a modern architecture might include all of these elements. The key to a modern data architecture is to apply the three-pronged strategy that you learned about earlier. *Modernize* the technology that you are using. *Unify* your data sources to create a single source of truth that can be accessed and used across the organization. And *innovate* to get higher value analysis from the data that you have.

Introduction to the Modern Data Architecture

The goal of the modern data architecture is to store data in a centralized location and make it available to all consumers to perform analytics and run AI/ML applications. But that doesn't mean that you have one data store—only that you have a single source of truth. As illustrated in Figure 1.4, a data lake provides the centralized repository of data and is integrated with the other types of data stores and data processing systems that were described in the previous section. Data might be queried directly from the lake, or it might be moved to and from other purpose-built tools for processing.

Figure 1.4 provides a conceptual look at the components of a modern data architecture and how they are connected to each other. The diagram doesn't reflect the actual architecture that accommodates these connections.

FIGURE 1.4   A conceptual diagram of a modern data architecture

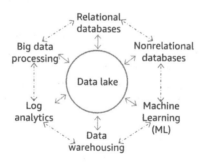

The movement of data among the lake and other integrated services falls into three general types: outside in, inside out, and around the perimeter.

Outside in is when an organization that stores data in purpose-built data stores, such as a data warehouse or a database, moves data into the lake to run analysis on it. For example, they copy query results for product sales in a given region from their data warehouse into their data lake to run product recommendation algorithms against a larger dataset by using ML.

Inside out is when an organization stores data in a data lake and then moves a portion of that data to a purpose-built data store to do additional ML or analytics. For example, they collect clickstream data from web applications directly into a data lake and then move a portion of that data out to a data warehouse for daily reporting.

Around the perimeter is when an organization moves data directly between the other data store components that are integrated with the data lake without needing to access the data lake. For example, they might copy the product catalog data stored in their database to their search service to make it easier to look through their product catalog and offload the search queries from the database.

The modern data architecture approach addresses the strategies of modernizing, unifying, and innovating with your data architecture, but it also introduces a lot of complexity to constructing your data pipeline. The main challenge with a data lake architecture is that raw data is stored with no oversight of the contents. In order for a data lake to make data usable, it needs to have defined mechanisms to catalog and secure data. Without these elements, data cannot be found or trusted, which results in a *data swamp*.

To build a successful modern data architecture, your design must incorporate the following features:

- The data lake should be able to easily scale as data grows. Use a scalable, durable data store that supports multiple ways to bring data in. For each component, select scalable services that balance the fastest performance at the lowest cost for the use case. Choose purpose-built tools. One of the key exam objectives is around choosing specific tools for specific use cases. You will continually assess options that could increase performance or reduce costs.

- Your design should also support the seamless data movement into and out of the data lake and around the perimeter—and, whenever possible, provide direct access to the data.

- Your design must also ensure the consistency of data across all components of the architecture. As data in your various data stores and data lake continues to grow, it becomes more difficult to move all of that data around securely and in a governed way. This is referred to as *data gravity*. In this architecture, it's critical to have robust mechanisms for authorization and auditing, with a centralized location to define policies and enforce them.

In the conceptual diagram shown in Figure 1.5, you see AWS services that map to the conceptual elements of the modern data architecture and support its key design considerations. You will learn more about each of these components throughout the book and will see how these connections are reflected in reference architectures that support this conceptual view.

Amazon Simple Storage Service (Amazon S3) provides storage for structured and unstructured data and is the storage service of choice to build a data lake on AWS. With Amazon S3, you can cost-effectively build and scale a data lake of any size in a secure environment with high durability. With Amazon S3, you can also use native AWS services to run big data analytics and AI/ML applications.

FIGURE 1.5   Modern data architecture on AWS

Amazon Athena is shown directly on the data lake to illustrate that it provides interactive querying of data directly in Amazon S3.

The architecture illustrates other AWS purpose-built services that integrate with Amazon S3 and map to each AWS service illustrated in Figure 1.5:

- Amazon Redshift is a fully managed data warehouse service.

- Amazon OpenSearch Service is a purpose-built data store and search engine that is optimized for real-time analytics, including log analytics.

- Amazon EMR provides big data processing and simplifies some of the most complex elements of setting up big data processing.

- Amazon Aurora provides a relational database engine that was built for the cloud.

- Amazon DynamoDB is a fully managed nonrelational database that is designed to run high-performance applications.

- Amazon SageMaker is an AI/ML service that democratizes access to ML processing.

To meet the goal of seamless data movement, Athena and Amazon Redshift both support federated queries and the ability to run queries across different data stores without needing to move the data between stores to perform the queries.

This chapter focuses mainly on streaming and batch ingestion. Figure 1.6 shows, at a high level, all the ingestion services available within the analytics ecosystem at the time of this writing, and also gives you a quick summary of which services to choose when. We'll discuss more of these later in the chapter.

FIGURE 1.6   Matching ingestion services to variety, volume, and velocity

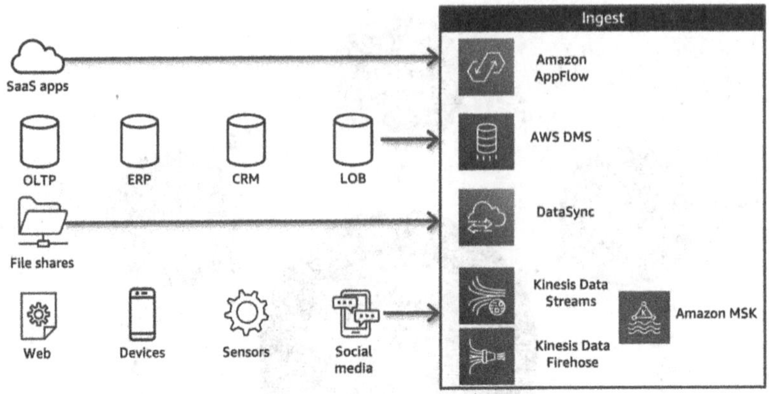

Introduction to Data Ingestion

Data ingestion, a critical phase in the data engineering lifecycle, involves collecting data from various sources and moving it to a platform where it can be stored, processed, and analyzed. This chapter delves into the nuances of data ingestion, focusing on AWS services, and covers key concepts such as throughput, latency, data ingestion patterns, and the intricacies of both streaming and batch data ingestion.

We'll use the data engineering lifecycle (Figure 1.7) to focus our energy on the key job requirements from a data engineering role, and explain how they relate to the exam requirements from the AWS Data Engineering – Associate certification exam. In essence, we would like to start working backward from the core objectives of data engineering and the end goal that needs to be achieved. If you look at a typical data engineering lifecycle, you move from the left-hand side of Figure 1.7 to the right, which is:

- Generation
- Storage
- Ingestion
- Transformation
- Serving

The layer below the dotted line includes critical components that will be relevant for the entire lifecycle, irrespective of the particular phase.

Throughout the book, we'll touch upon the different components of the data engineering pipeline.

Let's start by discussing data generation.

FIGURE 1.7   The data engineering lifecycle

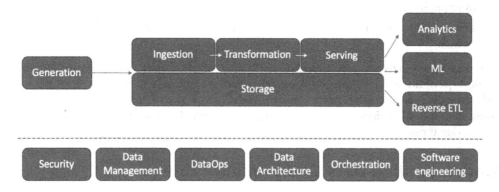

Data Generation

At the heart of data engineering is the process of data generation, where the journey of raw data begins. This stage is fascinating because it pulls in data from everywhere—like social media, online transactions, sensors, and user interactions—creating a huge, fast-moving, and diverse flow of information. Think of this as the data coming at us in all shapes, sizes, and speeds, challenging us with its sheer amount (volume), its rapid arrival rate (velocity), and its wide range (variety), from simple numbers to complex videos.

For a data engineer, this wild world of data is something they can't control. It's like trying to manage a river in flood; they can't control how much data is coming, how fast it's arriving, or what kind of data it is. But what they can do is quite remarkable: they can create systems to organize this chaos, making sure the data can be used effectively. They tackle the big waves of data (volume), keep up with its speed (velocity), and make sense of its many forms (variety). It's a mix of creativity and tech know-how, ensuring all this data is neatly collected, stored, and ready for the next steps.

Getting this right is crucial because it sets the stage for everything that follows in turning data into something valuable. Well-handled data can lead to insights that help make smart decisions and spark innovative ideas. But if it's not managed properly, opportunities are missed, and the data's potential is lost. The beginning phase of generating data, with all its challenges, is key to the whole data engineering process, affecting how data is stored, processed, analyzed, and visualized later on. How well a data engineer navigates this phase is essential for unlocking the value of the data, leading to powerful analytics, machine learning, and informed decisions that drive an organization forward. The exam will present you with simulated real-world situations, often actual customer problems, and present you with a list of solutions that might be suited for the particular scenario.

If you summarize the typical types of sources we work with, you will see data in three broad categories:

- Existing transactional systems (such as CRM systems or POS systems), which are typically based on databases like Aurora, MySQL, Oracle, Microsoft SQL Server: Data can arrive in batches or in a streaming fashion.

- Streaming data coming from IoT devices, sensors, and social media: Data mostly arrives in streaming fashion.
- Files coming from web servers (e.g., logs): Data can arrive in batches or in a streaming fashion.

Each of these sources can provide data with different volumes and velocities, depending on the type of the source. For example, existing transactional systems would typically provide structured data, which is pretty consistent in terms of its structure, whereas data coming from sensors and IoT devices can often change its structure based on the latest OS versions, application types, and so on.

Understanding Data Sources and Storage

Before ingesting data, it's essential to understand the origin and storage of the data. The data might originate from diverse sources like IoT devices, transactional databases, or online transaction processing systems. Recognizing how data is generated and stored, including the data's schema, frequency, and volume, is foundational for designing an effective ingestion strategy.

You need to ensure that you understand how the source system works, the way it generates data, the frequency and velocity of data, and the types of data being generated. Here are just a few questions to consider at this stage:

- What are the characteristics of the data (e.g., structured, semi-structured, unstructured, data types, data formats)?
- How is that data persisted in the source system (e.g., database, flat files, message queues)?
- Will there be any duplicates, what is the schema of that source data, and does that schema change?
- What is the volume of data being generated, and is it expected to grow over time?
- Are there any data quality issues or inconsistencies in the source data that need to be addressed?
- Are there any data governance or security requirements for the source data?
- Are there any dependencies or integrations with other systems that need to be considered?
- What are the data access and extraction mechanisms available for the source system?
- Are there any specific data transformation or cleansing requirements before loading the data into the target system?
- What are the expected service-level agreements (SLAs) or performance requirements for data extraction and loading?
- Are there any specific data retention or archiving requirements for the source data?

- Which error handling and recovery mechanisms are in place for the data extraction process?
- Are there any specific monitoring or auditing requirements for the data extraction process?

Ingestion Patterns and AWS Services

Ingestion patterns vary based on the nature and requirements of the data. Typically, data ingestion from source is broadly categorized into batch and streaming ingestion.

To generalize the characteristics of batch processing, batch processing is a data handling approach that involves the systematic execution of automated jobs that retrieve information from a source, transfer the resulting datasets to a secure storage location within the data pipeline, and then apply the necessary transformations tailored to the particular requirements of the given project. The scope of these transformations can vary significantly. For simpler use cases, it might involve basic cleansing and formatting to facilitate the integration of data into a data lake system. However, for more intricate objectives, such as those aimed at supporting extensive data queries, big data analytics, or machine learning (ML) applications, the process might encompass a more elaborate sequence of enrichment, augmentation, and intensive processing.

Batch jobs can be triggered in several ways: they may be initiated manually upon request, set to run according to a predetermined timetable, or launched automatically in response to certain triggers or events. The conventional extract, transform, and load (ETL) framework relies on batch processing techniques, though the alternative extract, load, and transform (ELT) approach may also employ batch processing methods.

One of the principal advantages of batch processing is its proficiency in handling vast volumes of accumulated transactional data over specific intervals. It excels particularly in executing complex tasks that require extended processing times. When immediate data analysis is not a pressing concern, batch processing becomes a particularly attractive option due to its cost-effectiveness and the relative simplicity of its management. This efficiency makes it an optimal choice for organizations looking to process large datasets without the need for real-time results.

In direct contrast to the batch processing model, stream processing activates a continuous flow of data. In this model, records are constantly fed into and transmitted through the stream. Consumers of this data, which can be systems or applications, then read and process these records in real time or near-real-time, within a dynamically moving time window. This method not only facilitates real-time analytics but also ensures that processed data can be promptly made available for immediate review and action. Furthermore, processed records may be stored in durable systems for subsequent use and analysis.

Streaming processing's standout feature is the ability to deliver processed results almost instantaneously, allowing for immediate action based on the data analyzed. This low-latency analysis is especially beneficial for handling high volumes of fast-moving, unstructured data streams. Stream processing is particularly designed to accommodate scenarios where the speed and immediacy of data processing are crucial.

AWS offers a range of services tailored for different ingestion needs, which we will discuss over the course of this chapter.

We have a lot of content to cover in this chapter, so the standard approach that we will take is to first introduce the different services covered in the exam, and then discuss their implications during the ingestion process.

Data Ingestion

There are two major types of data ingestion:

- **Batch ingestion:** This approach deals with data in finite sets. Jobs are often executed according to a predetermined schedule, such as hourly or nightly. It's akin to a bakery preparing dozens of loaves of bread at once and then selling them the next morning.

- **Streaming ingestion:** Here, data flows continuously, akin to a stream of water. This model is more suitable for tasks that require immediate attention, such as monitoring live financial transactions or managing the flow of data from millions of IoT devices.

The remainder of this chapter covers the AWS services that can be used for streaming and batch ingestion.

Streaming Ingestion

By 2025, IDC estimates there will be 175 zettabytes of data globally (that's 175 with 21 zeros), with 80% of that data being unstructured. As data grows exponentially, so does its velocity, necessitating tools that can swiftly capture, process, analyze, and derive actionable insights from this torrent of information.

Streaming data systems are particularly valuable because they can deliver ongoing insights with minimal delay, even when dealing with data influx that is both high in volume and variable in rate. The urgency of processing data is underscored by the concept that data's value diminishes as it ages—what's referred to as the *shelf life* of data. This concept doesn't imply that all data inevitably loses value, but it emphasizes that certain scenarios demand extremely low latency to maintain relevance. Figure 1.8 demonstrates the perishable nature of insights and the need to act upon the information quickly to realize optimal value.

Take, for instance, the scenario of fraud detection in credit card transactions. Here, the speed at which a fraudulent activity is identified is critical. Detecting fraud quickly not only positions a company to address and mitigate risks effectively but also prevents potential financial losses. Figure 1.8 explains how the value of data decreases over time in relation to decision-making. When time is of the essence and you have a time-sensitive situation at hand, Amazon Kinesis or Amazon MSK can demonstrate their strength. By enabling real-time data processing, streaming applications help organizations act swiftly, preserving the high value of immediate insights. The platform ensures that the valuable opportunity to act upon data at the peak of its relevance is not missed, as illustrated by the concept of the *perishable nature of insights*, which suggests that the sooner information is acted upon, the greater the benefit or value derived from it.

FIGURE 1.8   Information half-life in decision-making

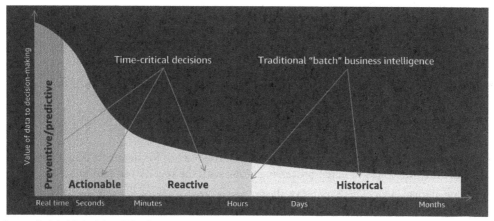

Source: Perishable Insights, Mike Gualtieri, Forrester

In summary, streaming services are designed to handle the complexities of high-velocity, unstructured data streams, providing businesses with the ability to process and analyze data in real time. This capability is not just a technical achievement but a strategic asset for any data-driven organization operating in today's fast-paced environment.

Now, let's delve into the nuances of stream processing and understand why it might be the superior choice in certain situations:

- **Decoupling data collection from processing:** Stream processing acts as a middle layer that separates the incoming flow of data (from producers) and the mechanisms that process this data (the consumers). This system acts like a flexible buffer zone, accommodating data at its own pace, which can be critical in managing variable data rates. Decoupling producers from consumers is a best practice when it comes to data management.

- **Unifying data streams:** Imagine a scenario with a million sensors each sending temperature data to be analyzed. Stream processing enables all these individual streams to converge seamlessly into a single, manageable channel.

- **Maintaining the order of events:** Certain sequences, such as bank transactions where the order of debit and credit is crucial, must be preserved. Stream processing ensures that the sequence remains unchanged from the moment it's sent to when it's processed.

- **Parallel processing:** Much like multiple lanes on a highway that allow cars to move simultaneously, stream processing allows for concurrent operations on the same dataset. This enables diverse applications to work side by side, each at its own pace, which can significantly accelerate time to market.

During the exam, you should look out for the following key attributes of stream processing applications to understand the use cases where a stream processing application make sense:

- **Ultra-low latency:** Stream processing is about speed, ensuring that data is processed almost as quickly as it's generated.

- **Guaranteed message delivery:** Just as a courier service ensures your parcel arrives, stream processing ensures data gets where it needs to go.

- **Support for the Lambda architecture:** This is a framework for data processing that provides the robustness of batch processing along with the speed of stream processing.

- **State management:** This capability allows you to keep track of the context of ongoing transactions within the data stream.

- **Time-based and count-based windows:** These windows help in organizing data for processing based on time intervals or quantities, which can be fixed or rolling.

- **Resilience to failure:** A stream processing system is designed to withstand problems, continuing to operate smoothly in the face of disruptions.

Despite these advantages, implementing streaming capabilities can be challenging, which is why organizations often struggle with setting up and scaling such systems. As data volumes skyrocket from thousands to billions of events, the complexity increases. Ensuring high availability and seamless integration with existing systems can also be challenging, not to mention the management complexities and maintenance costs.

In response to these challenges, AWS has expanded its offerings to simplify the streaming data ecosystem. This includes:

- **Amazon Kinesis:** A fully managed service designed to handle real-time data streams.

- **Amazon Managed Streaming for Kafka (MSK):** This service offers a managed environment for Apache Kafka, which is widely used for building real-time data pipelines and streaming apps.

- **Amazon Managed Flink:** A service that provides a managed environment for Apache Flink, an open-source stream processing framework.

These services are designed to abstract away the intricacies of stream processing, allowing businesses to leverage the power of real-time data analysis without the technical overhead.

Amazon Kinesis Introduction

Amazon Kinesis is AWS's flagship solution for real-time data streaming and analytics. It's designed to handle massive streams of data in real time, enabling businesses to analyze and respond to data quickly. The service is crucial for applications that require continuous data intake and processing, such as log and event data collection, real-time analytics, machine learning model inference, and more.

Amazon Kinesis provides multiple components, such as Amazon Kinesis Data Streams, Amazon Data Firehose (formerly Kinesis Data Firehose), and Amazon Managed Service for Apache Flink. Figure 1.9 shows the different streaming options on the Amazon Kinesis console page.

FIGURE 1.9   The Amazon Kinesis console page

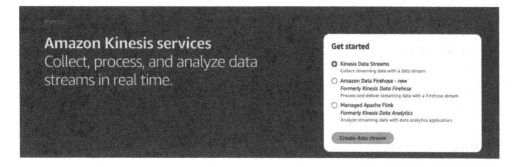

Let's dive into each service one by one. If you're preparing for an exam, it's crucial to understand the functions of these services, along with their capacity for handling data and their response times. Also, know when it's best to use them over alternatives, and be familiar with the methods for inputting and retrieving streaming data.

Amazon Kinesis Data Streams

Amazon Kinesis Data Streams is a massively scalable, near-real-time data streaming service that allows you to scale GBs of data per second from thousands of sources.

Imagine you have a bustling digital marketplace, much like a busy city center, but instead of people, you have a flood of data rushing in from every corner: clicks, video views, app activity, and more. Just as city planners manage traffic, you need a way to manage this data. This is where Amazon Kinesis Data Streams comes in—it's like a series of high-speed roadways designed for data.

Kinesis Data Streams is a service offered by Amazon Web Services that's built to handle massive waves of data in real time. Think of it as a set of superhighways for data that lets you collect, process, and analyze information as quickly as it comes in, allowing for instantaneous decision-making and action-taking. Whether it's temperature readings from air sensors or clicks on a website, Kinesis can handle it all with minimum configurations.

The service works by creating data streams, which you can picture as individual lanes on a highway. Each lane, or *shard*, as it's referred to in Kinesis, can carry a certain amount of data. If you need more capacity, you can add more shards. This makes Kinesis incredibly flexible and scalable—you can adjust the number of shards as the traffic of your data changes.

What sets Kinesis Data Streams apart is its ability to process and analyze data almost as soon as it's generated. So, if you're an online retailer, you can instantly track how customers are interacting with your site and adjust your strategies in real time. If you're a game developer, you can see how players are experiencing your game and fix issues immediately.

Amazon Kinesis was built to be accessible, and with some basic setup, you can start streaming data while paying only for what you use. You do not need to invest in heavy-duty servers or infrastructure, as Amazon Kinesis grows with your needs, whether you're a small startup or a large corporation.

In short, Amazon Kinesis Data Streams is like the traffic control system for data, ensuring that every bit of information gets where it needs to go quickly and efficiently, helping businesses make better decisions faster.

As Figure 1.10 illustrates, you have the ability to capture and store your data, after which you can direct it to a variety of applications for further processing. This includes leveraging services like Amazon Data Firehose, Amazon Managed Service for Apache Flink, employing Spark on Amazon EMR, or utilizing AWS Lambda for custom processing workflows. Once your data has been processed, you can bring it into your preferred business intelligence (BI) tool to create visualizations that can inform decision-making.

FIGURE 1.10   Kinesis Data Streams overview

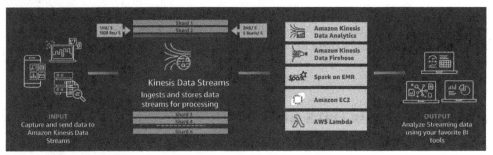

Source: Amazon Web Services, Inc.

Use Cases for Amazon Kinesis Data Streams

Amazon Kinesis Data Streams is adept at handling high-speed data collection and aggregation from multiple sources. It stands out in several key scenarios:

- **Quick capture and processing of log data:** Web and application servers, as well as IoT devices, generate a continuous flow of log data that needs to be gathered and processed quickly. Kinesis Data Streams offers a solution to capture this information with minimal delay, allowing for prompt data processing, which can help mitigate issues like server malfunctions or data loss.

- **Real-time metrics for business insight:** Businesses often require immediate visibility into their operations. For example, manufacturers may need to track the number of active machines on a shop floor and their output in real time. Delays in identifying issues could lead to costly downtime. Kinesis Data Streams provides the capability to monitor these metrics as they happen, which is crucial for timely decision-making and maintaining operational efficiency.

- **Immediate data analytics:** Kinesis Data Streams is particularly useful for scenarios requiring instant data analysis, such as identifying anomalies or detecting fraudulent transactions. By processing data as it's received, businesses can intervene rapidly when they detect unusual patterns that may indicate a problem.

- **Managing complex data flows:** In situations where data comes from various sources and needs to be combined—or aggregated—Kinesis Data Streams excels. It can handle the complexity of processing these diverse data streams, ensuring that they're orchestrated efficiently and effectively for downstream applications.

- **Integration with data warehousing:** A typical application of Kinesis Data Streams is to collect data and distribute it for further processing. One part of the system may transform the data or take immediate action based on its contents. Another part can group the data into batches and store it in a data lake, such as Amazon S3, from which it can be transferred to a data warehouse like Amazon Redshift for more in-depth analysis.

- **Enhancing search and analytics applications:** Logs from applications are vital for understanding user behavior and system performance. Kinesis Data Streams can funnel these logs into search and analytics platforms, such as OpenSearch. This enables rapid searching and visualization, and with tools like Kibana, you can create dashboards to track and display key events or trends.

In all these scenarios, Kinesis Data Streams acts as a powerful conduit for data, ensuring it is captured, processed, and made ready for whatever analysis or action is needed, swiftly and efficiently.

Kinesis Data Streams—Flow

As you may have understood by now, Amazon Kinesis Data Streams is a scalable service that scales elastically for near-real-time processing of streaming big data. The service stores large streams of data (gigabytes of data per second) in durable, consistent storage, reliably for near-real-time (few seconds) data processing by an elastically scalable fleet of data processing servers.

Streaming data processing has two layers: a storage layer and a processing layer (see Figure 1.11). The storage layer must support specialized ordering and consistency semantics that enable fast, inexpensive, and repayable reads and writes of large streams of data.

FIGURE 1.11   Kinesis Data Streams data flow

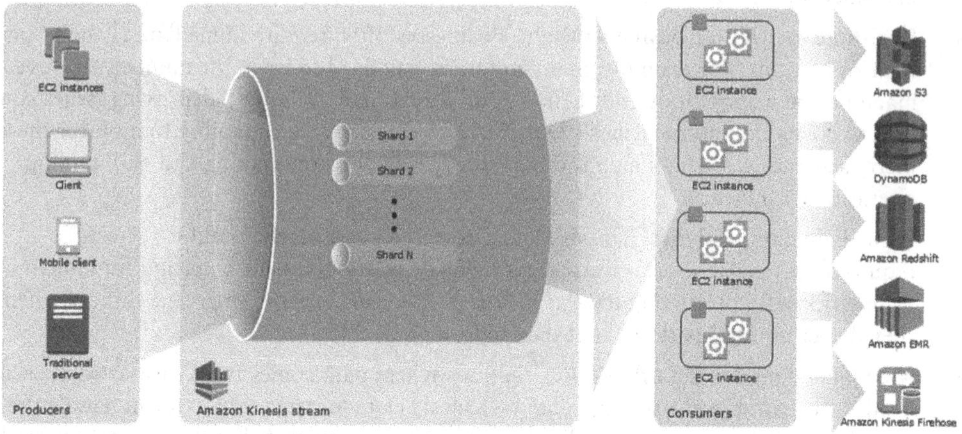

The processing layer is responsible for reading data from the storage layer, processing that data, and notifying the storage layer to delete data that is no longer needed.

Customers can compile the Amazon Kinesis library into their data processing application. Amazon Kinesis notifies the application (the worker) when there is new data to process. The control plane works with workers to solve scalability and fault tolerance problems in the processing layer.

Let's look at some of the key concepts of Kinesis Data Streams:

Kinesis Data Streams—Deep Dive

In this section, we'll take a close look at many aspects of Kinesis Data Streams.

What Is a Kinesis Data Stream?

We touched upon the concept of a "shard" earlier in the chapter. So, what is a "shard" actually? A shard is a logical concept that holds a series of data records in order, much like a queue. Every data record in this queue has a unique sequence number that Kinesis assigns to keep track of it. A Kinesis data stream is actually a collection of shards.

Data Record Basics

A data record is the smallest unit of information within a Kinesis data stream. Think of it as a packet of data that includes a sequence number (kind of like a tracking ID), a partition key (which helps organize the data), and a data blob. This blob is just a fancy term for a chunk of data, which can be as large as 1 MB. Kinesis doesn't peek into or alter this blob; it just stores it exactly as it receives it.

Choosing Your Stream's Capacity Mode

When setting up a Kinesis data stream, you'll decide on a capacity mode. This affects how the stream's capacity is managed and how you're billed. You can go with either on-demand or provisioned modes:

- **On-demand mode** means Kinesis automatically handles the stream's capacity to match your needs, billing you only for what you use. It's flexible and adjusts to your throughput requirements, whether they increase or decrease.

- **Provisioned mode** requires you to specify upfront how many shards you need. Your billing is based on the number of shards. You can adjust the shard count as your needs change.

Retention Period: How Long to Keep Data

By default, data in your stream is kept for 24 hours. However, you can extend this up to 365 days or shorten it back to the 24-hour minimum. Longer retention periods cost extra.

Producers and Consumers

While their names are self-explanatory, it is important to understand what producers and consumers are.

- **Producers** are sources that add records to your stream. For example, a web server logging activity could be a producer.

- **Consumers** take records from your stream to process them. They're typically applications designed to read and act on the streamed data.

Kinesis Data Streams Applications

These are specific consumers designed to work with the stream's data. They can be deployed across multiple EC2 instances and can feed data into another stream or AWS services.

Shard Details

A shard is like a lane in a highway; it directs a portion of the traffic. Each shard supports a certain number of transactions per second for both reading and writing data. The overall capacity of your stream depends on how many shards it has. You can adjust the number of shards based on your data traffic.

Partition Keys and Sequence Numbers

It's important to understand the role that partition keys and sequence numbers play:

- **Partition keys** help organize data into shards. Each record is tagged with a partition key, which Kinesis uses to determine which shard the record belongs to.

- **Sequence numbers** are unique identifiers for records within a shard, assigned by Kinesis after a record is added. They help keep track of the order of records.

Sequence numbers can't be used to categorize data within the stream. For organizing different sets of data, use partition keys or separate streams.

Working with the Kinesis Client Library

The Kinesis Client Library (KCL) helps your application process data from your stream efficiently and reliably. It ensures there's a process running for each shard, simplifying data consumption. The KCL uses a DynamoDB table for managing state information.

Naming Your Application

Each Kinesis Data Streams application needs a unique name within your AWS account and region. This name is used for DynamoDB table names and CloudWatch metrics.

Encrypting Your Data

Kinesis Data Streams supports automatic encryption for sensitive data as it enters the stream, using AWS Key Management Service (KMS) keys for security.

Example Code Snippets

Let's look at a couple of code snippets that deal with writing data to and reading data from Amazon Kinesis.

Adding a Record to a Stream

Here's how you can add a record to a stream:

```
import boto3
kinesis_client = boto3.client('kinesis', region_name='your-region')
# Create a data record
data = '{"example": "data"}'.encode('utf-8')
partition_key = 'examplePartitionKey'
# Put the record into the stream
response = kinesis_client.put_record( StreamName='yourStreamName', Data=data,
PartitionKey=partition_key )
print(response)
```

Consuming Records from a Stream

This example assumes you're using the Kinesis Client Library. The library abstracts away the details of fetching records from the stream, allowing you to focus on processing the data.

```
public class YourRecordProcessor implements IRecordProcessor {
    public void initialize(String shardId) {
        // Initialization logic here
    }

    public void processRecords(List<Record> records, IRecordProcessor
Checkpointer checkpointer) {
        for (Record record : records) {
            // Process each record
```

```
    }
}
```

```
  public void shutdown(IRecordProcessorCheckpointer checkpointer,
ShutdownReason reason)
```

Writing Data to Streams

To elaborate on writing data to Amazon Kinesis Data Streams and the considerations for ensuring efficient data transfer and processing, let's look at the different ways in which you can write data to Amazon Kinesis Data Streams and dive deeper into the methods and best practices for developing and managing Kinesis producers.

Producers in Amazon Kinesis Data Streams

A producer is essentially any application that sends data to Kinesis Data Streams. These can be built using the AWS SDK, specifically with Java in mind, and the Kinesis Producer Library (KPL), which offers a more streamlined interface for sending data to your streams.

The following are the different ways you can write data to an Amazon Kinesis Data Stream:

- Using the AWS SDK for Java and the Kinesis Producer Library (KPL):
  - Simplifies the development of producer applications.
  - Provides high write throughput, automated retries, record batching (aggregation), and seamless integration with the Kinesis Client Library (KCL).
- Directly using the Amazon Kinesis Data Streams API with the AWS SDK for Java:
  - Offers fine-grained control over stream operations, including creating streams, resharding, and managing records.
  - Requires handling of retries and record batching manually.
- Writing to Amazon Kinesis Data Streams using Kinesis Agent:
  - Kinesis Agent is a standalone Java software application that offers an easy way to collect and send data to Kinesis Data Streams.
  - It handles file rotation, checkpointing, and retries upon failures automatically.
  - It delivers data in a reliable, timely, and simple manner.
- Writing to Kinesis Data Streams using other AWS services:
  - AWS services like AWS Lambda, AWS IoT, Amazon CloudWatch Logs, and others can be configured to automatically write data to Kinesis Data Streams.
- Using third-party integrations:
  - Tools like Apache Flink, Fluentd, Logstash, and others support sending data to Kinesis Data Streams, expanding the ecosystem of data producers.

- Developing custom applications:
  - Custom applications developed using AWS SDKs in various programming languages can put data into Kinesis Data Streams.
  - These applications can run on EC2 instances, on-premises servers, or even as part of mobile or web applications.

Each method provides unique benefits and trade-offs in terms of simplicity, control, and integration with other AWS services or third-party tools.

Understanding Basic Requirements

To initiate data transfer to a stream, a producer must specify the following:

- **Stream name:** Identifies which stream the data should be sent to.
- **Partition key:** A key that determines the shard within the stream where the data is stored. The choice of partition key affects how data is distributed across shards and is crucial for optimizing data retrieval and processing.
- **Data blob:** The actual data payload you want to send to the stream.

The Importance of Partition Keys

Just like any distributed system where data distribution plays a key role in performance, partition keys play a vital role in data distribution across shards. The Kinesis service uses the partition key to assign the data to a specific shard. A well-thought-out partition key strategy is crucial to avoid uneven data distribution, which can lead to hot shards and affect the stream's ability to scale and process data efficiently.

Using the Kinesis Producer Library

The Kinesis Producer Library (KPL) simplifies the development of Kinesis producers by providing features such as high write throughput, automated retries, and data aggregation. This library batches multiple data records into a single Kinesis record, enhancing throughput and reducing the number of API calls needed. It's essential to monitor the KPL's performance and keep it updated to leverage improvements and bug fixes. We'll look at the KPL in more detail later in this section.

Monitoring and Troubleshooting

Amazon CloudWatch offers monitoring capabilities for tracking the operational metrics of your Kinesis producers. This is vital for identifying and resolving issues such as increased latency or throughput bottlenecks.

Advanced Topics for Kinesis Data Streams Producers

There are two advanced topics to understand about the KPL:

Handling Retries and Rate Limiting   The KPL automatically retries failed data records, using a strategy that considers both the time-to-live of the record and the maximum buffered time. Additionally, it implements rate limiting to prevent excessive retries from overloading the system. This is particularly important when dealing with partial failures and ensures that data is eventually written to the stream without overwhelming the shards.

KPL Aggregation   Aggregation is a powerful feature of the KPL that bundles multiple smaller records into a larger one, improving data transfer efficiency. However, this necessitates the use of de-aggregation logic on the consumer side to process the original records individually.

Key Considerations for Optimizing Producer Performance

When optimizing producer performance, you should know the following:

- **Security and IAM policies:** Ensure that producers have the necessary permissions to write to streams, which involves configuring IAM roles and policies correctly.
- **Optimal use of partition keys:** Design your partition key strategy to ensure a balanced distribution of data across shards, avoiding throttling and maximizing throughput.
- **Monitoring and analytics:** Utilize CloudWatch to monitor key metrics related to your producers and streams, allowing for proactive adjustments and optimization.
- **Update and maintain KPL:** Regularly update the KPL to benefit from performance improvements, new features, and bug fixes, ensuring your producers operate efficiently.

While AWS provides a simple interface to write data to an Amazon Kinesis stream, effectively writing data to data streams requires a comprehensive understanding of how producers work, optimal use of the KPL, and ongoing monitoring and optimization efforts to handle data at scale. The certification exam will typically have a couple of questions on KPL, so understanding it can help you with scoring those key certification points.

KPL Deep Dive

Think of the Kinesis Producer Library (KPL) as a smart assistant for your data. When you have a lot of information to send to different places, it can get tricky.

Maybe you're trying to:

- Send the same piece of information to several spots at once
- Keep trying to send data if it didn't work the first time
- Deal with a huge number of small bits of data all at once
- Make sure that the data is easy to use once it gets where it's going
- Keep track of how well the data sending and receiving is going

Doing all this manually can be a real headache. That's where KPL comes in to save the day. It's good at handling a lot of data all at once, and it does it quickly.

What's Great About the KPL?

Let's say you have a bunch of machines in a factory, and each one is sending tiny updates. You have to collect all these tiny updates and send them to a data stream. If you were to send each update one by one, it would take forever. The KPL helps you by grouping a lot of these tiny updates into one big update, allowing you to send multiple updates at once. This not only makes things faster but also ensures you don't hit the limits on how much data you can send at once.

With the KPL, you also don't have to worry about the details of making sure your data gets sent properly. It's smart enough to keep trying if there's a problem without you having to tell it to.

On the other side, when you want to use the data you've collected, the KPL makes that easier, too. It works well with the Kinesis Consumer Library (KCL), which is like KPL but for taking data out of the stream. If you're not using the KCL, you can still get your data out in a useful way with the KPL's tools.

The KPL also keeps an eye on how well your data is being sent and lets you see this information in CloudWatch. That means you can check on how fast and reliably your data is moving.

The KPL works in the background, so when you send data to it, it doesn't slow you down. It takes care of sending the data while you go on with other things. Later, it lets you know how it went.

In a nutshell, the KPL is like a behind-the-scenes wizard for your applications, making sure the data they create gets to the Kinesis data streams without a fuss.

Example of Using KPL

Here's how you might write some simple code to send data with KPL:

```
kinesis = KinesisProducer()

for i in range(100):
    data = ByteBuffer.wrap("myData".encode("UTF-8"))
    kinesis.addUserRecord("mystream", "mypartitionkey", data)
```

This little loop just sends the message "myData" to your stream a hundred times. The KPL takes care of the rest, making sure it all gets where it's meant to go.

Easily Send Data with Kinesis Agent

If you want to get your data into a stream without a fuss, Kinesis Agent is here to help. It's a program you can set up on your computer to do several helpful things:

- It watches your files and sends any new data to your Kinesis stream.
- It handles file rotation, which means it can switch to a new file when the old one gets too big or old.
- It remembers the last bit of data it processed, so it always knows where it left off.
- If there's a problem sending data, it tries again until it works.
- It also sends updates to CloudWatch so you can see how things are going.

Normally, Kinesis Agent looks for a new line (you know, when you press Enter on your keyboard) to figure out when one piece of data ends and the next begins. However, you can tweak it if your data is a bit more complex.

How to Get Your Data Flowing with Kinesis Agent

Here's how to install your agent and get it running:

Set Up the Agent   First, you have to install it. If you're using Amazon Linux, type the following in your computer's command line:

```
sudo yum install -y aws-kinesis-agent
```

For Red Hat Linux, it's a bit different. You'll download it directly from a web link like this:

```
bashCopy code
sudo yum install -y https://s3.amazonaws.com/streaming-data-agent/aws-
kinesis-agent-latest.amzn1.noarch.rpm
```

Or, if you like using GitHub, here's how to do it:

- Grab the agent from the awslabs/amazon-kinesis-agent page on GitHub.
- Install it with the following command:

```
sudo ./setup --install
```

Get the Agent Ready and Running   Now, you need to tell the agent what to do. There's a file you'll need to edit called /etc/aws-kinesis/agent.json. In this file, you'll set two main things:

- filepattern: This is how the agent knows which files to look at.
- kinesisstream: This is where you tell it which stream to send data to.

Kinesis Agent is smart enough to notice when you have new files, as long as they don't all pop up in the same second.

To start the agent, you can do it manually each time with:

```
sudo service aws-kinesis-agent start
```

Or, to make sure it starts whenever your computer does, you can set it up like this:

```
sudo chkconfig aws-kinesis-agent on
```

Once it's running, Kinesis Agent works quietly in the background, keeping an eye on the files you told it to and sending new data to your stream.

Using the AWS SDK for Java to Transmit Data to a Kinesis Stream

Leveraging the AWS SDK for Java presents a reliable method for pushing data to an Amazon Kinesis stream. The SDK provides two distinct operations to facilitate adding data to a stream: PutRecords, for batch data transmission, and PutRecord, for individual data record transmission.

PutRecords: Batch Data Transmission

The `PutRecords` operation permits the simultaneous transmission of multiple data records in a singular HTTP request. This approach is conducive to achieving higher data throughput to a Kinesis data stream.

The `PutRecords` operation is capable of handling up to 500 records per request, each record up to 1 MB in size, with the cumulative request size capped at 5 MB, partition keys inclusive.

Here is a conceptual demonstration of how you might use the `PutRecords` API in Java:

1. Initialize the Kinesis client builder with the appropriate regional settings and authentication credentials.

2. Construct a `PutRecordsRequest` and populate it with a list of `PutRecords RequestEntry` objects, each representing a data record.

3. Submit the `PutRecordsRequest` to the Kinesis stream and await the response to confirm successful data submission.

PutRecord: Individual Data Record Transmission

Compared to `PutRecords`, the `PutRecord` operation is designed to dispatch a single data record per HTTP request. Employing this operation, each data record is appended to the stream with a unique sequence number, an identifier assigned by Kinesis Data Streams. While the `PutRecord` operation is available, the use of `PutRecords` is generally advocated for efficiency, given its capacity for batch processing. Data within the stream is categorized using a partition key, which also determines the shard assignment within the stream.

The utilization of the aforementioned operations within the AWS SDK for Java streamlines the process of data integration into Kinesis streams, ensuring a seamless and efficient data management workflow.

Writing to Kinesis Data Streams Using Third-Party Options

If you're looking to funnel data into Kinesis Data Streams, you have several nifty third-party tools at your disposal that play well with Kinesis:

- **Apache Flink:** This is more than just a tool; it's a full-on framework for processing data streams, whether they're constantly flowing or just a finite batch. To connect it with Kinesis Data Streams, there's a specific connector you can use.

- **Fluentd:** Imagine a Swiss Army knife for log management—that's Fluentd. It helps you bring your logging game to the next level and can work in tandem with Kinesis to streamline data processing.

- **Debezium:** If you're into keeping tabs on your databases and reacting to every little change, Debezium is your go-to. It's all about capturing those changes, and you can pipe them straight into Kinesis Data Streams.

- **Oracle GoldenGate:** Need to shuffle data from one database to another? Oracle Golden-Gate is like a data-moving concierge that can also funnel your data right into Kinesis.

- **Kafka Connect:** Kafka's great at shuttling messages around, and Kafka Connect bridges the gap to Kinesis, making data transfer a breeze.

- **Adobe Experience Platform:** For those who are serious about enhacing the customer experience, Adobe's platform lets you centralize customer data and use it to create personalized experiences. And yes, it can send data to Kinesis, too.

- **Striim:** This platform is like a data relay race—it collects, transforms, analyzes, and sends data off in real time. It's another great way to get your data streaming smoothly into Kinesis.

- **Amazon Pinpoint:** Not just for marketing, Amazon Pinpoint can pinpoint (pun intended) the right data and send it over to Kinesis for further action.

Each of these tools has its own way of connecting to Kinesis Data Streams, so you'll want to check out the specific guides on how to set them up. Whether you're looking to capture changes as they happen, shuffle data between systems, or just make your logs more manageable, there's a solution that can help you get your data where it needs to go.

Reading Data from Kinesis Data Streams

Reading data from Amazon Kinesis Data Streams is a fundamental aspect of building streaming applications on AWS. The following sections provide an overview of the various ways to read data.

Data Viewer in the Kinesis Console

You can use the Data Viewer feature in the Kinesis console to quickly inspect the data in your stream. This is useful for debugging or verifying data ingestion. However, this method is not meant for processing large amounts of data or for use in production environments due to its limitations in throughput and the manual nature of the operation.

Querying Data Streams in the Kinesis Console

The Kinesis console provides a querying feature that allows you to run simple SQL-like queries against the stream. This is good for quick tests and inspections, but, similar to the Data Viewer, it's not designed for processing high volumes of data or complex queries.

Using AWS Lambda

Lambda functions can be set up to process Kinesis data streams. Here's an example of how to set up a Lambda function to process records from a Kinesis stream in Node.js:

```
exports.handler = async (event, context) => {
event.Records.forEach(record => {
 const payload =Buffer.from(record.kinesis.data,'base64').toString('ascii');
 console.log('Decoded payload:', payload);
});
return `Successfully processed ${event.Records.length} records.`;
};
```

Be mindful of the Lambda timeout and concurrency limits, and ensure that the batch size and window are configured properly to handle your stream's throughput.

Using Managed Service for Apache Flink

Amazon Kinesis Data Analytics is the easiest way to process data streams with Apache Flink. You write your stream processing applications in SQL or Java, and Kinesis Data Analytics takes care of everything required to run your queries continuously and automatically scales to match the volume and throughput of your incoming data.

Using Amazon Data Firehose

Amazon Data Firehose allows you to deliver data streams to destinations such as S3, Redshift, OpenSearch, and Splunk. The setup is straightforward and managed by AWS, so there is no need for custom coding or resource management. However, Firehose has throughput limits and buffering, which can introduce latency.

Using the Kinesis Client Library

The Kinesis Client Library (KCL) is a Java-based library provided by AWS to simplify the process of consuming and processing data from Kinesis data streams. The KCL handles complex issues such as fault tolerance, scaling in or out, distributing stream records among multiple consumers (workers), coordinating record processing, and checkpointing. By checkpointing, we mean that the KCL tracks the progress of record processing so that it can resume from the last point in case of failures.

The Relationship Between KCL and KPL

The Kinesis Producer Library (KPL) is a complementary library to KCL but for the opposite side of the data stream flow. While KCL is used for consuming data from Kinesis data streams, KPL is used for efficient and reliable production of data records to the stream. KPL allows for batching, retrying, and monitoring capabilities, enhancing the ability to publish data to Kinesis data streams at high throughput and with low latency. KPL aggregates records to increase throughput and manages the low-level details of sending data to Kinesis data streams.

Here's a snippet for a KCL 2.x consumer in Java:

```java
public class RecordProcessor implements ShardRecordProcessor {
    public void processRecords(ProcessRecordsInput processRecordsInput) {
        for (KinesisClientRecord record : processRecordsInput.records()) {
            String data = StandardCharsets.UTF_8.decode(record.data())
.toString();
            System.out.println(data);
        }
    }
    // Implement other interface methods...
}
```

Processing Multiple Data Streams with KCL 2.x for Java

KCL 2.x supports processing multiple Kinesis data streams within the same application. Each stream will have its own set of resources, and you can run multiple KCL applications within the same JVM process. Here's how you would configure a KCL application for processing multiple streams:

```
// For Stream 1
KinesisClientLibConfiguration kclConfig1 = new KinesisClientLibConfiguration(
        "applicationName1",
        "streamName1",
        credentialsProvider,
        workerId)
        .withInitialPositionInStream(InitialPositionInStream.TRIM_HORIZON);

// For Stream 2
KinesisClientLibConfiguration kclConfig2 = new KinesisClientLibConfiguration(
        "applicationName2",
        "streamName2",
        credentialsProvider,
        workerId)
        .withInitialPositionInStream(InitialPositionInStream.TRIM_HORIZON);

Worker worker1 = new Worker.Builder()
        .recordProcessorFactory(new RecordProcessorFactory())
        .config(kclConfig1)
        .build();

Worker worker2 = new Worker.Builder()
        .recordProcessorFactory(new RecordProcessorFactory())
        .config(kclConfig2)
        .build();

// Start workers for each stream in their own thread
new Thread(worker1).start();
new Thread(worker2).start();
```

Each application maintains its own checkpoints and operates independently, allowing for the concurrent processing of different streams.

Lease Tables

Lease tables are DynamoDB tables used by the KCL to track the assignment of shards to workers. They help synchronize the state across multiple instances of an application. Each record in a lease table represents a lease on a shard within the data stream. The lease owner, typically a KCL worker, is responsible for processing the records from that shard.

Tracking Processed Shards

You can use a lease table to track the shards processed by the KCL consumer application and thus KCL to achieve fault tolerance and load balancing. Here's what happens under the hood:

- **Lease acquisition:** When a KCL application starts, it attempts to acquire leases for the shards it will process.

- **Lease stealing:** In a multi-worker setup, if some workers are overloaded while others are idle, the KCL may redistribute the leases so the load is evenly balanced.

- **Lease renewal:** Each worker continuously renews its leases to prevent them from expiring and being taken over by other workers.

- **Lease checkpointing:** After successfully processing a batch of records, the worker check-points its progress by writing the sequence number of the last record processed into the lease table.

The KCL consumer application uses this lease information to resume processing from the last checkpointed position in case of a restart or failure. This ensures that no data is lost and the processing is exactly once or at least once, based on how you handle the checkpointing logic.

Here's how you might interact with the lease table in your application:

```
public class RecordProcessor implements ShardRecordProcessor {
    private Checkpointer checkpointer;

    @Override
    public void initialize(InitializationInput initializationInput) {
        checkpointer = initializationInput.checkpointer();
    }

    public void processRecords(ProcessRecordsInput processRecordsInput) {
        for (KinesisClientRecord record : processRecordsInput.records()) {
            String data = StandardCharsets.UTF_8.decode(record.data())
.toString();
            // Process record logic here
        }
        try {
            // Checkpoint once all records are processed
            checkpointer.checkpoint();
        }
```

Custom Consumers and Enhanced Fan-Out

Two more considerations are custom consumer applications and enhanced fan-out:

- **Developing custom consumers:** You can build your own consumer applications using the AWS SDK. This allows for shared throughput across multiple consumers but is subject to the stream's read limits.

- **Enhanced fan-out:** Enhanced fan-out is a key concept and often discussed during certification exam questions on streaming data involving Kinesis. This feature provides dedicated throughput to consumers by allowing them to receive records from a stream with lower latency and at a higher rate than standard consumers. When using KCL 2.x, you can create enhanced fan-out consumers, which offer improved performance.

```
// Example of creating an Enhanced Fan-Out consumer with KCL
ConsumerConfig consumerConfig = new ConsumerConfig.Builder()
        .streamName(streamName)
        .applicationName(applicationName)
        .enhancedFanOut()
        .build();
```

Limitations

There are several limitations to be aware of:

- Each method has its throughput limits, and it is important to understand these when architecting your solution.

- Lambda has payload size limits and execution duration limits, which may require additional batching logic.

- For the KCL, careful consideration must be given to worker distribution and check-pointing to avoid data loss.

Amazon Data Firehose

Processing data in a stream is achieved using Amazon Kinesis Data Streams and AWS Lambda in combination; however, often there is a need to persist the data for either long-term storage or further analysis. While Amazon Kinesis Data Streams was the first service that was built, the team soon realized that one of the most popular use cases for a streaming application was to capture data being emitted from these devices in real time and buffer it before storing it for longer-term analysis. Amazon, with its usual customer obsession, decided to build Amazon Data Firehose (previously known as Amazon Kinesis Data Firehose), a fully managed service, to allow users to deliver streaming data to a number of destinations, including Amazon S3, Amazon Redshift, Amazon OpenSearch Service, and a number of partner services like Coralogix, Datadog, Dynatrace, Elastic, custom destinations using an HTTP endpoint, Honeycomb, LogicMonitor, Logz.io, MongoDB Cloud, New Relic, Snowflake, Splunk, and Sumo Logic.

Amazon Data Firehose allows you to create a delivery stream, which can have the data written to it by various producers (max record length of 1,000 KB), and buffer the data (configurable parameter in MB or seconds) before delivering it to a target destination.

One of the most popular use cases is customers transforming the data arriving to a Data Firehose stream by fanning the transformed and raw data to different destinations (see Figure 1.12).

FIGURE 1.12   Data flow—S3 destination

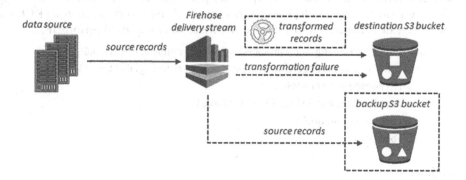

The process of streaming data varies depending on the destination due to the inherent characteristics and requirements of the target systems. For instance, when the target is an OpenSearch cluster, the data is directly streamed to the cluster, as it is designed to handle real-time data ingestion. However, in the case of Redshift, which is a data warehousing solution optimized for analytical workloads, the data is first delivered to an S3 bucket, and then a Copy command is executed to transfer the data from the S3 bucket to Amazon Redshift in a more efficient and optimized manner (refer to Figure 1.13 and Figure 1.14). This approach allows for better management and processing of large volumes of data before loading it into Redshift.

FIGURE 1.13   Amazon Redshift as a destination for Data Firehose

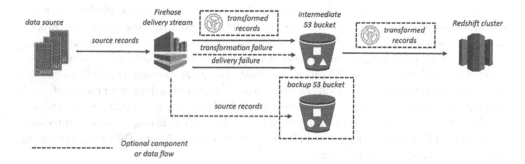

FIGURE 1.14   Amazon OpenSearch as a destination for Data Firehose

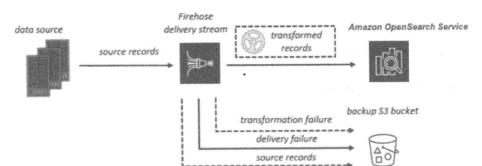

When the destination is Splunk, streaming data is delivered to Splunk but can also option-ally be backed to S3 (see Figure 1.15).

FIGURE 1.15   Splunk as a destination for Data Firehose

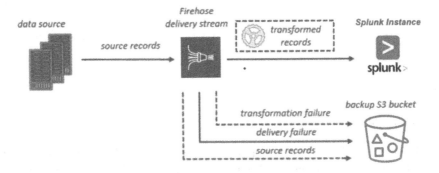

While Amazon Data Firehose supports multiple destinations, it also provides a number of different native sources on the platform that can write to the AWS Data Firehose (see Figure 1.16). Using the Kinesis API, you can also build connectors for new sources as well.

The native sources are as follows:

- **Kinesis Data Streams**
  - If your source Kinesis data stream has aggregation configured, Amazon Data Fire-hose will de-aggregate the records before delivering them to a destination.
  - When Kinesis Data Streams is used as a source for Data Firehose, the putRecord() and putRecordBatch() operations are disabled. If you want to use putRecord() or putRecordBatch(), you can use them on the Kinesis data stream itself.
  - Amazon Data Firehose starts reading records from the *latest* position of your Kinesis stream, and more than one Data Firehose delivery stream can read from the same Kinesis stream.

FIGURE 1.16   Native sources (console options) for Amazon Data Firehose

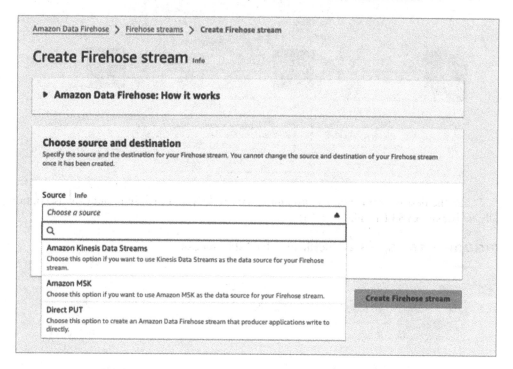

- **Amazon MSK**

    - Amazon Data Firehose also supports Amazon MSK as a data source. You can choose between MSK-provisioned and MSK-serverless clusters. With Amazon Data Firehose, you can effortlessly extract data from a chosen Amazon MSK cluster and topic, and then transfer it to a designated S3 destination.
        - Kinesis Agent
        - AWS SDK
        - CloudWatch Logs
        - CloudWatch Events
        - AWS IoT

Data Transformation with Amazon Data Firehose

While capturing data is critical, you will often need to perform data transformations for data streaming at high velocity. You can enable data transformation with Amazon Data Firehose. When you turn on data transformation in Firehose, it stores incoming data temporarily. The amount of data it can store before processing ranges from 0.2 MB to 3 MB. By default, it aims to gather 1 MB of data for processing for most destinations, but for Splunk and Snowflake, this default is smaller, at 256 KB. The time Firehose waits before sending data for processing ranges from 0 to 900 seconds, with a default of 60 seconds for most destinations. Snowflake is an exception, with a default wait time of 30 seconds.

To change these settings, use the `ProcessingConfiguration` option in the `CreateDeliveryStream` or `UpdateDestination` API, specifying the desired buffer size and time interval. Firehose then sends the data in batches to a Lambda function for processing. Once the data is processed, Firehose sends it to the final destination either when it accumulates enough data to meet the buffer size or when the specified time interval passes, whichever occurs first.

You can also use pre-built Lambda blueprints with Amazon Data Firehose. Amazon Data Firehose provides a number Lambda blueprints that you can use for the most common transformations, including but not limited to:

- **Process records sent to Amazon Data Firehose stream (Node.js, Python):** This blueprint shows a basic example of how to process data in your Firehose data stream using AWS Lambda.

- **Process CloudWatch logs sent to Firehose:** This blueprint is deprecated and will not appear in the exam.

- **Convert Amazon Data Firehose stream records in syslog format to JSON (Node.js):** This blueprint shows how you can convert input records in RFC3164 Syslog format to JSON.

AWS Serverless Application Repository contains a number of different blueprints you can use to simplify processing with Amazon Data Firehose. To view a list of available blueprints, visit `https://serverlessrepo.aws.amazon.com/applications` and search for "Firehose."

Converting Input Record Formats in Amazon Kinesis

One of the most common analytical requirements is to transpose data from row-based to columnar format to enhance query performance. Parquet and ORC are widely favored by users for this purpose due to their efficient data compression and superior analytical query execution. Amazon Data Firehose facilitates this transformation of JSON data into either Parquet or ORC formats. To accomplish the format conversion, Amazon Data Firehose requires the following three key components:

- **Deserializer:** This is employed to interpret the JSON structure of your incoming data. There are two options available for deserialization:
  - Apache Hive JSON SerDe
  - OpenX JSON SerDe

- **Schema definition:** To understand and map your data accurately, a schema is essential. AWS Glue can be utilized to automatically deduce a schema from your data and catalog it within the AWS Glue Data Catalog. Amazon Data Firehose will then consult this schema for data interpretation, which can also be applied across other AWS services that are schema-compatible.

- **Serializer:** For the final transformation into columnar storage, you can employ either ORC SerDe or Parquet SerDe.

By configuring these elements in Amazon Data Firehose, you can streamline your data for more effective analysis.

 If you enable record format conversion, you can't set your Amazon Data Firehose destination to be Amazon OpenSearch Service, Amazon Redshift, or Splunk. With format conversion enabled, Amazon S3 is the only destination that you can use for your Firehose stream.

Amazon Managed Service for Apache Flink

Now we'll examine Amazon Managed Service for Apache Flink.

What Is Apache Flink?

Apache Flink is an open-source stream processing framework for distributed, high-performing, always-available, and accurate data streaming applications. It is one of the most widely adopted open-source services and is used by companies like Netflix, Uber, Alibaba, Pinteret, and X (formerly Twitter).

Apache Flink stands out in the world of data processing for several compelling reasons.

It provides a suite of expressive APIs, including SQL API, Table API, DataStream API, and the ability to create stateful functions, offering flexibility and a rich set of functionalities for developers.

In terms of processing guarantees, Flink assures exactly-once state consistency, crucial for accurate data processing, and supports event-time processing and late data handling, enabling robust stream processing applications.

Its scale-out architecture allows it to adapt easily to the desired throughput, making it an ideal choice for applications that need to scale dynamically. This architecture can also support terabytes of state, facilitating the handling of large-scale data processing tasks.

Apache Flink boasts a vibrant open-source community that contributes to its continuous improvement and a broad set of connectors, enabling Flink to integrate with a wide variety of data systems, enhancing its interoperability and ease of use in diverse environments.

What Is Amazon Managed Service for Apache Flink?

Despite its robust capabilities in handling large-scale data processing, managing a Flink deployment introduces several complexities. These include ensuring high availability, managing consistent stateful computations across clusters, and scaling to meet fluctuating demands, all of which require substantial operational expertise and infrastructure management. Customers have often asked for an out-of-the-box offering of Apache Flink that is faster and easier to deploy, fully managed, and offers a pay-as-you-go model. To alleviate these challenges, Amazon introduced a managed Flink service known as Amazon Managed Service for Apache Flink (Managed Apache Flink).

This managed service abstracts away the operational toil, enabling developers to focus on application logic rather than infrastructure management. Consumers benefit from this offering through simplified operations, automatic scaling, adaptive resource provisioning, and a pay-as-you-go pricing model, which collectively lower the barrier to entry for implementing real-time analytics and complex event processing with Flink. It allows users to analyze streaming data interactively using managed Apache Zeppelin notebooks with Amazon Managed Service for Apache Flink Studio. You can use Amazon Managed Service for Apache Flink to build applications in SQL, Java, Python, or Scala, to perform joins, filters, and aggregations over time windows, and more.

Amazon Managed Service for Apache Flink doesn't directly handle data management itself. Instead, it focuses on processing the streaming data you provide. However, there are multiple ways to get data into an Apache Flink application running on Amazon Managed Service for Apache Flink:

- **AWS services:** You can configure your application to read data from various AWS services that act as sources for your streaming data. Some examples include Kinesis Data Streams, SQS, DynamoDB Streams, and MSK.

- **External sources:** You can also set up your application to receive data from external sources outside of AWS. This could involve messaging systems like Kafka or custom connectors built specifically for your data source.

How Does It Work?

Figure 1.17 shows how Amazon Managed Service for Apache Flink works.

FIGURE 1.17   An overview of Amazon Managed Service for Apache Flink

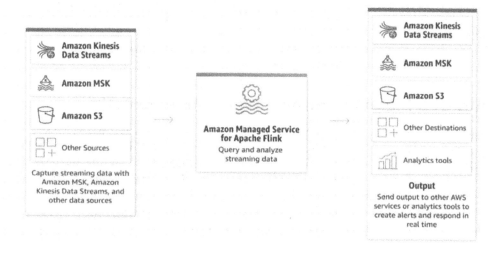

Integrations of Amazon Managed Service for Apache Flink

Amazon Managed Service for Apache Flink provides a number of connectors to a variety of sources, including but not limited to:

- Amazon Kinesis Data Stream
- Amazon Managed Streaming for Apache Kafka
- Rabbit MQ
- Apache Kafka
- Flink connectors

Destinations of the Managed Flink service (also known as sinks) include but are not limited to:

- Amazon Kinesis data streams
- Amazon Managed Streaming for Apache Kafka
- Amazon Daga Firehose
- Amazon S3
- Amazon DynamoDB
- RabbitMQ
- Apache Cassandra
- Elasticsearch

Pricing Model

Amazon Managed Service for Apache Flink has no upfront costs and there are no resources to provision. The service is priced using KPUs (Kinesis Processing Units). Each KPU is a virtual bundle of 1 vCPU compute capacity and 4 GB of memory. The usage of Managed Flink is an hourly billing rate based on the number of KPUs used to run the application, and the service automatically scales the number of KPUs required by your stream processing application.

For information about Managed Flink pricing, visit `https://aws.amazon.com/ managed-service-apache-flink/pricing/?`.

Amazon Managed Streaming for Apache Kafka

Amazon Managed Streaming for Apache Kafka, commonly known as Amazon MSK, is a fully managed service that emerged to simplify the provisioning and maintenance of Apache Kafka clusters in the cloud. Apache Kafka, originally developed by LinkedIn and later open-sourced as part of the Apache Software Foundation, is a distributed streaming platform designed to handle high volumes of data, enabling real-time data processing.

Recognizing the growing need for scalable data streaming solutions, Amazon Web Services incorporated Kafka into its robust ecosystem, offering a seamless experience that takes care of the underlying infrastructure management. Amazon MSK provides the same Kafka APIs that developers are familiar with, but without the overhead of cluster operations, allowing them to focus on building applications that efficiently handle data streams.

Some of the key benefits of Amazon MSK include:

- **Security, high availability, and accessibility:** Amazon Managed Streaming for Apache Kafka (Amazon MSK) transforms the open-source Apache Kafka into a robust, enterprise-grade streaming solution by providing comprehensive management capabilities and enhanced features. At its core, MSK handles all infrastructure management tasks, including automated cluster deployment, zero-downtime patching, and resource allocation, eliminating the operational burden from organizations. The service implements a sophisticated security architecture, featuring VPC isolation, AWS IAM integration, SASL/SCRAM authentication, and end-to-end encryption using AWS KMS and TLS 1.2. High availability is ensured through a multi-AZ architecture with automatic data replication, fault tolerance mechanisms, and disaster recovery options, including cross-region replication and point-in-time recovery. MSK seamlessly integrates with the broader AWS ecosystem, supporting various AWS services like Lambda, S3, and Kinesis, while maintaining compatibility with existing Kafka clients and tools. The service offers extensive monitoring and management capabilities through CloudWatch integration, custom metrics, and comprehensive APIs. Organizations benefit from flexible scaling options, including dynamic broker scaling and storage auto-scaling, along with cost optimization features such as pay-as-you-go pricing and resource optimization recommendations. MSK addresses compliance requirements through various certifications (SOC, PCI, HIPAA) and provides robust audit logging via CloudTrail. Performance optimization is achieved through configurable throughput limits, storage options, and continuous monitoring. The service includes 24/7 AWS enterprise support, proactive maintenance, and regular security updates, making it an ideal choice for organizations seeking to leverage Kafka's capabilities without the operational overhead. This comprehensive solution particularly benefits organizations requiring enterprise-grade streaming capabilities, strict security controls, high availability, and efficient scaling while significantly reducing the total cost of ownership and accelerating time-to-market for streaming applications. By bridging the gap between open-source Kafka and enterprise requirements, MSK enables organizations to focus on building applications and processing data streams rather than managing infrastructure, making it a valuable solution for businesses of all sizes.

- **Best practices:** Amazon MSK embeds industry best practices into its core design philosophy, automatically implementing optimal configurations and operational standards without requiring deep Apache Kafka expertise. The service intelligently sets default configurations based on proven production patterns, including appropriate partition counts, replication factors, and broker settings that ensure optimal performance and reliability. Through automation, MSK handles critical operational tasks such as broker placement across availability zones, network configuration, security group setup, and resource allocation according to established best practices. The service automatically implements crucial security measures, including encryption at rest and in transit, secure authentication methods, and proper network isolation. Performance optimization is built into the platform through automated monitoring, smart scaling decisions, and proactive maintenance scheduling. MSK's automated backup systems, failure detection, and recovery processes follow disaster recovery best practices, ensuring data durability and system availability. The service automatically manages cluster health through continuous monitoring and self-healing capabilities, applying patches and updates during maintenance windows that minimize impact on production workloads. Resource provisioning follows efficient sizing guidelines, with built-in alerts and recommendations when adjustments are needed. Additionally, MSK integrates logging, monitoring, and alerting best practices through its CloudWatch integration, providing meaningful metrics and actionable insights by default. These automated best practices extend to compliance and security configurations, ensuring that clusters meet regulatory requirements and security standards from the moment they're deployed. By embedding these best practices into the service's DNA, Amazon MSK significantly reduces the risk of misconfigurations, performance issues, and security vulnerabilities that often plague self-managed Kafka deployments, allowing organizations to focus on their business objectives rather than operational complexities.

- **Prioritize building applications:** Amazon MSK liberates developers from the complex, time-consuming tasks of managing Apache Kafka infrastructure by automating cluster provisioning, scaling, maintenance, and security configurations. This automation encompasses critical operational aspects like broker management, monitoring, patching, and backup processes, allowing development teams to concentrate their energy on building and enhancing their streaming applications rather than wrestling with infrastructure concerns. Moreover, the service's seamless integration with familiar AWS tools and services, combined with its support for standard Kafka APIs and tools, enables developers to maintain their existing workflows while benefiting from enterprise-grade reliability and security features without the associated operational overhead.

- **Eliminate cluster management:** MSK Serverless simplifies operations by removing the need for managing capacity, scaling, and partitioning.

Use Cases for Amazon MSK

Amazon MSK is essentially a managed Kafka offering and hence supports the use cases that are sweet spot for streaming services and applications. Customers typically use MSK for the following use cases. This is important to understand from an exam perspective so that you can align the right service to the right use case.

- Conducting analysis on web activity and logs as events occur.
- Capturing and storing sequences of events for transactional data.
- Facilitating communication between disconnected services through messages.
- Providing a flexible architecture by allowing services to operate independently.
- Enabling continuous data transformation and movement between systems.
- Gathering and synthesizing performance metrics and logs for systems.

Apache Kafka High-Level Architecture

Apache Kafka is structured as a distributed system for handling streaming data. At its core, data producers send records to the Kafka cluster, which consists of brokers responsible for maintaining published data. Each broker can act as a leader or follower in a process known as *replication*, ensuring high availability and fault tolerance. Data consumers then pull records from the brokers as needed. Underneath this architecture, Apache Kafka relies on Zookeeper for broker coordination and cluster management. This robust framework is designed to handle high-volume data streams in real time, making Kafka a vital component for applications that require reliable, fast, and scalable messaging solutions.

Figure 1.18 shows the Apache Kafka architecture at a high level.

FIGURE 1.18   Apache Kafka architecture

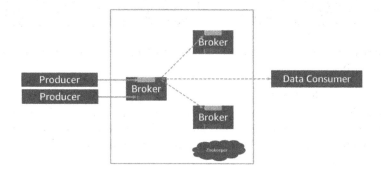

Apache Kafka—Anatomy of a Write

In the distributed architecture of Apache Kafka, data streaming is managed efficiently through the division of topics into multiple partitions. Each partition functions as an ordered, immutable sequence of records that are continually appended. For example, imagine a Kafka topic designated for tracking user activity on a website, segmented into three distinct partitions. Producers, which can be thought of as publishers, send records of data, such as user clicks or page views, to these partitions. The records are assigned to partitions typically based on certain criteria like a key value or round-robin assignment when no key is present.

Figure 1.19 shows a scenario where a user activity topic has three partitions. A producer responsible for user click events might send a new record to partition 1, which already contains records labeled with incremental offset numbers 0 through 5, indicating the order of arrival. If a second click event is sent without specifying a key, it may be assigned to partition 2 following the default partitioning logic, adding to the sequence of records in that partition. As new data flows in, Kafka maintains the order by appending each new piece of information to the end of the chosen partition, preserving the sequence in which events are produced. This allows consumer applications to process streams of data sequentially, thereby ensuring a coherent data history is maintained.

FIGURE 1.19   The anatomy of a Kafka write

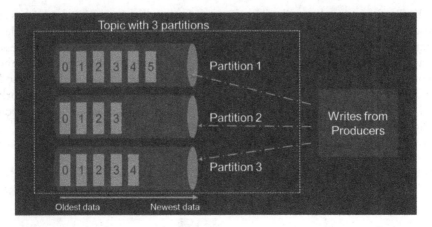

There are two main approaches for writing data to Amazon Managed Streaming for Apache Kafka (MSK):

- Using a producer application:
  - This method involves developing a producer application specifically designed to send data to your MSK cluster. You can write this application in any programming language with Kafka client libraries available. Popular choices include Java, Python, and Go.
  - The producer application will need to connect to your MSK cluster using the bootstrap servers and utilizing the Kafka Producer API to publish messages to your desired topics.
- Using streaming services:
  - AWS offers several services that can act as data sources and automatically push data into your MSK cluster. Here are a couple of options:
    - **Amazon Data Firehose:** This service allows you to configure data delivery from various sources like S3 buckets, CloudWatch logs, or even databases directly to your MSK cluster.
    - **Lambda functions:** You can develop Lambda functions that process data and then publish it to your MSK topics using the Kafka Producer library within the Lambda environment.

Apache Kafka—Anatomy of a Read

In the Apache Kafka ecosystem, the process of reading data is just as structured and well-organized as the process of writing it. To read the data efficiently, we have the concept of a consumer group. A consumer group is a powerful concept that enables scalable and fault-tolerant consumption of messages from Kafka topics. It consists of one or more consumer instances working together to process data from one or more topics (see Figure 1.20). This group structure allows for parallel processing, as multiple consumers can simultaneously read from different partitions of the same topic, significantly increasing throughput. Kafka automatically balances partitions across all consumers in a group, ensuring efficient load distribution. If a consumer fails, its partitions are reassigned to other active group members, maintaining processing continuity. Each consumer group manages its own offset in each partition it consumes, allowing different groups to process the same data at varying rates. This design supports scalability, as adding more consumers to a group can increase processing capacity up to the number of partitions in the topic.

Kafka guarantees at-least-once delivery to a consumer group unless the group's offset is explicitly modified. The system employs a group coordinator to manage membership, handle joins and leaves, and trigger rebalances when necessary. Each group is identified by a unique group.id, and multiple groups can independently read from the same topic, each maintaining its own offset. This flexible and robust architecture makes consumer groups essential for building scalable and resilient stream processing applications with Kafka.

In Figure 1.20, for example, a topic is divided into three partitions that correspond to different geographical regions' sales data. In this setup, we have three consumers in a consumer group, each tasked with consuming data from one partition. The consumer aligned with partition 1 will read sales records starting from the earliest unread message, marked by its next offset, say 0. As it reads and processes records, it advances to the next, ensuring that no data is missed and each record is processed once and only once by any consumer in the group.

Consumer 2, associated with partition 2, operates in tandem, perhaps beginning its read sequence from offset 1, if it has previously consumed the record at offset 0. Similarly, consumer 3 starts from its respective offset in partition 3. The consumers work independently and in parallel, yet cohesively, within the boundaries of their partitions. This parallel processing allows Kafka to manage vast streams of data, providing consumers with the ability to process data sequentially and in real time, ensuring that every message is acted upon swiftly, a key attribute for applications like live-tracking systems or real-time analytics.

Let's understand the concept of a consumer group with a simple everyday example. Imagine a bustling café with a long queue of orders. A consumer group is like a team of baristas, where each member is responsible for making specific types of drinks to ensure that all orders are fulfilled quickly and no two baristas make the same drink at the same time. In Kafka, each barista represents a consumer, and each type of drink corresponds to a partition within the topic. The consumer group ensures that all orders (messages) are processed, and by dividing the work (partitions) among the team members (consumers), it increases the speed and efficiency of order (message) processing.

Consumer groups are vital for Kafka's scalability, allowing multiple consumers to read in parallel and thereby handle a high volume of data. Additionally, if a consumer fails, Kafka can reassign the partitions to other consumers in the group, maintaining continuous processing without data loss. This mechanism is essential for distributed systems that require fault tolerance and scalability.

Figure 1.20 illustrates the anatomy of a Kafka read.

FIGURE 1.20 The anatomy of a Kafka read

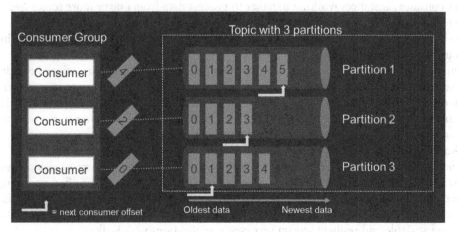

There are three different ways you can read data from Amazon Managed Streaming for Apache Kafka (MSK) topics:

- Using a consumer application:
  - This is the most common approach. You develop a consumer application specifically designed to read data from your MSK cluster. This application can be written in any programming language with Kafka client libraries available (e.g., Java, Python, etc.).
  - The consumer application connects to your MSK cluster using the bootstrap servers and utilizes the Kafka Consumer API to subscribe to specific topics.
  - Once subscribed, the consumer will receive a stream of messages from the chosen topics and process them as needed.
- Using streaming services: Similar to writing data, AWS provides services that can consume data from MSK and deliver it to other destinations for further processing or storage.
  - **Kinesis Data Streams:** You can configure Kinesis Data Streams to act as a consumer for your MSK topics. The data will be continuously streamed from MSK to Kinesis, where you can then process it using Kinesis applications or deliver it to other AWS services like S3 or Redshift.
  - **Amazon EMR:** If you're using Amazon EMR for big data processing, you can configure your EMR cluster to directly read data from MSK topics. This allows you to leverage EMR's capabilities like Spark or Hadoop to analyze the streaming data.
  - **AWS Lambda:** You can develop Lambda functions that subscribe to MSK topics and trigger upon receiving new messages. This allows for serverless processing of the streaming data within the Lambda environment.

- Monitoring tools:
  - Amazon CloudWatch provides integration with MSK, allowing you to monitor the health and performance of your cluster. While not directly reading data for processing, CloudWatch can display message throughput and consumer lag for each topic, helping you understand data flow within your MSK cluster.

Amazon MSK—Operating Modes and Key Features

Amazon MSK, a fully managed Apache Kafka service, offers two distinct deployment options to meet varying operational requirements: MSK Provisioned and MSK Serverless.

MSK Provisioned provides tiered storage for cost-effective scalability, allowing users to manage their Kafka clusters with greater control. This option is ideal for workloads with consistent and predictable demand, where manual environment control is preferred.

MSK Serverless automatically handles upgrades and partition rebalancing, significantly reducing management overhead. It introduces an adaptable model where the cluster scales automatically with application usage, making it suitable for unpredictable or variable workloads. MSK Serverless also features Graviton Support, enhancing both performance and cost efficiency.

Both options prioritize security, ensuring data protection across the platform. MSK Connect enables automatic scaling of Kafka clusters to meet demand, while providing comprehensive monitoring tools for system health and performance tracking.

The service integrates seamlessly with other AWS services, enhancing data workflows and analytics capabilities. It supports real-time analytics, enabling instant insights from streaming data.

Recent enhancements to Amazon MSK include:

- **Managed replication**: Amazon MSK streamlines data synchronization across different clusters or regions.
- **Glue schema registry integration**: Amazon MSK manages schema definition and versioning, improving data interaction capabilities.
- **Managed data delivery to Amazon S3**: Amazon MSK simplifies the process of storing large volumes of data, offering durable and cost-effective storage solutions.

MSK Serverless offers several unique advantages:

- Minimal base cost with pay-as-you-go pricing, making it cost-effective for smaller or sporadic workloads
- Automatic data replication at no additional charge, ensuring high availability without added complexity or cost
- Automatic partition placement and rebalancing, reducing operational overhead
- Compatibility with open-source Apache Kafka, maintaining expected features and performance
- Automatic distribution of resources across multiple Availability Zones, ensuring high availability without manual intervention

MSK Serverless is ideal for scenarios prioritizing ease of use, cost-effectiveness, and automatic scaling. It's particularly beneficial for users new to Kafka or with limited operational resources. MSK Provisioned, conversely, is better suited for environments requiring more manual control over consistent, predictable workloads.

Amazon MSK—Managed Replication

Amazon MSK's Managed Replication feature is like a bridge that connects your data across the world. Imagine you have a cluster of data in North Virginia, and you want to make sure that the same data can be accessed quickly and efficiently by your team in Ireland. Managed Replication does just that—it seamlessly duplicates your data from one Amazon MSK cluster to others across different regions (see Figure 1.21). This means your teams can write data in their local region and still share it globally without the wait, ensuring everyone has access to the same information at the same speed. It's not just about convenience; it's about building a system that's resilient, that can keep running smoothly even if one part faces an outage, and that respects the rules of data storage across borders.

FIGURE 1.21   MSK Managed Replication

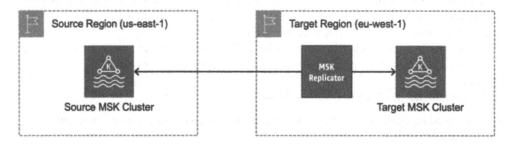

Amazon MSK—As a Long-Term Storage Engine

Consider a financial trading platform that offers algorithmic trading services. These services rely on the ability to make quick decisions based on historical trading patterns. For example, a trading algorithm might need to access historical trade and quote data at sub-second latency to execute a high-frequency trading strategy effectively. This strategy might involve analyzing patterns in the order book over the last few milliseconds to minutes to predict short-term market movements and place trades accordingly.

In such a scenario, accessing historical data with sub-second latency is crucial because even a delay of a few milliseconds could mean a significant financial difference.

In this scenario, you'd use Amazon MSK (Managed Streaming for Kafka) as the backbone of your data pipeline. Amazon MSK provides a managed Kafka service that handles real-time data feeds at a large scale. It offers the horsepower you need to process vast streams of social media events as they happen.

However, real-time analysis is only one part of your business. You also want to offer your clients the ability to look back at historical trends and events. Here's where the traditional setup might hit a snag—storage. Storing huge volumes of data for long periods can be costly and complex to manage, especially when you need to provide similar latencies on long-term stored data as the current dataset.

This is where Amazon MSK's Tiered Storage is helpful. It's a low-cost storage tier that lets you keep a more extended history of Kafka topics without breaking the bank. Amazon MSK Tiered Storage scales virtually unlimitedly, and you therefore don't have to worry about running out of space as your data grows. This storage solution also allows you to reprocess historical data in the exact order it was received, which is critical for accurate trend analysis.

The following are some of the pros and cons of MSK's Tiered storage feature:

Pros:

- Cost-efficient storage for large volumes of data.
- Scalable to handle growth without the need for constant provisioning.
- Retains data in Apache Kafka topics for as long as needed, surpassing the typical Kafka retention periods.
- Enables data reprocessing in the exact original order, which is crucial for consistent data analysis.
- Data transfer remains within the VPC, ensuring security and speed without exposure to the Internet.
- Speeds up partition rebalancing, which can be a performance bottleneck, especially with large datasets.

Cons:

- Could introduce complexity in managing another layer of storage.
- Potentially could have a learning curve for teams not familiar with tiered storage concepts.

Amazon MSK—Handling Scalability

Amazon MSK offers two types of scalability: horizontal and vertical.

Horizontal Scaling   Horizontal scaling involves adding more Kafka brokers to the existing system. When scaling horizontally, you should add brokers in multiples of the Availability Zones (AZs) being used to maintain high availability and fault tolerance. This scaling approach only supports "scaling out" operations, which means that you can add more brokers to handle increased load but not reduce them in this manner. Horizontal scaling also requires you to reassign partitions across the new set of brokers, which can be a manual or automated process depending on your setup.

Vertical Scaling   Vertical scaling is about changing the size or type of the Kafka brokers you're currently using. This could mean upgrading to more powerful instances or switching to a different family of instances that better suits your workload demands.

Vertical scaling allows both "scale-up" and "scale-down" operations, giving you the flexibility to adjust the resources depending on your current needs. A significant advantage of vertical scaling is that it typically doesn't involve any cluster I/O interruption, allowing for a seamless scaling process without downtime.

Both methods are crucial for accommodating the evolving data throughput requirements in a system, and the choice between horizontal and vertical scaling depends on the specific use cases and the growth pattern of the Kafka workload.

Sizing an MSK Cluster

When implementing Amazon MSK for analytics purposes, one of the most frequent challenges customer's face is determining the appropriate cluster size. This decision is crucial, as it directly impacts both performance and cost-effectiveness.

On the one hand, overprovisioning resources by setting up an excessively large cluster from the outset can quickly deplete your budget due to unnecessary expenses. On the other hand, starting with an undersized cluster may seem cost-effective initially but can lead to performance bottlenecks when scaling becomes necessary. It's important to note that expanding a cluster is not an instantaneous process; it requires careful planning and can temporarily affect performance during the scaling operation.

To achieve optimal performance and cost-efficiency, best practices for sizing an Amazon MSK cluster involve meticulous planning and a thorough assessment of resource requirements.

When discussing cluster sizing with our customers, we typically consider the following factors:

- **Partition counts per broker:** Depending on the broker type, you should adhere to the recommended partition limits. For example, a kafka.t3.small broker handles up to 300 partitions, while larger brokers like kafka.m5.4xlarge can handle up to 4,000 partitions. Exceeding these recommendations can lead to issues such as difficulties in updating the cluster configuration or the Apache Kafka version, and potential problems with Cloud-Watch metrics reporting.

- **Determining the number of brokers:** Use tools like the MSK Sizing and Pricing spreadsheet to get an initial estimate for the size of your MSK cluster and its costs. However, these should be treated as starting points, and actual performance should be validated through testing.

- **Throughput optimization for larger instances:** When utilizing larger instance types such as m5.4xlarge or m7g.4xlarge, fine-tuning specific configuration parameters can significantly enhance throughput. Two key parameters to focus on are

  - `num.io.threads`
  - `num.network.threads`

  These parameters are crucial for throughput optimization because they directly control the number of threads dedicated to I/O operations and network communication, respectively. Properly adjusting these values allows the system to more efficiently utilize the increased resources available in larger instances.

Best practices for tuning include the following:

- Prioritize increasing `num.io.threads` first, as this parameter governs the number of threads handling disk I/O operations, which are often the bottleneck in high-throughput scenarios.

- Exercise caution when increasing `num.network.threads`. While it can improve network handling capacity, setting it too high may lead to network congestion and diminishing returns.

- Incrementally adjust these parameters and monitor performance to find the optimal configuration for your specific workload and instance type.

- **Using the latest Kafka AdminClient:** To avoid issues like topic ID mismatches, especially with Kafka 2.8.0 or higher, use an AdminClient version that's up-to-date or ensure that you use the `--bootstrap-servers` flag instead of the deprecated `--zookeeper` flag for administrative tasks.

- **Building high availability:** Set up a Multi-AZ cluster with a replication factor of at least 3, and set `min.insync.replicas` to RF-1 to maintain high availability, especially during updates or when brokers are replaced.

- **Monitoring CPU usage:** Keep the total CPU utilization under 60% to allow for load redistribution when needed. Use CloudWatch alarms to monitor CPU usage, and scale up or out based on these metrics.

- **Broker resource monitoring:** Keep an eye on individual broker loads to ensure even distribution. Use tools like Cruise Control for ongoing load management.

- **Latency monitoring:** Track produce and consume latency, as they can increase with CPU usage.

- **Disk space management:** Set alarms to monitor disk usage, and have strategies in place to prevent running out of space, such as automatic scaling, adjusting retention policies, or deleting unused topics.

- **Log recovery:** Increase `num.recovery.threads.per.data.dir` to expedite log recovery post-unclean shutdowns.

- **Memory monitoring:** Watch the `HeapMemoryAfterGC` metric to avoid memory-related outages, and adjust configurations like `transactional.id.expiration.ms` to manage memory usage effectively.

- **Broker management:** Don't add non-MSK brokers using ZooKeeper commands, as it can lead to data loss and incorrect cluster information.

- **Encryption:** Always ensure that in-transit encryption is enabled for security.

- **Rebalancing partitions:** Use `kafka-reassign-partitions.sh` to move partitions and rebalance them across new brokers when scaling the cluster.

Comparison of Streaming Services

When deciding among AWS's streaming services, it is essential to understand how each service aligns with your specific needs. Kinesis Data Streams stands out for real-time custom data processing, offering robust integrations with many AWS services, making it an excellent choice for those looking for built-in AWS support. Amazon Data Firehose serves well as a streamlined data collection and delivery pipeline, ideal for gathering and preparing data for downstream analytics engines. Amazon Managed Streaming for Kafka (MSK) is the go-to option if your current environment is built around Apache Kafka or you require extensive integration capabilities with a variety of sources and targets. This knowledge can be incredibly useful, particularly when faced with questions about service selection in an exam setting.

Table 1.1 provides a quick comparison between the streaming services. I would highly recommend using this as an aid for your certification preparation.

TABLE 1.1   Comparison of AWS streaming services

Feature	Kinesis Data Streams	Amazon Data Firehose	Amazon MSK (Managed Streaming for Apache Kafka)
Record payload	Up to 1 MB per record	Up to 1 MB per record	Configurable, default max 1 MB
Operation size	1 MB per PutRecord, 5 MB per PutRecords (up to 500 records)	5 MB per Put RecordBatch (up to 500 records)	Configurable, typically up to 1 MB per message
Storage duration	24 hours to 365 days (configurable)	No storage (near-real-time delivery to destinations)	Configurable, typically 7 days by default
Throughput	1 MB/sec or 1,000 records/sec per shard	Automatically scales to match input	Configurable, can handle millions of records per second
Latency	Sub-second	Buffer time configurable (minimum 60 seconds)	Sub-millisecond
Processing	Custom processing with various stream processing frameworks	Minimal built-in processing, mainly for delivery	Custom processing with Kafka-compatible tools
Characteristics	Real-time streaming Custom processing Multiple consumers Durable storage	Fully managed Easy integration with AWS analytics services Automatic scaling-Data transformation capabilities	Fully managed Apache Kafka High throughput Multi-AZ replication BYOK encryption

Feature	Kinesis Data Streams	Amazon Data Firehose	Amazon MSK (Managed Streaming for Apache Kafka)
High availability	3 AZ	3 AZ	Configurable
Delivery (deduplication)	At least once	At least once	At least once (default), Exactly once (customisable)
Guaranteed ordering	Yes	No	Yes

Batch Ingestion

We've looked at a number of AWS services that support streaming ingestion. AWS offers a variety of services for batch-ingestion (e.g., AWS Glue, Amazon EMR, and even Amazon Redshift). This chapter focuses on AWS Glue, but we'll also touch upon other large scale data transfer solutions like the AWS Snow Family and AWS DataSync. We'll also discuss how DirectConnect can improve connectivity and simplify the data transfer process adding additional layer of security in the data transfer process.

AWS Glue

AWS launched AWS Glue, a fully managed extract, transform, and load (ETL) service, in 2016, with the intent of tackling the inherently complex and laborious nature of ETL processes. Despite the existence of numerous ETL tools and partners, a significant portion of ETL tasks were still being hand-coded, leading to brittle, error-prone, and maintenance-heavy code.

By providing a simple, serverless interface, AWS Glue automates much of the time-consuming data preparation tasks for analytics, such as data discovery, cataloging, and schema mapping. It allows users to discover and connect to various data sources, transform data to fit their analytics needs using a visual interface or custom code, and load it into AWS data stores like Amazon S3, Amazon RDS, and Amazon Redshift. With AWS Glue, you can create and run ETL jobs with less infrastructure to manage and at lower costs, thereby accelerating their data integration and analytics projects.

AWS Glue has improved a lot over the past eight years, and while it still retains its serverless nature, it now provides a comprehensive suite of capabilities to streamline the processing, governance, and management of data. It features a scalable data integration engine with built-in data transformations and a flexible execution engine, allowing users to transform and move data efficiently. Monitoring tools are included to keep track of ETL jobs and workflows.

Data governance is a key aspect of AWS Glue which centralizes data management tasks through the AWS Glue Data Catalog, AWS Glue Data Quality, and AWS Lake Formation integration. This ensures that data across various AWS services is cataloged, quality is maintained, and metadata management is unified.

A comprehensive ETL tool offers a variety of connectors, and hence Glue also simplifies the connection and ingestion of data through Glue connectors and the Glue connector marketplace, allowing seamless data flow from various sources. These connectors and various interfaces facilitate the integration of diverse datasets into AWS.

Furthermore, AWS Glue enhances user productivity with persona-specific tools tailored to different roles and responsibilities within data operations. Additional productivity tools and data ops tools are available to optimize the ETL process, allowing teams to customize their workflows and enhance efficiency.

Figure 1.22 shows the different components of AWS Glue and how a Glue job operates.

FIGURE 1.22   AWS Glue flow

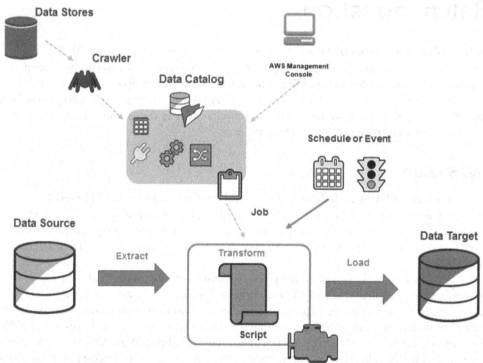

AWS Glue User Interfaces

AWS Glue is designed with all types of users in mind, which is why it is built to meet the needs of ETL developers, data engineers, business analysts, and data scientists with the following UI tools.

AWS Glue Studio

AWS Glue Studio is a visual interface that simplifies the creation, execution, and monitoring of ETL jobs. This powerful tool is designed to accommodate both experienced ETL developers and newcomers to data integration or Apache Spark.

Key features of AWS Glue Studio include:

- **Intuitive visual interface:** The platform offers a "boxes-and-arrows" approach, allowing users to design ETL workflows without writing complex code.

- **Versatile data management:** Users can easily transform and move data across various sources, leveraging AWS Glue's serverless, Spark-based ETL capabilities.

- **Comprehensive job run dashboard:** This feature provides a detailed overview of ETL operations, from execution metrics to resource utilization, enabling effective workflow monitoring and performance optimization.

- **Accessibility:** The user-friendly design makes it easier for professionals of all skill levels to harness the power of AWS Glue for data integration tasks.

- **Seamless integration:** As part of the AWS ecosystem, Glue Studio integrates smoothly with other AWS services, enhancing its capabilities and extending its usefulness in diverse data processing scenarios.

AWS Glue Studio empowers users to create and manage ETL jobs more efficiently, ultimately streamlining the data integration process within the AWS environment.

AWS Glue DataBrew

AWS Glue DataBrew is a visual data preparation tool specifically designed for data analysts and data scientists who need to clean and normalize data efficiently without writing code. This innovative solution addresses the often time-consuming and complex task of data preparation, allowing these professionals to focus more on analysis and insights rather than data wrangling.

Key features tailored for data analysts and scientists include:

- **Visual interface:** An intuitive, no-code environment that allows direct interaction with data from various sources, including data lakes, warehouses, and databases.

- **Built-in transformations:** Over 250 ready-to-use transformations that enable quick and easy data cleansing and normalization without requiring programming skills.

- **Data profiling:** Built-in capabilities to assess and profile data quality, helping analysts quickly understand their datasets.

- **Automation:** The ability to save and systematically apply transformations to new datasets, streamlining repetitive tasks.

- **Serverless architecture:** Eliminates the need for infrastructure management, allowing data professionals to focus on their core competencies.

- **Usage-based pricing:** Enables scalability without upfront costs, making it accessible for projects of all sizes.

AWS Glue DataBrew significantly reduces the time spent on data preparation. This allows these professionals to dedicate more time to extracting valuable insights and driving data-informed decisions within their organizations. Whether working on small-scale projects or large enterprise initiatives, data professionals can leverage DataBrew to enhance their productivity and effectiveness in the data preparation phase of their workflows.

AWS Glue Notebooks

AWS Glue Studio's notebooks are tailored for data engineers and ETL developers who prefer an interactive, code-centric approach to creating ETL jobs. This feature combines the familiarity of Jupyter Notebooks with the power of AWS Glue's serverless ETL capabilities, offering a seamless environment for those comfortable with writing and testing code.

Key features for data engineers and ETL developers include:

- **Interactive coding environment:** A Jupyter Notebook interface that allows for real-time code execution and output visualization.

- **Serverless infrastructure:** Eliminates the need for cluster management and configuration, allowing developers to focus solely on writing ETL logic.

- **AWS Glue ETL runtime consistency:** Ensures that code written in the notebook will behave identically when run as a full ETL job.

- **Seamless job conversion:** Easily transform notebook code into production-ready AWS Glue jobs without leaving the AWS Glue Studio interface.

- **Integrated development experience:** Write, test, and debug ETL code in a single environment, streamlining the development process.

- **Version control compatibility:** Save work as both notebooks and scripts, facilitating collaboration and version management.

AWS Glue Studio's notebooks cater to data engineers and ETL developers who value hands-on coding and iterative development. This tool allows them to leverage their programming skills while benefiting from the scalability and ease of management offered by AWS Glue's serverless architecture. Whether you are prototyping new ETL processes or refining existing ones, you can use the notebook interface to efficiently develop and deploy robust data integration solutions within the AWS ecosystem.

AWS Glue Interactive Sessions

AWS Glue's interactive sessions are primarily designed for data engineers and Spark developers who need to iteratively develop and test ETL jobs in a flexible, code-first environment. The key use case for these sessions is rapid prototyping and debugging of data processing tasks without the overhead of managing infrastructure or waiting for full job runs.

Key features supporting this use case include:

- **Real-time development:** Enables immediate execution and testing of ETL scripts, allowing for quick iterations and refinements.

- **Serverless Spark environment:** Provides access to Apache Spark's power without the need to manage clusters or infrastructure.

- **Flexible coding options:** Offers both a coding interface and a visual interface for constructing ETL scripts, catering to different developer preferences.

- **IDE integration:** Supports work in familiar development environments like Microsoft VS Code through Jupyter integration, enhancing productivity.

- **API access:** Allows programmatic creation and management of Spark applications, facilitating automation and integration with existing workflows.

- **Cost-effectiveness:** Pay only for compute resources used during active development, making it economical for iterative work.

AWS Glue's interactive sessions address the common challenge of lengthy development cycles in ETL job creation. They allow data professionals to quickly test ideas, troubleshoot issues, and optimize their data processing logic before committing to full production runs.

Crawlers/Classifiers

Imagine you're a librarian whose job is to organize a vast, ever-growing collection of books, which, in this case, are data files. You need to categorize them by genre, author, or content type. This is essentially what AWS Glue crawlers do for your data. They are the librarians of the data world, scanning through various data repositories, like a mix of modern e-books and classic hardcovers, which, in the data realm, are formats such as JSON, CSV, and data from relational databases housed in Amazon S3, Amazon RDS, and Amazon Redshift.

AWS Glue crawlers come with a set of pre-made classifiers—think of these as the rules of categorizing books by their covers or ISBNs. Sometimes, however, you get a unique book that doesn't fit the standard categories. For those, AWS Glue lets you create your own classifiers, like writing a new rule for a hybrid genre.

Once deployed, a crawler begins its journey through the data, applying these classifiers to understand what each file is—determining whether a column is a phone number, a date, or maybe a Social Security number. After this, it creates a detailed index card for each file, like a catalog entry, complete with all the schema details, and stores it in the AWS Glue Data Catalog. This catalog then acts as a guide for any data transformation processes you might need, ensuring that they are as accurate and efficient as possible.

Crawlers are also quite smart. When they revisit a previously scanned library section (or data store), they can spot if a new book has been added or if an existing one has changed editions (schema changes), and update the catalog accordingly, keeping everything current.

At this point, I would highly recommend you log in to the Glue console to create a crawler for your favorite data source. Perform the following step-by-step instructions:

1. Log in to the AWS Management Console and open the AWS Glue service.

2. Go to the Crawlers page and click Add Crawler.

3. Name your crawler—something that easily identifies the data it will catalog.

4. Specify the data store by choosing the type (S3, JDBC, etc.) and providing the path to your data.

5. Choose an IAM role that gives AWS Glue permissions to access your data.

6. Set up the schedule for the crawler. You can run it on demand or set it to crawl at regular intervals.

7. Configure the output by specifying the database in the AWS Glue Data Catalog where you want the tables to be created.

8. Review the settings, make any necessary adjustments, and then click Finish to create the crawler.

9. Run the crawler by selecting it from the list and clicking Run Crawler.

10. Monitor the crawler's progress and, once it's finished, check the AWS Glue Data Catalog to see your newly created tables.

Remember, as your data evolves, you might need to tweak the classifiers or adjust the crawler's schedule to keep your data catalog up to date. It's like the library's catalog that needs constant updates because new books keep arriving!

Data Catalog

The AWS Glue Data Catalog serves as a centralized metadata repository in the cloud for each AWS account, unique to each region. It's designed to scale, organizing data into databases and tables that represent your structured or semi-structured data stored across various services. It's essential for managing metadata from different systems, aiding in consistent data querying and transformation. It works hand-in-hand with AWS IAM and Lake Formation to fine-tune access, maintaining tight data security and compliance. For detailed governance features, including auditing with CloudTrail, check out the AWS documentation. The Data Catalog integrates with a host of AWS services, including Athena, Redshift Spectrum, and EMR, and is compatible with the Apache Hive metastore.

AWS Glue ETL and AWS Glue Jobs System

AWS Glue leverages the metadata stored in the Data Catalog to streamline ETL tasks by automatically generating scripts in Scala or PySpark with custom AWS Glue extensions. These scripts can be customized to perform a variety of data processing tasks, such as transforming a CSV file into a structured format suitable for analysis and storage in a service like Amazon Redshift.

AWS Glue offers a robust jobs system to manage your ETL workflow. You can automate your data processing by scripting AWS Glue jobs that handle the extraction, transformation, and relocation of your data. These jobs can be set to run on a schedule, in sequence, or in response to certain triggers, such as the arrival of new data. Detailed monitoring of these jobs ensures smooth execution, while the Jobs API allows for programmable interaction with the AWS Glue Jobs system.

This book is not a deep-dive on AWS Glue. I would highly recommend visiting the AWS documentation for in-depth guidance on AWS Glue's ETL capabilities and how to program Spark ETL scripts, including job monitoring and the API.

Streaming ETL in AWS Glue

AWS Glue facilitates ETL processes for streaming data, utilizing the Apache Spark Structured Streaming engine. It can handle data ingestion from sources like Amazon Kinesis, Apache Kafka, and Amazon MSK, supporting near-real-time data cleaning and transformations.

AWS Glue Streaming also supports a variety of data targets, including but not limited to Amazon S3, Amazon Redshift, MySQL, PostgreSQL, Oracle, MS SQL Server, Snowflake, Apache Iceberg, Delta, and Apache Hudi, any database connectable via JDBC, and a number of AWS Glue Marketplace connectors.

Glue Streaming is suited for various real-time data processing scenarios, including near-real-time analytics, fraud detection, social media and sentiment analysis, IoT data processing, clickstream analysis, log monitoring, recommendation systems, and handling of event-driven data workloads. It allows for precise schema management and also supports schema auto-detection during streaming ETL jobs, accomodating both AWS Glue-specific and Apache Spark native transformations for comprehensive data processing.

If you are preparing for a certification exam, I would highly recommend you go through the following tutorial, which walks you through the process of creating a streaming ETL job using AWS Glue studio: `https://docs.aws.amazon.com/glue/latest/dg/ streaming-tutorial-studio.html`.

You will likely see questions on the exam that ask about the best streaming service given a particular scenario. We've already covered Kinesis and Kafka, so you need to know when AWS Glue Streaming would be more suitable.

AWS Glue Streaming is particularly useful when you're already using AWS Glue or Spark for batch processing and want to leverage your existing setup for real-time stream processing without learning a new framework. It's also beneficial when you need a unified service to manage batch and real-time workloads, have complex transformations to perform, prefer visual job building, or are working with transactional data lakes like Apache Iceberg, Apache Hudi, or Delta Lake. Conversely, you'd directly use MSK or Kinesis when you need specialized streaming or queue management that might not require the additional ETL capabilities of AWS Glue.

AWS Glue Data Quality

AWS Glue Data Quality, utilizing the DeeQu framework, allows for advanced monitoring and measurement of data quality, which is essential for reliable business decisions. It uses DQDL for rule definition, offering machine learning for anomaly detection, and simplifies rule creation with auto recommendations.

This serverless solution supports data across AWS Glue and the Data Catalog, ensuring comprehensive data integrity with minimal setup. AWS Glue Data Quality comes with more than 25 out-of-the-box DQ rules to start from, allowing you to create the rules that suit your specific need, and helps you track bad data by identifying exact records that might have caused your overall data quality scores to drop.

How Does Glue Data Quality Work?

AWS Glue helps check if your data is up to scratch by keeping track of useful statistics. Let's say you want to know how many different values are in your dataset and if that number matches what you expect. AWS Glue does that by calculating these unique values and checking them against the standards you've set.

It's not just a one-off thing, either. AWS Glue keeps an eye on these stats continuously, which allows it to spot unusual trends. Think of it like it's getting smarter over time, learning what's normal for your data and pointing out anything odd. These little nudges, or "observations," are like hints from AWS Glue's machine learning brain, suggesting new rules to keep your data in line with what you're looking for.

To get the most out of it, you should run your checks regularly, like every hour or every day. If you're a bit hit-and-miss with when you run these jobs, the insights you get might not be as helpful.

Figure 1.23 shows the typical data flow with Glue Data Quality and indicates how the observations can lead to building better data quality tools over time.

FIGURE 1.23   AWS Glue Data Quality flow

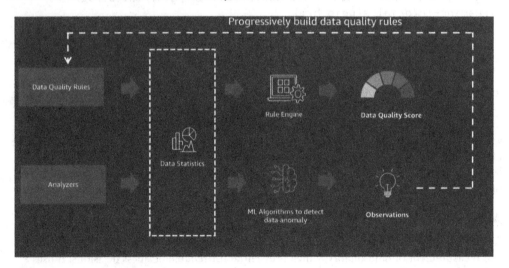

AWS Glue Data Quality offers two unique entry points for the Data Catalog and ETL jobs, accommodating various data sources and integration needs, with support for dynamic and ML-based rules for nuanced data quality analysis.

- **Data Quality for AWS Glue Data Catalog:** This AWS Glue Data Catalog's Data Quality feature offers a straightforward approach for those without coding experience, like data stewards and business analysts, to establish data quality guidelines. This is ideal for scenarios where you need to assess data quality in already cataloged datasets. This feature is accessible through the AWS Glue management console and its APIs.

- **Data Quality for AWS Glue ETL jobs:** This feature is for proactive data quality tasks, to help you filter out bad data before loading datasets into a data lake. The typical use cases are when you want to incorporate data quality tasks into your ETL jobs, write code that defines data quality tasks in ETL scripts, or manage the quality of data that flows in your visual data pipelines. Typically, these data quality operations are performed from AWS Glue Studio, AWS Glue Studio notebooks, and AWS Glue interactive sessions. You also have the option to use AWS Glue libraries for ETL scripting and using AWS Glue APIs.

Change Data Capture with Glue Bookmarks

Quite often we need to capture data from sources in a variety of ways, such as full data extracts from the source or identifying delta records. Identifying delta records is often complicated because you need to ensure that only the updated data from the data source is captured, hence simplifying the remaining ETL pipeline and improving overall performance and reduce the total end-to-end runtime. AWS Glue uses Glue bookmarks to track the processed data from previous runs of an ETL job by persisting the state information from the job run.

This persisted state information is called a *job bookmark*. Job bookmarks help AWS Glue maintain state information and prevent the reprocessing of old data. Job bookmarks allow you to process new data when rerunning on a scheduled interval. A job bookmark is composed of the states for various elements of jobs, such as sources, transformations, and targets. For example, your ETL job might read new partitions in an Amazon S3 file. AWS Glue tracks which partition(s) the job has already processed successfully to prevent duplicate processing and duplicate data in the job's target data store.

Job bookmarks are implemented for some of the most common file formats on Amazon S3, including JSON, CSV, Apache Avro, XML, Parquet, and ORC.

While AWS Glue's job bookmarking feature works seamlessly for Amazon S3 input sources, it has certain limitations when dealing with relational data sources accessed through JDBC connections. The bookmarking mechanism's ability to capture changes (deltas) in relational sources is constrained by specific conditions.

For relational data sources, job bookmarks are only supported if the table's primary keys are sequentially ordered. This sequential ordering is crucial for the bookmarking system to accurately track changes. Additionally, job bookmarks can detect new rows added to the table, but they cannot identify updated rows. This limitation arises because bookmarks rely on primary keys, and if a primary key already exists in the target, AWS Glue cannot distinguish whether the corresponding row has been modified in the source.

It's important to note that at the time of writing this, the AWS Glue team was actively working on addressing this limitation, aiming to enhance the bookmarking capabilities for relational data sources.

Conversely, when Amazon S3 serves as the input source for AWS Glue jobs, the job bookmarking mechanism operates efficiently. In this scenario, the bookmarks track the last modified timestamps of the objects (files) in the input data source. During subsequent job runs, AWS Glue compares the current timestamps of the input files against the bookmarked timestamps from the previous run. Any input file with a more recent modification timestamp is flagged for reprocessing, ensuring that only the changed files are subjected to additional computations.

This intelligent approach optimizes resource utilization and minimizes redundant processing, as unchanged files are skipped during job execution. The bookmarking feature for Amazon S3 input sources streamlines the data processing workflow, enabling efficient handling of incremental updates to the input data while avoiding unnecessary overhead.

Amazon Data Migration Service

AWS Data Migration Service (DMS) is a versatile tool and has already been used to migrate millions of databases to AWS. While originally built for database migration, it now supports a wide array of data sources and targets, which can be classified into different categories, such as relational databases, NoSQL, analytics, and data warehouses. This makes it a great tool for data ingestion as well.

- **Relational databases:** AWS DMS can handle a range of popular relational databases both as sources and targets. This includes heavyweight databases such as Oracle, SQL Server, PostgreSQL, MySQL, MariaDB, and SAP ASE. It also supports databases hosted on cloud platforms like Amazon RDS, GCP MySQL, and SQL Azure, as well as on-premises databases. For databases running on AWS, it can interact with Amazon Aurora and those running on Amazon EC2 instances.

- **NoSQL:** When dealing with NoSQL databases, AWS DMS supports MongoDB and Amazon DocumentDB as sources, allowing for migrations from these flexible schema systems. For targets, apart from MongoDB and DocumentDB, it can also migrate data to Amazon DynamoDB, which is designed to handle large-scale, high-traffic NoSQL data, and Amazon Neptune, which is a fast, reliable graph database service. Moreover, DMS can interact with Amazon Elasticsearch Service for search and analytics purposes and Amazon ElastiCache for in-memory data caching, which is often used to enhance the performance of existing databases.

- **Analytics:** From an analytics standpoint, AWS DMS can move data into Amazon S3, which serves as a centralized storage that can be used for big data analytics, and AWS Snowball, a data transport solution for transferring terabytes to petabytes of data into and out of AWS. These services are essential for handling vast datasets required for analytics workflows.

- **Data warehousing:** For data warehousing needs, which are integral to analytics because they provide centralized storage and retrieval of large volumes of structured data optimized for query and analysis, DMS supports a range of targets. These include traditional data warehouses such as Oracle, SQL Server, Greenplum, Teradata, Vertica, and Netezza, as well as modern cloud-based solutions like Amazon Redshift and Azure Synapse. Amazon Redshift, in particular, is a fast, scalable data warehouse that makes it simple and cost-effective to analyze all your data across your data warehouse and data lake.

- **Streaming data**: In terms of real-time analytics and streaming data, AWS DMS can target Amazon Kinesis Data Streams, which enables real-time processing of streaming data at scale, and Amazon Managed Streaming for Kafka (Amazon MSK), which is a fully managed service that makes it easy to build and run applications that use Apache Kafka to process streaming data.

The ability to migrate and replicate data across such a diverse range of sources and targets makes AWS DMS a powerful tool in the analytics space. It enables organizations to aggregate data from disparate databases into a central repository where it can be used for comprehensive analytics. The flexibility of DMS allows it to fit into various analytics architectures, whether you're moving legacy database data into a modern data warehouse for historical analysis or streaming real-time data into an analytics platform for instant insights. This capability to integrate various data forms into a single coherent system is vital for data-driven decision-making and is at the heart of modern analytics strategies.

Key Components of DMS

AWS Database Migration Service (DMS) is a tool that helps you move your data to AWS. It's like a moving truck for your data, taking it from where it is now to where you want it to be in AWS. Here's a breakdown of the different parts that make up AWS DMS:

- **Finding databases**: DMS can discover the databases you have and help you figure out what's there.
- **Changing database formats**: If your databases speak different languages (e.g., Oracle or SQL), DMS can translate them so they understand each other.
- **The replication machine**: This is like the engine of the moving truck. It's where the actual moving happens.
- **Starting and ending points**: These are like the old and new homes for your data. DMS connects to where your data is coming from and where it's going to.
- **The moving task**: This is the to-do list for your move, telling DMS exactly what to move and how to move it.

Let's look at the different components that help you achieve all of the aforementioned functionalities:

- **Discovering your databases with DMS Fleet Advisor**: DMS Fleet Advisor takes a look at all your database systems and gives you a report. It works with different types of databases, such as Microsoft SQL Server and Oracle, and you don't have to install it everywhere—just in one place.
- **Changing database schemas with DMS Schema Conversion**: When you're moving from one type of database to another, DMS Schema Conversion helps you change the database design and code to fit the new place. It's like making sure your furniture will fit through the door of your new house.

- **The replication instance:** The replication instance is where the magic happens. It's a special place in AWS that does the heavy lifting of moving your data. You can pick different sizes of this replication instance depending on how big your move is. Figure 1.24 shows the workings of a replication instance. Note that it runs multiple replication tasks to connect between a variety of source and target endpoints.

FIGURE 1.24   AWS DMS replication instance running replication tasks

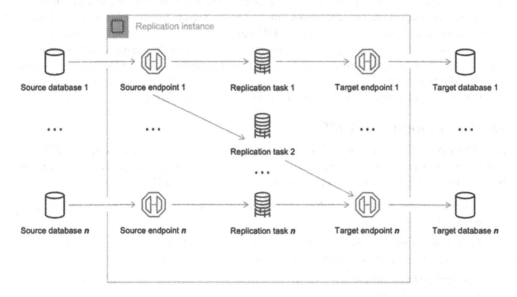

- **Storage and high availability:** Your replication instance has storage space for your data during the move. If you're moving a lot, you might need more space. DMS also makes sure that there's a backup ready in case something goes wrong, so your data is safe.

- **Endpoints:** Endpoints are the old and new homes for your data (i.e., they are like the addresses for your old and new data homes). You tell DMS where to pick up your data and where to drop it off. DMS checks to make sure it can get into both places before starting the move.

- **The replication task:** The replication task is your moving plan. It tells DMS what data to pack up, how to handle special items, and where everything goes. You can also tell DMS to keep an eye on your data as it moves to make sure nothing gets lost or broken. Figure 1.25 shows the inner workings of a replication task and how it uses the Source Unload/Target load mechanism to move data from the sources to the targets while maintaining change caches and DMS logs.

In simple terms, AWS DMS is like a super-fast and simple moving service for your databases, helping you plan the move, pack up your data, and get it safely to its new home in AWS.

FIGURE 1.25   Functions of a DMS replication task

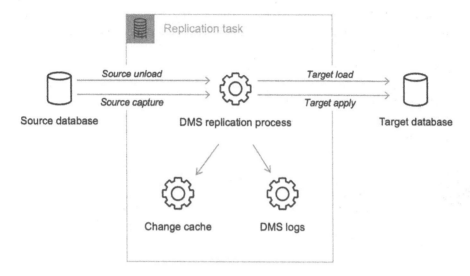

Ongoing Replication, or Change Data Capture (CDC) with DMS

AWS DMS supports three migration options, each having its own nuances.

- Existing data
    - AWS DMS creates files or tables in the target database.
    - AWS DMS populates the tables with data from the source.
    - Existing data migration is available via 'Migrate Existing Data' in the Console or 'Full Load' via API.
    - AWS DMS captures changes on the source during migration.
    - Once the initial migration completes, changes are applied to the target as units of completed transactions.
    - Full data migration plus ongoing replication is available via 'Migrate Existing Data and Replicate Ongoing Changes' in the Console or 'full-load-and-cdc' via API.
- Replicate changes only
    - AWS DMS reads the recovery file on the source database.
    - AWS DMS optimizes change replication by buffering and batch-applying grouped transactions to the target.
    - Ongoing changes replication is available via 'Replicate Data Changes Only' in the Console or 'cdc' via API.

For target preparation, you can choose between the following options with AWS DMS:

- **Do nothing:** In Do Nothing mode, AWS DMS assumes target tables are pre-created. In Full Load mode or Full Load Plus CDC mode, ensure that the target tables are empty before starting the migration.

- **Drop Tables On Target:** In Drop Tables On Target mode, AWS DMS drops the target tables and re-creates them before starting the migration. This ensures that the target tables are empty when the migration starts.

- **Truncate:** In Truncate mode, AWS DMS truncates all target tables before the migration starts.

From an exam perspective, it is important to know that DMS can actually be used to load data to Amazon S3, Amazon OpenSearch, Amazon Kinesis Data Streams, Amazon Kafka, and Amazon Redshift (Provisioned and Serverless). In addition, it gives better flexibility when it comes to capturing delta records.

AWS DataSync

While working with AWS customers, we see that customers want to migrate more and more workloads to the cloud, and the size of the datasets gets increasingly larger as well. I have yet to come across an organization where datasets are decreasing, and hence, there's a need for tools to help move the data quickly and efficiently. There are many open-source tools available for little or no cost that can move data to AWS.

Transferring a few files here and there is pretty easy to do. But when you start looking at copying large amounts of data, there are a lot of factors to consider. Many of our customers initially look at using DIY tools, which makes sense because many of these DIY tools are often "free" to use. It's also possible to write your own tools to do this on your own, but it takes a significant amount of work.

Tools that may initially appear to be "free" can actually cost enterprises a lot of money—and time—when applied to larger-scale migrations.

Most importantly, you don't want to find out that the files that took hours or days to transfer are corrupted, especially when you have a tight project timeline. This is where tools like AWS DataSync can help by performing data integrity checks both in transit and at rest to ensure data written to your destination matches the data read from your source.

AWS has a habit of always working backward from customer problems. After hearing from our customers about some of the challenges they were facing with trying to transfer data into AWS, we realized there was an opportunity to help them by removing a lot of the undifferentiated heavy lifting that comes with building your own migration tools, which is why we built AWS DataSync, a fully-managed service for online transfer of data to and from AWS.

Performance is critical to any migration tool, and DataSync has been built for performance. In fact, based on our internal tests, it runs up to 10x faster than common open-source tools, utilizing compression, parallel transfer, and other optimizations to get your data to the cloud as fast as possible. In particular, DataSync was purpose built to handle the challenge of migrating millions or even billions of small files, a task that can be particularly difficult for do-it-yourself solutions. We also wanted to make DataSync easy to use by allowing customers to get up and running quickly, focusing on the task of getting their data to the cloud.

Security is and has always been our top priority at AWS, and we built DataSync to transfer data securely and reliably. DataSync encrypts data in-flight and supports encryption at rest on S3 and EFS. In addition, DataSync provides a number of options for validating your data, making sure that all data was transferred successfully.

DataSync integrates with common cloud management tools such as CloudWatch, CloudTrail, IAM, and others.

We also wanted DataSync to be cost-effective since customers want to keep the costs minimum. While exact pricing is not part of exam questions, you are often asked about finding a solution that is simple or cost-effective. DataSync can offer both simplicity and lower costs.

The following are some of the key characteristics of AWS DataSync:

- **Supports fast data transfer:** Up to 10 times faster than common open-source tools, using compression and parallel transfer
- **Easy to use:** Supports NFS and SMB protocols, installable on-premises or in-cloud
- **Secure and reliable:** Encryption in transit, encryption at rest on S3, EFS, and FSx, and built-in verification
- **Cloud integrated:** S3, EFS, FSx, CloudWatch, IAM, CloudTrail, etc.
- **Cost-effective:** 1.25 cents per GB transferred, pay only for the data copied

How Does DataSync Work?

The DataSync software agent connects to your Network File System (NFS) and Server Message Block (SMB) storage, so you don't have to modify your applications. To get started, all you have to do is deploy the DataSync agent, connect it to your file system, select your AWS storage resources, and start moving data between them. DataSync is managed centrally from the AWS Management Console.

Since security and logging are key parts of data migrations, DataSync also integrates with other key AWS tools such as: AWS Key Management Service (KMS), AWS Identity and Access Management (IAM), AWS CloudTrail, and AWS CloudWatch.

From an architectural standpoint, DataSync has two major components:

- DataSync Discovery
- DataSync Transfer

The Deep-Dive into DataSync Discovery

You can start the data migration process with AWS DataSync by deploying the DataSync agent, a software application that facilitates the secure transfer of data between on-premises storage systems and AWS services. The agent software communicates with the local storage management system in a secure way, using port 443. After establishing a successful connection, the agent starts a discovery process to identify and understand the details and structure of the on-premises storage system.

Following the data collection phase, the DataSync agent transmits the gathered dataset descriptors to the DataSync Discovery service. This transfer occurs over a secure, public service endpoint, ensuring that the metadata related to the storage environment is relayed to AWS without compromising security.

DataSync Discovery, utilizing the ingested metadata, performs an analysis to identify the most suitable AWS storage targets for the customer's dataset. This recommendation process is informed by the specific requirements and configurations of the on-premises storage system. DataSync Discovery serves as a decision-support component, providing users with insights into optimal AWS storage solutions to facilitate an efficient migration pathway tailored to the customer's infrastructure. Figure 1.26 shows the three steps of the DataSync Discovery process.

FIGURE 1.26   DataSync Discovery

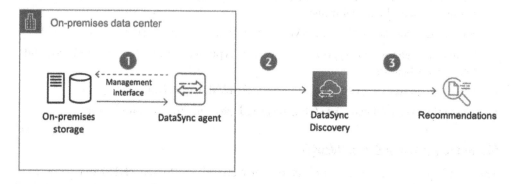

DataSync Transfer

DataSync can be used to transfer data between on-premises storage and AWS, between AWS storage services, and even between cloud storage systems and AWS storage services.

Transferring Data Between On-Premises Storage and AWS

The architecture diagram in Figure 1.27 illustrates how AWS DataSync facilitates the transfer of data from on-premises storage to AWS cloud storage services.

Here's how the process unfolds:

1. The journey begins with the DataSync agent, a specialized software deployed within your on-premises environment. This agent securely connects to your local storage systems' management interface, typically through the well-established port 443, ensuring a secure path via TLS (Transport Layer Security) encryption. This is similar to packing your valuables into a secure, armored truck for transportation.

2. From there, the data embarks on its journey to the AWS Region, where the cloud resources are waiting. The DataSync agent transfers the data across the Internet, ensuring that it remains encrypted and secure during transit.

3. Upon reaching the AWS Region, the data is then distributed to the appropriate AWS storage services based on the recommendations. These services could include Amazon S3 buckets for object storage, Amazon EFS for file storage, or Amazon FSx or Windows File Server for specific Windows-based storage needs.

This architecture is particularly relevant for several use cases, such as:

- **Disaster recovery**: Regularly syncing critical data to AWS, ensuring that in the event of a disaster, your data is securely stored and readily available in the cloud.

- **Data archiving**: Moving large amounts of infrequently accessed data from on-premises storage to the cloud for long-term retention and compliance.

- **Content distribution**: Syncing content repositories to the cloud to serve global audiences with lower latency and higher availability.

- **Data lakes**: Aggregating data from various on-premises systems into a centralized AWS data lake for advanced analytics and machine learning.

- **Cloud migration**: As part of a broader cloud migration strategy, incrementally moving on-premises workloads and datasets to AWS services for enhanced scalability and innovation.

The AWS DataSync service streamlines and accelerates the data transfer process, simplifying what would otherwise be a complex and resource-intensive problem, allowing organizations to focus on deriving value from their data rather than the logistics of moving it.

FIGURE 1.27   Transferring between on-premises and AWS

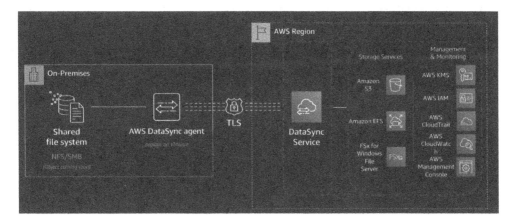

Transferring Data Between AWS Services

The architecture diagram in Figure 1.28 represents a setup using AWS DataSync to transfer data between different AWS storage services within an AWS Region. At the core of this setup, we see the DataSync service, depicted as the central node that orchestrates the data flow. On either side of the DataSync node, there are AWS storage services represented, which could include Amazon S3 buckets, EFS file systems, or FSx for Windows File Server instances.

In a typical use case, you might have an application running in one part of AWS that generates large amounts of data—for example, a web application storing user data on EFS. You may want to back up this data to S3 or require processing with another service that requires the data to be in a different storage service, like FSx. DataSync automates the movement of data between these services securely and efficiently, using TLS to encrypt the data in transit, ensuring that your data is protected.

Here are some example scenarios where this architecture is applied:

- **Disaster recovery:** Replicating data across different storage services to ensure that in the event of a failure, the data remains available and the applications continue to function with minimal disruption.

- **Data lakes:** Consolidating data from various sources into a single S3-based data lake, enabling advanced analytics and machine learning processes on a centralized dataset.

- **Content distribution networks (CDNs):** Synchronizing multimedia content across multiple storage locations to provide low-latency access to users distributed geographically.

- **Database backup and restoration:** Periodically backing up database snapshots to a secure storage service for recovery purposes, ensuring business continuity.

- **Hybrid storage environments:** Bridging on-premises storage systems with cloud storage to facilitate a gradual migration to the cloud or to extend the on-premises data storage capabilities.

By configuring DataSync within your environment, you can maintain a high-throughput, low-latency data sync mechanism, optimizing your cloud storage strategy for operational efficiency, cost, and performance.

FIGURE 1.28 Transferring data between AWS storage services

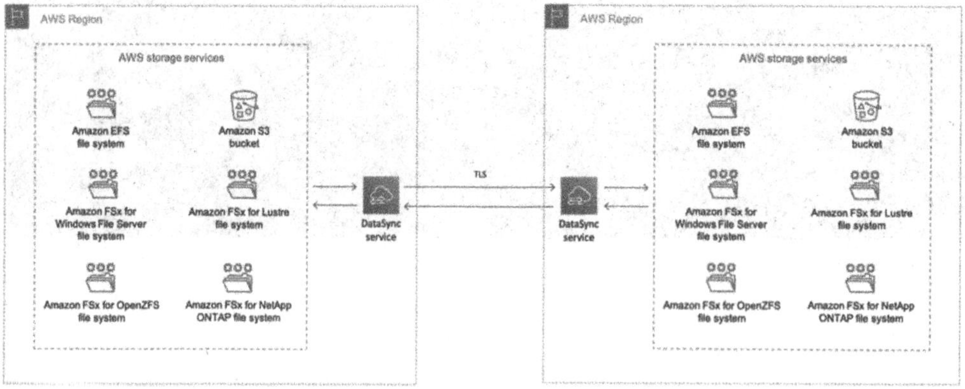

Transferring Data Between Cloud Storage Systems and AWS Storage Services

The architecture diagram in Figure 1.29 depicts the setup for AWS DataSync used to transfer data between cloud storage systems (Azure Blob Storage) and AWS storage services within an AWS Region. The process is anchored by the DataSync service, positioned as the operational node, ensuring data is transferred securely and efficiently.

To the left of the DataSync node, we see a cloud storage system that represents the source of the data. It might be an existing AWS service, like an S3 bucket or EFS file system that you're using to store your data for various applications, or even object storage from Azure or GCP. The data from this cloud storage passes through the DataSync node, which handles all aspects of the transfer securely, thanks to the TLS (Transport Layer Security) protocol that encrypts the data in transit, adding a layer of security as it moves across the network.

On the right side of the DataSync node are the AWS storage services, which can be a variety of different AWS offerings, depending on your needs. Data might be directed to another S3 bucket, an EFS file system, or an FSx for Windows File Server. The target destination is determined based on the desired outcome of the transfer.

A typical use case for this architecture might be consolidating data from various cloud storage locations to a single data lake for analytics and processing. For instance, a company might be using multiple S3 buckets across different departments to store data and now wants to centralize this into a single S3 bucket or EFS file system for unified access and easier management. DataSync can seamlessly handle this consolidation, moving large datasets swiftly and securely, while the company pays only for the data transferred.

Another use case could involve transferring regularly updated datasets from ongoing operations to a dedicated analytics environment. Suppose a financial institution stores transaction data across various cloud storage services and wants to perform timely risk analysis. In that case, DataSync can be used to aggregate this data to a centralized storage location where complex analytics operations are executed.

FIGURE 1.29   Transferring data between cloud storage services and AWS services

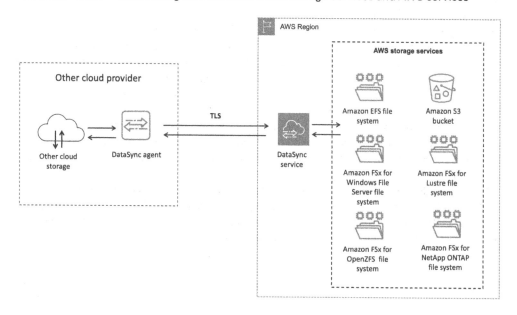

AWS DataSync is a bridge that simplifies the movement of data across different storage services within the AWS ecosystem, optimizing for performance, cost, and ease of use in various data management scenarios.

Large-Scale Data Transfer Solutions

We have seen a number of different technologies that allow you to collect data from different data sources when the volumes are low to moderate. However, when you come across situations when you need to migrate large data volumes, such as when data sizes are over multiple terabytes or petabytes, transferring the data over an Internet connection could take a very long time. Those are the scenarios in which you need large-scale data transfer options like the AWS Snow Family, which offers specially designed devices that provide a secure and economical way to transfer massive amounts of data, up to petabytes, offline.

You can lease a Snow device according to your needs and easily move your data to the cloud. These devices are built to withstand even the toughest conditions, ensuring that your data is protected with high security no matter where you need to take it. With a range of devices offered by AWS, you can choose the best fit for environments where space or weight is a concern, for easy portability, or for a variety of networking needs. Whether you're working in a remote location or in a bustling city, the AWS Snow Family has a data transfer solution to match your situation.

AWS Snowcone

AWS Snowcone is a compact, tough device designed to help you move a lot of data (up to petabytes) to AWS without needing the Internet. It's super portable and can handle rough conditions, making it perfect for use almost anywhere—from remote work sites to busy offices. Snowcone is light enough for one person to carry and can even fit in a standard mailbox or be delivered by drone! Whether you're offline by sending the device back to AWS or online using AWS DataSync, Snowcone makes moving your data easy. It supports both edge computing with Amazon EC2 and local storage, even in challenging environments.

Snowcone comes in two types: one with a hard disk drive (HDD) offering 8 TB of storage, and another with a solid-state drive (SSD) with 14 TB of storage. It's about the size of a tissue box, weighs roughly 4.5 pounds, and is durable enough for any setting. Compared to its bigger cousin, AWS Snowball, Snowcone is much lighter and smaller.

For offline data transfer, you just load your data onto a Snowcone and ship it to AWS. Online transfers are smooth, too, thanks to AWS DataSync pre-installed on the device for easy data import/export with AWS storage services. Snowcone works well with file-based applications and connects to both wired and wireless networks. It's powered through a USB-C connection, compatible with standard adapters, and can even run on a battery for mobile uses.

Once your data job is done, Snowcone's built-in E Ink shipping label ensures it gets back to AWS safely. AWS takes care of all the shipping logistics, and the device is securely erased, following NIST standards after your data is transferred. Figure 1.30 shows a Snowcone device, which is built to make your big data transfers simple, secure, and efficient.

FIGURE 1.30 An AWS Snowcone device

AWS Snowball

AWS Snowball is a rugged device designed to handle large data transfers and perform computing tasks at the edge, where data is generated and used. It comes in two varieties:

- **Snowball Edge Compute Optimized:** This version is packed with computing power, making it suitable for tasks like machine learning and video analysis. It has 104 virtual CPUs, 416 GB of memory, and an optional NVIDIA Tesla V100 GPU for graphics-intensive work. It also offers 28 TB of solid-state storage.

- **Snowball Edge Storage Optimized:** This version focuses on providing massive storage capacity for large data migrations. It can offer up to 80 TB of hard drive storage or 210 TB of solid-state storage, making it perfect for moving huge amounts of data. Despite their differences, both Snowball devices are built to operate in remote or challenging environments like oil rigs or military bases.

Snowball devices are not just about storage and computing; they also offer fast and secure network connectivity, supporting speeds from 10 to 100 Gbps. All data is encrypted on the device itself to ensure security and speed up the transfer process. If you need even more power or space, you can connect multiple Snowball devices together in a cluster. Additionally, if you're using Kubernetes, you can set up an Amazon EKS Anywhere cluster on Snowball devices.

For data storage, Snowball works with Amazon S3-compatible storage, allowing applications to read and write data as if they were directly interacting with S3. For block storage needs, Snowball supports attaching volumes to EC2 instances running on the device, enabling you to develop applications in the cloud and run them on the edge without any changes.

Security is a top priority with Snowball. All data is encrypted, and the devices meet stringent standards like HIPAA and FedRAMP, making them suitable for sensitive environments. Managing Snowball is also easy, thanks to AWS OpsHub, which allows you to manage your devices without an Internet connection.

When you're ready to move your data, you can ship the Snowball device back to AWS, where your data will be securely transferred to the cloud. AWS handles all the shipping details, and with the device's innovative E-Ink shipping label, tracking is straightforward. After the job is completed, AWS ensures that the device is wiped clean according to strict standards, maintaining your data's privacy from start to finish.

Figure 1.31 shows the entire process of AWS Snowball.

AWS Direct Connect

In the AWS Data Engineering exam, you may encounter scenarios related to AWS Direct Connect (see Figure 1.32), a cloud service solution that simplifies the establishment of a dedicated network connection from your on-premises infrastructure to AWS. Understanding AWS Direct Connect and its use cases is crucial for the exam and proper AWS architecture.

FIGURE 1.31   The AWS Snowball process

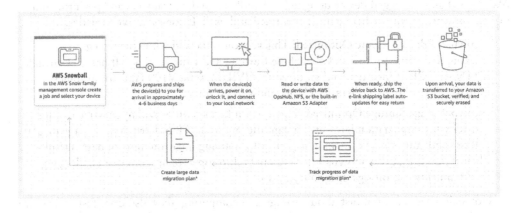

AWS Direct Connect allows you to create private connectivity between AWS and your data center, office, or colocation environment. This dedicated connection can often reduce network costs, increase bandwidth throughput, and provide a more consistent network experience compared to internet-based connections.

As shown in Figure 1.32, AWS Direct Connect enables you to establish a dedicated network connection between your network and one of the AWS Direct Connect locations. Leveraging industry-standard 802.1q VLANs, this dedicated connection can be partitioned into multiple virtual interfaces. This partitioning allows you to use the same connection to access public resources, such as objects stored in Amazon S3, using public IP address space, and private resources, like Amazon EC2 instances running within an Amazon Virtual Private Cloud (VPC) using private IP space, while maintaining network separation between the public and private environments. These virtual interfaces can be reconfigured at any time to meet your changing needs.

The key benefits of AWS Direct Connect, which may be relevant in the AWS Data Engineering Exam, include:

- **Reduced bandwidth costs:** By establishing a dedicated network connection, you can potentially reduce the costs associated with transferring large amounts of data over the Internet.

- **Consistent network performance:** AWS Direct Connect provides a more reliable and consistent network experience compared to Internet-based connections, which can be crucial for data engineering workloads that require predictable performance.

- **Compatibility with all AWS services:** AWS Direct Connect seamlessly integrates with various AWS services, enabling you to leverage the full range of AWS offerings for your data engineering needs.

- **Private connectivity to your Amazon VPC:** AWS Direct Connect allows you to establish private connectivity to your Amazon VPC, ensuring secure and isolated communication between your on-premises infrastructure and AWS resources.

- **Elastic scaling between 1 Gbps to 10 Gbps:** AWS Direct Connect offers flexible bandwidth options, allowing you to scale your dedicated connection from 1 Gbps to 10 Gbps, accommodating your evolving data transfer and processing requirements.

In the AWS Certified Data Engineering Associate exam, questions related to AWS Direct Connect may focus on scenarios involving large-scale data transfers, secure connectivity between on-premises and AWS environments, or optimizing network performance for data-intensive workloads. Understanding the capabilities and benefits of AWS Direct Connect can help you effectively address such scenarios and make informed decisions in the exam.

FIGURE 1.32   AWS DirectConnect overview

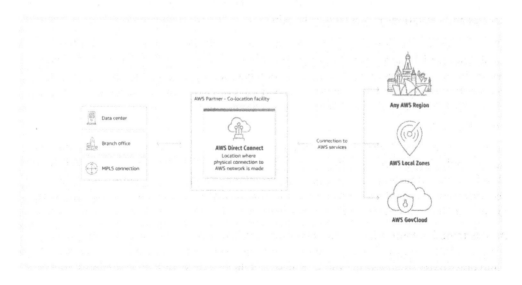

Summary

This chapter discussed the various components of the data pipeline when it comes to ingesting data onto the AWS cloud. We looked at ingesting data from a variety of sources using AWS services that are purpose-built for streaming and batch ingestion. We looked at streaming services like Amazon Kinesis, Amazon Managed Streaming for Kafka, Managed Streaming for Apache Flink, and AWS Glue Streaming. We also discussed batch ingestion using AWS Glue and AWS Data Migration Service, and we touched upon some large-scale data transfer solutions like the Amazon Snowball Family of devices for data transfers that are too huge to be transmitted over a standard Internet connection, and AWS Direct Connect for direct connectivity between your data center and AWS.

While we touched on the theoretical concept of different services, the AWS Certified Data Engineering Associate exam expects practical knowledge of these services. I would highly recommend that you open up these AWS services and run some of the workshops provided in the References section of this chapter.

Exam Essentials

Understand the core streaming data services and their use cases   Know the differences between Amazon Kinesis Data Streams, Amazon MSK, and Amazon Managed Service for Apache Flink. Kinesis is ideal for real-time data processing with sub-second latency; MSK suits Apache Kafka workloads requiring high throughput and retention; and Managed Flink excels at complex stream processing with SQL or Java. Understanding these services' characteristics and limitations is crucial for choosing the right streaming solution.

Know the batch ingestion services and when to use them   Fully understand AWS Glue's capabilities for ETL jobs, including crawlers, job bookmarks for incremental loads, and data quality features. Understand AWS DMS for database migration and replication, and when to use AWS DataSync for transferring large volumes of data between on-premises and AWS storage services. Know how to handle schema changes and data transformations during batch ingestion.

Be able to implement large-scale data transfer solutions   Understand when to use the AWS Snow Family devices versus AWS Direct Connect for large data transfers. Snow devices are ideal for offline transfer of massive datasets with limited connectivity, while Direct Connect provides dedicated network connections for consistent, secure data transfer. Know the capacity limits and security features of each solution.

Be able to design fault-tolerant data ingestion architectures   Know how to implement replication, partitioning, and error handling in streaming and batch ingestion pipelines. Understand how to use enhanced fan-out in Kinesis, configure MSK for high availability, and implement proper retry mechanisms in AWS Glue jobs. Master the configuration of monitoring and alerting for ingestion pipelines.

Know how to optimize performance and costs in data ingestion   Understand the throughput limits, scaling options, and cost implications of different ingestion services. Know how to choose between on-demand and provisioned capacity modes, implement proper partitioning strategies, and optimize buffer sizes and intervals for optimal performance and cost efficiency.

Review Questions

1. A data engineering team is designing a real-time data processing system for a social media analytics company. The system needs to ingest and process millions of social media posts per minute, with the ability to scale automatically based on incoming data volume. The processed data should be available for real-time dashboards and stored for future analysis. Which combination of Amazon Kinesis services would best meet these requirements? (Choose two.)

    A. Amazon Kinesis Data Streams for data ingestion

    B. Amazon Data Firehose for data delivery to storage

    C. Amazon Kinesis Video Streams for data ingestion

    D. Amazon Kinesis Data Analytics for real-time processing

    E. Amazon SQS for message queuing

2. A data engineering team is building a system to analyze IoT sensor data from thousands of devices in real time. The data needs to be processed as it arrives and then stored for long-term analysis. The team wants to minimize the operational overhead and ensure that no data is lost during processing. Which Amazon Kinesis configuration would best meet these requirements?

    A. Use Kinesis Data Streams with enhanced fan-out consumers and configure the stream to use Provisioned Throughput mode.

    B. Implement Amazon Data Firehose with dynamic partitioning and deliver data directly to Amazon S3.

    C. Set up Kinesis Data Streams with standard consumers and use On-Demand capacity mode.

    D. Deploy Kinesis Data Analytics with tumbling windows and connect it directly to IoT Core.

3. A data engineering team is designing a real-time data streaming solution using Amazon Managed Streaming for Apache Kafka (Amazon MSK). They need to ensure that their Kafka cluster can handle sudden increases in traffic without manual intervention. Which feature should they enable to meet this requirement?

    A. MSK Connect

    B. MSK Serverless

    C. MSK Auto Scaling

    D. MSK Cruise Control

4. A company is using Amazon MSK for its data streaming needs and wants to integrate it with its existing AWS Identity and Access Management (IAM) setup for authentication and authorization. Which of the following methods should they use to achieve this integration?

    A. Enable SASL/SCRAM authentication and create IAM users for each Kafka client.

    B. Use SSL certificates for authentication and IAM roles for authorization.

    C. Enable IAM access control for the MSK cluster and use IAM roles or users for client authentication.

    D. Implement Kerberos authentication and map Kerberos principals to IAM roles.

5. A company is using Amazon Data Firehose to deliver streaming data to Amazon S3. They want to ensure that the data is encrypted at rest in the S3 bucket. Which of the following methods provides the highest level of control over the encryption keys while still allowing Amazon Data Firehose to encrypt the data?

   A. Enable encryption in transit for Amazon Data Firehose.

   B. Use AWS Key Management Service (KMS) customer-managed keys.

   C. Use client-side encryption before sending data to Amazon Data Firehose.

   D. Use S3-managed encryption keys (SSE-S3).

6. A data engineering team needs to build an ETL pipeline to process large volumes of semi-structured JSON data stored in Amazon S3 and load it into an Amazon Redshift data warehouse. The team wants to minimize the amount of custom code they need to write and maintain. Which AWS service should they choose for this task?

   A. Amazon EMR

   B. AWS Glue

   C. AWS Lambda

   D. Amazon Redshift Spectrum

7. A company wants to build a data lake solution that can automatically discover and catalog data from various sources, including on-premises databases and cloud storage. It needs a solution that can handle schema changes automatically and provide a searchable catalog of its data assets. Which AWS service should they use as the core component of this solution?

   A. Amazon Athena

   B. AWS Data Pipeline

   C. AWS Glue

   D. AWS Lake Formation

8. A large e-commerce company is planning to migrate its on-premises Oracle database to Amazon Aurora PostgreSQL. The database is approximately 5 TB in size and experiences high transaction volumes during business hours. The migration needs to be performed with minimal downtime, and the company wants to ensure that any data changes occurring during the migration process are captured and applied to the target database. Additionally, the company needs to transform some of the data during the migration process, including encrypting sensitive customer information and restructuring some tables to optimize for the new database engine. The migration also needs to handle large BLOB data stored in the Oracle database. Which AWS service or combination of services would be most suitable for this migration task?

   A. Use AWS Glue to extract data from Oracle, transform it, and load it into Aurora PostgreSQL.

   B. Employ AWS DataSync to transfer the data and use AWS Lambda for data transformation.

   C. Utilize Amazon EMR with custom scripts for data extraction, transformation, and loading.

   D. Implement AWS Database Migration Service (DMS) with custom transformations.

9. A genomics research institute has accumulated 80 TB of raw sequencing data stored in their on-premises data center. They want to transfer this data to AWS for analysis using various AWS analytics services. The institute is located in a remote area with limited Internet connectivity, with a maximum bandwidth of 100 Mbps. They need to complete the data transfer within two weeks and ensure the security of the sensitive genetic data during transit. Additionally, they want to minimize the impact on their daily operations and internet usage. Which AWS service or solution should they use for this data transfer?

   A. Set up an AWS Direct Connect connection and transfer the data over a private network.

   B. Use AWS DataSync with a DataSync agent installed on-premises to transfer the data to Amazon S3.

   C. Implement AWS Snowball devices for offline data transfer to AWS.

   D. Utilize Amazon S3 Transfer Acceleration with multipart uploads for faster data transfer.

10. A retail company wants to ingest large volumes of daily sales data (approximately 500 GB per day) from its operational database into its Amazon Redshift data warehouse for analytics. The data is currently exported as CSV files and stored in Amazon S3. The company needs a solution that can quickly load this data into Redshift tables, perform basic transformations like data type conversions, and handle occasional schema changes. They also want to ensure optimal performance and cost-efficiency. Which method should it use for this data ingestion process?

   A. Use AWS Glue to extract data from S3, transform it, and load it into Redshift.

   B. Implement DistCp with Amazon EMR to copy data from S3 to Redshift.

   C. Utilize Sqoop with Amazon EMR to transfer data from S3 to Redshift.

   D. Employ the Amazon Redshift COPY command to load data directly from S3.

Chapter

2

Building Automated Data Pipelines

**THE AWS CERTIFIED DATA ENGINEER –
ASSOCIATE EXAM OBJECTIVES COVERED
IN THIS CHAPTER MAY INCLUDE, BUT ARE
NOT LIMITED, TO THE FOLLOWING:**

✓ **Domain 1: Data Ingestion and Transformation**

  ▪ 1.3 Orchestrate data pipelines

  ▪ 1.4 Apply programming concepts

✓ **Domain 3: Data Operations and Support**

  ▪ 3.3 Maintain and monitor data pipelines

Introduction

By now you are already familiar with how the chapters are distributed based on the tasks corresponding to each domain discussed in the *AWS Certified Data Engineer Associate Exam Guide* (https://d1.awsstatic.com/training-and-certification/docs-data-engineer-associate/AWS-Certified-Data-Engineer-Associate_Exam-Guide.pdf). Let's do a quick walkthrough of which tasks are covered in this chapter. This chapter covers two tasks from Domain 1: Data Ingestion and Transformation and one task from Domain 3: Data Operations and Support.

There is a reason we have created a separate chapter for Automation of the data pipelines, because this is a huge topic on its own. To help you align with the *AWS Certified Data Engineer Associate Exam Guide*, let's first summarize what will be covered in this chapter corresponding to the individual task.

Please note that we will be mentioning a handful of AWS services during the following sections, but don't be overwhelmed by it just now, as we will be covering these services in detail during the latter part of this chapter.

> **Task Statement 1.3: Orchestrate Data Pipelines with AWS**   This task revolves around orchestrating data pipelines using AWS services to efficiently manage ETL (extract, transform, and load) processes. Key knowledge areas include understanding event-driven architecture and configuring AWS services based on schedules or dependencies. It involves skilled use of AWS Lambda, Amazon EventBridge, AWS Step Functions, and AWS Glue, including leveraging AWS Glue workflows, and also orchestrating pipelines through Amazon Managed Workflows for Apache Airflow (Amazon MWAA). These pipelines should be designed for performance, availability, scalability, resiliency, and fault tolerance. Also crucial are maintaining serverless workflows and utilizing AWS notification services such as Amazon SNS and Amazon SQS for efficient alerting mechanisms.

> **Task Statement 1.4: Apply Programming Concepts with AWS**   This task emphasizes the application of programming concepts in the deployment and management of AWS-based data pipelines. It requires knowledge of CI/CD processes, SQL queries for data handling, and infrastructure as code (IaC) practices with AWS Cloud Development Kit

(AWS CDK) and AWS CloudFormation. Skills include optimizing AWS Lambda for concurrency and performance, managing data transformations using SQL queries within Amazon Redshift and Amazon Athena, and employing the AWS Serverless Application Model (AWS SAM) for the deployment of serverless data pipelines that might include Lambda functions, AWS Step Functions, and Amazon DynamoDB tables. Also essential are understanding distributed computing principles, data structures, and algorithms, and leveraging Git for source control management.

Task Statement 3.3: Maintain and Monitor Data Pipelines with AWS   This task focuses on the maintenance and monitoring of data pipelines, utilizing a comprehensive suite of AWS services for operational efficiency and security. Knowledge areas include logging with Amazon CloudWatch, security monitoring with Amazon Macie, and audit trails with AWS CloudTrail. Skills necessary for this task involve extracting and analyzing logs for audits using Amazon Athena and Amazon CloudWatch Logs, deploying AWS-based logging and monitoring solutions for comprehensive auditability and traceability, and troubleshooting performance issues with tools like Amazon EMR and AWS Glue. Additionally, maintaining and monitoring data pipelines involves utilizing Amazon SNS and Amazon SQS for notification services, and understanding Amazon OpenSearch Service for advanced log analysis and insights, ensuring the pipelines remain performant, secure, and reliable.

Introduction to Automated Data Pipelines

We have been referencing the data engineering lifecycle throughout this book. Let's try to map what will be covered in this chapter.

Figure 2.1 shows the highlighted sections that will be covered when talking about the data engineering lifecycle.

FIGURE 2.1   The data engineering lifecycle

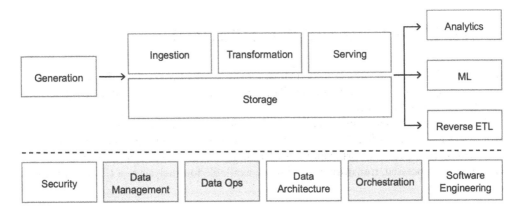

Let's break down the highlighted boxes in Figure 2.1. *Orchestration* is straightforward, as it's one of the task statements that will be covered in this chapter. Automating data pipelines and orchestration is like a city's traffic system, where automation installs traffic lights for smooth flow, and orchestration acts as the traffic control center, ensuring all parts work together efficiently.

Figure 2.2 shows the AWS Step Functions workflow for a successful ETL pipeline, from the Step Functions Inspector panel.

Data management, which encompasses the three task statements (orchestration, application of programming concepts, and maintenance and monitoring of data pipelines) involves the integration of AWS services to efficiently move, transform, and store data, ensuring data accuracy and availability through orchestration tools like AWS Lambda, AWS Step Functions, Amazon Managed Workflows for Apache Airflow (MWAA), and AWS Glue. Programming practices, such as CI/CD and infrastructure as code (IaC) with AWS Cloud-Formation, play a crucial role in deploying and managing data infrastructure consistently. Moreover, maintaining data integrity and performance is achieved through meticulous monitoring and logging with services like Amazon CloudWatch and AWS CloudTrail, alongside optimizing data storage and retrieval processes in services like Amazon S3 and Amazon Redshift. This holistic approach to data management ensures secure, efficient, and scalable handling of data across its lifecycle, underpinning the reliability and effectiveness of data-driven decisions and processes.

DataOps, adopting an agile methodology from DevOps for data analytics, emphasizes the automation, integration, and continuous delivery of data to enhance decision-making processes. It involves automating data pipelines using AWS services like AWS Lambda, AWS Step Functions, and AWS Glue for efficient data flow management; applying agile programming concepts, such as CI/CD, IaC with AWS CDK and AWS CloudFormation, and SQL query optimization, to enable rapid and iterative development; and maintaining and monitoring these pipelines with tools like Amazon CloudWatch and AWS CloudTrail for performance tuning and error minimization. This holistic approach streamlines data operations, significantly reducing cycle times for analytics, improving data quality, and fostering a culture of continuous improvement and collaboration among data teams, ensuring data insights are timely, accurate, and aligned with business goals.

Now let's dive deep into the orchestration piece.

Data Pipeline Orchestration

In order to design any orchestration pipeline, we can think of it as a flow diagram, which has a starting point and an ending point. The start of the flow diagram can be triggered on a schedule or due to an event.

Orchestration for data pipelines involves the automation and management of complex workflows and tasks within the data processing lifecycle—from extraction, transformation, and loading (ETL) to monitoring and error handling. It is crucial for ensuring that data is accurately processed, transformed, and made available for analysis in a timely and efficient manner.

FIGURE 2.2   Orchestrate an ETL pipeline with AWS Step Functions

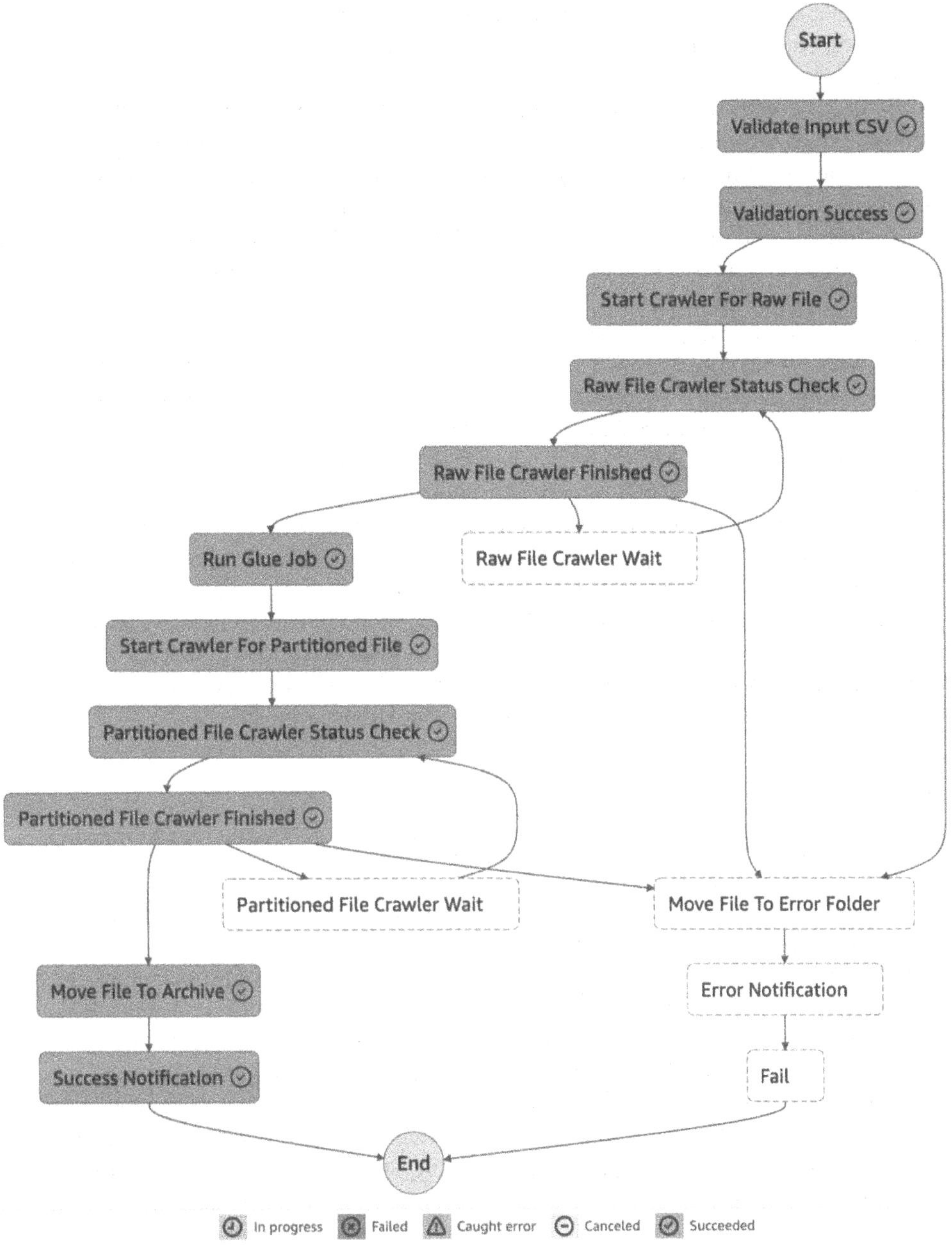

Source: Amazon Web Services / https://docs.aws.amazon.com/pdfs/
prescriptive-guidance/latest/patterns/prescriptive-guidance
.pdf#orchestrate-an-etl-pipeline-with-validation-transformation-
and-partitioning-using-aws-step-functions, last accessed on 19
December 2024.

Imagine a scenario where you have multiple data sources, such as databases, streaming data, and cloud storage. These data sources need to be processed, transformed, and integrated in a specific sequence to derive meaningful insights. This is where data pipeline orchestration comes into play, directing the flow of data through various stages of the pipeline.

AWS offers services like AWS Data Pipeline, AWS Glue, AWS MWAA, and AWS Step Functions, which serve as the orchestration tools. These services allow you to define and schedule data processing tasks, manage dependencies, and handle error conditions, ensuring that each process is triggered at the right time and in the right order.

Furthermore, data pipeline orchestration enables you to break down complex data workflows into modular components, allowing for reusability and scalability. These components can be easily swapped or modified.

The beauty of the multiple orchestration tools that AWS provides lies in its ability to integrate with a wide range of AWS services and third-party tools, creating a harmonious ecosystem where data flows seamlessly from one stage to another. This integration allows for advanced data processing techniques, such as machine learning and real-time analytics, enabling you to extract deeper insights and make data-driven decisions.

This chapter delves into the most widely recognized AWS services, emphasizing those frequently encountered in certification exams. By understanding these services and their use cases, you will be better equipped to determine the appropriate service for specific scenarios.

We begin with AWS Step Functions, a prominent orchestration service known for its versatility and integration across the AWS ecosystem. Step Functions enables developers to coordinate multiple AWS services into seamless workflows, simplifying complex processes. Its state machine-based approach ensures reliability and transparency, making it a cornerstone for automation and orchestration within cloud-native architectures.

AWS Step Functions

AWS Step Functions is a serverless workflow service that allows you to coordinate and manage the components of distributed applications and microservices using visual workflows. It provides a reliable way to orchestrate and sequence various AWS services, making it an ideal choice for building and managing data pipelines.

Step Functions offers a visual interface to design and manage workflows, making it easier to understand and maintain complex data pipelines. Workflows are defined using Amazon States Language, a JSON-based language that describes the states (tasks) and transitions (flow) of the workflow. One of the key advantages of Step Functions is its seamless integration with various AWS services, such as AWS Lambda, AWS Batch, AWS Glue, Amazon ECS, Amazon SNS, and Amazon SQS, allowing you to orchestrate and coordinate these services within your data pipeline. Additionally, Step Functions supports parallel execution of tasks, enabling efficient processing of large datasets or performing multiple operations concurrently.

Step Functions also provides built-in error handling and retry mechanisms, ensuring reliable execution of your data pipelines and minimizing the need for manual intervention.

Furthermore, it integrates with Amazon CloudWatch, allowing you to monitor and log the execution of your workflows, providing visibility into the progress and performance of your data pipelines. Step Functions can be used for orchestrating ETL (extract, transform, and load) pipelines, where you can extract data from various sources, transform it using AWS services like AWS Glue or AWS Lambda, and load it into data warehouses or data lakes. It can also be used for managing data processing workflows, coordinating and sequencing various data processing tasks, such as data validation, enrichment, and analysis, using a combination of AWS services like AWS Batch, AWS Lambda, and Amazon EMR. Additionally, Step Functions can be employed for managing machine learning pipelines, including data preprocessing, model training, evaluation, and deployment, leveraging services like Amazon SageMaker and AWS Lambda. Finally, it can be used for event-driven pipelines, triggering and orchestrating data pipelines based on events from various sources, such as Amazon S3, Amazon Kinesis, or Amazon SNS, enabling real-time data processing and analysis.

Key Features of AWS Step Functions for Data Pipeline Orchestration

Table 2.1 describes the AWS Step Functions features you can use for data pipeline orchestration.

TABLE 2.1   Key features of AWS Step Functions for data pipeline orchestration

Feature	Description
Visual Workflow Designer	Provides a visual interface to design and manage workflows, making it easier to understand and maintain complex data pipelines.
State Machine Definition	Workflows are defined using Amazon States Language, a JSON-based language that describes the states (tasks) and transitions (flow) of the workflow.
Integration with AWS Services	Seamlessly integrates with various AWS services, such as AWS Lambda, AWS Batch, AWS Glue, Amazon ECS, Amazon SNS, and Amazon SQS, allowing you to orchestrate and coordinate these services within your data pipeline.
Parallel Processing	Supports parallel execution of tasks, enabling efficient processing of large datasets or performing multiple operations concurrently.
Error Handling and Retry Mechanisms	Provides built-in error handling and retry mechanisms, ensuring reliable execution of your data pipelines and minimizing the need for manual intervention.
Monitoring and Logging	Integrates with Amazon CloudWatch, allowing you to monitor and log the execution of your workflows, providing visibility into the progress and performance of your data pipelines.

Use Cases for Data Pipeline Orchestration

Table 2.2 shows the AWS Step Functions use cases for data pipeline orchestration.

TABLE 2.2 Use cases for data pipeline orchestration with AWS Step Functions

Use Case	Description
ETL (Extract, Transform, and Load) Pipelines	Orchestrates the extraction of data from various sources, transforms it using AWS services like AWS Glue or AWS Lambda, and loads it into data warehouses or data lakes.
Data Processing Workflows	Coordinates and sequences various data processing tasks, such as data validation, enrichment, and analysis, using a combination of AWS services like AWS Batch, AWS Lambda, and Amazon EMR.
Machine Learning Pipelines	Manages the end-to-end lifecycle of machine learning workflows, including data preprocessing, model training, evaluation, and deployment, leveraging services like Amazon SageMaker and AWS Lambda.
Event-Driven Pipelines	Triggers and orchestrates data pipelines based on events from various sources, such as Amazon S3, Amazon Kinesis, or Amazon SNS, enabling real-time data processing and analysis.

Designing Data Pipelines with AWS Step Functions

When designing data pipelines with AWS Step Functions, the first step is to define the workflow by breaking down your data pipeline into individual tasks or steps, and identify the AWS services or custom code (AWS Lambda functions) required for each task. Next, create a state machine definition using the Amazon States Language to define the state machine, which represents the workflow of your data pipeline. This includes specifying the states (tasks), their order of execution, and any branching logic or parallel processing requirements. Integrate the necessary AWS services into your state machine definition, such as AWS Glue for data transformation tasks, AWS Batch for batch processing, Amazon S3 for data storage, and AWS Lambda for custom code execution. Define the input data sources for your data pipeline, such as Amazon S3 buckets or Amazon Kinesis streams, and specify the output destinations for the processed data, like Amazon S3 or Amazon Redshift.

Implement error handling and retry mechanisms within your state machine definition to ensure reliable execution and recovery from failures. Set up monitoring and logging for your Step Functions workflow using Amazon CloudWatch, providing visibility into the execution of your data pipeline and helping in troubleshooting and performance optimization. Test your data pipeline workflow locally or in a non-production environment before deploying it to production, as Step Functions supports versioning, allowing you to manage and roll back changes if needed. Optionally, you can automate and schedule the execution of your data pipeline using AWS services like Amazon EventBridge or AWS Data Pipeline, ensuring that your data processing workflows run at the desired intervals or in response to specific events.

To help you understand this better, let's go through the general steps here:

1. **Define the workflow:** Start by breaking down your data pipeline into individual tasks or steps. Identify the AWS services or custom code (AWS Lambda functions) required for each task.

2. **Create a state machine definition:** Use the Amazon States Language to define the state machine, which represents the workflow of your data pipeline. This includes specifying the states (tasks), their order of execution, and any branching logic or parallel processing requirements.

3. **Integrate AWS services:** Incorporate the necessary AWS services into your state machine definition. For example, you can use AWS Glue for data transformation tasks, AWS Batch for batch processing, Amazon S3 for data storage, and AWS Lambda for custom code execution.

4. **Configure input and output:** Define the input data sources for your data pipeline, such as Amazon S3 buckets or Amazon Kinesis streams. Additionally, specify the output destinations for the processed data, like Amazon S3 or Amazon Redshift.

5. **Implement error handling and retries:** Configure error handling and retry mechanisms within your state machine definition to ensure reliable execution and recovery from failures.

6. **Monitor and log:** Set up monitoring and logging for your Step Functions workflow using Amazon CloudWatch. This will provide visibility into the execution of your data pipeline and help in troubleshooting and performance optimization.

7. **Test and deploy:** Test your data pipeline workflow locally or in a non-production environment before deploying it to production. Step Functions supports versioning, allowing you to manage and roll back changes if needed.

8. **Automate and schedule:** Optionally, you can automate and schedule the execution of your data pipeline using AWS services like Amazon EventBridge or AWS Data Pipeline, ensuring that your data processing workflows run at the desired intervals or in response to specific events.

In the example shown in Figure 2.3, the data pipeline is represented as a state machine in AWS Step Functions using simple sequential state machine. Each task (e.g., Extract Data, Task1, Task2, Task3, Task4) is a state in the state machine, and the arrows represent the transitions or flow between the tasks. This visual representation helps in understanding and managing the complex data pipeline workflow. Apart from support for AWS Native service integrations directly or indirectly by using AWS Lambda Function as a step, AWS Step Functions supports the flow-related states shown in Table 2.3.

FIGURE 2.3 Orchestrating an ETL pipeline with AWS Step Functions

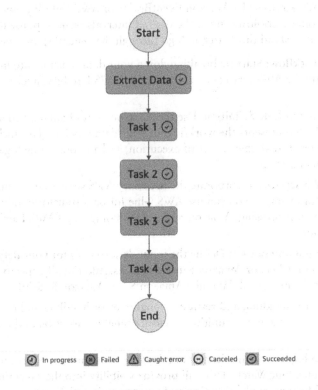

TABLE 2.3 Flow-related states of AWS Step Functions

State	Description
Task	A state that performs a single unit of work, such as invoking an AWS Lambda function, running an AWS Batch job, or calling a third-party API.
Choice	A state that provides branching logic based on the input data or the result of the previous state. It allows you to control the flow of execution based on specified conditions.
Wait	A state that delays the execution of the state machine for a specified period or until a specified condition is met.
Parallel	A state that initiates multiple branches of execution in parallel, allowing you to run multiple tasks concurrently.
Map	A state that iterates over an array of items and runs a set of steps for each item in the array.
Success	A terminal state that successfully completes the state machine execution.

State	Description
Fail	A terminal state that stops the state machine execution and marks it as a failure.
Pass	A state that simply passes its input to its output, allowing data to flow through the state machine without performing any work.
Catch	A state that catches and handles errors that occur in other states within the same branch of execution.
Retry	A state that retries the execution of a failed state or task a specified number of times, with optional delay and backoff strategies.

By leveraging AWS Step Functions for data pipeline orchestration, you can build reliable, scalable, and maintainable data processing workflows. Step Functions' visual interface, integration with various AWS services, and built-in error handling and monitoring capabilities make it a powerful tool for managing complex data pipelines in the cloud.

Orchestrating Large-Scale Parallel Data Processing with AWS Step Functions

In the previous sections, we explored how AWS Step Functions enables you to orchestrate and coordinate various AWS services and custom code into serverless workflows. We discussed the visual workflow designer, state machine definitions, and the different states available, such as Task, Choice, Wait, and Parallel.

However, as your data processing requirements grow, you may encounter scenarios where you need to process large datasets in a highly parallel and scalable manner. This is where the new Distributed Map state in AWS Step Functions comes into play.

The Distributed Map state is a powerful extension of the existing Map state, designed to handle large-scale parallel data processing workloads. It allows you to iterate over millions of objects stored in Amazon Simple Storage Service (Amazon S3), launching up to 10,000 parallel workflows to process the data concurrently.

Imagine you have a vast collection of log files, images, or CSV data stored in an S3 bucket, and you need to perform complex transformations or analysis on each individual item. With the Distributed Map state, you can seamlessly orchestrate this process, leveraging the scalability and parallelism offered by AWS Step Functions and other AWS services.

One of the key advantages of the Distributed Map state is its native integration with Amazon S3. You can configure the S3 bucket and prefix where your data resides directly within the distributed map configuration. This tight coupling with S3 streamlines the data ingestion process, eliminating the need for complex data staging or preprocessing steps.

Unlike the original Map state, which is limited to processing JSON arrays, the Distributed Map state supports a wide range of input sources, including JSON arrays, JSON files,

CSV files, and even Amazon S3 inventory. This flexibility allows you to work with diverse data formats and structures, ensuring that your data processing workflows can adapt to your specific requirements.

To process the data, you can compose any service API supported by AWS Step Functions, such as invoking AWS Lambda functions, running AWS Batch jobs, or making API calls to other AWS services. This integration with various AWS services empowers you to leverage the power of serverless computing, containerization, and managed services, enabling you to build highly scalable and cost-effective data processing pipelines.

Whether you're processing log files for analysis, transforming image data for machine learning models, or performing complex calculations on financial data, the Distributed Map state in AWS Step Functions provides a powerful and scalable solution for orchestrating large-scale parallel data processing workloads in the cloud.

For further information on this new state to help with large-scale parallel processing, please refer to the AWS blog post *Step Functions Distributed Map – A Serverless Solution for Large Scale Parallel Data Processing* (`https://aws.amazon.com/blogs/aws/ step-functions-distributed-map-a-serverless-solution-for-large-scale- parallel-data-processing`).

Amazon Managed Workflows for Apache Airflow

Another popular orchestration service is Amazon Managed Workflows for Apache Airflow (Amazon MWAA), which is a fully managed service that allows you to easily set up and operate Apache Airflow environments in the AWS Cloud. Apache Airflow is an open-source platform for programmatically authoring, scheduling, and monitoring workflows. With Amazon MWAA, you can leverage the power of Apache Airflow to build and automate data pipelines on AWS without the overhead of managing the underlying infrastructure.

Amazon MWAA provisions and manages the Apache Airflow environment, including the web server, scheduler, and worker nodes, ensuring high availability and scalability. It seamlessly integrates with various AWS services, such as Amazon S3, Amazon Redshift, AWS Glue, Amazon EMR, and Amazon SageMaker, enabling you to orchestrate and automate data pipelines across these services. Amazon MWAA provides access to the Apache Airflow web interface and APIs, allowing you to author, schedule, monitor, and manage your data pipelines using the familiar Airflow tooling.

Amazon MWAA is designed to be secure and compliant, with features like AWS Private-Link for private network access, integration with AWS Identity and Access Management (IAM) for access control, and support for AWS Key Management Service (KMS) for data encryption. It automatically scales the Apache Airflow environment based on your workload demands, ensuring high availability and performance for your data pipelines. Additionally, Amazon MWAA integrates with Amazon CloudWatch, providing comprehensive monitoring and logging capabilities for your Apache Airflow environments and data pipelines. Amazon MWAA can be used for orchestrating and automating ETL (extract, transform, and load) pipelines, leveraging AWS services like Amazon S3, AWS Glue, and Amazon Redshift for data extraction, transformation, and loading. It can also be used for automating data lake ingestion and processing, ingesting, and processing data from various sources into a data lake on Amazon S3, using Apache Airflow workflows and AWS services like Amazon Kinesis and Amazon EMR. Furthermore, Amazon MWAA can be employed for building and managing end-to-end machine learning pipelines, including data preprocessing, model training, evaluation, and deployment, using Apache Airflow and AWS services like Amazon SageMaker. Finally, it can be used for event-driven data pipelines, triggering and orchestrating data pipelines based on events from various sources, such as Amazon S3, Amazon Kinesis, or Amazon SNS, enabling real-time data processing and analysis.

Key Features of Amazon MWAA for Data Pipeline Automation

Table 2.4 describes the Amazon MWAA features you can use for data pipeline automation.

TABLE 2.4   Key features of Amazon MWAA for data pipeline automation

Feature	Description
Managed Apache Airflow Environment	Provisions and manages the Apache Airflow environment, including the web server, scheduler, and worker nodes, ensuring high availability and scalability.
Integration with AWS Services	Seamlessly integrates with various AWS services, such as Amazon S3, Amazon Redshift, AWS Glue, Amazon EMR, and Amazon SageMaker, enabling you to orchestrate and automate data pipelines across these services.
Airflow User Interface and APIs	Provides access to the Apache Airflow web interface and APIs, allowing you to author, schedule, monitor, and manage your data pipelines using the familiar Airflow tooling.
Secure and Compliant	Designed to be secure and compliant, with features like AWS Private-Link for private network access, integration with AWS Identity and Access Management (IAM) for access control, and support for AWS Key Management Service (KMS) for data encryption.
Scalability and High Availability	Automatically scales the Apache Airflow environment based on your workload demands, ensuring high availability and performance for your data pipelines.
Monitoring and Logging	Integrates with Amazon CloudWatch, providing comprehensive monitoring and logging capabilities for your Apache Airflow environments and data pipelines.

Use Cases for Amazon MWAA in Data Pipeline Automation

Table 2.5 shows the Amazon MWAA use cases for data pipeline automation.

TABLE 2.5   Use cases for Amazon MWAA in data pipeline automation

Use Case	Description
ETL (Extract, Transform, and Load) Pipelines	Orchestrate and automate complex ETL workflows, leveraging AWS services like Amazon S3, AWS Glue, and Amazon Redshift for data extraction, transformation, and loading.
Data Lake Ingestion and Processing	Automate the ingestion and processing of data from various sources into a data lake on Amazon S3, using Apache Airflow workflows and AWS services like Amazon Kinesis and Amazon EMR.
Machine Learning Pipelines	Build and manage end-to-end machine learning pipelines, including data preprocessing, model training, evaluation, and deployment, using Apache Airflow and AWS services like Amazon SageMaker.
Event-Driven Data Pipelines	Trigger and orchestrate data pipelines based on events from various sources, such as Amazon S3, Amazon Kinesis, or Amazon SNS, enabling real-time data processing and analysis.

Building Data Pipelines with Amazon MWAA

When building data pipelines with Amazon MWAA, the first step is to create an Amazon MWAA environment, which provisions and manages the Apache Airflow infrastructure for you. Configure the environment settings, such as networking, security, and logging. Next, use the Apache Airflow Python scripting interface to define your data pipelines as directed acyclic graphs (DAGs). DAGs represent the sequence of tasks and dependencies within your data pipeline. Incorporate the necessary AWS services into your Airflow DAGs using the provided operators and hooks. For example, you can use the AWS Glue operator for data transformation tasks, the Amazon EMR operator for batch processing, and the Amazon S3 operator for data storage and retrieval. Define the dependencies between tasks within your Airflow DAGs, ensuring that tasks are executed in the correct order and that data flows seamlessly through your pipeline.

Use Airflow's scheduling capabilities to define the execution schedule for your data pipelines, or trigger them based on specific events or conditions. Leverage the Apache Airflow web interface and APIs to monitor the execution of your data pipelines, view logs, and manage tasks and workflows. Configure error handling and retry mechanisms within your Airflow DAGs to ensure reliable execution and recovery from failures. Utilize Amazon CloudWatch to monitor and log the execution of your Apache Airflow environments and data pipelines, providing visibility into performance and enabling troubleshooting. Take advantage of Amazon MWAA's automatic scaling capabilities to ensure that your Apache Airflow environment can handle increasing workloads and data pipeline demands.

1. **Set up an Amazon MWAA environment:** Create an Amazon MWAA environment, which provisions and manages the Apache Airflow infrastructure for you. Configure the environment settings, such as networking, security, and logging.

2. **Define Airflow DAGs:** Use the Apache Airflow Python scripting interface to define your data pipelines as directed acyclic graphs (DAGs). DAGs represent the sequence of tasks and dependencies within your data pipeline.

3. **Integrate AWS services:** Incorporate the necessary AWS services into your Airflow DAGs using the provided operators and hooks. For example, you can use the AWS Glue operator for data transformation tasks, the Amazon EMR operator for batch processing, and the Amazon S3 operator for data storage and retrieval.

4. **Configure task dependencies:** Define the dependencies between tasks within your Airflow DAGs, ensuring that tasks are executed in the correct order and that data flows seamlessly through your pipeline.

5. **Schedule and trigger pipelines:** Use Airflow's scheduling capabilities to define the execution schedule for your data pipelines, or trigger them based on specific events or conditions.

6. **Monitor and manage pipelines:** Leverage the Apache Airflow web interface and APIs to monitor the execution of your data pipelines, view logs, and manage tasks and workflows.

7. **Implement error handling and retries:** Configure error handling and retry mechanisms within your Airflow DAGs to ensure reliable execution and recovery from failures.

8. **Integrate with AWS services for monitoring and logging:** Utilize Amazon CloudWatch to monitor and log the execution of your Apache Airflow environments and data pipelines, providing visibility into performance and enabling troubleshooting.

9. **Automate and scale:** Take advantage of Amazon MWAA's automatic scaling capabilities to ensure that your Apache Airflow environment can handle increasing workloads and data pipeline demands.

By leveraging Amazon MWAA, you can streamline the process of building and automating data pipelines on AWS. With its managed Apache Airflow environment, seamless integration with AWS services, and robust monitoring and logging capabilities, Amazon MWAA simplifies the orchestration and management of complex data pipelines in the cloud.

AWS Glue

AWS Glue is a fully managed ETL service that simplifies preparing and loading data for analytics. It provides a serverless environment for running Apache Spark ETL jobs and supports Python shell jobs for lightweight scripting and transformations. With its ability to handle both batch and streaming ETL workflows, AWS Glue enables the seamless processing of diverse data sources. Integrated tightly with other AWS services, it offers a versatile and scalable solution for automating and managing data pipelines across the AWS platform.

When it comes to building and automating data pipelines with AWS Glue, you can follow these general steps:

1. **Discover and catalog data sources:** AWS Glue provides a Data Catalog, which is a persistent metadata store that allows you to discover and catalog data sources across

various AWS services, such as Amazon S3, Amazon RDS, and Amazon Redshift. This step involves crawling your data sources and creating metadata tables in the Data Catalog.

2. **Define ETL jobs:** Use AWS Glue's visual editor or Apache Spark scripts to define your ETL jobs. These jobs specify the transformations and processing steps that need to be applied to your data sources. AWS Glue supports a wide range of data formats and provides built-in transformations, as well as the ability to write custom transformations using Apache Spark.

3. **Create data pipelines:** AWS Glue allows you to create and manage data pipelines, which are workflows that orchestrate and schedule the execution of your ETL jobs. Data pipelines can include multiple jobs, as well as dependencies and branching logic.

   - Data pipelines can be triggered based on various events, such as the arrival of new data in Amazon S3 or a scheduled time.

   - You can define retry policies and error-handling mechanisms to ensure reliable execution of your pipelines.

4. **Monitor and manage pipelines:** AWS Glue integrates with Amazon CloudWatch, allowing you to monitor the execution of your data pipelines and ETL jobs. You can view logs, set up alerts, and track performance metrics.

   - AWS Glue also provides APIs and SDKs for programmatically managing and automating your data pipelines.

5. **Optimize and scale:** AWS Glue automatically provisions and scales the Apache Spark environment based on the workload requirements of your ETL jobs and data pipelines.

   - You can configure worker types and scaling policies to optimize performance and cost.

   - AWS Glue supports modern tools and technologies by offering near-current versions of runtime versions. For example, AWS Glue 5.0 includes Apache Spark 3.5.3, closely aligned with the (at the time of writing) current release, Spark 3.5.4, enabling access to cutting-edge features and performance improvements while maintaining stability and security.

AWS Glue offers several advantages when building and automating data pipelines on AWS:

- **Serverless architecture:** AWS Glue is a fully managed service, eliminating the need to provision and manage infrastructure for running your ETL jobs and data pipelines.

- **Integrated with AWS services:** AWS Glue seamlessly integrates with other AWS services, such as Amazon S3, Amazon RDS, Amazon Redshift, and Amazon Athena, enabling you to build end-to-end data pipelines on the AWS platform.

- **Apache Spark integration:** AWS Glue provides a serverless Apache Spark environment, allowing you to leverage the power of Apache Spark for data processing and transformation.

- **Data Catalog:** The AWS Glue Data Catalog simplifies data discovery and metadata management, making it easier to understand and work with your data sources.

- **Scalability and flexibility:** AWS Glue automatically scales the Apache Spark environment based on your workload demands, ensuring efficient and cost-effective execution of your data pipelines.

- **Monitoring and logging:** AWS Glue integrates with Amazon CloudWatch, providing comprehensive monitoring and logging capabilities for your ETL jobs and data pipelines.

By leveraging AWS Glue, you can streamline the process of building and automating data pipelines on AWS. Its serverless architecture, integration with AWS services, and Apache Spark support make it a powerful tool for orchestrating and managing complex data processing workflows in the cloud.

FIGURE 2.4   AWS Glue data pipeline architecture

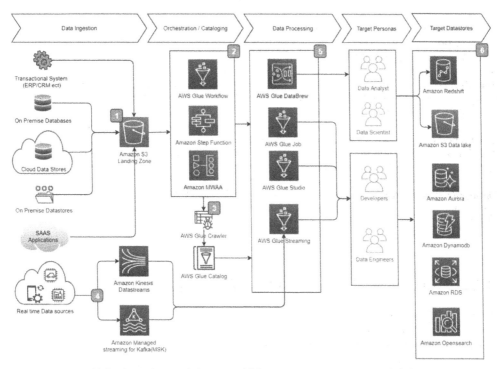

Source: Amazon Web Services / https://docs.aws.amazon.com/whitepapers/ latest/aws-glue-best-practices-build-efficient-data-pipeline/ reference-architecture-with-the-aws-glue-product-family.html, last accessed on 19 December 2024.

Figure 2.4 shows the creation of a data pipeline using the AWS Glue product family. AWS Glue Data Catalog is used to discover and catalog data sources. ETL jobs are defined using AWS Glue's visual editor or Apache Spark scripts. These ETL jobs are then orchestrated and scheduled using AWS Glue data pipelines. The execution of these pipelines and jobs is monitored and managed using Amazon CloudWatch for logs and metrics.

Table 2.6 shows the advantages of using AWS Glue for building data pipelines.

TABLE 2.6   Advantages of AWS Glue for building and automating data pipelines

Advantage	Description
Serverless Architecture	AWS Glue is a fully managed service, eliminating the need to provision and manage infrastructure for running ETL jobs and data pipelines.
Integration with AWS Services	AWS Glue seamlessly integrates with other AWS services, such as Amazon S3, Amazon RDS, Amazon Redshift, and Amazon Athena, enabling end-to-end data pipelines on the AWS platform.
Apache Spark Integration	AWS Glue provides a serverless Apache Spark environment, allowing you to leverage the power of Apache Spark for data processing and transformation.
Data Catalog	The AWS Glue Data Catalog simplifies data discovery and metadata management, making it easier to understand and work with your data sources.
Scalability and Flexibility	AWS Glue automatically scales the Apache Spark environment based on your workload demands, ensuring efficient and cost-effective execution of your data pipelines.
Monitoring and Logging	AWS Glue integrates with Amazon CloudWatch, providing comprehensive monitoring and logging capabilities for your ETL jobs and data pipelines.

AWS Glue Workflows for Data Pipeline Orchestration

AWS Glue Workflows is a feature within the AWS Glue service that allows you to orchestrate and manage complex data processing pipelines. It provides a visual interface for defining and scheduling workflows, enabling you to coordinate the execution of various AWS Glue jobs, crawlers, and triggers. See Table 2.7 for an overview of the key components.

TABLE 2.7   Key components of AWS Glue Workflows

Component	Description
Jobs	Apache Spark ETL jobs for data transformation and processing
Crawlers	Crawlers that discover and catalog data sources in the AWS Glue Data Catalog
Triggers	Triggers that initiate workflow runs based on events or schedules
Workflows	Visual representations of the data processing pipelines, including dependencies and branching logic

Creating AWS Glue Workflows

Here is how to create AWS Glue workflows:

1. **Define AWS Glue jobs:** Create Apache Spark ETL jobs using AWS Glue's visual editor or Apache Spark scripts to perform data transformations and processing tasks.

2. **Configure crawlers:** Set up crawlers to discover and catalog data sources in the AWS Glue Data Catalog.

3. **Set up triggers:** Define triggers to initiate workflow runs based on events (e.g., new data arrival in Amazon S3) or schedules.

4. **Design workflows:** Use the AWS Glue Workflows visual interface to design and orchestrate your data processing pipelines, specifying the order of execution, dependencies, and branching logic.

Figure 2.5 is from the AWS documentation on building AWS Glue workflows to build and orchestrate ETL pipelines directly in the AWS Glue console. An AWS Glue crawler discovers and catalogs data sources. A trigger (e.g., new data arrival) initiates the AWS Glue workflow, which orchestrates the execution of three AWS Glue jobs—for data extraction, data transformation, and data loading.

When to Use What (AWS Step Functions, Amazon MWAA, or AWS Glue)

When it comes to building and automating data pipelines on AWS, you have several powerful services at your disposal: AWS Step Functions, Amazon Managed Workflows for Apache Airflow (Amazon MWAA), and AWS Glue. Each service has its own strengths and use cases, and choosing the right one depends on your specific requirements and the nature of your data pipeline.

FIGURE 2.5   An AWS Glue workflow

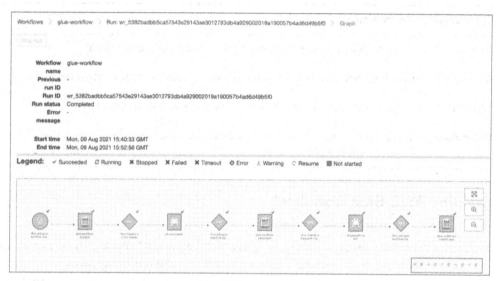

Source: https://aws.amazon.com/blogs/architecture/field-notes-how-to-build-an-aws-glue-workflow-using-the-aws-cloud-development-kit

AWS Step Functions   AWS Step Functions is like a versatile multi-tool that can handle a wide range of tasks. It's a serverless workflow service that allows you to orchestrate and coordinate various AWS services and custom code. Step Functions is particularly well suited for building and managing data pipelines that involve multiple steps, branching logic, and parallel processing.

Use AWS Step Functions when:

- Your data pipeline involves orchestrating multiple AWS services and custom code.
- You need to implement complex branching logic or parallel processing.
- Your data pipeline requires event-driven or long-running workflows.
- You want a visual representation of your workflow for easier understanding and maintenance.

Amazon MWAA   Amazon MWAA is like a specialized power tool designed specifically for managing Apache Airflow workflows. It provides a fully managed Apache Airflow environment, allowing you to focus on building and automating data pipelines without worrying about the underlying infrastructure.

Use Amazon MWAA when:

- You have existing Apache Airflow expertise or prefer the Airflow workflow management approach.
- Your data pipelines involve complex scheduling and dependency management.
- You need to integrate with a wide range of AWS services and third-party tools.
- You require robust monitoring, logging, and scalability for your Apache Airflow environment.

AWS Glue   AWS Glue is like a specialized tool designed for extract, transform, and load (ETL) operations. It provides a serverless Apache Spark environment and a data catalog for managing metadata, making it an ideal choice for building and automating data pipelines focused on data transformation and loading.

Use AWS Glue when:

- Your data pipeline primarily involves ETL operations, such as data extraction, transformation, and loading.
- You need to work with a wide range of data formats and sources.
- You want to leverage the power of Apache Spark for data processing and transformation.
- You require a centralized data catalog for metadata management and data discovery.

To better understand when to use each service, consider Table 2.8.

TABLE 2.8   Service strengths and use cases

Service	Strengths	Use Cases
AWS Step Functions	Orchestration, visual workflows, branching logic, parallel processing	Complex multi-service pipelines, event-driven workflows, long-running workflows
Amazon MWAA	Managed Apache Airflow, scheduling, dependency management, scalability	Preference over managed service for widely used open-source technologies, ETL pipelines, data lake ingestion, machine learning pipelines, complex scheduling
AWS Glue	ETL operations, Apache Spark integration, data catalog, serverless	Data transformation, data loading, working with diverse data formats

It's important to note that these services can also be used in combination to build more comprehensive data pipelines. For example, you could use AWS Glue for ETL operations, AWS Step Functions for orchestrating the overall pipeline, and Amazon MWAA for managing specific Apache Airflow workflows within the pipeline.

To illustrate with an analogy, imagine you're building a house. AWS Glue would be like the tools used for framing, cutting, and assembling the structure (data transformation and loading). AWS Step Functions would be the blueprint and project management tool, orchestrating the various construction tasks and ensuring that everything is coordinated (orchestrating multiple services and workflows). Amazon MWAA would be like a specialized subcontractor responsible for handling complex plumbing and electrical work (managing Apache Airflow workflows for specific tasks).

In Figure 2.6, the different AWS services (AWS Step Functions, Amazon MWAA, and AWS Glue) are depicted as tools in a carpenter's toolbox. Just as a carpenter would choose the right tool for a specific job, you need to select the appropriate AWS service based on the complexity, scale, and requirements of your data pipeline.

FIGURE 2.6   AWS services analogy—a carpenter's toolbox

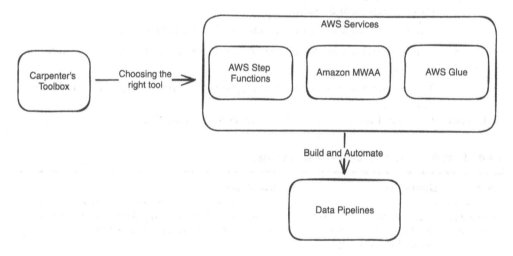

By understanding the strengths and use cases of each service, you can choose the right tool (or combination of tools) to build efficient, scalable, and reliable data pipelines on AWS.

Best Practices for Data Pipelines Orchestration

Data pipelines are the backbone of modern data-driven applications, enabling the seamless flow of data from various sources to its destination for analysis and decision-making. Orchestrating these pipelines effectively is crucial for ensuring data integrity, reliability, and scalability.

Here are some best practices to consider when building and orchestrating data pipelines:

- **Modular design:** Adopt a modular approach to pipeline development, breaking down complex processes into smaller, reusable components. This promotes code reusability, maintainability, and testability.

- **Idempotency:** Ensure that your pipeline components are idempotent, meaning they can be executed multiple times without causing unintended side effects. This is particularly important for handling failures and retries.

- **Monitoring and alerting:** Implement robust monitoring and alerting mechanisms to track pipeline performance, identify bottlenecks, and promptly address issues. This can be achieved through logging, metrics, and alerting tools.

- **Error handling and retries:** Design your pipelines to gracefully handle errors, and implement retry mechanisms for transient failures. This enhances resilience and reduces the need for manual intervention.

- **Scalability and parallelization:** Architect your pipelines to scale horizontally and leverage parallelization techniques to handle increasing data volumes and workloads efficiently.

- **Data lineage and provenance:** Maintain comprehensive data lineage and provenance information to track the origin, transformations, and dependencies of your data. This aids in troubleshooting, auditing, and ensuring data quality.

- **Versioning and testing:** Implement versioning for your pipeline code and data artifacts, and establish robust testing practices to ensure pipeline integrity and catch regressions early.

- **Documentation and collaboration:** Document your pipelines thoroughly, including their purpose, components, dependencies, and configurations. Foster collaboration among team members to promote knowledge sharing and collective ownership.

- **Security and access control:** Implement appropriate security measures—such as encryption, access controls, and secure data transfer protocols—to protect sensitive data and ensure compliance with relevant regulations.

- **Automation and scheduling:** Automate pipeline execution and scheduling to ensure timely and consistent data processing. This can be achieved through orchestration tools or workflow management systems.

In Figure 2.7, the data pipeline orchestrates the flow of data from multiple sources through various stages, including ingestion, staging, cleaning, enrichment, and finally, loading it into the data sink. Each stage represents a modular component that can be independently developed, tested, and scaled as needed. The orchestration ensures that these components are executed in the correct order, with proper error handling, monitoring, and scheduling mechanisms in place.

By following these best practices, you can build robust, scalable, and maintainable data pipelines that deliver reliable and valuable insights to drive your business forward.

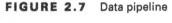

FIGURE 2.7   Data pipeline

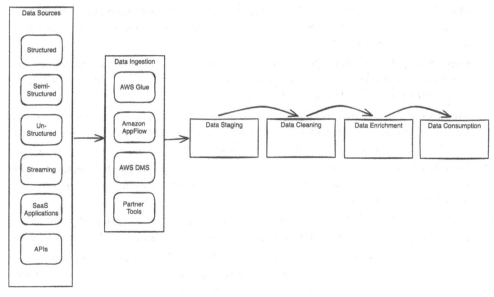

Supporting AWS Services for Enhanced Orchestration

In the following sections, we'll examine supporting AWS services for enhanced orchestration.

AWS Lambda

AWS Lambda is a serverless computing service that allows you to run code without provisioning or managing servers. It automatically scales and manages the underlying compute resources, making it a powerful and flexible tool for building and automating data pipelines on AWS. AWS Lambda can be seamlessly integrated with various AWS services, including AWS Step Functions, Amazon Managed Workflows for Apache Airflow (Amazon MWAA), and AWS Glue, to enhance and extend their capabilities.

AWS Lambda Functions Limitations

Here are some limitations of AWS Lambda functions:

- **Execution time limit:** AWS Lambda functions have a maximum execution time limit of 15 minutes. If your function takes longer than 15 minutes to complete, it will be terminated. This limitation can be a challenge for long-running or computationally intensive tasks.

- **Memory allocation:** The maximum memory allocation for a Lambda function is 10,240 MB (10 GB). While this is generally sufficient for most use cases, memory-intensive applications or those requiring large in-memory data processing may face limitations.

- **Disk space:** AWS Lambda functions have a temporary disk space of 512 MB in the /tmp directory. This space is used for storing temporary files and data during function execution. If your function requires more disk space, you'll need to leverage other storage services, such as Amazon S3 or Amazon EFS, which will be discussed in the next section.

- **Concurrent executions:** AWS imposes a default limit of 1,000 concurrent executions per account (region-specific), which can be increased upon request.

- **Deployment package size:** The deployment package size for a Lambda function, including code and dependencies, is limited to 50 MB when uploaded directly via the console, Lambda API, or SDKs. For larger files, you can upload them using Amazon S3. The uncompressed contents of a deployment package cannot exceed 250 MB. If using an AWS Lambda container image, the maximum image size is 10 GB.

- **VPC networking:** When running a Lambda function within a virtual private cloud (VPC), there are additional considerations and limitations related to network configuration, security group rules, and Internet access.

- **Cold start latency:** Lambda functions may experience higher latency during "cold starts," which occur when a new instance of the function needs to be initialized. This can impact the overall performance of your application, especially for time-sensitive workloads.

- **Language support:** While AWS Lambda supports a variety of programming languages (e.g., Python, Node.js, Java, C#, and Go), it may not support all versions or features of a particular language or runtime.

- **External dependencies:** If your Lambda function relies on external dependencies or libraries, you'll need to include them in the deployment package, which can increase the package size and potentially impact cold start performance.

- **Stateless architecture:** AWS Lambda functions are designed to be stateless, meaning they cannot maintain state between invocations. If you need to maintain state or share data between function invocations, you'll need to use external storage services like Amazon DynamoDB or Amazon ElastiCache.

While AWS Lambda Functions have these limitations, AWS provides various services and techniques to mitigate or work around them, such as AWS Step Functions for long-running workflows, AWS Batch for batch processing, and AWS Lambda Layers for managing dependencies. Additionally, AWS continuously works on improving and expanding the capabilities of AWS Lambda to address emerging use cases and requirements.

Using and Mounting Storage in Lambda Functions

AWS Lambda functions, by default, have a limited temporary storage capacity (/tmp directory) and are designed to be stateless. However, when building and orchestrating data pipelines that involve processing large datasets or require access to persistent storage, you can leverage the ability to mount storage volumes from within Lambda functions. This feature allows you to access and process data stored in Amazon Elastic File System (Amazon EFS) or Amazon Simple Storage Service (Amazon S3), enabling more efficient and scalable data processing workflows. Imagine you're a chef preparing a multi-course meal for a large event. Just as you would need access to a well-stocked pantry and refrigerator to store and retrieve ingredients, mounting storage volumes within Lambda functions provides your data pipeline with access to a vast storage space for data retrieval and processing.

Table 2.9 shows the mounting methods for different storage services.

TABLE 2.9 Mounting storage volumes in Lambda functions

Storage Service	Mounting Method
Amazon EFS	Specify the EFS file system ID and mount point in the Lambda function configuration.
Amazon S3	Use the AWS Lambda File System library to mount an S3 bucket as a file system.

Example: Mounting an Amazon EFS Volume

Here is an example of mounting an Amazon EFS volume:

```python
import os

def lambda_handler(event, context):
    # Access data from the mounted EFS volume
    data_path = "/mnt/efs/data/input_data.csv"
    with open(data_path, "r") as f:
        data = f.read()

    # Process the data
    processed_data = process_data(data)

    # Write the processed data back to the EFS volume
    output_path = "/mnt/efs/data/output_data.csv"
    with open(output_path, "w") as f:
        f.write(processed_data)
```

In this example, the Lambda function mounts an Amazon EFS volume at the /mnt/efs path. It reads input data from the mounted volume, processes the data, and then writes the processed data back to the mounted volume.

AWS Lambda and AWS Step Functions

AWS Lambda functions can be used as tasks within AWS Step Functions state machines, enabling you to execute custom logic and perform specific operations as part of your data pipeline workflows. This integration allows you to:

- Implement custom data processing or transformation logic using AWS Lambda functions

- Invoke AWS Lambda functions to interact with other AWS services or third-party APIs

- Leverage AWS Lambda functions for data validation, enrichment, or filtering tasks within your data pipelines

- Use AWS Lambda functions to handle error conditions, retries, or fallback scenarios in your Step Functions workflows

AWS Lambda and Amazon MWAA

While Amazon MWAA provides a managed Apache Airflow environment, you can extend its functionality by integrating with AWS Lambda. This integration enables you to:

- Create custom Airflow operators or sensors using AWS Lambda functions, allowing you to interact with AWS services or third-party APIs directly from your Airflow workflows

- Implement custom data processing or transformation logic within your Airflow directed acyclic graphs (DAGs) using AWS Lambda functions

- Leverage AWS Lambda functions for data validation, enrichment, or filtering tasks within your Airflow-based data pipelines

- Use AWS Lambda functions to handle error conditions, retries, or fallback scenarios in your Airflow workflows

AWS Lambda and AWS Glue

AWS Glue provides built-in integration with AWS Lambda, allowing you to extend the capabilities of your ETL jobs and data pipelines. This integration enables you to:

- Implement custom data transformation logic using AWS Lambda functions within your AWS Glue ETL jobs

- Invoke AWS Lambda functions to interact with other AWS services or third-party APIs as part of your ETL processes

- Use AWS Lambda functions for data validation, enrichment, or filtering tasks within your AWS Glue ETL jobs

- Leverage AWS Lambda functions to handle error conditions, retries, or fallback scenarios in your AWS Glue data pipelines

By integrating AWS Lambda with services like AWS Step Functions, Amazon MWAA, and AWS Glue, you can extend their capabilities and build more flexible and customized data pipelines. AWS Lambda functions can be used to perform a wide range of tasks, such as data processing, transformation, validation, enrichment, and integration with other AWS services or third-party APIs.

Here are some examples of how AWS Lambda can support these services in building and automating data pipelines:

- **Data transformation and enrichment:** You can create AWS Lambda functions to perform custom data transformations or enrichment tasks that are not natively supported by the services. For example, you could use a Lambda function to apply complex business rules, perform data cleansing, or integrate with external APIs to enrich your data.

- **Event-driven pipelines:** AWS Lambda functions can be triggered by events from various AWS services, such as Amazon S3, Amazon Kinesis, or Amazon SNS. This allows you to build event-driven data pipelines that automatically process and transform data as it arrives, enabling real-time data processing and analysis.

- **Custom operators and sensors:** In the case of Amazon MWAA, you can create custom Airflow operators or sensors using AWS Lambda functions. This allows you to extend the functionality of your Airflow workflows and interact with AWS services or third-party APIs in a more customized manner.

- **Error handling and retries:** AWS Lambda functions can be used to implement custom error handling and retry mechanisms within your data pipelines. For example, you could use a Lambda function to capture and process errors, perform retries, or trigger fallback actions in case of failures.

- **Parallel processing:** AWS Lambda functions can be invoked in parallel, enabling you to process large datasets or perform multiple operations concurrently within your data pipelines. This can significantly improve the performance and efficiency of your data processing workflows.

By leveraging the serverless nature and flexibility of AWS Lambda, you can build more powerful, customized, and scalable data pipelines that integrate seamlessly with services like AWS Step Functions, Amazon MWAA, and AWS Glue. AWS Lambda functions act as building blocks, allowing you to extend the capabilities of these services and tailor your data pipelines to your specific requirements.

Now, for any orchestration pipeline to truly be asynchronous, you need to use events and queues to be able to trigger the subsequent task. With MWAA and AWS Step Functions, this is managed for you under the hood. However, there are cases where you might want to leverage event streaming to do additional custom tasks. For such cases, AWS has a service called Amazon EventBridge. It's a fully managed, serverless event bus service that enables you to build event-driven architectures by reacting to events from various AWS services, as well as your own applications and third-party sources.

Let's take a closer look at Amazon EventBridge.

Amazon EventBridge

As previously mentioned, Amazon EventBridge is a serverless event bus service that helps you to build event-driven architectures supporting events from various AWS services, as well as your own applications and third-party sources. It acts as a central hub for routing and processing events, making it a powerful tool for building and automating data pipelines on AWS. Amazon EventBridge can be seamlessly integrated with services like AWS Step Functions, Amazon Managed Workflows for Apache Airflow (Amazon MWAA), and AWS Glue, enabling you to build advance event-driven data pipelines and streamline your data processing workflows.

Amazon EventBridge and AWS Step Functions

AWS Step Functions allows you to orchestrate and coordinate various AWS services and custom code using visual workflows. By integrating it with Amazon EventBridge, you can trigger and automate your Step Functions state machines based on events from various sources, enabling event-driven data pipelines. This integration allows you to:

- Trigger Step Functions workflows in response to events from AWS services (e.g., Amazon S3, Amazon Kinesis, Amazon SNS) or custom applications

- Build event-driven data pipelines that automatically process and transform data as it arrives, enabling real-time data processing and analysis

- Implement complex event patterns and rules to filter and route events to the appropriate Step Functions workflows

- Leverage the visual representation of Step Functions workflows to manage and maintain event-driven data pipelines more effectively

Amazon EventBridge and Amazon MWAA

Amazon MWAA provides a fully managed Apache Airflow environment for building and automating data pipelines. By integrating it with Amazon EventBridge, you can trigger and schedule your Airflow DAGs based on events from various sources, enabling event-driven and dynamic scheduling of your data pipelines. This integration enables you to:

- Trigger Airflow DAGs in response to events from AWS services (e.g., Amazon S3, Amazon Kinesis, Amazon SNS) or custom applications

- Build event-driven data pipelines that automatically process and transform data as it arrives, enabling real-time data processing and analysis

- Implement complex event patterns and rules to filter and route events to the appropriate Airflow DAGs

- Leverage Airflow's scheduling capabilities and dependency management to orchestrate event-driven data pipelines more effectively

Amazon EventBridge and AWS Glue

As discussed earlier, AWS Glue is a fully managed ETL service that allows you to prepare and load data for analytics. By integrating it with Amazon EventBridge, you can trigger and automate your AWS Glue ETL jobs and data pipelines based on events from various sources, enabling event-driven data processing and loading. This integration allows you to:

- Trigger AWS Glue ETL jobs and data pipelines in response to events from AWS services (e.g., Amazon S3, Amazon Kinesis, Amazon SNS) or custom applications

- Build event-driven data pipelines that automatically extract, transform, and load data as it arrives, enabling real-time data processing and analysis

- Implement complex event patterns and rules to filter and route events to the appropriate AWS Glue ETL jobs and data pipelines

- Leverage AWS Glue's serverless Apache Spark environment and Data Catalog to process and transform data within event-driven data pipelines

By integrating Amazon EventBridge with services like AWS Step Functions, Amazon MWAA, and AWS Glue, you can build more flexible and responsive data pipelines that react to events in real time. This event-driven approach enables you to process and transform data as soon as it becomes available, reducing latency and enabling more efficient data processing workflows.

Here are some examples of how Amazon EventBridge can support these services in building and automating data pipelines:

- **Real-time data processing:** You can use Amazon EventBridge to trigger data pipelines in response to events from data sources like Amazon S3, Amazon Kinesis, or Amazon SNS. For example, when new data is uploaded to an S3 bucket, an event can trigger an AWS Glue ETL job or an AWS Step Functions workflow to process and transform the data in real time.

- **Scheduled data pipelines:** Amazon EventBridge supports scheduled events, allowing you to trigger data pipelines at specific times or intervals. This can be useful for batch processing or periodic data ingestion and transformation tasks.

- **Event-driven workflows:** With Amazon EventBridge, you can build event-driven workflows that span multiple services. For example, an event from Amazon S3 could trigger an AWS Step Functions workflow, which in turn invokes AWS Glue ETL jobs and Amazon MWAA Airflow DAGs to process and transform the data.

- **Complex event patterns:** Amazon EventBridge allows you to define complex event patterns and rules, enabling you to filter and route events based on specific conditions or combinations of events. This can be useful for building more sophisticated event-driven data pipelines that react to specific scenarios or data patterns.

- **Centralized event management:** Amazon EventBridge acts as a central hub for managing and routing events, providing a unified interface for integrating with various AWS services and custom applications. This simplifies the management and monitoring of event-driven data pipelines.

By leveraging the power of Amazon EventBridge, you can build more responsive, event-driven data pipelines that seamlessly integrate with services like AWS Step Functions,

Amazon MWAA, and AWS Glue. This integration enables real-time data processing, dynamic scheduling, and event-driven orchestration, allowing you to build efficient and scalable data processing workflows on AWS.

Now, for any data pipeline, notification and queuing services are key. Why, you might ask? They provide the eyes and ears to closely monitor the data pipeline. You can get notifications in case of failures, when a job completes, or even in cases where you want to send an automated report. Let's dive into these scenarios a bit.

Notification and Queuing Services

Building and orchestrating data pipelines often involves multiple components and services working together to process and transform data. In such complex environments, it's crucial to have a robust notification and alerting system in place to ensure timely communication of events, failures, or critical updates. Amazon Simple Notification Service (Amazon SNS) and Amazon Simple Queue Service (Amazon SQS) are two powerful services that can be integrated into your data pipelines to provide reliable and scalable notification and alerting capabilities.

Amazon Simple Notification Service

Amazon SNS is a fully managed messaging service that enables you to send notifications from the cloud. It provides a highly available, durable, and secure way to send messages to various endpoints, such as email addresses, mobile devices, or AWS Lambda functions. Amazon SNS can be used in data pipelines to send alerts and notifications about various events, such as:

- Pipeline execution status (success, failure, or warning)
- Data quality issues or anomalies detected during processing
- Completion of critical tasks or milestones
- Errors or exceptions encountered during data transformation or loading

By integrating Amazon SNS with your data pipeline orchestration tools (e.g., AWS Step Functions, Amazon MWAA, or AWS Glue), you can configure notifications to be sent to relevant stakeholders or systems, ensuring timely awareness and enabling prompt action when needed.

Amazon Simple Queue Service

Amazon SQS is a fully managed message queuing service that enables you to decouple and scale microservices, distributed systems, and serverless applications. In the context of data pipelines, Amazon SQS can be used to queue and process notifications or alerts generated by various components of your pipeline. This approach can be particularly useful when you need to:

- Decouple the notification generation from the processing or handling of alerts
- Handle bursts of notifications or alerts during peak periods

- Implement retry mechanisms or dead-letter queues for failed notifications
- Integrate with third-party monitoring or alerting systems

By leveraging Amazon SQS, you can build a scalable and reliable notification system for your data pipelines, ensuring that alerts and notifications are not lost or dropped, even during periods of high load or temporary failures.

Integrating notification services like Amazon SNS and Amazon SQS into your data pipelines can provide several benefits:

- **Real-time alerting:** Receive timely notifications about critical events, failures, or milestones in your data pipelines, enabling prompt action and minimizing potential data loss or downstream impacts.

- **Centralized notification management:** Consolidate notifications from various components of your data pipelines into a centralized system, simplifying management and monitoring.

- **Scalability and reliability:** Amazon SNS and Amazon SQS are fully managed services that automatically scale to handle high volumes of notifications or alerts, ensuring reliable delivery even during peak loads.

- **Integration with third-party systems:** Easily integrate with third-party monitoring, alerting, or incident management systems by leveraging the messaging capabilities of Amazon SNS and Amazon SQS.

- **Customizable delivery:** Configure notifications to be delivered to various endpoints, such as email addresses, mobile devices, or AWS Lambda functions, enabling flexible and customized alerting mechanisms.

Here's an example of how you could integrate Amazon SNS and Amazon SQS into your data pipeline orchestration:

1. Configure Amazon SNS topics to receive notifications from your data pipeline orchestration tools (e.g., AWS Step Functions, Amazon MWAA, or AWS Glue).

2. Subscribe Amazon SQS queues to the Amazon SNS topics to receive and queue the notifications or alerts.

3. Implement AWS Lambda functions or other components to process the messages from the Amazon SQS queues, performing actions such as sending emails, triggering incident management workflows, or integrating with third-party monitoring systems.

4. Optionally, configure dead-letter queues or retry mechanisms in Amazon SQS to handle failed notifications or alerts.

By leveraging the power of Amazon SNS and Amazon SQS, you can build a robust and scalable notification and alerting system for your data pipelines, ensuring timely communication of critical events and enabling prompt action when needed. This integration can help improve the reliability, monitoring, and overall management of your data processing workflows.

Applying Programming Concepts

The following sections explore applying programming concepts.

CI/CD

Continuous integration and continuous delivery (CI/CD) practices are essential for building and automating reliable and scalable data pipelines. CI/CD enables you to streamline the development, testing, and deployment processes, ensuring that changes to your data pipelines are thoroughly tested and deployed in a consistent and automated manner.

Continuous Integration

Continuous integration (CI) involves regularly merging code changes into a central repository, followed by automated builds and testing. In the context of data pipelines, CI can be implemented by:

- Maintaining your data pipeline code (e.g., AWS Step Functions state machines, Amazon MWAA DAGs, AWS Glue ETL scripts) in a version control system like AWS CodeCommit or GitHub.
  - Example: Store your AWS Glue ETL scripts and AWS CloudFormation templates in an AWS CodeCommit repository.
- Configuring a CI pipeline using services like AWS CodePipeline or GitHub Actions to automatically build and test your data pipeline code whenever changes are pushed to the repository.
  - Example: Set up an AWS CodePipeline that triggers automated tests and validation checks whenever new code is pushed to your AWS CodeCommit repository.
- Implementing automated testing frameworks and tools to validate the functionality, data quality, and performance of your data pipelines.
  - Example: Use Apache Airflow's built-in testing utilities to write and run unit tests for your Amazon MWAA DAGs.
- Leveraging infrastructure-as-code tools like AWS CloudFormation or Terraform to provision and configure the necessary resources for your data pipelines in a consistent and repeatable manner.
  - Example: Define and manage your AWS Glue Data Catalog, AWS Glue jobs, and AWS Step Functions state machines using AWS CloudFormation templates.

Continuous Delivery

Continuous delivery (CD) extends the CI process by automatically deploying the tested and validated changes to production or staging environments. For data pipelines, CD can be achieved by:

- Integrating your CI pipeline with deployment tools like AWS CodeDeploy or AWS CloudFormation to automatically deploy your data pipeline code and configurations to the target environments.
  - Example: Use AWS CodeDeploy to deploy your AWS Glue ETL scripts and AWS Step Functions state machines to different environments (e.g., development, staging, production).

- Implementing blue/green or canary deployment strategies to minimize downtime and reduce the risk of introducing breaking changes to your production data pipelines.
  - Example: Use AWS CodeDeploy's blue/green deployment strategy to deploy a new version of your AWS Glue ETL jobs alongside the existing version, allowing for seamless traffic switching and rollback if needed.

- Automating the creation and management of environments (e.g., development, staging, production) using infrastructure-as-code tools and environment management services like AWS Cloud9.
  - Example: Use AWS CloudFormation to provision and configure separate environments for development, staging, and production, including the necessary resources like Amazon S3 buckets, AWS Glue Data Catalogs, and Amazon MWAA environments.

- Configuring monitoring and alerting mechanisms to detect and respond to issues or failures during the deployment process.
  - Example: Set up Amazon CloudWatch alarms and Amazon SNS notifications to receive alerts if your AWS Step Functions workflows or AWS Glue ETL jobs encounter errors or failures during deployment.

- Implementing rollback strategies to revert to a previous stable version of your data pipelines in case of deployment failures or critical issues.
  - Example: Leverage AWS CodeDeploy's rollback capabilities to automatically revert to the previous version of your AWS Glue ETL jobs or AWS Step Functions state machines if the new deployment fails or encounters critical issues.

Figure 2.8 illustrates a typical CI/CD pipeline for data pipelines, showcasing the integration of various AWS services.

In this example, code changes to data pipeline components (e.g., AWS Glue ETL scripts, AWS Step Functions state machines) are pushed to an AWS CodeCommit repository. An AWS CodePipeline CI pipeline is triggered, which builds, tests, and validates the changes using automated testing frameworks and tools. If the tests pass, the changes are deployed to a staging environment provisioned and managed by AWS CloudFormation. After successful testing in the staging environment, the changes are deployed to the production environment, also managed by AWS CloudFormation.

FIGURE 2.8   A typical CI/CD pipeline

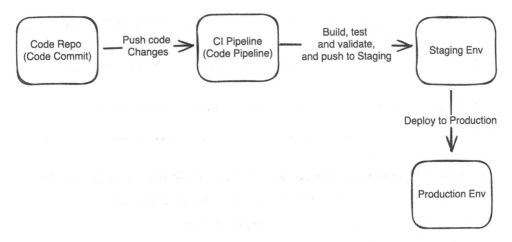

By adopting CI/CD practices with examples like these and leveraging relevant AWS services, you can build and automate data pipelines with greater efficiency, reliability, and confidence, enabling you to deliver high-quality data processing workflows that meet the evolving needs of your organization.

Using AWS SAM for Serverless Data Pipeline Deployment

The AWS Serverless Application Model (AWS SAM) is an open-source framework that simplifies the packaging, deployment, and management of serverless applications on AWS. When building and orchestrating data pipelines that leverage serverless components like AWS Lambda functions, AWS Step Functions, and Amazon DynamoDB tables, AWS SAM can streamline the deployment process and ensure consistent and repeatable deployments across different environments.

Imagine you're a logistics manager responsible for coordinating the delivery of packages across multiple cities. Just as you would need a standardized system to efficiently package and route the packages to their destinations, AWS SAM provides a structured approach to packaging and deploying your serverless data pipeline components to the AWS Cloud.

Table 2.10 provides an overview of the AWS SAM components.

TABLE 2.10   AWS SAM components

Component	Description
template .yaml	The AWS SAM template file that defines the serverless resources and their configurations
code/	The directory containing the source code for your Lambda functions or other components
tests/	The directory for unit tests and integration tests for your serverless components
samconfig .toml	The configuration file for customizing AWS SAM CLI options and settings

Example: Deploying a Serverless Data Pipeline with AWS SAM

Here's an example of deploying a serverless data pipeline with AWS SAM:

1. Define your serverless resources in the `template.yaml` file:

```
Resources:
  DataPipelineFunction:
    Type: AWS::Serverless::Function
    Properties:
      CodeUri: code/
      Handler: app.lambda_handler
      Runtime: python3.9
      # ... (additional function configuration)

  DataPipelineStateMachine:
    Type: AWS::Serverless::StateMachine
    Properties:
      DefinitionUri: statemachine/data_pipeline.asl.json
      # ... (additional state machine configuration)
```

2. Package and deploy your serverless application using the AWS SAM CLI:

```
$ sam build
$ sam deploy -guided
```

3. The AWS SAM CLI will guide you through the deployment process, prompting for parameters and creating or updating the necessary resources on AWS.

Analogy: Logistics and Package Delivery

Imagine you're a logistics manager responsible for coordinating the delivery of packages across multiple cities. AWS SAM can be likened to a standardized packaging and routing system:

- `template.yaml`: The package manifest that describes the contents and destination of each package.
- `code/`: The actual contents or items being packaged and delivered.
- `tests/`: Quality assurance checks to ensure the packages are properly packed and ready for delivery.
- `samconfig.toml`: Routing instructions and delivery preferences for the packages.

Benefits of Using AWS SAM for Serverless Data Pipelines

Here are the benefits:

- **Simplified deployment:** AWS SAM abstracts away the complexities of packaging and deploying serverless components, allowing you to focus on building and orchestrating your data pipelines.
- **Consistent deployments:** By defining your serverless resources in a standardized template, AWS SAM ensures consistent and repeatable deployments across different environments.
- **Infrastructure as code:** AWS SAM templates enable you to treat your serverless infrastructure as code, facilitating version control, collaboration, and automated deployments.
- **Local testing and debugging:** AWS SAM provides tools for locally testing and debugging your serverless components before deploying them to AWS.
- **Integration with AWS Services:** AWS SAM seamlessly integrates with various AWS services, enabling you to build and orchestrate serverless data pipelines that leverage multiple AWS services.

By leveraging AWS SAM, you can streamline the deployment and management of your serverless data pipelines, ensuring consistency, repeatability, and efficient collaboration across your development team, just like a standardized packaging and routing system enables efficient and reliable package delivery across multiple destinations.

SQL Queries in Data Pipeline Orchestration

When building and orchestrating data pipelines, SQL queries play a crucial role in extracting data from various sources and performing transformations on the data. These queries can be integrated into different stages of the data pipeline, enabling efficient data processing and transformation.

Data Source Queries

In the extraction stage of a data pipeline, SQL queries are used to retrieve data from relational databases or other data sources that support SQL. This can be achieved by incorporating SQL queries into the pipeline orchestration tools or services, such as AWS Step Functions, Amazon MWAA, or AWS Glue.

For example, in an AWS Glue ETL job, you can use SQL queries to extract data from an Amazon Redshift data warehouse or an Amazon RDS database instance:

```
SELECT column1, column2, column3
FROM schema.table_name
WHERE condition;
```

Data Transformations

SQL queries can also be used for data transformations within the data pipeline. These transformations can include filtering, sorting, aggregating, joining, and reshaping data to meet specific requirements.

- AWS Glue ETL Jobs
  - SQL queries can be embedded within AWS Glue ETL scripts written in Python or Scala to perform data transformations using Apache Spark SQL.
  - Example: Joining and aggregating data from multiple sources.
- Amazon MWAA (Apache Airflow)
  - SQL queries can be executed within Apache Airflow tasks or operators, such as PostgresOperator or MySqlOperator.
  - Example: Filtering and sorting data before loading it into a data warehouse.
- AWS Lambda Functions
  - SQL queries can be executed within AWS Lambda functions using database connectors or libraries like psycopg2 (for PostgreSQL) or pymysql (for MySQL).
  - Example: Transforming data and storing the results in an Amazon S3 bucket.

Data Pipeline Orchestration

SQL queries can be integrated into the orchestration of data pipelines using services like AWS Step Functions, Amazon MWAA, or AWS Glue. These services provide mechanisms to invoke SQL queries at specific stages of the pipeline, enabling efficient data extraction, transformation, and loading.

For example, an AWS Step Functions state machine can orchestrate the following steps, as shown in Figure 2.9:

1. Invoke an AWS Lambda function to execute a SQL query and extract data from a database.

2. Pass the extracted data to an AWS Glue ETL job for transformation using SQL queries.

3. Load the transformed data into an Amazon Redshift data warehouse using another SQL query.

FIGURE 2.9   AWS Step Functions

By integrating SQL queries into the orchestration of data pipelines, you can leverage the power and flexibility of SQL for data extraction, transformation, and loading. This approach enables efficient and scalable data processing, ensuring that data is accurately extracted, transformed, and loaded into the desired targets.

Infrastructure as Code for Repeatable Data Pipeline Deployments

Infrastructure as code (IaC) is a practice of managing and provisioning infrastructure resources through machine-readable definition files, rather than manual processes. When building and orchestrating data pipelines, IaC plays a crucial role in ensuring consistent and repeatable deployments across different environments (e.g., development, staging, and production).

Imagine you're a chef responsible for setting up and managing multiple restaurant kitchens across different locations. Without a standardized approach, each kitchen might have different equipment, layouts, and processes, leading to inconsistencies in food preparation and service quality. IaC for data pipelines is like having a detailed blueprint or recipe for setting up and configuring your kitchen infrastructure consistently across all locations.

AWS CloudFormation

AWS CloudFormation is a popular IaC service provided by AWS. It allows you to define and provision AWS resources using JSON or YAML templates. These templates describe the desired state of your infrastructure, including resources like Amazon S3 buckets, AWS Glue jobs, AWS Step Functions state machines, and Amazon MWAA environments.

Here's an example CloudFormation template for an AWS Glue job:

```
Resources:
  GlueJobRole:
    Type: AWS::IAM::Role
    Properties:
      # Role definition...
```

```
GlueJob:
  Type: AWS::Glue::Job
  Properties:
    Name: my-etl-job
    Role: !Ref GlueJobRole
    Command:
      Name: glueetl
      ScriptLocation: s3://my-bucket/scripts/etl.py
```

AWS Cloud Development Kit

The AW Cloud Development Kit (AWS CDK) is an open-source software development framework that allows you to define and provision AWS resources using familiar programming languages like Python, TypeScript, Java, C#, and Go. It provides a higher-level abstraction over CloudFormation templates, making it easier to write and maintain IaC code.

Here's an example AWS CDK code for an AWS Step Functions state machine:

```python
from aws_cdk import Stack, aws_stepfunctions as sfn


class DataPipelineStack(Stack):
    def __init__(self, scope, id, **kwargs):
        super().__init__(scope, id, **kwargs)

        # Define state machine tasks
        start = sfn.Pass(self, "Start")
        extract_data = sfn.Task(self, "ExtractData", ...)
        transform_data = sfn.Task(self, "TransformData", ...)
        load_data = sfn.Task(self, "LoadData", ...)

        # Define state machine definition
        definition = start.next(extract_data) \
                          .next(transform_data) \
                          .next(load_data)

        # Create the state machine
        sfn.StateMachine(self, "DataPipeline",
                        definition=definition,
                        timeout=Duration.minutes(60))
```

Benefits of IaC for Data Pipeline Deployments

IaC provides several benefits for data pipeline deployments:

- **Consistent and repeatable deployments:** IaC ensures that your data pipeline infrastructure is deployed consistently across different environments, reducing the risk of configuration drift and human errors, just like having a standardized kitchen setup across all restaurant locations.

- **Version control:** IaC definition files can be stored in version control systems like Git, allowing you to track changes, collaborate with team members, and roll back to previous versions if needed, similar to maintaining a recipe book for your kitchen.

- **Automated deployments:** IaC tools like AWS CloudFormation and AWS CDK support automated deployments, enabling you to integrate them into your CI/CD pipelines for faster and more reliable deployments, akin to streamlining the process of setting up new restaurant kitchens.

- **Modular and reusable components:** IaC definitions can be modularized and reused across multiple projects or environments, promoting code reuse and reducing duplication, similar to having a set of standard recipes that can be used across different restaurant locations.

- **Documentation and visibility:** IaC definition files serve as documentation for your infrastructure, providing visibility into the resources and configurations used in your data pipelines, much like having a detailed kitchen manual for reference.

By adopting IaC practices with tools like AWS CloudFormation and AWS CDK, you can streamline the deployment and management of your data pipeline infrastructure, ensuring consistency, repeatability, and scalability across different environments, just like having a standardized and well-documented kitchen setup across all restaurant locations.

Data Structures and Algorithms

In the realm of data engineering, where handling massive volumes of data is the norm, efficient data structures play a pivotal role in ensuring smooth and optimized operations. From storing and retrieving data to processing and analyzing it, data structures are the backbone that enable seamless data management and extraction of valuable insights.

Let's embark on a journey through the applications of data structures in data engineering:

- **Data storage and retrieval:** Databases and file systems rely on B-trees for indexing and data partitioning, enabling fast data retrieval. Hash tables and binary search trees facilitate caching and indexing, ensuring rapid access to frequently accessed data.

- **Data processing and pipelines:** In batch processing, arrays and linked lists handle tabular data and data pipelines efficiently. For stream processing, linked lists and queues are indispensable for processing continuous data streams and event processing.

- **Data analysis and machine learning:** Binary trees and binary search trees form the foundation of decision trees and random forests, enabling powerful predictive modeling. Graph data structures, along with graph traversal algorithms like BFS (Breadth-First Search) and DFS (Depth-First Search), unlock insights from complex networks, powering social media analysis and recommendation systems.

- **Distributed systems and big data processing:** Heaps and priority queues facilitate task scheduling and top-k queries, ensuring efficient resource allocation and prioritization. Tries (prefix trees) enable autocomplete features, IP routing, and data compression, optimizing storage and retrieval in distributed environments.

- **Generative AI and vector storage:** With the rise of generative AI models like large language models and diffusion models, efficient vector storage and retrieval have become crucial. Data structures like k-d trees, ball trees, and vector indexes based on techniques like product quantization and scalar quantization enable fast nearest neighbor search and similarity calculations on high-dimensional vector embeddings, powering applications like text generation, image generation, and semantic search.

Underpinning these applications are the fundamental data structures: linear (arrays, linked lists, and queues) and non-linear (trees, graphs, hash tables, heaps, and tries). Each structure offers unique strengths and trade-offs in terms of time and space complexity, making them suitable for specific use cases.

Understanding how these data structures fit into real-world data and AI applications is crucial for preparing for data engineering certification exams. In your day-to-day work as a data engineer, you would need to dive deeper into these algorithms to fully utilize them and build efficient and scalable systems.

Optimizing Code to Reduce Runtime for Data Ingestion and Transformation

In the context of data pipelines, optimizing code for data ingestion and transformation is crucial to ensure efficient and timely processing of data. Just as a well-tuned engine can improve a vehicle's performance, optimized code can significantly reduce the runtime of your data pipelines, leading to faster insights and better resource utilization.

Imagine you're a race car mechanic responsible for tuning and optimizing the performance of high-speed vehicles. Just as you would carefully analyze and fine-tune various components to extract maximum performance, optimizing code for data pipelines involves identifying and addressing bottlenecks, leveraging efficient algorithms, and utilizing available resources effectively.

Code Optimization Techniques

There are a number of code optimization techniques:

- Parallelization and distributed processing:
  - Leverage parallel processing frameworks like Apache Spark or Dask to distribute computations across multiple cores or nodes.
  - Example: Splitting a large dataset into partitions and processing them in parallel using Apache Spark's RDD or DataFrame operations.
- Efficient data formats and compression:
  - Use columnar data formats like Apache Parquet or ORC for efficient storage and retrieval of large datasets.
  - Leverage compression techniques like Snappy or LZO to reduce data transfer and storage costs.

- Indexing and partitioning:
  - Implement indexing strategies on frequently queried columns to improve query performance.
  - Partition large datasets based on common filtering criteria to reduce the amount of data scanned.
- Caching and memorization:
  - Cache intermediate results or frequently accessed data to avoid redundant computations.
  - Implement memorization techniques to store and reuse the results of expensive function calls.
- Vectorization and SIMD instructions:
  - Leverage vectorized operations and SIMD (Single Instruction Multiple Data) instructions for efficient data processing.
  - Example: Using NumPy or Pandas vectorized operations for numerical computations in Python.
- Profiling and bottleneck identification:
  - Utilize profiling tools like Apache Spark's Web UI, AWS Glue's Job Metrics, or Python's cProfile to identify performance bottlenecks.
  - Analyze and optimize the identified bottlenecks through code refactoring, algorithm optimization, or resource allocation.

Example: Optimizing an ETL Job

Consider an ETL job that reads data from Amazon S3, performs transformations, and loads the results into an Amazon Redshift data warehouse. Here's an example of how you could optimize the code:

```
# Read data from S3 using Parquet format
data = spark.read.parquet("s3://bucket/data/*.parquet")

# Partition and cache the data for efficient processing
partitioned_data = data.repartition("partition_column").cache()

# Perform transformations in parallel using Spark's DataFrame operations
transformed_data = partitioned_data.filter(...).join(...).select(...)

# Write the transformed data to Redshift using the optimized Redshift
JDBC writer
transformed_data.write.format("io.github.spark_redshift_community.spark
.redshift") \
                .option("tempdir", "s3://temp-bucket/") \
```

```
            .mode("overwrite") \
            .option("forward_spark_s3_credentials", "true") \
            .jdbc("jdbc:redshift://redshift-cluster:5439/database",
"table", properties)
```

In this example, we leverage Apache Parquet for efficient data storage, partition and cache the data for faster processing, perform transformations using Spark's parallel DataFrame operations, and utilize the optimized Redshift JDBC writer for efficient data loading into Amazon Redshift.

Benefits of Code Optimization

Code optimization provides several benefits:

- **Reduced runtime:** Optimized code can significantly reduce the runtime of data ingestion and transformation tasks, enabling faster delivery of insights and better utilization of resources.

- **Improved scalability:** By leveraging techniques like parallelization and distributed processing, optimized code can scale more effectively to handle larger datasets and higher workloads.

- **Cost savings:** Efficient code can reduce the compute resources required for data processing, leading to cost savings in cloud environments like AWS.

- **Enhanced maintainability:** Optimized code is often more readable, modular, and easier to maintain, facilitating future enhancements and modifications.

By optimizing code for data ingestion and transformation, you can build efficient and high-performing data pipelines, much like a well-tuned race car that delivers exceptional performance on the track.

Structuring SQL Queries to Meet Data Pipeline Requirements

In the context of data pipelines, SQL queries play a crucial role in extracting, transforming, and loading data from various sources. Structuring these queries effectively is essential to ensure efficient and reliable data processing. Just as a well-designed blueprint is crucial for constructing a sturdy building, structuring SQL queries appropriately can help build robust and scalable data pipelines.

Imagine you're an architect responsible for designing and constructing a skyscraper. Just as you would carefully plan and structure the building's components to meet specific requirements, such as load-bearing capacity, energy efficiency, and aesthetic appeal, structuring SQL queries involves considering factors like performance, maintainability, and adherence to data pipeline requirements.

Structuring SQL Queries for Data Pipelines

There are several significant aspects of structuring SQL queries for data pipelines:

- Modularization and reusability:
  - Break down complex queries into smaller, reusable components (e.g., views, common table expressions [CTEs], or user-defined functions).
  - Example: Creating a view or CTE to encapsulate a frequently used data transformation or filtering logic.

- Performance optimization:
  - Structure queries to leverage database indexing, partitioning, and other performance optimization techniques.
  - Example: Adding appropriate indexes or partitioning keys to improve query performance.

- Data quality and validation:
  - Incorporate data quality checks and validation rules within SQL queries to ensure data integrity.
  - Example: Using CASE statements or user-defined functions to validate data and handle exceptions or null values.

- Parameterization and dynamic queries:
  - Use parameterized queries or dynamic SQL to build flexible and reusable queries that can adapt to changing requirements or configurations.
  - Example: Parameterizing date ranges or filtering conditions to make queries more dynamic and configurable.

- Readability and maintainability:
  - Structure queries using proper formatting, comments, and naming conventions to improve readability and maintainability.
  - Example: Using descriptive column aliases and breaking complex queries into multiple steps with comments explaining each step.

- Incremental processing and idempotency:
  - Structure queries to support incremental processing and idempotency, ensuring that data pipelines can handle failures and restarts gracefully.
  - Example: Using window functions or partitioning techniques to process data incrementally and avoid duplicates or inconsistencies.

Example: Structured SQL Query for Data Transformation

Consider a data pipeline that processes sales data from multiple sources and loads it into a data warehouse for analysis. Here's an example of a structured SQL query that performs data transformation and validation:

```
-- Step 1: Extract and union data from multiple sources
WITH source_data AS (
```

```
  SELECT * FROM source1
  UNION ALL
  SELECT * FROM source2
  UNION ALL
  SELECT * FROM source3
)


-- Step 2: Perform data transformations and validations
, transformed_data AS (
  SELECT
    COALESCE(TRIM(product_name), 'Unknown Product') AS product_name,
    CASE
      WHEN sale_amount < 0 THEN 0
      ELSE sale_amount
    END AS valid_sale_amount,
    CASE
      WHEN sale_date < '2022-01-01' THEN NULL
      ELSE sale_date
    END AS valid_sale_date
  FROM source_data
)


-- Step 3: Load data into the target table
INSERT INTO data_warehouse.sales_fact
SELECT *
FROM transformed_data;
```

In this example, we use CTEs to modularize the query into distinct steps: data extraction, transformation, and loading. The transformations include handling null values, validating sale amounts, and filtering out invalid sale dates. The structured approach improves readability, maintainability, and the ability to extend or modify the query as needed.

Benefits of Structuring SQL Queries

Structuring SQL queries provides several benefits:

- **Improved performance:** Well-structured queries can leverage database optimization techniques, leading to faster data processing and reduced runtime.

- **Enhanced data quality:** Incorporating data validation and quality checks within SQL queries helps ensure the integrity and reliability of data flowing through the pipeline.

- **Increased maintainability:** Modular and well-documented SQL queries are easier to understand, modify, and maintain over time, facilitating collaboration and future enhancements.

- **Flexibility and adaptability:** Parameterized and dynamic queries can adapt to changing requirements or configurations, reducing the need for extensive code changes.
- **Scalability and reliability:** Structuring queries to support incremental processing and idempotency can improve the scalability and reliability of data pipelines, enabling graceful handling of failures and restarts.

By structuring SQL queries effectively, you can build efficient, maintainable, and reliable data pipelines that meet specific requirements, just as a well-designed and structured skyscraper meets its intended purpose while adhering to safety, efficiency, and aesthetic standards.

Using Git Commands for Data Pipeline Development

In the world of data pipeline development, version control systems like Git play a crucial role in managing code changes, collaborating with team members, and maintaining a reliable and traceable development process. Git commands allow you to perform various actions on your code repositories, enabling efficient collaboration and code management.

Imagine you're an architect overseeing the construction of a large building project. Just as you would need a system to track and coordinate the work of different teams, manage changes to the blueprints, and maintain a record of the building's evolution, Git provides a similar framework for managing the development of your data pipelines.

Table 2.11 shows common Git commands.

TABLE 2.11 Common Git Commands

Command	Description
git init	Initializes a new Git repository in the current directory
git clone	Creates a local copy of a remote repository
git add	Stages changes for the next commit
git commit	Records staged changes to the local repository
git push	Uploads local commits to a remote repository
git pull	Downloads changes from a remote repository and merges them
git branch	Lists, creates, or deletes branches
git checkout	Switches between branches or restores files
git merge	Combines changes from one branch into another

Example: Managing a Data Pipeline Repository

Here's how you can manage a data pipeline repository:

1. Initialize a new Git repository for your data pipeline project:

   ```
   $ git init
   ```

2. Create a new branch for a feature or bug fix:

   ```
   $ git checkout -b new-feature
   ```

3. Stage and commit changes to your local repository:

   ```
   $ git add .
   $ git commit -m "Implemented new feature"
   ```

4. Push your local commits to a remote repository:

   ```
   $ git push origin new-feature
   ```

5. Create a pull request for code review and merge the changes into the main branch. Update your local repository with the latest changes from the remote:

   ```
   $ git checkout main
   $ git pull
   ```

Figure 2.10 shows an example of managing a data pipeline repository with Git commands.

FIGURE 2.10 Data pipeline development with Git commands

Benefits of Using Git for Data Pipeline Development

Using Git for data pipeline development provides several benefits:

- **Collaboration:** Git enables multiple team members to work on the same codebase simultaneously, facilitating collaboration and code sharing.

- **Version control:** Git maintains a detailed history of all changes made to the codebase, allowing you to track and revert changes if needed.

- **Branching and merging:** Git's branching and merging capabilities enable parallel development, code reviews, and controlled integration of changes.

- **Reproducibility:** By maintaining a version-controlled codebase, you can ensure the reproducibility of your data pipelines across different environments.

- **Backup and recovery:** Git repositories serve as a backup for your code, allowing you to recover from accidental deletions or system failures.

By leveraging Git commands and following best practices for version control, you can streamline the development and orchestration of your data pipelines, fostering collaboration, maintaining code integrity, and enabling efficient management of changes and updates.

Testing and Debugging Techniques

When building and orchestrating data pipelines, implementing robust testing and debugging techniques is crucial to ensure the reliability and correctness of your data processing workflows. Just as a mechanic would thoroughly inspect and test an engine before putting it into service, testing and debugging your data pipelines can help identify and resolve issues before they impact your production systems. Imagine you're a quality assurance engineer responsible for ensuring the smooth operation of a complex manufacturing line. Testing and debugging techniques in data pipelines can be likened to the various quality control measures and diagnostic tools employed to identify and resolve potential issues before they disrupt the production process.

See Table 2.12 for testing techniques you can use with data pipelines.

TABLE 2.12   Testing and debugging techniques

Technique	Description
Unit Testing	Testing individual components or functions of your data pipeline, such as AWS Lambda functions or Apache Spark transformations
Integration Testing	Testing the integration and interaction between different components of your data pipeline, such as AWS Glue jobs and AWS Step Functions workflows
End-to-End Testing	Testing the entire data pipeline from start to finish, simulating real-world scenarios and data flows
Data Quality Testing	Validating the quality and integrity of the data processed by your data pipeline, ensuring it meets expected standards and requirements
Debugging Tools	Utilizing tools like AWS X-Ray, AWS CloudWatch Logs, and Apache Spark's Web UI to debug and troubleshoot issues within your data pipelines

Example: Testing an AWS Glue ETL Job

Here's an example of testing an AWS Glue ETL job:

```
# Unit test for a data transformation function
def test_transform_data():
    input_data = [{"id": 1, "value": 10}, {"id": 2, "value": 20}]
    expected_output = [{"id": 1, "value": 20}, {"id": 2, "value": 40}]

    output_data = transform_data(input_data)
    assert output_data == expected_output
```

Analogy: Quality Control in Manufacturing

Imagine you're a quality assurance engineer responsible for ensuring the smooth operation of a complex manufacturing line:

- **Unit tests:** Inspecting individual components or subassemblies for defects or issues before they are integrated into the larger system

- **Integration testing:** Testing the interaction and compatibility between different components or subsystems to ensure they work together as intended

- **End-to-end testing:** Simulating the entire manufacturing process from start to finish, testing the final product under real-world conditions

- **Data quality testing:** Performing quality checks on the raw materials, components, and final products to ensure they meet specified standards and requirements

- **Debugging tools:** Using diagnostic tools, sensors, and monitoring systems to identify and troubleshoot issues within the manufacturing line

Just as quality control measures and diagnostic tools are essential for identifying and resolving potential issues in a manufacturing line, implementing robust testing and debugging techniques is crucial for building reliable and high-quality data pipelines. By employing techniques such as unit testing, integration testing, end-to-end testing, data quality testing, and leveraging debugging tools, you can ensure the smooth operation and accuracy of your data processing workflows.

Logging, Monitoring, and Auditing for Data Pipeline Orchestration

Effective logging, monitoring, and auditing practices are essential for ensuring the reliability, traceability, and performance of your data pipelines. Just as a pilot relies on various instruments and logs to monitor and troubleshoot the aircraft's systems, implementing robust logging and monitoring solutions can help you gain visibility into your data pipelines, identify and resolve issues, and maintain compliance with auditing requirements.

Extracting Logs for Audits

Logs serve as a valuable source of information for auditing purposes, providing a record of activities, events, and potential issues within your data pipelines. To facilitate audits, you can extract logs from various sources, such as:

- **AWS CloudTrail:** Captures API calls made to AWS services, including those related to your data pipelines (e.g., AWS Glue, Amazon EMR, AWS Step Functions).

- **Amazon CloudWatch Logs:** Centralized log management service for capturing application logs, including those generated by your data pipeline components (e.g., AWS Lambda functions, Amazon MWAA tasks).

- **Application-specific logs:** Logs generated by your custom applications or third-party tools involved in your data pipelines.

Deploying Logging and Monitoring Solutions

To facilitate auditing and traceability, you can deploy logging and monitoring solutions that integrate with your data pipelines. Table 2.13 shows some examples.

TABLE 2.13   Examples of logging and monitoring solutions

Solution	Description
Amazon CloudWatch	Provides monitoring and logging services for AWS resources and applications, including metrics, logs, and alarms.
AWS CloudTrail	Records API calls made to AWS services, enabling auditing and compliance monitoring.
Amazon OpenSearch Service	A managed OpenSearch service for log analytics, search, and visualization.
Third-Party Logging/ Monitoring Tools	Solutions like Datadog, Splunk, or Elasticsearch can be integrated for advanced log management and monitoring.

Example: Logging in an AWS Lambda Function

Here's an example of logging in an AWS Lambda function:

```
import logging
import boto3

logger = logging.getLogger()
logger.setLevel(logging.INFO)

def lambda_handler(event, context):
    # Log the incoming event
    logger.info(f"Received event: {event}")

    # Perform data processing
    processed_data = process_data(event["data"])
```

```
# Log the processed data
logger.info(f"Processed data: {processed_data}")

# Send logs to CloudWatch Logs
logs_client = boto3.client("logs")
logs_client.put_log_events(
    logGroupName="/aws/lambda/my-function",
    logStreamName=context.log_stream_name,
    logEvents=[
        {
            "timestamp": int(round(time.time() * 1000)),
            "message": f"Processed data: {processed_data}",
        }
    ],
)
```

In this example, the Lambda function logs the incoming event and processes data using the Python logging module. Additionally, it sends the log events to Amazon CloudWatch Logs using the AWS SDK for Python (Boto3).

You can see how the Lambda function works in Figure 2.11.

FIGURE 2.11   The AWS Lambda function

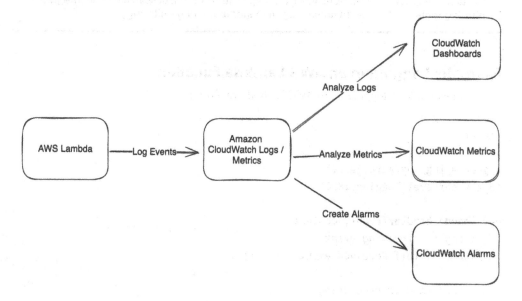

Using Notifications for Alerts

Monitoring solutions often provide mechanisms for sending notifications or alerts based on predefined conditions or thresholds, delivered through various channels. Amazon SNS supports notifications for both application-to-application (A2A) and application-to-person (A2P) interactions.

For application-to-application (A2A) notifications, Amazon SNS integrates with AWS Lambda, Amazon SQS, AWS EventBridge, Amazon Kinesis Data Firehose and HTTPS-based webhooks. For anything else that does not directly integrate with SNS, you can route messages through intermediaries like Lambda or SQS.

For application-to-person (A2P) notifications, Amazon SNS supports SMS, email, mobile push notifications, notifications to Slack, AWS Chime, or Teams, etc. via AWS Chatbot, and, last but not the least, PagerDuty to deliver operational insights to on-call teams.

Figure 2.12 shows an example of configuring an Amazon CloudWatch alarm to send an SNS notification when a specific metric exceeds a threshold.

FIGURE 2.12   Configuring notifications with Amazon CloudWatch

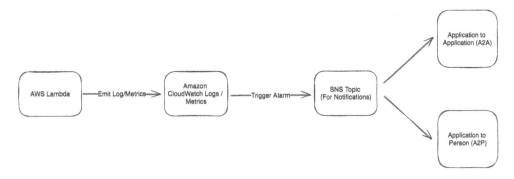

Just as a detective relies on detailed logs and evidence trails to understand the sequence of events, motives, and potential issues in a case, logging application data in your data pipelines provides valuable insights into the execution flow, performance, and potential problems. By capturing and analyzing log events from various components of your data pipelines, you can effectively monitor, debug, and troubleshoot any challenges that may arise, ensuring the smooth and reliable operation of your data processing workflows.

Amazon OpenSearch, the managed OpenSearch service by AWS, can be integrated as a logging destination for advanced log management and analysis. It provides powerful search, visualization, and analytics capabilities, allowing you to gain deeper insights into your application logs and optimize your data pipelines accordingly.

Case Studies and Real-World Examples

Now let's examine several case studies and real-world examples.

Case Study 1: Batch Data Processing Pipeline for Financial Transactions

A financial institution needs to process large volumes of transaction data from various sources (e.g., online banking, ATMs, point-of-sale systems) on a daily basis. The processed data needs to be loaded into a data warehouse for reporting and analysis.

Figure 2.13 shows the solution architecture, which includes the following points:

- Transaction data from various sources is deposited into Amazon S3.
- AWS Glue ETL jobs extract, transform, and load the data.
- Processed data is loaded into Amazon Redshift for reporting and analysis.

FIGURE 2.13   Batch data processing pipeline for financial transactions

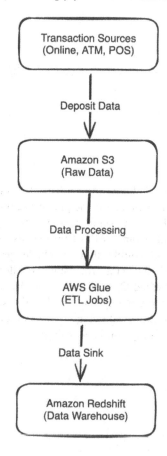

Example: An AWS Glue ETL job written in Apache Spark can perform data transformations such as:

```
from pyspark.sql.functions import col, sum, avg

# Read transaction data from S3
transactions = spark.read.csv("s3://bucket/transactions/*.csv")

# Calculate daily totals and averages
daily_stats = transactions.groupBy("date") \
                    .agg(sum("amount").alias("total_amount"),
                        avg("amount").alias("avg_amount"))

# Write processed data to Redshift
daily_stats.write.format("io.github.spark_redshift_community.spark
.redshift") \
                .option("tempdir", "s3://temp-bucket/") \
                .mode("overwrite") \
                .jdbc("jdbc:redshift://redshift-cluster:5439/database",
"daily_stats", properties)
```

Case Study 2: Real-Time Streaming Data Pipeline for IoT Sensor Data

A manufacturing company wants to build a real-time data pipeline to ingest and process sensor data from thousands of IoT devices deployed across their production facilities. The goal is to monitor equipment performance, detect anomalies, and trigger predictive maintenance workflows.

Figure 2.14 shows the solution architecture, which includes the following points:

- IoT devices publish sensor data to AWS IoT Core.
- Data is streamed to Amazon Kinesis Data Firehose for ingestion.
- Raw data is stored in Amazon S3 for archival and batch processing.
- Processed data is stored in Amazon OpenSearch for analytics and visualization.

Case Study 3: Data Lake Ingestion and Processing Pipeline

An e-commerce company wants to build a data lake to store and analyze customer behavior data, product catalogs, and sales data. The data needs to be ingested from various sources, processed, and made available for analytics and machine learning workloads.

FIGURE 2.14   Real-time streaming data pipeline for IoT sensor data

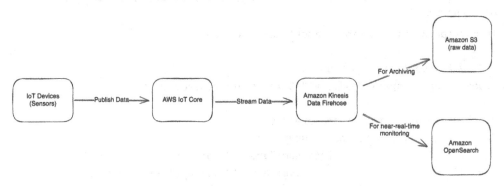

Figure 2.15 shows the solution architecture, which includes the following points:

- Data from various sources is ingested into Amazon S3 as the data lake.
- AWS Glue is used to process, discover, and catalog the data.
- Amazon Athena is used for ad hoc querying and analytics.
- Amazon SageMaker is used to build and deploy machine learning models.

FIGURE 2.15   Data lake ingestion and processing pipeline

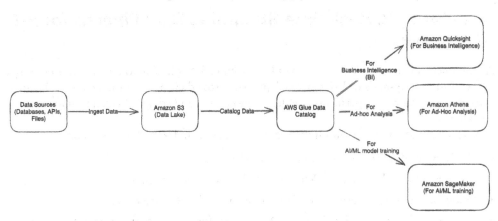

Case Study 4: Machine Learning Pipeline for Image Classification

A computer vision company wants to build a machine learning pipeline to train and deploy image classification models. The pipeline should handle data preprocessing, model training, evaluation, and deployment.

Figure 2.16 shows the solution architecture, which includes the following points:

- Image data is stored in an Amazon S3 bucket.
- AWS Step Functions orchestrates the machine learning pipeline.
- AWS Lambda functions preprocess the image data.
- Amazon SageMaker is used for model training.
- AWS Lambda functions evaluate the trained model.
- If accuracy is > 90%, the model is used for batch transform job.
- Otherwise, Admins are notified for Model Accuracy too low.

FIGURE 2.16   Machine learning pipeline for image classification

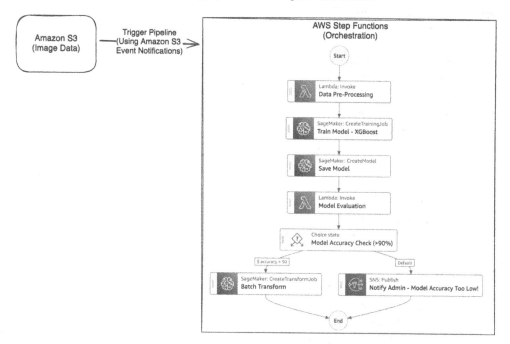

Example: An AWS Step Functions state machine definition (Amazon States Language) for the pipeline:

```
{
  "StartAt": "PreprocessData",
  "States": {
    "PreprocessData": {
      "Type": "Task",
```

```
    "Resource": "arn:aws:lambda:us-west-2:123456789012:function:Preprocess
Data",
      "Next": "TrainModel"
    },
  "TrainModel": {
    "Type": "Task",
    "Resource": "arn:aws:states:::sagemaker:createTrainingJob.sync",
    "Parameters": {
      "TrainingJobName": "image-classification-training",
      "RoleArn": "arn:aws:iam::123456789012:role/SageMakerRole",
      "AlgorithmSpecification": {
        "TrainingImage": "811284229777.dkr.ecr.us-west-2.amazonaws.com/
image-classification:latest",
        "TrainingInputMode": "File"
      },
      "OutputDataConfig": {
        "S3OutputPath": "s3://bucket/output"
      },
      "ResourceConfig": {
        "InstanceCount": 1,
        "InstanceType": "ml.m5.xlarge",
        "VolumeSizeInGB": 10
      },
      "StoppingCondition": {
        "MaxRuntimeInSeconds": 3600
      },
      "InputDataConfig": [
        {
          "ChannelName": "training",
          "DataSource": {
            "S3DataSource": {
              "S3DataType": "S3Prefix",
              "S3Uri": "s3://bucket/input/training",
              "S3DataDistributionType": "FullyReplicated"
            }
          },
          "ContentType": "application/x-image",
          "CompressionType": "None"
        }
```

```
        ]
      },
      "Next": "EvaluateModel"
    },
    "EvaluateModel": {
      "Type": "Task",
      "Resource": "arn:aws:lambda:us-west-2:123456789012:function:Evaluate
Model",
      "Next": "DeployModel"
    },
    "DeployModel": {
      "Type": "Task",
      "Resource": "arn:aws:states:::sagemaker:createModel",
      "Parameters": {
        "ModelName": "image-classification-model",
        "ExecutionRoleArn": "arn:aws:iam::123456789012:role/SageMakerRole",
        "PrimaryContainer": {
          "Image": "811284229777.dkr.ecr.us-west-2.amazonaws.com/image-
classification:latest",
          "ModelDataUrl": "s3://bucket/output/model.tar.gz"
        }
      },
      "End": true
    }
  }
}
```

Case Study 5: ETL Pipeline for Data Warehouse Loading

A retail company wants to build an ETL pipeline to extract data from various sources (e.g., point-of-sale systems, e-commerce platforms, CRM systems), transform the data, and load it into a data warehouse for reporting and analysis.

Figure 2.17 shows the solution architecture, which includes the following points:

- Data from various sources is deposited into Amazon S3.
- AWS Glue ETL jobs extract, transform, and load the data.
- Processed data is loaded into Amazon Redshift as a data warehouse.
- Amazon QuickSight is used for reporting and business intelligence.

FIGURE 2.17   ETL pipeline for data warehouse loading

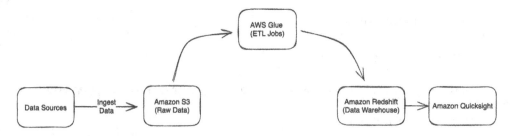

Example: An AWS Glue ETL job written in PySpark to transform and load data:

```
from pyspark.sql.functions import col, sum, avg

# Read data from S3
sales_data = spark.read.json("s3://bucket/sales/*.json")
product_data = spark.read.csv("s3://bucket/products/*.csv", header=True)

# Join and transform data
sales_with_products = sales_data.join(product_data, "product_id") \
                                .select("order_id", "product_name", "quantity",
"price")

# Calculate revenue and load into Redshift
revenue = sales_with_products.select("order_id",
                                     (col("quantity") *
col("price")).alias("revenue"))

revenue.write.format("io.github.spark_redshift_community.spark.redshift") \
          .option("tempdir", "s3://temp-bucket/") \
          .mode("overwrite") \
          .jdbc("jdbc:redshift://redshift-cluster:5439/database",
"revenue", properties)
```

Summary

Effective data pipeline orchestration requires a holistic approach that combines AWS services to automate workflows, manage resources, handle errors, and ensure data is processed efficiently and accurately. AWS Step Functions, Amazon MWAA, AWS Lambda, Amazon EventBridge, and AWS Glue stand out as key services for orchestrating data pipelines, supported by other AWS services like Amazon SNS, Amazon SQS, AWS CloudFormation, AWS CDK, and Amazon CloudWatch for comprehensive management, monitoring, and execution of data processing tasks.

Exam Essentials

Understand the use cases and key features of AWS Step Functions, Amazon MWAA, and AWS Glue for orchestrating and automating data pipelines.   AWS Step Functions is ideal for coordinating distributed workflows with visual monitoring. Amazon MWAA (Managed Workflows for Apache Airflow) provides a managed solution for Airflow-based workflows, while AWS Glue combines ETL capabilities with data cataloging for seamless pipeline orchestration.

Know how to integrate AWS Lambda functions to extend the capabilities of data pipelines with custom data processing or transformation logic.   AWS Lambda can be used to perform custom data transformations or trigger downstream processes, providing flexibility to extend pipeline capabilities without managing additional infrastructure.

Leverage Amazon EventBridge to build event-driven data pipelines that can be triggered and automated based on events from various sources.   Amazon EventBridge allows pipelines to be triggered by events such as changes in data storage or API activity, enabling seamless automation and real-time data processing.

Implement robust monitoring, logging, and notification mechanisms using services like Amazon CloudWatch and Amazon SNS for effective management and alerting of data pipelines.   Amazon CloudWatch provides detailed metrics and logs for pipeline performance monitoring, while Amazon SNS can be used to send alerts and notifications for failures or thresholds exceeded.

Adopt best practices for data pipeline orchestration, such as modular design, error handling, scalability, and data lineage tracking.   Design pipelines in smaller, reusable modules to enhance maintainability and scalability, while implementing error handling to manage failures gracefully. Tracking data lineage ensures traceability and compliance.

Apply programming concepts like infrastructure as code with AWS CloudFormation or AWS CDK for consistent and repeatable deployments of data pipelines across different environments.   IaC tools like AWS CloudFormation and AWS CDK enable automated, consistent deployment of pipeline resources, reducing manual errors and ensuring uniform environments.

Utilize version control systems like Git for collaborative development, code management, and maintaining a reliable and traceable development process for data pipelines.   Version control with Git enables collaboration, tracks changes, and maintains a reliable history for debugging or rolling back to previous versions of the pipeline.

Structure SQL queries effectively for efficient data extraction, transformation, and loading within data pipelines, considering factors like performance optimization, data quality validation, and incremental processing.   Optimize SQL queries with indexes, filters, and partitioning to handle large datasets efficiently, while ensuring data quality validation and supporting incremental data loads.

Implement testing and debugging techniques, such as unit testing, integration testing, and data quality testing, to ensure the reliability and correctness of data pipelines.   Unit testing validates individual pipeline components; integration testing ensures end-to-end workflows function correctly; and data quality testing verifies the accuracy and consistency of processed data.

Understand the strengths and use cases of different AWS services (Step Functions, MWAA, Glue, Lambda, EventBridge, etc.) and when to use each service or a combination of services for building and orchestrating data pipelines.   Step Functions excels in workflow orchestration; MWAA suits complex Airflow-based workflows; and Glue is optimal for ETL operations. Combining services like Lambda and EventBridge can create versatile, event-driven pipelines tailored to specific use cases.

Review Questions

1. Which AWS service allows you to create and manage visual workflows to orchestrate AWS services and custom code?

    A. AWS Lambda

    B. AWS Step Functions

    C. AWS Glue

    D. Amazon MWAA

2. What is the primary purpose of Amazon Managed Workflows for Apache Airflow (Amazon MWAA)?

    A. To provide a fully managed Apache Airflow environment for building and automating data pipelines

    B. To orchestrate AWS Lambda functions

    C. To perform data transformations using Apache Spark

    D. To create and manage data lakes

3. Which AWS service provides a serverless Apache Spark environment and a Data Catalog for building and automating ETL pipelines?

    A. AWS Step Functions

    B. Amazon MWAA

    C. AWS Glue

    D. AWS Lambda

4. What is the purpose of Amazon EventBridge in the context of data pipeline orchestration?

    A. To trigger and automate data pipelines based on events from various sources

    B. To perform data transformations

    C. To store and manage data lakes

    D. To provide a managed Apache Airflow environment

5. Which AWS service can be used to send notifications and alerts for data pipeline events, such as failures or completion?

    A. Amazon SNS

    B. AWS CloudTrail

    C. Amazon CloudWatch

    D. AWS Glue

6. What is the purpose of infrastructure as code (IaC) in the context of data pipeline deployments?

   A. To ensure consistent and repeatable deployments across different environments

   B. To perform data transformations

   C. To orchestrate data pipelines

   D. To send notifications and alerts

7. Which AWS service can be used to implement custom data processing or transformation logic within data pipelines?

   A. AWS Step Functions

   B. AWS Lambda

   C. Amazon MWAA

   D. Amazon EventBridge

8. What is the purpose of using Git commands in data pipeline development?

   A. To perform data transformations

   B. To orchestrate data pipelines

   C. To manage code changes, collaborate with team members, and maintain version control

   D. To send notifications and alerts

9. Which technique can be used to validate the quality and integrity of the data processed by a data pipeline?

   A. Unit testing

   B. Data quality testing

   C. Debugging tools

   D. Logging and monitoring

10. What is the purpose of using Amazon CloudWatch in the context of data pipeline orchestration?

   A. To perform data transformations

   B. To orchestrate data pipelines

   C. To provide monitoring and logging capabilities for data pipelines

   D. To manage code changes and version control

Chapter

3

Data Transformation

**THE AWS CERTIFIED DATA ENGINEER –
ASSOCIATE EXAM OBJECTIVES COVERED
IN THIS CHAPTER MAY INCLUDE, BUT ARE
NOT LIMITED, TO THE FOLLOWING:**

✓ **Domain 1: Data Ingestion and Transformation**

  ▪ 1.2 Transform and process data

✓ **Domain 3: Data Operations and Support**

  ▪ 3.4 Ensure data quality

Introduction to Data Integration

Toward the end of the last millennium, the data management landscape underwent a significant transformation. Powered by relational databases, online transactional processing (OLTP) systems emerged as the workhorse for storing and managing real-time operational data. These systems prioritized speed and transactional integrity (*ACID* properties) to reflect the reliable record of the business's activity. This directly created the need to analyze the data for insights, resulting in the creation of online analytical processing (OLAP) systems around the mid-1990s. OLAP relied on data warehouses for historical data analysis to support business intelligence and data-driven decision-making. Both OLTP and OLAP operated in distinct realms with distinct design patterns. To bridge the gap between the current state (OLTP) and historical tapestry (OLAP), specialized extract, transform, and load (ETL) processes were developed. These processes form the foundation of the data transformation pipeline, which ensures the continuous and seamless flow of data from operational systems to the analytical world. While the ETL process offers a foundational approach to data integration, its challenges in handling complex data formats and real-time processing have driven the evolution of various ETL methods, such as ELT, micro-batching, reverse ETL, each offering distinct advantages for specific use cases.

This chapter discusses various mechanisms to transform and process the ingested data based on requirements using AWS services such as AWS Lambda, Amazon Athena, Amazon Elastic MapReduce (Amazon EMR), AWS Glue, Amazon Redshift, Amazon Data Firehose, and Amazon Managed Service for Apache Flink. You will learn how to optimize container usage for performance needs, optimize costs, and improve performance while implementing data transformation services.

This chapter will also cover how to run data quality checks and apply validation rules while processing the data.

Data Transformation

Data transformation is the process of reshaping data from its initial state into a format that downstream applications can understand and utilize. So, which tools are available to make raw data consumable for downstream stakeholders? The task dictates the tool.

Some of the AWS services and ingestion tools can do light transformations when they write the data out in Parquet format. For example, Amazon Data Firehose can write data in Parquet format; Amazon AppFlow can help you with data transformations like masking, filtering, validations; and Data Migration Service allows you to perform basic transformations while replicating the records from the source to the target system. However, for heavier transformations using distributed computing, you can process and prepare your data using AWS Lambda, Amazon EMR, AWS Glue, and Amazon Redshift.

The upcoming sections delve into each service and give you a comprehensive overview of their functionalities. We will then culminate with a comparative analysis highlighting the most suitable service for various use cases.

AWS Lambda

One of the major benefits of cloud computing is its ability to abstract the infrastructure layer. Traditionally, application development involved provisioning, configuring, and maintaining servers. This consumed valuable developer resources and limited scalability during peak loads. Serverless computing provides you with that abstraction, allowing you to focus on the code for your applications without spending time building and managing the underlying infrastructure. AWS Lambda is a serverless compute service that allows you to run code without provisioning or managing servers. Within Lambda, your code is stored in a code deployment package and contains an event handler. It works on the pay-as-you-go model. You are charged based on the number of invocations for your functions and the duration it takes for your code to execute.

AWS Lambda automatically scales your code to handle any volumes of requests, ensuring smooth performance even during traffic spikes. It provides built-in code monitoring and logging via Amazon CloudWatch. By eliminating server management, AWS Lambda accelerates faster development by allowing developers to write code and deploy the applications quickly. AWS Lambda supports a variety of programming languages, including C#, Java, Go, PowerShell, Node.js, Python, and Ruby. Each AWS Lambda function runs in its own isolated environment with its own resources and file system view.

Unlike traditional servers, Lambda functions do not run constantly. At the time of writing this book, Lambda functions are purposefully limited to a maximum execution time of 15 minutes (https://docs.aws.amazon.com/lambda/latest/dg/gettingstarted-limits.html). An event triggering in Lambda could be from either an HTTP request via Amazon API Gateway, a schedule managed by Amazon EventBridge, or an Amazon S3 notification.

Reference Architectures and Use Cases

Event-Driven Architecture

AWS Lambda and Amazon S3 static hosting offer a cost-effective approach for websites. The web frontend resides on Amazon S3, with content delivery accelerated by Amazon CloudFront caching (a content delivery network). Lambda functions handle application logic and persist data in managed databases, such as Amazon RDS (relational) or Amazon DynamoDB (non-relational).

Figure 3.1 showcases a classic example of event-driven architecture, where the customer connects to a web UI application hosted on Amazon S3. Amazon API Gateway receives user requests from the web application, and these requests are forwarded to AWS Lambda to calculate the best trip options based on the user's prerequisites. The result is then efficiently stored in an Amazon Neptune graph database. Different parallel streams of Lambda are spun to also ingest the data from on-premises databases and send customer bookings through the customer ordering system.

The following reference blog showcases more use cases of event-driven architectures using AWS Lambda:

```
https://aws.amazon.com/blogs/architecture/ibm-consulting-creates-
innovative-aws-solutions-in-french-hackathon
```

FIGURE 3.1   IBM-designed AWS solution of event-driven architecture

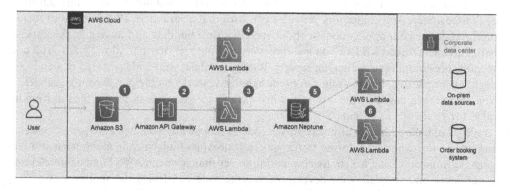

To learn more about the event-driven architecture pattern, please refer to following site:

```
https://stackoverflow.blog/2020/03/16/how-event-driven-
architecture-solves-modern-web-app-problems
```

Real-Time File Processing

When a new file is uploaded in Amazon S3, you can invoke AWS Lambda to trigger a process and facilitate on-the-fly document conversion for various formats (e.g., PDF, HTML, etc.) based on the user's needs. You can also convert the files to the Parquet format during the ETL process, eliminating the need for static storage of multiple document versions. Parquet is a columnar storage format that is optimized for analytical queries and minimizes I/O operations by reading only the columns needed for a query. This speeds up query execution.

Real-Time Stream Processing

For applications handling large volumes of real-time streaming data (telemetry, click stream analytics, log analytics), Lambda functions can be designed to process the required information without impacting the main application's performance. If you are building a pipeline to ingest IoT (Internet of Things) data securely in near real-time, one of the solutions would be to use Amazon Data Firehose to ingest the streaming data to Amazon S3, also creating a Lambda function to remove any personal identifiable information (PII) and to transform the data before storing it in the S3 bucket.

Lambda functions can also be built to analyze AWS CloudTrail or Amazon CloudWatch logs in real time, searching for specific events and sending notifications via Amazon Simple Notification Service (Amazon SNS) or custom hooks to Slack, Zendesk, or any other systems.

Polling and Batching

For real-time data processing with Amazon Kinesis Data Streams, Lambda reads records from the data stream and invokes your function synchronously through a polling mechanism. Unlike asynchronous processing, Lambda waits for your function's execution to complete before fetching the next batch of records. This ensures that all processing logic within your function is finished before moving to the next dataset. By default, Lambda polls each Kinesis shard at least once per second. To optimize data processing efficiency, you can configure Lambda to retrieve records from Kinesis in batches. At the time of this writing, you can configure a batching window (up to 5 minutes), which allows Lambda to accumulate records before invoking your function. Before invoking the function, Lambda continues to read records from the event source until it has gathered a full batch (i.e., the batching window expires or the batch reaches a payload limit of 6 MB).

To handle high data volumes effectively, Lambda can process multiple batches from a single Kinesis shard concurrently. This parallelism is controlled by the `Parallelization Factor` setting, which allows you to specify the number of concurrent batches that Lambda can process from a single shard.

Visit the following AWS documentation to learn more about the retries, reliability, and error handling for real-time data processing with Amazon Kinesis Data Streams and Lambda: `https://docs.aws.amazon.com/lambda/latest/dg/with-kinesis.html`.

Lambda event source mappings process each event at least once, and duplicate processing of batches can occur. Also, stream polling during event source mapping creation and updates exhibits eventual consistency. This means that it might take a few minutes for Lambda to begin processing events from a newly created or updated stream. To ensure that no data is lost during this period, it is recommended to use the `TRIM_HORIZON` (process all records in the stream), `LATEST` (process only new records that are added to the stream) or `AT_TIMESTAMP` (process records starting from a specific time) options for the stream's starting position.

Replace *Cron*

Scheduled Lambda events are ideal for routine tasks within AWS accounts, including backups, resource checks, and report generation. This is a more cost-effective solution than running a cron job on an Amazon EC2 (Elastic Cloud Compute) instance.

> While AWS Lambda supports emulating cron jobs through scheduled expressions in Amazon EventBridge, this approach should be exercised cautiously. Batch processing tasks scheduled with Amazon EventBridge carry the risk of exceeding the 15-minute Lambda timeout if the volume of the transactions spikes unexpectedly. Instead, the recommended approach for scalability is to configure Amazon S3 to directly invoke the Lambda function upon each new object upload. This ensures near-real-time processing and eliminates the risk of exceeding Lambda's execution time limits.

To get a complete list of services that integrate with AWS Lambda, visit the AWS official documentation:

`https://docs.aws.amazon.com/lambda/latest/dg/lambda-services.html`

Best Practices and Anti-Patterns

In the serverless architecture, especially when you are dealing with services like AWS Lambda, ensuring data consistency becomes paramount. These services are designed for fault tolerance—they handle failures gracefully and often involve retries. However, this introduces a potential pitfall. What if the same event triggers your Lambda function multiple times, causing duplications? This is where the principle of idempotency assumes significance. An idempotent function guarantees that no matter how many times it is invoked with the same input, the output remains consistent beyond the initial execution. This ensures data integrity.

 Real World Scenario

Consider a restaurant analogy to explain the concept of idempotency. Imagine you are at your favorite pizza restaurant and tell the waiter your order (event). He heads to the kitchen, but unfortunately, there is a power outage, and he may not remember if he already placed the order (multiple invocations). If he places it again, you end up getting two pizzas! This is a scenario with no idempotency. Now, when you apply idempotency in action, the waiter checks a table—like Amazon DynamoDB (non-relational)—to see if your orderID (unique identifier) exists. If it does not, he places the order and adds your orderID to the table with a timer (TTL [Time to Live]). The orderID here takes care of the duplication and ensures data integrity. TTL is used to expire the items to limit the storage space.

Anti-Patterns

The following are anti-patterns to consider:

Long-Running Applications   Lambda functions have a 15-minute execution timeout. If your application demands longer processing times, consider alternatives like Amazon

EC2, Amazon EKS (managed Kubernetes), or Amazon ECS (container orchestration) for extended workloads.

Lambda as an Orchestrator   For complex tasks, instead of chaining multiple Lambda functions and increasing the complexity to handle errors and retries, consider using AWS Step Functions to orchestrate these workflows.

Dynamic Websites   While Lambda can handle static websites, it's not ideal for highly dynamic and high-traffic websites. These require more robust resources to handle frequent updates and user interactions. Amazon EC2, Amazon EKS, or Amazon ECS in conjunction with AWS CloudFormation will be recommended.

Stateful Applications   Lambda functions operate in a "stateless" manner. This means that they don't maintain any memory between invocations. This makes them unsuitable for applications that require persistent state, like remembering user preferences or keep track of ongoing processes. For such scenarios, store your data in external services like Amazon S3 or Amazon DynamoDB.

Lambda Monolith   Migrating an entire application as monolithic Lambda functions can be tempting, but it leads to inefficiencies. These "monoliths" become cumbersome (e.g., large package size), pose security challenges (e.g., broad IAM roles), and hinder maintenance (e.g., difficult upgrades and testing). The recommended approach is to decompose them into microservices (smaller packages)—one function per each well-defined task. This results in improved performance and simplified maintenance.

Synchronous Waiting within a Single Lambda Function   One consideration for billing calculation while executing a Lambda function is the duration. When function code makes a blocking call, you are billed for the time it waits to receive a response. Avoid lengthy synchronous tasks within the same Lambda function. Try to arrange the independent tasks to run in parallel for better efficiency and optimized costs. For example, if the first function writes to S3, trigger the second function asynchronously via S3 events, thereby minimizing the wait times. Also consider using AWS Step Functions as an orchestrator of the workflow. When using standard workflow within the AWS Step Functions, you are billed for each state transition within the workflow rather than the total duration of the entire workflow. Also, you can move out the logic of retry, wait, callback mechanism, and error handling from Lambda into the state condition of the AWS Step Functions so that your Lambda function only focuses on the business logic.

Recursive Patterns   Lambda functions can trigger infinite loops if they both receive input from and send output to the same AWS service (e.g., Amazon S3). Imaging using a Lambda function to write to an S3 bucket, which triggers the same function again, resulting into a loop. To avoid this, it is recommended to keep input and output services separate. If you must write back to the same service that triggered the function, use safeguards like positive triggers (unique identifiers) or reserved concurrency limits to prevent such loops. Additionally, CloudWatch monitoring can alert you to sudden spikes in the concurrency, allowing you to intervene before the resource exhaustion occurs.

Wasting Invocations   Processing every message in a queue or stream can be expensive if you only care about a subset of the data. An example would be triggering an invocation only when the temperature drops below 30 degrees Celsius. Traditionally, Lambda code would filter messages within the function itself, wasting resources processing irrelevant data. The recommended approach is to leverage Lambda event filtering (see `https://docs.aws.amazon.com/lambda/latest/dg/invocation-eventfiltering.html`). By defining filters during event source mapping, you can ensure that Lambda is invoked only for events that meet your criteria, reducing unnecessary processing costs.

Cold Starts   When Lambda receives a request to run a function, it first prepares an environment (downloads code, sets up memory, etc.). If the invocations are synchronous, this initial startup time—often referred to as a *cold start*—adds to the execution time. Lambda reuses warmed environments for a limited time after an invocation based on the frequent calls, which helps reduce the cold starts on production workloads. However, the most effective and recommended approach is to have a provisioned concurrency. This ensures a pre-decided set number of always-available warmed environments, minimizing cold starts and guaranteeing low latency. To learn more about how to improve the performance while using AWS Lambda, please refer to the AWS blog: `https://aws.amazon.com/blogs/compute/operating-lambda-performance-optimization-part-1`.

To delve deeper into the intricacies of anti-patterns and explore additional examples, please refer to the official AWS documentation on the best practices of AWS Lambda: `https://docs.aws.amazon.com/lambda/latest/operatorguide/anti-patterns.html`

AWS Lambda—File Systems Mounting

While Lambda itself is serverless, your functions often need to store and access data. As Lambda functions handle various tasks, from image processing to data analysis, each use case has different storage requirements. Some functions need temporary storage for processing, while others require persistent data sharing across invocations. Lambda offers a range of storage solutions:

- **Amazon S3:** Ideal for large, infrequently accessed data such as backups or logs

- **Temporary storage:** Ideal for short-lived data used within a single function execution

- **Lambda layers:** Efficient for sharing common libraries across functions without bloating deployments

- **Amazon EFS:** Enables persistent data sharing and access to frequently used files

To understand the comparisons of each storage solution and the maximum size limits, visit the AWS blog: `https://aws.amazon.com/blogs/compute/choosing-between-aws-lambda-data-storage-options-in-web-apps`

 At the time of writing this book, AWS Lambda allows you to configure ephemeral storage (/tmp) between 512 MB and 10,240 MB, in 1-MB increments.

AWS Glue

AWS Glue is a serverless, fully managed data integration service that provides capabilities to discover, prepare, and combine data for analytics, machine learning, and application development. It provides development environments catered to multiple personas with different skillsets: a visually rich GUI using AWS Glue Studio for data engineers, notebook style interactive code development for data scientists, and no-code development for data analysts using AWS Glue DataBrew.

Here is a breakdown of what AWS Glue offers:

- **Serverless environment:** AWS Glue eliminates the need to manage any infrastructure for your ETL jobs. It automatically provisions and scales resources based on your workloads.

- **Ease of use:** It provides a visual interface for building ETL workflows. It also supports writing scripts in PySpark or Scala for more complex tasks.

- **Variety of data sources and destinations:** AWS Glue can access data from various sources, including Amazon S3, relational databases, and streaming services like Amazon Kinesis Data Streams and Apache Kafka. It also supports loading data into various targets, including Amazon Redshift, data lakes and so on.

- **Built-in transformations:** AWS Glue offers a library of built-in transformations for data manipulation tasks, including sorting, joining, data cleaning, and filtering.

- **Scheduling and triggering:** You can schedule ETL jobs to run on a regular basis or trigger them based on events such as new data arrival.

- **Incremental loading:** AWS Glue supports loading data incrementally from the data sources. This helps you read and process only the newly added data and process late-arriving data as part of the ETL runs.

- **Monitoring and logging:** AWS Glue provides job monitoring and logging capabilities to track the progress and performance of the ETL workloads.

- **Cost-effective:** Since AWS Glue is serverless, you only pay for the resources used by your ETL jobs. This eliminates the cost of managing and maintaining the infrastructure.

- **Cataloging and discovery of data:** It offers a central repository to store the metadata about your data sources, transformations, and targets. AWS Glue also provides automated schema discovery.

Next, we'll look at the AWS Glue components that help you achieve these functionalities.

Key Components of AWS Glue

Figure 3.2 shows an AWS representation of how AWS Glue enables you to modernize your data architecture.

FIGURE 3.2   AWS Glue high-level overview

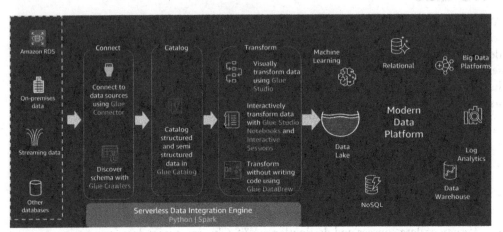

AWS Glue Connectors

AWS Glue connectors act like a bridge between your data sources and transformation component (in this case, AWS Glue Studio). They allow you to connect to various data sources and extract, transform, and load your data. There are three main connector offerings from AWS Glue:

- **Built-in connectors:** AWS Glue supports a number of built-in connectors for popular data sources, such as relational databases (JDBC), Amazon S3, and others.

- **Custom connectors:** If you do not find the built-in connectors for your data sources, you can develop your own custom connectors. These connectors are written in code and use Spark, Athena, or JDBC interfaces to interact with your data source.

- **Marketplace connectors:** For non-natively supported data stores, you can also subscribe to connectors in AWS Marketplace.

Connections created using custom or AWS Marketplace connectors in AWS Glue Studio appear in the AWS Glue console with type set to UNKNOWN. Please refer to the official AWS documentation to learn in depth about how to develop custom connectors:

https://docs.aws.amazon.com/glue/latest/dg/connectors-chapter.html

AWS Glue Crawlers and Classifiers

Imagine a huge data warehouse with information scattered everywhere. AWS Glue crawlers act like watchguards, tracking every data movement, finding and listing all the data, keeping track of the changing in the inventory (schema evolution, partition changes), and checking for updates and missing entries (data freshness and monitoring). Glue crawlers help you automatically discover new data sources, define the schema, and keep data organized, tracked, and flowing smoothly for tasks like data processing (ETL automation).

A classifier reads the data in the data store and recognizes the format of the data (CSV, JSON). AWS Glue provides a set of built-in classifiers, but you can also create your own custom classifiers.

AWS Glue Catalog

AWS Glue Data Catalog is your technical, persistent metadata store. It stores information about what data you have and where it resides. Imagine AWS Glue crawlers and AWS Glue Data Catalog working together. Crawlers help you to automatically find and analyze your data sources from silos. They use classifiers to understand the data structure, define the schema and then later deposit the extracted metadata into the AWS Glue Catalog. Consider the AWS Glue Catalog as a central index, which indexes all this information, making it easy to find specific data. We will delve deeply into the functionalities, including advanced configuration, in Chapter 6.

AWS Glue ETL Jobs

Based on the business logic and the skill set of the persona, AWS Glue provides three options for building the ETL data pipelines and transforming your data: Glue Studio (for data engineers), Glue DataBrew (for data analysts), and Glue Notebooks (for data scientists). AWS Glue enables you to perform ETL operations on both batch and streaming (real-time) data.

Glue Studio is a visual development environment for building and managing ETL workflows. You can use the drag-and-drop functionality to build these ETL pipelines.

Glue DataBrew is a low-code/no-code visual tool specifically designed for data analysts, enabling them to clean and transform data with built-in transformations.

Glue Notebooks leverages familiar Jupyter notebooks for interactive custom coding, allowing data scientists to perform complex data transformations with Python or Scala. It provides more flexibility and control for advanced users familiar with coding.

For streaming use cases, you can leverage AWS Glue Streaming ETL, which is built on the Apache Spark Structured Streaming engine.

Glue Workflows

Glue workflows play a crucial role in orchestrating complex ETL activities. They act as a central hub for managing multiple Glue crawlers, Glue ETL jobs, and triggers. Chapter 2 discusses Glue workflows in more depth.

Glue Data Quality

Glue Data Quality is a feature within AWS Glue that helps you ensure the accuracy, completeness, data validation, and consistency of your data by implementing data quality checks at rest (on your catalog tables) and in transit (during the ETL runs). We will cover this further later in this chapter.

In this chapter, we will focus on the transformation and processing aspects using AWS Glue.

AWS Glue DataBrew

Data preparation can feel like a tedious and mysterious job to those without any coding experience. Imagine business users or data analysts needing to clean and organize the messy data before they can use it for their business requirements, but feeling constrained because they don't know how to write code in Python or Scala. This is where AWS Glue DataBrew comes in as a lifesaver. It's a no-code serverless ETL tool designed specifically for people with little or no coding skills. Imagine a user friendly, visual interface that allows you to tackle data preparation tasks without writing a single line of code. It empowers the audience to focus on extracting valuable insights from your data. AWS Glue DataBrew offers a library of over 250 built-in transformations that address common data quality issues such as filtering anomalies, data masking, correcting invalid values, and so on.

AWS Glue DataBrew supports various data sources, such as Amazon S3, Amazon Redshift, Amazon Aurora, and Amazon RDS databases, or data sources using *JDBC* (Java Database Connectivity) drivers. Once the data is connected, it empowers the users to transform the data through a rich visual interface. You can build data processing workflows by simply dragging and dropping the pre-built transformations. You can apply data quality rules to perform conditional checks based on your business needs. Additionally, AWS Glue DataBrew allows you to preview the impact of the transformations before applying them to the entire dataset. This ensures that you understand the impact and ramifications of each step on your data. Once the data transformations are complete, AWS Glue DataBrew stores the cleaned and prepared dataset back into Amazon S3. This curated data can be integrated with data visualization tools, such as Amazon QuickSight, or other BI platforms, such as Tableau.

Architecture Core Components

Figure 3.3 illustrates the high-level architecture of AWS Glue DataBrew. With AWS Glue DataBrew, you can connect directly from various data sources and visually prepare, clean, and normalize the data using over 250 built-in transformations. The results are then published to downstream applications for further insights.

Let's take a closer look at a few of those concepts, along with projects, datasets, and jobs:

Projects   Imagine projects as your dedicated workspace for each data preparation task. This is where you manage all the ingredients—the data itself, the transformation it needs, and even the automated processes you can schedule.

Datasets   Datasets are the raw and unprocessed records that are available after connecting to various data sources.

Recipes   Recipes are the step-by-step instructions for transforming your data. Using AWS Glue DataBrew, you can define multiple steps and actions to transform the data. You can download a copy of the recipe steps so that you can reuse the recipe in other projects or other transformations. You can also publish multiple versions of a recipe.

Jobs   A job instructs AWS Glue DataBrew to execute the recipe on your chosen dataset. You can even run jobs on-demand or schedule them to run automatically, ensuring that data is always prepared and up-to-date.

Data Lineage   Data lineage provides a visual map, like following a recipe backwards, showing the data's origin, its journey through various processes, and its final storage location (see Figure 3.4).

Data Profile   Before diving into transformation, it's useful to understand the data's current state. As shown in Figure 3.5, a data profile acts like a detailed report, outlining the data's structure, content context, and any relationship between different elements.

FIGURE 3.3   AWS Glue DataBrew high-level architecture

AWS Glue DataBrew integrates with Amazon CloudWatch alarms to monitor metrics and receive notifications via Amazon SNS. Additionally, AWS CloudTrail logs user actions and API calls made within AWS Glue DataBrew, providing a detailed audit history. Glue Data-Brew secures data both in transit and at rest. For data in transit, Glue DataBrew uses SSL/TLS for secure communication, and at rest, it leverages AWS Key Management Service to encrypt and decrypt data.

Handling PII

In today's data-driven world, companies face the challenge of ever-increasing volumes of sensitive data. Identifying and protecting PII at scale can be a complex and time-consuming process. Data privacy regulations like *CCPA* and *GDPR* also add additional layers of complexity and compliance. AWS Glue DataBrew allows you to streamline the identification and protection of sensitive data with different techniques, including masking, encryption, and redaction. When you run a profile job on your dataset, you have the option to enable PII statistics. This helps you identify PII columns and apply specific transformations on them.

FIGURE 3.4   Data lineage with AWS Glue DataBrew

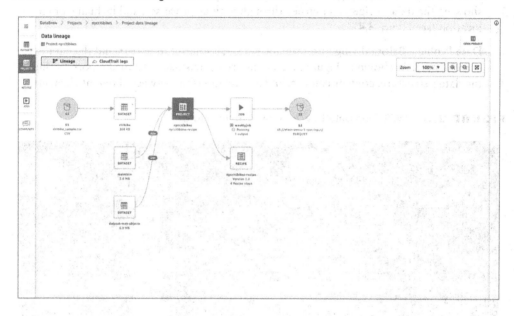

FIGURE 3.5   Data profiling with AWS Glue DataBrew

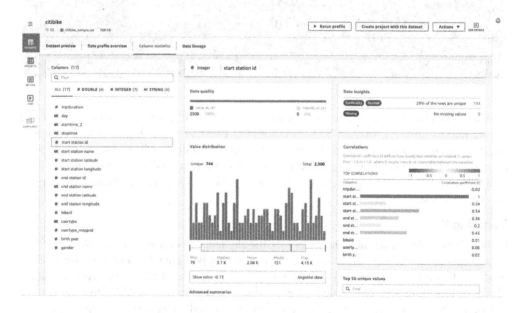

With respect to the transformation and handling of PII data, AWS Glue DataBrew uses the following data masking techniques:

- **Substitution**: It replaces PII with realistic-looking values, ideal for maintaining data integrity while masking sensitive information.

- **Shuffling**: It re-arranges PII values within the same column across different rows, further obfuscating sensitive information.

- **Encryption (deterministic)**: It ensures the same PII value always encrypts to the same ciphertext, facilitating decryption when needed for authorized access.

- **Encryption (probabilistic)**: It encrypts PII values differently each time, offering an extra layer of security. Data cannot be decrypted back to its original form.

- **Decryption**: It decrypts previously encrypted data for processing when authorized access is required.

AWS Glue DataBrew also offers additional options, such as nulling out, deletion, masking specific portions, or hashing for PII handling, allowing you to tailor the approach to your specific needs.

For more detailed steps and instructions on how to handle and identify PII data using AWS Glue DataBrew, refer to this blog: `https://aws.amazon.com/blogs/big-data/introducing-pii-data-identification-and-handling-using-aws-glue-databrew`.

AWS Glue ETL Jobs

AWS Glue runs your ETL jobs in a serverless environment with the engine of your choice, Spark or Ray. AWS Glue on Apache Spark supports three flavors for data transformation: Spark, Spark Streaming, and Python Shell. Spark is the workhorse for the data transformation; Spark Streaming handles real-time data pipelines; and Python Shell is used to run arbitrary Python scripts without a Spark cluster. Python Shell is mostly suitable for small-to-medium ETL jobs and triggering long-running queries on Amazon Redshift, Amazon Athena, Amazon EMR, and more.

AWS Glue on Apache Spark

Apache Spark is a distributed system for in-memory processing of large datasets, making it incredibly fast. It is written in Scala but offers front-ends in Python (PySpark), Java, R, and SQL. AWS Glue Spark jobs are essentially serverless Spark clusters where you can run Python or Scala code for data transformation. Spark operates on the distributed system model, where it distributes the data across multiple machines (cluster nodes), enabling parallel processing and faster results. Let's focus specifically on PySpark.

PySpark offers three primary data structures for data manipulation at different levels of abstraction.

RDD (Resilient Distributed Dataset)   The code building block, an RDD is a distributed list of lists spread across the cluster nodes for fault tolerance. There are two ways to create an RDD:

1. Parallelize an existing collection in your driver program.
2. Reference a dataset in an external storage system, such as Amazon S3, HDFS, HBase, or any data source offering a Hadoop InputFormat. For example:

```
data =[1,2,3,4,5] distData =sc.parallelize(data)
```

DataFrame   DataFrame allows you to add column labels to the RDD for easier data access and manipulation. It is similar to the Pandas DataFrames commonly used by Python developers. Consider DataFrame as a high-level API for RDDs.

DynamicFrame (Glue-Specific)   This layer sits on top of DataFrame and offers additional functionalities like advanced transformation and integration with Glue Data Catalog for data discovery. DataFrame and DynamicFrame can be easily converted to each other using the `fromDF` and `toDF` functions. This conversion does not involve any data copying and hence there is no performance impact to consider.

These data structures are immutable, meaning you cannot modify the existing data. Each transformation creates a new data structure.

Glue uses dy_ to indicate DynamicFrame and df_ to indicate DataFrame usage.

Glue DynamicFrame and Spark DataFrame

Imagine you have a library with a massive collection of books. Spark DataFrame and Glue DynamicFrame are akin to different ways to organize these books on shelves.

Spark DataFrame   Spark DataFrames are like pre-built bookshelves with fixed compartments. They work well if all your books are the same size and format. But if you have oddly shaped books, DataFrames become limiting. They require you to know the exact format of each book (data) beforehand (schema).

Glue DynamicFrame   Glue DynamicFrames are like adjustable bookshelves with flexible dividers. They can accommodate any type of book, regardless of size, shape, or binding (data). They can even figure out the format of each book (data) as they are placed on the shelf (schema and schema evolution). This makes them perfect for diverse use cases.

Glue DynamicFrames natively interact with the Glue connectors, thereby simplifying the data ingestion and data transformation tasks across multiple data sources. They natively support the AWS Glue Data Catalog. They leverage Glue's query optimization capabilities to enhance the data processing speed and resource utilization. Glue DynamicFrame provides a high-level API that simplifies complex data transformations. DynamicFrame refers to the entire data, and DynamicRecord refers to a single row of a data.

As shown in Figure 3.6, DynamicFrame infers the schema on-the-fly, enabling the transformations in a single pass. One of the unique features of DynamicFrame is the Choice type. Using the `resolveChoice`, DynamicFrame allows you to leave multiple type possibilities open for a later decision. In this case, the *deviceid* column has both `long` and `string` data types. With DataFrame being conformed to the fixed schema, if more than one data type were present, the processing would be interrupted. With the `resolveChoice` execution, you have the possibility to project every type to given type (`project`), cast to single type (`cast`), keep both types in two separate columns (`make_cols`), or create a structure that contains each data type (`make_struct`).

FIGURE 3.6 AWS Glue DynamicFrame using the Choice type

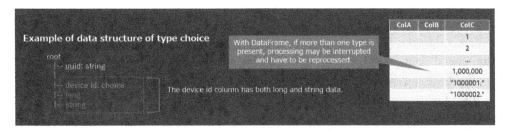

One of the key advantages of using AWS Glue DynamicFrame is its ability to handle complex nested data structures. Using `relationalize`, it automatically converts semi-structured data (like JSON) into relational database tables. Figure 3.7 depicts an example of how it flattens the corresponding schema with rows and columns, making it suitable to query and analyze.

FIGURE 3.7 AWS Glue DynamicFrame for relational schema

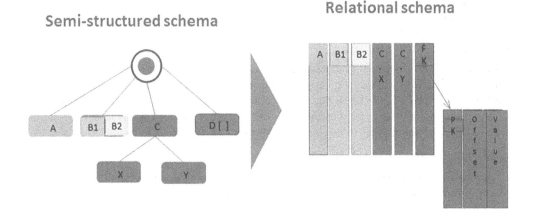

Please refer to this site for the complete list of PySpark transforms using AWS Glue: https://docs.aws.amazon.com/glue/latest/dg/aws-glue-programming-python-transforms.html.

Working with PySpark in Glue

A typical PySpark transformation script in Glue involves these steps:

1. **Initialize connection:** Establish a connection to the Spark cluster using `GlueContext`.

2. **Read data:** Use `GlueContext` to read data from various data stores using the Glue Data Catalog.

3. **Transform data:** Perform transformations on the data using DataFrame or DynamicFrame.

4. **Write data:** Use `GlueContext` to write the transformed data to the destination in a specific format (e.g., Parquet).

Migrating Apache Spark Programs to AWS Glue

If you have existing Spark programs, you can migrate them to AWS Glue to benefit from its features and managed environment. Here are the steps and breakdown of the process:

1. **Spark version compatibility:** Ensure that your Spark program version is compatible with the supported version in your chosen AWS Glue release.

2. **Third-party libraries:** Include the necessary libraries using *JARs* for Scala as well as Wheel and source code for Python.

3. **Data source credentials:** Manage the data source's credentials using AWS Glue connections. This simplifies connecting to various data stores.

4. **Apache Spark configuration:** Use `SparkSession` to configure Spark runtime settings within your Glue job.

5. **Custom configuration:** Set custom configurations through job parameters accessible within your code.

6. **Java code migration:** Provide the fully qualified name of a class with a `main` method in a dependency as a job argument (`--class`) to use it as the entry point for your Glue Scala job.

Custom Visual Transforms

Custom visual transforms let you define, reuse, and share business-specific ETL logic among your teams. The Glue Studio UI gives you the flexibility to use the built-in transformations while building the ETL pipelines. You can combine these with the custom transforms during data processing. In order to use custom transforms in AWS Glue Studio, you will need to create two files and upload them to Amazon S3 buckets.

- **Python file:** Contains the transform function (`myTransform.py`).

- **JSON file:** Describes the transform function. This is also known as the config file that is required to defined the transform (`myTransform.json`).

AWS Glue Studio will automatically match them using their respective file names. These custom transforms will appear in the drop-down when the data engineers use Glue Studio for building the ETL pipelines. It will import these files as modules (`import myTransform`) in your job script.

AWS Glue for Ray

AWS Glue for Ray is a processing engine that supports large datasets with Python and popular Python libraries. Before the release of Glue for Ray, AWS Glue used to process the ETL jobs using either Apache Spark's distributed processing engine for large workloads or Python's single-node processing engine for smaller workloads. But customers who liked Python for its ease of use and rich collection libraries found it difficult to scale beyond a single compute node. Glue for Ray is designed to address this specific need of Python developers working with big data. Unlike Glue Spark, which uses Apache Spark, Glue Ray focuses on Python. Glue Ray utilizes Ray, an open-source framework built for scaling Python code. This means that you can distribute your Python data processing tasks across multiple machines and improve the performance. Glue for Ray also reduces the need to learn new programming languages by using existing Python libraries like Panda. You can create a Ray job from the AWS Glue console or the AWS SDK. You can use AWS Glue for Ray with Glue Studio Notebooks, a local notebook, SageMaker Studio Notebook, or an IDE of your choice. Figure 3.8 depicts the core architecture for AWS Glue for Ray.

FIGURE 3.8   AWS Glue for Ray architecture

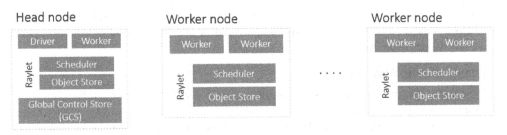

At the heart of Glue for Ray lies two key components:

Ray Core   This open-source framework is the maestro of distributed computing. It seamlessly distributes your Python code across multiple machines and coordinates the entire processing symphony. This significantly boosts your performance for larger datasets.

Ray Dataset   Imagine this as the data workhorse. Built on Apache Arrow, a high-performance columnar data format, Ray Dataset efficiently manages and distributes your data across the cluster. It acts as a counterpart to Spark DataFrames. It facilitates efficient data manipulation and analysis within your Python code.

When you run a Ray job using Glue for Ray, AWS automatically provisions a Ray cluster for you. This cluster consists of two key types of nodes:

Head Node   This acts as a conductor, overseeing the entire operation. It manages the cluster and runs the Ray driver process, which essentially initiates your Python application. Interestingly, the head node is functionally identical to worker nodes, except for these additional responsibilities.

Worker Node   These are the workhorses that carry out the actual data processing tasks. They submit and execute the distributed Python functions based on your code.

Raylets are the schedulers that keep things organized. These processes, running on each node, ensure efficient allocation among concurrent running jobs. Additionally, a shared memory object store resides within each worker node, enabling efficient data exchange during the processing.

Global Control Store is the central nervous system of the cluster. The head node houses a critical component called the Global Control Store. It keeps track of all the worker nodes. Similar to how Apache Spark treats workers as nodes, the Global Control Store views each machine in the cluster as a node, managing cluster-level metadata for optimal operation.

Glue for Ray comes pre-equipped with toolkits like the Modin (Distributed Pandas) library, which lets you distribute your existing Pandas applications across the Ray cluster without modifications, thus ensuring a smoother transition. The AWS SDK for Pandas act as an abstraction layer to simplify data access from various AWS services, such as Amazon S3, Amazon Redshift, and DynamoDB, using familiar Pandas syntax.

To learn more about AWS Glue for Ray, please refer to the AWS blog at `https://aws .amazon.com/blogs/big-data/introducing-aws-glue-for-ray-scaling-your-data-integration-workloads-using-python`.

Glue Costs and Anti-Patterns

AWS Glue uses a pay-as-you-go pricing model wherein you only get charged for the resources that you use. The primary unit for measuring the processing power in AWS Glue is the DPU (data processing unit). Think of DPUs as virtual machines with a set amount of CPU and memory. One DPU provides 4 vCPUs and 16 GB of memory. AWS Glue charges you based on the DPUs used and the duration of their use. For AWS Glue crawler and AWS Glue ETL jobs, you are charged at an hourly rate per second used. For Data Catalog storage and access, there is a free tier for the first million objects stored and accessed each month. After that, you pay a flat monthly fee. If you use an interactive environment to develop your data processing code, you are charged an hourly rate per second utilized. For AWS Glue DataBrew, interactive sessions are billed per session, while the jobs are billed per minute used. There is no charge for the Glue Schema Registry.

While AWS Glue offers so much flexibility to build ETL pipelines for multiple personas, there are some scenarios where using AWS Glue as an ETL engine may prove to be anti-pattern. Glue is built on Apache Spark, so if you need other engines, such as Hive or Pig, or want a mix of engines, consider Amazon EMR for more flexibility. AWS Glue is a managed service with limited configuration options. If your use case requires heavy Spark configurations, Amazon EMR or EKS would be the recommended choice.

Reference Architectures and Use Cases

Let's examine the reference architectures and use cases.

Incremental Processing

Customers often have different data processing requirements that involve merging multiple datasets with varying data ingestion frequencies. Processing this data stream can be a daunting task when you have to reprocess the entire data from scratch. Also, this adds to the cost. Incremental processing helps you focus only on the new and updated data since the last processing run. Less processing translates to less resource consumption and potentially lower costs for services like AWS Glue. By skipping unchanged data, it reduces processing time, especially for massive datasets. AWS Glue utilizes a feature called *job bookmarks*, which enable you to define specific columns in your data source (bookmark keys) that uniquely identify each record. During a job run, Glue can keep the track of the last processed values in these columns. In subsequent runs, the Glue job automatically resumes the processing from the point it left off, focusing only on the data with values exceeding the previously processed bookmark values. Glue also supports using multiple columns as bookmark keys. This provides you with more granular control over what constitutes "new data."

Figure 3.9 shows an AWS architecture representation of incremental loading from a relational database where one or more source columns can be specified as bookmark keys to process the incremental data. AWS Glue ingests and processes only the new records from the data source and stores the data to Amazon S3.

FIGURE 3.9   Incremental processing with AWS Glue

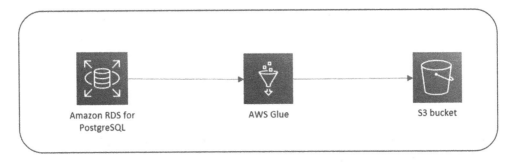

Amazon RDS for PostgreSQL → AWS Glue → S3 bucket

For Amazon S3, once you enable Glue job bookmarks, it automatically tracks the new objects that land in the data lakes. For databases, when you read from JDBC, you can specify the column names to use as bookmark keys. As shown in Figure 3.10, `jobBook markKeys` and `jobBookmarkKeysSortOrder` are used to identify the unique record. By default, if you do not specify these parameters, Glue job bookmarks takes the primary key of the table, provided that is sequentially increasing or decreasing (with no gaps). The `transformation_ctx` parameter serves as a key to search the bookmark state for a specific source in your script. If you need to reprocess a specific set of data, you can rewind or reset your bookmarks.

FIGURE 3.10 AWS Glue job bookmarks code snippet

```
Script   Job details   Runs   Data quality   Schedules   Version Control   Upgrade analysis - preview
```

Script Info

```
1   import sys
2   from awsglue.transforms import *
3   from awsglue.utils import getResolvedOptions
4   from pyspark.context import SparkContext
5   from awsglue.context import GlueContext
6   from awsglue.job import Job
7
8   args = getResolvedOptions(sys.argv, ['JOB_NAME'])
9
10  sc = SparkContext()
11  glueContext = GlueContext(sc)
12  spark = glueContext.spark_session
13  job = Job(glueContext)
14  job.init(args['JOB_NAME'], args)
15
16  datasource0 = glueContext.create_dynamic_frame.from_catalog(
17      database = "hr",
18      table_name = "emp",
19      transformation_ctx = "datasource0",
20      additional_options = {"jobBookmarkKeys":["empno"],"jobBookmarkKeysSortOrder":"asc"}
21  )
22
23  applymapping1 = ApplyMapping.apply(
24      frame = datasource0,
25      mappings = [("ename", "string", "ename", "string"), ("hrly_rate", "decimal(38,0)", "hrly_rate", "decimal(38,0)"),
26          ("comm", "decimal(7,2)", "comm", "decimal(7,2)"), ("hiredate", "timestamp", "hiredate", "timestamp"),
27          ("empno", "decimal(5,0)", "empno", "decimal(5,0)"),
28          ("sal", "decimal(7,2)", "sal", "decimal(7,2)")],
29      transformation_ctx = "applymapping1"
30  )
31
32  datasink2 = glueContext.write_dynamic_frame.from_options(
33      frame = applymapping1,
34      connection_type = "s3",
35      connection_options = {"path": "s3://hr/employees"},
36      format = "csv",
37      transformation_ctx = "datasink2"
38  )
39  job.commit()
```

Taking Advantage of Both DynamicFrame and DataFrame During ETL

Now that we have seen the difference between DataFrame and DynamicFrame, how do we take advantage of both these data structures during ETL processing? As shown in Figure 3.11, while loading the data as a DynamicFrame, AWS Glue optimizes the data loading using AWS Glue Catalogs, loading only differential data and cleaning the semi-structured data as part of the pre-processing step. Since DataFrame is better at table operations, such as JOIN and Filter, the DynamicFrame is converted to DataFrame using the toDF function. Once the table operations of data is done, it is converted back to DynamicFrame using the fromDF function. DynamicFrame is used to write the data back to the target destination and is also leveraged to update the data catalogs during the writes to destination table.

FIGURE 3.11   Using DataFrame and DynamicFrame in AWS Glue ETL

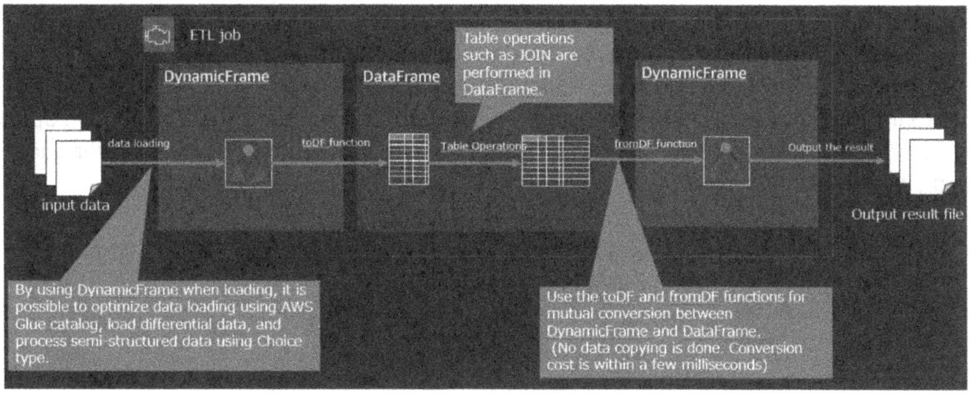

Building Transactional Data Lakes

The modern data landscape relies heavily on two giants: data lakes and data warehouses. Data lakes store vast amounts of structured, unstructured and semi-structured raw data, while data warehouses offer a more optimized and processed environment for analysis. However, keeping the data consistent between these two systems can be a challenge. While data lakes offer great flexibility, they have limitations such as data reliability, query performance due to large number of small files ingested and resulting into unnecessary disk reads, improper indexing, deletion of data for *GDPR* and *CCPA* compliance and maintaining historical versions. Transactional data lakes address these limitations by leveraging open table formats like Apache Hudi, Apache Iceberg and Delta Lake. These formats offer features like *ACID* (*atomicity*, *consistency*, *isolation*, and *durability*) transactions, Schema Enforcement and Evolution, Incremental processing and Change Data Capture. They also offer techniques like small file compaction, caching mechanism, data skipping and optimized indexing that help to enhance the query performance. Transactional data lakes also help to perform UPSERTS (Updates, Delete, Merge) on the data similar to a table simplifying the compliance with GDPR and CCPA regulations. Figure 3.12 shows an architecture representation of building a Transactional Data Lakes using Apache Iceberg and AWS Glue. In this example, in Figure 3.12, data is ingested into the data lake in raw format. The raw data is then cataloged and processed with AWS Glue and the final target data is loaded in Iceberg format applying MERGE technique to remove any duplications. The processed data is consumed using Amazon Athena for interactive querying by the end users. For fine grain access control, AWS Lake Formation is used to provide granular control, restrictive and secure access on the data for different users and roles.

Real- and Near-Real-Time Data Processing

AWS Glue can be used to ingest data from streaming services like Amazon Kinesis Data Streams and Amazon Managed Streaming for Apache Kafka (Amazon MSK). It can then process the data using Apache Spark Structured Streaming. Another example of using AWS

Glue in streaming use cases is to join the streaming data with reference data stored in a database like Amazon DynamoDB. This can be useful for enriching the streaming data with additional information. You can also use AWS Glue to develop and debug streaming ETL jobs in AWS Glue Studio notebooks and interactive sessions. In Figure 3.13, Amazon MSK Serverless, a managed Kafka service, is used to simplify the data ingestion, and IAM is used for secure authentication. AWS Glue is used to process the data in near-real time using Spark Structured Streaming. The final processed data is stored in Amazon S3 (data lake) for querying with Amazon Athena.

FIGURE 3.12   AWS Reference Architecture for Transactional data lakes with AWS Glue

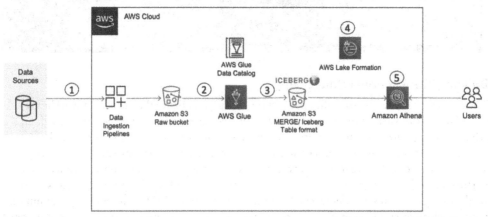

Source: Amazon Web Services / `https://aws.amazon.com/blogs/big-data/build-a-transactional-data-lake-using-apache-iceberg-aws-glue-and-cross-account-data-shares-using-aws-lake-formation-and-amazon-athena`, last accessed on 19 December 2024.

Serverless Event-Driven Workflows

Data pipelines traditionally rely on schedules or external triggers. This can prove to be inefficient for data that needs immediate processing. There is also a high possibility that you may not be able to fully predict the arrival of new files from the upstream systems into the data lakes. To cater to this requirement, AWS Glue event-driven workflows offer data processing on real-time events delivered by Amazon EventBridge. As shown in the architecture in Figure 3.14, developers can start AWS Glue workflows (consisting of AWS Glue crawlers or AWS Glue ETL jobs) based on the events delivered by Amazon EventBridge. Any new files that land on an Amazon S3 data lake generates an event. If this event matches with the rule pattern configured in Amazon EventBridge, it triggers the AWS Glue workflow.

Performance Tuning and Cost Optimization

Now let's look at ways to monitor and optimize costs and tune performance.

FIGURE 3.13 AWS reference architecture for near-real time processing with AWS Glue

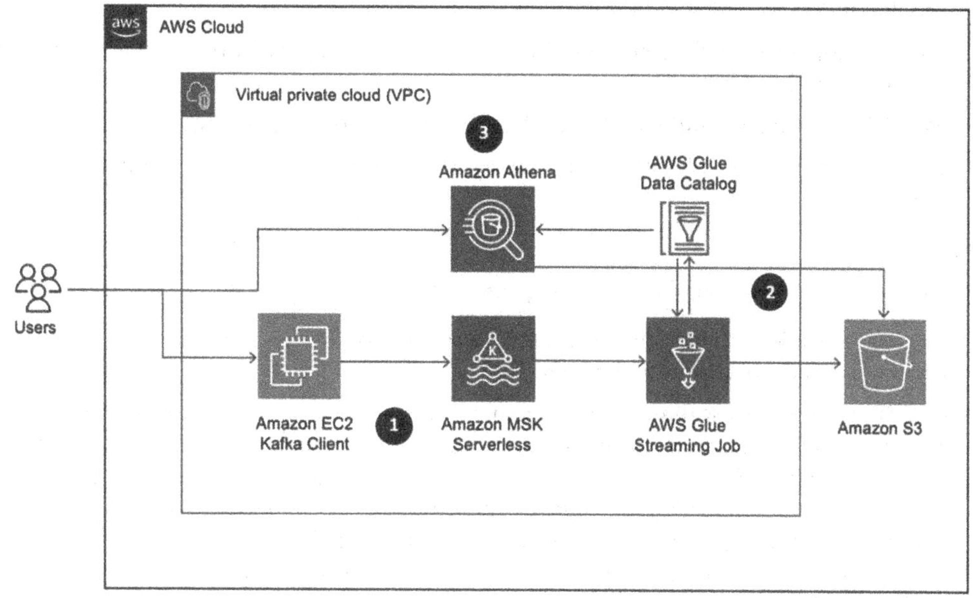

Source: Amazon Web Services / https://aws.amazon.com/blogs/big-data/securely-process-near-real-time-data-from-amazon-msk-serverless-using-an-aws-glue-streaming-etl-job-with-iam-authentication, last accessed on 19 December 2024.

FIGURE 3.14 AWS reference architecture for event-driven workflows with AWS Glue

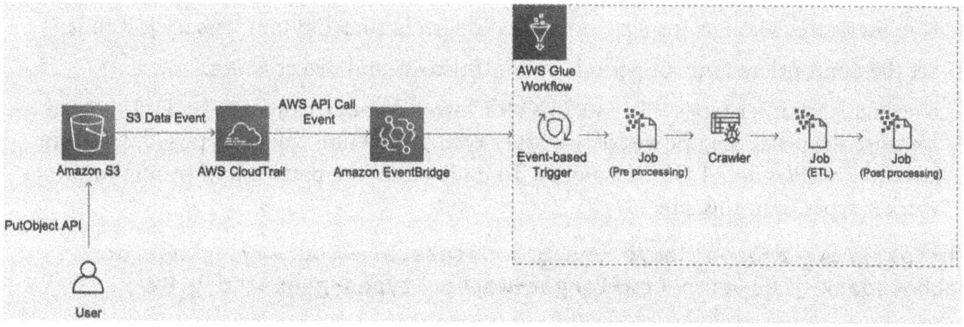

Source: Amazon Web Services / https://aws.amazon.com/blogs/big-data/build-a-serverless-event-driven-workflow-with-aws-glue-and-amazon-eventbridge, last accessed on 19 December 2024.

Monitoring Cost

You can monitor costs in several ways:

- You can monitor overall costs and individual job costs using AWS Cost Explorer and AWS Glue Studio.
- AWS Glue version 2.0 and later have a 1-minute billing for DPU hours.
- You can also use AWS CloudFormation templates to integrate the cost monitoring with AWS CloudWatch.

Optimizing Cost

You have a variety of options for optimizing costs:

- It is recommended to upgrade to the latest version of AWS Glue to benefit from performance improvements and new features.
- You can use the auto-scaling feature to dynamically adjust resources based on workload. The auto-scaling feature can be used for both batch and streaming use cases. There will be cases when you do not have constant volume of data and therefore will not have the same capacity requirements over time. If you provision your capacity to meet the SLA at peak times, this capacity will be underutilized and wasted during the low volume periods. Using the auto-scaling feature, you can set the maximum capacity required and let the AWS Glue job decide how to automatically adjust to the needs and reduce the cluster size when not needed to save on cost.
- Consider using AWS Glue Flex job for non-time-sensitive workloads to reduce costs. With Flex, an AWS Glue job runs on spare compute capacity instead of dedicated hardware. The start and runtimes of the jobs using Flex can vary based on the fact that spare compute resources are not readily available and can be reclaimed during the job runs.
- Use interactive sessions for development and testing to avoid unnecessary job runs.
- Set the appropriate timeout periods to control costs and detect issues.
- Use smaller worker types (like G0.25X) for low-volume streaming jobs. DPU is used to measure the processing power of a worker type. AWS Glue worker type G0.25X translates to 2 vCPUs and 4 GB of memory. To understand the pattern and scaling for other worker types, visit this site:

  ```
  https://aws.amazon.com/blogs/big-data/scale-your-aws-glue-for-
  apache-spark-jobs-with-new-larger-worker-types-g-4x-and-g-8x
  ```

Performance Tuning

When it comes to performance tuning, you have several options:

- Analyze bottlenecks using CloudWatch metrics and use the Spark UI to identify areas for improvement.
- Reduce costs by scanning less data. Use job bookmarks for incremental data processing, prune partitions for partitioned data, and predicate pushdown. Predicate pushdown is

a function that reads only the blocks that hit the filter or where clause for the columns that are not used as partition columns. You can apply this predicate pushdown on S3 by using the push_down_predicate parameter. This approach allows you to selectively list and read necessary data. It also helps the Glue job to not run into OOM errors during ETL processes.

- Parallelize tasks to improve processing speed, such as using JDBC reads in parallel.

- Minimize the data I/O load by reading the data you need. This can be achieved using Apache Parquet. Apache Parquet is a columnar format, which means that the data in the same column is stored in the same chunk as much as possible, and aggregation is often performed on column-by-column basis. This format is highly recommended for analytical use cases. Since the data in the same column often has the regularity in the data arrangement, compression is better than row-by-row storage. Additionally, Parquet stores metadata such as data type and number of records together with the data. This allows you to skip over unnecessary data and use metadata for aggregation.

- When reading a DataFrame from AWS Glue Data Catalog from a data source with many partitions consisting of multiple partition keys, setting the partition index will reduce the time to fetch the read partition. If no partition indexes are present on the table, AWS Glue loads all the partitions of the table, and then filters on the loaded partitions using the query expression. The query takes more time for execution without any indexes. With Partition Index, it will only fetch a subset of the partitions instead of loading all partitions in the table.

- Use groupSize and groupFiles to read a large number of small files in Amazon S3. These properties enable the ETL task to read a group of input files into a single in-memory partition. Grouping files together reduces the memory footprint on the Spark driver. Without grouping, each Spark application must process each file using a different Spark task. Too many small files spun into multiple Spark tasks may cause the Spark driver to crash, resulting in an out-of-memory exception.

- AWS Glue also provides an optimized mechanism to list files on S3 while reading data into a DynamicFrame. When you set the S3ListImplementation parameter to True, the Glue S3 Lister only iterates over the final list of filtered files to be read.

 To learn more about how to optimize memory management in AWS Glue, visit this blog:

https://aws.amazon.com/blogs/big-data/optimize-memory-management-in-aws-glue

Amazon Athena

Amazon Athena is a serverless, interactive analytics service built on open-source Trino and Presto engines, as well as the Apache Spark framework, with no provisioning or configuration effort required. It provides a simplified way to analyze data from an Amazon S3 data lake and over 30 data sources, including on-premises data sources and other cloud systems, using SQL or Python. Some of the use cases where Amazon Athena can be used include interactive data exploration for machine learning (ML) and AI, business intelligence (BI) reporting, and ad hoc querying. For the end user, Amazon Athena abstracts the information of storage and how the files are placed in the data lakes. It supports many data formats, including CSV, JSON, Parquet, ORC, and more. Athena also helps you analyze unstructured, semi-structured, and structured data on your data lakes.

Here are few use cases where Amazon Athena shines:

- You can integrate Athena with Glue Data Catalog. This allows you to connect to the catalog tables and run ad hoc queries using ANSI SQL to query your data in-place in Amazon S3.

- Athena also integrates with Amazon QuickSight for easy data visualization.

- You can use JDBC or ODBC drivers to connect to other business intelligence tools and SQL clients.

- You can query staging data on data lakes with Athena before loading into Amazon Redshift (data warehouse).

- Athena can be used to analyze logs from Amazon CloudTrail, Amazon CloudFront, Amazon Virtual Private Cloud (VPC), and Elastic Load Balancing (ELB) stored in data lakes.

- You can integrate Athena with Jupyter, Zepplin, Rstudio notebooks.

Workload Management

Athena workgroups provide a mechanism to manage workgroups, access, and costs within your Athena environment. Some of the key benefits of workgroups include:

- **Separation of duties:** Isolate queries for different teams, applications, or workloads. This promotes organization and improves security by controlling access to specific datasets.

- **Cost management:** Enforce cost constraints through per-query and per-workgroup data scan limits. This helps prevent unexpected charges and keeps costs predictable.

- **Query tracking:** Maintain independent query history and saved queries for each workgroup. This simplifies retrieval of past queries specific to a theme or a project.

- **Monitoring and alerting:** Track query-related metrics in Amazon CloudWatch for each workgroup. Set thresholds and alarms to trigger actions, such as SNS notifications, when usage reaches predefined limits.

- **Workgroup settings:** Define workgroup-wide settings, such as the Amazon S3 location for storing query results, encryption configurations, and control over objects written to the results bucket. These settings can be enforced, ensuring that all queries within the workgroup adhere to them. In nutshell, each workgroup can have its own query history, data limits, IAM policies, and encryption settings.

Athena for Spark

Amazon Athena for Apache Spark allows you to run Apache Spark workloads directly within Athena. This eliminates the need to provision and manage Spark infrastructure for interactive data exploration. You can use familiar Jupyter notebooks as the interface to perform data processing and programmatically interact with Spark applications using Athena APIs. Amazon Athena integrates with AWS Glue Data Catalog, enabling it to work with any data source in AWS Glue Data Catalog. Athena for Spark uses Firecracker (a lightweight micro-virtual machine) for sub-second startup times, eliminating the need to maintain warm pools of resources.

With the support for Apache Spark, you can use both Spark SQL and PySpark in a single notebook to generate application insights or build models. Some of the use cases for Athena for Spark include performing complex data analysis, such as regression tests and time series forecasting. Apache Spark with Python allows you to take advantage of a rich ecosystem of libraries, including data visualization in Matplotlib, Plotly, and Seaborn.

SQL-Based ETL Processes

Despite being old-fashioned, SQL is still widely used by many organizations. I remember a conversation with one of my customers where he said he preferred SQL for its simplicity more than programming languages like Python and Scala. To paraphrase Winston Churchill, "SQL is the worst query language, except for all others that have been tried."

For users who want to perform SQL-based ETL processes and data transformation, Amazon Athena provides Create Table as Select (CTAS) and INSERT INTO statements in addition to SELECT operations to perform the ETL processing. When you run the CTAS query, the tables and the partitions created are automatically added to the AWS Glue Data Catalog, making them immediately available for subsequent queries. You can orchestrate and automate Amazon Athena queries by building an ETL pipeline using the AWS Step Functions orchestrator.

The following code snippet shows an example of a CTAS query written in Amazon Athena that converts data into Parquet format while writing to the destination:

```
CREATE TABLE tmp_ctas_001 WITH (
    format='PARQUET',
    external_location = 's3://<bucket>/amazon_reviews_partitioned/product_
category=Toys/'
)
AS SELECT marketplace, customer_id, review_id, product_id, product_parent,
product_title, star_rating, helpful_votes, total_votes, vine, verified_
purchase, review_headline, review_body, review_date, year, product_category
FROM amazon_reviews_tsv
WHERE product_category = 'Toys'
```

Athena Costs and Anti-Patterns

Athena works on a pay-as-you-go model. For SQL queries, there are two billing options. Per-Query Billing is where you only pay for the data scanned by the queries you run. You are charged for the number of bytes scanned per query. There is no charge for DDL (CREATE, ALTER, DROP) or failed queries. Canceled queries are billed for the total amount of data scanned when the query is cancelled. Athena also runs SQL queries with Provisioned Capacity. In this mode, you purchase DPUs (compute units) and assign them to the workloads. You pay a flat hourly rate for the active DPUs (with a 1-hour minimum). One DPU is 4 vCPUs and 16 GB of memory. In this mechanism, there is no charge for the data scanned. This is good for consistent workloads or users who prefer flat-rate pricing. Please refer to the official AWS documentation for more information on pricing: https://aws.amazon.com/athena/pricing.

While Amazon Athena is a powerful tool for interactive data analysis, there are a few use cases where other services might be a better fit for your business requirements. For complex, high-speed analytical queries that generate business reports, Amazon Redshift is a more suitable option. If you are dealing with ETL workloads with extremely large datasets and require extensive data processing with big data frameworks (Spark, Hadoop, Presto, HBase), consider either using AWS Glue or Amazon EMR. Athena is not a transactional or relational database; therefore, it is not meant to be a replacement for SQL engines like MySQL or Postgres.

Reference Architectures and Use Cases

When it comes to Amazon Athena, there are several reference architectures and use cases to consider.

Federation

Werner Vogels, CTO and VP of Amazon.com, once said, "Seldom can one database fit the needs to multiple distinct use cases." Today, organizations build highly distributed applications using purpose-built databases—in a sense, choosing right tool for the right job. As the number of data stores and applications grows over time, integrating the data and drawing consolidated insights from these multiple data sources can be quite challenging.

Federated queries in Amazon Athena allow users to query data stored in various data sources using a single SQL query. This eliminates the need to move data or learn new tools for different data sources. The data sources can be either running on-premises or hosted in the cloud. Athena executes federated queries using data source connectors that run on AWS Lambda. These Lambda functions, written in languages such as Python, Java, Rust, etc., are code that translates between Athena and the specific data source. AWS provides connectors for various data sources, but you also have the flexibility to build your own connectors using the Athena Query Federation SDK. Once you deploy a data source connector, it is associated with a catalog name, which you can specify in your SQL queries.

Certain connectors also support push down predicates while querying. When a query is submitted against a data source, Athena invokes the corresponding connector to identify the parts of the tables that need to be read, manages parallelism, and pushes down filter predicates. Since the connectors are run on Lambda, customers benefit from the Athena's serverless architecture.

Each data connector is composed of two Lambda functions, each specific to a data source: one for metadata and one for record reading. When a query runs on federated data source, Athena fans out the Lambda invocations, reading metadata and data in parallel. Recall that we previously talked about the limits on Lambda executions. This applies here too. The number of parallel invocations depends on the Lambda concurrency limits enforced in your account. For example, if you have a limit of 50 concurrent Lambda invocations, Athena can invoke 50 parallel Lambda functions for record reading. For two queries in parallel, Athena invokes twice the number of concurrent executions.

Figure 3.15 shows how Athena federated queries work. When you submit a federated query to Athena, Athena invokes the right Lambda-based connectors to connect with your data source. Athena fans out Lambda invocations to read metadata and data in parallel. However, every Lambda function has a response limit of 6 MB. In Trino, there is a concept of *spill to disk*, which allows intermediate operation results to be offloaded to disk during memory-intensive tasks. If a Lambda function's response size exceeds 6 MB, it needs a S3 bucket to spill the data. However, if the required query amount of the SQL syntax is less than the limit size, then the operation on the spill bucket will not happen. This is why, in additional to writing query results to the Athena query results location in Amazon S3, data connectors also need to have a reference to write to a spill bucket in Amazon S3 when the response size is exceeded.

FIGURE 3.15   AWS architecture for Amazon Athena federated queries

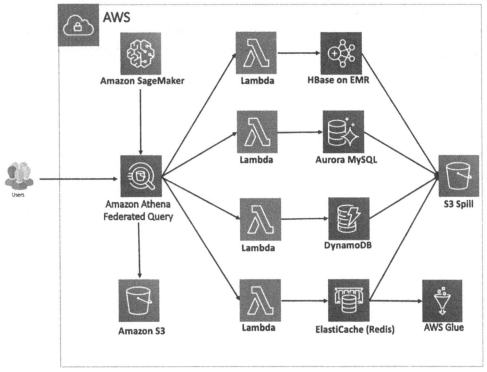

Source: Amazon Web Services / https://aws.amazon.com/blogs/big-data/extracting-and-joining-data-from-multiple-data-sources-with-athena-federated-query, last accessed on 19 December 2024.

Multi-Cloud Data Lake Analytics

Many organizations operate data lakes spanning across multiple cloud data stores. In such cases, the primary requirement is to have an integrated and unified query interface to seamlessly run analytical queries across these cloud stores. Amazon Athena offers connectors to efficiently query data residing in Azure Data Lake Storage (ADLS) Gen2, Google Cloud Storage (GCS), SAP Hana, Google BigQuery, Azure Synapse, and so on. To view the entire list, please visit the AWS official documentation here: `https://docs.aws.amazon.com/athena/latest/ug/connectors-sap-hana.html`.

In the blog located at `https://aws.amazon.com/blogs/big-data/multicloud-data-lake-analytics-with-amazon-athena`, Athena connectors are used to query the data from ADLS Gen2 and GCS alongside data residing in Amazon S3. An Athena connector is an extension of the Athena query engine. When a query runs on a federated data source using a connector, Athena invokes multiple AWS Lambda functions to read the data sources in parallel, optimizing performance. Cost allocation tags are used to track the costs associated with Athena workgroups, Lambda functions, and S3 storage for query results and spills.

Self-Service BI Applications with Amazon Athena

Amazon QuickSight is a serverless, cloud-based business intelligence service from AWS that brings data insights to end users through ML-powered dashboards and data visualizations. Figure 3.16 illustrates an end-to-end reference architecture where the data from the source is ingested into Amazon S3. The raw data is then processed using AWS Glue, and the final curated data is stored in Amazon S3. This curated data is then crawled using an AWS Glue crawler and cataloged using AWS Glue Data Catalog. Amazon QuickSight connects to the Athena data source connector and queries these Glue Data Catalog tables to visualize the data and build rich dashboards.

FIGURE 3.16   Visualizing data with Amazon QuickSight using Amazon Athena

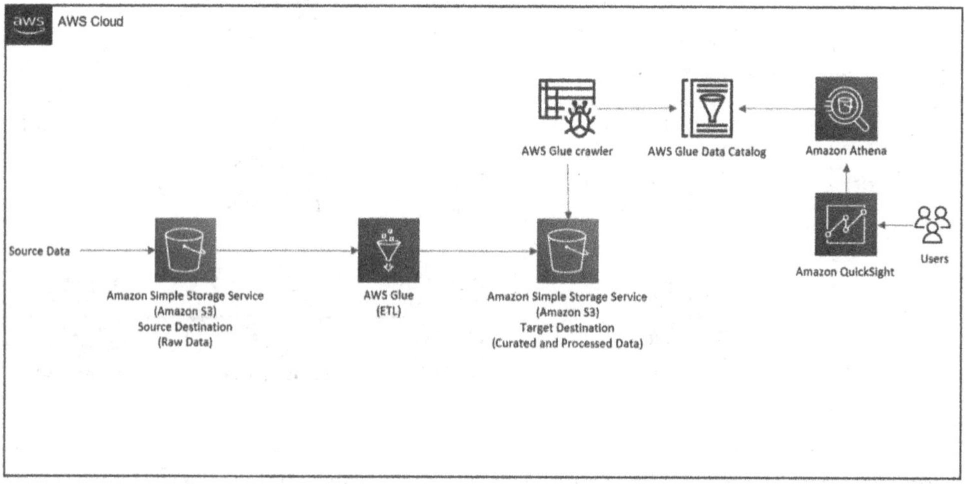

Building Transactional Data Lakes Using Athena

We have already established the benefits of transactional data lakes while discussing AWS Glue. Apache Iceberg is one of the open table formats that manage large collections of files as tables and support data lake operations at the record level, including insert, update, delete, and time travel queries. Amazon Athena supports read, time travel, write, and DDL queries for Apache Iceberg tables that use the Apache Parquet format for data and AWS Glue Data Catalog as their metastore.

The following code snippet shows an example of creating an Iceberg table with Amazon Athena:

```
CREATE TABLE iceberg_table (
  id int,
  data string,
  category string)
PARTITIONED BY (category, bucket(16,id))
LOCATION 's3://DOC-EXAMPLE-BUCKET/iceberg-folder'
TBLPROPERTIES (
  'table_type'='ICEBERG',
  'format'='parquet',
  'write_compression'='snappy',
  'optimize_rewrite_delete_file_threshold'='10'
)
```

To learn more about schema evolution and time travel using Apache Iceberg and Amazon Athena, please refer to the AWS official documentation: https://docs.aws.amazon.com/athena/latest/ug/querying-iceberg.html.

Performance Tuning and Cost Optimization

There are multiple strategies to optimize query performance and minimize costs when using Amazon Athena. Let's look at two strategies where you can focus on performance tuning and costs.

Data Storage Optimization

There are several aspects involved in data storage optimization. Let's look at each of them.

Partitioning Your Data

Organize the data into partitions based on frequently used query filters (e.g., region, date). This allows Athena to focus only on relevant data by restricting the amount of data scanned by the query. A common question asked by customers is how to choose the right column to partition by.

Some factors to consider when deciding on partition columns include an even distribution of data to ensure no skewing, choosing the column that is widely queried or accessed, and not creating multiple levels of partitions that result in too many small files. (This causes overhead in retrieving and processing partition metadata.)

We have already established the advantages of data partitions. With a partition index, instead of retrieving all the partitions' metadata, only the metadata for the partition value in the query's filter is retrieved from the catalog. You can set the property `partition_filtering.enabled` to `true` in AWS Glue or set the parameter by running an `ALTER` statement in AWS Athena.

Bucketing

Distribute the records within partitions based on specific column values (e.g., user ID). This is useful for queries that look up specific values and can significantly improve performance for high-cardinality columns.

Compression

Reduce the data size scanned from S3 by compressing your data (e.g., using gzip, Snappy, or LZO). Reducing the data scanned from Amazon S3 results in lower storage costs. Compressing your data also speeds up the queries by reducing the network traffic from Amazon S3 to Amazon Athena. Note that when Amazon Athena reads the data, it assigns different ranges of files to different nodes in order to maximize the parallel processing of the data. Each range is known as a *split*, and files that can be read in parallel are referred to as *splittable*. Columnar data formats like Parquet and ORC are splittable. This is because, unlike CSV and JSON, Parquet files are binary files that contain metadata about their contents. So, without needing to read/parse the contents of the files, Spark can simply rely on the header/metadata to determine the column names and data types. Also, there is a trade-off between compression rate and compression/decompression speed (e.g., bzip2 is splittable and provides good compression, but it has a slow processing speed).

Please refer to this site to learn more about the compression formats: `https://docs.aws.amazon.com/athena/latest/ug/compression-formats.html`.

Optimize the File Size

Aim for a balance between the number of files and their size. Too many small files can lead to overhead, while extremely large files might not be processed efficiently in parallel. An optimum file size is around 128 MB.

Use Columnar File Formats

Use columnar formats like Parquet or ORC instead of row-based formats like CSV or JSON. Athena can selectively read only the required columns, thereby improving efficiency.

Predicate Pushdown

Predicate pushdown is a database optimization technique wherein the query performance can be improved by filtering the data before transfer. This reduces the amount of data processed and retrieved during the query execution. When submitting a query on the front end (e.g., BI dashboard), if the query involves filtering conditions or predicates, they are normally evaluated after the data is fetched. This means that the query engine performs a full table scan. Predicate pushdown reorganizes the execution process so that filters are pushed down closer to the data sources (the source tables) before the data is retrieved.

Without predicate pushdown on the database: `SELECT column_1 FROM table_name`
With Predicate Pushdown on the database: `SELECT column_1 FROM table_name`
`WHERE [...]`

Depending on the data source connectors, Athena can push filter predicates to the source for processing. Some of the data source connectors that support predicate pushdown include Amazon S3, Amazon Athena DynamoDB connectors, Amazon Athena JDBC connectors (Amazon Redshift, MySQL, Postgres), and so on.

Cost-Based Optimizers

Traditionally, Athena determined the order of joins and how to process the queries based on a set order (tables listed in the query) and internal rules. This might not always be the most efficient way. Cost-based optimizers (CBO) improve Athena queries by using the column statistics stored in the AWS Glue Data Catalog. This allows the CBO to make smarter decisions about how to run queries, such as reordering joins and pushing aggregations down.

Query Tuning

When it comes to query tuning, there are several techniques you can employ.

Optimize

The Athena SQL engine is built on the open-source distributed engines Trino and Presto. Athena uses distributed sort to run the sort operation in parallel on multiple nodes. Instead of using `ORDER BY`, use the `LIMIT` clause to reduce the cost of the sort operation when looking for Top N or Bottom N values.

Choosing the right join is critical for query performance. Specify the larger table on the left side of the join and the smaller table on the right for better performance. For joins based on equality conditions, Athena builds a lookup table from the table on the right and distributes it to the worker nodes. It then streams the table on the left, joining rows by looking up matching values in the lookup table. So, if you are fitting one of the tables into the memory, it's probably best to choose the smaller table to use as the lookup table. This method of join is called the *distributed hash join*. To understand more about the detailed functionalities of the join, please refer to `https://trino.io/episodes/9.html`.

While performing aggregations, include only the necessary columns in the `GROUP BY` clause and avoid redundant columns. This is to reduce the amount of CPU and memory required. Consider using the `ARBITRARY` function to avoid unnecessary columns. In the following code snippet, there is only one `username` for a corresponding `userid`. Hence, instead of aggregating on both columns, we use `ARBITRARY(username)` to speed up the performance of the queries.

```
SELECT userid,arbitrary(username), sum(sales)
FROM "advworks"."products"
group by userid  ;
```

Select and Use the Approximate Functions

For exploring larger datasets, consider using `approx_distinct` instead of `COUNT (DISTINCT column)` for approximate distinct value counts. This can be faster with a small trade-off in accuracy.

Select only the required columns in the final query to limit the needed columns, thereby reducing the data processing and result size.

Partition Projection

Use partition projection for highly partitioned tables to minimize the overhead by calculating partition information instead of retrieving it from the metastore.

UNLOAD

Split large result sets into multiple files in S3 using UNLOAD to reduce the write time. Specify the desired compression and file format (e.g., Parquet, ORC, Avro).

Query Result Reuse

For frequently run queries with static data, use Query Result Reuse to potentially retrieve cache results instead of recomputing them. When you enable Query Result Reuse, Athena looks for a previous execution of the query within the same workgroup. If it finds the corresponding stored results, it directly points to the previous result location or fetches data from it. This boosts the performance when multiple users execute same query, specifically when the results do not change within a specific time frame. You have the option to configure the age for reusing the query results. Athena uses the stored result as long as it is not older than the age that you specify. At the time of this writing, the age ranges from a minimum of 1 minute to a maximum of 7 days.

Connectivity Using JDBC and ODBC Drivers

In some use cases, you may need to connect to different data sources using Java Database Connectivity (JDBC) and Open Database Connectivity (ODBC). This is applicable to use cases that do not support direct connectivity options (e.g., connectivity to Power BI dashboards).

JDBC is a JAVA API for connecting and interacting with the relational databases. In AWS, to connect to a data source using JDBC, first prepare the JDBC driver for the specific database you want to connect to. Athena offers two JDBC drivers: version 2.x and 3.x. Version 3.x is newer and offers better performance and compatibility. Next, once the driver is prepared, configure the needed security groups with inbound rules to access the necessary ports for the database. In your Java application, use the JDBC driver to establish a connection to the database by providing the appropriate connection credentials, such as the URL, username, and password. The connection URL typically includes the database hostname, IP address, port, and database name. After the connection is established, you can use JDBC's APIs to execute SQL statements and perform queries, updates, and other database operations.

ODBC is a standardized API for connecting to various data sources, including relational databases. First, select an ODBC driver that corresponds to the data source to which you are connecting. Athena offers two ODBC drivers, version 1.x and 2.x, and supports Linux, macOS, and Windows. Then, install the ODBC driver on the system you will be connecting to the data source. Once this task is done, set up an ODBC data source name, which contains relevant connection details such as hostname, port, authentication credentials. Specify the DSN and establish the connection to the data source.

Athena supports SAML 2.0-based authentication with various identity providers, including Azure AD, Okta, and PingFederate. To learn more about driver federation, please refer to the AWS official documentation here: `https://docs.aws.amazon.com/athena/ latest/ug/athena-bi-tools-jdbc-odbc.html`.

Amazon Redshift

Amazon Redshift is a fully managed petabyte-scale data warehouse service in the cloud. We will be discussing the architecture, data modeling, and data storage of Amazon Redshift in Chapter 5. In this chapter, we will focus on the processing part of the data warehouse.

Amazon Redshift has two querying mechanisms: one that performs ELT operations after loading the data into the Redshift data warehouse, and another that queries the data directly from files on Amazon S3. The latter is performed using Amazon Redshift Spectrum. Amazon Redshift Spectrum, as shown in Figure 3.17, is a feature within Amazon Redshift that enables you to query the data directly in Amazon S3 data lakes without having to load the data or duplicate your infrastructure. Using Amazon Redshift Spectrum, you can query open file formats such as Apache Parquet, ORC, JSON, Avro, and CSV.

FIGURE 3.17 Amazon Redshift Spectrum query pattern

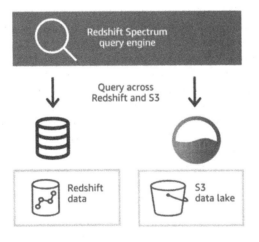

There are two common design patterns when moving the data from source to data warehouse. The fundamental difference between the two patterns is where the actual transformation happens. The first pattern is the traditional extract, transform, and load (ETL), wherein the transformation takes place *before* the data gets loaded into the data warehouse. In this pattern, data processing is done with tools such as AWS Glue or Amazon EMR.

Figure 3.18 shows an ETL mechanism where the raw data from source or data lakes is cleansed using ETL operations. The curated data is then loaded into Amazon Redshift either using the COPY command or via Amazon Redshift Spectrum.

FIGURE 3.18   AWS ELT pattern for Amazon Redshift Spectrum

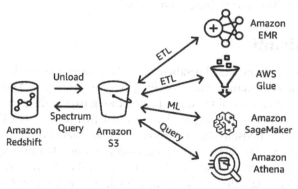

Source: Amazon Web Services / `https://aws.amazon.com/blogs/big-data/etl-and-elt-design-patterns-for-lake-house-architecture-using-amazon-redshift-part-1`, last accessed on 19 December 2024.

The second pattern is the extract, load, and transform (ELT), wherein the data transformation engine is built into the data warehouse for SQL workloads and data transformation is done *after* the data loading. This pattern uses the highly optimized and scalable data storage and compute power of a massively parallel processing (MPP) architecture.

ELT works well when you have only data warehouse use case and all the users either consume the data from BI dashboards or query on the data warehouse engine. But what if you have consumers who want to consume data from the data lakes or use the interactive query engine Amazon Athena? Also, if the data is not frequently used for reporting, storing massive amount of unused data in Amazon Redshift might prove costly. A possible solution is to perform post-data processing in Amazon Redshift, where the final aggregated result is offloaded back to Amazon S3 (data lakes) for other use cases. This also helps you to store the infrequent data for a longer time (cold data) in the data lakes at low cost. The frequently used data (hot data) will be queried within Amazon Redshift.

As part of the ELT operation, you can also use the COPY command to load the data from raw layer of Amazon S3 to Amazon Redshift to perform data modeling and transformations within the data warehouse.

Transformations Using Amazon Redshift RSQL

Amazon Redshift RSQL is a powerful tool for interacting with Amazon Redshift data warehouses and performing ETL operations. It offers a familiar command-line interface similar to PostgreSQL's psql but with additional functionalities specifically designed for Redshift. It supports conditional statements and looping constructs for building ETL workflows with branching logic and error handling. It also facilitates exporting data from Redshift to local files with various formatting options. RSQL scripts can be integrated with shell scripting to automate the ETL process. By scheduling the script execution via cron jobs, you can ensure regular data extraction, transformation, and loading tasks without manual intervention. For users migrating from Teradata and using Basic Teradata Query (BTEQ) scripts for ETL, Amazon Redshift RSQL offers a smoother transition. The AWS Schema Conversion Tool (AWS SCT) can automatically convert the BTEQ scripts to RSQL scripts, minimizing script rewriting efforts. For more details on this, visit the blog here: `https://aws.amazon.com/blogs/big-data/perform-etl-operations-using-amazon-redshift-rsql`.

Apart from this, Amazon Redshift also integrates with Visual Studio Code (VSCode), a popular free and open-source code editor. This integration allows you to write and run SQL queries within VSCode using a notebook interface.

Transformations Using the Redshift Data API

The Amazon Redshift Data API allows you to programmatically access and interact with your Redshift data warehouse from web services or applications.

Here are few specific scenarios where the Redshift Data API shines:

Integration with Web Services   If you are building applications or workflows that rely on Redshift data, the Data API allows seamless integration with services like AWS Lambda, SageMaker notebooks, and Cloud9. This enables you to design and trigger event-driven applications, analyze results, and automate tasks based on your Redshift data.

Ad Hoc Analysis and Reporting   If you need to run on-demand queries or generate reports from your Redshift data, the Data API facilitates this by allowing you to send SQL statements directly from your code or applications. This method is useful when user interaction or dynamic report generation is required.

Data Pipelines and Automation   The Redshift Data API can be incorporated into data pipelines to automate data processing tasks. You can use either Lambda functions or AWS Step Functions SDK integration to invoke the Redshift Data API. One of the benefits of the latter is that it allows direct calling of AWS services like the Redshift Data API from the state machine without writing any code. This reduces complexity while performing orchestration.

Securing the Connection   If you want to decouple your application logic from directly managing Redshift connections and credentials, the Redshift Data API offers a secure solution. You can leverage AWS Secrets Manager to keep the sensitive information separate from your application code.

Short-Lived Queries   The Redshift Data API's pay-per-use model makes it cost-effective for short queries or infrequent data access needs. By default, the Redshift Data API runs asynchronously. Also, the Data API has a maximum query duration of 24 hours. So, this may not be ideal for long-running queries.

EL(T) with dbt on Redshift

Data Build Tool (dbt) is an open-source command-line tool that helps analysts and engineers simplify data transformation workflows by replacing complex SQL scripts with modular and reusable data models. It enforces best practices for writing SQL code and facilitates collaboration by centralizing data transformations in a version-controlled repository. Data Build Tool focuses on the "transform" part of ELT and ETL. It automatically generates documentation for your data models, including descriptions, lineage, and dependencies, making it easier for users to understand how your data is being transformed and where it originated. To delve deep into the implementation of dbt with Redshift, please visit this blog: `https://aws.amazon.com/blogs/big-data/implement-data-warehousing-solution-using-dbt-on-amazon-redshift`.

Cost and Anti-Patterns

Amazon Redshift comes in two flavors: Provisioned and Serverless. The cost for Amazon Redshift provisioned is based on the instance type, number of nodes, and usage time. Redshift Serverless operates on a pay-as-you-go model, where the query is metered on a per-second basis, with a minimum charge of 60 seconds of resource usage. Redshift Spectrum within the flavor of Redshift provisioned is charged per terabyte of data scanned. For a more nuanced breakdown on the costs, visit the official AWS documentation: `https://aws.amazon.com/redshift/pricing`.

One of the common anti-patterns I encounter during my customer discussions is Redshift being used as a transactional system. Amazon Redshift is an OLAP engine. A common rule of thumb is to avoid row-by-row, cursor-based processing and to have hundreds and thousands of single record inserts, updates, and deletes. Frequent updates, inserts, and deletes are more suitable to an OLTP transactional database. Amazon Redshift is more performant if we stage those records for bulk updates, inserts, and delete similar to a batch operation.

Another anti-pattern is the usage of unstructured data and blob data. Amazon Redshift does not support an arbitrary schema structure for each row. It is recommended to process this data using ETL tools and load the curated data into Amazon Redshift. If you plan to store large blob files like videos or images, it is recommended to store them in data lakes (Amazon S3) and reference their location in Amazon Redshift. The data itself will be stored in S3; however, Amazon Redshift will keep track of the metadata of these files.

Reference Architectures and Use Cases

During my interactions with customers, I often sense an underlying fear of data getting locked into the data warehouse. Surrendering all data to the data warehouse creates challenges such as increased storage costs, complexity during migration, and the inability for other technologies and services to use the data for their use cases, resulting in lack of innovation. Whether the data warehouse is on-premises or in the cloud, this challenge still exists, and the problem statement does not change.

This is where the concept of the modern data warehouse comes into its own. Rather than being a monolithic engine just meant for traditional use cases like BI reports, the modern data warehouse breaks the silos and enables you to unlock new possibilities for diverse applications like real-time analytics, running ML inferences, and querying data in data lakes and on-premise databases. Figure 3.19 showcases the modern data warehouse architecture of AWS using Amazon Redshift for different use cases, such as operational analytics, real-time querying, data lake querying, machine learning and advanced analytics, data sharing, and third-party collaboration. The numbers in the figure represent the individual use cases discussed in the following sections.

FIGURE 3.19   Amazon Redshift architecture patterns

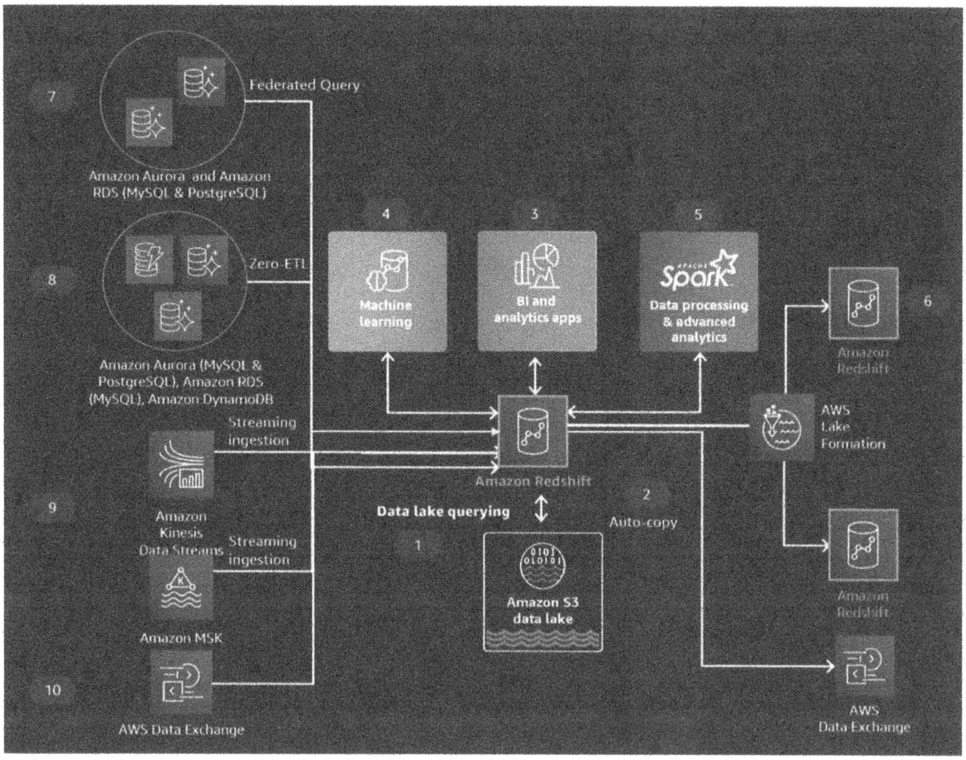

Use Case 1: Data Lake Querying

This use case demonstrates how to implement a hot and cold pattern using Amazon Redshift Spectrum. Hot data is classified as the frequently queried data, and cold data is the infrequently queried data. I remember a use case where the customer said that all their data was classified as hot data. My immediate follow-up question was how many months' data was frequently queried by users. If the data usage pattern spans over the last 2 years or 6 months, then why keep rest of the 5 or 10 years of data in the data warehouse, thereby inflating the costs. Instead, store the data in the cold layer—in this case, data lakes—and when needed, interactively query the data in your data lakes using Redshift Spectrum. Redshift Spectrum allows you to query data that sits in Amazon S3 without loading it into the Amazon Redshift. By utilizing Redshift for hot data and Redshift Spectrum for cold data, you can leverage the best of both worlds—performance for hot data and reduced costs for cold data.

Use Case 2: Auto Copy

We already discussed the ELT part, where data from the source is ingested and then transformed in the data warehouse. However, to copy data from a data lake to Redshift, you either need to use an ETL tool like AWS Glue or initiate a Lambda function that, upon receiving a notification from Amazon S3, copies the data from the data lake to Redshift. Now, this COPY statement can be stored in a COPY job, which automatically loads the new files detected in the specified Amazon S3 path. It tracks the previously loaded files and excludes them from the ingestion process. This eliminates the need for any ETL tools like AWS Glue or Lambda as an intermediate step to track and load the incremental files from Amazon S3 to Redshift.

Use Case 3: BI and Analytics Applications

Amazon Redshift seamlessly integrates with traditional business intelligence (BI) tools and workflows. This empowers organizations to leverage their existing BI investment and infrastructure to analyze data stored in a Redshift data warehouse.

Use Case 4: Redshift ML

Machine learning (ML) has become an indispensable tool for unlocking hidden patterns and extracting valuable insights from data. However, building and deploying ML models can be complex and often requires specialized skills and infrastructure. Redshift ML is a feature within Amazon Redshift that makes it easy for SQL users to create, train, and deploy ML models using familiar SQL commands. Business analysts and users with SQL knowledge can harness the power of ML and run inferences on the dataset without venturing outside their comfort zone. Redshift ML also supports using Bring Your Own Models (BYOM) for local or remote inference.

Use Case 5: Amazon Redshift Integration with Apache Spark

We discussed distributed processing with Apache Spark earlier in the chapter when describing ETL processing with AWS Glue. Amazon Redshift's integration with Apache Spark makes it easy to build and run Spark applications on Redshift. Traditionally, interacting with Redshift data from Spark involved cumbersome data movements or relying on separate tools. This new integration removes those barriers, allowing you to seamlessly process the Redshift data directly within your Spark application. Redshift integration leverages pushdown optimization techniques. This means that Spark intelligently pushes the supported operations like filters, aggregations, and joins down to Redshift for execution. This reduces the data movement between Redshift and Spark, leading to improved performance. The integration allows data engineers to use familiar Spark APIs (SQL, Data Frames, Datasets) for interacting with Redshift data.

Use Case 6: Data Share

When data is spread in different silos and lines of business, organizations tend to leverage shared data to gain deeper insights and make data-driven choices. Traditionally, the concept of the data sharing involved copying data or building necessary ETL pipelines. Setting up and maintaining a dedicated infrastructure for data transfer proved to be expensive and cumbersome. Standardized protocols and procedures for data sharing were often absent, leading to confusion and inconsistencies. The ETL pipelines built for this very specific purpose often lead to issues with data staleness and duplication.

Amazon Redshift data sharing allows you to share data within and across organizations and AWS regions without moving or copying it. Redshift data sharing provides a secure way to share live data for read across Amazon Redshift clusters. With this approach, users can isolate their workloads, and share and collaborate frequently on the data to drive innovation. You can share data at many levels, including database, schema, views, tables, columns and SQL-based user-defined functions.

Use Case 7: Federated Queries

We previously discussed querying data lakes using Amazon Redshift without loading the data into Redshift. A similar mechanism, Redshift federated queries, helps users to break the data silos by querying the data from their transactional OLTP databases without loading it into Redshift. Federated queries combine queries from live data in external databases, such as Amazon RDS and Amazon Aurora, with queries across Redshift and Amazon S3 (data lake) for a unified view.

Use Case 8: Zero-ETL

As businesses increasingly rely on big data and analytics, the traditional ETL process can become a bottleneck. The time taken to move the data from the source to the target involves complex data pipelines, which induces latency, maintenance, and custom coding. Any change in the data source necessitates updates in these pipelines, further delaying analysis. From a data engineering perspective, instead of maintaining such fragile pipelines, Zero-ETL comes in like a breath of fresh air, eliminating any need for intermediate steps and moving data directly from the source to the target. Zero-ETL is a type of integration that acts as a data replication tool without the usual processing hurdles. There are multiple integration use cases where the change data capture from transactional OLTP databases can be immediately replicated into Redshift. The emphasis on direct data movement allows for speedy data transfers and swift migrations. The elimination of data movement tools like AWS Glue or AWS Lambda leads to minimal learning curves and a reduction in costs and implementation expenses. Data is available often in near-real-time to real time in target applications, as long as the data needs minimal data cleansing.

Having said this, does this mean that ETL is no longer needed? Zero-ETL is excellent for use cases that require quick replication and mirroring of data from transactional databases or streaming sources. However, it comes with its own caveats. Zero-ETL doesn't induce any transformation capabilities on its own. Hence, after replicating the data into the target system (data warehouse), the absence of curated data or processed data may hinder the ability to cater to most data reporting needs. Traditional ETLs are equipped with safeguards and controls to ensure the integrity of the data. In the case of Zero-ETL, integrity relies solely on the systems that transfer the data.

Use Case 9: Streaming

The use case for streaming data directly into Redshift is another flavor of Zero-ETL. Using this simplified ingestion mechanism, you can directly ingest streaming data into your data warehouse with Amazon Kinesis Data Streams and Amazon Managed Service for Kafka without the need to stage the data in Amazon S3.

Use Case 10: Data Monetization

Why does data monetization matter? Organizations generate vast amounts of data, but many fail to capitalize on it. Data monetization can improve profitability, revenue growth, and innovation. It enhances customer experience, boosts worker productivity, and reduces costs. An excellent book on data monetization, *Data Is Everybody's Business*, written by MIT CISR researchers, explains the different approaches to data monetization.

AWS Data Exchange is a service that adopts the data monetization strategy of value realization from selling. AWS Data Exchange is a data marketplace where you can easily find third-party datasets and subscribe and consume them to enrich your own insights. You can easily license your data in Amazon Redshift through AWS Data Exchange. Subscribers can easily find your data and subscribe to your dataset. Once the subscription grants are fulfilled, they can quickly query, analyze, and build applications using the third-party dataset.

Performance Tuning Techniques

There are a few mechanisms you can use during your ELT process to improve the performance of queries on Amazon Redshift.

- Throughput is a measure of how much work a cluster can do in a period of time. Automatic WLM (workload management) improves throughput with query priorities and concurrency scaling.

- Invest in the latest version of Amazon Redshift JDBC or ODBC drivers for best performance improvement.

- Amazon Redshift leverages materialized views to precompute the results of frequently used queries.

- Concurrency scaling allows you to add capacity dynamically, and elastic resize allows you to quickly increase or decrease the number of compute nodes of your cluster.

- Use Amazon Redshift Advisor to identify recommendations to improve the cost efficiency and performance of your cluster.

- Amazon Redshift has short query acceleration feature that uses machine learning algorithms to run short-running jobs in their own queue, thereby improving the performance of long-running queues.

- Use the COPY command to perform data loads and compress your data files wherever possible.

To learn more about performance tuning, visit this blog: `https://aws.amazon.com/blogs/big-data/top-10-performance-tuning-techniques-for-amazon-redshift`.

Amazon Elastic MapReduce

Amazon Elastic MapReduce (Amazon EMR) is a managed cluster platform that simplifies running big data frameworks like Apache Hadoop and Apache Spark on AWS. Using these frameworks, you can process and analyze massive amounts of data for analytics and business intelligence workloads. Amazon EMR also helps you perform transformations and move data in and out of AWS data stores and databases.

To provide these capabilities, Amazon EMR integrates seamlessly with other AWS services.

- EMR relies on Amazon EC2 instances to create the virtual machines that make up your cluster.
- Amazon Virtual Private Cloud (Amazon VPC) allows you to configure a secure virtual network for your cluster.
- Amazon S3 is used to provide a scalable storage solution for your cluster's input, output, and intermediate data.
- Amazon CloudWatch keeps an eye on your cluster's performance and lets you set up alerts.
- IAM controls who can access and managed your cluster resources.
- AWS CloudTrail logs all API calls made to EMR for better tracking and auditing.
- Orchestration tools like Amazon Managed Workflows for Apache Airflow (MWAA) and AWS Step Functions help you schedule and automate the launch of your EMR clusters, as well as to schedule jobs for processing the data.
- AWS Lake Formation helps you discover, catalog, and secure the data stored in an S3 data lake, making it easier to use with EMR.

Key Components

This section discusses the key components of Amazon EMR.

Cluster and Nodes

The central component of Amazon EMR is the cluster. An EMR cluster is a group of virtual machines (EC2 instances) working together. Each machine (node) has a specific role:

- **Primary node:** Manages the cluster and coordinates the tasks among other nodes. It tracks the status of the tasks and monitors the health of the cluster.
- **Code node:** Stores the data and runs processing tasks.
- **Task node (optional):** Runs processing tasks without storing the data.

Figure 3.20 shows a cluster with one primary node and four core nodes.

FIGURE 3.20   A cluster with nodes

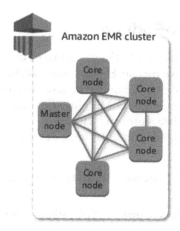

Source: Amazon Web Services / `https://docs.aws.amazon.com/emr/latest/ ManagementGuide/emr-overview.html`, last accessed on 19 December 2024.

> Every cluster has primary node, and it is possible to create a single-node cluster with only the primary node.

Submitting Work to a Cluster

You can submit work(steps) to Amazon EMR clusters in two ways: First, by defining all processing steps upfront when launching a temporary cluster that automatically terminates upon completion. Second, by maintain a long-running cluster where you can continuously submit new processing jobs using tools like the Amazon EMR console, Amazon EMR API, or AWS CLI.

Processing Data

EMR supports various frameworks, including Apache Hadoop, Apache Spark, Apache Hive, Apache HBase, Apache Spark, Presto, and other big data workloads. You can choose the applications and framework needed during cluster creation. Data processing involves submitting jobs directly to applications or running steps within the cluster. Steps are ordered units of work that instruct the cluster on how to manipulate the data. Steps typically involve input data (from S3 or *HDFS*), processing using tools like Pig or Hive, and writing output data to a location like Amazon S3. Steps are run sequentially, with each step's state changing from PENDING to RUNNING to COMPLETED as it progresses. In case of failures, you can define how subsequent steps behave (cancel, continue, or terminate the cluster). An illustration of step sequence execution and change of state is shown in Figure 3.21.

FIGURE 3.21   Step sequence execution and change of state

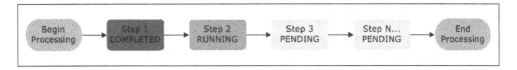

Cluster Lifecycle

An EMR cluster goes through the following distinct phases:

- STARTING: EC2 instances are provisioned based on your configuration.

- BOOTSTRAPPING: Custom applications and configurations are installed on each node.

- RUNNING: After bootstrap actions are completed, native applications such as Hadoop, Spark, Hive are installed, and the cluster is ready to work. Steps are executed sequentially.

- WAITING: The cluster is idle after completing the submitted steps.

- TERMINATING/TERMINATED: The cluster is shut down either automatically (after steps) or manually. Failures can also lead to termination. Data stored on the cluster is lost unless retrieved before termination.

Storage

EMR clusters rely on different storage options to manage data during processing.

Hadoop Distributed File System

Hadoop Distributed File System (HDFS) is a built-in file system that distributes data across clusters for scalability and fault tolerance. It stores multiple copies of data on different instances to ensure that no data is lost if an individual instance fails. HDFS is ideal for the temporary storage of intermediate results during processing or workloads with frequent reads/writes. However, data is lost when the cluster terminates.

EMR File System

Using the EMR File System (EMRFS), Amazon EMR extends Hadoop to add the ability to directly access data stored in Amazon S3 like a regular file system. This is useful for storing large datasets, such as input and output data, while HDFS handles the intermediate processing results.

Local File System

The local file system refers to the disk storage (instance store) attached to each virtual machine (EC2 instance) in the cluster. However, the data stored here is temporary and will disappear when the cluster terminates.

EMR Deployments

You can deploy your workloads to EMR using Amazon EC2, Amazon Elastic Kubernetes (EKS), or on-premises AWS Outposts. Amazon EMR Serverless is an alternate deployment option that provides a serverless runtime environment. You can run and manage the workloads with the EMR Console, API, SDK, or CLI. For an interactive experience, you can use EMR Studio or SageMaker Studio.

EMR on EC2 is the most common deployment option. It offers full control and optimization over your cluster configuration. For the best price performance for your workload, you can choose from a wide range of instance types.

EMR on EKS leverages Kubernetes for containerized workloads. It integrates well with the existing EKS deployments. With this deployment option, you can focus on running analytics workloads while EMR on EKS builds, configures, and manages containers for open-source applications. It also gives you the flexibility to consolidate multiple versions of Spark on the same EKS cluster. This deployment option improves resource utilization by sharing resources across different applications. However, it requires familiarity with Kubernetes concepts for management.

EMR on Outposts brings EMR to your on-premises environment. It is ideal for workloads with strict data residency or latency requirements.

EMR Serverless is the serverless option where AWS manages the infrastructure. It helps you avoid over- or under-provisioning resources for your data processing jobs. You can specify a different IAM role for each job, allocate costs by department, and apply cost controls.

EMR Serverless

With EMR Serverless, you don't need to set up or manage clusters. It automatically scales resources based on your workload. EMR Serverless uses concepts such as applications, job runs, and workers. An EMR Serverless application defines the open-source framework, such as Spark or Hive, and the version you want to use. A job run is a request submitted to the application to process data. You can run multiple jobs concurrently in an application. EMR Serverless uses workers to run these jobs. EMR Serverless also pre-initializes workers to improve the startup times for the jobs. By default, each application uses workers with 4 vCPUs, 30 GB of memory, and 20 GB of local storage per worker. These default values are engine-specific and can be modified by setting the `initialcapacity` parameter of an application. You can start your EMR Serverless application and pre-initialize the pool of workers as soon as a user starts the application. This is suitable for interactive use cases such as data exploration and SQL queries. If processing the user requests requires more workers than what has been pre-initialized, EMR Serverless automatically adds more workers up to the maximum concurrent limits that you specify. Therefore, by controlling the number of workers to pre-initialize and the maximum concurrent workers, you can optimize user experience and costs for your interactive applications.

Figure 3.22 illustrates how EMR Serverless works.

FIGURE 3.22   AWS EMR Serverless architecture

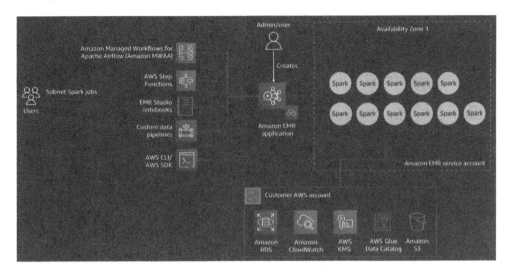

EMR on EKS

With EMR on EKS, you can run applications on a common pool of resources without having to provision a separate infrastructure. Applications are independent of the infrastructure. When you submit a job to Amazon EMR, your job definition contains all the application-specific parameters. EMR uses these parameters to instruct Amazon EKS about which pods and containers to deploy. Amazon EKS, as shown in Figure 3.23, then provisions resources from Amazon EC2 or AWS Fargate to run the job.

Let's understand a few concepts related to Amazon EMR on EKS.

Amazon EKS uses Kubernetes namespaces to divide cluster resources between multiple users and applications. The namespaces are the foundation for multi-tenant environments. A Kubernetes namespace can have either Amazon EC2 or AWS Fargate as the compute provider.

A virtual cluster is a Kubernetes namespace registered with EMR for running jobs and hosting endpoints. Multiple virtual clusters can share a physical EKS cluster.

A virtual cluster is a Kubernetes namespace registered with EMR for running jobs and hosting endpoints. Multiple virtual clusters can share a physical EKS cluster.

A job run is a unit of work—such as a PySpark script, SparkSQL query, or Spark jar—that you submit to Amazon EMR on EKS. A job run should specify a virtual cluster, job name, execution role, EMR release, and job artifacts. Logs are uploaded to Spark History Server and optionally to Amazon CloudWatch and Amazon S3. The API name for Amazon EMR on EKS is Amazon EMR Containers.

FIGURE 3.23   AWS EMR on EKS architecture

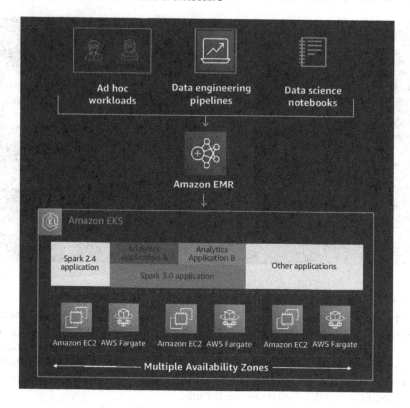

As shown in Figure 3.24, Amazon EMR integrates with EKS to simplify running Spark jobs on containerized environments. By registering EMR with a namespace in your EKS cluster, you essentially create a virtual cluster for EMR to manage. When you submit a Spark job, EMR instructs the EKS scheduler to create pods (containers) for your job. These pods include an Amazon Linux base image, Apache Spark, and other dependencies. Each job runs in its own pod, downloads the container image (or uses as cached version if available), and then executes the job. After the job finishes, the pod terminates. EMR even allows you to debug these completed jobs using the Spark application UI within the console.

Having understood each of these flavors, it is important to understand the differences between these deployment models. Table 3.1 provides a comparison of the differences among EMR on EC2, EMR on EKS, and EMR Serverless.

FIGURE 3.24   AWS EMR on EKS job workflow

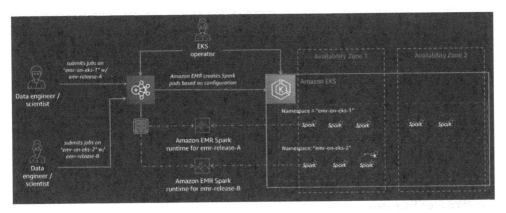

TABLE 3.1   Feature comparison of EMR deployment models

Feature	Amazon EMR Serverless	Amazon EMR on EC2	Amazon EMR on EKS
Support of latest open-source revisions	Yes	Yes	Yes
Resilience to Availability Zone (AZ) failures	Yes (automated job redirection)	No (clusters run in a single AZ)	Yes (with multi-AZ EKS clusters)
Automatically scale resources up and down as needed	Yes	Yes	Yes
Encryption for data at rest	Yes	Yes	Yes
Open-source frameworks supported	Spark, Hive, and Presto	Spark, Hive, Presto, Flink, and Trino	Spark
Support for fine-grain authorization using AWS Lake Formation	Yes	Yes	Yes
Support for Apache Hudi and Apache Iceberg	Yes	Yes	Yes
Integration with Apache Ranger for table- and column-level permission control	No	Yes	No

TABLE 3.1   Feature comparison of EMR deployment models *(continued)*

Feature	Amazon EMR Serverless	Amazon EMR on EC2	Amazon EMR on EKS
Customize open-source framework installed, load additional libraries and dependencies	Yes	Yes	Yes
Connect to self-hosted Jupyter notebooks	No	Yes	Yes
Build and orchestrate pipelines using Apache Airflow, MWAA, and AWS Step Functions	Yes	Yes	Yes
Ability to allocate costs	Per application or per Job	Per cluster	Per application
Ability to use EC2 Spot	No	Yes	Yes
Pricing	By vCPU and memory used	By instance and EBS volume added	By instance type used along with vCPU and memory
Startup time	~2–3 minutes Few seconds in warm pool	~7–12 minutes	~10 seconds if EKS is running ~2 minutes if EKS is scaled to 0

Cost and Anti-Patterns

EMR pricing on AWS follows a pay-per-second model. You are charged for each second your EMR cluster is running, with a one-minute minimum billing increment. This ensures fairness regardless of whether you run a cluster for a few minutes or several hours. The cost depends on the type and number of virtual machines (EC2 instances) used in your cluster. Different instance types have varying costs based on processing power, memory, and storage capacity. The storage used by your cluster also impacts the cost. Data stored in Amazon S3 has its own pricing structure separate from the EMR charges. To learn more about the EMR pricing model, visit https://aws.amazon.com/emr/pricing.

Amazon EMR is built for massively parallel processing. If the dataset is small or requires only a single thread processing, then it is recommended to use other ETL tools.

Reference Architecture and Use Cases

Let's examine the reference architecture and use cases.

Build Incremental Data Pipelines

Transactional data lakes store historical data in its entirety, offering a complete picture of past events. Using open table formats like Apache Hudi, Apache Iceberg, and Delta Lake format, you can efficiently handle inserts, updates, and deletes within the data lake itself. This eliminates the need to completely rewrite the historical data and also benefits from de-duplication of records.

Figure 3.25 illustrates how to manage a data lake with continuously changing data. The architecture uses AWS Database Migration Service (DMS) to capture the historical and incremental (CDC) data changes from the database and stream them into an Amazon S3 data lake. Amazon EMR Serverless runs Spark jobs to transform the data and write it into the Delta tables within S3. Delta tables efficiently handle inserts, updates, and deletes. The curated data is then further cataloged using AWS Glue Data Catalog, making it accessible for interactive querying in Amazon Athena and Amazon Redshift.

FIGURE 3.25   Building data pipelines using Amazon EMR

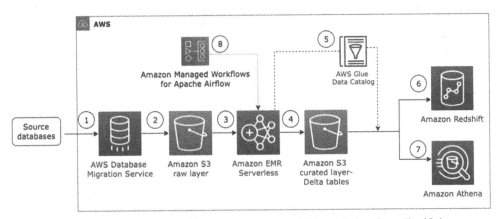

Source: Amazon Web Services / `https://aws.amazon.com/blogs/big-data/build-incremental-data-pipelines-to-load-transactional-data-changes-using-aws-dms-delta-2-0-and-amazon-emr-serverless`, last accessed on 19 December 2024.

Accelerate HiveQL to Spark SQL Migration

Businesses using Hive for data warehousing want to leverage Spark's benefits (faster processing, cost savings) in the cloud. However, the manual migration from Apache Hive to Apache Spark involves writing scripts and managing Spark job configurations, which is time-consuming and error-prone. One solution is to migrate Hive with Oozie workloads to Spark SQL and run them on Amazon EMR. Visit the following blog for more detailed steps:

```
https://aws.amazon.com/blogs/big-data/accelerate-hiveql-with-oozie-to-spark-sql-migration-on-amazon-emr
```

Performance Tuning Techniques

There are several performance tuning techniques you can use.

Persistent vs. Transient Clusters

There are two cluster types used by EMR: persistent and transient. Transient clusters are designed for short-lived jobs and ideal for one-time data processing tasks or workflows that do not require the cluster to be continuously available. Additionally, transient clusters are easier to upgrade and restart the jobs. An example of using transient cluster is when you have batch processing job that pulls web logs from Amazon S3 and processes the data once a day. Launching a transient cluster typically takes less time as compared to a persistent cluster. Data stored on the cluster's local file system (EMRFS) is lost when the cluster terminates. Hence, you need to store the data in a persistent location like S3 for later access. Utilize transient clusters for cost optimization and pay only for the resources used during the job execution.

A persistent cluster is designed for continuous operation. It is suitable for recurring jobs to handle scheduled jobs or continuous data pipelines. Data stored on the cluster's local file system (EMRFS) persists even after job completes, allowing access for subsequent jobs. Since the cluster remains active, subsequent jobs can start processing data faster without waiting for the cluster launch. One key consideration here is that you incur charges even when the cluster is idle.

Instance Fleets

When you create a cluster and specify the configuration of primary node, core, and task node, you have two configuration options: instance groups and instance fleets.

In case of instance groups, you need to manually add instances of the same type to the existing groups. You can set up automatic scaling based on CloudWatch metrics. It is ideal for scenarios where you have a well-defined cluster configuration with specific instance types for different node groups. With instance groups, it is easier to manage the individual instance groups, and you can have granular control over instance types for each node group. However, it also poses rigidity for dynamic scaling requirements. Instance groups are limited to a single instance type per node group.

On the other hand, instance fleets are well suited for clusters with dynamic resource needs or cost optimization goals. They are ideal for task nodes where Spot instances can be utilized. Instance fleets enable you to mix on-demand and Spot instances within them, offering flexibility, cost savings, and fault tolerance. They also support multiple instance types for a node group, allowing EMR to choose the optimal option based on availability and cost.

Table 3.2 gives a quick reference to node type purchasing options and configurations based on various application scenarios.

TABLE 3.2 Choosing the right purchase option for the scenario

Application Scenario	Master Node Purchase Option	Core Node Purchase Option	Task Node Purchase Option
Long-running clusters	On-demand	On-demand or Instance Fleet Mix	Spot or Instance Fleet Mix
Cost-driven workloads	Spot	Spot	Spot
Critical workloads	On-demand	On-demand	Spot or Instance Fleet Mix
Application testing	Spot	Spot	Spot

 Spot instances can be taken at any time, so they should not be used for time-sensitive jobs that require predictable completion time or have service-level agreements (SLAs).

Amazon S3 Partitions, Compression, and File Formats

With S3 as your persistent data store, it is important to understand how the data is partitioned. Effective partitioning helps to read only the files the query needs and reduces the amount of data scanned. Additionally, if the data is compressed and in columnar file formats like Parquet, partitioning increases performance on reads. Data compression lowers the storage costs by reducing the data storage footprint. It also lowers the bandwidth costs by moving less data from the source to the destination.

Choosing the Right Instance Type

When you are configuring an EMR cluster, it is important to consider the right EC2 instance that will represent the cluster nodes. The primary node typically does not have large computational requirements. However, for clusters with applications that are specifically deployed on the primary node (JupyterHub, Hue), a larger primary node may be required for optimal cluster performance. The computational needs of the core and task nodes depend on the type of processing the application performs. Many jobs can be run on general-purpose instance types (M5 and M4 family), which offer balanced performance in terms of CPU, disk space, and input/output. Database and memory-caching applications may benefit from running on high-memory instances like the R4 family.

Using the Latest Versions

Use the latest EMR upgrades to get performance benefits. Some of the benefits of upgrading Amazon EMR include:

- You can achieve increased productivity and lowered costs by leveraging the newest features.

- Updated applications run faster.

- Up-to-date bug fixes provide a stable infrastructure.

- The latest security patches strengthen security.

- It provides up-to-date access to open-source software features.

EMR Managed Scaling

With EMR Managed Scaling, you can specify minimum and maximum compute limits for clusters. Amazon EMR follows a dynamic scaling strategy and computes the actual cluster requirements and automatically resizes to reach the correct scale directly for best performance and resource utilization. EMR Managed Scaling continuously monitors key metrics based on the workload and optimizes the cluster size for best resource utilization. You can view high-resolution metrics at 1-minute granularity to visualize how Managed Scaling is reacting to the incoming workload. Amazon EMR automatically detects the need to scale up or down without specific cooldown periods.

For more details about EMR Managed Scaling, see https://aws.amazon.com/blogs/big-data/introducing-amazon-emr-managed-scaling-automatically-resize-clusters-to-lower-cost.

Optimizing Spark Performance

EMR with Apache Spark provides multiple performance optimization features for Apache Spark. A few of them are listed here.

Adaptive Query Execution   Adaptive Query Execution (AQE) is a framework for re-optimizing the query plans based on runtime statistics. Adaptive Join Conversion switches from sort-merge-join operations to broadcast-hash-join operations to improve query performance. Adaptive coalescing of shuffle partitions groups small shuffle partitions to avoid overhead from having too many tasks, improving distribution.

Dynamic Partition Pruning   Dynamic Partition Pruning (DPP) reads only relevant partitions from tables based on the query's needs, reducing data processing time.

Optimized Subquery Handling and Joins   This optimization flattens specific subqueries for more efficient aggregation. Optimized joins improve join performance using techniques like filtering with bloom filters and reordering joins for better execution plans.

Deciding Between Amazon EMR and AWS Glue

Now that we have comprehensive insights from both Amazon EMR and AWS Glue, let's look at how to choose the right service for your big data workloads.

Both Amazon EMR and AWS Glue are AWS services for big data processing. Although they have some similarities, they serve different purposes. The key lies in understanding what sets them apart and what are the distinctive features and differences between the two.

Amazon EMR supports Apache Hadoop and other popular frameworks, such as Apache Spark, HBase, and Trino, making the "lift and shift" scenario to rehost your on-premises big data applications in the cloud easier with minimum modifications. EMR is extremely flexible when you want to customize and add optimizations to Apache Spark along with custom libraries. You can also run Spark on Kubernetes using EMR on EKS. This gives you the flexibility to select a specific version of Spark and choose specific infrastructure (catering to performance and cost) to run the desired workloads.

AWS Glue is a serverless data integration service that does not require you to provision or manage servers. With AWS Glue, you can generate Python or Scala code to perform ETL tasks. While AWS Glue doesn't provide the same elasticity as Amazon EMR, its serverless nature offers operational efficiency and scalability. AWS Glue is recommended for workloads where you want to migrate from legacy ETL platforms and also would like to use the built-in connectors and transformations while performing data processing. AWS Glue offers a fully managed data solution that supports all phases of data integration—ingestion, connectors, authoring, transformation and data quality, job monitoring, cataloging, and data management.

In conclusion, the decision to use either Amazon EMR or AWS Glue comes down to your specific ETL needs, business and scaling requirements, and level of skills and management.

Stream Processing

Traditional batch-processed data analytics leads to delays in gaining insights. Streaming analytics, in contrast, delivers real-time insights for faster decision-making for organizations. Some of the benefits of streaming real-time analytics include gaining insights from various data sources to understand customer behavior and respond quickly, analyzing trends and identifying opportunities ahead of competitors, discovering opportunities for cost reduction, monitoring data streams for breaches and ensuring compliance with regulations, introducing platform modernization by moving from monoliths to microservices, performing change data capture from transactional systems, detecting anomalies, conducting log analytics, analyzing clickstream data, and more.

Most common use cases for streaming workloads undergo this lifecycle, where data is collected from various sources, such as sensors, applications, and social media, at high velocity. The data is ingested into the storage, a purpose-built engine, where it is stored in the order it was received for a set duration of time and can be replayed indefinitely during this time. Once you store the data in a streaming storage, you can use libraries, processing frameworks, or other tools to read the data. This data can either be used for generating real-time alerts or can be sent to destinations such as data lakes, databases, or data warehouses for analytics and insights.

The process of ingestion and collection is explained in Chapter 1. In this chapter, we will focus on the processing part of the streaming workloads.

For processing the streaming workloads, you can use Amazon Data Firehose and Amazon Managed Service for Apache Flink.

Amazon Data Firehose

Amazon Data Firehose acts as a one-stop shop for capturing, transforming, and delivering data streams to your destination, as shown in Figure 3.26.

FIGURE 3.26   AWS representation of a high-level streaming workflow with Amazon Data Firehose

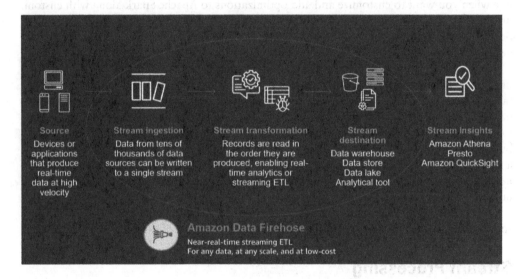

Firehose a fully managed service that makes it easy to load massive volumes of streaming data from multiple sources into Amazon S3, Amazon Redshift, Amazon OpenSearch Service, generic HTTP endpoints, and service providers like Datadog, New Relic, MongoDB, and Splunk. You can send data to the delivery stream by calling the Firehose API or by running the Linux agent that you provide on the data source. Figure 3.27 illustrates the streaming workflow and gives you an overview of the list of the sources and targets supported by Amazon Data Firehose.

Firehose offers built-in data transformation features that enable you to apply on-the-fly transformations, eliminating the need for coding or managing servers. Firehose transforms and processes your data streams as they arrive. It automatically scales to match the throughput of your data. Amazon Data Firehose can also batch, compress, and encrypt your data streams before loading them into the destination, minimizing storage costs and increasing security.

Additionally, Firehose uses AWS Lambda (as shown in Figure 3.28) to prepare and transform incoming raw data in your Firehose stream to Parquet format before loading to the target applications. The transformed records in Parquet format are delivered to Amazon S3. Additionally, if the Lambda invocation fails due to transformation errors, network timeout, or invocation limit, Amazon Data Firehose retries the invocation three times by default. If they still do not succeed, then the skipped records are captured in a separate S3 bucket. Firehose also allows you to capture the source records in their raw state (pre-transformation stage) and store them in different S3 bucket as a backup.

FIGURE 3.27   Amazon Data Firehose overview

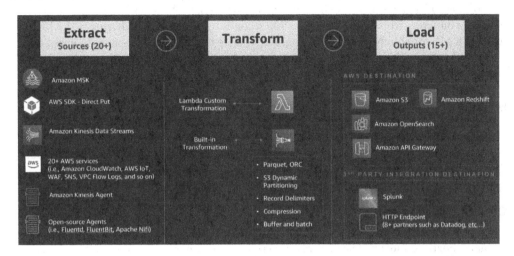

FIGURE 3.28   AWS Amazon Data Firehose architecture

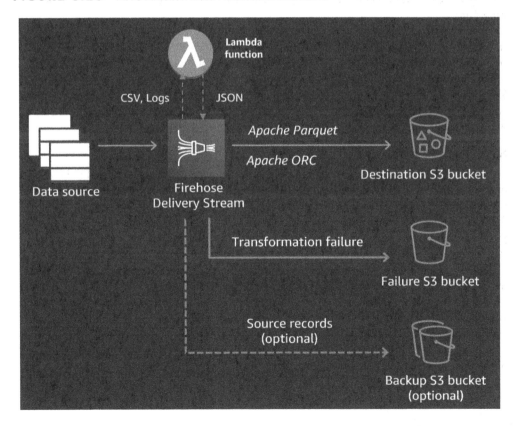

When you enable the Firehose data transformation, it buffers the incoming data. At the time of this writing, in order to deliver the data to data lakes (Amazon S3), you can configure the buffering from 0 seconds up to 900 seconds for time-based buffering or 1 MB up to 128 MB for volume-based buffering. Buffering is flushed to the destination based on either buffer threshold or whichever comes first (volume-based buffering or time-based buffering). Splunk destinations are buffered for 5 MB or 1 min.

Buffering hints are ideal when you want to deliver optimally sized files to Amazon S3 and get better performance from data processing applications.

Amazon Data Firehose also enables you to automatically convert the incoming JSON data in the stream to Apache Parquet or Apache ORC format using record transformation/record format conversion. Amazon Data Firehose seamlessly integrates with AWS Glue Data Catalog. During record format conversion, you can select the AWS Glue Catalog table to specify the schema for your source records.

Cost and Anti-Patterns

Amazon Data Firehose works on pay-as-you-go pricing model where you are charged for the amount of data you ingest. The key cost drivers are ingestion, format conversion, delivery data to VPC endpoint, and dynamic partitioning. For more details on the cost, visit the official AWS documentation here: `https://aws.amazon.com/kinesis/data-streams/pricing`

Amazon Data Firehose is meant for near-real-time use cases considering the buffering time based on time and size. It is a fully managed service with integrated data transformations and can deliver streaming data to destinations without writing code. Data is not stored in Amazon Data Firehose. The recommended services for storing streaming data are Amazon Kinesis Data Streams and Amazon Managed Service for Kafka. If the use case demands more complex data processing with lower latency and high throughput, the recommendation is to use other streaming services like Amazon Managed Service for Apache Flink.

Reference Architectures

We saw a couple of architecture patterns during the overview of Amazon Data Firehose ingestion to Amazon S3 and various other destinations. One of the use cases where Firehose can be leveraged is to ingest data from Amazon Virtual Private Cloud (VPC) flow logs into Splunk for analysis. The architecture pattern in Figure 3.29 illustrates how Firehose enables you to monitor and analyze machine data from VPC flow logs in Splunk for better operational intelligence.

Amazon API Gateway is a fully managed service that allows developers to create, publish, maintain, monitor, and secure APIs at any scale. Figure 3.30 illustrates the architecture where the data is streamed and ingested into Amazon Data Firehose, which is further integrated with Amazon API Gateway. Amazon API Gateway acts as a front end (single entry point) for different API-based microservices and web application assets like Amazon DynamoDB, Amazon SNS, HTTP end points, and so on. This allows you to expose a single web API domain without exposing the underlying implementation.

FIGURE 3.29   Amazon Data Firehose and Splunk integration

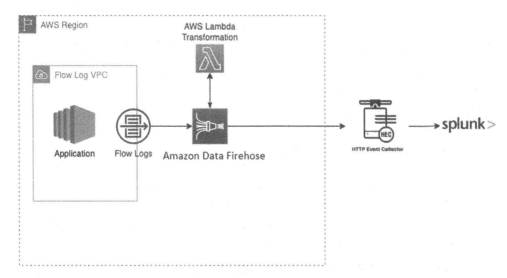

FIGURE 3.30   Amazon Data Firehose and Amazon API Gateway integration

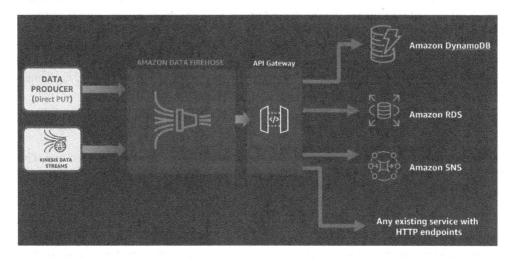

Performance Tuning Techniques

Firehose supports built-in data format conversion from raw data or JSON into formats like Apache Parquet or Apache ORC. In terms of compression, it supports gzip, Snappy, zip, and Hadoop-compatible Snappy data compression.

We already saw the performance tuning practices for Athena. We discussed that the data needs to be partitioned and bucketed. Firehose allows you to dynamically partition your streaming data before delivery to S3 using static or dynamically defined keys like `customer_id` or `order_id`. Dynamic partitioning is the process of automatically organizing data into separate folders or partitions based on the values of certain attributes. Firehose groups data by these keys and delivers it into key-unique S3 prefixes to enable high-performance analytics in S3 when using Athena, Redshift Spectrum, or a BI tool.

Dynamic partitioning offers several advantages for managing and analyzing streaming data in Amazon Data Firehose.

- Data is organized efficiently, allowing you to target specific subsets for analysis, resulting in improved query performance.

- By eliminating redundant data within partitions, storage and data transfer costs are optimized. This aids to further cost optimization while processing the data streams.

- Grouping the related data together simplifies data management tasks like retention policies, tracking changes, and maintaining data integrity.

- Dynamic partitioning seamlessly scales with growing data volumes. You can easily adapt your partitioning strategy based on changing needs.

Amazon Managed Service for Apache Flink

Apache Flink is a framework and distributed processing engine for stateful computations over bounded and unbounded data streams. Examples of data generated as a stream include sensor measurements, user interactions on a website, machine logs, and credit card transactions.

Unbounded data streams have a start but no defined end. They are like continuously flowing rivers of data with no foreseeable stopping point. Unbounded streams must be continuously processed; it is not possible to wait for all input data to arrive. Another challenge is that the processing of unbounded streams requires that events be ingested in a specific order—such as the order in which events occurred—to be able to reason about its result completeness. An example of an unbounded stream would be processing a live stream of social media posts.

Unlike unbounded data streams, bounded data streams have a defined start and end. The data streams can be processed by ingesting all data before performing any computations on them. Hence, ordered ingestion is not required to process bounded streams because a bounded data set can always be sorted. An example of a bounded data stream, also known as batch processing, is processing a day's worth of website logs or a set of financial transactions for a particular day.

Apache Flink excels at processing both bounded and unbounded datasets. It is designed to run stateful streaming applications at any scale. Its asynchronous and incremental checkpoint algorithm ensures minimal impact on processing latencies while at the same time guaranteeing exactly-once state consistency. Figure 3.31 illustrates where Apache Flink sits in AWS's data streaming services.

Now, the question is where can we deploy Apache Flink on AWS? The first option is the fully managed and serverless service, Amazon Managed Service for Apache Flink. The second option is to deploy Apache Flink applications on an Amazon EMR cluster, which can be configured for high availability. However, you have to manage how you want to scale your application. The third option is to run self-managed Flink applications on Amazon Elastic Kubernetes Service (Amazon EKS).

FIGURE 3.31   Amazon Managed Service for Apache Flink

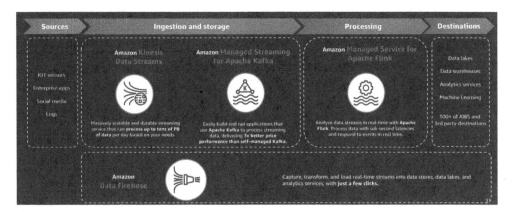

Amazon Managed Service for Apache Flink (MSF) enables you to write Flink applications in Java, Scala, Python, or SQL, and leverage open-source Flink libraries. The service manages the underlying infrastructure, including provisioning resources, handling fault tolerance and automatic scaling. MSF supports sub-second latencies for stream processing. You can choose between building applications in your preferred IDE (interactive development environment) or using interactive Flink Studio for real-time querying and development. Figure 3.32 helps you decide between Amazon Managed Service for Apache Flink and Amazon Managed Service for Apache Flink Studio based on your use case. Amazon Managed Service for Apache Flink is ideal for long-running applications, like streaming ETL, or continuous processing. You can develop Flink applications directly in your IDE using Flink APIs. You can also leverage the familiar *SDLC* practices like Git versioning, *CI/CD*, and unit testing. However, if you are interested in interactive data exploration, real-time querying, and private dashboards, Managed Service for Apache Flink Studio is the recommended option. SQL users can deploy long-running applications directly from Studio. MSF Studio also integrates with AWS Glue Data Catalog.

While Studio notebooks can be promoted to long-running applications, for full SFDC integration and development practices, using Flink with a traditional IDE is recommended.

With regards to monitoring, MSF integrates with Amazon CloudWatch, allowing you to configure CloudWatch metrics and logs for Flink applications. You can monitor application performance and error condition using CloudWatch logs. You can also use the Apache Flink Dashboard to monitor the running jobs.

FIGURE 3.32   AWS reference chart for MSF

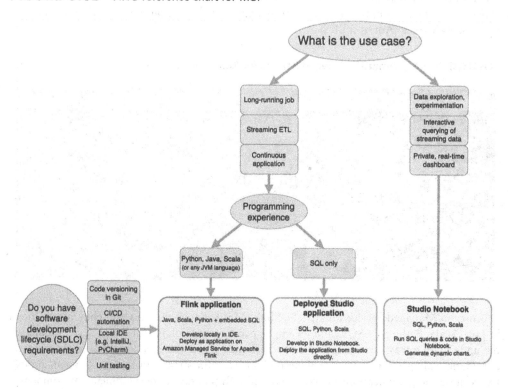

Choosing a Flink API

Flink offers four levels of API abstraction: Flink SQL, Table API, Data Stream API, and Process Function. Figure 3.33 illustrates these four APIs and the difference in the levels of abstraction.

Flink SQL offers the highest level of abstraction with a concise and familiar syntax for querying data streams. It uses SQL queries and offers easy integration with the Table API.

The Table API is a declarative DSL centered on tables. It focuses on table manipulation using a relational model with schemas and operations like select, join, and group by. Table API programs also go through an optimizer, which applies optimization rules before execution.

It is advisable to start with a higher level of abstraction wherever possible; however, some Flink features are available only with the DataSet or DataStream APIs (Core APIs). With the DataStream API, you can create your applications in Java, Python, or Scala. The DataStream API is designed to work with common processing building blocks, such as transformations, joins, aggregations, and windowing. These APIs work with bounded or unbounded data streams. The Data Set API offers additional primitives on bounded datasets, such as loops and iterations.

FIGURE 3.33   AWS reference chart for Flink API

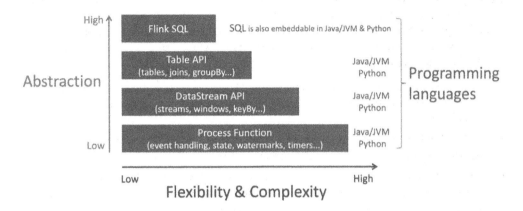

The lowest level abstraction simply offers stateful and timely stream processing. It is embedded into the DataStream API via the ProcessFunction operation and allows you to freely process events from one or more streams. Using these, you can register event time, processing time callbacks, watermarks, timers and other sophisticated computations.

Amazon Managed Service for Apache Flink integrates with various data sources and destinations. Figure 3.34 illustrates the integration of MSF with services such as Amazon Kinesis Data Stream, Amazon Managed Service for Apache Kafka (MSK), Amazon Open-Search Service, Amazon DynamoDB, JDBC connectors, and so on.

FIGURE 3.34   AWS architecture on MSF integrations

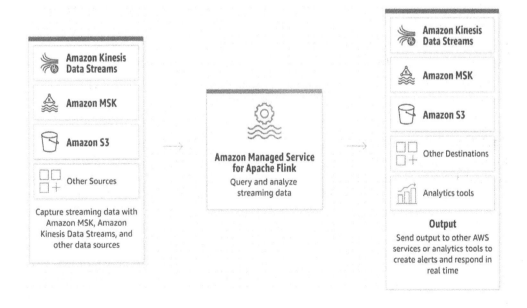

Data Transformation in Flink

In Flink, the transformation operator converts one or more DataStreams into a new DataStream. The new DataStream allows you to chain these transformations together to create complex pipelines. DataStream uses different data manipulation techniques, such as aggregation and filtering, to achieve specific needs.

Please refer to the article at https://datafans.medium.com/flink-commonly-used-operator-transformation-8832a3490d47, which lists a few examples of common transformations used with Apache Flink:

- Map: Applies a function to each element in a DataStream, creating a new element in the output stream. It is useful for tasks like data cleaning, format changes, or basic calculations.

- Filter: Filters elements in a DataStream based on a user-defined function. Only elements that meet the condition pass through to the output stream.

- FlatMap: Similar to Map, it applies a function to each element. However, FlatMap can output zero, one, or multiple elements for each input element. You can use FlatMap when you want to split or expand your DataStream.

- KeyBy: Groups elements in a DataStream based on a specific key field. It is useful for operations that require grouping of data, such as aggregations or joins.

- Reduce: Applies a user-defined function to pairs of elements within a group created by KeyBy. It iteratively combines elements until a single result remains for each group. This is useful for summarizing data within groups.

- Join: Combines elements from multiple DataStreams based on matching keys.

- Aggregate: Applies an aggregate function—such as count, sum, or average—to elements within the groups defined by KeyBy.

- Window: Groups elements within a defined time window or based on other criteria. This allows you to perform calculations or aggregations on the data chunks within the window.

- Project: Selects fields from elements in a DataStream, creating a new stream with a reduced set of fields.

To learn more about the Flink data transformations, please refer to https://nightlies.apache.org/flink/flink-docs-release-1.14/docs/dev/dataset/transformations.

Real-Time Anomaly Detection

Real-time anomaly detection is crucial for timely decision-making in various scenarios, such as fraud detection, predictive maintenance, and so on. However, the challenge is to handle massive data streams arriving at high speed, as well as constantly drifting ML models as the data patterns change over time.

Random Cut Forest (RCF) is an algorithm known to mitigate these challenges and is widely used for anomaly detection use cases. With MSF, you can run an online RCF algorithm within a Flink job to detect anomalies.

Costs and Anti-Patterns

With MSF, you only pay for the resources you use, eliminating the upfront costs. The pricing is based on Kinesis Processing Units (KPUs). At the time of this writing, charges are applied at an hourly rate based on the number of KPUs used by the application. One KPU equals to 1 vCPU and 4 GB of memory. For more details on the pricing, please refer to the AWS official documentation: `https://aws.amazon.com/managed-service-apache-flink/pricing`.

Using MSF to process pure batch data, where you only need to process 100 records a day, is a counterproductive approach. Services like AWS Glue or AWS Lambda can be considered.

Reference Architectures

Let's examine the reference architectures for Amazon Flink.

Telemetry Data Analytics in Real Time

In the automotive industry, fleet management for vehicles is essential to collect, process, and analyze high-velocity traffic data and react in real time to control and reroute traffic. Figure 3.35 shows an example of how to analyze the telemetry data of a taxi fleet in real time to optimize fleet operations using Amazon Managed Service for Apache Flink. The telemetry data is ingested into the Amazon Kinesis Data Streams. The application reads the timestamp attribute of the stored events and replays them as though they occurred in real time. The telemetry data is processed using MSF. During processing, if it breaches the threshold, it can generate alerts using AWS Lambda and Amazon SNS so that the engineering team can take action on it. The aggregated metrics post-processing are pushed to Amazon OpenSearch to derive insights. Amazon Data Firehose also captures the raw telemetry data and sends it to Amazon OpenSearch to perform complex searches on massive amount of data.

FIGURE 3.35 AWS reference architecture on telemetry data analytics

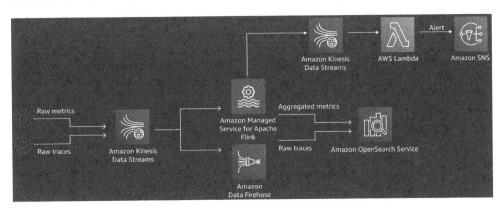

Device Sensors Real-Time Anomaly Detection

Figure 3.36 illustrates how an organization can use Amazon Managed Service for Apache Flink to monitor sensor data from their vehicles in real time. AWS IoT Gateway ingests sensor data and feeds it to Amazon Kinesis Data Streams. Apache Flink analyses the data stream for temperature anomalies and triggers alerts to Lambda functions and SNS. Regular sensor data is also stored in the data lakes in Amazon S3 via Amazon Data Firehose for further analysis using Amazon Athena and Amazon QuickSight. Long-term data can be archived in Glacier using S3 Lifecycle policies. The architecture diagram is referenced from `https://docs.aws.amazon.com/pdfs/whitepapers/latest/streaming-data-solutions-amazon-kinesis/streaming-data-solutions-amazon-kinesis.pdf`.

FIGURE 3.36   AWS reference architecture on anomaly detection

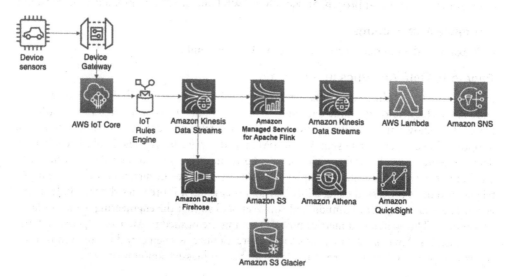

Change Data Capture with MSF

Amazon Flink directly ingests changes coming from different databases using change data capture (CDC). CDC connectors for Apache Flink are a set of source connectors that support reading database snapshots and continue to read transaction logs with exactly-once processing. As shown in Figure 3.37, an Amazon EventBridge rule triggers a Lambda function that simulates CDC data in the RDS database. Only the changed records will be captured and consumed using the Apache Flink application using Amazon Managed Service for Flink Studio. Within Studio, once the data is consumed and processed, the results are written into Amazon S3 using Apache Hudi to eliminate the duplicates for the same record key. By using Apache Hudi, you can perform ACID transactions on top of the data lakes, which can later be queried using Amazon Athena. Flink CDC connectors eliminate the need for you to manage Debezium connectors or any other tools.

FIGURE 3.37   AWS reference architecture of MSF for change data capture

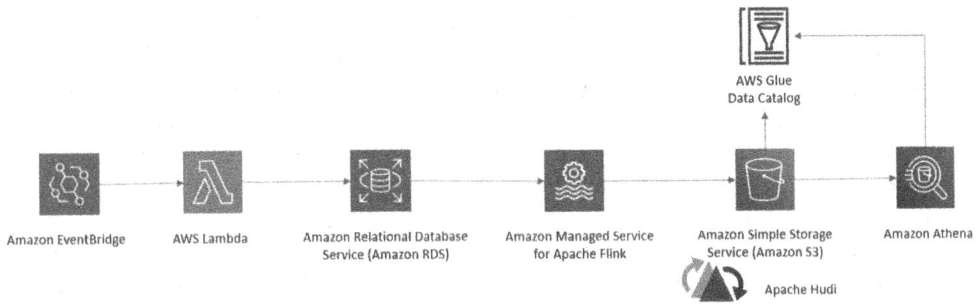

Please refer to this GitHub site to delve more into this use case: https://github.com/aws-samples/streaming-data-lake-flink-cdc-apache-hudi?tab=readme-ov-file

Checkpoints and Savepoints

Checkpoints are automatic, periodic snapshots of your application's state taken by Flink itself. They happen at regular intervals to ensure that you do not lose too much progress in case of any failure. Consider checkpoints as automatic backups in the background. Flink can then use these checkpoints to recover your application's state and resume processing from where it left off.

Savepoints are manual snapshots that you, the user, can explicitly trigger. They provide a way to pause your application, create a consistent state representation, and then potentially resume later, restart with a different configuration, or even migrate to a different cluster. Think of them as user-controlled backups that you can create at specific points for various purposes. Unlike checkpoints, savepoints are not automatically cleaned by Flink, so you will need to manage their lifecycle,

Performance Tuning Techniques

Now, let's examine the performance tuning techniques for Amazon Flink.

Fault Tolerance   Use checkpoints for automatic, periodic backups of your application's state to recover from failures with minimal data loss. Leverage savepoints for user-controlled backups at specific points in time for upgrades, maintenance, or debugging.

Performance and Parallelism   Set parallelism appropriately for each operator in your application to distribute the workload and optimize resource utilization. Consider using in-memory processing for stateful applications whenever possible for low latency.

Development   Avoid overly complex functions within stateful functions. Break down the complex logic into separate user-defined functions (UDFs) for better maintainability. Consider higher-level abstractions like Flink's Table or SQL APIs for simpler development and tasks.

Backpressure   Backpressure usually occurs when the job cannot process the data quickly enough. This means that the operator struggles to keep up processing the message volume it receives. There can be several reasons; for example, the operator may require more CPU resources, or it might be waiting for the I/O operations to complete. This causes the upstream operators to slow down, which further propagates the backpressure to the source, resulting in a delay in the overall throughput of the application. Backpressure information is exposed through the Flink Dashboard, which helps you to identify which operators in an application are slow. It is recommended, during troubleshooting, to start from the sink and work backwards. In most of the cases where customers run into performance issues, it is when the sinks are not able to handle the amount of traffic being generated by the Flink application. One of the reasons might be throttling, where the Flink application is not able submit the records, causing a trickle effect all the way back to the source operator, which starts to consume fewer records.

Troubleshooting and Monitoring   Leverage the Flink Dashboard and CloudWatch alarms to detect an application's issues and troubleshoot errors.

Data Skew   Flink's monitoring dashboard allows you to track metrics like the number of records received/sent by individual subtasks (instances of the same operator). This helps you identify partitions with imbalanced data volumes (skew).

While choosing a partition key, aim for the key with a high number of distinct values (high cardinality) to distribute the workloads evenly across partitions. Avoid situations where some partitions receive significantly more data than others, leading to bottlenecks.

Visit the AWS official documentation to understand tips and tricks on troubleshooting problems that you might encounter during development and runtime with MSF: `https://docs.aws.amazon.com/managed-flink/latest/java/troubleshooting.html`

Micro-batching vs. Continuous Streaming

In the big data world, Apache Flink and Apache Spark are two of the most popular frameworks for distributed processing. Flink's unique point is its checkpointing and savepointing mechanisms. These mechanisms are the central backbone of its exactly-once delivery model. Flink was developed as a "streaming-first" engine, whereas Apache Spark uses a "batch-first" approach. By contrast, Spark treats data streams as micro-batches (simulating streaming with tiny batches) rather than as a continuous stream. This results in an at-least-once delivery model (meaning there could be duplicates) and induces longer latencies (measured in seconds) than Flink. Flink, on the other hand, offers true continuous processing, reacting to events as they arrive.

Having said this, there are also hybrid workloads that involve both real-time and batch processing with Flink and Spark together. The best choice of framework depends on the specific needs and priorities of the use case. However, it is important to consider the trade-offs between real-time processing speed, developer experience, and existing infrastructure when making the decision.

Please refer to the AWS blog, which gives a comparative study of Flink and Spark processing: `https://aws.amazon.com/blogs/big-data/a-side-by-side-comparison-of-apache-spark-and-apache-flink-for-common-streaming-use-cases`

Now that we have explored the data transformation aspects, let's shift gears and explore a different approach: leveraging containers for data processing. Containers offer a lightweight, portable, and modular way to build and deploy data pipelines.

Introduction to Containers

The concept of containers has been around for decades, but they gained significant popularity in the early 2000s with the introduction of technologies like Docker. Simply put, with containerization, developers can write applications once and run them anywhere. Phrases like, "Oh, when I tested on my machine, it worked" started to become history.

In simple words, a container is a self-contained unit that packages an application's code and all its dependencies (libraries, configuration files) together. Think of it as a portable box containing everything your application needs to run, regardless of the underlying environment. These containers share the host operating system kernel, making them lightweight and efficient.

Containerization is the process of creating and managing containers. It involves building the container image (the blueprint for the container), running the container instances, and managing their lifecycle. It is like having an assembly line for creating and deploying these portable application packages.

One of the benefits of containerization is "build once, deploy everywhere." Developers can use containerization to deploy applications in multiple environments without rewriting the program code.

On AWS, you have choice of fully managed container services, including Amazon Elastic Container Service (ECS) and Amazon Elastic Kubernetes Service (EKS).

Amazon ECS

Amazon ECS is a fully managed container service that helps you deploy, manage, and scale containerized applications. It is integrated with both AWS and third-party tools, such as Amazon Elastic Container Registry (ECR) and Docker.

There are three layers in Amazon ECS:

- **Capacity:** Capacity is the infrastructure where your containers run. ECS offers different choices for the infrastructure that underpins your containerized applications, such as Amazon EC2, AWS Fargate, and on-premises servers and virtual machines (VMs).

- **Controller:** Controller deploys and manages the applications that run on the containers. The Amazon ECS scheduler is the software that manages your application.

- **Provisioning:** Provisioning refers to the tools that you can use to interface with the scheduler to deploy and manage your applications and containers. There are multiple options for provisioning ECS, including AWS CLI, AWS SDK, AWS Management Console, Copilot, and AWS CDK.

You specify the infrastructure (capacity) when you create a cluster. This could be Amazon EC2 instances (where you manage the servers), AWS Fargate (serverless option), or even on-premises servers/virtual machines you already own (within Amazon ECS Anywhere). Within your task definition, you specify how individual tasks will be launched. This involves selecting the same "launch type" you chose for your cluster. This launch type essentially determines the infrastructure your containers will utilize when you run them as standalone tasks or deploy them as part of larger service. After you choose the launch type, Amazon ECS verifies that the task definition parameters you configure work with the launch type. ECS Service manages how many tasks should run simultaneously in an ECS cluster. Figure 3.38 illustrates the architecture of Amazon ECS.

FIGURE 3.38 Amazon ECS constructs

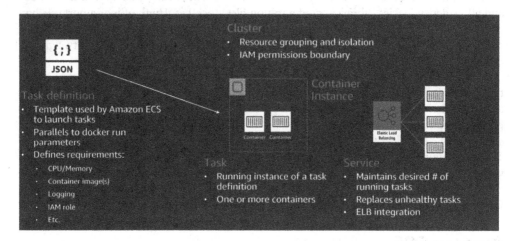

With the Fargate launch type, there are no instances to maintain. It is serverless and works on a pay-as-you-go model. All you need to do is create a task definition and define which cluster you want to run your applications on. AWS will create the ECS tasks based on the RAM and CPU needs. With Fargate, you get more flexibility in choosing the exact CPU and memory that your application needs. Fargate handles scaling out your capacity, so you don't have to worry about spikes in traffic. It is suitable for small workloads that have occasional bursts, batch workloads, or large workloads that require less operational overhead.

The EC2 launch type is suitable for large workloads that must be price-optimized. In this case, you must provision and maintain the infrastructure (i.e., EC2 instances). Each EC2 instance must run the ECS agent to register with the ECS cluster. When using the EC2 launch type, group related containers with a common purpose into separate task definitions. This allows you to scale each component independently (e.g., separate front-end, back-end, and data store services) for maximum efficiency. You can then combine these task definitions into services to manage their availability and scaling.

Amazon ECS tasks can leverage Amazon Elastic File System (EFS) for Multi-AZ persistent storage. EFS offers scalable storage that automatically adjusts capacity based on your needs. Tasks running in any Availability Zone will share the same data in the EFS file system. This functionality works seamlessly with both Fargate and EC2 instances running your ECS tasks.

 Amazon S3 cannot be mounted as a file system.

Amazon Elastic Container Registry

Amazon Elastic Container Registry (ECR) is used to store and manage Docker images on AWS. You can store Docker images publicly or privately. Amazon ECR is fully integrated with Amazon ECS and Amazon EKS and is backed by Amazon S3. All you need to do is specify the Amazon ECR repository in your task or pod definition for Amazon ECS or Amazon EKS to retrieve the relevant images for your applications. Amazon ECR uses AWS IAM to control and monitor the access control of your container images.

Amazon Elastic Kubernetes Service

Amazon Elastic Kubernetes Service (EKS) is a managed service that eliminates the need to install, operate, and maintain your own Kubernetes control plane on AWS. Kubernetes is an open-source system for automatic deployments, scaling, and management of containerized applications. A common use case for Amazon EKS is when users are already using Kubernetes on-premises or in another cloud and would like to migrate to AWS using Kubernetes.

Amazon EKS aligns with the general cluster architecture of Kubernetes. As shown in Figure 3.39, each EKS cluster has its own control plane spread across multiple Availability Zones. Amazon takes care of managing this plane. In addition to the control plane, an Amazon EKS cluster has set of worker machines called *nodes*. You can choose your worker nodes either to run on EC2 instances or Fargate (serverless option). EKS also offers tools like Karpenter for auto-scaling and managed node groups for simplified management of EC2 instances. AWS takes care of tasks like patching, updating, and scaling nodes, easing the operational aspect. Additionally, for full control over your EC2 instances, EKS offers self-managed nodes, wherein you have the full control over the underlying infrastructure. Custom kubelet arguments are supported to allow you to fine-tune certain aspects, such as resource management (CPU, memory), pod priority, and eviction policies.

Similar to ECS, EKS also supports various data volume options, such as Amazon EBS and Amazon EFS (https://docs.aws.amazon.com/eks/latest/userguide/storage .html).You need to specify a `StorageClass` manifest on your EKS cluster. Amazon EKS also leverages the Container Storage Interface (CSI) compliant driver to create Kubernetes persistent volumes for persistent disks attached during the instance startup.

FIGURE 3.39   A high-level view of an Amazon EKS cluster

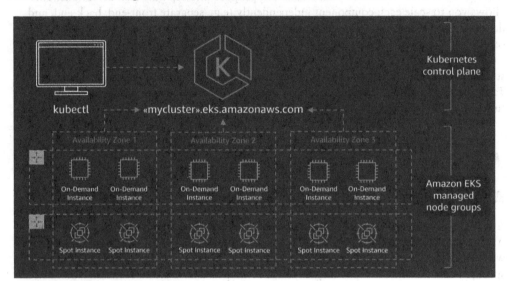

Optimizing Container Usage

When it comes to AWS containers, we discussed the use cases where individual container services shine. You can strike a fine balance between cost efficiency and high performance by considering the following:

Choosing the Right Service

- Consider your workload's needs (scalability, fault tolerance).
- Understand service capabilities (container types, networks, storage).
- Pick a deployment model (serverless, cluster-based, self-managed).
- Ensure smooth integration with other AWS services.
- Choose a service that fits your budget.
- Optimize the container images.
- Use Spot instances for cost savings.

Optimizing Container Images

- Reduce the size of the container image (remove unnecessary files, use a minimal base image).
- Leverage multi-stage builds for efficiency.
- Implement caching to speed up the builds.
- Prioritize security (scan for vulnerabilities, avoid sensitive PII data).
- Test and validate the images before deployment.

Implementing Security

- Secure base images and keep them updated.
- Limit access to containers and images to authorized users and services only.
- Implement access controls with RBAC.
- Secure container networking (network policies, encryption, firewalls).

Monitoring Container Performance

- Collect and analyze metrics (CPU, disk I/O, network, memory).
- Set up alerts for key performance metrics.
- Use a centralized logging mechanism for easier troubleshooting.
- Use auto-scaling to handle varying workloads.
- Monitor the health of containers.

Now that we have harnessed the power of containers for creating isolation and managing individual tasks within your data workloads, how do you bridge the gap between these containerized services and the outside world? In the next section, we will explore how you can leverage API Gateway to create and manage APIs and use it as single-entry point for your applications and services.

API-Driven Data Pipelines on AWS

Imagine you own a popular restaurant chain with multiple locations. You want to create a mobile app that allows customers to:

- Browse your menu and see item descriptions and prices (GET request).
- Place orders for takeaway or delivery (POST request).
- View their order history and past receipts (GET request).

This is where API Gateway comes in. In building applications, an API helps simplify programming by abstracting the underlying implementation and exposing only the necessary objects or actions you need. API Gateway acts as a front-end service and enables clients to access your data securely with controlled access.

Instead of building separate APIs for each functionality (one for menu, one for orders, one for receipts), you can create a single API using API Gateway. This simplifies the development. It also simplifies and handles tasks like traffic management, access control, and error handling. During peak hours, your app might receive a surge of orders. API Gateway can handle this volume of traffic efficiently, ensuring your restaurant's backend systems are not overloaded. API Gateway can also implement authentication mechanisms to ensure that only authorized users can place orders. When you add new features to your app (e.g., online reservations), you can use API Gateway's canary deployments to gradually roll out the updated

API to a small group of users before making it available to everyone. This minimizes the risk and allows for bug detection before a wider release. In a nutshell, API Gateway acts a front door for your mobile app to interact with your restaurant's backend services.

Amazon API Gateway

Amazon API Gateway is a fully managed, serverless service that makes it easy for developers to create, publish, maintain, monitor, and secure APIs at scale. These APIs can access data and functionality from various AWS services or from your own web applications. Figure 3.40 illustrates how the APIs you build in Amazon API Gateway provide you with an integrated developer experience for building AWS serverless applications. API Gateway acts as a "front door" for applications to access data and business logic from your backend services, such as workloads running on Amazon Elastic Compute Cloud (EC2), code running on AWS Lambda, or any web application or real-time communication applications.

FIGURE 3.40   AWS API Gateway architecture

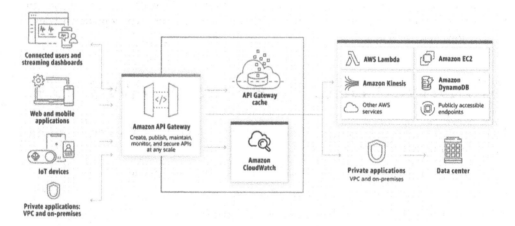

Types of APIs

API Gateway lets you create different types of APIs for your applications, including REST APIs, HTTP APIs, and WebSocket APIs.

REST APIs

An API Gateway REST API is made up of resources and methods. Imagine a restaurant menu. Each dish (resource) has options (methods), like adding it to your order (POST), or checking its availability (GET). The app interacts using commands (HTTP verbs) and API Gateway translates them for the kitchen (backend). A resource here translates to a logical entity, and a method corresponds to a REST API request submitted by the user of your API and the response returned to the user. The app doesn't know where the requested data is stored or fetched from on the backend. In API Gateway REST APIs, the frontend is encapsulated by method requests and method responses.

HTTP APIs

HTTP APIs are similar to REST APIs, but they are faster and cheaper. Think of placing a simple takeout order (express lane order). The app sends the request through API Gateway, which efficiently routes to the right restaurant's system.

You can create an HTTP API that integrates with a Lambda function on the backend. When a client calls your API, API Gateway sends the request to the Lambda function and returns the function's response to the client.

WebSocket APIs

In a WebSocket API, both the client and the server can send messages to each other at any time. Think of enabling a real-time live chat with a customer service representative.

In APIs, an endpoint is typically a URL that provides the location of the resource on the server. Endpoints are the doorways to the application's data. The API endpoint type can be edge-optimized, regional, or private, depending on where the majority of your API traffic originates from.

API Gateway Endpoints

There are several types of API Gateway endpoints to be aware of.

Edge-Optimized API Endpoints

An edge-optimized API endpoint (the default for REST APIs) is best for geographically distributed users. It routes requests to the nearest *CloudFront* location for faster performance. Any custom domain name that you use for an edge-optimized API applies across all regions.

Regional API Endpoints

A regional API endpoint is ideal for clients within the same region, especially for APIs serving a small number of high-demand clients in a specific region. It reduces connection overheads. Custom domain names are specific to the deployment region and can be the same across regions if deployed in multiple regions.

Private API Endpoints

A private API endpoint is accessible only from within your VPC using an interface VPC endpoint. It is useful for APIs with sensitive data or for internal use cases.

Data Transformations

Amazon API Gateway can perform basic request validations. It can verify one or both of the following conditions:

- The required request parameters in the URL, query string, and headers of an incoming request are included and not blank.
- The applicable request payload adheres to the configured JSON schema request of the method.

In some use cases, you may need to map the incoming payload to match the downstream service contract. In situations like this, your first reaction might be to add a Lambda function after Amazon API Gateway to transform the payload information and reformat it before ingesting into the downstream service. However, Lambda can be costly for small transformations. Cold starts can significantly increase latency and affect the overall performance. Additionally, concurrency and scaling of an API changes if you have an additional Lambda function in the execution path of the request. If your workload experiences sharp spikes of traffic, a direct integration with your persistence layer can lead to better ability to handle such spikes.

So, is there way to achieve the data transformations we need without the Lambda function?

One of the key features of API Gateway is mapping templates. These templates can be used to modify or validate the incoming request to a specification that is required by your backend services. For simpler data manipulations, mapping templates can be a more lightweight and cost-effective alternative to Lambda functions. They can extract specific data from request bodies or headers, modify and reformat data before sending to backend service, and transform responses from backend services into the format expected by your clients.

A mapping template is a script expressed in Velocity Template Language (VTL). Figure 3.41 illustrates the workflow of API Gateway and VTL. Apache Velocity has a number of operators that can be used when an expression is evaluated. These operators allow you to implement transformations and business logic in your Velocity templates.

FIGURE 3.41   API Gateway transformation mapping

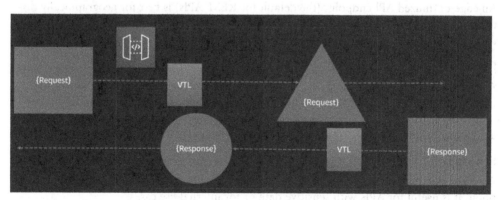

During the early stages of the development, Lambda provides more flexibility for data manipulation and logic. Writing code in Lambda allows for quicker adjustment and shortens the feedback loop for changes and developer experience. In this scenario, Lambda can be a starting point and VTL templates can be an optimization step for stable APIs to reduce cost and potentially improve performance. Please refer to this site to see examples of VTL templates:

```
https://docs.aws.amazon.com/apigateway/latest/developerguide/set-up-
data-transformations-in-api-gateway.html
```

Reference Architecture

Consider an online bookstore application. As with any modern full-stack web application, this application has multiple use cases, including a product catalog, product search, a best-sellers list, and social recommendations. For these diverse use cases, one database can seldomly fit the needs. Many organizations today build highly distributed applications using a variety of purpose-built databases.

Figure 3.42 shows how to build modern application with purpose-built databases.

FIGURE 3.42   Building modern applications with purpose-built databases

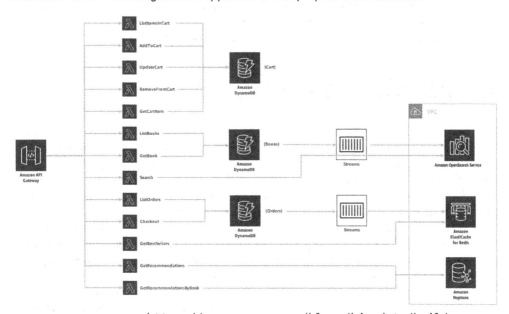

Source: Amazon Web Services / `https://aws.amazon.com/blogs/big-data/build-incremental-data-pipelines-to-load-transactional-data-changes-using-aws-dms-delta-2-0-and-amazon-emr-serverless`, last accessed on 19 December 2024.

The core of the bookstore's online store is its product catalog. This catalog contains details like descriptions, prices, quantities, and locations. The method for retrieving these types of attributes is often a key-value lookup based on the product's unique identifier. This use case makes Amazon DynamoDB ideal as the durable storage to maintain bookstore's product catalog.

The second use case is to enable customers to search the product catalog and find the next great read. Amazon OpenSearch Service helps provide this information and is ideal for fast and efficient searching based on keywords and faceted navigation. Whenever a product is added, updated, or removed from the catalog's product table in DynamoDB, the change needs to be reflected in the search index of Amazon OpenSearch Service. An easy way to do this is to use Amazon DynamoDB Streams to update the index every time a change is made to the catalog. This integration is activated via Zero-ETL integration between Amazon DynamoDB and Amazon OpenSearch Service.

The third use case is to enable users to see the best-sellers list or "Top 20" purchased books. This requires a database to maintain a leaderboard without having to do expensive summation queries across all purchases each time a user refreshes the web page. Amazon ElastiCache for Redis provides built-in, in-memory data structures, such as sorted sets, that allow the bookstore to create a best-sellers list quickly and effectively.

The fourth use case is to provide social recommendations to help customers find more contextually appropriate content—in this case, content based on what their friends have purchased. Amazon Neptune is a natural fit to navigate links in the data, enabling recommendations based on related purchase activity and social connections.

In order to fetch and update all of this information, the web storefront makes a series of different API calls. This is orchestrated through Amazon API Gateway, which acts as a central hub for handling API calls to these different backend services.

Introduction to Data Quality

In the age of artificial intelligence (AI), where algorithms are revolutionizing industries and shaping our future, a crucial element often remains hidden: data quality—the unsung hero of AI. While the capabilities of AI models grab the headlines, the foundation upon which they stand—the very data they learn from—is often overlooked. Imagine building a skyscraper on a foundation of sand. No matter how beautifully designed or meticulously constructed, the entire structure is at risk of collapse. Similarly, projects built on low-quality data are inherently unstable, leading to unreliable results, wasted resources, and potentially disastrous consequences. In fact, I have seen many projects of data warehousing and business intelligence fail due to the low engagement of key business users and stakeholders. These low engagements were the direct result of a lack of trust in the data.

There are many definitions of "data quality," but according to Wikipedia (https://en.wikipedia.org/wiki/Data_quality), data is generally considered high quality if it is "fit for [its] intended uses in operations, decision making and planning, and data is deemed of high quality if it correctly represents the real-world construct to which it refers." Data quality is one of the crucial components of data governance. However, one of the common mistakes people make is to consider data quality and data governance synonymous. Many organizations, when asked about data governance implementation, proudly proclaim, "Yes, we have data quality!" While this enthusiasm is commendable, it often reveals a misunderstanding of the true scope of data governance.

Data quality is the fuel that powers the engine of data governance. Let me explain with an example. Imagine a recipe of your favorite dish (your data). Data quality is like having fresh, high-quality ingredients (accurate and reliable data), which are essential for creating a satisfying and tasty dish. Data governance is like following the recipe meticulously (established practices to ensure data integrity). It also goes a step further by addressing potential issues beyond the initial data state, encompassing factors like the following:

- **Standardization:** Ensuring consistent formatting and units throughout the data, akin to using the correct measuring cups and spoons in the recipe

- **Documentation:** Providing clear instructions and ingredient information, similar to the recipe notes that guide the cooking process
- **Access control:** Limiting who can access and modify the ingredients, analogous to keeping pets or children away from sensitive kitchen tools
- **Monitoring and lineage:** Tracking data usage and origin, similar to keeping track of ingredient usage and substitutions throughout the cooking process

Data governance provides a holistic approach to ensure long-term data integrity. It is this synergetic relationship that empowers organizations to make informed decisions based on reliable information.

Data Quality Challenges to Overcome

Data quality issues come in various forms, hindering the effectiveness of data analysis. Here are the prominent challenges to address:

Incompleteness   This encompasses missing values, incomplete cases, and gaps in the data feeds. These gaps can impede analysis and lead to skewed results.

Inconsistency   This includes inconsistent formats, units of measure, references, and property mappings. Inconsistencies introduce confusion and hinder the ability to draw meaningful insights.

Inaccuracy   This refers to invalid values, corrupted data, and errors in data collection.

Duplication   This involves redundant data entries that lead to skewed analysis and wasted storage space.

Lack of Standardization   This stems from the absence of unified data collection processes and data format standards.

Timeliness   This refers to the data being current, relevant, and updated within an appropriate timeframe.

Lack of Time to Analyze Data and Identify Errors   Lack of time to analyze data mainly highlights a resource constraint rather than a specific data quality issue. While it is not directly related to data quality itself, it can significantly impact how well data is utilized for decision-making. Insufficient time for analysis can lead to rushed or incomplete evaluation, potentially overlooking crucial insights and missing opportunities for improvement.

 Real World Scenario

An example of data quality challenges can be seen in an article published in *PubMed* by Kristin Hirata and colleagues (https://pubmed.ncbi.nlm.nih.gov/28976456), where they determined that the incorrect or absent recording of patient weights could lead to medication dosage errors. Hirata and her colleagues examined the frequency and consequences of weight errors that occurred across 79,000 emergency department encounters of children under the age of 5 years. They revealed that, although weight errors were relatively rare (0.63%), a large proportion of weight errors led to subsequent medication-dosing errors (34%). By investing in data quality initiatives, healthcare organizations can minimize the risk of errors and ensure the safety and well-being of their patients.

Having established the significance of data quality and the challenges it presents, let's now shift our focus to practical solutions. We will delve into the implementation of data quality strategies and best practices, equipping you with the knowledge and tools to transform your data landscape from a potential quagmire into a reliable and valuable asset.

We already established earlier in this chapter on how AWS Glue helps to provide a unified approach by integrating from multiple data sources and facilitates efficient data transformation. Let's now look at how AWS Glue Data Quality can address the challenges associated with data quality, encompassing data profiling, data cleansing, and data validation.

AWS Glue Data Quality

AWS Glue Data Quality is a feature of AWS Glue, Amazon's fully managed extract, transform, and load (ETL) service. AWS Glue Data Quality builds on the robust foundation of the open-source framework *DeeQu*. Developed and utilized by Amazon to ensure the quality of large production datasets, DeeQu provides the underlying technology for AWS Glue Data Quality. Additionally, AWS Glue Data Quality leverages the Data Quality Definition Language (*DQDL*), a specialized language designed specifically for defining data quality rules. This combination empowers users to effectively harness the power of open-source technology and tailor data quality checks to their specific needs.

Figure 3.43 illustrates how AWS Glue Data Quality rules can be broadly categorized into four dimensions: consistency, completeness, accuracy, and integrity.

AWS Glue Data Quality offers the following key features and benefits:

- **Comprehensive data quality monitoring**: AWS Glue Data Quality allows you to apply data quality rules to both data at rest (in datasets and data lakes) and data in transit (flowing through ETL pipelines). This ensures that data quality is maintained throughout its lifecycle.

- **Scalability and cost-effectiveness**: Built on serverless architecture, AWS Glue Data Quality scales automatically to handle fluctuating data volumes without requiring infrastructure management. You only pay for the resources you use, making it cost efficient for various data sizes.

- **Open source foundation**: AWS Glue Data Quality leverages the robust DeeQu framework, ensuring flexibility and portability.

- **Data profiling and rule creation:** You can gain insights into your data structure and quality using the built-in profiling tools. AWS Glue Data Quality offers more than 25 out-of-the-box rules to help you get started; however, you can also define custom rules to address specific data quality needs.

- **ML-based data quality detection:** AWS Glue Data Quality leverages machine learning (ML) capabilities to identify both common and hard-to-detect data quality issues. This proactive approach helps ensure that your data remains accurate and reliable.

- **Rapid onboarding:** You can get started quickly with minimal effort. AWS Glue Data Quality automatically analyzes your data and suggests tailored data quality rules, saving valuable time and effort compared to manual configuration.

- **Alerts and monitoring:** AWS Glue Data Quality issues alerts when it detects anomalies and discrepancies, enabling timely intervention to ensure the health and integrity of stakeholder data.

- **Integration with other AWS services:** While powerful in its own right, AWS Glue Data Quality shines even brighter when integrated with the broader ecosystem of AWS services. Data ingested through AWS Glue can be automatically subjected to quality checks using AWS Glue Data Quality. This ensures data integrity before it is transferred to downstream services like *Amazon Redshift* for analytics and data warehousing use cases, or *Amazon S3* for storing golden and curated/processed records, thereby preventing the propagation of errors. The *metadata* generated by AWS Glue Data Quality can be leveraged to construct tables with *Amazon Athena*. This facilitates powerful analysis and reporting capabilities, providing valuable insights into data quality trends and overall data health. Stakeholders can build reconciliation dashboards to compare the total records ingested into the source versus records ingested into the target.

FIGURE 3.43   A representation of AWS Glue Data Quality rule types

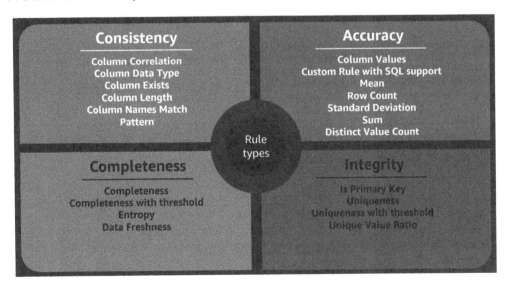

However, before embarking on this journey, its crucial to understand its structure – the blueprint for crafting effective data quality checks through Data Quality Definition Language.

 AWS Glue Data Quality checks can be applied at rest on catalog tables. This feature will be covered in Chapter 6.

Data Quality Definition Language

To find data quality issues in transit, you will write rules using a domain-specific language created by AWS called Data Quality Definition Language (DQDL). DQDL is case-sensitive and contains a ruleset that groups individual data quality rules. To construct a ruleset, you must create a list of rules that contain one or more comma-separated DQDL rules.

```
Rules = [
    IsComplete "col_A",
    IsUnique "col_B"
]
```

The structure of a DQDL rule depends on the rule type, but it generally fits the following format:

```
<RuleType> <Parameter> <Parameter> <Expression>
```

The RuleType parameter specifies the case-sensitive name of the rule category you want to create. Examples include IsComplete, IsUnique, and CustomSql. Each rule type has its own unique set of parameters that define its specific behavior. To view the complete list of rule types, see this page:

```
https://docs.aws.amazon.com/glue/latest/dg/dqdl.html#dqdl-rule-types
```

You can also combine the rules using the "and" and "or" are logical operators.
The following example illustrates how DQDL rules can be combined:

```
(IsComplete "id") and (IsUnique "id")
(RowCount "id" > 50) or (IsPrimaryKey "id")
```

However, you cannot combine the logical operators into a single expression.
The following is an example of an invalid DQDL rule:

```
(Mean "Star_Rating" > 2) and (Mean "Order_Total" > 550) or (IsComplete
"Order_Id")
```

This demonstrates how to find data quality issues with static rules, thereby establishing baseline expectations for data quality. Static data quality rules are the cornerstones of ensuring consistent clean information. However, as data landscapes evolve and become more complex, there is a shift toward dynamic rules, and analyzers become essential. Let's explore this with an example.

Real World Scenario

Imagine you're an engineer monitoring a river's health. Static rules, like fixed checkpoints, might tell you if the water level is currently above or below a certain point. But what if there is a drought or sudden downpour? Static rules would not catch these changes, potentially leading to problems downstream. This is where dynamic rules and analyzers come in—they are like smart sensors for your data!

Dynamic rules are like having a sensor that considers past water levels. It can tell you, "Hey, the water level is rising faster than usual compared to the last few weeks. This might be a flood!"

Analyzers are like a network of sensors that constantly monitor various aspects of the river, such as temperature, flow rate, and even the presence of pollutants. They gather this information for the dynamic rules to analyze.

In essence, dynamic rules and analyzers make your data quality checks smarter and more adaptable. They help you understand the *why* behind your data, not just the *what*.

With AWS Glue Data Quality, you can apply dynamic rules to check the data quality in transit. Dynamic rules compare current metrics produced by your rules with their historical values. For example, the dynamic rule RowCount > avg(last(5)) will check whether the current dataset's row count is strictly greater than the average of the last five row counts for the same dataset.

DQDL rules use functions called analyzers to gather information about your data. Analyzers generate statistics that can be used to detect anomalies. They can independently exist without rules.

```
Rules = [
    RowCount > avg(last(10))
],
Analyzers = [
    DistinctValuesCount "Country",
    ColumnLength "Country"
]
```

In this example, the DistinctValuesCount analyzer records the number of distinct values in the dataset's "Country" column. The ColumnLength analyzer tracks the minimum and maximum "Country" size over time.

DQDL also detects anomalies for a given DeeQu rule. Every execution of the Detect Anomalies rule results in saving the evaluated value for the given rule. When there is enough data gathered, the anomaly detection algorithm takes all the historical data for that given rule and runs anomaly detection. The DetectAnomalies rule fails when the anomaly is detected. Here is the syntax to detect anomalies for a given rule:

```
DetectAnomalies <RULE_NAME> <RULE_PARAMETERS>
```

An example to illustrate the usage would be to detect anomalies in the number of records. We provide RowCount as a rule name:

```
DetectAnomalies "RowCount"
```

Now that we have established the format of DQDL and its features, we'll turn to applying DQDL rules while building ETL pipelines (data quality in transit) and apply proactive measures to improve the quality of the dataset.

Data Quality in Transit

Once an AWS Glue job is defined, data quality checks can be integrated within the ETL job. This can be done by creating data quality rules in AWS Glue. Figure 3.44 illustrates how AWS Glue Data Quality can be applied in AWS Glue Studio during the ETL process.

FIGURE 3.44   The AWS Glue Studio interface with the transformation step of data quality

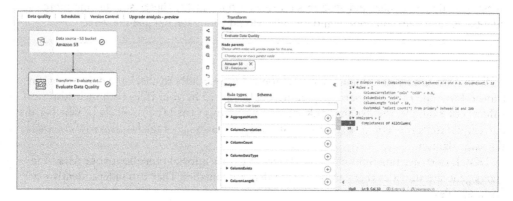

Once the evaluation happens, data quality node provides two output options: rowLevelOutcomes and ruleOutcomes. rowLevelOutcomes provides additional columns, such as:

- DataQualityRulesPass: Provides an array of rules that passed a data quality check

- DataQualityRulesFail: Provides an array of rules that failed a data quality check

- DataQualityRulesSkip: Provides an array of rules that skipped a data quality check

- DataQualityEvaluationResult: Provides a Passed or Failed status at the row level

Note that the overall result can be displayed as Failed, but a certain record within the dataset might pass.

Once you get the evaluation results, you can choose to output the configured results to Amazon S3 for further analysis and alternately proceed with the ETL job with failed data quality result. On enabling the output for Data Quality Results, as shown in the Figure 3.45, ruleOutcomes is added to the data pipeline.

FIGURE 3.45   Configuring data quality results output to Amazon S3

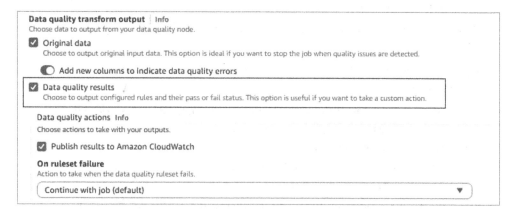

The output of `ruleOutcomes` can then be sent to Amazon S3 or be viewed from the AWS Glue Studio Console, as illustrated in Figure 3.46. For every ETL job run, AWS Glue Data Quality will evaluate the dataset and provide a data quality score.

FIGURE 3.46   Data validation of a data quality score on the AWS Management Console

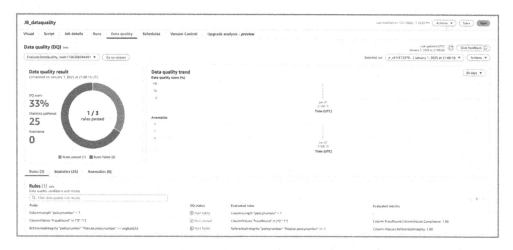

Coming back to our culinary-inspired adventure, let's build a data pipeline that utilizes DQ checks and separates the good data from the bad, ensuring that only the finest ingredients reach our applications. The list of the ingredients is as follows:

Raw Data   Our "unsorted" data, like a basket of vegetables, could contain inconsistencies, errors, and missing values.

Data Quality Rules   These act as our recipe, defining the criteria for "good" data. Think of them as instructions like "tomatoes must be red and firm." This helps to select the highest quality ingredients from the basket.

AWS Glue Data Quality   This is our "data inspector," meticulously examining the raw data against the defined rules.

Amazon S3   This serves as our "pantry," storing the results of the DQ checks for later use.

Map the steps to the numbering given in the data pipeline in Figure 3.47.
Here are the steps:

- Gather the raw data: Ingest the source data from the data lakes (Amazon S3) (1).

- Inspection: Apply AWS Glue Data Quality rules on the source data. It scrutinizes the data against the established rules (2).

- Sorting the goods: The results from the data quality check are sent to the `ruleOutcomes` (3a), and the evaluation result is stored in Amazon S3 (4).

- The original data, along with the four additional columns that we discussed— `DataQualityRulesPass`, `DataQualityRulesFail`, `DataQualityRulesSkip` and `DataQualityEvaluationResult`—is captured in `rowLevelOutcomes` (3b).

- Based on the evaluation, the original data is split into two streams, where the "good" data is separated from the "bad" data (5). Imagine separating the fresh tomatoes from the wilted ones.

- The separation criteria are based on the status of `DataQualityEvaluationResult`. If the status is `Passed`, then the "good" data is sent to downstream applications (6a). The data is fine-tuned further by changing the schema, such as dropping the irrelevant columns (7), before finally being pushed to the curated data lake (8).

- If the status is `Failed` (6b), then the "bad" data is sent to the Invalid Folder in S3 for further examination (9).

Similar to AWS Glue Studio, AWS Glue Data Quality checks can also be applied with AWS Glue DataBrew and Glue Studio Notebooks. In AWS Glue DataBrew, once the ruleset is defined, you can add it to a profile job for validation. You can define more than one ruleset for a dataset. AWS Glue DataBrew also provides rule recommendations based on the dataset's profile. This accelerates and simplifies the process of creating essential checks, empowering users to create more comprehensive checks over time.

Please refer to the blog `https://aws.amazon.com/blogs/big-data/enforce-customized-data-quality-rules-in-aws-glue-databrew` to learn more about how to enforce customized data quality rules in AWS Glue DataBrew.

You can programmatically access using AWS Glue Data APIs (`https://docs.aws.amazon.com/glue/latest/dg/aws-glue-api-data-quality-api.html`) to integrate data quality checks into custom applications, workflows, and scripts.

To facilitate automated deployment and configuration of data quality checks, AWS Glue Data Quality also offers infrastructure as code (`https://docs.aws.amazon.com/AWSCloudFormation/latest/UserGuide/aws-resource-glue-dataqualityruleset.html`).

FIGURE 3.47 A representation of an ETL data pipeline with data quality checks in transit

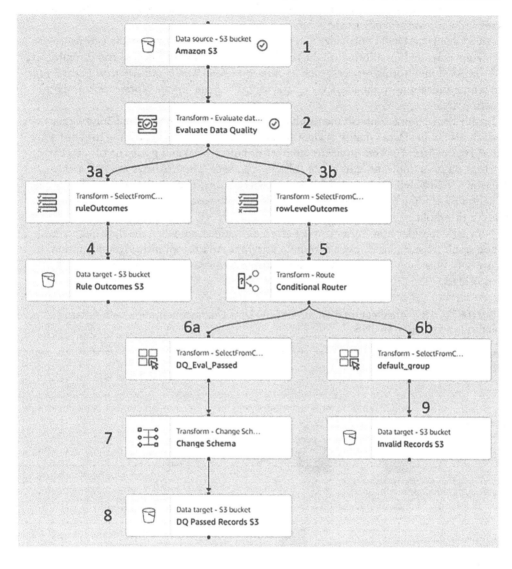

Alerts and Monitoring

Why do we need to monitor and perform automation on data quality checks? Data riddled with inconsistencies and errors can have a cascading effect in the downstream applications and impact the overall system reliability. Data quality alerts function as an early warning system, notifying stakeholders of potential problems before they manifest and snowball into significant problems. If the data quality is continuously monitored without the benefit of alerts, imagine the significant investment of resources both in terms of time and personnel.

Data quality alerts can help streamline this process by focusing attention only on situations that deviate from predefined quality standards. This helps the data teams prioritize critical issues and address them efficiently.

AWS Glue Data Quality provides you with the flexibility to take proactive measures by setting up alerts and monitoring on the results of the data quality checks. You can integrate with the AWS monitoring services, such as *Amazon CloudWatch* and *Amazon EventBridge*, and send notifications to the users via emails using *Amazon Simple Notification Service (Amazon SNS)*.

Enable the option to publish the results of the data quality to Amazon CloudWatch.

Each AWS Glue Data Quality evaluation metric emits a pair of metrics: `glue.data` `.quality.rules.failed` (indicates number of failed rules) and `glue.data.quality` `.rules.passed` (indicates number of rules that passed). These metrics are visible in Amazon CloudWatch, which can be used to create alarms. The alarm state can then trigger an action by sending mail via Amazon SNS and alert the users if the data quality run falls below a threshold.

Now let's consider how a user can get an email notification when the data quality evaluation result fails or falls below a threshold using the Amazon EventBridge integration. Figure 3.48 illustrates how you can set up alerts and notifications using Amazon EventBridge.

FIGURE 3.48 Architecture diagram of Glue Data Quality integration with Amazon EventBridge and Amazon SNS

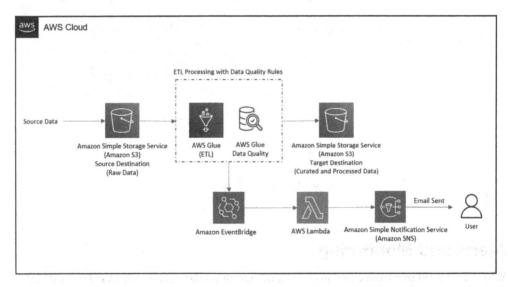

The architecture diagram illustrates the scenario where the raw data is ingested into Amazon S3 in the source destination. This would be treated as the landing zone where raw

data from multiple sources systems and applications can be collected. The source data is then transformed, and the necessary data quality checks are applied using AWS Glue and AWS Glue Data Quality. The processed ("good") data is sent to the target destination in Amazon S3. Upon the completion of the data quality evaluation run, Amazon EventBridge receives a notification event that contains the outcomes. You can apply specific rules in Amazon Event-Bridge to capture specific jobs in the ETL run. The event is examined by Amazon Event-Bridge and activates a Lambda function to handle the notification. The Lambda function dispatches an SNS alert with data quality metrics to the specified email address.

The following code snippet illustrates how to configure the event rules in Amazon EventBridge:

```
{
  "source": ["aws.glue-dataquality"],
  "detail-type": ["Data Quality Evaluation Results Available"],
  "detail": {
    "context": {
      "contextType": ["GLUE_JOB"],
      "jobName": ["JB_dataquality"]
    },
    "state": ["FAILED"]
  }
}
```

For more details on configuring rules and extracting information using the `get_data_quality_result` API, visit this page:

https://docs.aws.amazon.com/glue/latest/dg/data-quality-alerts
.html#data-quality-alerts-eventbridge

It is not mandatory to use AWS Lambda in the architecture. You can directly push the notification from Amazon EventBridge to the target email address via Amazon SNS. However, while sending the email notification to the stakeholder, you can format the output of the email using AWS Lambda. In this manner, you can send customized messages in a more readable format. Please refer to the code in the aforementioned web page for more about formatting the email with AWS Lambda.

If users seek a more streamlined approach, it is recommended to use Amazon EventBridge for data quality alerts, as it requires only a one-time setup to alert users. However, we recognize that some users might prefer using Amazon CloudWatch due to their familiarity with the service. To cater to these preferences, AWS offers integration with Amazon CloudWatch.

Extended Use Cases

There are a couple of extended use cases that are helpful to know about.

Visualization and Data Reconciliation   While we established that high-quality data serves as a bedrock for building a robust data governance framework, data quality results can also be incorporated into the business intelligence dashboards to visualize the data flow (e.g., ingested records vs. target records).

Data Monetization   When data is being shared to internal and external parties, both within and outside the organization, for monetization, embedding data quality as a core feature builds consumer trust and ultimately drives product adoption. This also leads to increased incentives for the data producer to maintain high-quality data.

Summary

This chapter provided a comprehensive overview of data transformation techniques on AWS. We began by exploring the history of ETL, its various mechanisms, and the different approaches, including traditional ETL and Zero-ETL.

We then delved into various AWS services for data transformation, such as AWS Lambda, Amazon Athena, Amazon Redshift, AWS Glue, Amazon EMR, Amazon Managed Service for Apache Flink (MSF), and Amazon Data Firehose. We compared and contrasted batch processing and stream processing, helping you choose the right service for your specific use case.

We discussed Apache Spark and Apache Flink, recommending when to use each framework. The sections also included performance optimizations and cost-saving strategies for each of the data transformation services used.

We also covered data access techniques using JDBC and ODBC connections. Looking beyond data transformation, we discussed API Gateway, which acts as a secure frontend service, allowing controlled client access to data. We also compared and contrasted Docker, virtual machines, ECS, EKS, and ECR.

Additionally, we explored low-code/no-code data transformations using AWS Glue Data-Brew. Finally, we concluded the chapter by discussing how AWS Glue Data Quality helps improve the quality of both in-transit and at-rest data.

Exam Essentials

Be able to select the right AWS services to apply data transformations.   AWS Lambda is a serverless compute service for running code without provisioning servers. It supports multiple programming languages and is ideal for event-driven and short-running tasks. AWS Glue ETL is a fully managed ETL service that supports batch and streaming workloads.

It uses Apache Spark and Ray for processing. It also integrates with AWS Glue Data Catalog for metadata management. It offers both code- and visual-based job creation. Amazon Athena is a serverless query service for analyzing data in Amazon S3 and is useful for ad hoc queries and data exploration. You can run SQL-based queries or Apache Spark analytics workloads using Amazon Athena. Amazon Redshift is a fully managed, petabyte scale data warehouse that uses columnar storage for optimized query performance. It offers Redshift Spectrum for querying data directly in S3. For streaming workloads, Amazon Managed Service for Apache Flink supports real-time processing and complex event processing. Amazon Data Firehose supports data transformation using Lambda services. It delivers real-time streaming data to destinations such as Amazon S3, Amazon Redshift, Amazon OpenSearch, Splunk, and custom HTTP endpoints.

Know the benefits of container services on AWS.   Amazon ECS is a fully managed container orchestration service that supports Docker containers. It offers two launch types: EC2 and AWS Fargate. Amazon EKS is a fully managed Kubernetes service that simplifies the development, management, and scaling of containerized applications using Kubernetes on AWS. It provides a highly available and secure Kubernetes control plane while allowing users to run Kubernetes worker nodes on EC2 instances or in a serverless environment using AWS Fargate. Amazon ECS is a fully managed Docker container registry that makes it easy to store, manage, and deploy container images. It integrates seamlessly with Amazon ECS and Amazon EKS to provide secure and scalable storage for Docker images, and provides private repositories with fine-grained access controls.

Understand API-driven data pipelines.   Amazon API Gateway is a fully managed service for creating, publishing, and securing scalable APIs, supporting REST and WebSocket protocols.

Know the methods and services to apply data validation checks.   AWS Glue Data Quality integrates seamlessly with AWS Glue ETL jobs and allows you to define, run, and monitor data quality rules as part of the data processing workloads.

Review Questions

1. A data engineer uses an AWS Glue job to process many small JSON files from Amazon S3. Today, the job also outputs many small files to S3. The data engineer would like to create large partitions in S3 while rewriting the job without significantly impacting the processing time. Which solution will meet the requirements?

    A. Set the groupSize parameter of the AWS Glue job to a larger value.

    B. Configure workload partitioning on the AWS Glue job using the boundedSize parameter.

    C. Choose a different worker type with higher DPUs and rerun the AWS Glue job.

    D. Perform a repartition in the AWS Glue job before writing to Amazon S3.

2. A data engineer needs to apply ETL transformations only on the latest ingested files in Amazon S3. Which service can he choose to achieve this with the *least* operational overhead?

    A. AWS Step Functions

    B. AWS Glue

    C. AWS Lambda

    D. Amazon EMR

3. A data engineer attempts to run an AWS Glue job to read data from Amazon S3. However, after a few minutes, the job fails with an out-of-memory error. Which solution will resolve the error?

    A. Increase the MaxRetries variable in the AWS Glue job definition.

    B. Increase the timeout limit in the AWS Glue job definition.

    C. Enable autoscaling.

    D. Define predicate pushdowns in the AWS Glue job.

4. A company using an on-premises Hadoop cluster for various batch processing jobs (Spark, TensorFlow, MXNet, Hive, Presto) anticipates a data surge. They want to migrate to AWS for scalable and durable storage. However, they want to reuse their existing jobs. Which solution will meet these requirements *most* cost effectively?

    A. Migrate to Amazon EMR. Store the data in Amazon S3. Launch transient EMR clusters when jobs need to run.

    B. Migrate to Amazon EMR. Store all the data in HDFS. Add more core nodes on-demand.

    C. Re-architect the solution with the serverless offering of AWS Glue.

    D. Migrate to Amazon Redshift. Use Amazon Redshift RA3 instances for frequently used data and Amazon S3 for infrequent data access and to optimize the storage cost.

5. You are tasked with implementing data quality checks for a massive dataset stored in Amazon S3. However, cost efficiency is a major concern. Which approach would be *most* suitable using AWS Glue Data Quality?

    A. Create a long-running AWS Glue ETL job that continuously scans the entire S3 dataset for quality issues.

    B. Leverage an AWS Glue data pipeline with a full data transformation and cleaning job, ensuring complete data checks.

    C. Configure Amazon Athena with the S3 bucket and write complex data queries to identify issues.

    D. Create an AWS Glue ETL job and leverage Glue job bookmarks to incrementally scan newly arriving data. Apply data quality checks on the incremental dataset and periodically run the Glue job at scheduled interval.

6. In an oil and gas company, a data analyst needs to implement anomaly detection on the pressure sensor data stream collected by Kinesis Data Streams. While Lambda can trigger the valve actions, the focus is on cost-effective anomaly detection within the data stream. Which of the following solutions would be recommended?

    A. Launch a Spark streaming application using Amazon EMR cluster and connect to Amazon Kinesis Data Streams. Use an ML algorithm to identify the anomaly. Spark will send an alert to open the valve if an anomaly is discovered.

    B. Use the RANDOM_CUT_FOREST function in the Amazon Managed Service for Apache Flink to detect the anomaly and send an alert to open the valve.

    C. Use Amazon Data Firehose and choose Amazon S3 as the data lake storage of the sensors data. Create a Lambda function to schedule the query of Amazon Athena in S3 query. The Lambda function will send an alert to open the valve if an anomaly is discovered.

    D. Provision an EC2 fleet with the KCL application to consume the stream and aggregate the data collected by the sensors to detect the anomaly.

7. A game retailer stores massive amounts (several TBs) of user purchase data in a 3-month window on a MySQL RDS instance. The retailer analyzes this recent data frequently. However, older historical data is needed for quarterly trend reports, requiring joins with the recent data. What is the most cost-effective and performant solution for this scenario?

    A. Use AWS Glue to perform the ETL and incrementally load a year's worth of data into Amazon Redshift. Regularly run queries against Redshift. Catalog the data in Amazon S3 and use Amazon Athena to join the historical and current data to generate the reports.

    B. Set up a Multi-AZ RDS database and run automated snapshots on the standby instance. Configure Amazon Athena to run historical queries on an S3 bucket containing automated snapshots.

    C. Use an RDS read replica to sync a year's worth of data. Export the older historical data into Amazon S3 for long-term storage. From the data in S3 and Amazon RDS, create a data catalog using AWS Glue and use Amazon Athena to join historical and current data to generate the reports.

    D. Schedule the export of your data from Amazon RDS to Amazon S3 every day. Load a year's worth of data in Amazon Redshift and use it for regular queries. Join the historical data and current data using Amazon Redshift Spectrum to generate the trend reports.

8. A travel and media company wants to build a data lake on Amazon S3. The raw data needs to undergo data transformations for the data analysts to create reports. Daily scheduled transformations will handle 500 GB of mixed-format data, while one-time transformations will handle terabytes of archived data. The company seeks a cost-effective solution that meets the requirement. How can it achieve this? (Choose three.)

    A. Run data transformations on daily incoming data using AWS Glue.

    B. Scan and identify the schema of daily incoming data using Amazon Athena.

    C. Instantiate an Amazon EMR cluster to perform a one-time data transformation on the archived data.

    D. Run data transformations on daily incoming data using Amazon Redshift.

    E. Use an Amazon SageMaker notebook instance to perform data transformation on the archived data.

    F. Scan and identify the schema of daily incoming data using an AWS Glue crawler.

9. A data scientist is developing a REST API for internal applications. Currently, every API call that is made to the application is logged in JSON format to an HTTP endpoint. What is the recommended low-code approach to stream the JSON data into S3 in Parquet format?

    A. Set up Kinesis Data Stream to ingest the data and use Amazon Data Firehose as the delivery stream. Once the data is ingested into S3, use an AWS Glue job to convert the JSON data to the Parquet format.

    B. Use Amazon Data Firehose as the delivery stream. Enable a record transformation that references a table stored in Apache Hive Metastore in EMR.

    C. Use Amazon Data Firehose as the delivery stream. Enable a record transformation that references a table stored in AWS Glue Data Catalog, defining the schema for your source records.

    D. Use Amazon EMR to process streaming data. Create a Spark job to convert the JSON to Parquet using Apache Hive Metastore to determine the schema of the JSON data.

10. A data engineer must create a solution where they need to move the data from Amazon S3 to a standalone Amazon Redshift database for analysis. Then, the data needs to be transferred back to Amazon S3 for archiving purposes. Which solution meets this requirement?

    A. Use AWS DMS to transfer the data between Amazon S3 and Amazon Redshift.

    B. Use the Amazon Redshift COPY command to load the data from S3 to Redshift. Use the UNLOAD command to load the data back to Amazon S3.

    C. Use Amazon Redshift Spectrum to load the data from Amazon S3 to Amazon Redshift. Use the UNLOAD command to load the data back to Amazon S3.

    D. Use Amazon S3 Transfer Acceleration to transfer the data between Amazon S3 and Amazon Redshift.

11. For compliance reasons, a company needs to delete records from an Amazon S3 data lake once it reaches its retention limit. Which solution will meet the requirement with the *least* operational overhead?

    A. Copy the data from Amazon S3 to Amazon Redshift to delete the records.

    B. Configure the tables by using the Apache Hudi format and use Amazon Athena to delete the records.

C. Configure the tables by using the Apache Iceberg format and use Amazon Redshift Spectrum to delete the records.

D. Configure the tables by using the Apache Iceberg format and use Amazon Athena to delete the records.

12. A marketing firm manages the social media activity for a client. The posts are collected in Amazon Kinesis Data Streams, and its shards are partitioned based on the username. Posts from each user need to be validated in the same order they are received before being transferred to an Amazon OpenSearch cluster. Recently, a data analyst observed a delay in the display of the posts in the OpenSearch service, with posts taking more than 30 minutes to appear during peak hours. What should the data analyst do to reduce the latency issues?

A. Use AWS Lambda functions to process the data from Kinesis Data Streams using the Parallelization Factor feature.

B. Reshard the stream to increase the number of shards and change the partition key to social media post views.

C. Use an HTTP/2 stream consumer instead of the standard data stream iterator.

D. Use Amazon Data Firehose to read and validate the posts before transferring them to Amazon OpenSearch.

13. A company has moved its data transformation job to an Amazon EMR cluster with Apache Pig. The cluster uses on-demand instances to process large datasets. The output is critical to operations. It usually takes 1 hour to complete the job, and the company must ensure that the whole process adheres to the SLA of 2 hours. The company is looking for a solution that will provide cost reduction and negligibly impact availability. Which combination of solutions can be implemented to meet the requirements? (Choose two).

A. Add a task node that runs on a Spot instance.

B. Configure an EMR cluster that uses instance groups.

C. Use a Spot instance for all node types.

D. Configure an EMR cluster that uses instance fleets.

E. Assign Spot capacity for all node types and enable the switch to the on-demand instance option.

14. A company needs a data analyst to prepare and clean the data from an Amazon RDS PostgreSQL database. The data will be used for visualizations. The data processing involves finding the missing values, filtering the data records, and masking the PII data. The data analyst needs to do these modifications with minimal effort in the code. Which of these services would be recommended as a low-code/no-code data processing solution for the analyst?

A. AWS Glue

B. Amazon EMR

C. Amazon Athena

D. AWS Glue DataBrew

15. A data engineer has custom Python scripts that perform common formatting logic, which is used by many Lambda functions. If there is any need to modify the Python scripts, the data engineer must manually update all the Lambda functions. Which solution will meet the requirement, requiring less manual intervention to update the Lambda functions?

    A. Package the common Python script into Lambda layers. Apply the Lambda layers to the Lambda functions.

    B. Assign aliases to the Lambda functions.

    C. Store a pointer to a custom Python script in environment variables in a shared S3 bucket.

    D. Combine multiple Lambda functions into one Lambda function.

16. A data engineer needs to analyze the quality and consistency of a dataset before it is ingested into the data warehouse. The data engineer wants to use AWS Glue DataBrew to also run the profiling on the dataset. Which solution will meet these requirements with the *least* operational overhead?

    A. Use outlier detection to flag unusual data points.

    B. Use the PyDeequ framework to apply data quality rules on the dataset.

    C. Use data quality rules to validate the threshold values and define constraints.

    D. Use data quality checks for value distribution statistics to calculate the metrics such as standard deviation.

17. A financial services company stores its data in Amazon Redshift. A data engineer wants to run real-time queries on financial data to support a web-based trading application. The engineer would like to run the queries from within the trading application. Which solution offers the *least* operational overhead?

    A. Unload the data to Amazon S3 and use S3 Select to run the queries.

    B. Configure and set up JDBC connection to Amazon Redshift.

    C. Establish WebSocket connections to Amazon Redshift.

    D. Use Amazon Redshift Data API.

    E. Unload the data to Amazon S3 and use Amazon Athena to run the queries.

18. A data engineer needs to schedule a workflow that runs a set of Glue jobs every day. However, these workloads are not time-sensitive. Which is the *most* cost-effective solution?

    A. Choose the STANDARD execution class in the Glue job properties.

    B. Use the Spot instance type in the Glue job properties.

    C. Choose the FLEX execution class in the Glue job properties.

    D. Enable the Auto scaling mode in the Glue job properties.

19. A marketing team is building a data pipeline using AWS Glue to ingest customer clickstream data from various web applications. The data is stored in JSON format on Amazon S3. The team wants to ensure the data quality before feeding it into the marketing analytics dashboard. Which of the following functionalities within AWS Glue can be used to define data quality rules and monitor the quality of the customer clickstream data before it reaches the dashboard? (Choose two).

   A. AWS Glue Data Catalog

   B. AWS Glue DataBrew

   C. AWS Glue Crawler

   D. AWS Glue Workflows

20. A company is planning to migrate a legacy Hadoop cluster running on-premises to AWS. The cluster must use the latest EMR release and include its custom scripts and workflows during the migration. The data engineer must reuse the existing Java application code on-premises in the new EMR cluster. Which of these solutions is the recommended approach?

   A. Submit a `PIG` step in the EMR cluster and compile the Java program using the version of the cluster.

   B. Submit a `STREAMING` step in the EMR cluster and compile the Java program using the version of the cluster.

   C. Submit a `spark-submit` step in the EMR cluster and compile the Java program using the version of the cluster.

   D. Submit a `CUSTOM_JAR` step in the EMR cluster and compile the Java program using the version of the cluster.

Chapter

4

Storage Services

**THE AWS CERTIFIED DATA ENGINEER –
ASSOCIATE EXAM OBJECTIVES COVERED
IN THIS CHAPTER MAY INCLUDE, BUT ARE
NOT LIMITED TO, THE FOLLOWING:**

✓ **Domain 2: Data Store Management**

- Task 2.1 Choose a data store

- Task 2.3 Manage the lifecycle of data

Introduction to Data Stores

Choosing a data store is a critical phase in the data engineering lifecycle that follows the data ingestion phase, when data has been collected and now requires a platform where it can be stored, processed, and analyzed. This chapter focuses on AWS storage services and their characteristics, how to choose and configure them for performance based on use case/access patterns, and aligning them with data migration requirements.

Storage Platforms

Storage infrastructure is one of the key components of a data platform. There are three main cloud storage types, each with its own use cases and advantages: object storage, file storage, and block storage.

Object Storage

Object storage stores and manages data in an unstructured format called objects. The AWS object store is called Amazon S3. The benefits of object storage include its unlimited scalability, together with the low cost of storing large volumes of data for various use cases such as data lakes, log files, machine learning, and analytics. When working with data, it is important that you do not lose data, and, in the event that something happens, you are able to recover it successfully (resilience). Furthermore, you must be able to keep the data in good condition over a long period (durability). This is another benefit offered by object storage, which is achieved by storing the data on multiple devices, across multiple systems, and across multiple data centers and regions.

Object storage is the main storage of the cloud, which is suitable for data lakes that require an architecture capable of supporting large amounts of data where each data piece is stored as an object that can be easily identified by the object metadata. Object metadata is information that describes and explains the (object) data that is stored, and is used for discovery and identification. Object metadata explains the origin of the data, its nature, and its lineage. Without having seen the data, from the metadata, you will be able to know its origin, type, and lineage. A good metadata analogy is a book, where the data is the content of the book, while the metadata is the title, the subject, the format, the publication date, and the author.

Data lakes are an important part of a data lake architecture, and object storage is the ideal type for them. Object storage is able to deliver an architecture for large amounts of data where each data piece is stored as an object, with the object metadata providing a unique identifier for it. This removes the scaling limitations that are common with traditional file types.

Object Storage Importance

As the storage of the cloud, object storage is critical to a modern data architecture, as it supports the growth requirements of businesses that manage rapidly expanding data pools from many sources. This data is used by many applications, end users, and business processes. It is mostly unstructured, comes in different formats, and does not ordinarily fit into a central repository. Because of this, the data is inaccessible for analytics, machine learning, or cloud native applications, which slows down innovation and adds complexity. This is where object storage performs well, as it breaks down the many silos caused by the different source systems and provides a central, scalable, and cost-effective storage system that can store all data types in their native formats. It delivers unlimited storage capacity, scalability, and high durability at low per-gigabyte prices while making the data accessible from anywhere.

Use Cases

This section discusses some common use cases for object storage.

Analytics

Object stores allow you to store an unlimited amount of data of any type in the cloud, enabling you to perform big data analytics to get insights about customers, operations, or the market you are serving.

Data Lake

As a central repository for structured and unstructured data, a data lake requires a storage medium that is highly scalable, which an object store is able to provide. The object store allows the data lake to have access to unlimited capacity, and an organization can have one single place that meets their data storage requirements.

Backup and Recovery

Object stores provide a suitable environment to store backup data from your applications. You can configure the object store to replicate data so that if there's a failure in the source system, the duplicate object store becomes available and applications can run without interruptions. You can also replicate data in object stores across data centers and geographical regions to make it available closer to customers and your internal users in the desired geographical region.

Data Archiving

Cloud object storage is suitable for long-term storage and can be used to replace your current on-premises solutions. It's a cost-effective archive that allows you to retain large amounts of data at low costs and ensures that regulatory requirements are adhered to. It provides solutions that offer better data durability, reduce the effort required to manage additional hardware and software, are more secure, and provide better accessibility for advanced analytics and business intelligence.

Machine Learning

Machine learning models typically require millions or billions of example data items to train and produce inferences and predictions. Cloud object storage provides the storage platform for this large amount of data at a low cost while being highly scalable.

Cloud-Native Application Data

Object storage provides data management for cloud native applications that use technologies such as serverless and containerization to meet customer expectations. Customers demand flexibility and speed from these applications, which are typically made of independent, small, loosely coupled architectures called *microservices* that benefit from object storage to support quick deployment and greater customer reach.

Rich Media

Media files, such as music, video, and digital images, are normally large, costly to store, and slow to render across the Internet. Object storage allows you to overcome these restrictions by enabling you to create a global architecture that renders media files to users using the different storage classes and replication features found with object stores.

For a good summary of object storage, see `https://aws.amazon.com/what-is/ object-storage`.

Block Storage

Applications that require efficient, fast, and reliable data access normally use block storage. Block storage works by taking data and then dividing it into blocks of equal sizes. This data block is then stored by the block storage system on underlying physical storage that optimizes it for faster access and retrieval. With this type of storage, you have direct access to the data, while file storage has a file system as a layer to process before the data can be accessed.

Benefits of Block Storage

This section discusses the benefits of block storage.

Performance

As previously explained, metadata is additional data that describes the primary data. Think of a book's title, subject, format, and author as metadata, while the book's content is the actual data. Metadata relies on unique identifiers assigned to each block for read/write operations. Unlike object stores, block storage uses limited metadata, allowing for efficient data access and retrieval. This limited metadata enables block storage to deliver very low latency, which is required for high-performance workloads. An additional feature of block storage architecture is that it provides multiple paths to data, making it the preferred storage for high-performance applications.

Flexibility and Scalability

Block storage allows individual blocks to be configured for different operating systems, such as Linux and Windows, and is not constrained to specific network environments, making it highly flexible. The architecture is also highly scalable, as it allows developers to add new blocks as additional capacity needs arise.

Frequent Modification

Block storage supports frequent data writes without affecting performance, as it only rewrites the selected block with new data, not the entire file. It does this by identifying the block that needs to be modified and then rewriting the data in that block.

Granular Control

Block storage allows developers to optimize performance by grouping the fast-changing data on specific blocks and storing static files on other files. This results in improved system performance, as updates only affect the small number of blocks being modified, not an entire file. To achieve performance gains, you can use tiering, whereby you store fast-changing data on high-performance solid state disks (SSDs) while putting warm or colder data on lower-cost (and slower) hard drives (HHDs).

Block Storage Key Use Cases

The unique characteristics of block storage make it a preferred option for transitional, mission-critical, and I/O-intensive applications. A variety of applications, including relational databases, time series databases, containers, boot disks and hypervisor file systems, are suitable for block storage. This section discusses the key use cases of block storage.

Storage Area Networks

Most organizations implement a SAN architecture, which is a specialized high-speed network that connects multiple storage devices to provide a centralized storage infrastructure. Developers often deploy block storage as part of a SAN architecture that is accessible to multiple applications/servers simultaneously. This ensures that data is retrieved quickly and efficiently, which improves business operations.

Containers

Block storage is also used to store containerized applications in cloud environments, as it provides flexibility, scalability, and the efficiency required for container deployments. Block storage allows developers to migrate containers seamlessly between servers, locations, and operating system environments.

Transactional Workloads

Block storage is also used to set up robust, scalable transactional databases that are highly efficient, as each block is a self-contained unit that can be hosted on different servers. These blocks provide databases with storage for processing time-sensitive and mission-critical stores that require low latency, high capacity, and fault tolerance. To protect against data loss and ensure data redundancy, organizations implement Redundant Array of Independent Disks (RAID) to secure the block storage. The RAID systems back up data in secondary storage to ensure data recover in the event of a disk failure. For mission-critical applications, data loss is not tolerated. Imagine losing transaction data for your online retailer business.

Analytics and Data Warehousing

Block storage is also used with Hadoop Distributed File System (HDFS) to store data as independent units, enabling high performance for Hadoop and Kafka analytics applications.

Virtual Machines

Another usage of block storage is in supporting virtual machines (VMs), allowing users to install computing resources such as operating systems and file systems on block storage volumes. These volumes can be easily increased, decreased, or transferred between hosts.

For a good summary of block storage, see `https://aws.amazon.com/what-is/block-storage`.

Cloud File Storage

This method of storing data in the cloud provides applications and servers with access to data through shared file systems. This type of storage is ideal for workloads that rely on shared file systems, such as web serving, content management, analytics, development tools, media and entertainment, home directories, database backups, and storage for containers.

An important feature of a cloud file system is that it provides shared access to file data, allowing users to create, modify, access, or delete files. This feature of allowing shared access to modify the same file enables collaboration, which improves productivity and innovation. An ideal cloud file storage system must be fully managed, provide high performance, integrate easily with other applications, and be secure, highly available, and cost-effective.

AWS provides several fully managed cloud file storage services, including Amazon Elastic File System (Amazon EFS), Amazon FSx for NetApp ONTAP, Amazon FSx for Lustre, Amazon FSx for OpenZFS, and Amazon FSx for Windows File Server.

For a good summary of cloud file storage, see `https://aws.amazon.com/what-is/cloud-file-storage`.

Comparison of Storage Types

For a quick comparison of the differences between object storage, block storage, and file storage, see Figure 4.1.

FIGURE 4.1   The differences between object, block, and file storage

Summary of differences: object vs. block vs. file storage

	Object storage	Block storage	Cloud file storage
File management	Store files as objects. Accessing files in object storage with existing applications requires new code and the use of APIs.	Can store files but requires additional budget and management resources to support files on block storage.	Supports common file-level protocols and permissions models. Usable by applications configured to work with shared file storage.
Metadata management	Can store unlimited metadata for any object. Define custom metadata fields.	Uses very little associated metadata.	Stores limited metadata relevant to files only.
Performance	Stores unlimited data with minimal latency.	High-performance, low latency, and rapid data transfer.	Offers high performance for shared file access.
Physical storage	Distributed across multiple storage nodes.	Distributed across SSDs and HDDs.	On-premises NAS servers or over underlying physical block storage.
Scalability	Unlimited scale.	Somewhat limited.	Somewhat limited.

Data Storage Formats

Data can be stored in different types of file formats, each impacting workload efficiency. It is important that you select the file format that gives the best performance for your workload and data pipeline. Choosing the correct file format type can impact whether you wait for milliseconds for an answer or you wait for minutes.

One key aspect to note when dealing with organizing data is that it can be stored either in row format (which is the common format) or in columnar format. Each format has its use cases, with the most common being that row format is suitable for OLTP databases, while columnar storage is suitable for OLAP databases.

Some of the common file formats are JSON, CSV, TXT, Avro, Parquet, and Optimized Row Columnar (ORC). For big data workloads, the common file formats include Avro, Parquet, and OCR due to their superior performance capabilities, which are required when dealing with very large amounts of data. With that said, Parquet is the most common file type for big data analytics workloads.

When choosing file formats, it is important that you consider the following

- Choose a file format based on write frequency.

- Choose a file format based on your data access patterns.

- You must utilize a compression technique that decreases storage requirements and also enhances I/O efficiency. This can improve performance, as there are fewer bytes transferred between the disk and the compute layers. Note, however, that when you compress data, you require more compute to compress and decompress the data.

- You must partition your data to enable data pruning, which reduces the need to read unnecessary files and hence improves the performance of your applications.

Table 4.1 provides a comparison of the three common file types used with big data workloads.

TABLE 4.1   Big data workload file types

	Avro	ORC	Parquet
Format Type	Row-based	Columnar	Columnar
Year Introduced	2009	2013	2013
Self-describing	Yes	No	Yes
Schema Evolution	Supports	Supports	Supports
Compression	Good	Excellent	Excellent
Splitable	Yes	Yes	Yes
Ideal Use Case	Write-heavy operations	Read-heavy operations, Hive workloads	Analytics, complex nested data
Language Support	Language-neutral	Primarily Hive	Multiple (Java, C++, Python)
Compression Options	Uncompressed, Snappy, Deflate, Bzip2, XZ	Snappy, zlib	Multiple flexible options
ACID Support	No	Yes (with Hive)	No
Predicate Pushdown	No	Yes	Yes
Data Skipping	No	Yes	Yes
Complex Data Types	Supports	Supports	Supports
Optimization For	Hadoop ecosystem	Hive	Spark, various query engines

	Avro	ORC	Parquet
Storage Efficiency	Good	Very Good	Very Good
Query Performance	Good	Very Good	Excellent

To learn more about the differences between row and columnar storage on a database table, see `https://docs.aws.amazon.com/redshift/latest/dg/c_columnar_storage_disk_mem_mgmnt.html`.

Storage Services and Configurations for Specific Performance Demands

AWS offers a wide range of storage services that you can use to store, access, protect, and analyze your data. These services provide reliability, scalability, and security for your data, making it easy to match your storage methods with your needs. It is important to select a storage service that aligns with your access patterns to ensure that you get the performance required to meet your SLAs. Figure 4.2 provides an overview of data storage solutions on AWS, and Table 4.2 examines which services or tools are suited for each type of storage.

FIGURE 4.2   Overview of data storage solutions on AWS

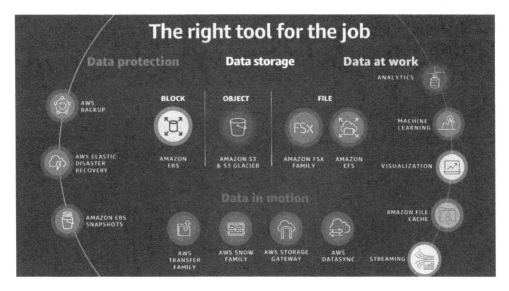

TABLE 4.2   Storage services and tools for storage types

Storage Type	Optimized For	Storage Services or Tools
Block	Block storage is optimized for low latency and high performance. It is easy to use and scales quickly to meet high performance requirements. It is typically attached to single Amazon EC2 instances or containers and is suitable for applications such as databases and ERP systems. It can also be used as local storage for instances.	Amazon EBS, Amazon EC2 instance store
File system	The file system storage type is optimized for workloads and applications that require shared read and write access across multiple hosts. It supports both cloud and on-premises hosts, such as Amazon EC2 instances or containers, as well as multiple on-premises servers. This makes it suitable for team file shares, analytics workloads, machine learning training, and highly available enterprise applications.	Amazon EFS, Amazon FSx, Amazon FSx for Lustre, Amazon FSx for NetApp ONTAP, Amazon FSx for OpenZFS, Amazon FSx for Windows File Server, Amazon S3 File Gateway, Amazon FSx File Gateway
Object	Object storage is ideal for read-heavy workloads such as content delivery, big data analytics, web hosting, and machine learning processes. It excels in scenarios where large volumes of data need to be stored, accessed, and distributed globally over the internet, making it a versatile solution for businesses with diverse data management needs. Consider this option when you need an affordable and very large, centralized data store that allows you to store all sorts of data types.	Amazon S3
Cache	Cache storage is a high-speed, fully managed, and scalable caching solution used for processing file data. It seamlessly integrates with diverse storage locations, which can be either on-premises or cloud-based. It works with on-premises NFS file systems, cloud-based file systems (such as Amazon FSx for OpenZFS and NetApp ONTAP), and object storage (like Amazon S3).	Amazon File Cache
Hybrid/ edge	Hybrid/edge storage is optimized to provide low-latency data access between on-premises and cloud environments for on-premises applications. These applications also gain access to cloud-backed storage.	AWS Storage Gateway Tape Gateway, AWS Storage Gateway Volume Gateway

Source: https://docs.aws.amazon.com/decision-guides/latest/storage-on-aws-how-to-choose/choosing-aws-storage-service.html

Amazon Simple Storage Service

Amazon Simple Storage Service (Amazon S3) is an object storage service used by customers of all sizes and industries. It offers scalability, data availability, security, and performance. It can be used to store and protect any amount of data for multiple use cases, such as data lakes, websites, backups, archives, applications, IOT devices, and big data analytics. Some of the key features of S3 include:

- As an object store, Amazon S3 stores objects in buckets.
- An object is a file and any metadata that describes the file.
- A bucket is a container for objects.
- To store data in S3, you must first create a bucket and specify the bucket name and AWS Region. Then you upload your data to the bucket as objects.
- Each object has a key (key name), which is a unique identifier within the bucket.
- S3 buckets and the objects in them are private by default and can be accessed only if you explicitly grant access permissions.
- Access permissions are granted using bucket policies, AWS Identity and Access Management (IAM) policies, access control lists (ACLs), and S3 access points.

  Figure 4.3 provides an overview of how Amazon S3 works.

FIGURE 4.3   How Amazon S3 works

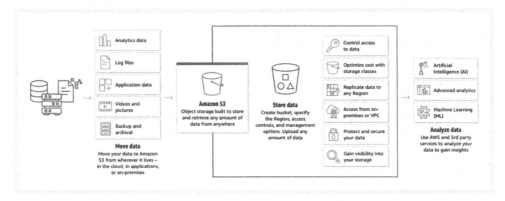

Source: Amazon Web Services / `https://docs.aws.amazon.com/AmazonS3/latest/userguide/Welcome.html`, last accessed on 19 December 2024.

The following sections dive deeper into the features of Amazon S3.

S3 Storage Classes

Amazon S3 offers different storage classes for different use cases. The classes provide you with different capabilities, such as retrieval performance, cost optimizations, and data durability, and also suitability to different access patterns. The needs of organizations for their data storage vary and are not the same for the different systems and applications that require the data.

For example, archive data required for regulatory purposes and accessed only once a year does not require storage that gives millisecond access, whereas data used in a data warehouse or web application would require fast access storage. Additionally, there may be some applications that only require access to a copy of the data temporarily to execute processes, and then the copy can be deleted. This copy does not need to be in highly durable storage offering a Multi-AZ setup. It can be in a Single-AZ storage class, which could be cheaper than the Multi-AZ environment, as losing this copy of the data would not be impactful since you can restore it from an existing copy.

Table 4.3 explores in more detail the features and functionalities of the different storage classes.

Amazon S3 Store Management

Amazon S3 provides four storage management features that allow organizations to manage their data, enabling them to enforce some business requirements. With these management features, organizations can ensure that they can meet regulatory requirements (such as preventing objects from being deleted), reduce latency, manage costs, and save multiple distinct copies of data depending on the need. Table 4.4 explores these management features.

Access Management and Security

Security is a top priority for Amazon, and we ensure that this extends to the services we provide for our customers. Amazon S3 provides various features that can be used for auditing and access management of buckets and objects. By default, Amazon S3 buckets and objects inside them are private . You only have access to the S3 resources that you create unless explicit permissions are granted for access to other resources. To grant additional resource permissions for specific use cases and audit permissions, the features presented in Table 4.5 are available.

TABLE 4.3 Storage class features

Storage Class	Description	Designed For	Durability (designed for)	Availability (designed for)	AZs	Min storage duration	Min billable object size	Other considerations
S3 Standard	Default storage class; high durability, availability; performance	Frequently accessed mission-critical production data (more than once a month) with millisecond access	99.999999999%	99.99%	>= 3	None	None	None
S3 Express One Zone	High-performance; single-zone storage; lowest latency	Single-digit milli-second data access for latency-sensitive applications within a single AWS Availability Zone; data that needs the fastest possible access	99.999999999%	99.95%	1	None	None	S3 Express One Zone objects are stored in a single AWS Availability Zone that you choose.
S3 Standard-IA	Infrequently accessed data; lower cost than Standard	Long-lived, infrequently accessed data (once a month) with millisecond access; long-term storage, backups; disaster recovery files	99.999999999%	99.9%	>= 3	30 days	128 KB	Per-GB retrieval fees apply.

TABLE 4.3 Storage class features *(continued)*

Storage Class	Description	Designed For	Durability (designed for)	Availability (designed for)	Min storage duration AZs		Min billable object size	Other considerations
S3 One Zone-IA	Stores data in a Single AZ; lower cost than Standard-IA	Re-creatable, infrequently accessed data (once a month) with millisecond access	99.999999999%	99.5%	1	30 days	128 KB	Per-GB retrieval fees apply. Not resilient to the loss of the Availability Zone.
S3 Glacier Instant Retrieval	Lowest-cost storage for long-lived data accessed once per quarter	Long-lived, archive data needing immediate access that is accessed once a quarter with millisecond access	99.999999999%	99.9%	>= 3	90 days	128 KB	Per-GB retrieval fees apply.
S3 Glacier Flexible Retrieval	Very low-cost storage for archive data accessed 1–2 times per year	Long-lived archive data (backups) accessed once a year, with retrieval times of minutes to hours	99.999999999%	99.99% (after you restore objects)	>= 3	90 days	NA*	Per-GB retrieval fees apply. You must first restore archived objects before you can access them.

Storage Class	Description	Designed For	Durability (designed for)	Availability (designed for)	Min storage AZs duration	Min billable object size	Other considerations
S3 Glacier Deep Archive	Lowest-cost storage class for data accessed less than once per year	Long-lived/long-term archive data accessed less than once a year, with retrieval times of hours	99.99999999%	99.99% (after you restore objects)	>= 3 180 days	NA**	Per-GB retrieval fees apply. You must first restore archived objects before you can access them.
S3 Intelligent-Tiering	Automatically moves data between access tiers	Data with unknown, changing, or unpredictable access patterns	99.99999999%	99.9%	>= 3 None	None	Monitoring and automation fees per object apply. No retrieval fees.
RRS (not recommended)		Noncritical, frequently accessed data with millisecond access	99.99%	99.99%	>= 3 None	None	None

TABLE 4.4 Amazon S3 storage management features

Feature	Description
S3 Life-cycle	This feature allows you to configure lifecycle rules for objects in Amazon S3, managing them cost-effectively throughout their lifecycle. You can transition objects between storage classes based on business needs, and delete or expire objects when they are no longer required (end of lifetime).
S3 Object Lock	This feature enables you to prevent S3 objects from being overwritten or deleted, whether by mistake or intentionally. It can be used as an additional protection layer against deletions and can also facilitate regulatory compliance that requires write-once-read-many (WORM) storage.
S3 Replication	This feature allows you to automatically copy (replicate) your data (objects), along with their metadata and tags, between S3 buckets in the same or different regions. It is useful for regulatory compliance, reducing latency, and improving security.
S3 Batch Operations	This feature provides a simplified and scalable way to manage large amounts (billions) of objects using a single API request or a few steps in the Amazon S3 console. You can perform operations such as invoking AWS Lambda functions, restoring billions of objects, and copying data (COPY).

TABLE 4.5 Amazon S3 permissions features

Feature	Description
S3 Block Public Access	This is a very important security feature that blocks public access to S3 buckets. It is turned on at the bucket level by default. As a security measure, we recommend keeping this feature enabled unless you have a clear use case that requires turning it off.
AWS Identity and Access Management (IAM)	IAM (Identity and Access Management) is used to secure and control access to AWS resources, including Amazon S3. It serves as a central point to manage permissions for accessing resources. IAM allows you to control who can sign in (authentication) and what permissions they have (authorization) to use the resources.
Bucket policies	This feature allows you to use the Identity and Access Management (IAM) policy language to configure resource-based permissions for your S3 buckets and their objects.
Amazon S3 access points	This feature allows you to create named access points (network endpoints) with specific policies to manage large-scale data access for shared datasets in Amazon S3.

Feature	Description
Access control lists (ACLs)	This capability grants authorized users in other accounts read and write permissions to individual buckets and objects. As a best practice, we advise that you use S3 resource-based policies or IAM user policies for access control, and we recommend that you keep ACLs disabled. There are scenarios where you would want to use ACLs, such as if a bucket owner allows other AWS accounts to upload objects. In these cases, permissions to these objects can only be managed using object ACL by the AWS account that owns the object. Some other limitations of ACLs are that you can't explicitly deny permissions or grant permissions to users in your account.
S3 Object Ownership	This bucket-level feature is designed to simplify and streamline access control for S3 buckets and objects. It addresses complexities that can arise when objects in a bucket are owned by different AWS accounts. It can be used to enable or disable ACLs, which are by default disabled. Disabling ACLs gives ownership of all the bucket objects to the bucket owner, allowing them to manage access exclusively by using access management policies.
IAM Access Analyzer for S3	This is a security feature that provides the capability to review and monitor S3 bucket access policies. It enables you to ensure that your policies have granted access as per intent, helping to identify and rectify any unintended public or cross-account access to your S3 resources.

Data Processing

Automatic data processing involving data transformations, and initiating workflows at scale is a key aspect of the role. Amazon S3 provides the following features to facilitate this at scale:

- **S3 Object Lambda:** This enables you to add your own code to S3 GET, HEAD, and LIST requests. With this capability, you can modify and process data as it is returned to an application. Some of the actions you can do include returning only specific rows through filtering, resizing images dynamically, and, as a key security feature, redacting confidential data.

- **Event notifications:** These are very useful, as they can be used to initiate workflows that use AWS Lambda, Amazon Simple Notification Service (Amazon SNS), and Amazon Simple Queue Service in response to changes made to your data. This can be a useful monitoring mechanism, especially to detect and respond to actions from bad actors or when there are actions that you want to take once a data update is made legally.

Storage Logging and Monitoring

When you manage resources, it is important that you are able to monitor and control how they are used. Amazon S3 provides both automated and manual monitoring tools to assist you in effectively managing your Amazon S3 resources and understanding how they are being used.

- **Automated monitoring tools:**
  - Amazon CloudWatch metrics for Amazon S3: This functionality enables you to monitor and assess the operational status of your Amazon S3 resources in real time. With these operational metrics, you can then configure alerts when defined thresholds are breached, allowing you to take responsive action.
  - AWS CloudTrail: This records bucket- and object-level API actions of AWS resources, such as a user, a role, or a service in Amazon S3.

- **Manual monitoring tools:**
  - Server access logging: This provides records for all requests that are made to an Amazon S3 bucket. The server access logs serve many purposes, including security and auditing. You can also use them to gain insights about your customer base and dive deeper into your Amazon S3 bill.
  - AWS Trusted Advisor: This allows you to analyze your account using AWS best practices to achieve cost and performance optimizations, improve security and resilience, and operate your environment at scale. AWS Trusted Advisor uses best practice checks and then provides recommendations to close gaps when there is deviation.

Analytics and Insights

As a data engineer, it is important to have visibility into your storage usage so that can you analyze and optimize it. This can lead to cost and performance benefits. Amazon S3 offers the following features to facilitate this:

- **Amazon S3 Storage Lens:** This provides you with organization-wide visibility into object storage usage and activity trends. It also provides actionable recommendations that can be used to optimize your storage and achieve cost reduction. With Amazon S3 Storage Lens, you can track more than 60 metrics across multiple accounts and buckets via an interactive dashboard in the S3 console.

- **Storage Class Analysis:** This enables you to analyze storage access patterns over time, which can help you decide when to transition the right data to the right storage class to achieve both improved performance and cost savings. To configure Storage Class Analysis, you use the Amazon S3 console, the AWS CLI, the REST API, or the AWS SDKs.

- **S3 Inventory with inventory reports:** This feature enables you to manage your storage by creating lists that you can audit and report on. You can create these lists of objects on a defined schedule, which are then published to a destination bucket in CSV, ORC, or Parquet files. An example of when this can be useful is to report on the replication status of the objects in your bucket.

Strong Consistency

As a distributed system, where data is often replicated across multiple nodes—sometimes in real time—and can be accessed by multiple processes concurrently, one of the challenges posed is maintaining data consistency. There are different consistency models that balance data consistency and system performance. Some of these models are

- **Strong consistency**: In this model, every read operation must return the most recent write operation.

- **Eventual consistency**: The system is allowed to be temporarily inconsistent, with the promise that eventually all reads will return the same most recent write operation.

- **Causal consistency**: This is a middle ground between eventual consistency and strong consistency, where related events are seen by all processes in the same order while unrelated events can be seen in any order.

According to the AWS User Guide, Amazon S3 provides "strong read-after-write consistency for PUT and DELETE requests of objects in your Amazon S3 bucket in all AWS Regions. This behavior applies to both writes of new objects as well as PUT requests that overwrite existing objects and DELETE requests. In addition, read operations on Amazon S3 Select, Amazon S3 access control lists (ACLs), Amazon S3 Object Tags, and object metadata (for example, the HEAD object) are strongly consistent." (Source: `https://docs.aws` `.amazon.com/AmazonS3/latest/userguide/Welcome.html#ConsistencyModel`)

Another important characteristic to note is that updates to a single key are atomic (i.e., they either complete or don't complete); hence, there is never any partiality, where it partially completes. For example, if you make a PUT request to an existing key from one process and then perform a GET request on the same key from a second process concurrently, you will either:

- Get the old data or new data.

- You will never get partial or corrupted data.

Let's take a look at some examples that show this behavior in action:

- A process writes a new object to Amazon S3 and immediately lists keys within its bucket. The new object appears in the list.

- A process replaces an existing object and immediately tries to read it. Amazon S3 will return the new data.

- A process deletes an existing object and immediately tries to read it. Amazon S3 will not return any data, as the object has been deleted.

- A process deletes an existing object and immediately lists keys within its bucket. The object does not appear in the listing.

- Amazon S3 doesn't support object locking for concurrent writers. If two PUT requests are made simultaneously to the same key, only the request with the latest timestamp will be successful.

- Updates are based on single keys, and you cannot make atomic updates across keys. In practice, this means that you can't make an update to key2 dependent on an update to key1.

Bucket configurations have an eventually consistent model, which means that:

- When you delete a bucket and immediately list all buckets, the deleted bucket might still appear.

- Enabling versioning on a bucket for the first time can take a short while for the changes to be fully applied, and a 15-minute wait is encouraged before issuing PUT or DELETE requests on objects in the bucket.

Let's take a look at a few examples that illustrate the behavior of concurrent applications. The example in Figure 4.4 shows that we have two writes W1 (write 1) and W2 (write 2) that finish before the start of the reads R1 (read 1) and R2 (read 2). As mentioned earlier, since S3 is strongly consistent, the two reads will both return color = ruby.

FIGURE 4.4   Concurrent applications behavior—example 1

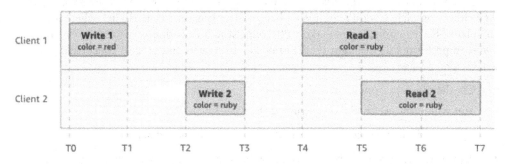

In the example in Figure 4.5, W2 is still writing when R1 starts. Therefore, R1 can return either color = ruby or color = garnet. However, because W1 and W2 finish before the start of R2, R2 will return color = garnet.

In the example in Figure 4.6, W2 starts before W1 has completed and received an acknowledgement, which means the two writes are considered as concurrent. In such situations, S3 internally uses last-writer-wins semantics to determine which write takes precedence. What then provides a challenge is that the order of S3 receiving the requests and the order in which the applications receive the acknowledgment cannot be predicted due to possible factors such as latency (i.e., if the two hosts are in different regions). In this case, it is best to determine the final value after both W1 and W2 have been acknowledged.

FIGURE 4.5   Concurrent applications behavior—example 2

Domain = MyDomain, Item = StandardFez

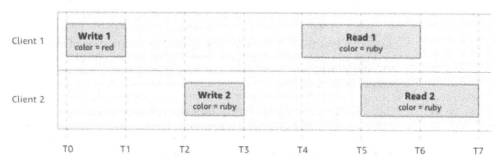

FIGURE 4.6   Concurrent applications behavior—example 3

Domain = MyDomain, Item = StandardFez

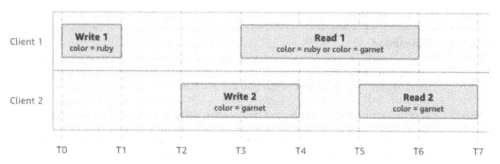

Accessing S3

Table 4.6 lists the various methods that can be used to access S3.

TABLE 4.6   S3 access methods

Access Method	Description
AWS Management Console	This is a web-based user interface for managing Amazon S3, where users sign in via the AWS Management Console and access the Amazon S3 console.
AWS Command Line Interface (AWS CLI)	Allows users to issue commands or build scripts at the command line to perform AWS tasks, including Amazon S3 operations.

TABLE 4.6   S3 access methods *(continued)*

Access Method	Description
AWS SDKs	AWS provides SDKs (software development kits) consisting of libraries and sample code for various programming languages and platforms. The AWS SDKs provide a convenient way to create programmatic access to Amazon S3.
Amazon S3 REST API	The architecture of Amazon S3 is designed to be programming language-neutral, using AWS-supported interfaces to store and retrieve objects. Users can access S3 and AWS programmatically by using the Amazon S3 REST API, which is an HTTP interface.

Table 4.7 lists the various S3 objects.

TABLE 4.7   S3 Objects

Component	Description
Key	This is the name that you assign to an object in an Amazon S3 bucket and is used to retrieve the object when you are accessing it.
Version ID	This is a string that is generated by Amazon S3 when you add an object to a bucket. The object key and version ID uniquely identify an object in the bucket. With versioning, you can keep multiple variants of an object in a bucket. This feature can be used to preserve, retrieve, and restore every version of every object stored in your bucket. This feature can be useful for regulatory compliance requirements that might require you to keep track of changes made to objects. Note that buckets can be in one of three versioning states: • Unversioned (the default state) • Versioning-enabled • Versioning-suspended Versioning is enabled and suspended at the bucket level. Once versioning is enabled, it can never return to an un-versioned state, but it can be suspended.
Value	This is the actual data (content) that you are storing in the bucket. Its size can range from zero to 5 TB. In addition, the object value can be any sequence of bytes.

Component	Description
Metadata	Amazon S3 provides two different kinds of object metadata: system-defined metadata and user-defined metadata. System-defined metadata is defined automatically and includes an object's creation date, size, and storage class. The user adds user-defined metadata when an object is uploaded. User-defined metadata cannot be modified once the object has been uploaded. To edit metadata for an existing object, you use the COPY action (copy to the same destination) and specify the new metadata you want to apply, which replaces the old metadata for the object.
Subresources	Subresources are resources that are subordinate to objects, which means that they do not exist on their own and are always associated with an object or a bucket. An example of a subresource is an access control list.
Access control information	The Amazon S3 resources that you create (e.g., buckets and objects) are private by default, meaning you must explicitly grant permissions for others to access them. To control access to the objects, you can use resource-based access control lists (such as ACLs) and user-based access control lists. For an in-depth analysis of access control, see `https://docs.aws.amazon.com/AmazonS3/latest/userguide/security_iam_service-with-iam.html`
Tags	Tags are key-value pairs that can be used to categorize resources, including storage. Tags can be added to new objects when you upload them, or you can add them to existing objects. Some things to note about tags: • You can associate a maximum of 10 tags with an object. • The keys and values in the key-value pairs are case-sensitive. • A tag key has a maximum length of 128 Unicode characters, while tag values have a maximum length of 256 Unicode characters.

Source: Amazon Web Services / `https://docs.aws.amazon.com/AmazonS3/latest/userguide/UsingObjects.html`, last accessed on 19 December 2024.

Table 4.8 lists and provides a description of the currently avialable S3 object subresource.

TABLE 4.8 S3 object subresource

Subresource	Description
acl	An access control list (ACL) is a subresource that allows you to manage access to buckets and objects. As a subresource, an ACL cannot exist without a bucket or object. An ACL defines the accounts and groups that have access, as well as the type of access they have been granted. To update an ACL, you have to replace the existing ACL.

Source: Amazon Web Services / `https://docs.aws.amazon.com/AmazonS3/latest/userguide/UsingObjects.html`, last accessed on 19 December 2024.

Paying for Amazon S3

Amazon S3 is designed to charge you only for what you use, and there are no hidden fees or overage charges. The cost components for Amazon S3 are storage pricing, request and data retrieval pricing, data transfer and transfer acceleration pricing, data management and insights feature pricing, replication pricing, and transformation and query feature pricing. For an in-depth understanding of S3 pricing, see https://aws.amazon.com/s3/pricing.

Getting Started with S3 Buckets

When you're using S3, you'll be working with buckets. Here are the basic steps to create an S3 bucket:

1. **Sign in to the AWS Management Console:** Open the Amazon S3 console at https://console.aws.amazon.com/s3.
2. **Choose an AWS Region:** Select the Region where you want to create the bucket.
3. **Navigate to Buckets:** In the left navigation pane, choose Buckets.
4. **Start the bucket creation:** Choose Create bucket.
5. **Enter a bucket name:** The name must be unique within a partition, 3–63 characters long, and can contain lowercase letters, numbers, dots, and hyphens.
6. **Choose a bucket type:** Select General Purpose.
7. **Configure object ownership:** Choose ACLs Disabled (Bucket owner enforced) or ACLs Enabled.
8. **Set Block Public Access settings:** It is recommended to keep all settings enabled.
9. **Configure bucket versioning:** Choose to Enable or Disable versioning.
10. **Add tags (optional):** Add key-value pairs to categorize storage.
11. **Configure default encryption:** Choose between Amazon S3 Managed Key (SSE-S3) or AWS Key Management Service key (SSE-KMS).
12. **Configure advanced settings (optional):** Enable S3 Object Lock if needed.
13. **Create the bucket:** Review the settings and choose Create Bucket.

For more details on creating and using buckets, see https://docs.aws.amazon.com/AmazonS3/latest/userguide/creating-bucket.html.

Amazon Elastic Block Storage

Amazon Elastic Block Storage (EBS) is a scalable and high-performance block storage specifically designed for Amazon EC2. EBS allows you to create volumes and attach them to

Amazon EC2 instances. Once they are attached, you can create a file system on top of the volumes, run a database, or do any other use case for block storage. EBS volumes are placed on a single Availability Zone (AZ) and are automatically replicated to protect from failure of a single component. All EBS volumes offer snapshot capabilities that are durable and designed to offer high availability. Amazon EBS provides a feature that allows you to dynamically increase capacity, tune performance, and change instance type or volumes that are in use without experiencing downtime or having a negative impact on performance, enabling you to right-size applications or the agility to respond to performance changes.

As a block storage, its use cases include building mission-critical, I/O-intensive cloud applications. EBS is suitable for migrating on-premises storage area network (SAN) workloads to the cloud. EBS is also suitable for deploying and scaling relational or NoSQL databases, including SAP HANA, PostgreSQL, Microsoft SQL Server, MySQL, Oracle, MongoDB, and Cassandra. EBS can also be used with clusters for big data analytics engines, such as Hadoop and Spark, where you can freely attach and reattach volumes depending on your requirements.

EBS makes available multiple volume types, which provide you with both storage and cost optimization options. These volumes are divided into two: SSD-based, which are suitable for transactional workloads such as databases and boot volumes, and HDD-based, which are suitable for intensive analytics workloads such as MapReduce and log processing.

Figure 4.7 provides an overview of Amazon Elastic Block Storage (EBS).

FIGURE 4.7   Amazon Elastic Block Storage (EBS) overview

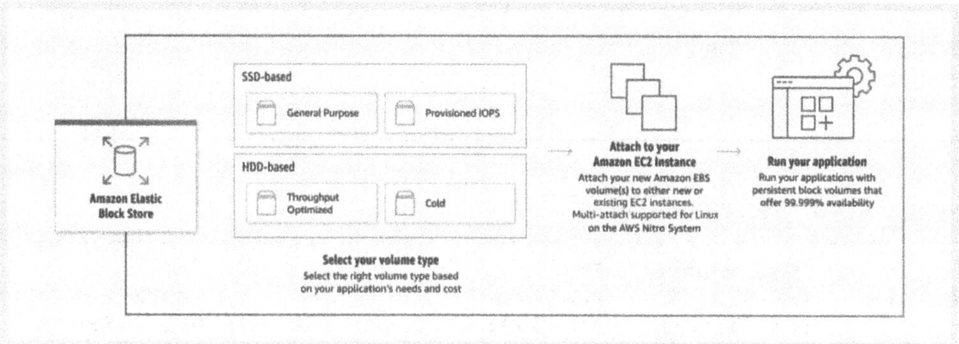

EBS Volume Types

Let's take a closer look at the two volume types. Table 4.9 presents the specifics of HDD-based volumes, and Table 4.10 presents the specifics of SSD-based volumes.

TABLE 4.9   HDD-based volumes

EBS Volume Type	Throughput Optimized HDD (st1)	Cold HDD (sc1)
Short Description	Low-cost HDD volume designed for frequently accessed, throughput-intensive workloads	Lowest cost HDD volume designed for less frequently accessed workloads
Durability	99.8% – 99.9%	99.8% – 99.9%
Use Cases	Big data; data warehouses; log processing	Colder data requiring fewer scans per day
API Name	st1	sc1
Volume Size	125 GB – 16 TB	125 GB – 16 TB
Max IOPS**/Volume	500	250
Max Throughput***/ Volume	500 MB/s	250 MB/s
Max Throughput/ Instance	12,500 MB/s	7,500 MB/s
Price	$0.045/GB-month	$0.015/GB-month
Dominant Performance Attribute	MB/s	MB/s

TABLE 4.10   SSD-based volumes

EBS Volume Type	EBS Provisioned IOPS SSD (io2 Block Express)	EBS Provisioned IOPS SSD (io1)	EBS General Purpose SSD (gp3)	EBS General Purpose SSD (gp2)
Short Description	Highest performance SSD volume designed for business-critical, latency-sensitive transactional workloads	Highest performance SSD volume designed for latency-sensitive transactional workloads	Lowest cost SSD volume that balances price performance for a wide variety of transactional workloads	General-purpose SSD volume that balances price performance for a wide variety of transactional workloads

EBS Volume Type	EBS Provisioned IOPS SSD (io2 Block Express)	EBS Provisioned IOPS SSD (io1)	EBS General Purpose SSD (gp3)	EBS General Purpose SSD (gp2)
Durability	99.999%	99.8% – 99.9%	99.8% – 99.9%	99.8% – 99.9%
Use Cases	Largest, most I/O-intensive, mission critical deployments of NoSQL and relational data-bases, such as Oracle, SAP HANA, Microsoft SQL Server, and SAS Analytics	I/O-intensive NoSQL and relational databases	Virtual desktops; medium-sized single-instance databases, such as Microsoft SQL Server and Oracle; latency-sensitive interactive appli-cations, boot vol-umes, and dev/test environments	Virtual desktops; medium-sized single-instance databases, such as Microsoft SQL Server and Oracle; latency-sensitive interactive appli-cations, boot vol-umes, and dev/test environments
API Name	io2	io1	gp3	gp2
Volume Size	4 GB – 64 TB	4 GB – 16 TB	1 GB – 16 TB	1 GB – 16 TB
Max IOPS/ Volume	256,000	64,000	16,000	16,000
Max Throughput*/ Volume	4,000 MB/s	1,000 MB/s	1,000 MB/s	250 MB/s
Max IOPS/ Instance	420,000	420,000	260,000	260,000
Max Throughput/ Instance	12,500 MB/s	12,500 MB/s	12,500 MB/s	7,500 MB/s
Latency	Sub-millisecond	Single-digit millisecond	Single-digit millisecond	Single-digit millisecond

TABLE 4.10 SSD-based volumes *(continued)*

EBS Volume Type	EBS Provisioned IOPS SSD (io2 Block Express)	EBS Provisioned IOPS SSD (io1)	EBS General Purpose SSD (gp3)	EBS General Purpose SSD (gp2)
Price	$0.125 per GB-month	$0.125 per GB-month	$0.08 per GB-month	$0.10 per GB-month
	$0.065 per provisioned IOPS-month for up to 32,000 IOPS	$0.065 per provisioned IOPS-month	3,000 IOPS free; $0.005 per provisioned IOPS-month over 3,000	
	$0.046 per provisioned IOPS-month for 32,001 to 64,000 IOPS		125 MB/s free; $0.04 per provisioned MB/s-month over 125	
	$0.032 per provisioned IOPS-month for greater than 64,000 IOPS			
Dominant Performance Attribute	IOPS, throughput, latency, capacity, and volume durability	IOPS	IOPS	IOPS

In summary:

- SSD-based volumes (io2 Block Express, io1, gp3, gp2) are suitable for transactional, latency-sensitive workloads.
- HDD-based volumes (st1, sc1) are optimized for throughput-intensive, less frequently accessed workloads.

Data Protection

Amazon EBS provides you with the ability to save point-in-time snapshots of your volumes to Amazon S3. These snapshots are stored incrementally so that only blocks that have changed since the last snapshot are saved. Snapshots can be used to create multiple new volumes, expand volume size, or move volumes across AZs. When creating a new volume, you have the option of creating it based on an existing snapshot.

For an overview of Amazon EBS and its features, see https://aws.amazon.com/ebs/features.

Amazon Elastic File System

Amazon Elastic File System (EFS) is another storage service in AWS that is designed to provide you with serverless, fully elastic file storage, which enables you to share file data without the overhead of provisioning storage capacity and performance. It is built to scale (to petabytes) without applications experiencing disruptions and can be used both with AWS services and on-premises resources. EFS use cases include storage for containerized and serverless applications, big data analytics, web serving, content management, database backups, and application development and testing.

Figure 4.8 provides an overview of Amazon EFS.

FIGURE 4.8 Amazon Elastic File System (EFS) overview

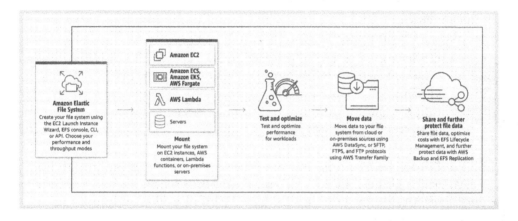

Amazon EFS Features

Amazon EFS offers a range of features that deal with storage management, performance and scale, storage classes, accessibility, data protection and security, and data transfer.

- Store management:
  - Amazon EFS is a fully managed service that provides network file sharing (NFS) and shared file system storage for Linux workloads.
  - It is very quick to create and configure file systems without the need to manage file systems and the overhead of configuring software, updating hardware, or performing backups.
  - To create a fully managed file system within seconds, you can use the AWS Management Console, AWS SDK, or the AWS Command Line Interface (CLI).

- EFS offers two file types to meet your specific needs (availability and durability):
  - EFS Regional file systems offer the highest level of durability and availability for storing data and cover multiple Availability Zones.
  - EFS One Zone file systems store data in a single AZ. This has the downsize of potential data unavailability during a fault within the AZ.
- **Performance and scale:**
  - Amazon EFS storage is fully elastic and highly scalable by default and grows and shrinks automatically to suit your needs. You are billed for what you use.
  - The default EFS Elastic Throughput mode ensures that your file system will automatically scale throughput. This is the recommended mode if you are unsure of your maximum peak throughput requirements of your application and want to benefit from automatic scaling to meet demand.
- **Storage classes:**
  - Amazon EFS offers three storage classes:
    - EFS Standard: Use this for frequently accessed data that has higher performance needs. EFS Standard is SSD-powered and delivers sub millisecond latencies.
    - EFS Infrequent Access: This is suitable for infrequently accessed data and provides low double-digit millisecond latencies. EFS Infrequent Access is suitable for data accessed a few times per quarter and offers up to 95% lower costs than EFS Standard.
    - EFS Archive: This is suitable for infrequently accessed data and provides low double-digit millisecond latencies. EFS Archive is suitable for data accessed a few times a year and offers up to 50% lower costs than EFS Archive.
  - EFS provides EFS Lifecycle Management, which can be enabled to tier files between storage classes based on access patterns. The default policy moves unused files from Standard to EFS IA after 30 days of consecutive non-usage and to EFS Archive after 90 consecutive days of non-access. EFS intelligent tiering can be enabled to reverse the process.
- **Accessibility:**
  - Amazon EFS supports access to Amazon Elastic Compute Cloud (EC2) instances, AWS containers, and serverless compute services.
  - It supports on-premises services using a traditional permissions model and file locking using the NFS v4 protocol.
  - Amazon EC2 instances can support access to your file systems across AZs and Regions.
  - On-premises servers can access Amazon EFS via AWS Direct Connect or AWS VPN services.

- Amazon EFS provides applications running on EC2, AWS Fargate, Amazon Elastic Kubernetes Service (EKS), or AWS Lambda with access to a shared file system for stateful workloads.

- **Data protection and security:**
  - Amazon EFS helps organizations that have regulatory requirements for storing data hundreds of miles away by replicating copies of file system data to a region of their choosing. It also provides a Recovery Point Objective (RPO) and Recovery Time Objective (RTO) of minutes.
  - Amazon EFS backups are automatically managed by AWS Backup, which is fully managed.
  - Amazon Virtual Private Cloud (VPC) security group rules are used to control network access to your file systems in conjunction with Identity Access Management (IAM) and Amazon EFS access points.
  - Data at rest is transparently encrypted using encryption keys managed by the AWS Key Management Service (KMS). Data in transit in secured using Transport Layer Security (TLS).

- **Data transfer:**
  - To transfer and move data between on-premises storage and Amazon EFS, you can use AWS DataSync, a managed data transfer service that transfers data over the Internet, or AWS Direct Connect.
  - You can use AWS Transfer Family to transfer files directly into and out of Amazon EFS. The supported protocols include Secure File Transfer Protocol (SFTP), File Transfer Protocol (FTP), and File Transfer Protocol over SSL (FTPS).

Amazon File Cache

Amazon File Cache (`https://aws.amazon.com/filecache`) is a fully managed, scalable, high-speed or high-performance cache on AWS that is used for processing file data stored in disparate locations, including on-premises. To create a high-performance cache, you can use the AWS Management Console, Command Line Interface, or an API. Amazon File Cache is a managed service, so you do not have to worry about managing cache hardware or tuning performance. In addition, you do not have to manage and monitor free space, as this is done automatically by releasing less frequently used data when your cache needs additional storage.

Figure 4.9 provides an overview of Amazon File Cache.

FIGURE 4.9   Amazon File Cache overview

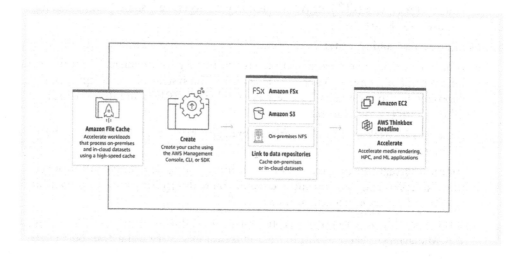

Amazon File Cache Features

Amazon File Cache offers the following features:

- Performance and scale:
  - Data in Amazon File Cache can be accessed from EC2 instances, ECS, and EKS container instances with sub-millisecond average first-byte latencies, up to hundreds of GB/s of throughput, and millions of IOPS.
- Data sources:
  - Amazon File Cache supports the creating of a high-speed cache linked to one or more on-premises NFS file systems.
  - Amazon File Cache supports creating high-speed caches linked to one or more AWS file systems or Amazon S3 buckets.
- Security:
  - Amazon Virtual Private Cloud (VPC) is used to isolate your cache in its own virtual network and allows access to the cache from endpoints.
  - AWS Identity and Access Management (IAM) integrates with Amazon File Cache, allowing you to control the actions that IAM users and groups can take to manage your caches. Tags are also supported by Amazon File Cache, which can be used to control the actions that IAM users and groups can take based on the tags.
- Use cases:
  - Amazon File Cache Bursting enables visual effects (VFX) rendering and transcoding workloads on AWS to meet peak compute needs during media production.

- Amazon File Cache accelerates high-performance computing (HPC) cloud-bursting workloads with scalable cache performance designed to support hundreds of thousands of compute cores.

- Amazon File Cache provides access to on-premises and in-cloud datasets to maximize throughput to training instances.

- Amazon File Cache allows you to run advanced analytics efficiently on petabytes of on-premises data by caching only the required subsets that need to be processed.

Amazon FSx

Amazon FSx is a file system service that lets you launch, run, and scale feature-rich, high-performance cloud file systems that are reliable, secure, and scalable. Because Amazon FSx is a managed service, it removes the need for you to manage and provision hardware, patch software, and run and manage backups, which is a key differentiator of cloud services and allows you to focus on differentiating your offering.

Amazon FSx offers four widely used file systems that you can choose from for your use case based on familiarity with a given file system or by matching the file system's feature sets, performance profiles, and data management capabilities. The four options are NetApp ONTAP, OpenZFS, Windows File Server, and Lustre.

The benefits of Amazon FSx include its high availability, durability, cost-effectiveness, and support for industry-standard protocols that offer connectivity to Windows, Linux, and macOS users and applications. It also delivers sub-second latencies and high throughput, helping you meet the performance needs of your most demanding workloads. An additional benefit is that you can migrate and synchronize data from on-premises to AWS and have it available immediately to a wide range of integrated AWS services.

Common use cases of Amazon FSx include:

- Amazon FSx makes it easy to adopt cloud storage agility and scalability for your applications without modifying your application code.

- Amazon FSx supports machine learning, analytics, and HPC applications that require highly performant and scalable storage to support large clusters of compute resources and large volumes of data.

- Amazon FSx allows you to quickly spin up test and development environments, which allows you to reduce release cycles.

- Amazon FSx provides the scalability required for delivering media and entertainment projects, which require high-performance storage.

- Amazon FSx enables you to securely manage backups and archive or replicate on-premises file storage to AWS to meet regulatory or disaster recovery requirements.

To help choose the version of Amazon FSx suitable for your use case, see https://aws .amazon.com/fsx/when-to-choose-fsx.

Implementing the Appropriate Storage Services for Specific Cost and Performance Requirements

Table 4.11 provides an overview of how to configure some of the AWS services to use the storage services discussed in the previous sections.

TABLE 4.11   Configuring AWS storage options

AWS Service	Storage Options	How to Configure
Amazon Redshift	Amazon S3	Specify an S3 bucket as the data repository when creating or configuring a Redshift cluster.
Amazon EMR	Amazon S3	Use S3 as the default file system when launching an EMR cluster. Specify S3 locations for input, output, and log data.
AWS Lake Formation	Amazon S3	Integrate AWS Lake Formation with an S3 data lake. Specify the S3 locations to be managed by AWS Lake Formation.
Amazon RDS	Amazon EBS	Choose the appropriate EBS volume type and size when launching or modifying an RDS instance. Attach additional EBS volumes to the RDS instance as needed.
DynamoDB	DynamoDB (Managed Service)	DynamoDB is a fully managed NoSQL database service, so the storage is handled by the service.
Amazon Kinesis Data Streams	Amazon S3	Configure Kinesis Data Streams to deliver data to an S3 bucket for long-term storage and processing.
Amazon MSK	Amazon S3 Amazon EBS	Specify S3 locations for storing data and logs when creating an MSK cluster. Attach EBS volumes to the MSK broker instances for additional storage.

Aligning Data Storage with Data Migration Requirements

As an additional task to choosing a storage service, you also need to decide how to migrate your data from the source system to your chosen service. AWS offers different options depending on whether the data migration needs to be offline or online.

Online migration means that the data is transferred over the Internet while it is still running in your on-premises source environment. One benefit of online migration is it can be more efficient since downtime is minimized and you are able to use your cloud resources sooner. For online migration, you need a stable Internet connection, meaning it cannot always be suitable for transferring large amounts of data or mission-critical applications, which can be impacted by an unstable Internet connection. Choose an online migration where speed is critical.

Offline migration involves moving data to the cloud without the need for an Internet connection. The data is physically transferred on external media, such as a hard drive or other storage medium, to the data center of your cloud provider. This method is used primarily for transferring large amounts of data, when there is limited bandwidth or Internet connectivity, or when there are concerns about the security or privacy of the data if it is sent over the Internet.

I encourage you to watch this three-minute video about the AWS Snowmobile, an actual truck that you can use to move exabytes of data to the AWS cloud: `https://www.youtube.com/watch?v=8vQmTZTq7nw`.

Table 4.12 provides a comparison of when to use the online and offline migration options.

TABLE 4.12   Migration Options

Migration Option	When Speed Is the Priority	When Bandwidth Is Important
Online	An online migration is one that is suitable when there are frequent updates made to the data. Use this migration option for ongoing workloads or time-critical workloads. Online migrations allow for continuous data replication, which minimizes downtime and ensures that the most recent data is always available at the destination.	You should consider running the migration during hours when there is minimal network usage, which will give you sufficient bandwidth for the migration. Weekends and late nights are some of the time periods to consider.
Offline	An offline migration is suitable for one-off uploads, such as when you are moving the initial data from the source system. It can also be used for periodic uploads, such as weekly or monthly uploads. This is the migration option to use when there is no requirement to update the data while it is in transit.	You should use this migration option when only minimal bandwidth is required.

Determining the Appropriate Storage Solution for Specific Access Patterns

When choosing the appropriate storage solution, it is important to consider the workloads' access patterns and the characteristics of the available storage options. Different types of workloads have different requirements regarding how the data will be accessed, which influences the suitability of the storage options discussed previously.

Database workloads have different access patterns than, for example, the need to archive data in long-term storage for regulatory requirements or to store data for access for your favorite streaming service. Consider the following criteria when choosing your storage type based on access patterns:

Protocols Block storage: Use block storage for applications that require fast and consistent I/O operations. It offers high-performance storage that is directly attached to a compute instance with low-latency access.

File-based storage: Choose file-based storage for workloads that need access to shared data across multiple compute instances. File-based storage is natively mountable from any operating system using standard industry protocols such as SMB and NFS.

Object storage: Choose object storage when you have read-heavy workloads (such as streaming applications and services). It is easily accessible over the Internet through an application programming interface (API).

Client Types It's very important to consider the type of operating systems that will be used by the clients accessing the data to ensure easy access and data sharing across various workloads. Avoid compatibility issues by selecting the right file systems.

Performance This is a critical factor when choosing a storage service, as most organizations aim to optimize operations. Considerations include whether the workload is sensitive to latency, whether it is read/write heavy, and whether throughput and bandwidth are important.

Managing the Lifecycle of Data

Data has what is referred to as a *lifecycle*, which is its lifetime from creation/data entry to its destruction. As data moves through the various stages, it is important that you follow a data lifecycle management (DLM) approach that will ensure structure and organization to your organization's data, ensuring that key organizational goals such as data security and data availability are always met.

This section discusses the important reasons for managing the lifecycle of data, and then we move on to guidelines and best practices.

Legal and Compliance Requirements

Today's business environments are highly regulated, which means that, as a data engineer, compliance should be at the forefront of your data management strategy. Complying with industry regulations through the implementation of proper data lifecycle management practices helps organizations maintain customer trust by ensuring the proper protection of customer data, demonstrating compliance during audits, responding quickly to legal or regulatory requests, and avoiding noncompliance penalties.

There are different regulations that apply to different situations, with some of these being industry-specific. Examples include:

- Healthcare (Health Insurance Portability and Accountability Act—HIPAA in the United States)
- Data Protection (General Data Protection Regulation—GDPR in the EU)
- Data retention requirements, which specify the minimum retention periods
- Audit trails

To understand more about compliance at AWS, please refer to this page: `https://aws.amazon.com/compliance`.

Cost Optimization

When you store your data efficiently based on access patterns, you will benefit from cost reductions. Storage platforms, such as S3 allow you to move infrequently accessed data to cheaper storage tiers, which leads to cost savings. Furthermore, it is important to delete unnecessary or duplicate data to free up storage space and reduce costs.

Performance Improvement

Your applications can benefit from better performance if you move frequently accessed data to high-performance storage. In addition, you must remove old or irrelevant data, which can improve query performance.

Data Security

Security is "priority zero" at AWS, and as a data engineer you need to ensure that your lifecycle management includes security measures at all stages. This ensures that risk is reduced by properly protecting sensitive data and deleting it when it is no longer needed.

Disaster Recovery and Business Continuity

It is important to select the storage solution that is appropriate for your use case. Next, we will look at the guidelines you need to consider.

Selecting the Appropriate Storage Solutions for Hot and Cold Data

For hot data (frequently accessed), you should consider using the following services:

- **Amazon S3 Standard:** This is designed for frequently accessed data, low latency, and high throughput. It is ideal for big data analytics, content distribution, and dynamic websites.

- **Amazon EBS (Elastic Block Store):** This provides block-level storage for compute (EC2) instances and is suitable for databases, file systems, and applications that require frequent updates.

- **Amazon RDS (Relational Database Service):** This is a managed relational database for frequently accessed structured data, supporting various database engines, including MySQL, PostgreSQL, Oracle, SQL Server, and Aurora.

- **Amazon ElastiCache:** This is an in-memory caching service for extremely low-latency data access. It is suitable for real-time applications and caching layers.

- **Amazon DynamoDB:** This is a NoSQL database for high-performance applications and provides single-digit millisecond latency. It is suitable for e-commerce web applications.

For cold data (infrequently accessed), you must consider the following:

- Amazon S3 Standard-Infrequent Access (S3 Standard-IA)
- Amazon S3 Intelligent-Tiering
- S3 One Zone-Infrequent Access (S3 One Zone-IA)
- Amazon S3 Glacier storage classes

For a deeper explanation on selecting the appropriate S3 storage class for hot or cold data, please refer to `https://aws.amazon.com/s3/storage-classes`.

Optimizing Storage Costs Based on the Data Lifecycle

As part of managing the lifecycle of data, you must also implement best practices to optimize storage costs. The aim is that you pay the minimal amount for your storage costs while still achieving performance that meets your SLAs.

Please start this section by watching this video: `https://youtu.be/IVzf4gNIoTQ`. The following are the best practices that you can use to optimize storage costs:

- Use S3 Lifecycle policies to automatically transition objects between storage classes, which will result in cost savings.

- Implement S3 Intelligent-Tiering for automatic cost optimization.

- Use AWS Storage Gateway for hybrid cloud storage optimization.

- Leverage Amazon EFS Lifecycle Management for file system data.

Deleting Data to Meet Business and Legal Requirements

Here are the best practices:

- Use S3 Lifecycle policies for automatic deletion of objects.
- Implement AWS Config Rules to enforce deletion policies.
- Use AWS Macie for data discovery and classification to identify sensitive data.
- Leverage AWS Organizations for centralized policy management across accounts.

Implementing Data Retention Policies and Archiving Strategies

Here are the best practices:

- Use S3 Glacier for long-term archival storage.
- Implement S3 Object Lock for WORM (write once, read many) compliance.
- Use AWS Backup for centralized backup management.
- Leverage AWS DataSync for efficient data transfer to archive storage.

Protecting Data with Appropriate Resiliency and Availability

Here are the best practices:

- Use S3 Cross-Region Replication (CRR) for geographic redundancy.
- Implement Multi-AZ deployments for RDS and EBS.
- Use AWS Backup for comprehensive data protection.
- Leverage Amazon S3 versioning to protect against accidental deletions.
- Implement AWS Shield for DDoS protection.

Summary

This chapter covered a very important section of the exam: storage platforms such as object, block, and cloud file storage, and their characteristics and use cases. We specifically spent a lot of time on the AWS object Store Amazon S3, which forms the foundation of data lakes/lake houses in a modern data architecture.

In the second part of the chapter, we looked at data lifecycle management, together with the different considerations that you have to make as a data engineer, such as legal/compliance requirements, cost considerations, data security, and business continuity and disaster recovery.

Exam Essentials

Understand the importance of storage in your data environment. This includes knowing why choosing the right storage platform, configured according to best practices, can enable you to have a secure, performant, and resilient data platform and applications.

Understand data lifecycle management. This includes knowing how to implement the data lifecycle using best practices to help your organization achieve its business goals.

Know the different storage solutions provided by AWS, their characteristics, and their use cases. These storage options are object storage, cloud file storage, and block storage. You must know the different data storage formats and which ones are useful for achieving high performance for your use cases.

Be able to select the appropriate storage platform based on the relevant use case. This includes considering specific access patterns and performance demands.

Be able to configure your storage environment. Know the best configuration practices to achieve security, high performance, resilience, agility, and business continuity.

Review Questions

1. A media company needs to store large video files that are accessed frequently in the first month after upload, but rarely afterward. The company wants to optimize storage costs while maintaining quick access for the first month. Which Amazon S3 storage solution should they implement?

    A. Use S3 Standard for all storage. Create custom AWS Lambda functions that will monitor object access patterns and manually move objects to S3 Standard-IA after 30 days of no access. Schedule the Lambda function to run daily to check and move objects as needed.

    B. Store all data in S3 Glacier Deep Archive to minimize costs. Implement a custom application that will track object ages and retrieve objects from Glacier when accessed, caching them in S3 Standard temporarily. This approach requires significant development effort but may offer cost savings.

    C. Use S3 Intelligent-Tiering for all objects. Configure S3 Intelligent-Tiering to use a 30-day threshold for moving objects to the infrequent access tier. Monitor storage costs and access patterns using S3 Storage Lens to ensure the automated tiering is functioning as expected.

    D. Implement a lifecycle policy to store data in S3 Standard for 30 days, then transition to S3 Standard-IA for long-term storage. Use S3 Inventory to regularly audit object storage classes and ensure the lifecycle policy is working correctly. Enable S3 Storage Lens to monitor usage patterns and costs across storage classes.

2. A research institution needs to process large genomic datasets using high-performance computing clusters. They require a file system that can provide high throughput and low-latency access across multiple EC2 instances. Which AWS storage service should they use?

    A. Use Amazon EFS and configure it in Max I/O performance mode. Implement EFS access points to manage application-specific entry points to the file system. Set up automatic backups using AWS Backup to ensure data durability.

    B. Implement Amazon FSx for Lustre, configuring it for the highest available performance. Use data compression to optimize storage efficiency and cost. Set up FSx for Lustre linked to an S3 bucket for long-term data storage and easy data import/export.

    C. Utilize Amazon S3 with S3 Select for efficient data retrieval. Implement S3 Transfer Acceleration to improve upload and download speeds. Use S3 Intelligent-Tiering to automatically optimize storage costs based on access patterns.

    D. Deploy multiple Amazon EBS volumes in a RAID 0 configuration attached to a single large EC2 instance. Use EBS Multi-Attach to allow multiple EC2 instances to access the same EBS volume simultaneously. Implement regular EBS snapshots for data protection.

3. A retail company wants to implement a data lake solution on AWS to analyze customer behavior patterns. It needs a storage solution that can handle diverse data types, scale easily, and provide cost-effective long-term storage. Which service should it choose?

- **A.** Use Amazon RDS with a Multi-AZ deployment to store structured customer data. Implement read replicas for improved query performance. Use RDS Proxy to manage database connections efficiently and reduce failover times.

- **B.** Store Deploy Amazon EFS with lifecycle management to automatically move infrequently accessed files to EFS IA storage class. Use EFS access points to create application-specific entry points to the file system. Implement AWS DataSync for efficient data transfer from on-premises systems.

- **C.** Implement Amazon S3 as the foundation for the data lake. Use S3 storage classes to optimize costs based on data access patterns. Implement S3 Select and Glacier Select for efficient querying of specific data. Use AWS Glue for data catalog and ETL processes.

- **D.** Utilize Amazon DynamoDB with on-demand capacity mode to handle unpredictable workloads. Implement DynamoDB Streams to capture data changes and trigger real-time analytics. Use DynamoDB Accelerator (DAX) for read performance optimization.

4. A steel manufacturing company needs to store and analyze IoT sensor data from its production lines. It expects to generate millions of small files daily and require fast query performance. Which data storage format should it use in its Amazon S3 data lake?

- **A.** Store data in CSV files, using AWS Glue to catalog and transform it. Implement Athena for SQL-like queries on the CSV files. Use S3 Intelligent-Tiering to automatically optimize storage costs based on access patterns.

- **B.** Utilize JSON files to maintain the hierarchical structure of the sensor data. Implement Amazon Kinesis Data Firehose to stream the data directly into S3. Use Amazon Elasticsearch Service for fast, flexible querying of the JSON data.

- **C.** Use Parquet files for efficient compression and query performance. Use AWS Glue to convert incoming data to Parquet format. Leverage Athena or Redshift Spectrum for high-performance queries. Implement S3 lifecycle policies to transition older data to Glacier.

- **D.** Store data in plaintext files, using AWS Lambda to process and aggregate the data in real time as it's uploaded to S3. Use Amazon QuickSight for visualizations and basic analysis of the aggregated data.

5. A data analytics firm needs to perform complex queries on large datasets stored in Amazon S3. It wants to minimize data transfer and compute costs while maximizing query performance. Which service should it use in conjunction with S3?

- **A.** Use Amazon Redshift Spectrum to query data directly in S3 without loading it into Redshift. Create external tables in Redshift to map to S3 data. Implement a columnar format like Parquet for improved query performance. Use Redshift Workload Management (WLM) to optimize query execution.

- **B.** Implement Amazon Athena to run ad hoc queries on S3 data without managing infrastructure. Use AWS Glue to catalog and transform data into optimized formats. Set up Athena workgroups to control query access and cost management. Utilize an Athena federated query to join data from multiple sources.

C. Deploy Amazon EMR clusters to process large datasets using Hadoop ecosystem tools. Use EMR File System (EMRFS) to directly access S3 data. Implement EMR notebooks for interactive analysis. Configure EMR automatic scaling to handle varying workloads efficiently.

D. Utilize Amazon RDS with a PostgreSQL engine to load and query data from a relational database. Implement AWS Database Migration Service (DMS) to continuously replicate data from S3 to RDS. Use RDS read replicas to scale read performance for complex queries.

6.   A financial services company needs to store sensitive customer data to meet regulatory compliance requirements. It needs the ability to prevent any modifications or deletions of the data for a fixed period. Which Amazon S3 feature should it use?

A. Enable S3 Versioning to maintain multiple versions of each object. Implement custom IAM policies to restrict delete and overwrite permissions. Use AWS CloudTrail to audit all access and changes to the objects, ensuring compliance with regulatory requirements.

B. Implement S3 Object Lock in Governance mode to restrict object deletion. Create custom IAM roles with specific permissions to override the lock when necessary. Use AWS Config rules to monitor and alert any changes to the Object Lock settings.

C. Configure S3 Object Lock in Compliance mode to enforce retention periods. Set up AWS CloudWatch alarms to monitor any attempts to modify or delete locked objects. Implement regular audits using AWS Macie to detect any sensitive data that may not be properly protected.

D. Utilize S3 access points to control access to specific datasets. Create separate VPC endpoints for different user groups, and use bucket policies to enforce strict access controls. Implement S3 event notifications to track all data access and modifications in real time.

7.   A global e-commerce company needs to replicate its product catalog data stored in Amazon S3 across multiple AWS regions for improved performance and disaster recovery. Which S3 feature should it implement to achieve this?

A. Enable S3 Versioning in all regions to maintain multiple versions of objects. Use AWS Lambda functions to manually sync data between regions on a scheduled basis. Implement S3 event notifications to trigger updates when objects change.

B. Configure S3 Cross-Region Replication (CRR) to automatically replicate data to specified regions. Set up IAM roles for S3 replication. Use replication metrics and S3 event notifications to monitor the replication process and ensure data consistency across regions.

C. Implement S3 Transfer Acceleration to speed up data transfers between regions. Use AWS Global Accelerator to route users to the nearest S3 bucket. Manually sync data between regions, using the AWS CLI, on a regular schedule.

D. Utilize S3 Intelligent-Tiering in each region to optimize storage costs. Implement AWS DataSync to periodically copy data between S3 buckets in different regions. Use AWS Config rules to ensure bucket configurations are consistent across regions.

8. A startup is developing a mobile app that allows users to upload and share photos. It needs a storage solution that can handle unpredictable traffic spikes and provide low-latency access to images worldwide. Which AWS service should it use?

A. Use Amazon EFS with mount targets in multiple Availability Zones. Implement cross-region replication using AWS DataSync. Configure AWS Global Accelerator to route users to the nearest EFS mount target for low-latency access.

B. Implement Amazon S3 with Transfer Acceleration for fast uploads. Use S3 event notifications to trigger Lambda functions for image processing. Set up Amazon CloudFront distributions with S3 as the origin for low-latency global content delivery.

C. Deploy Amazon EBS volumes in multiple regions, attached to EC2 instances running a custom image server. Use Amazon Route 53 with latency-based routing to direct users to the nearest EC2 instance. Implement Auto Scaling to handle traffic spikes.

D. Utilize Amazon FSx for Windows File Server with Data Deduplication enabled to optimize storage for similar images. Implement AWS Storage Gateway to cache frequently accessed files in on-premises locations for faster access.

9. A media streaming service needs to store and serve large video files to users globally with minimal latency. The streaming service also needs to ensure high durability of its content. Which S3 storage class and additional service should it use.

A. Use an S3 Standard storage class for high durability and availability. Implement Amazon CloudFront for content delivery, creating a CloudFront distribution with S3 as the origin. Use CloudFront Field Level Encryption to protect sensitive data. Implement Lambda@Edge for personalized content delivery and dynamic content at the edge.

B. Utilize S3 Intelligent-Tiering with AWS Global Accelerator for improved latency. Configure S3 Transfer Acceleration for faster uploads of new content. Use S3 Batch Operations to manage large-scale changes to objects. Implement S3 Object Lock to prevent accidental deletions of important content.

C. Deploy S3 One Zone-IA with Amazon Route 53 for DNS-based routing. Use S3 Multipart Upload for efficient uploading of large video files. Implement S3 Inventory to track object metadata and S3 Storage Lens to analyze storage usage patterns. Use AWS Elemental Media Convert for video transcoding.

D. Implement S3 Glacier with S3 Select for retrieving specific portions of video files. Use S3 Glacier Vault Lock to enforce compliance controls. Implement S3 Batch Operations to restore sets of objects from Glacier. Use Amazon Kinesis Video Streams for real-time video ingestion and playback.

10. A government agency needs to store sensitive documents securely, ensuring they cannot be modified or deleted for a specified retention period. It also needs to provide evidence of compliance with data protection regulations. Which S3 feature should it implement?

A. Enable S3 Versioning to maintain a history of all object versions. Implement S3 lifecycle policies to expire old versions after the retention period. Use S3 server-side encryption with AWS KMS for data encryption. Implement AWS CloudTrail to log all S3 API calls for auditing purposes.

B. Configure S3 Object Lock in Governance mode with a specified retention period. Use S3 Inventory to track objects and their retention settings. Implement S3 access points for fine-grained access control. Use AWS Config rules to monitor and enforce compliance with retention policies.

C.   Implement S3 Object Lock in Compliance mode with a specified retention period. Enable S3 Versioning to maintain object history. Use S3 Inventory and S3 Storage Lens to monitor object retention and compliance. Implement AWS CloudTrail and AWS Config for comprehensive auditing and compliance monitoring.

D.   Utilize S3 Access Points to restrict access to the sensitive documents. Implement custom Lambda functions to enforce retention periods by denying delete operations. Use AWS Key Management Service (KMS) with customer managed keys for encryption. Implement AWS Macie for sensitive data discovery and classification.

Chapter

5

Databases and Data Warehouses on AWS

**THE AWS CERTIFIED DATA ENGINEER –
ASSOCIATE EXAM OBJECTIVES COVERED
IN THIS CHAPTER MAY INCLUDE, BUT ARE
NOT LIMITED TO, THE FOLLOWING:**

✓ **Domain 2: Data Store Management**

- 2.1: Choose a data store
- 2.3: Manage the lifecycle of data
- 2.4: Design data models and schema evolution

Introduction

This chapter will teach you about databases and data warehouses on the AWS platform. Databases and data warehouses are crucial technologies for storing and processing data in an analytics system. They are designed to handle various types of data, including structured and semi-structured data, as well as different types of queries. These can range from highly selective queries fetching one or a few rows to complex analytics queries on massive datasets that return aggregated results.

No single technology can efficiently handle this variety of data and querying patterns. Therefore, AWS believes in "using the right tool for the job" and provides different services for each use case rather than trying to cover all use cases poorly in one service.

In this chapter, you will learn about the following AWS services and their use cases:

- Amazon DocumentDB (with MongoDB compatibility)
- Amazon DynamoDB
- Amazon Keyspaces (for Apache Cassandra)
- Amazon MemoryDB for Redis
- Amazon Neptune
- Amazon RDS
- Amazon Redshift

This chapter covers storage, ingestion, and serving from the data engineering lifecycle (see Figure 5.1).

Amazon Redshift

Amazon Redshift is a fully managed cloud data warehouse that can handle data volumes up to the petabyte scale. It uses a massively parallel processing (MPP) architecture to process complex analytics and business intelligence (BI) queries on massive datasets with high performance. Redshift uses SQL to analyze structured and semi-structured data and supports integration into data lakes and operational databases.

FIGURE 5.1 The data engineering lifecycle

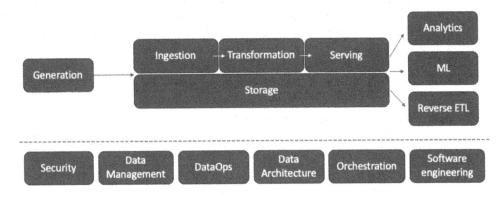

What Is a Data Warehouse?

A *data warehouse* is a centralized repository that stores data from various sources, including a company's internal operational systems (such as ERP and CRM applications), databases, log files, and external sources (such as web analytics providers and social media platforms). Organizations utilize this data collection for business intelligence and analytical analysis, which helps provide visibility and insights into their operational performance. By consolidating data in one place, storing a history of the data, and allowing users to query all of this data quickly, a data warehouse provides a powerful means for a business to gain insights into how it has performed in the past and to make informed decisions for the future.

The process of loading a data warehouse involves ETL, which stands for extract, transform, and load. In the ETL process, data is first extracted from various sources. After extraction, the data goes through a transformation stage, where business rules are applied, the data is cleaned, and the data is restructured to enhance performance for querying while also making it more intuitive for non-technical users. The transformed data is then loaded into the data warehouse, making it available for the business to consume with dashboards, reports, ad hoc SQL queries, and other downstream processes.

At its core, a data warehouse is a database specifically designed for this use case: to store large amounts of data and execute complex SQL queries with high performance. Another term for this use case is *online analytical processing* (OLAP). Typically, businesses use two main types of processing in their data systems: online transactional processing (OLTP) and online analytical processing (OLAP). An OLTP workload's primary purpose is to record events or transactions that occur in the real world and store them quickly and efficiently.

A simplified example is a sales transaction in which a customer buys a product at a specific time. An OLTP database is designed to rapidly retrieve details of the customer and the product they purchased and save a single sales record.

OLTP workloads are typically handled by a company's "front-end" or operational databases, which persist data from applications like point-of-sale systems. While OLTP databases excel at quickly collecting and efficiently storing transactions, they are not designed to analyze vast numbers of them. This is the use case for which OLAP systems are designed and where they shine. Amazon Redshift is AWS's purpose-built data service for data warehousing and OLAP workloads.

Refer to Table 5.1 for a detailed breakdown of the differences between OLTP and OLAP.

TABLE 5.1   Differences between OLTP and OLAP

Aspect	OLTP	OLAP
Primary Use	Managing transactional data; day-to-day operations	Analytical processing; decision support systems
Data	Highly normalized to reduce data redundancy	Typically denormalized to optimize for query speed
Queries	Short, simple transactions	Complex queries involving aggregations and joins
Database Design	Optimized for read/write speed and data integrity	Optimized for query performance and analysis speed
Typical Operations	INSERT, UPDATE, and DELETE frequently used	Predominantly SELECT queries
Transaction Volume	High number of transactions, typically smaller in size	Lower number of transactions, but often large and complex
Users	Operated by clerks, DBAs, or automated scripts	Used by analysts, managers, decision-makers
Response Time	Very fast, aiming for milliseconds to seconds	Can range from seconds to minutes depending on the query complexity
System Focus	ACID properties (atomicity, consistency, isolation, durability)	High throughput for complex analytical queries
Examples	Banking systems, retail transactions, reservations systems	Data warehouses, business reporting systems, data mining

Redshift Architecture

Redshift has two different architectures: provisioned and serverless. The following sections explain the details of the architectures and which use cases are best suited for each type.

Redshift Provisioned

The main component of the Redshift provisioned architecture is a *cluster* (see Figure 5.2). A cluster contains multiple nodes, one called the *leader node*, and one or many others are called *compute nodes*. The leader node can be considered the "brain" of the cluster. It accepts external connections from SQL clients via JDBC or ODBC and the Data API and coordinates query execution across the compute nodes. There is only one leader node in every cluster.

Compute nodes can be considered the "brawn" of the cluster and are responsible for the heavy-lifting part of query processing by scanning and aggregating data across large datasets and sending the result to the leader node for final merging and aggregation. You can have a single compute node in a cluster, but this is only recommended for functional testing. The true power of Redshift happens when multiple compute nodes process a query in parallel; this is known as *massively parallel processing* (MPP).

FIGURE 5.2   Redshift architecture

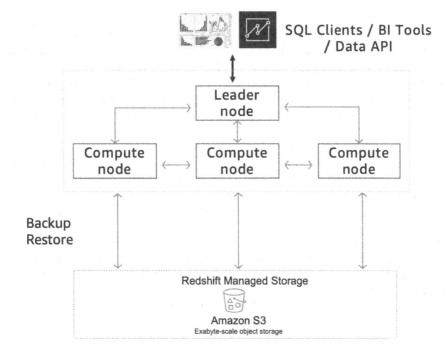

Compute nodes are partitioned into units called *slices*. A slice contains a portion of the node's memory and disk space and processes a portion of the work when you run a query. Slices provide intra-node parallelism, allowing Redshift to break queries down to a finer level and run them in parallel across the slices and the compute nodes. The number of slices per node depends on the node type.

Redshift currently has two classes of node type: RA3 (Redshift Architecture 3) and DC2 (Dense Compute 2). Another class, DS2 (Dense Storage 2), has been deprecated and will not be covered in this book.

DC2 is an older generation node type. One of its main characteristics is that storage and compute are combined in the compute nodes. The disadvantage of this design is that increasing the amount of storage space on a cluster also requires expanding the compute (i.e., adding more compute nodes), which is an inflexible and expensive way of adding more storage. Figure 5.3 shows the two DC2 node types.

FIGURE 5.3   DC2 node types

Node type	vCPU	RAM (GiB)	Default slices per node	Storage per node	Node range	Total capacity
dc2.large	2	15	2	160 GB NVMe-SSD	1–32	5.12 TB
dc2.8xlarge	32	244	16	2.56 TB NVMe-SSD	2–128	326 TB

RA3 is a newer generation node type and is the recommended option for provisioned clusters. RA3 has Redshift Managed Storage (RMS), which separates the storage and compute by storing data on Amazon S3 in a unique file format optimized for Redshift. On RA3 clusters, the compute node's hard drives are caches between the RMS storage and the node's compute. When a query is run, Redshift will return the data from the compute node's storage cache if it is available or move the data from RMS storage into the cache over a high-speed network.

RA3 nodes with RMS storage provide advantages, such as the separation of storage and compute, allowing you to grow your storage easily and cost-effectively without also having to increase your compute; high data resiliency and availability, with S3 replicating the data across three availability zones; and the ability for Redshift to introduce new features, like data sharing, which enables multiple clusters to read and write to the same storage. Figure 5.4 shows RA3's node types.

Redshift provisioned clusters have two pricing models: on-demand and reserved instances (RIs). On-demand is a pay-as-you-go model, and you are charged by the hour for the time you run a cluster, with partial hours charged in one-second increments. With reserved instances, you reserve cluster capacity for a one- or three-year term. Reserved instances provide significant discounts over on-demand pricing and can be a cost-effective model to use once you have confirmed your cluster sizing.

FIGURE 5.4   RA3 node types

Node type	vCPU	RAM (GiB)	Default slices per node	Managed storage limit per node [1]	Node range with create cluster	Total managed storage capacity [2]
ra3.large (single-node)	2	16	2	1 TB	1	1 TB[3]
ra3.large (multi-node)	2	16	2	8 TB	2-16	128 TB
ra3.xlplus (single-node)	4	32	2	4 TB	1	4 TB[3]
ra3.xlplus (multi-node)	4	32	2	32 TB	2-16[4]	1024 TB[4]
ra3.4xlarge	12	96	4	128 TB	2-32[5]	8192 TB[5]
ra3.16xlarge	48	384	16	128 TB	2-128	16,384 TB

Redshift Serverless

Redshift Serverless is the latest generation of Redshift architectures and has two main components: *workgroups* and *namespaces*. Workgroups are compute resources, and namespaces are storage resources.

With Serverless, you don't need to choose a node type or the number of nodes for your cluster, as you do with provisioned clusters. Instead, you select a base workgroup capacity in Redshift Processing Units (RPUs). One RPU provides 16 GB of memory, and, at the time of writing, a workgroup can be configured to have between 8 and 1,024 RPUs in increments of 8, with a default setting of 128. Increasing the base RPU capacity will improve the performance of complex queries on large datasets.

A namespace contains database objects such as tables, views, stored procedures, and users. When you create a workgroup, you associate it with a namespace. Currently, there is a one-to-one relationship between workgroups and namespaces. Therefore, a workgroup can only be associated with one namespace, and a namespace can only be associated with one workgroup.

Redshift Serverless automatically scales out during periods of high concurrency. Concurrency is a measure of the number of queries being run simultaneously. For example, it is common for a data warehouse to have high concurrency on Monday mornings when business users start work, and they all open dashboards to see the results from the weekend. This sudden burst in the number of queries being run simultaneously puts a heavy load on the data warehouse. It can cause the system to reach its maximum ability to run any more queries in parallel. When this happens, a data warehouse or database will usually put queries not currently running onto a queue and wait for a concurrency slot to become available before the query can be run.

Redshift Serverless will automatically detect when queries start queuing and will scale outward, increasing the overall concurrency of the system to run any waiting queries.

Once the burst of queries has been completed, Redshift Serverless will automatically scale back in to conserve resources and control costs. Redshift provisioned clusters have similar behavior with a feature called Concurrency Scaling, which we will discuss later in the chapter. With Redshift Serverless, you are charged based on the duration of your workloads, with a 60-second minimum. To conserve costs, Redshift Serverless automatically pauses during periods of no activity and restarts when queries are run.

AI-Driven Scaling

With AI-driven scaling, Redshift Serverless can scale up base workgroup resources (RPUs) to handle complex workloads that process large amounts of data, as well as scale out to handle periods of high concurrency. The feature automatically monitors workloads on a workgroup and applies AI processing to determine when and how much to scale up and, of course, when to scale back down.

Instead of setting a base RPU amount for the workgroup, you choose a price performance target by adjusting a slider control to determine whether you want the workgroup to prioritize cost savings or performance (see Figure 5.5). Redshift will then scale to best meet this target for your workloads.

FIGURE 5.5   Redshift Serverless AI-driven scaling slider control

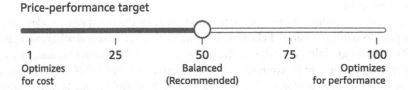

An example of AI-driven scaling in action is: let's say you have a large ETL load that runs every Sunday at midnight. AI-driven scaling will monitor the workgroup and learn this workload pattern. It will then automatically scale up the workgroup before the large load on Sunday and automatically scale it back down once the load has been completed. See the following blog post for examples of AI-driven scaling:

```
https://aws.amazon.com/blogs/big-data/optimize-your-workloads-with-
amazon-redshift-serverless-ai-driven-scaling-and-optimization
```

Provisioned or Serverless?

Which version of Redshift should you choose, and what are the trade-offs? Serverless has the advantage of not worrying about choosing a node type or number of nodes; instead, you select a base RPU amount or a price-performance target, allowing users to get up and running quickly. You pay based on the duration of your workloads, so you only pay for what you use, making it more cost-effective for periodic loads (e.g., an ETL load that runs once per hour). Additionally, there are fewer options to tweak, simplifying administration.

With provisioned clusters, you have the advantage of significant discounts with reserved instances (RIs), which can make them more cost-effective for 24/7 loads. You also have more ability to configure functionality, such as adding queues with priorities for workload management.

For a more extensive data warehouse, both serverless and provisioned clusters can be used in the same system with the data sharing feature (which will be discussed later in this chapter). This allows you to split your workloads across different clusters, using a combination of serverless and provisioned clusters depending on the workload type (e.g., periodic and constant loads).

Redshift Spectrum

Redshift Spectrum is a feature of Redshift that is available in both provisioned and serverless clusters, although it is not referred to as Redshift Spectrum on serverless. It enables you to query your data lake in Amazon S3 directly from Redshift and even join data from S3 with data stored in Redshift's local storage in the same query.

Redshift Spectrum provides a seamless experience, with data lake tables (files) appearing as regular tables that can be queried like local tables stored in Redshift RMS storage. Spectrum works in combination with the AWS Glue Data Catalog. The Glue Data Catalog stores metadata about files in the S3 data lake, and Redshift uses this metadata when it parses and runs queries on the data lake files. This includes metadata about S3 partitions and Glue statistics, allowing the Redshift optimizer to run efficient queries on the data lake.

Spectrum enables what AWS calls the Modern Data Architecture, or Lake House Architecture, and allows you to manage the data lifecycle. Not all data has equal value, and the performance requirements for accessing data often depend on its value. High-value data can be described as data that is accessed often and must be retrieved with high performance; this type of data is also known as *hot data*. Low-value data is rarely accessed and is not required to be retrieved quickly; it is also known as *cold data*. There is a spectrum between hot and cold data, but data usually falls into categories of hot, warm, and cold.

You can keep your hot and warm data stored in Redshift RMS storage to provide the best possible query performance and leave your cold data in your S3 data lake to be queried with Spectrum when needed. This lets you keep your Redshift cluster lean and optimizes storage costs. Data usually moves from hot to cold as it ages, and a typical lifecycle pattern is to keep recent data in Redshift storage and move older data into S3. For example, you could keep the most recent 12 months of data in your sales fact table in Redshift storage and, each month, move the oldest month of data into S3. To give seamless access to data stored in both places, you can create a database view that selects both from the table in Redshift and the data in S3. The Redshift optimizer is clever enough to scan only the data filtered by a query using the view; therefore, you won't be charged Spectrum costs if you select only from Redshift storage.

In addition to allowing users to run queries on an S3 data lake, Spectrum can also be used to ingest data into Redshift in an ETL load. In particular, it is helpful for incremental loads, where you only load new or changed data (deltas). This is because, with Spectrum, you are running a query on your source data and have the flexibility to filter the data you want to load, as opposed to using the COPY command to ingest data where you have to load an entire table or partition. Another advantage of Spectrum is that you can select specific columns to load into Redshift without having to load all columns, as you do with the COPY command.

Redshift Spectrum is one of only three features with an extra charge for use on provisioned clusters (Concurrency Scaling and ML are the other features) and is charged 5 USD per terabyte scanned. With compressed data, you are charged for the compressed size, not the uncompressed size. Therefore, you can optimize costs by partitioning and compressing the data files in S3. Redshift Serverless has no extra charge; the Spectrum cost is bundled into the RPU cost. Run the following lab to learn how to use Redshift Spectrum:

```
https://catalog.workshops.aws/redshift-immersion/lab4
```

Federated Queries

The *federated query* feature lets you directly query external databases from Redshift. This allows you to see live data from your front-end operational databases and join the live data with data stored locally in Redshift without needing to load it using an ETL process, enabling real-time dashboards and analytics.

For example, you could build and store a Customer 360 dataset in Redshift on an hourly or daily basis and federate a query to your sales application database to return live information on customer sales. Both datasets can be joined in a SQL query, possibly stored in a database view, and used by a dashboard to show real-time customer sales and precalculated marketing attributes from the Customer 360.

This concept can be taken further by adding data from your data lake to your dashboard using Redshift Spectrum. You could have large amounts of website log data stored in your S3 data lake and want your dashboard to have information about the history of customer visits to your site. With Spectrum, you can write a SQL query to read the logs from your data lake and combine the query in the same view as the Customer 360 query for local Redshift data and the federated query for live sales data. This provides an integrated view of customer data from three different systems.

The federated query feature currently supports Amazon RDS for PostgreSQL, Amazon Aurora PostgreSQL, Amazon RDS for MySQL, and Amazon Aurora MySQL.

To use federated queries, you create an external schema in Redshift that exposes the tables from an external database. You can then query the exposed tables, and Redshift sends the query to the external database for running. Once the query has been completed, the external database sends the result set back to Redshift. Any filters on the query are "pushed down" to the external database, reducing the amount of data sent back to Redshift to optimize the query performance.

Be aware that when the query is run on the external database, it will use its resources, and heavy queries could slow down the system, which you don't want to do on a front-end operational database that your company website or application could use. Therefore, ensure that the federated queries are efficient and tested in this situation.

Columnar Storage

An essential feature of Redshift is the way it internally stores data. A traditional OLTP database physically stores data on disk in rows, meaning all columns from the row are stored together on disk. This makes retrieving and processing a whole row of data—a common use case in OLTP—efficient. With business intelligence (BI) and analytics queries, retrieving and processing entire rows of data from a table is less common. Instead, it is more common to select a few columns, usually some textual dimension attributes (e.g., sale_date, region, shipping_status), and some numeric measures that are aggregated by the dimension attributes (e.g., SUM(sales_amount), SUM(tax_amount)).

To facilitate the efficient retrieval and processing of BI and analytics queries, where typically only a few columns in a table are selected, instead of storing data in rows on disk, Redshift stores each column separately on disk. Specifically, Redshift stores the values from a column in dedicated blocks rather than a whole row in a single block (or multiple blocks). This significantly reduces I/O because only blocks related to the columns selected need to be read, not the blocks containing other columns in the table. See these compared in Figures 5.6 and 5.7.

FIGURE 5.6   Row-based storage

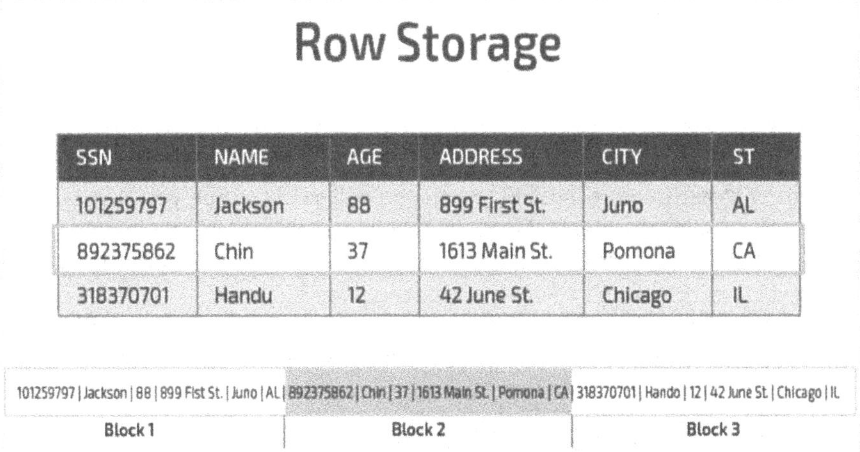

Row Storage

SSN	NAME	AGE	ADDRESS	CITY	ST
101259797	Jackson	88	899 First St.	Juno	AL
892375862	Chin	37	1613 Main St.	Pomona	CA
318370701	Handu	12	42 June St.	Chicago	IL

101259797 | Jackson | 88 | 899 Fist St. | Juno | AL | 892375862 | Chin | 37 | 1613 Main St. | Pomona | CA | 318370701 | Hando | 12 | 42 June St. | Chicago | IL

Block 1	Block 2	Block 3

An additional advantage is that because each block contains the same data type, each column can use a different compression algorithm. This allows you to optimize the compression of each column, reducing the amount of storage used and I/O when the data is queried.

Data API

You have multiple options for connecting to Redshift. Typically, you will connect to a SQL client tool or BI application, such as a dashboard, via JDBC or ODBC. This gives you a synchronous connection to Redshift; however, you can also connect to Redshift asynchronously with the *Data API*. The Data API gives you asynchronous, programmatic access to Redshift, making it helpful to use with web service-based applications.

FIGURE 5.7   Columnar storage

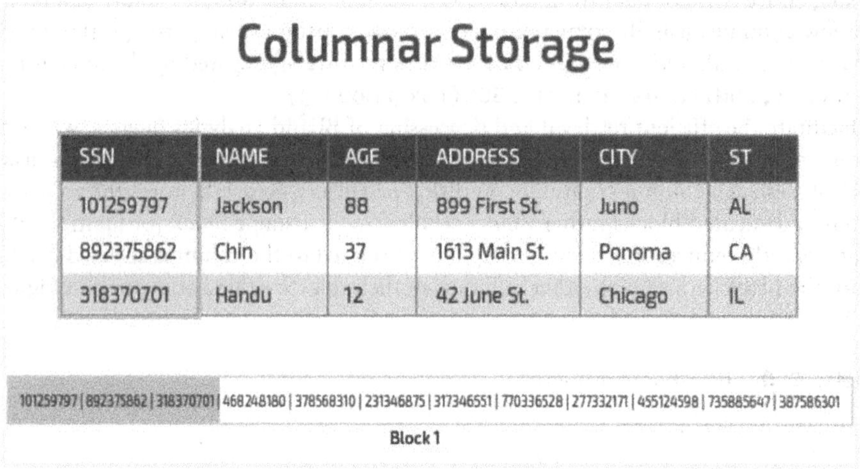

To use the Data API, you issue commands to a secure HTTP endpoint with a supported programming language via the AWS SDK. For example, you can run a SQL query by issuing the `ExecuteStatement` command. This command will send the query to Redshift, run it, and collect the results server-side. Then, you would run the `GetStatementResult` command to retrieve the results and return them to the client once the query has been completed.

In addition to being useful with web service-based applications, the Data API is a useful way to execute steps in an ETL process from a workflow tool like AWS Step Functions or Apache Airflow, as demonstrated in the following blog post:

```
https://aws.amazon.com/blogs/big-data/etl-orchestration-using-
the-amazon-redshift-data-api-and-aws-step-functions-with-aws-sdk-
integration
```

Refer to the API Reference for full details of the actions and data types:

```
https://docs.aws.amazon.com/redshift-data/latest/APIReference/
Welcome.html
```

Data Distribution

As previously mentioned, Redshift is a massively parallel processing (MPP) system that runs queries in parallel across multiple compute nodes and slices and can process queries on large amounts of data much faster than a traditional OLTP database could. Specifically, the way this processing works on Redshift is as follows:

1. A SQL client, BI tool, or the Data API sends a query to the leader node.

2. The leader node creates an execution plan for the query and compiles it into a C++ file.

3. The leader node sends the C++ file down to each of the compute nodes.

4. Each compute node then runs the query on its slices.

5. When each compute node has finished running the query, it returns the result set to the leader node.

6. The leader node performs the final processing steps, such as merging each dataset into one set and running any required aggregation or sorting.

7. The leader node sends the final result set to the client.

The key to MPP performance is step four, where the query runs on multiple compute nodes and slices in parallel. The efficiency of this processing depends mainly on how the data is distributed across the compute nodes (i.e., which node the data is stored on). For example, if you have a four-node cluster and all of the data is stored on only the fourth node, then when a query is run, that node will be doing all the processing, while the other three nodes would have no work to do. This is known as having data skewed across the cluster and is a significant cause of poor performance in an MPP system.

In Redshift, the *distribution style* (DISTSTYLE) determines how a table's data is distributed across a cluster. A distribution style is a table setting that has four possible types:

ALL   The entire table is copied to every compute node.

EVEN   Each table row is distributed across the nodes in a round-robin fashion.

KEY   A single column in the table is designated as the key, and rows are distributed across the nodes by a hash algorithm run on the column.

AUTO   Redshift automatically sets the table to use either ALL, EVEN, or KEY based on its attributes, such as its size and the queries that are run on it.

The DISTSTYLE can be set on a new table with the CREATE TABLE statement or changed on an existing table with the ALTER TABLE statement. Be aware that altering the DISTSTYLE is a synchronous process; if the table is large, it may take a long time to finish.

You can learn more about CREATE TABLE here:

https://docs.aws.amazon.com/redshift/latest/dg/r_CREATE_TABLE_NEW.html

You can learn more about ALTER TABLE here:

https://docs.aws.amazon.com/redshift/latest/dg/r_ALTER_TABLE.html

DISTSTYLE AUTO is the default when you create a table and the recommended setting; however, Redshift allows you to manually set distribution keys if you prefer to fine-tune the model. The following lists some general recommendations on how to manually set distribution keys:

DISTSTYLE KEY   Use DISTSTYLE KEY on table columns that are frequently joined on and have a high cardinality. Cardinality is a measure of the number of unique values in a dataset. Having a high-cardinality column means that a high number of unique values are stored in that column. Setting DISTSTYLE KEY on high-cardinality columns helps reduce a table's rows from being skewed across the nodes. A primary-key column is an excellent example of a high-cardinality column. Typically, temporal columns (DATE or TIMESTAMP data types) are not good examples of high-cardinality columns because the data values are often inconsistent (e.g., an e-commerce website may have more orders during lunchtime on workdays).

Setting the KEY distribution style on tables commonly joined co-locates the same data values on each compute node; therefore, when you run a query that joins these tables, Redshift can process the matching rows on each node. If the matching rows were not co-located, Redshift would have to move data around the nodes to process the joins; this process, known as *redistribution*, negatively affects a query's performance.

For example, if you have a customer table that joins to an orders table on a customer_id column and you set DISTSTYLE KEY on the customer_id column, then all customer_id values of 100 will be stored on the same node, and all values of 101 will also be stored on the same node. (This may or may not be the same node as 100.) When Redshift processes the query and runs the join, it can join all the rows on each node without having to move (redistribute) any rows around the cluster.

DISTSTYLE ALL   Use DISTSTYLE ALL on small dimension tables (parent tables). Because DISTSTYLE ALL creates a full copy of the table on each node, this guarantees rows will be co-located. Note, however, that multiple table copies will increase the storage used.

DISTSTYLE EVEN   If there are no good candidate columns for a KEY distribution and the table is too large for an ALL distribution, set the table to DISTSTYLE EVEN. With an EVEN distribution, each row will be created across the nodes in a round-robin pattern, ensuring the data is evenly distributed and is not skewed.

Data Sorting

How data is physically sorted in a table is another crucial concept in Redshift performance. Unlike OLTP databases, which are designed to process small amounts of data (one or a small group of rows) very quickly and can quickly look up a small number of rows using B-tree indexes, Redshift does not have traditional indexes. This is because Redshift is designed for business intelligence (BI) and analytics queries, and with these types of queries, you are most commonly scanning large amounts of data and aggregating the result, such as a management dashboard that shows daily sales amounts and not processing only one or a few rows.

Instead of traditional indexes, Redshift has *sort keys*. A sort key is a table setting that determines how a table's rows—specifically its blocks—are physically sorted on disk. Redshift stores data in blocks, and each block's min and max values are stored in a Redshift metadata construct called a *zone map*. By using sort keys and zone maps, Redshift can perform what's called a *range-bound scan* and "prune off" blocks outside a query's filter range. By "pruning off" blocks, Redshift can skip reading blocks outside the query's range, decreasing the amount of I/O required and increasing the query's performance.

For example, suppose you have a sales order table with a sort key on the `order_date` column. The table will be physically sorted on disk in ascending order of the values in the `order_date` column. (Getting the rows sorted may require the VACCUM command to be run; this will be covered later in the chapter). Now, if you run a query on the table with a filter on the `order_date` column of `WHERE order_date BETWEEN '2024-03-01' AND '2024-03-07'`, then, using the zone maps, Redshift can identify which blocks do not contain data between March 1 and 7 and skip over these blocks, reducing the number of rows that need to be read and processed, which improves the query performance.

There are two types of sort keys: compound and interleaved. A compound sort key contains one or more columns and sets the table to be sorted in the order the columns are specified in the `CREATE TABLE/ALTER TABLE` statement. You can have up to 400 columns in a compound sort key, but having more than four columns is not advised, because adding more columns will give you diminishing returns in performance.

An interleaved sort key gives equal weight to each column in the sort key and can help improve performance if you have many different queries that filter on different columns. Interleaved sort keys require more maintenance when data in the table is changed; however, and for this reason, they should only be used for specialized cases where it is determined that a compound sort key is insufficient and the extra maintenance is justified for the performance improvement.

Like distribution styles, sort keys can be automatically set by Redshift or manually set. A sort key can be manually set on a new table with the `CREATE TABLE` statement or changed on an existing table with the `ALTER TABLE` statement.

The underlying functionality driving the automated distribution styles, sort keys, and encoding is the automatic table optimization (ATO) feature. For a deep dive into ATO, see the following blog post:

https://aws.amazon.com/blogs/big-data/automate-your-amazon-redshift-performance-tuning-with-automatic-table-optimization

Vacuum

Vacuuming a table is an important maintenance activity in Redshift. It serves two main purposes: first, to free up space by removing any logically deleted records, and second, to sort a table according to its sort key.

In Redshift, when you delete a row, it is not immediately removed from the table's underlying storage. Instead, the record is logically deleted (i.e., marked for delete but not visible) and continues to consume space. An update to a row in Redshift performs a delete and insert under the covers, therefore also leaving logically deleted rows. By running a vacuum, any logically deleted rows are removed from the table, and the table is reorganized to free the consumed space.

As described in the previous section, Redshift can do a range-bound scan to improve a query's performance when a filter is applied to a column with a sort key. However, the table must be mostly sorted so that Redshift can perform a range-bound scan. If rows have not been inserted into a table in the order of the sort key, a vacuum operation is required to sort and reorganize the table.

Redshift's autonomics feature, Auto Vacuum, will automatically identify unsorted tables and tables with unreclaimed space and vacuum them. However, if the cluster is constantly busy, there may not be any spare resources to run the Auto Vacuum, so you might need to run the vacuum manually.

To run a vacuum manually, use the VACUUM command, which you can learn more about here:

https://docs.aws.amazon.com/redshift/latest/dg/r_VACUUM_command.html

The command has the options shown in Table 5.2 to control its behavior.

TABLE 5.2 VACUUM command options

Vacuum Command	Description
VACUUM FULL table_name	Sorts the whole table and removes logically deleted rows, reclaiming consumed disk space. VACUUM FULL is the default, and it's not necessary to use the FULL keyword.
VACUUM SORT ONLY table_name	Sorts the table but does not reclaim space from logically deleted rows.
VACUUM DELETE ONLY table_name	Reclaims space from logically deleted rows but does not sort the table.
VACUUM REINDEX table_name	Analyzes interleaved sort keys and runs a full vacuum. Only required on tables with an interleaved sort key.
VACUUM RECLUSTER table_name	Sorts and reclaims space from portions of the table. Doesn't perform a full table reorganization, shortening the vacuum time. Is effective on frequently loaded large tables where only recent data is queried.

Compression Encoding

As previously discussed, Redshift is a columnar database. This allows the encoding (compression) to be set at the column level rather than the row level, like in more traditional databases. Redshift has 12 different encoding types suitable for various data types:

- AZ64
- BYTEDICT

- DELTA
- DELTA32K
- LZO
- MOSTLY8
- MOSTLY16
- MOSTLY32
- RAW (no compression)
- RUNLENGTH
- TEXT255
- TEXT32K
- ZSTD

See the *Redshift Database Developer Guide* for full details of each type. You can manually specify the encoding type for each column in the CREATE TABLE/ALTER TABLE statement; otherwise, Redshift will automatically select an appropriate encoding with ATO, which is the recommended option. Columns assigned as sort keys should be set to RAW (uncompressed) because compressing sort key columns causes the sort key to be less effective.

SQL Query Optimization

Optimizing SQL queries is a deep topic in any database. In this book, we'll cover the primary best practices on Redshift and some of the system tables you can use to help with optimization.

Best Practices for Writing Queries on Redshift

Here are some best practices for writing queries:

- Avoid using SELECT *. Include only the columns you specifically need.
- Use a CASE expression to perform complex aggregations rather than selecting from the same table multiple times.
- Don't use cross-joins unless absolutely necessary. (Joining tables without a join condition creates a Cartesian product.)
- Avoid non-equijoins—joins that don't use an equals sign (=).
- Use subqueries in cases where one table in the query is used only for predicate conditions and the subquery returns a small number of rows (fewer than ~200), instead of joining.
- Use predicates (filters) to restrict the dataset as much as possible.
- Avoid using functions in query predicates.

- If possible, use a WHERE clause to restrict the dataset and ensure that at least the leading column in the Sort Key is part of the WHERE selection.

- Add predicates to filter tables participating in joins, even if the join condition filters the same data.

- If you use both GROUP BY and ORDER BY clauses, ensure that the columns are in the same order in both clauses.

System Tables for Query Behavior

As shown in Table 5.3, Redshift has several system tables that help identify performance problems with SQL queries.

TABLE 5.3   Redshift system tables for performance tuning

System Table	Description
SYS_QUERY_HISTORY	Provides details of running and completed queries, including DDL, DML, COPY, UNLOAD, and Spectrum queries.
SYS_QUERY_DETAIL	Provides in-depth details of a query at the processing step level.
SYS_QUERY_TEXT	Provides the full SQL text of all queries.
STL_EXPLAIN	Explain plan of queries that have been submitted for execution.
STL_ALERT_EVENT_LOG	Logs potential performance issues identified in queries by the query optimizer with suggested solutions (e.g., missing statistics, nested loop joins, large distribution, etc.). This table is not available on serverless clusters, only on provisioned clusters.

Workload Management (WLM)

Redshift is a multiuser system and, therefore, needs to handle many different workloads running simultaneously. These could include ETL processes for loading and transforming new data, business users running dashboards, and analysts running ad hoc SQL queries. Redshift's *workload management* (WLM) feature efficiently divides up the resources of a cluster and allocates them to each running workload.

Redshift provisioned clusters have two types of WLM: manual and auto. Auto is the recommended setting for most clusters. Manually configuring WLM can be used in specialized situations; however, it takes skill and effort and may need to be adjusted over time as workloads change. Therefore, auto WLM is the right choice for most use cases, and this book does not cover manual WLM in detail.

Redshift Serverless has automated workload management but currently does not allow you to configure separate queues or set priorities on queues.

Auto WLM

With auto WLM on provisioned clusters, you can create up to eight separate queues to which you can then assign a priority and assign users either directly or via a group or a role. When a user runs a query, the query is sent to the queue the user is assigned to, and auto WLM determines the number of resources to provide the query. Auto WLM manages query concurrency (the number of queries run simultaneously) and memory across the cluster using machine learning algorithms that determine how best to provision the cluster's resources depending on what is currently running on the cluster and using statistics from workloads that have been run in the past.

This is a significant advantage over manual WLM, where you must specify a fixed amount of memory and concurrency per queue. Therefore, even if a queue has no queries running on it, resources (memory and concurrency) are still assigned to it and will be wasted. Auto WLM can move those resources to a queue (or multiple queues) with queries running on them, ensuring that a cluster's resources are efficiently used.

The priority of a queue can be set to the following values, from highest to lowest:

- HIGHEST
- HIGH
- NORMAL
- LOW
- LOWEST

A higher-priority queue will have more memory and concurrency dedicated to the queries running on it. Auto WLM can also kill queries on lower priority queues to free up concurrency for queries waiting on a higher-priority queue.

Short Query Acceleration (SQA)

Short query acceleration (SQA) is a feature that helps prevent "short" running queries from getting stuck queueing behind "long" running queries. When SQA is enabled, any queries that WLM's ML algorithms consider to be short-running are sent to a special SQA queue, where they are sent to run ahead of any long-running queries. SQA is not a queue-specific feature and works across all queues.

Query Monitoring Rules (QMR)

Another useful and powerful feature of WLM is *query monitoring rules* (QMRs). With QMRs, you can assign rules on a queue to perform actions when a condition on a metric is met. For example, you can create a QMR rule to kill any queries running for more than 30 minutes, or you can create a rule to log a row into a system table for any queries processing more than 1 billion rows in a join step.

QMRs allow you to put "safety guardrails" on a cluster to prevent users from misusing resources. For example, if a user writes a query and misses a join condition in the WHERE clause, the query will create a huge Cartesian product that consumes many resources, slowing down other queries and workloads. A QMR rule can automatically catch and abort this type of query before it degrades the cluster's overall performance. Table 5.4 lists some examples of the available metrics that can be used in a QMR.

TABLE 5.4   Example Redshift QMR metrics

Metric	Name
Query execution time	query_execution_time
Rows joined	join_row_count
Return row count	return_row_count

To see the full list of QMR metrics that you can create a condition on, refer to the following documentation:

```
https://docs.aws.amazon.com/redshift/latest/dg/cm-c-wlm-query-
monitoring-rules.html#cm-c-wlm-query-monitoring-metrics
```

Table 5.5 lists the possible actions a QMR can take on auto WLM.

TABLE 5.5   Redshift QMR actions

Action	Description
Log	Information about the query is written to the STL_WLM_RULE_ACTION system table.
Abort	The action is logged, and the query is cancelled.
Change priority	The query's priority is changed.

Each WLM queue can have up to 25 rules, allowing you to control resource usage across the cluster at a detailed level. It is generally recommended to have more rules and tighter controls on queues where users have free reign to write and run any queries, and less control is needed on queues where the queries have been tested and proven to have acceptable performance.

A useful script is available on the Redshift Utils GitHub that analyzes a cluster and gives a list of candidate QMRs for the cluster's workloads:

```
https://github.com/awslabs/amazon-redshift-utils/blob/master/src/
AdminScripts/wlm_qmr_rule_candidates.sql
```

Concurrency Scaling

Concurrency Scaling is a feature that allows Redshift provisioned clusters to scale out automatically during periods of high concurrency (the number of queries run simultaneously). It is common for a DW to experience an uneven concurrency load and have periods when there is a sudden "burst" in the number of queries being run. Monday mornings are a typical example, when users log in and run their dashboards to see the results from the weekend, creating many queries that hit the DW simultaneously. This is a situation in which legacy DWs struggled because they had no way of scaling to handle the change in workload.

On Redshift, when a cluster has reached its concurrency limit and queries start to wait, Redshift pulls in additional clusters from a warm pool in the cloud and routes the waiting queries to the new clusters to run. Once the queries have completed running, the additional clusters are sent back to the warm pool.

Concurrency Scaling works for both writes and reads; therefore, the feature will handle any burst of ETL workloads running INSERTs, UPDATEs, DELETEs, etc.

Concurrency Scaling needs to be enabled on provisioned clusters in order for it to work and can be individually enabled or disabled on each WLM queue. You can also set the maximum number of Concurrency Scaling clusters that will be activated at any time, up to 10. Concurrency Scaling is an extra-cost feature on provisioned clusters and is charged using the on-demand rates for the cluster size, with one hour of free usage for every 24 hours the cluster is running.

Serverless clusters have similar functionality called Autoscaling, which is always enabled. To control costs, the MaxRPU setting, which can be adjusted in the console or via the Redshift API, limits the amount a serverless cluster can scale out to.

Example Auto WLM Setup

Table 5.6 shows an example auto WLM setup.

TABLE 5.6 Example Redshift auto WLM setup with SQA = TRUE

Queue Number	Queue Name	Priority	Concurrency Scaling	QMR Rules	
				Condition	Action
1	Dashboards	HIGH	Auto	Query execution time (seconds) > 1,800	Log
2	ETL	NORMAL	Auto		
3	Adhoc Queries	LOW	Off	Query execution time (seconds) > 1,800	Abort
				Rows joined (rows) > 1,000,000,000	Abort
				Return row count (rows) > 1,000,000	Abort

This WLM setup defines three different queues, one for each workload. It gives the highest priority to the Dashboards queue to dedicate more resources to running dashboards to keep users happy. Concurrency Scaling is set to Auto so Redshift can scale out during periods of high concurrency, like the Monday morning rush.

The ETL queue has a lower priority, and Concurrency Scaling is set to Auto to help with any burst of write activity.

The Adhoc Queries queue has been given the lowest priority, and Concurrency Scaling is set to Off. This is because it is meant as a "sandbox" type environment, where analysts are free to experiment and run any SQL query and, therefore, could use all the cluster's resources with poorly written or particularly large queries. The QMR rules on the Adhoc Queries queue are also the strictest.

Short query acceleration (SQA) has also been enabled at the cluster level and will apply to all queues.

Data Sharing

With Redshift's *data sharing* feature, you can run multiple clusters (or serverless workgroups) on the same storage. This allows you to break away from a monolithic architecture with all your workloads running on the same compute resources and provides a more scalable, modern multi-cluster architecture that isolates your compute workloads and allows you to right-size the resources for each workload.

With data sharing, one cluster is designated as a producer, and one (or multiple) cluster(s) is defined as a consumer (see Figure 5.8). The producer cluster creates a data share, adds database objects like tables, views, and functions, and then authorizes other clusters to access the share.

Authorized clusters can then consume the data share, which creates a new database on the consumer cluster containing the shared objects. The shared objects can then be read from and written to on the consumer cluster. Data sharing across clusters is "zero-copy," meaning that the data is not duplicated on each consumer cluster; it is read from the shared RMS storage. RMS storage makes data sharing possible; therefore, the feature is only available for RA3 node types on provisioned clusters and Serverless workgroups.

FIGURE 5.8   Redshift data sharing

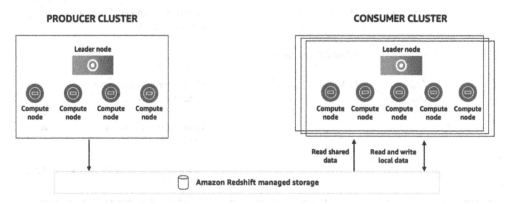

Some common architectures that use this feature are hub-and-spoke and data mesh. In a Redshift hub-and-spoke architecture, you typically have a producer cluster for ETL processing and multiple consumer clusters for data consumption. The consumer clusters could be used for different use cases, such as dashboards, data science, and ad hoc queries, or they could be dedicated to business units in an organization, such as sales, marketing, and finance. By dedicating a cluster to a business unit, you can charge back the cost of the cluster to that business unit, allowing you to have a decentralized cost structure.

In Figure 5.9, the ETL cluster is the producer, and the three other clusters are the consumers. Notice how each cluster is a different size (node type and the number of nodes). The producer or any of the consumers could also have been a Serverless cluster.

FIGURE 5.9   Data sharing in a hub-and-spoke architecture

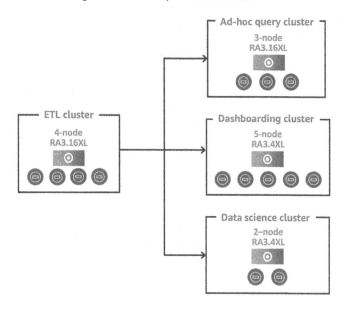

In a data mesh-style architecture, each cluster typically hosts a "data product," which could align with a business unit. That data product shares its data with other data products (see Figure 5.10).

Run the following lab to learn how to set up and use data sharing:

```
https://catalog.workshops.aws/redshift-immersion/lab14
```

Cluster Resizing

Another benefit of Redshift is that a cluster can be easily and quickly resized. You can resize a cluster up or down by adding or removing compute nodes and changing the node type.

This ability to resize can be used to grow a cluster over time as workloads increase and for one-off or periodic workloads requiring more processing power to complete within a given timeframe. Resizing allows you to scale the cluster up on demand and back down once the workload is complete.

FIGURE 5.10 Data sharing used in data mesh-style architecture

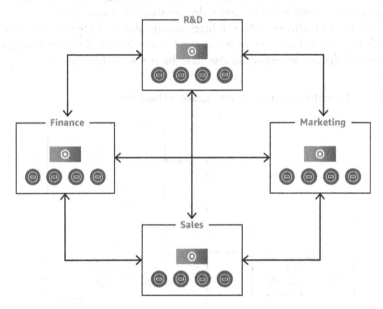

On Serverless, you can resize a workgroup by changing the base RPU amount, or AI-driven scaling will automatically resize it based on the workload. There are two methods for resizing provisioned clusters: elastic resize and classic resize.

Elastic Resize

An elastic resize takes an average of 10 minutes to complete. It can add or remove compute nodes from a cluster (known as an *in-place resize*) or change the node type. Any connected sessions will be held during the resize process for in-place resizes, but some may be dropped. When changing the node type, all queries will be dropped.

An elastic resize is the fastest way to resize a cluster. It works by moving data slices onto and off compute nodes. Compute nodes are partitioned into slices that contain memory and disk space. When you elastic resize a cluster up, Redshift adds new compute nodes and then moves slices from the original nodes onto the new nodes. The reverse happens when you resize the cluster down; slices are moved off of the nodes that will be removed and moved onto the remaining nodes. Redshift can add or remove compute by moving the slices around without redistributing the data across the new compute node arrangement.

However, this method limits the number of configurations you can resize to. For example, if you have a cluster with two nodes of RA3.xlplus, each node has two slices by default; therefore, you can resize up to a maximum of four nodes, with each node now having one data slice. The Redshift Console will list what configurations you can resize up and down to. You can also use the `describe-node-configuration-options` AWS CLI command with the `action-type resize-cluster` option.

Classic Resize

A classic resize differs from an elastic resize in that there are no limitations on the configurations you can resize to. This is because, unlike an elastic resize, a classic resize does redistribute the data.

A classic resize works by creating a new cluster with the chosen configuration, which could be for an in-place resize or a change of node type. Any tables with a distribution style of KEY are created on the new cluster with a distribution style of EVEN. Data and metadata are then migrated to the new cluster, and the original cluster's endpoint is assigned to the new cluster. This process takes a few minutes, and any connected sessions are dropped.

Once this part of the resize is finished, the new cluster is opened and is available for reads and writes. In the background, any tables that initially had a distribution style of KEY and were changed to EVEN in the resize are redistributed back to the original KEY style. This is the second stage of the resize and can take hours to days, depending on the amount of data and number of tables.

Be aware that as the distribution style of some tables has changed, queries can take longer to run until this phase has been completed. It is not advised to run a classic resize on a very busy cluster, and you should reduce the workloads or plan an outage to ensure that the cluster has enough free resources to complete this stage as quickly as possible. Concurrency Scaling can also help reduce the performance impact.

Loading Data into Redshift

Data can be ingested into Redshift in batches or near-real-time via streaming.

Batch Ingestion

For batch ingestion, the recommended method is to use the *COPY command* to load files into Redshift. The COPY command is recommended over the INSERT command because it can load files in parallel directly via the compute nodes, enabling much faster loading performance. Ingestion via the INSERT or MERGE command must traverse the leader node, serializing the load.

The COPY command can load many different file types, including:

- CSV
- Fixed-width
- Avro
- JSON
- PARQUET
- ORC
- SHAPEFILE (geolocation data)

Files can also be compressed with the following formats:

- BZIP2
- GZIP
- LZOP
- ZSTD

The COPY command loads files into Redshift directly via the compute nodes in parallel by utilizing the compute nodes' slices. Each slice can load one file at a time. Therefore, if your cluster has 32 slices, it can load all 32 files in parallel in one batch. For the following file types, Redshift can automatically split the files to match the slice count of the cluster:

- Uncompressed CSV files
- BZIP compressed CSV files
- Columnar files (Parquet/ORC)

For other file types that cannot be automatically split, you can optimize your file loading performance by making the number of files you are ingesting in a batch a multiple of the number of data slices on your cluster. For example, if you have two nodes of RA3.4xl and, therefore, eight slices. (The RA3.4xl node type has four slices per node.) You will get the best ingestion performance if you split your files into multiples of 8 (e.g., 16, 32, 64, etc.), with the size of each file being between 1 MB and 1 GB after compression.

Redshift Spectrum for Ingestion

Redshift Spectrum can also be used to ingest data into Redshift. Spectrum is more flexible than the COPY command because, with Spectrum, you query your S3 data lake with a SQL query. This allows you to manipulate the data before loading it into Redshift (e.g., you can filter data you do not want to ingest, remove columns, aggregate result sets, etc.). However, with the COPY command, you have much less ability to manipulate/transform the data, and you have to load the whole file/all of the files in the S3 prefix.

Spectrum is helpful for incremental loads, i.e., only loading new or changed (delta) data, as you can select and load just the delta rows with a filter. Spectrum incurs an additional cost, however. Therefore, using the COPY command is a better option for ingesting large amounts of data, such as a complete history load, where you are loading a whole table with all the data from your source.

Best Practices for Batch Data Ingestion

The best practices for batch data ingestion include the following:

- Use the COPY command.
- If you cannot use COPY, use a multi-row INSERT command instead of a single-row INSERT command.
- Match the number of files in a batch to the cluster's slice count for file types that Redshift cannot automatically split.

- Keep the file size between 1 MB and 1 GB after compression.
- Use a single COPY command to load multiple files under the same S3 prefix, not a COPY command per file.
- Consider using Redshift Spectrum for incremental (delta) loads.

Streaming Ingestion

Batch ingesting data files is not the only way to load data into Redshift. Data can also be streamed into Redshift to allow near-real-time analytics suitable for sources that generate data continuously, such as IoT devices or clickstream data. You can stream data into Redshift with either the Redshift streaming ingestion feature or Amazon Firehose.

Redshift Streaming Ingestion

With the *Redshift streaming ingestion* feature, data can be streamed directly into Redshift from Amazon Kinesis Data Streams and Amazon Managed Streaming for Apache Kafka.

Redshift streaming ingestion consumes data from a Kinesis or Kafka stream and loads it into a materialized view in Redshift. For instance, a JSON event on a Kinesis stream can be loaded into a materialized view in a SUPER data type (the native data type for semi-structured data) column. When the materialized view is refreshed, new data is pulled from the stream and inserted into the SUPER column. The JSON can then be queried using the PartiQL SQL syntax extensions. The streaming materialized view can either be manually refreshed (the default) or can be set to pull new events from the queue as they arrive automatically.

Amazon Firehose

Data can also be streamed into Redshift via *Amazon Firehose*. The main difference with the Redshift streaming ingestion feature is that Firehose uses a push method. In contrast, streaming ingestion uses a pull method and pulls events off a queue and into a materialized view. Firehose drops the data into a file on S3 and then uses the COPY command to push data to a Redshift table, in effect doing a mini-batch load.

Firehose also incurs additional costs, so it is recommended that you use the streaming ingestion feature if you are using Kinesis or Managed Kafka. However, Firehose does support more sources and can be used if you are not using Kinesis or Managed Kafka.

Unloading Data from Redshift

In addition to loading data into Redshift from S3 using the COPY command, you can do the opposite and unload data from Redshift into S3 with the *UNLOAD command*. The UNLOAD command extracts the results of a SELECT statement into delimited text, JSON, or Apache Parquet files on S3.

If you have a large amount of data to unload from Redshift, using the UNLOAD command is recommended rather than selecting large numbers of rows through JDBC/ODBC or the Data API. This is because, like COPY, UNLOAD processes data in parallel across the compute nodes, allowing you to rapidly extract data from Redshift's RMS storage to S3.

By unloading data from Redshift into your S3 data lake, you can keep your cluster lean by archiving off older and less valuable data, and you can make data that you have transformed and refined in Redshift available to other parts of your organization through open file formats like Apache Parquet.

Transforming Data in Redshift

As well as being a fast database for running BI and analytics queries, Redshift can also be used as a powerful transformation engine in an ELT (extract, load, and transform) architecture. ELT processing differs from ETL (extract, transform, and load) processing, in that instead of using an external technology such as AWS Glue to transform the data first and then load the transformed dataset into the data warehouse, the data is first loaded into the data warehouse in its raw state and then transformed with SQL using the power of the data warehouse engine. Redshift is commonly used in ELT architectures, and with its MPP architecture, it can efficiently transform vast amounts of data.

Stored Procedures

When transforming data on Redshift, you use SQL to modify the data with statements such as INSERT, UPDATE, MERGE, and DELETE. You can run these statements individually as part of a workflow from a tool like AWS Step Functions. However, you can also group related statements into a stored procedure, which, as the name implies, is stored inside Redshift and, when executed, runs each of its SQL statements in the given order. Stored procedures also include typical programmatic features like variables, conditional and looping expressions to control logic flow, exception handling, and transaction control.

Stored procedures are an excellent way to modularize your ELT code to make it more understandable and maintainable. Run the following lab to learn how to use stored procedures in an ELT ongoing load:

```
https://catalog.workshops.aws/redshift-immersion/lab13
```

Materialized Views

A *materialized view* is a database object that stores precomputed query results in a "materialized" (i.e., persisted) dataset. Subsequent queries can use the precomputed results from the materialized view, skipping the expensive tasks of reading the underlying tables and performing joins and aggregates, thereby improving query performance.

Materialized views are not just a simple cache, however. When data changes are applied to the underlying tables, materialized views can be refreshed automatically or manually with a full or incremental refresh, and other similar queries can use them, not just the query used to create the materialized view.

Also, with the query rewrite feature, user queries on base tables can be automatically and transparently rewritten by the database engine to use one or more materialized view, improving the performance of dashboards and queries without the user even needing to be aware that the materialized views exist.

A common use of materialized views is to create aggregate tables (also known as summary tables). As the name implies, an aggregate table aggregates a dataset to reduce the overall amount of data, improving the performance of queries. For example, when reporting on sales data, it is typical to report on the total sales amount per day rather than every sales transaction and its sales amount. Instead of recalculating a daily amount every time you run a query, you can calculate the daily totals once and persist them in a materialized view to be used by any other queries requiring this information.

Figure 5.11 is a simple example of a materialized view (mv_loc_sales) created from two base tables (store_info and sales). The materialized view joins the two base tables and aggregates the total_sales amount by the location (loc) column.

FIGURE 5.11   A materialized view (mv_loc_sales) created from two base tables (store_info and sales)

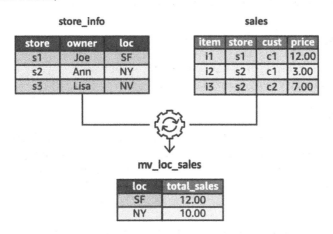

Materialized views can be refreshed either with a full or incremental refresh. A full refresh replaces all data in the materialized view and completely reloads it from the base tables. An incremental refresh tracks modifications to the base tables (inserts, updates, deletes) and modifies only the changed rows in the materialized view. Not all materialized views can be incrementally refreshed; it depends on the underlying SQL query. Certain SQL elements, including OUTER JOIN and window functions, are currently not supported for incremental refreshes.

A materialized view refresh can be manually run or set to run automatically when Redshift has spare resources.

Automated Materialized Views

An innovative feature of Redshift is its *Automated Materialized Views* (AutoMV). Redshift monitors queries on a cluster and, using machine learning algorithms, determines if a query—or multiple queries—could be served by a materialized view and if the performance gain from a materialized view would be worth the cost of the processing power and disk space to build and maintain it.

If Redshift determines that the performance benefit is worth the cost, it automatically creates a materialized view in the background and redirects queries on the base tables to the materialized view using the query rewrite feature. This process is completely transparent to the user, who should only notice that their query's performance has improved.

Redshift then keeps the state of the materialized view in sync with the base tables using automatic incremental refreshes. It will finally drop the materialized view if it is no longer being used or cannot be refreshed, which could happen if the structure of the base tables is changed.

For a deep dive into AutoMV, see the following blog post:

```
https://aws.amazon.com/blogs/big-data/optimize-your-amazon-redshift-
query-performance-with-automated-materialized-views
```

Data Modeling on Redshift

Redshift supports various types of data models, the main types being star schemas, snowflake schemas, and highly denormalized/flat models.

Star Schema

The most common data model used in Redshift and data warehousing is the *star schema*, also known as a dimensional model. A star schema contains two main types of tables: fact tables and dimension tables. A star schema has a fact table joined to and surrounded by multiple dimension tables, giving it a "star-like" appearance (see Figure 5.12).

Fact Tables

There are different types of *fact tables*. For this book, we'll discuss the most common type: the transactional fact table. As the name implies, a transactional fact table stores data at the transaction level, such as a row per sales order, per shipment, etc. The columns of the fact table store numeric information about the transaction, such as the sales amount and the number of items ordered, along with foreign keys that join to the dimension tables. Fact tables are the largest tables in a star schema in terms of size (number of rows/data volume); however, as they ideally only contain numeric columns (there are exceptions in the real world), they are narrow (less space used for a row), which optimizes the amount of storage they consume.

Dimension Tables

Dimension tables store textual information that describes the fact transactions, such as what products were part of the order, which customer made the order, which website the order was made on, etc. Dimension tables are usually wide (a lot of long text columns). Still, they optimize storage by normalizing the entity (e.g., one row per product in the product dimension), rather than repeating the product details per transaction row.

FIGURE 5.12 A star schema data model with a central fact table surrounded by dimension tables

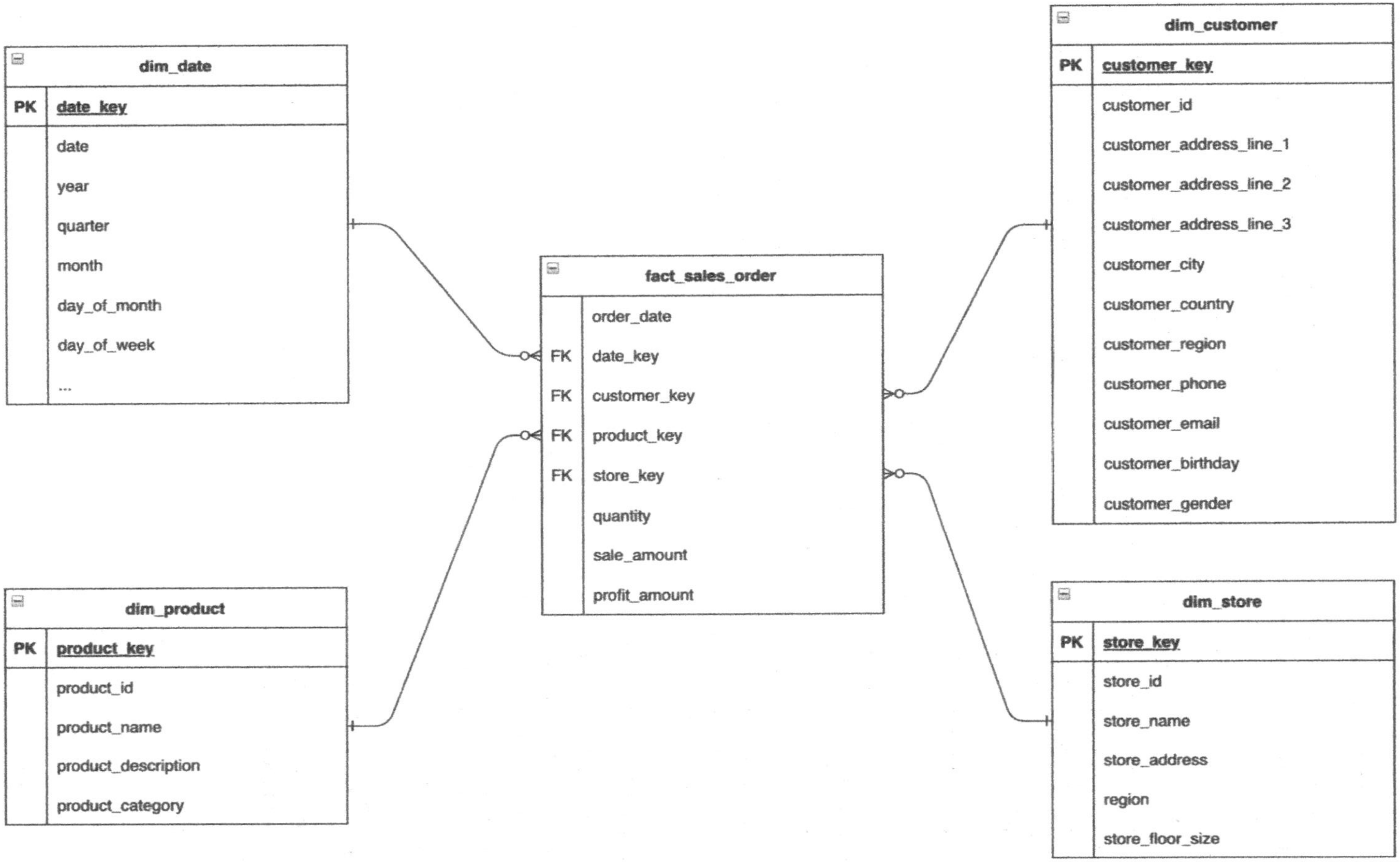

Snowflake Schema

Snowflake schemas are star schemas with normalized dimensions (see Figure 5.13). Any repeating attribute is normalized into its own dimension, which is joined to the original dimension.

For example, if a product dimension has a product category attribute and one of the product categories is "Hardware," then products in this category would have "Hardware" repeated in every row. In a snowflake schema, you would create a new dimension, `dim_product_category`, which would join to the product dimension and have a single row for the Hardware category.

Snowflake schemas use less storage than star schemas; however, they are not as easy to use, and the extra joins involved can affect performance. Therefore, a star schema is preferred.

Highly Denormalized/Flat

A third type of data model commonly used in Redshift is the *highly denormalized,* or "flat," table (see Figure 5.14). Instead of normalizing out the dimensions, all the entities are denormalized and pre-joined into a single wide table. In this model, queries can perform better because Redshift doesn't need to do the expensive processing step of joining tables; however, it can increase the amount of storage used because long text columns will be repeated for every row. The performance of updates on dimension columns can also be affected because every row needs to be updated, whereas in a star schema dimension, only a single row would need to be updated.

Semi-Structured Data

Traditionally, data warehouses stored and processed mainly structured data; however, modern data warehouses also need to be able to handle semi-structured data such as JSON. In Redshift, semi-structured data is dealt with using the SUPER data type. SUPER is a native data type that stores schemaless JSON, which can be queried directly with SQL using the PartiQL extension language. Redshift Spectrum also allows you to query semi-structured data from objects stored in your S3 data lake.

Data Security in Redshift

In this section, we will focus on two key areas of data security: database security and AWS Lake Formation security.

FIGURE 5.13 A snowflake schema data model with a central fact table surrounded by normalized dimension tables

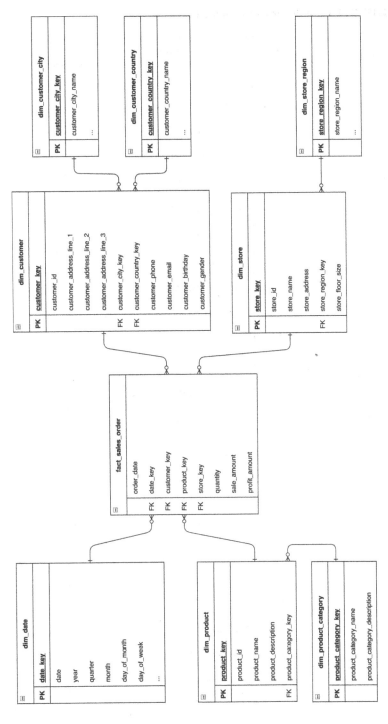

FIGURE 5.14   A denormalized/flat table

sales_order_flat
order_date
product_id
product_name
product_description
product_category_name
product_category_description
customer_id
customer_address_line_1
customer_address_line_2
customer_address_line_3
customer_city_name
customer_country_name
customer_phone
customer_email
customer_birthday
customer_gender
store_id
store_name
store_address
store_region_name
store_floor_size
quantity
sale_amount
profit_amount

Database Security

Redshift has a layout similar to other relational databases and includes the following objects:

- Databases
- Schemas
- Users
- Groups
- Roles

At the top level is the database, the main container. Users, groups, and roles are defined at this level. The database is then divided into schemas. A schema holds the main objects, such as tables, views, materialized views, UDFs, and stored procedures.

By default, the user who creates the database object is the owner and can grant permission to other users to access the object either with a direct grant on the object or by granting permission to either a group or role and then granting the group or role to a user. Groups and roles are similar in their functionality. The difference is that a role can be assigned to another role, which cannot be done with a group, making roles a more powerful way to organize permissions. It's recommended to use roles rather than groups.

When a Redshift cluster is launched, a superuser, the admin user, is created. A superuser has full permissions over all databases and database objects on the cluster and can create other superusers.

Column-Level Security

Access can be granted at the column level, allowing you to hide sensitive data like personality identifiable information (PII) or credit card details from particular users and groups/roles. Access to columns is set by GRANT and REVOKE statements, similar to how table-level permissions are set.

Row-Level Security

Security can also be set at the row level in Redshift, meaning users can only see rows in a table depending on their permissions. For example, rows in a sales transactions table could be secured by country, with sales managers only able to see sales made in their country. Redshift does this by dynamically appending a WHERE clause filter to queries as they are run, making the process fully transparent to users and not requiring additional views or different tables to be created and stored.

To set row-level security (RLS) on a table in Redshift, you create a policy object that defines a column filter (e.g., country = 'New Zealand'). You then attach the policy to a table and users and roles. If a user who has this RLS policy attached runs the following query:

```
SELECT country, SUM(sales_amount)
FROM sales;
```

Redshift will rewrite the query to the following before it is run, ensuring that the user only sees the `sales_amount` for New Zealand:

```
SELECT country, SUM(sales_amount)
FROM sales
WHERE country = 'New Zealand';
```

Multi-tenant applications are an excellent use case for RLS. Instead of having multiple copies of your data model, one for each customer/tenant, which adds a lot of extra development, maintenance, and administration work, you can add a column to each table that identifies which tenant the row belongs to (e.g., `tenant_id`). You can then create an RLS policy for each tenant and assign it to them (e.g., `'tenant_id = 1'`, `'tenant_id = 2'`, etc.). Each tenant will now only see their data when they query the database.

Dynamic Data Masking

With the *dynamic data masking* (DDM) feature, you can obfuscate data at the column and cell level, protecting sensitive information like email addresses, credit card numbers, and other PII data. The masking is dynamic, meaning the data is obfuscated when queried and does not require different versions of the data set to be created and stored.

Data in a column can be completely masked (e.g., credit card numbers shown as XXXX-XXXX-XXXX-XXXX) or partially masked (e.g., XXXX-XXXX-XXXX-1234), or it can be masked based on complex rules; however, it's recommended not to make the masking logic too complex, as this may affect performance on large datasets.

To apply DDM to a table, you create a policy object that applies custom masking rules using user-defined functions in SQL, Python, or Lambda. You then attach the policy to the table and assign the policy to a user or role. By having different masking policies on the same table and assigning the policies appropriately to users and roles, you can secure sensitive information at various levels. For example, general users will only see fully masked credit card numbers, call center operators will see partially masked credit card numbers, and the fraud protection team will see the full unmasked credit card numbers.

AWS Lake Formation Security

Redshift integrates with AWS Lake Formation via Spectrum and data sharing. Spectrum can query data in S3 registered with an AWS Glue Data Catalog and managed by Lake Formation. With Lake Formation, you can establish security policies for table-, column-, row-, and cell-level permissions. Lake Formation then enforces security on queries made from Redshift via Spectrum.

Furthermore, Lake Formation can handle security for data sharing, allowing you to centrally define table-, column-, and row-level access across data shares.

Amazon DynamoDB

Amazon DynamoDB is a fully managed NoSQL database with unmatched scalability, performance, availability, and durability. It allows you to run web-based applications with vast numbers of requests and seamlessly scale up and down to match the incoming load while automatically replicating data across multiple Availability Zones, ensuring high availability and durability. Common use cases for DynamoDB are Internet-scale web, mobile, and gaming applications, such as e-commerce shopping carts, user session and profile management, and leaderboards.

What Is a NoSQL Database?

Unlike traditional OLTP databases, which store data in a relational format, NoSQL databases store data in a more flexible, non-relational way. This allows them to efficiently store and process semi-structured and unstructured data, making them well suited for modern applications like web, mobile, and gaming that require high performance at a massive scale.

As the name implies, you generally don't use SQL to interact with a NoSQL database. Instead, you use APIs that work nicely with programming languages, easing the development effort and increasing developer efficiency.

NoSQL databases typically use a distributed architecture, allowing them to scale out easily, quickly, and cost-effectively by adding more nodes. A traditional relational OLTP database often can only scale up, requiring you to increase the size of your base server (this is known as *vertical scaling*), which is a less flexible and usually more expensive way to scale.

DynamoDB Main Concepts

This section discusses the elements that are fundamental to how DynamoDB operates:

Tables Like most databases, DynamoDB's main "container" for storing data is the table, usually modeled on an entity such as a Customer or Sales table. A fundamental difference between tables in DynamoDB and a relational database is that you don't join multiple tables together in DynamoDB; instead, each table is designed to serve a predefined set of queries.

Items Tables hold items. An item is similar to a row or record in a relational database and uniquely identifies an entity, such as a particular customer or sale. Unlike a row in a relational database, however, an item does not have a predefined schema and can contain different attributes. The primary key attributes of a table do need to be the same for every item.

Attributes An item contains at least one attribute. An attribute is similar to a column in a relational database and stores information that describes the item (e.g., for Customer: CustomerID, Name, Address, etc.). Attributes can be scalar (i.e., have only one value) or be nested.

Primary Keys, Partition Keys, and Sort Keys Each table must have a primary key that uniquely identifies items in that table. A primary key comprises a partition key and, optionally, a sort key. The first attribute in an item is a partition key. This is a single scalar attribute used by DynamoDB to determine which partition (a subset of the storage) the item will be stored in. DynamoDB uses an internal hash function to choose an item's partition.

A composite primary key has a second attribute: the sort key. The sort key orders all items stored in the same partition. In tables with a composite primary key, it's possible to have multiple items with the same partition key as long as each has a different value for the sort key.

 The partition key of an item is also called a *hash attribute*, and the sort key of an item is also called a *range attribute*. When you create a table in DynamoDB, you define the KeyType as HASH or RANGE.

Here is an example of a Customer table in DynamoDB:

Customer

```
{
    "CustomerID": 990,
    "JoinDate": "2024-04-06"
    "LastName": "Ash",
    "FirstName": "Damien",
    "EmailAddress": "damien.ash@example.com"
}
{

    "CustomerID": 991,
    "JoinDate": "2024-08-15"
    "LastName": "Jones",
    "FirstName": "Tom",
    "HomeAddress": {
                "HouseNo": "32",
                "Street": "Main St",
                "City": "Huntsville",
                "State": "Alabama"
            }
}
{
    "CustomerID": 992,
    "JoinDate": "2024-10-20"
    "LastName": "Fabian",
    "FirstName": "Chris",
    "PhoneNo: "1-678-3343"
    "DeliveryAddress": {
                "POBoxNo: "1033",
                "City": "Los Angeles, CA"
            }
}
```

This *table* has a composite *primary key* comprising the `CustomerID` (*partition key*) and `JoinDate` (*sort key*) attributes. Each *item* is delimited in curly brackets and uniquely identified by the primary key. Notice that the structure of each item is different; this shows the flexibility of a schema-less data model in DynamoDB, with the primary key attributes only required to be in each item.

Querying DynamoDB

As previously mentioned, you usually don't write to or read from (query) a NoSQL database with SQL; instead, you use the provided API. Table 5.7 lists some of the main API calls.

TABLE 5.7 Example DynamoDB API calls

API Call	Description
`CreateTable`	Creates a table and optionally creates secondary indexes, or can enable DynamoDB Streams on a table.
`DeleteTable`	Removes (drops) a table.
`PutItem`	Writes (inserts) a single item into a table. You must specify the primary table but not other attributes.
`GetItem`	Returns (selects) a single item from the table. You must specify the primary key.
`Scan`	Returns all items from a table or index.
`UpdateItem`	Modifies (updates) one or many items in the table. You must specify the primary key.
`DeleteItem`	Removes (deletes) a single item from a table. You must specify the primary key.

> DynamoDB does provide a SQL-like alternative to using the API. PartiQL is a SQL-compatible query language that can interact with DynamoDB. It allows you to perform the API actions in a more SQL way. For example, to query a single item from the Customer table, you can use the API or PartiQL as follows:

API
`GetItem`

{

```
    TableName: "Customer",
    Key: {
        "CustomerID": 990,
        "JoinDate": "2024-04-06"
    }
}
```

The following call will return all the item's attributes because no attributes were specified.

PartiQL

```
SELECT *
FROM Customer
WHERE CustomerId=990
AND JoinDate='2024-04-06'
```

Run the following lab to learn how to set up and run basic operations on DynamoDB:

```
https://catalog.workshops.aws/dynamodb-labs/hands-on-labs
```

Secondary Indexes

Primary keys provide an efficient way to return an item from a table, but what if you want to return an item via an attribute that's not the primary key? This is where *secondary indexes* help. A secondary index is a DynamoDB object that contains a different primary key than the original (base) table and a subset of attributes from that table. Secondary indexes are read-only and maintained by DynamoDB, with any changes (item adds, modifies, deletes) on the base table automatically copied to the index. You query a secondary index the same way you would query a table.

DynamoDB has two types of secondary index:

Global Secondary Index   A global secondary index (GSI) has a different partition key than the base table and a different sort key, which is optional. GSIs are "global," as they are not tied to the base table partitions, and are implemented like a "shadow" table. They don't conflict with or use any resources from the base table, can be created when a table is created or added and dropped later, and only support eventual consistency. Up to 20 GSIs are supported on a table. (This is a soft limit that can be changed by AWS support.)

Local Secondary Index   A local secondary index (LSI) has the same partition key as the base table but a different sort key. LSIs are considered "local" because their partition scope is the same as the base table. They consume capacity from the base table because they don't have a "shadow" table. They must be created when the table is created and can't be added or dropped later, and support eventual or strong consistency chosen at query time. Up to five LSIs are supported on a table.

Time to Live

Time to Live (TTL) is a convenient feature for managing the lifecycle of data on DynamoDB. You enable TTL on a table and create a timestamp attribute on each item in the Unix epoch time format that defines when the item should be deleted. When that timestamp has been reached, DynamoDB will automatically delete the item within a few days. The timestamp attribute can be updated or removed before the delete date.

An example of how you could use the feature is to calculate the date several days into the future from the date the item was created (for example, 30 days) and write that timestamp to the TTL attribute. Then, if the item is updated, you calculate a new date from the update date and overwrite the TTL attribute with the new value.

TTL can be enabled on a table through the DynamoDB console or via an API.

DynamoDB Streams

In many database applications, the ability to track and audit data changes is required. Another name for this process is *change data capture* (CDC). DynamoDB simplifies CDC with its streams feature. With *DynamoDB Streams*, you can track changes to items in a table in near-real time, such as adding, modifying, and deleting items.

When you enable DynamoDB Streams on a table, any item modifications are saved as stream records to a separate log (the stream) and held for 24 hours before they are removed. A stream record contains the primary key of the modified item and information about the modification, including a before-and-after image for updated items and a before image for deleted items. Stream records are held in the stream in the order the changes were made.

DynamoDB Streams can be accessed via an API or integrated with Lamba functions, allowing you to build near-real-time applications triggered by changes to items in a table. For example, you may have a table storing delivery information for online orders, and you want to warn customers when delivery dates have changed. You can enable a DynamoDB stream on the table and configure a Lamba function to trigger when the delivery date attribute changes. Then, you can email the customer using the Amazon Simple Email Service (Amazon SES). You could also, for example, filter for high-priority customers and update a customer services application with Amazon Simple Notification Service (Amazon SNS), alerting a representative to call the customer.

DynamoDB Streams Kinesis Adapter

Another recommended way to consume DynamoDB Streams is to use the DynamoDB Kinesis Adapter (see Figure 5.15). The DynamoDB Streams API is low-level and requires your application to deal with the ordering of stream shards (collections of stream records). The Kinesis Adapter handles this for you, simplifying your coding. The Kinesis Client Library (KCL) further simplifies coding with other useful abstractions and design patterns to process DynamoDB Streams shards and stream records.

FIGURE 5.15   DynamoDB Streams interacting with the Kinesis Adapter and Kinesis Client Library

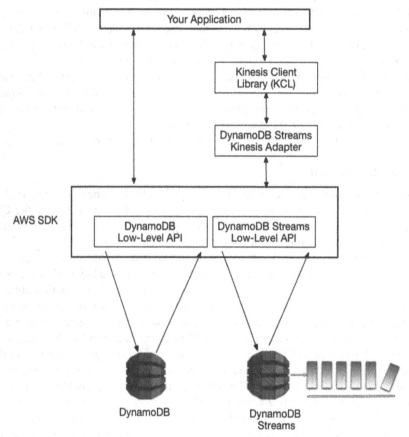

DynamoDB Read Consistency

Unlike most relational databases that always return the most up-to-date data when queried, DynamoDB has two different consistency types for reads: eventually consistent reads and strongly consistent reads.

Eventually Consistent Reads

By default, DynamoDB tables and indexes have *eventually consistent reads*. This means that a subsequent read may not return the most up-to-date data after new writes on a table. The latest data will be returned if you wait a short time and rerun the read request. You might wonder why you would want to use a consistency model that has a chance of returning stale data. This is because eventually consistent reads maximize throughput and minimize costs (eventually consistent reads are half the cost of strongly consistent reads), and immediately having the most recent data may not be a strong requirement for your application.

Strongly Consistent Reads

With *strongly consistent reads*, the most up-to-date data is always returned and reflects the updates from all prior successful write operations. Read API calls like GetItem and Scan have an optional ConsistentRead parameter; however, strongly consistent reads are only supported on tables and local secondary indexes, not global secondary indexes or DynamoDB Streams.

Global Tables

DynamoDB *global tables* enable you to create multi-region and multi-active applications without building a custom replication solution. You choose the regions where you want a replica of the global table, and DynamoDB automatically creates the tables and replicates data between them. Any changes to global table replicas are replicated to all other replicas, usually within one second. Existing single-region tables can be converted to global tables, and regions can be added or removed from existing global tables. Reads on global tables are eventually consistent. Some use cases for global tables include:

- Applications with globally dispersed users
- Low latency reads from multiple geolocations
- Disaster recovery across different regions
- Easy migrations across regions

DynamoDB Read/Write Capacity

DynamoDB has two modes to manage the read and write capacity of tables: provisioned mode and on-demand mode.

Provisioned Mode

With provisioned mode, the default mode, you manually set the capacity on a table and are charged for it whether you use it or not. You can enable auto-scaling and set an upper and lower capacity limit, and DynamoDB will scale up and down within those bounds based on demand. Provisioned mode allows you to control your costs and prevent unexpected cost overruns. You can further optimize by purchasing reserved capacity in advance for a lower overall cost. Provisioned mode is suitable for the following use cases:

- Predictable workloads
- Workloads with a steady demand or gradual increases
- Workloads with a known demand profile—can be cost-optimized by reserving capacity

Read/Write Capacity Units

When you create a table in provisioned mode, you need to specify the throughput capacity in terms of *read capacity units* (RCUs) and *write capacity units* (WCUs), determining the amount of data your application needs to read or write per second.

One RCU is the equivalent of one strongly consistent read, or two eventually consistent reads, per second for an item up to 4 KB. One WCU is the equivalent of one write per second for an item up to 1 KB. If your application exceeds the table's RCU or WCU limit, it will be throttled by DynamoDB and will receive an HTTP 400 (Bad Request | ProvisionedThroughputExceededException) error code.

The throughput capacity of a table can be changed at any time with the update-table API command. You can use the capacity calculator in the DynamoDB table creation console to calculate the required capacity for a table.

DynamoDB can also dynamically manage provisioned throughput with auto-scaling for tables and GSIs. You can define an upper and lower range for read and write capacity units and a target utilization percentage within that range. DynamoDB will scale to maintain the target utilization. With auto-scaling, you benefit from provisioned capacity while handling sudden traffic spikes without throttling your application.

On-Demand Mode

With on-demand mode, DynamoDB manages table capacity automatically. You don't have to plan capacity, provision, or set reservations. You simply use DynamoDB and pay for what you use. DynamoDB will scale to meet the load, scaling down to zero when there are no requests. On-demand mode is suitable for the following use cases:

- New workloads where you don't know the required capacity
- Unpredictable "spikey" workloads
- Periodic workloads that are often idle

Read/Write Request Units

Read and write request units determine how you are charged in on-demand mode. One *read request unit* is the equivalent of one strongly consistent read, or two eventually consistent reads, per second for an item up to 4 KB. One *write request unit* is the equivalent of one write per second for an item up to 1 KB.

By default, the on-demand mode throughput rate is limited by the per-table quota of 40K read request units and 40K write request units, which AWS Support can adjust. There are no account-level throughput quotas with the on-demand mode.

You can also set a maximum read/write throughput per second for on-demand tables and GSIs. Requests that exceed the maximum limit are throttled. This is recommended to prevent unexpected surges that cause bill shock, giving you more predictable costs.

On-demand Scaling and Throttling

On-demand mode automatically scales a table's throughput capacity to meet changes in traffic demand. A new on-demand table starts with a capacity of 4K writes per second and 12K reads per second. As the traffic volume on a table grows, on-demand mode will automatically scale to twice the table's previous traffic peak.

Let's say your application traffic hits a peak on a table of 100K reads per second; when this peak is reached, the on-demand capacity mode will instantly scale to a capacity of 200K reads per second. Then, you hit a peak of 200K reads per second, and the on-demand capacity mode will scale to a capacity of 400K reads per second, and so on.

Note, however, that throttling can occur if your application traffic exceeds double the previous peak within 30 minutes. In the preceding example, if the application traffic increases from 100K to *over* 200K requests per second within 30 minutes, DynamoDB can throttle requests. To prevent this throttling from happening, you can either space out your traffic growth over at least 30 minutes or pre-warm the table. Pre-warming a table involves converting an on-demand table to a provisioned table, setting the required write capacity for your peak, and then converting the table back to on-demand mode after several minutes.

DynamoDB Accelerator

With effective primary keys, DynamoDB can provide very fast query response times in milli-seconds. However, this performance can degrade as data volumes increase, and for some use cases, millisecond latency is not fast enough. To address this, AWS provides an in-memory caching service for DynamoDB: *DynamoDB Accelerator* (DAX). DAX provides microsecond read response times and has a DynamoDB-compatible API requiring only minimal changes to your existing applications. DAX is best suited for primarily read-heavy applications rather than write-heavy ones, and applications that require eventually consistent rather than strongly consistent reads.

Amazon Relational Database Service

Amazon Relational Database Service (Amazon RDS) is a managed service that helps to remove the administrative burden required to set up and maintain commercial and open-source relational databases. It automates many complex and time-consuming tasks, including deploying databases, scaling compute and storage, patching, and backups. It also allows you to easily improve the availability and durability of your databases with multi-AZ deployments and increase the read performance with read-replica instances. Amazon RDS currently covers the following relational database engines:

- Db2
- MariaDB
- Microsoft SQL Server
- MySQL
- Oracle
- PostgreSQL
- Aurora (MySQL Compatible)
- Aurora (PostgreSQL Compatible)

Typical use cases for Amazon RDS include online transactional processing (OLTP) applications with structured (i.e., relational) data. This includes enterprise resource planning (ERP), customer relationship management (CRM), financial systems, and Software as a Service (SaaS) applications. The following sections describe the main features of Amazon RDS.

RDS Scalability

The three main topics you'll want to know about regarding RDS scalability are read replicas, vertical scaling, and storage autoscaling.

Read Replicas

With RDS *read replicas*, you can easily scale out your database with additional read-only instances to provide enhanced performance on read-heavy workloads and lessen the load on your primary DB instance, so heavy reads don't affect its ability to serve your applications. You can create up to 15 read replicas per source DB instance, which can be deployed in different Availability Zones (AZ), adding durability to your system (see Figure 5.16).

When you create a read replica, RDS uses a snapshot of the primary DB instance and creates a read-only clone in a different AZ. Any data changes made on the primary DB instance are replicated *asynchronously*, using the database's native replication functionality, to the read replicas. This ensures that any delay in committing to the read replica doesn't affect the primary DB instance.

Each read replica has its own endpoint to which connections can be directed. A read replica can also be promoted to a full read/write DB instance, providing disaster recovery if the primary DB instance fails.

If your company doesn't have a data warehouse and you want to run reporting or BI queries against your database, read replicas are well suited for this use case and will prevent the extra load from running on your production DB; however, they should not be considered a replacement for a properly designed data warehouse running on technology specially designed for that purpose, like Amazon Redshift.

FIGURE 5.16   An Amazon RDS read replica deployment

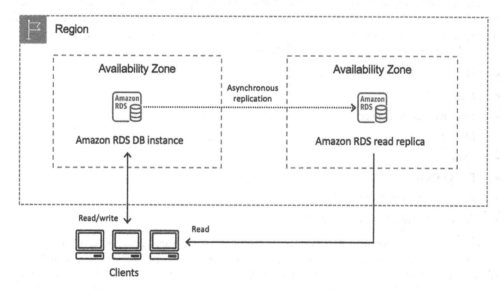

Vertical Scaling

Vertical scaling means to increase or decrease the size of your DB instance server. This may be required to handle an increase in your workloads or to reduce costs if you have over-provisioned the instance size. RDS allows you to change the *DB instance class* (type and size of server) from the console, the AWS CLI, or the RDS API. The process takes 10–15 minutes to complete and can be done on primary DB instances and read replicas. A resize can be run immediately or set to be processed during the next maintenance window.

Storage Auto Scaling

If you cannot determine the amount of storage your database will require ahead of time, RDS can automatically grow the storage when necessary. The *RDS* Storage Auto Scaling feature monitors storage usage, and when it detects that space is running low, it allocates more storage up to a maximum threshold you set.

RDS Availability

RDS offers two types of multiple Availability Zone (AZ) deployments to provide database durability and high availability: Multi-AZ DB instances and Multi-AZ DB clusters.

Multi-AZ DB Instance

The first and more basic type is a *Multi-AZ DB instance* (see Figure 5.17). With a Multi-AZ DB instance, a standby instance is created in a different AZ, and changes to data on the primary DB instance are replicated synchronously to the standby. This means that a transaction won't be committed until it is written to both the primary and standby instances. This is an essential distinction from the asynchronous read replica replication, as it can add latency to transactions on the primary instance; however, AWS has fast network connections between AZs to mitigate this issue.

If the primary DB instance fails (e.g., due to a hardware failure or in the unlikely event the whole AZ goes down), the standby instance is automatically promoted to the primary instance, and a new standby instance is created in a different AZ. Clients continue to connect to the same endpoint, which will be automatically changed to point toward the new primary instance in the other AZ. This gives clients a seamless experience without having to change their connection settings.

A Multi-AZ DB instance is an active-passive deployment with no client read access to the standby instance; therefore, it cannot be used to increase throughput for read-heavy workloads like a read replica.

Multi-AZ DB Cluster

The second type of multi-AZ deployment is a *Multi-AZ DB cluster* (see Figure 5.18). This type differs from a Multi-AZ DB instance in that it has two readable DB instances along with the read/write primary instance and spans three AZs. Replication from the primary DB instance to both the reader DB instances is *semi-synchronous,* meaning a transaction must be written to at least one reader instance before it's committed. Due to this behavior, the write latency is usually lower than that on a Multi-AZ DB instance deployment.

FIGURE 5.17 An Amazon RDS a Multi-AZ DB instance deployment

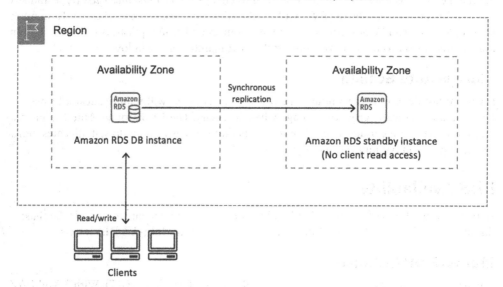

If the primary writer DB instance fails, the cluster will automatically failover to one of the secondary reader DB instances, switching to the instance with the most recent changes.

A Multi-AZ DB cluster offers several advantages over a Multi-AZ DB instance. It provides higher availability and durability with three Availability Zones (AZs) instead of two. Additionally, it has lower write latency due to semi-synchronous replication and can handle higher read capacity since the secondary DB instances are readable. However, the downside is the increased cost of having an additional DB instance.

FIGURE 5.18 An Amazon RDS a Multi-AZ DB cluster deployment

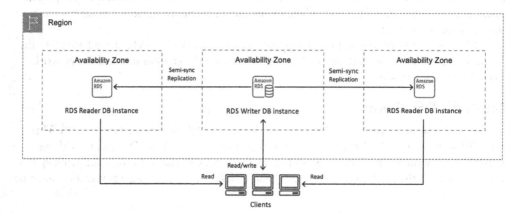

Run the following lab to learn how to set up and run basic operations on Amazon RDS for MySQL:

```
https://catalog.us-east-1.prod.workshops.aws/workshops/0135d1da-9f07
-470c-9845-44ead3c78212
```

Amazon Aurora

Amazon Aurora (Aurora) is another relational database engine included in RDS. It is an AWS native service fully compatible with MySQL and PostgreSQL. Aurora provides high performance (five times the throughput of MySQL and three times that of PostgreSQL), high availability, scalability, and global deployment at one-tenth the cost of commercial databases.

What is the difference between running MySQL or PostgreSQL on RDS and running them on Aurora? The following sections will cover the main differences in detail.

Aurora Topology

As shown in Figure 5.19, Aurora has a cluster topology with a single writer DB instance and up to 15 reader instances spanning multiple Availability Zones (AZs). The number of reader instances is automatically scaled based on throughput demand. If the writer instance fails, Aurora automatically promotes one of the reader instances to become the new writer. Aurora has two default endpoints for incoming connections: one for the writer and one for the readers. The reader endpoint serves as a load balancer between the reader instances, and the writer endpoint is automatically updated to point to the new writer instance in the case of a failover.

Distributed Storage

Other RDS databases, such as RDS MySQL or RDS PostgreSQL, utilize Amazon Elastic Block Store (EBS) attached storage. In contrast, Aurora employs a unique storage subsystem separate from the compute nodes, featuring a distributed and shared architecture. This design enables the independent scaling of both storage and compute resources.

On Aurora, data is stored in a storage volume accessible by all of the cluster's DB instances as a single global volume. Backups are continuously streamed from the storage volume to Amazon S3. A cluster storage volume consists of hundreds of virtual storage nodes with locally attached solid state drives (SSDs). These nodes are distributed across three Availability Zones (AZs), with six copies of the data (two per AZ), providing highly durable storage.

Serverless Configuration

Like other RDS databases, Aurora can be configured with a provisioned setup using different DB instance classes; however, it also supports a serverless configuration. With Aurora serverless, compute is automatically scaled up and down based on the workload, and you only pay for what you use. This allows you to meet the peak demand of your workloads and optimize for cost by not needing to over-provision a server that is not always fully utilized. Aurora scales "in-place." This means a running query will be granted more CPU and memory instantly and in a nondisruptive way.

FIGURE 5.19   The topology of Amazon Aurora

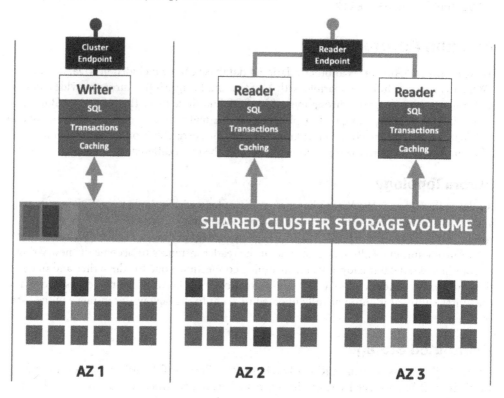

The capacity of a serverless instance is measured in *Aurora capacity units* (ACUs). One ACU is the equivalent of 2 GBs of memory. When you create a serverless instance, you set a minimum and maximum ACU within the range of 0.5 to 128 ACUs, and Aurora then scales in fine-grained increments, as small as 0.5 of an ACU.

Global Databases

If your application has global reach, you need low-latency reads from multiple geolocations, or you require full disaster recovery, Aurora *global databases* can meet your requirements (see Figure 5.20).

Global databases consist of a primary Aurora cluster in a single region (the primary region) and additional read-only clusters in up to five different secondary regions. Data replication from the primary to the secondary regions is done at the storage layer across AWS' high-speed backbone, with most transactions being replicated within a second. The read-only clusters can be created in regions close to your customer base, ensuring fast reads for your application. Database writes can be sent back to the primary cluster with the *write forwarding* feature.

FIGURE 5.20   Amazon Aurora global database

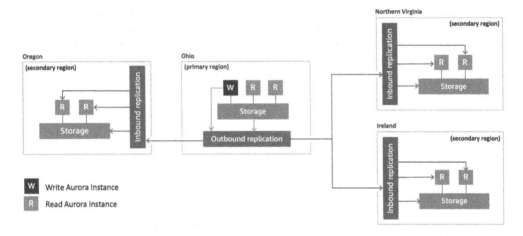

If the performance of a primary region deteriorates, or even if the entire region has an outage, you can perform a managed failover of the primary cluster to a different region; this promotes the secondary cluster in the new region into the primary write cluster. This promotion typically happens in less than one minute, providing fast and effective disaster recovery.

Amazon Neptune

Amazon Neptune is a fully managed, high-performance, highly available *graph database* and AWS's purpose-built data store for highly connected data. It can store billions of relationships, query them in milliseconds, and scale to hundreds of thousands of queries per second.

Like Amazon RDS, Neptune supports read replicas for scaling read throughput that can be created in multiple AZs. In the case of a primary instance or AZ failure, a read replica can be promoted to the primary writer, providing high availability and durability.

Neptune use cases include fraud detection, Customer 360 queries, industrial parts management, social networking applications, and recommendation engines.

What Is a Graph Database?

Some datasets are *highly connected* in nature. Think of the data behind one of the popular social or business networking sites where each user connects to other users as a "friend" or "connection." With this type of dataset, the *relationships* between the users are of interest, and being able to traverse the relationships efficiently and at high speed is crucial.

A common use case in this type of business is to display personalized advertisements to users based on their interests. One way to accomplish this is by examining things they have "liked." To gather a wide-ranging dataset, social networking companies also look at the interests of that user's friends and the friends of that user's friends.

A large social networking company could have millions, or even billions, of users, with each user having multiple "friend" relationships with other users. Trying to run a query on a relational database to find out the interests of a user's friends and the friends of their friends would be very complex and perform badly, requiring multiple tables with "many to many" joins, and it could not scale to this size. This is the type of query a graph database is designed to handle.

What Is a Graph?

A graph is a mathematical construct. It comprises nodes, also known as vertices, which represent real-world objects, and edges, also known as relationships, which represent connections between the nodes. A node or edge can also have properties (attributes) associated with it. For example, you could have a graph of a user node connected to another user node with an edge representing a friend relationship. The user node could have properties against it, such as the user's name and zip code. The friend edge could also have properties against it, such as the date the friendship was created (see Figure 5.21).

FIGURE 5.21   A simple graph

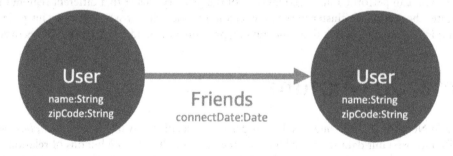

A graph database stores its data internally in a graph format, making it much easier to write queries such as "Who are the friends of a user's friends?" and much more efficient at processing these types of queries. To write a query on Neptune, you use special querying languages (Gremlin, openCypher, and SPARQL) that allow you to transverse highly connected datasets effectively and elegantly (see Figure 5.22).

Run the following lab to learn how to perform basic admin tasks and run queries on Amazon Neptune:

```
https://catalog.workshops.aws/neptune-deep-dive
```

FIGURE 5.22 A knowledge graph

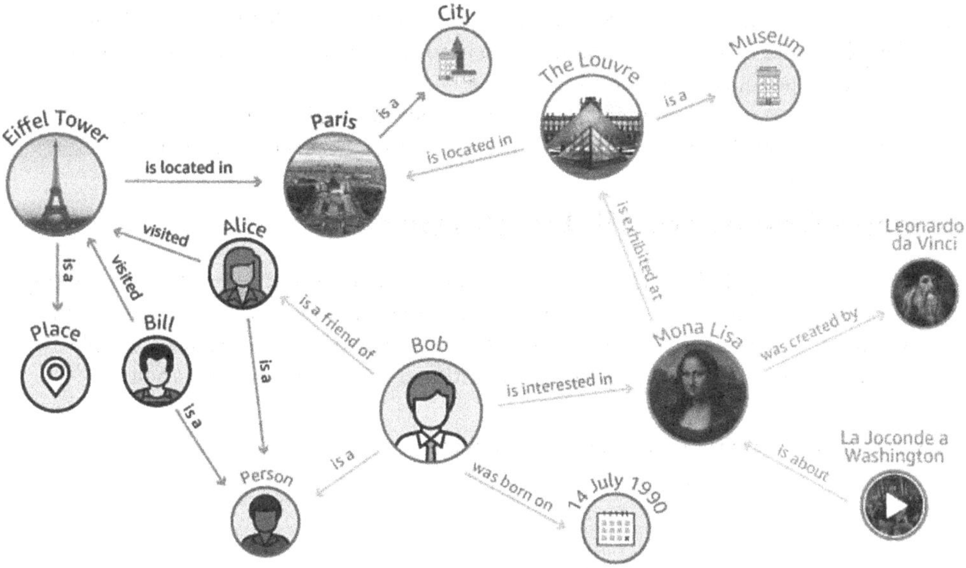

Amazon DocumentDB (with MongoDB Compatibility)

Amazon DocumentDB is a fully managed, highly available, fast, and reliable MongoDB-compatible *document database*. It is optimized to store and manage JSON documents and can scale to millions of requests per second and petabytes of storage. Like other AWS purpose-built databases, Amazon DocumentDB is fully managed, removing the undifferentiated, time-consuming, and complex database management tasks, such as capacity planning, deploying servers, patching servers, running backups, and setting up high availability and disaster recovery operational plans and resources.

What Is a Document Database?

A document database stores and processes semi-structured data in the form of documents. Each *document* is typically an object with associated metadata and can be seen as roughly equivalent to a row in a relational database. Documents can be grouped into a *collection*, which is roughly analogous to a table in a relational database. Documents can be stored in formats like JSON, BSON, and XML; however, Amazon DocumentDB exclusively uses JSON.

Unlike rows in a relational database, documents in a document database don't have a strict structure imposed on them. Therefore, different documents can have different metadata, such as different field-value pairs and arrays. This makes a document database much more flexible and easy for application developers to work with and can improve read performance, as no joins are required for queries.

Use cases for Amazon DocumentDB include mobile and web applications, content management systems, Internet of Things (IoT) solutions, and profile management.

Amazon DocumentDB Architecture

An Amazon DocumentDB cluster comprises a single primary instance for reads and writes and up to 15 replicas for reads (see Figure 5.23). Storage is separated from compute and held in a distributed storage volume that can be scaled up to 128 TB. Writes are replicated six ways across three Availability Zones for additional availability and durability.

FIGURE 5.23   Amazon DocumentDB architecture

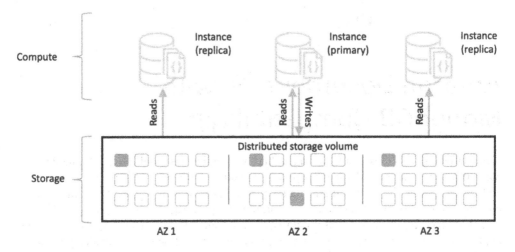

Connecting to Amazon DocumentDB

Amazon DocumentDB is compatible with the MongoDB API (a popular third-party document database); therefore, you can use MongoDB applications, tools, and drivers to connect to and develop on Amazon DocumentDB. To connect via Python, you can use the PyMongo library. Run the following lab to learn how to set up and run basic operations on Amazon Amazon DocumentDB:

```
https://catalog.us-east-1.prod.workshops.aws/workshops/464d6c17-
9faa-4fef-ac9f-dd49610174d3
```

Amazon MemoryDB for Redis

Amazon MemoryDB for Redis is a Redis-compatible *in-memory database* with the following features:

- Ultra-fast performance with microsecond reads and single-digit millisecond writes
- Multi-AZ transactional log for storage consistency and durability
- Highly scalable storage and compute with 99.99% availability
- Fully managed deployment, patching, monitoring, and snapshots
- Integration with other AWS services like Amazon Cloudwatch and Amazon EKS

What Is Redis?

Redis (Remote Dictionary Server) is a popular open-source in-memory NoSQL key-value store. Rather than storing data on disk like typical databases, Redis stores data in memory, allowing it to have super-fast read and write performance. It is mainly used as a cache or document database.

What Is Amazon MemoryDB?

Amazon MemoryDB is the AWS cloud-based implementation of Redis that simplifies the deployment and operation of a Redis database and ensures full data durability by storing data across multiple Availability Zones.

The prominent use cases for memory DB are new applications that require a durable database with ultra-fast performance, current applications that use Redis but want durability to avoid the risk of data loss, and any applications that currently use a cache on their database for low latency and want to simplify the architecture.

Some typical systems and applications that use MemoryDB include microservices-based systems, chat and messaging applications, real-time geospatial analysis for ride-hailing and food delivery, and session data management (login information and cookies) for large-scale Internet applications. Run the following lab to learn about Amazon MemoryDB for Redis:

```
https://catalog.us-east-1.prod.workshops.aws/workshops/23394eff-
66dd-421a-9513-efe12b9197d0
```

Amazon Keyspaces (for Apache Cassandra)

AWS's next NoSQL database offering is *Amazon Keyspaces* (for Apache Cassandra), a Cassandra-compatible wide-column store database. As with AWS's other NoSQL database services, they have integrated a popular open-source product into their cloud infrastructure, making a technology that is often difficult to deploy and manage easily deployable with a few clicks and managed automatically, removing much of the administrative burden and need for specialized expertise.

What Is Apache Cassandra?

Apache Cassandra is an open-source, NoSQL, distributed, wide-column store database designed for large-scale applications that require fast reads and writes. It was initially created by Facebook for their inbox search feature and made open source in July 2008. Being distributed, it was built to run on multiple low-cost servers (nodes), allowing it to scale easily under periods of high usage and provide data durability in the event of losing a node.

To run queries, Cassandra uses its own language called Cassandra Query Language (CQL), which is similar to SQL. Like other NoSQL databases, you cannot join tables together in Cassandra. Therefore, all the information you need in a query must be structured into a single table. This makes it essential to deeply understand your required access patterns when modeling tables in Cassandra or Amazon Keyspaces.

What Is a Wide-Column Store Database?

Wide-column store databases store data in columns and rows, similar to a relational database. However, the table structure is more flexible. In contrast to a relational database, where each row has the same set of columns with the same data types, a wide-column store database allows for a different number of columns on each row, with different column names and data types.

What Is Amazon Keyspaces?

Amazon Keyspaces is AWS's implementation of Apache Cassandra and includes many features to simplify management and administration and to add security, including:

- Managed provisioning, upgrades, patching, and backups
- Auto-scaling of throughput and storage
- Built-in monitoring with Amazon CloudWatch
- High availability and durability with tables replicated across three separate Availability Zones
- Multi-region replication
- Table encryption
- Automatic continuous backups with no performance impact on the application
- Integration with other AWS services like AWS IAM and AWS KMS

Amazon Keyspaces is Apache Cassandra compatible, meaning existing Cassandra drivers and tools can be used along with the CQL query language. Therefore, to update your existing Cassandra applications, you only need to point them to a Keyspaces endpoint.

Standard use cases for Amazon Keyspaces include low-latency applications, player profiles, time series data, and Internet of Things (IoT) device information. Run the following lab to learn how to connect to and use Amazon Keyspaces (for Apache Cassandra):

`https://catalog.workshops.aws/unlocking-amazonkeyspaces`

AWS Database Comparison

Table 5.8 compares the different AWS databases and their use cases and formats.

TABLE 5.8   AWS database summary comparison

Database	Type	OLTP/ OLAP	Use Cases	Data Format
Amazon Redshift	MPP data warehouse	OLAP	Business intelligence, analytics queries	Primarily structured but can also store semi-structured (JSON)
Amazon DynamoDB	NoSQL database	OLTP	Web, mobile, and gaming applications	Semi-structured (key-value)
Amazon RDS	Relational database	OLTP	Enterprise resource planning (ERP), customer relationship management (CRM), and financial systems	Structured
Amazon Neptune	Graph database	OLTP	Fraud detection, social networking applications, and recommendation engines	Graph
Amazon DocumentDB	Document NoSQL database	OLTP	Web/mobile applications, content management systems, and profile management	Semi-structured (document)
Amazon MemoryDB	In-memory NoSQL key-value store	OLTP	Chat and messaging applications, real-time geospatial analysis, and session data management	Semi-structured (key-value)
Amazon Keyspaces	Wide-column store NoSQL database	OLTP	Low-latency applications, player profiles, and time series data	Structured but more flexible than a relational database

Summary

This chapter covered the various database and data warehouse services provided by AWS. As mentioned previously, AWS's philosophy is that you use the right tool for the job, and they offer several different databases to ensure that each use case is covered in the most effective and highly performant way.

We explained the different types of databases, including relational and NoSQL, and the various types of workloads, such as OLTP and OLAP. We then dived into Amazon Redshift and covered how its MPP architecture provides fast querying and processing for data warehouse use cases.

Next, we covered AWS's other database services, including NoSQL databases like Amazon DynamoDB and its ability to scale to huge Internet volumes, the relational database service Amazon RDS, which provides fully managed versions of popular commercial databases, and AWS's own MySQL- and PostgreSQL-compatible database, Aurora.

Then, we looked at some of the more specialized databases like Amazon Neptune, a graph database for handling highly connected data, and Amazon MemoryDB for ultrafast reads and writes. Lastly, we looked at two of AWS's NoSQL-compatible databases: Document DB (with Mongo DB compatibility) and Amazon Keyspaces (for Apache Cassandra), which allow you to run your existing applications and tools with the power of the AWS infrastructure managing your database and providing high availability and durability.

Exam Essentials

Understand the different types of databases and when to use them.   Understand the difference between a relational database and a NoSQL database. Know the difference between an OLTP workload for front-end applications and an OLAP data warehousing workload. Understand the use cases for graph, document, and in-memory databases.

Know the correct way to get data into and out of Amazon Redshift.   The COPY command is the best way to load data into Redshift. To unload large amounts of data, use the UNLOAD command to write the data to S3 rather than running a query via JDBC/ODBC. Both commands process the data in parallel across the compute nodes, improving performance. To programmatically and asynchronously query Redshift and paginate results, use the Redshift Data API.

Know the Redshift features for querying external data   Redshift Spectrum allows you to query your S3 data lake. Federated queries let you directly query external databases from Redshift, including Amazon RDS for PostgreSQL, Amazon Aurora PostgreSQL, Amazon RDS for MySQL, and Amazon Aurora MySQL.

Be able to optimize a Redshift table for query performance.   Redshift is a massively parallel processing (MPP) system, and how a table's data is distributed across its nodes affects query performance. Understand the different distribution styles (ALL, EVEN, KEY, AUTO) and when to use them. Know that a sort key defines how a table's rows are sorted and that filtering on a sort key column can improve query performance by eliminating block reads.

Understand Redshift materialized views and when to use them.   Redshift materialized views precompute and persist the results of a query. The materialized view can then be queried instead rerunning expensive operations such as joins and aggregations.

Know the Redshift data sharing feature and when to use it.   Redshift data sharing lets you read and write live data across clusters with zero copying, allowing you to isolate your workloads and run multi-cluster architectures.

Understand Amazon DynamoDB throughput management and throttling.   DynamoDB can throttle requests when read capacity units (RCUs) and write capacity units (WCUs) are exceeded. DynamoDB auto scaling can prevent throttling by automatically adjusting throughput capacity.

Know the DynamoDB Time to Live (TTL) feature.   The TTL feature manages the lifecycle of data on DynamoDB and automatically deletes items from a table based on a timestamp attribute. DynamoDB deletes items older than the timestamp within a few days.

Understand DynamoDB Streams and when to use them.   DynamoDB Streams track data updates on DynamoDB tables and store the changes in a log (stream). Streams can be consumed via API and combined with Lambda functions to trigger an action after a data change.

Know the suitable data models for Redshift and NoSQL databases like DynamoDB.   The most common data model in Redshift is a star schema. NoSQL databases like DynamoDB typically model all required data for a query into a single table.

Know the Amazon RDS high availability features.   Amazon RDS offers two types of multiple Availability Zone (AZ) deployments to provide database durability and high availability: Multi-AZ DB instances and Multi-AZ DB clusters.

Review Questions

1. You are designing an ingestion process for a client using Amazon Redshift. The client has large amounts of data loaded into files in S3 once a day. What is the most efficient and cost-effective way to load the data into Redshift?

    A. Load the data into Amazon RDS MySQL using the native loader, and then use a Redshift Federated Query to ingest the data into Redshift.

    B. Use Redshift Spectrum to select data from S3, and them load it into Redshift with an `INSERT` statement.

    C. Use the Redshift `COPY` command to load the data into Redshift.

    D. Use the Redshift Data API to asynchronously select data, and then load it into Redshift with an `INSERT` statement.

2. The Data Warehousing team of a large retail company has been asked to provide a periodic export of large amounts of data from Redshift into files in S3 so it can be used for machine learning models by the Data Science team. What is the most efficient and effective way to export the data?

    A. Use AWS Glue to select the data from Redshift and write it into files on S3.

    B. Use the Redshift `UNLOAD` command to write files to S3.

    C. Use AWS Data Pipeline to select data from Redshift via JDBC, and then call a Python script to write the results into files on S3.

3. An application development team wants to build a front-end application that displays data stored in the company's Redshift data warehouse. They need to paginate the data and connect to Redshift asynchronously. They also want a simple way to manage connections to Redshift. Which method best suits their requirements?

    A. Directly connect each application user to Redshift via JDBC/ODBC.

    B. Set up an application load balancer in front of Redshift to automatically manage the connections.

    C. Use a Lamba function to connect to Redshift via JDBC/ODBC and paginate the result sets.

    D. Use the Redshift Data API to asynchronously query Redshift and paginate the result sets.

4. A customer is experiencing poor performance with a query in Redshift. The query joins two large tables on a single column key and aggregates the result. Each table has hundreds of millions of rows. What would be the best distribution style to use on each table?

    A. Use the `ALL` distribution style to create a copy of each table on every compute node.

    B. Use the `EVEN` distribution style to distribute rows round-robin to each compute node.

    C. Use the `KEY` distribution style and set the columns used in the join as distribution keys.

5. Your company has a website application running on Amazon RDS for MySQL and a data warehouse on Amazon Redshift. The analytics team has a requirement to show real-time information from the application on a dashboard, along with historical data from Redshift. What approach would you advise the team to use that would involve the least amount of effort?

    A. Use the RDS MySQL native export functionality to unload data to S3, and then load it in parallel into Redshift with the `COPY` command.

    B. Implement Athena federated queries to query across the RDS MySQL database and Redshift.

    C. Utilize a Redshift federated query to directly query the MySQL RDS database, and then combine the results with historical Redshift data in a database view.

    D. Use the RDS MySQL native export functionality to unload data to S3, and then query the data using Redshift Spectrum. Combine the data from the Spectrum query and historical data stored in Redshift in a database view.

6. A gaming company operates a mobile application running on Amazon DynamoDB. It has an unpredictable workload with variations in throughput and have started getting throttling errors during periods of high user activity. What is the most effective way to scale its DynamoDB capacity to cope with the variable load, which involves the least operational effort and optimizes costs?

    A. Set the read/write capacity units to handle the maximum throughput DynamoDB needs to handle.

    B. Utilize the DynamoDB auto scaling feature to adjust capacity based on load.

    C. Use a Lambda function to monitor Amazon CloudWatch metrics and call the DynamoDB API to adjust capacity units based on the throughput.

    D. Manually change capacity units depending on the system load.

7. You are working for a company as a data architect that runs an online web store on Amazon DynamoDB with high throughput volumes. You want to send customers an email when their order status has changed to "Shipped." What would be the best approach to handle this requirement?

    A. Set up a DynamoDB stream on the Orders table with a Lambda trigger that sends an email via the Amazon Simple Email Service (Amazon SES) when the order status has changed to "Shipped."

    B. Export the Orders table into S3 once an hour to maintain a complete history. Run an AWS Glue job to identify orders whose status has changed to "Shipped," and then send an email via Amazon SES.

    C. Set up a nightly extract into Amazon Redshift using the `COPY` command. Run a lambda function to check for any status changes to "Shipped," and then send an email via Amazon SES.

8. You've been asked to recommend the right database solution for a customer with relational data who requires strong durability, high availability, and disaster recovery. Which overall solution will best suit their requirements?

   A. Amazon DocumentDB with additional replicas for enhanced read performance

   B. Amazon DynamoDB with its automatic replication across multiple availability zones

   C. Amazon RDS with a Multi-AZ DB instance deployment

   D. Amazon Neptune to optimize instances of highly connected data with additional read replicas for high availability

9. An online gaming company wants to build a leaderboard application for its platform and needs to choose a storage service. The application needs to efficiently handle large volumes of requests with high read and write throughput, low latency, and semi-structured data in JSON format. What would be a suitable service for this task?

   A. Amazon DynamoDB

   B. Amazon Redshift

   C. Amazon RDS

   D. Amazon Neptune

10. An online retailer is developing a recommendation engine for its web store. The engine will provide personalized product recommendations to customers based on their past purchases and browsing history. The engine must efficiently navigate a highly connected dataset with low latency. This involves complex queries to identify products similar to those purchased by the customer and find products bought by other customers who have purchased the same item. Which solution best addresses this use case?

   A. Use Amazon RDS for PostgreSQL with the Apache AGE (graph database) extension.

   B. Use Amazon DocumentDB (with MongoDB compatibility) to efficiently handle semi-structed data.

   C. Use Amazon Neptune to efficiently traverse graph datasets.

   D. Use Amazon MemoryDB for Redis for ultra-fast query performance.

Chapter 6

Data Catalogs

THE AWS CERTIFIED DATA ENGINEER - ASSOCIATE EXAM OBJECTIVES COVERED IN THIS CHAPTER MAY INCLUDE, BUT ARE NOT LIMITED TO, THE FOLLOWING:

✓ **Domain 2: Data Store Management**

  ▪ 2.2 Understand data cataloging systems

✓ **Domain 3: Data Operations and Support**

  ▪ 3.4 Ensure data quality

Data Catalogs

A data catalog is the dictionary for your business data. Imagine you are visiting the Louvre Museum in Paris. You are overwhelmed by the vast collection of artworks—paintings, sculptures, and artifacts—spread across seemingly endless galleries. How do you find the Venus de Milo statue you have always wanted to see? This is where a museum catalog comes in. It acts as a directory, providing you with information about the museum's collection—what pieces are there, where they are located, and their history and significance.

Similarly, a data catalog functions as a central repository for information about an organization's data assets. Just as a museum catalog helps you navigate a vast art collection, a data catalog helps you find the specific data you need within your organization.

Benefits of Data Catalogs

There are some key benefits that make data catalogs absolutely indispensable:

Enhancing Data Discovery By meticulously organizing and indexing your data, you significantly enhance its discoverability. Data analysts can quickly locate relevant datasets through intuitive search functions, saving valuable time on scavenging information.

Building Trust and Ensuring Compliance Data governance is paramount for any organization. A well-maintained data catalog acts as a central hub for data policies and access controls. Metadata and versioning within the catalog provide a clear audit trail, ensuring the data's origin and that any changes align with legal and regulatory compliance. This transparency fosters trust in the data's accuracy, leading to more reliable decision making.

Breaking Down Silos and Fostering Collaboration Data silos—isolated pockets of information within individual departments—are a common challenge. They lead of miscommunication, inefficiencies, and missed opportunities. Data catalogs act as a bridge, creating a unified and comprehensive view of all data assets across departments. By breaking down data siloes, the catalog unleashes the true value of your data by making it accessible and usable across the entire organization.

Streamlining Data Management   Data analysts no longer have to navigate through disparate systems to locate relevant data. This streamlined approach optimizes data usage, allowing teams to focus on the analysis itself rather than the logistics of data retrieval. Additionally, with a clear understanding of data usage patterns within the catalog, you can prioritize data quality initiatives and optimize resource allocation for data management tasks.

Now that we have established the significance of data catalogs, let's explore two specific data catalog implementations: Apache Hive Metastore and AWS Glue Data Catalog.

Hive Metastore is a core component of Apache Hive that stores metadata for Hive tables, such as the location of data files, table schemas, and partition structures. The metadata storage is used by Hive to keep track of the data being analyzed. AWS Glue Data Catalog is the go-to service for data cataloging within AWS. Unlike Hive Metastore, AWS Glue Data Catalog acts as a central hub for metadata across a wider range of data sources. Another key difference is that AWS Glue Data Catalog is serverless, so there is no additional administrative overhead in managing the infrastructure.

In this chapter, we will dive deep into the creation of AWS Glue Data Catalogs using AWS Glue crawlers, build and reference data catalogs, synchronize partitions with a data catalog, and implement data quality checks at rest on AWS Glue Data Catalogs.

AWS Glue Data Catalog

AWS Glue Data Catalog is a persistent metastore for data assets. It enables you to catalog metadata information about datasets, which can be stored anywhere on AWS, on-premises, or with a third-party provider. In this chapter, you will learn how to create Glue Data Catalogs using AWS Glue.

AWS Glue Data Catalog can be integrated with Amazon Athena, Amazon Redshift Spectrum, Amazon EMR, AWS Lake Formation, and Amazon SageMaker. Amazon Redshift automatically mounts the AWS Glue Data Catalog, allowing you to query the data lake tables in Amazon S3 with three-part notation in Amazon Redshift Query Editor v2. This integration eliminates the need to load the data from the data lake to data warehouse.

AWS Glue Data Catalog comprises the following components:

Databases   A database can be considered as a logical collection of metadata tables in AWS Glue. When tables are created, you can group them under a specific database. A table cannot be present in more than one database.

Tables   A table within AWS Glue Data Catalog is a resource that holds the metadata information of the dataset. As shown in Figure 6.1, the catalog contains information such as schema of the dataset, location of the data files, compression formats, input and output format, table properties, Serializer-Deserializer (SerDe) information, serialization library, and SerDe class parameters.

FIGURE 6.1   Metadata information on the AWS Management Console

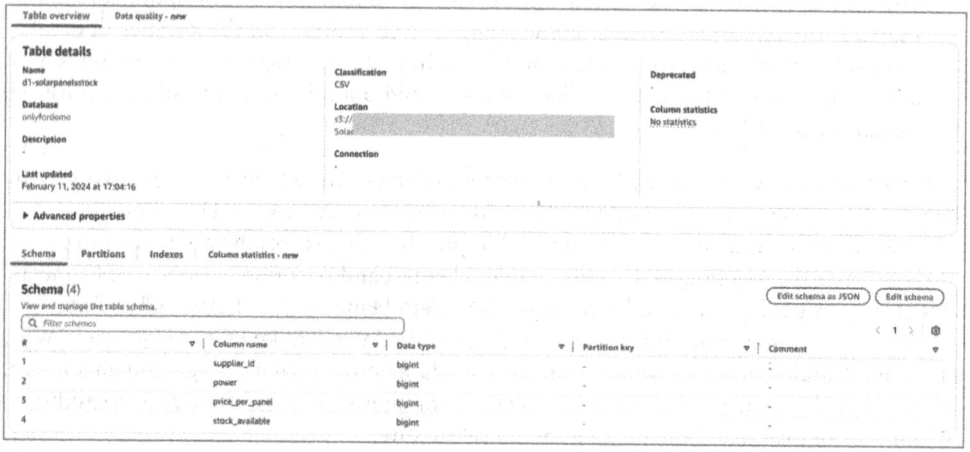

You can create data catalogs manually. However, as data volumes grow, manually maintaining a data catalog becomes increasingly difficult. AWS Glue crawlers can automatically infer the schema of the datasets and update changes in the data sources, thereby reducing the overhead of manually managing and keeping the metadata up-to-date.

AWS Glue Crawlers and Classifiers

AWS Glue crawlers help you keep your data catalogs organized and up-to-date. They automatically scan various data stores, such as Amazon S3 buckets, to understand the structure and organization of your data. They are also able to determine the schema, the data types of each column, and how the data is partitioned. Crawlers can also be used to add, update, and delete tables and partitions. This information is then stored in the Glue Data Catalog (central index repository) for your data lakes. To understand data formats like JSON or CSV, they use built-in or custom classifiers. Glue crawlers can be scheduled periodically so that metadata is always up-to-date and in sync with the underlying data. Incremental crawls are also an efficient way to add new partitions to existing tables with stable schemas. Let's look at how a crawler decides when to create partitions.

In Figure 6.2, the crawler examines the folders and determines the "root" table and its partitions based on the folder structure. You specify the starting folder to crawl with the "Include path." If the folders within a level have similar schemas, the crawler creates a partition within a single table. In this example, Sales is the root folder, and "Include path" is set to Sales – s3://sales/.

In this example, a single table will be created with partition keys *year*, *month*, and *day*. To create separate tables for folders with distinct schemas, define separate data stores (Include paths) for the crawler, each pointing to the root folders of a desired table. This is important for Amazon Athena queries, as they rely on prefixes to identify the tables. Separate Include paths ensure that tables with different schemas are recognized correctly.

FIGURE 6.2   AWS Glue crawler execution on an Amazon S3 folder

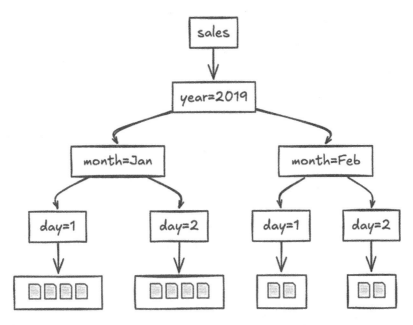

Figure 6.3 shows the AWS Management Console view of creating AWS Glue crawlers.

1. Represents the Include path where the crawler examines the root folder provided.

2. Represents the option of incremental crawls for newly added partitions.

   When the option of "Crawl new sub-folders only" is turned on, it will first run a complete crawl on the dataset to allow the crawler to record the initial schema and partition structure. During the recrawl, only the new partitions will be added to the existing table. This reduces the cost of scanning the entire dataset. With this option, no schema changes are made, and no new tables will be added to the Glue Data Catalog after the initial crawl run.

3. Represents the option to crawl on S3 event-based notification.

   Instead of listing the objects from an Amazon S3 or Data Catalog target, you can configure the crawler to use Amazon S3 events to find any changes. The crawler consumes S3 events from an SQS queue based on its schedule. There are no charges if there are no new events, making it more efficient.

AWS Glue crawlers have several configuration options that affect how they update the Data Catalog. These options fall under the categories of catalog update behavior, catalog deletion behavior, and table schema inheritance, as shown in Figure 6.4.

FIGURE 6.3 The AWS Management Console view for AWS Glue crawlers

Add data source
Data source
Choose the source of data to be crawled.
S3
Network connection - optional
Optionally include a Network connection to use with this S3 target. Note that each crawler is limited to one Network connection so any other S3 targets will also use the same connection (or none, if left blank).
Clear selection
Add new connection
Location of S3 data
In this account
In a different account
S3 path
Browse for or enter an existing S3 path.
s3://bucket/prefix/object
View
Browse S3
All folders and files contained in the S3 path are crawled. For example, type s3://MyBucket/MyFolder/ to crawl all objects in MyFolder within MyBucket.
Subsequent crawler runs
This field is a global field that affects all S3 data sources.
Crawl all sub-folders
Crawl all folders again with every subsequent crawl.
Crawl new sub-folders only
Only Amazon S3 folders that were added since the last crawl will be crawled. If the schemas are compatible, new partitions will be added to existing tables.
No schema changes are made or no new tables will be added to the Data Catalog after the first crawl run.
Crawl based on events
Rely on Amazon S3 events to control what folders to crawl.
Sample only a subset of files
Exclude files matching pattern
Cancel
Add an S3 data source
1
2
3

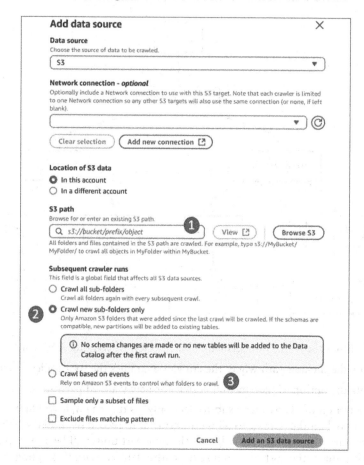

FIGURE 6.4 Updating and deleting Data Catalog behavior on the AWS Management Console

When the crawler detects schema changes in the data store, how should AWS Glue handle table updates in the data catalog?
Update the table definition in the data catalog
Add new columns only
Ignore the change and don't update the table in the data catalog
New partitions are added, but existing partitions are not updated
Update all new and existing partitions with metadata from the table
Partitions inherit metadata properties — such as their classification, input format, output format, SerDe information, and schema — from their parent table.
How should AWS Glue handle deleted objects in the data store?
Delete tables and partitions from the data catalog
Ignore the change and don't update the table in the data catalog
Mark the table as deprecated in the data catalog
If you run a job that references a deprecated table, the job might fail. Edit jobs that reference deprecated tables to remove them as sources and targets. We recommend that you delete deprecated tables when they are no longer needed.
Create partition indexes automatically
Enable creation of a separate Partition Index for every Catalog table providing efficient lookup for specific partitions.

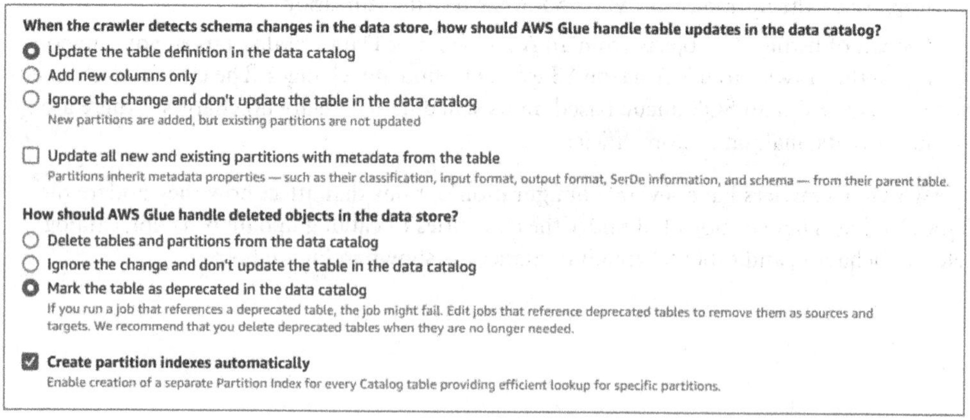

The options in the catalog update behavior category determine how the crawler handles changes to existing tables. You can choose to update the entire table definition, add only new columns, or ignore changes entirely.

The options in the catalog deletion behavior category determine what happens when the crawler encounters objects that are no longer present in the data source. You can choose to delete these objects from the Data Catalog, ignore them, or mark them as deprecated.

The options in the table schema inheritance category determine how the crawler handles the schema of a table's partitions. By default, the partitions are assumed to have the same schema as the table itself. However, you can configure the crawler to update the schema of the partitions to match the schema of the table.

Next, we'll discuss why updating partitions matters. Also, are crawlers the only way to update the partitions on your catalog tables?

Capturing and Synchronizing Incremental Metadata

When the end user consumes a query from Amazon Athena, it uses partitions to efficiently scan the relevant data based on the query. Without updated partitions, Athena scans the entire dataset, resulting in slow query performance. Faster queries during data processing also translate to reduced cost. Updating partitions ensures that Amazon Athena recognizes new data immediately, allowing you to generate BI reports based on the latest information.

There are multiple options to update partitions. We already saw one possibility using an AWS Glue crawler. Here are some additional options:

AWS Glue ETL Jobs   While performing your ETL transformations using AWS Glue ETL jobs, you can add new partitions, update schemas, and create tables using the `enableUpdateCatalog` argument within your ETL script. This allows you to include new partitions in the Data Catalog immediately after the job finishes, without waiting for a separate crawler to run.

For more information on adding partitions, updating schemas, and creating tables, please refer to the AWS official documentation at `https://docs.aws.amazon.com/glue/latest/dg/update-from-job.html`.

MSCK REPAIR TABLE Command   You can run the `MSCK REPAIR TABLE` query in Athena to identify and create partitions for new data added to S3. The query can be triggered manually or automated using S3 events and Lambda functions. An example of the command would be

```
MSCK REPAIR TABLE table_name;
```

ALTER TABLE ADD PARTITION Command   You can run the SQL command `ALTER TABLE ADD PARTITION` in Athena to add the partition by altering the tables. This process can be automated or triggered manually using S3 events and Lambda functions. An example of the command would be

```
ALTER TABLE table_name ADD IF NOT EXISTS PARTITION[…];
```

Boto3 SDK   Lambda functions are serverless and cost-effective. You can create a Lambda function and configure it to watch for S3 file-created events, as shown in Figure 6.5. When the file is dropped into S3 via a PUT event, the Lambda function triggers and extracts the partitions from the S3 object, creating a partition in the Glue Data Catalog.

FIGURE 6.5   Updating partitions using AWS Glue ETL

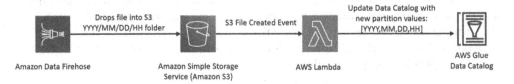

MSCK REPAIR TABLE can be a costlier option compared to ALTER TABLE ADD PARTITION. This is because MSCK needs to scan the table's sub-tree in the file system (S3 bucket). Multiple levels of partitioning and traversing additional sub-directories increase costs. For adding new partitions to the existing table, ALTER TABLE ADD PARTITION may prove to be more efficient. The execution time for the latter is measured in seconds, compared to MSCK REPAIR, which takes minutes. Both methods are executed using Amazon Athena, where there is a possibility of running into Athena Service quota limits. Using an AWS Glue crawler is the most comprehensive and recommended solution for automatically detecting data schema changes and creating partitions. However, it can be slow and expensive. If cost is a consideration and the schema is fixed and stable, then the Boto3 SDK is the recommended approach.

Glue Data Catalogs with Amazon Athena

In Chapter 3, you learned how to create SQL-based ETL processes and perform data transformation using Amazon Athena. When you create a CTAS query, the table creation process registers the dataset with Athena. This registration occurs in AWS Glue Data Catalog, which enables Athena to run queries. In Athena Query Editor, this catalog is referred to with the label AWSDataCatalog.

The difference between using an AWS Glue crawler and Amazon Athena to create Data Catalogs is that AWS Glue Crawler has the capability to automatically detect schema changes. When you create DDLs in Amazon Athena using SQL CTAS, it does not have the ability to infer the schema or automatically update any changes to the schema.

Versioning

Automated metadata management, while convenient, may introduce unintended consequences. Human errors or unexpected changes can break pipelines relying on the catalog. AWS Glue Data Catalog safeguards metadata by employing a robust versioning mechanism for its tables. Every edit, even one replicating an existing definition, triggers the creation of a new version. These versions are assigned unique identifiers, typically starting from 1 and incrementing sequentially. Only one version of the table can be active at a time. This active version will be available for querying and data manipulation. Past versions remain preserved to facilitate change history tracking, allowing you to understand who made modifications to the table definition, when they were made, and how they were implemented. For more information on understanding and comparing schema versions, please refer to the official documentation: https://docs.aws.amazon.com/glue/latest/dg/console-tables.html.

You can also migrate your existing tables in the Glue Data Catalog to use open table formats like Apache Iceberg, Apache Hudi, and Delta Lake. To understand how to read and write the open table format with AWS Glue Data Catalog, please refer to this documentation: https://docs.aws.amazon.com/glue/latest/dg/aws-glue-programming-etl-datalake-native-frameworks.html.

Open table formats with AWS Glue Data Catalogs introduce features like ACID transactions, enabling security and atomicity when multiple users query and insert into the Data Catalog tables. In the event of a failed transaction, both data and metadata can be rolled back to the previous desired state. Open table formats like Apache Iceberg maintain a version history of each table. Every write operation—whether adding, updating, or deleting data—creates a new version in the history. This version contains the data files written and the corresponding metadata snapshot. Apache Iceberg also supports time-based and snapshot-based queries for historical data analysis. Time-based queries allow you to specify a specific point in time to access the data as it existed at that moment. Snapshot-based queries leverage version identifiers to access the data from a particular historical version.

Data Lineage

Data lineage plays a pivotal role in data lakes, acting as a roadmap that illuminates the flow of data from its origin to its final destination. This understanding is essential for data engineers and analysts, enabling them to trace transformations, pinpoint potential issues, and ensure data quality throughout the processing pipelines. Chapter 3 described how AWS Glue DataBrew captures the trace during ETL processing.

Alternately, you can leverage open-source frameworks such as OpenLineage project, which provides a technology-agnostic metadata model for capturing the data lineage. You can also automate data lineage on Amazon Managed Workflows for Apache Airflow (Amazon MWAA) with OpenLineage. OpenLineage provides a plug-in for Apache Airflow that extracts data lineage from directed acyclic graphs (DAGs). For more details on the architecture and implementation, please refer to this blog: https://aws.amazon.com/blogs/big-data/automate-data-lineage-on-amazon-mwaa-with-openlineage.

Query Performance and Cost Savings

AWS Glue Data Catalog also provides several query performance and cost benefits.

Column-Level Statistics

AWS Glue Data Catalog supports column-level statistics for AWS Glue tables. It helps you to understand data profiles by getting insights about the values within a column, such as minimum value, maximum value, nulls, total distinct values, average length of value, and so on. AWS analytic services like Amazon Redshift Spectrum and Amazon Athena can use these column statistics to generate query execution plans and choose the optimal plan to improve the query performance. To learn more about how to schedule the runs to generate the column statistics with AWS Lambda and Amazon EventBridge scheduler, please visit: https://aws.amazon.com/blogs/big-data/enhance-query-performance-using-aws-glue-data-catalog-column-level-statistics.

Partition Indexes

Tables are organized into partitions. Table partitioning is a data organization technique that involves splitting a large table into smaller, manageable segments based on specific criteria. These segments, called partitions, are stored and accessed independently. While AWS Glue supports automatic partition updates and additions, very large data lakes with millions of partitions can encounter performance issues. When you use GetPartitions API to retrieve specific data segments using a filter expression, the performance of the query can get slow.

To mitigate this bottleneck of slow query performance and latency issues, AWS Glue uses partition indexes for partition keys. Without partition indexes, the Data Catalog retrieves all partitions from the table and then filters them based on your expression. This process becomes time-consuming as the number of partitions grows. Partition indexes act like specialized mini catalogs within the Data Catalog, allowing the GetPartitions API to efficiently identify the relevant partitions to match your filter expressions without doing a full table scan. This results in increased query performance, increased concurrency as a result of fewer GetPartitions API calls, and cost savings on query time and data scanned.

If AWS Glue Data Catalogs are created using an AWS Glue crawler, a partition index will also be created by default, eliminating the need to create it manually. The creation of partition indexes benefits the analytic workloads running on Amazon Athena, Amazon Redshift Spectrum, AWS Glue, and Amazon EMR.

Automatic Compaction for Apache Iceberg Tables

As data is added and updated, Apache Iceberg creates numerous small data files in the underlying S3 storage. These small files can lead to inefficiencies when running queries. Traditionally, organizations would need to build custom pipelines to periodically compact these small files into large ones. This process was not only time-consuming but also added infrastructure management costs. AWS Glue Data Catalog's automatic compaction eliminates the need for custom pipelines. Once enabled, it continuously monitors the data writes and automatically triggers compaction jobs in the background. This optimizes the S3 storage layout by reducing the number of small files, leading to faster read performance for data lake queries.

Data Quality at Rest

Building on the foundation established in Chapter 3, this chapter delves deeper into the realm of data quality with AWS Glue Data Catalogs.

As a reminder, Chapter 3 explored the distinction between data quality and data governance and why data quality is important for organizations. You then learned about DQDL, domain-specific rules that AWS Glue Data Quality uses to perform the data quality checks. We covered the process of data quality checks in transit for real-time validations and separating out invalid records prior to sending them to downstream applications. You also learned how to apply alerts and monitor data quality through Amazon CloudWatch or Amazon EventBridge, as well as how to send notifications to data engineers.

This chapter shifts the focus to data quality checks on AWS Glue Data Catalog tables at rest.

Here are the steps to perform data quality checks on AWS Glue Data Catalog tables at rest:

1. Generate rule recommendations (optional).
2. Monitor the rule recommendations (optional).
3. Edit the recommended rule (optional).
4. Create a ruleset.
5. Run the ruleset to evaluate the data quality.
6. View the data quality scores and results.

Rule Recommendations

AWS Glue Data Quality removes the guesswork by helping you to define data quality rules automatically by analyzing your data's characteristics. It suggests rules based on different aspects of your data, such as missing values, uniqueness, valid value ranges of a column, and so on. These suggested rules can be a good starting point to ensure your data quality.

The AWS Glue console further allows you to manage these recommendations. You can see the progress of ongoing recommendations, add suggested rules to your framework with a single click, and even view past recommendations for reference. Recommendation runs are automatically deleted after 90 days.

To generate recommendations, as shown in Figure 6.6, select the IAM Role, allocate the number of workers to run the recommendation, and set the runtime for this task. The default is 120 minutes.

Data Quality rule recommendations are an optional starting point, ideal for data stewards who are new to AWS Glue Data Quality. This feature helps them get acquainted with Data Quality Definition Language and understand the potential data quality checks without manually writing rules from scratch. While recommendations offer a valuable head start, you can always review and refine the suggested rules to perfectly align with your specific data quality needs.

FIGURE 6.6   Data quality recommendation on the AWS Management Console

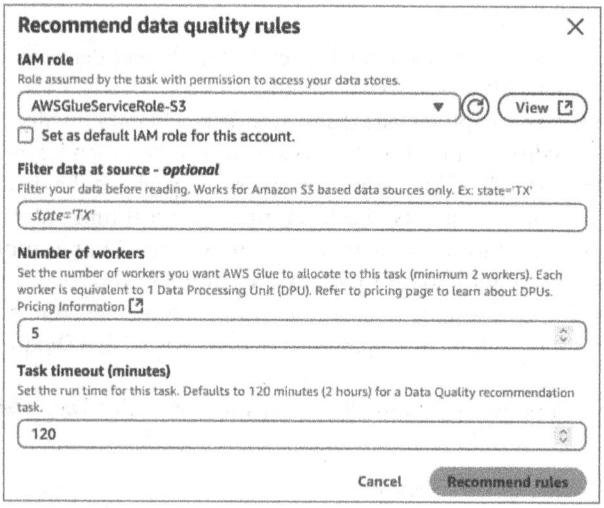

Data Quality Rules

Once the recommendations are generated, you can insert the relevant rules into your data quality framework. The collection of recommendation rules written as part of the framework is called a *ruleset*. Once these recommended rules are incorporated, save the ruleset and configure the details of the run, as shown in Figure 6.7.

As illustrated in Figure 6.7, you can publish the metrics to Amazon CloudWatch and send the output of the data quality results to an Amazon S3 location. The data quality runs can be scheduled at specific intervals or can be run on-demand.

In the Evaluation Run Details section, as shown in Figure 6.8, you will see the output of the data quality evaluation results. The difference between data quality checks in transit and at rest is that AWS Glue Data Catalog data quality results (at-rest) do not give you record-level information.

As of the writing of this book, anomaly detection, dynamic rules, support for Flex, and autoscaling are not supported for data quality checks at rest. To get more insights into the comparison of data quality checks at rest and in transit, please visit the AWS documentation: `https://aws.amazon.com/blogs/big-data/getting-started-with-aws-glue-data-quality-from-the-aws-glue-data-catalog`.

As shown in Figure 6.9, the Historical View pane provides extended information where you can monitor the progress of data quality runs and recommendations.

Please refer to the 6-part blog series to understand more on AWS Glue Data Quality: `https://aws.amazon.com/blogs/big-data/getting-started-with-aws-glue-data-quality-from-the-aws-glue-data-catalog`.

FIGURE 6.7   Ruleset Run Details Configuration on the AWS Management Console

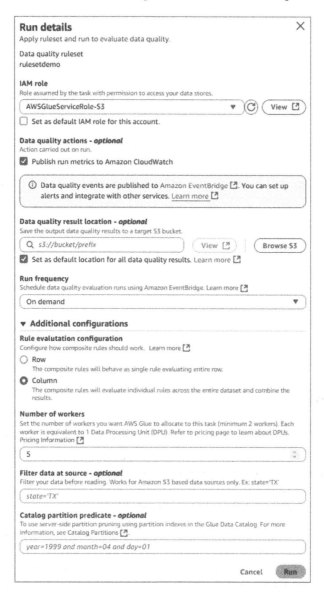

AWS Glue Data Quality also offers APIs to programmatically manage and interact with data quality aspects of your data pipeline. It offers functionalities for data types, ruleset management, recommendation runs, and data quality evaluations. To get more information on the APIs, please visit this documentation: `https://docs.aws.amazon.com/glue/latest/dg/aws-glue-api-data-quality-api.html`.

FIGURE 6.8   Evaluation results of data quality at rest on the AWS Management Console

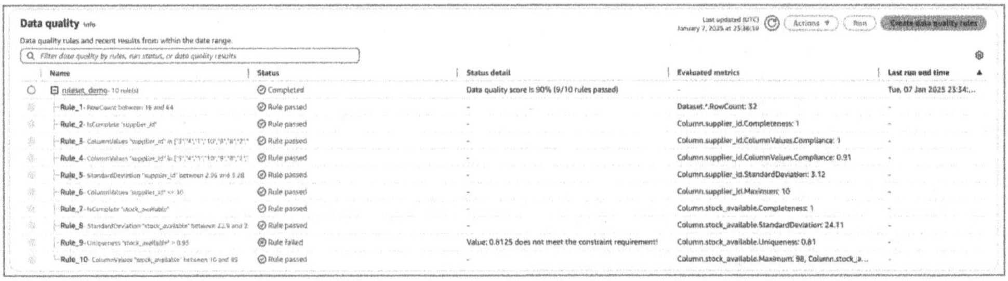

FIGURE 6.9   Monitoring data quality runs on the AWS Management Console

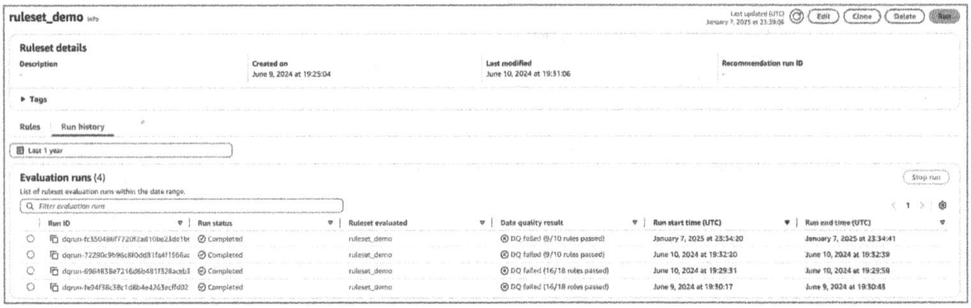

Summary

This chapter covered the essential aspects of managing metadata, such as AWS Glue Data Catalog and how it stores the metadata. We also discussed automated techniques to discover and infer schemas using AWS Glue crawlers. We addressed the challenges of metadata maintenance and proposed solutions for keeping metadata up-to-date and improving the query performance. This chapter also delved into metadata versioning and rollbacks to rectify problematic changes.

Additionally, we described how to ensure the integrity and reliability of your data at rest using AWS Glue Data Quality. Automated rule recommendations analyze your data and suggest DQDL rules to identify potential issues, simplifying rule creation for beginners. You can define a collection of DQDL rules as a ruleset to check various aspects of data quality for a specific table. AWS Glue Data Quality allows you to monitor the status of the recommendation rules (in progress or complete). For programmatic control, you can leverage APIs to manage the data quality checks.

Exam Essentials

Understand the importance of data catalogs   While both AWS Glue Data Catalog and Apache Hive Metastore serve as central repositories for metadata, AWS Glue Data Catalog is a managed service offered by AWS, eliminating the need for manual setup and maintenance. AWS Glue Data Catalog provides a unified metadata repository across a variety of data sources and data formats, integrating with Amazon EMR, Amazon RDS, Amazon Redshift, Redshift Spectrum, Athena, and any application compatible with Apache Hive Metastore. Data catalogs act as the central nervous system for your data ecosystem, providing a single source of truth about your data assets. They enhance discoverability, governance, data quality, integration, performance, and overall data management efficiency.

Understand the difference in data quality checks at rest and in transit   Data quality (DQ) checks at rest are performed on AWS Glue Data Catalog tables, whereas DQ checks in transit are performed during AWS Glue ETL job runs. This chapter discussed a few key differentiators unique to AWS Glue Data Catalogs. AWS Glue data quality at rest can automatically recommend the data quality rules based on your data in the Data Catalog. However, it does not support identifying records that fail these checks. This feature is only available while performing DQ checks on ETL jobs. Additionally, features such as dynamic rules, anomaly detection, autoscaling, and support for Spot Instances (Flex) are only available for AWS Glue ETL. It is also essential to understand integration of Data Quality with alerts and monitoring services like Amazon EventBridge and Amazon CloudWatch. The results of the data quality checks can also be sent to Amazon S3 for further analysis.

Review Questions

1. A company seeks a data catalog with the *least* amount of operational overhead to manage metadata across various data sources in their AWS environment. The data stores include structured sources such as Amazon RDS and Amazon Redshift, and semi-structured sources such as JSON files and .xml files stored in Amazon S3. The company seeks a solution to update the data catalog on a regular basis and detect changes to the source metadata. Suggest an option with the least amount of operational overhead.

   A. Use Amazon DynamoDB as the data catalog. Create custom AWS Lambda functions that will connect to the data catalog and gather metadata information from diverse sources. Schedule the Lambda functions to periodically update the data catalog.

   B. Use Amazon Aurora as the data catalog. Create custom AWS Lambda functions that will connect to the data catalog and gather metadata information from diverse sources. Schedule the Lambda functions to periodically update the data catalog.

   C. Use Amazon Redshift as the data catalog. Create custom AWS Lambda functions that will connect to the data catalog and gather metadata information from diverse sources. Schedule the Lambda functions to periodically update the data catalog.

   D. Use AWS Glue Data Catalog as a central metadata repository. Use AWS Glue crawlers to connect to diverse sources and update the Data Catalog with metadata changes. Schedule the crawlers to run periodically to update the metadata catalog.

2. You work as a data analytics specialist for a retail company that uses an Amazon EMR cluster to ingest and provide query capabilities for its massive amounts of shipment and delivery information. You need the metastore for the EMR cluster to be persistent. Which option gives you the best metastore option with the *least* amount of effort?

   A. Save your metastore information in your Hive MySQL database on the master node file system.

   B. Save your metastore information in an external metastore in Amazon Aurora.

   C. Save your metastore information in an external metastore in AWS Glue Data Catalog.

   D. Save your metastore information in an external metastore in Amazon DynamoDB tables.

3. A company is setting up a system to manage all of the datasets it stores in Amazon S3. The company wants to automate the transformation jobs on the data and maintain a catalog of the metadata concerning the datasets. Recommend a solution that requires the *least* amount of setup and maintenance.

   A. Create an Amazon EMR cluster with Apache Hive installed. Then, create a Hive metastore and a script to run transformation jobs on a schedule.

   B. Create an AWS Glue crawler to populate the AWS Glue Data Catalog. Then, create an AWS Glue ETL job and set up a schedule for data transformation jobs.

   C. Create an Amazon EMR cluster with Apache Spark installed. Then, create an Apache Hive metastore and a script to run transformation jobs on a schedule.

   D. Create an Amazon SageMaker Jupyter notebook instance that transforms the data. Then, create an Apache Hive metastore and a script to run transformation jobs on a schedule.

4. A large retail company uses AWS Glue Data Catalog to manage metadata for their data lake stored in Amazon S3. The data catalog has grown significantly over the past few years, containing millions of tables and billions of partitions. Analysts are experiencing slow query performance when running reports on specific datasets. Which approach would *most* effectively improve query performance without requiring significant changes to existing ETL pipelines?

   A. Implement AWS Glue Data Catalog encryption for improved security.

   B. Utilize AWS Glue Data Catalog statistics to optimize query planning.

   C. Migrate the data lake to a different data storage service.

   D. Increase the number of compute resources allocated to the data catalog.

5. Your company is migrating its data warehouse to an Amazon S3 data lake. You need a central service to manage metadata for various data sources, such as CSV files, JSON objects, and relational databases. How would you leverage AWS Glue Data Catalog for this solution?

   A. Configure Amazon Athena with the S3 bucket and use its built-in data catalog.

   B. Implement a custom solution using scripts to manage and track metadata for the data sources.

   C. Use AWS Glue crawlers to automatically discover and infer the schema information for the various data sources and store metadata information in AWS Glue Data Catalog.

   D. Set up AWS Lake Formation to manage the data lake.

6. You manage a data lake on Amazon S3 containing financial transaction data. You are concerned about the data quality and want to implement automated checks to identify missing values and inconsistencies. However, keeping costs under control is also a critical factor. Which of the following AWS services would be the *most* cost-effective solution for identifying data quality issues in your S3 data lake?

   A. AWS Glue

   B. Amazon EMR

   C. Amazon Athena

   D. Amazon Redshift Spectrum

7. A retail company maintains a vast data lake on Amazon S3. The company would like to analyze the data using diverse tools such as Amazon Athena, Amazon QuickSight, Amazon Redshift. What is the *most* efficient method to integrate this data with these analytics tools to minimize the development efforts and costs?

   A. Connect and configure each analytics tool to Amazon S3 separately.

   B. Use AWS Glue to catalog the data and make it accessible to each analytics tool.

   C. Export the data from data lake to each analytics tool.

   D. Use Amazon Redshift to catalog the data and make it accessible to each analytics tool.

8. A startup stores inventory and historical transaction records in an Amazon S3 bucket integrated with AWS Glue Data Catalog. The customer sales report data is sent and stored every night in an Amazon Redshift cluster. To complete the processing, the data analyst needs to combine the historical transactions with the sales report data. Suggest an option to the data analyst who is looking for the *least* configuration effort to reduce the workload of the cluster.

    A. Migrate the historical transaction records from Amazon S3 to Amazon Redshift using AWS Glue.

    B. Unload the customer sales report from Amazon Redshift to Amazon S3 using AWS Lambda. Query the data using Amazon Athena by combining the historical transaction records with the customer sales data.

    C. Use Amazon Redshift Spectrum to query the AWS Glue Data Catalog, which is automatically mounted on the Amazon Redshift cluster. Query the historical transaction records stored in Amazon S3 using Amazon Redshift Spectrum, and then combine them with the native customer sales report in Amazon Redshift.

    D. Create an AWS Glue ETL pipeline to move the customer sales report data to AWS Glue Data Catalog.

9. Which AWS Glue feature enables you to detect and fix data quality issues across your datasets?

    A. Data quality rules

    B. Data cleansing recipes

    C. Data lineage

    D. Data profiling

10. A data analyst would like to collect and store statistical information about table data in order to understand the nature of the data without running queries. Which feature from Glue Data Catalog will you recommend to the data analyst?

    A. Table versioning

    B. Schema evolution

    C. Partition indexing

    D. Column statistics

11. Which open table format is natively supported by AWS Glue Data Catalog for registering and managing table metadata, allowing for improved query performance and schema evolution?

    A. Apache Hudi

    B. Apache Iceberg

    C. Delta Lake

    D. All of the above

12. A data engineer would like to create an automated process to organize a data lake by cataloging the data in Amazon S3. The solution should support potential schema changes as well as record the history of the changes using the *least* amount of operational overhead. Which AWS service will meet these requirements?

A. AWS Lambda

B. Amazon Athena

C. An AWS Glue crawler

D. AWS Step Functions

13. A data engineer uses an AWS Glue ETL job to process data at 15 minute intervals. The final curated data is copied to Amazon S3. To improve the performance of the query, AWS Glue Data Catalog partitions need to be updated automatically after each job run. Which solution will meet these requirements *most* cost-effectively?

A. Use Apache Hive metastore to manage the data catalog. Update AWS Glue ETL code to include `enableUpdateCatalog` and `partitionKeys` arguments.

B. Use AWS Glue Data Catalog to manage the data catalog. Update AWS Glue ETL code to include `enableUpdateCatalog` and `partitionKeys` arguments.

C. Use AWS Glue Data Catalog to manage the data catalog. Create an AWS Glue Workflow and define a trigger within the workflow to start the crawler once the AWS Glue ETL job completes.

D. Use AWS Glue Data Catalog to manage the data catalog. Use AWS Glue Studio for ETL job and use the feature that supports updates to AWS Glue Data Catalog during the job runs.

14. A data analyst creates a table from a recordset stored in Amazon S3. The data is then partitioned using `year=2024/month=12/day=06/` format. Although the partitioning was successful, no records were returned when the SELECT* query was executed. What could be the possible reason?

A. The analyst did not run the `MSCK REPAIR TABLE` command after partitioning the data.

B. The analyst did not run the `MSCK REPAIR TABLE` command before partitioning the data.

C. The newly created table does not have read permissions.

D. The S3 bucket where the sample data is stored does not read permissions.

E. The analyst needs to use the `CTAS` command `CREATE TABLE AS SELECT` while creating the table in Amazon Athena.

Chapter 7

Visualizing Your Data

THE AWS CERTIFIED DATA ENGINEER – ASSOCIATE EXAM OBJECTIVES COVERED IN THIS CHAPTER MAY INCLUDE, BUT ARE NOT LIMITED TO, THE FOLLOWING:

✓ **Domain 3: Data Operations and Support**

   ▪ 3.2 Analyze data by using AWS services

Introduction

By now, you are already familiar with how the chapters are distributed based on the tasks corresponding to each domain mentioned in the AWS Certified Data Engineer Associate Exam Guide (https://d1.awsstatic.com/training-and-certification/docs-data-engineer-associate/AWS-Certified-Data-Engineer-Associate_Exam-Guide.pdf). This chapter covers the following task from Domain 3: Data Operations and Support, which focuses on analyzing your data:

> **Task Statement 3.2: Analyze data by using AWS services** In my opinion, this is the most interesting part of data engineering. At this stage, your data is loaded and most likely in a curated format. Now comes the time to analyze and visualize the data. AWS offers multiple services for this, and we will cover these services individually to help you prepare for the exam. If you look at the task statement in the *AWS Certified Data Engineer Associate Exam Guide*, you will find that it requires you to understand the trade-offs between provisioned and serverless services. You should also have a solid understanding of running SQL queries, visualizing data for analysis, knowing when and how to apply cleaning techniques, using data aggregation, rolling averages, grouping, and pivoting techniques.

Introduction to Data Visualization

Data visualization is a critical skill for data engineers and analysts, enabling them to transform raw data into meaningful insights and compelling visual narratives. This comprehensive guide focuses on analyzing and visualizing data using AWS services, as outlined in the *AWS Certified Data Engineer Associate Exam Guide*.

In today's data-driven world, the ability to effectively visualize data is more important than ever. It allows us to:

- Identify patterns and trends quickly
- Communicate complex information clearly

- Support data-driven decision-making
- Detect anomalies and outliers
- Tell compelling stories with data

This guide will equip you with the knowledge and skills needed to excel in data visualization on the AWS platform, preparing you for the AWS Certified Data Engineer Associate exam and real-world data engineering challenges.

We can categorize any field of a dataset into either a *dimension* or a *fact* (often referred to as a *measure*). A dimension can be easily understood as a category. For instance, if you have a monthly sales and profit table, you will have dimensions such as order date, sales region, sales country, sales person, and so on, which you can use to slice and dice your data. But the same table will have fields such as total sales, total profit, total cost, and so on. These are numerical values and referred to as *measures* or *facts*.

Types of Data Visualizations

Understanding different types of visualizations is crucial for choosing the right representation for your data. In the following sections, we'll explore the types of data visualizations.

Bar Charts

This is one of the most common visual types. There are multiple variants of bar charts, such as single measure, multi-measure, clustered, or stacked. You can also choose between vertical bars and horizontal bars.

Regardless of the type of visual you choose, the main goal of bar charts is to compare multiple categories. As shown in Figure 7.1, a typical example would be quarterly sales by region.

Histograms

Although histograms look similar to bar charts, they are very different. In fact, the only similarity is their appearance because they use bars. On a histogram, each bar is called a *bin* or a *bucket*. It displays the distribution of values in your data to understand more about the data distribution. An example of this is sales distribution across different price ranges.

Line Charts

This is another popular chart that you come across in your day-to-day activities. Choosing between a line chart and bar chart is often a personal choice. However, in some cases, such as forecasting, it makes more sense to use a line chart than a bar chart.

A line chart is mostly a preferrable choice for showing trends over time. A typical example of a line chart is for stock price fluctuations over a year.

FIGURE 7.1 Quarterly sales by region

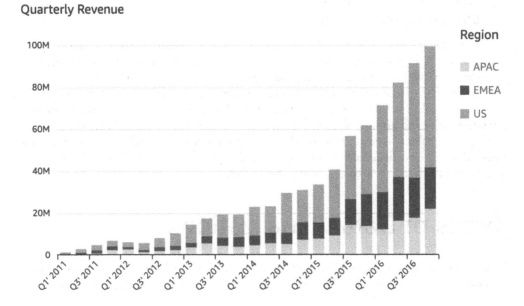

Quarterly Revenue

Scatter Plots

Scatter plots can be very powerful when your goal is to show relationships between two or three measures across two dimensions. Each bubble on the scatter plot represents one or two dimension values. The X and Y axes represent two different measures that apply to the dimension. A bubble appears on the chart at the point where the values for the two measures for an item in the dimension intersect. Optionally, you can also use bubble size to represent an additional measure.

Let's walk through an example. As shown in Figure 7.2, we want to analyze the relationship between three measures:

1. Sales ($): Represented on the Y-axis
2. Marketing Costs ($): Represented on the X-axis
3. Profitability ($): Represented by the size of the bubble

For this example, I analyzed the relationship between the marketing costs across product categories (Electronics, Clothing, and Food). With this plot, I can see that as my marketing costs increase, my sales also increase, along with overall profits.

Pie and Donut Charts

A pie chart is another common visual type, typically used when you want to show composition or proportions. For instance, you might want to see the market share of different companies.

FIGURE 7.2   A scatter plot

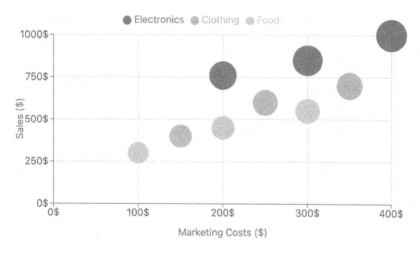

A variation of a pie chart is a donut chart. A donut chart is often used when you want to show the totals in the center of the donut. Choosing between a donut or a pie chart is often based on user preference; there is no hard and fast rule of choosing one over the other.

Use pie or donut charts to compare values for items in a dimension. The best use for this type of chart is to show a portion of total sales, as shown in Figure 7.3.

FIGURE 7.3   A pie chart in Amazon QuickSight

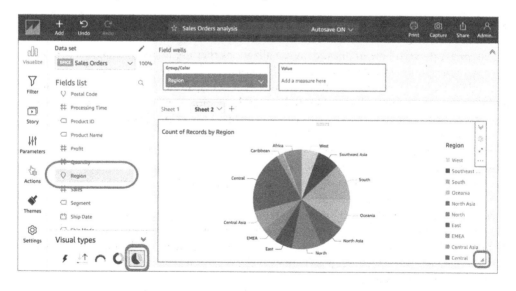

Heatmaps

Heatmaps are powerful visualization tools that use color-coding to represent data values in a two-dimensional matrix. They are particularly useful for identifying patterns, trends, and outliers in large datasets. Amazon QuickSight supports the creation of heatmaps, enabling data engineers to effectively communicate complex data relationships and help stakeholders make data-driven decisions based on visually intuitive representations of large-scale data patterns (see Figure 7.4).

FIGURE 7.4 A heatmap in Amazon QuickSight

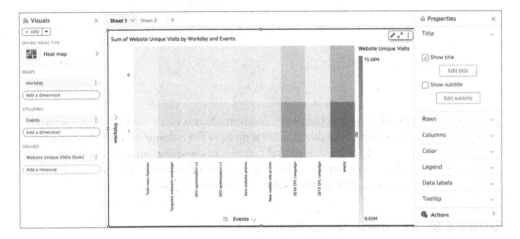

Treemaps

Treemaps are powerful hierarchical data visualizations that use nested rectangles to represent complex, multilevel data in a space-efficient manner, as shown in Figure 7.5. Each rectangle's size is proportional to the quantity it represents, allowing for quick visual comparisons between different data points and categories. Colors can be used to denote different categories or to represent an additional dimension of the data. This visualization type is particularly effective for displaying large datasets where space is at a premium, as it can show thousands of items simultaneously on a single screen. Treemaps excel at revealing patterns, outliers, and proportional relationships within hierarchical data structures. They are commonly used to visualize data such as file system usage, budget allocations, stock market performance, or population demographics.

While treemaps can effectively show the relative sizes of categories and subcategories, they may not always clearly display the hierarchical structure of the data, especially for deeply nested hierarchies. Despite this limitation, treemaps remain a valuable tool for analysts and data engineers seeking to gain quick insights into the composition and distribution of large, hierarchical datasets.

FIGURE 7.5   A treemap in Amazon QuickSight

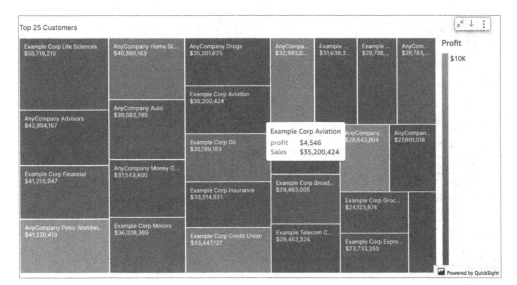

Geospatial Maps

Geospatial maps are powerful visualization tools that display data in a geographical context, allowing users to understand spatial relationships and patterns within their data. These maps use location-based information, typically latitude and longitude coordinates, to plot data points or regions on a map of the Earth or a specific area. Geospatial maps can represent various types of data, from simple point locations to complex overlays of multiple data layers. They are particularly effective for visualizing trends, clusters, and distributions that may not be apparent in traditional charts or tables. Common types of geospatial visualizations include point and filled maps, bubble maps, where the size of markers represents data magnitude (see Figure 7.6), and heat maps showing density (see Figure 7.7). These maps are widely used in fields such as sales distribution, urban planning, environmental science, logistics, and market analysis to provide insights into location-based phenomena, optimize resource allocation, and support decision-making processes.

Principles of Effective Data Visualization

In the realm of data engineering, the ability to effectively visualize data is crucial for conveying insights and supporting decision-making processes. Several key principles guide the creation of impactful data visualizations.

FIGURE 7.6 A geospatial map in Amazon QuickSight

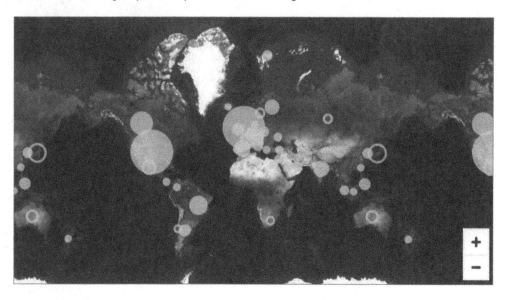

FIGURE 7.7 A geospatial heat map in Amazon QuickSight

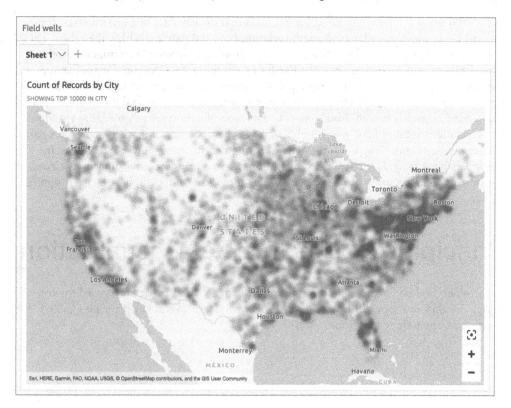

First and foremost is *clarity*—a well-designed visualization should be easily comprehensible at a glance, allowing viewers to quickly grasp the main message without confusion. This principle emphasizes the importance of clean, uncluttered designs and intuitive layouts.

Accuracy is another fundamental principle, as it ensures the integrity of the information being presented. Data visualizations must represent information truthfully, without distortion or misrepresentation. This involves careful consideration of scale, proportion, and context to avoid misleading interpretations.

Alongside accuracy, *efficiency* in visualization is crucial. This concept, often associated with Edward Tufte's data-to-ink ratio principle introduced in his book *The Visual Display of Quantitative Information*, advocates for maximizing the amount of information conveyed relative to the graphic elements used. In practice, this means eliminating unnecessary decorative elements and focusing on those that directly contribute to understanding the data.

The *aesthetic* aspect of data visualization should not be overlooked. While the primary goal is to convey information, the use of design principles can significantly enhance the appeal and engagement of visualizations. This includes thoughtful use of color, typography, and layout to create visually pleasing and professional-looking charts and graphs. However, aesthetics should never compromise the clarity or accuracy of the data representation.

Lastly, *relevance* is a critical principle in effective data visualization. Every element included in a visualization should serve a purpose in conveying the intended message. This principle encourages data engineers to be selective, including only the most pertinent information and avoiding the temptation to overcrowd visualizations with extraneous details. By adhering to these principles—clarity, accuracy, efficiency, aesthetics, and relevance—data engineers can create powerful visualizations that effectively communicate complex data insights, aiding in better understanding and decision-making within organizations.

Trade-offs Between Provisioned and Serverless Services

In the AWS ecosystem, data visualization services span a spectrum from fully provisioned to completely serverless offerings. This range provides data engineers with flexible options to meet diverse visualization needs.

Serverless services such as Amazon Athena, AWS Glue, and Amazon QuickSight have revolutionized the approach to data processing and visualization:

- Amazon Athena offers a serverless, interactive query service that makes it easy to analyze data directly in Amazon S3 using standard SQL. It's excellent for ad hoc visualization needs and can be a cost-effective solution for intermittent workloads.

- AWS Glue provides a fully managed extract, transform, and load (ETL) service that makes it simple to prepare and load data for analytics. Its serverless nature makes it ideal for data preparation tasks preceding visualization.

- Amazon QuickSight, as a fully managed, serverless business intelligence service, allows you to create and publish interactive dashboards that can be accessed from any device. Its serverless architecture ensures automatic scaling and pay-per-session pricing, making it highly flexible for various visualization scenarios.

These serverless options offer several advantages:

- Automatic scaling based on demand
- Pay-only-for-what-you-use pricing models
- Reduced operational overhead
- Rapid setup and deployment

However, they may face challenges with cold starts or cost predictability for high-volume, consistent workloads.

On the other hand, traditionally provisioned services such as Amazon EMR and Amazon Redshift now offer serverless options alongside their original provisioned models:

- Amazon EMR (both provisioned and serverless) allows analysts to process vast amounts of data using open-source tools such as Apache Spark, Hive, and many others. The serverless option automatically starts, scales, and shuts down resources as needed.
- Amazon Redshift (both provisioned and serverless) provides data warehousing capabilities. The serverless option automatically scales compute and memory resources for demanding and unpredictable workloads.

These hybrid offerings combine the robust capabilities of provisioned services with the flexibility of serverless architectures.

When choosing between these options for data visualization tasks, consider the following:

- **Workload predictability:** For consistent, high-volume visualization needs, provisioned options may offer advantages in performance predictability. For variable demands, serverless options like Athena or QuickSight can provide greater flexibility.
- **Cost sensitivity:** Analyze your usage patterns. Serverless options such as Athena and QuickSight can be economical for intermittent use, while provisioned services might be more cost-effective for high-utilization scenarios.
- **Operational overhead:** Fully serverless options such as Glue, Athena, and QuickSight significantly reduce management overhead, which can be beneficial for teams focused on creating visualizations rather than managing infrastructure.
- **Performance requirements:** For visualizations requiring consistent, high-performance query capabilities, provisioned services or their serverless counterparts (such as EMR Serverless or Redshift Serverless) might be preferable. However, services such as Athena and QuickSight have made significant strides in performance for many use cases.
- **Scalability needs:** Serverless options excel in scenarios where visualization demands can spike unexpectedly. QuickSight, for instance, automatically scales to accommodate varying numbers of users and query complexities.

- **Data preparation needs:** If your visualization workflow involves significant data preparation, consider using AWS Glue in conjunction with visualization tools for a fully serverless ETL and visualization pipeline.

- **Hybrid approaches:** Many organizations find success in hybrid approaches—for example, using Athena for ad hoc queries, Glue for data preparation, QuickSight for general business intelligence, and Redshift for high-performance analytical queries.

The choice between provisioned, serverless, or hybrid approaches for data visualization in AWS requires careful consideration of your specific use cases, workload patterns, budget constraints, and operational preferences. By understanding the strengths of each service—from the fully serverless nature of Athena, Glue, and QuickSight to the flexible options offered by EMR and Redshift—data engineers can craft visualization solutions that are powerful, insightful, efficient, and cost-effective.

AWS Services for Data Analysis and Visualization

In the following sections, we'll take a closer look at Amazon QuickSight, AWS Glue Data-Brew, Amazon Athena, and Amazon SageMaker Data Wrangler.

Visualizing Data with Amazon QuickSight

In the realm of data visualization and business intelligence, Amazon QuickSight stands out as a powerful, fully managed, serverless solution. As data engineers, understanding how to leverage QuickSight's capabilities is crucial for delivering impactful insights to stakeholders across your organization.

What Is Amazon QuickSight?

Amazon QuickSight is AWS's answer to the growing demand for easy-to-use, scalable business intelligence tools. It's designed to make it simple for anyone in an organization to build interactive dashboards and perform ad hoc analysis, all without the need for complex infrastructure or deep technical expertise.

Key Features of Amazon QuickSight

Amazon QuickSight has several key features:

- **SPICE (Super-fast, Parallel, In-memory Calculation Engine):** At the heart of QuickSight lies SPICE, a robust in-memory engine that allows for lightning-fast data processing. SPICE automatically replicates data for high availability and enables QuickSight to scale to thousands of users without performance degradation.

- **Machine learning insights:** QuickSight doesn't just visualize your data; it helps you understand it. With built-in ML capabilities, it can automatically detect anomalies and generate forecasts, bringing predictive analytics to your fingertips.

- **Embedded analytics:** QuickSight allows you to embed dashboards and visualizations directly into your applications, extending the power of data analytics to your end users seamlessly.

- **Pay-per-session pricing:** Unlike traditional BI tools with fixed licensing costs, QuickSight offers a flexible pricing model. You only pay for what you use, making it cost-effective for organizations of all sizes.

- **Broad data integration:** QuickSight can connect to a wide array of data sources, from AWS services like S3, Redshift, and RDS to on-premises databases and SaaS applications.

Real-World Use Cases for Amazon QuickSight

To truly appreciate the power of QuickSight, let's explore some common use cases:

- **Executive dashboards:** Imagine that you're tasked with creating a dashboard for your company's C-suite. With QuickSight, you can pull data from various sources (sales figures from Redshift, customer feedback from RDS, and marketing metrics from third-party APIs) into a single, comprehensive view. Executives can get a real-time pulse on the business at a glance.

- **Sales performance analysis:** For a sales team spread across different regions, QuickSight can be a game-changer. You can create interactive maps showing sales by territory, drill-down capabilities to analyze performance by product or salesperson, and trend lines to spot seasonal patterns. The ML Insights feature can automatically highlight unusual spikes or dips in sales, prompting timely action.

- **Real-time website analytics:** If you're managing an e-commerce platform, QuickSight can help you monitor website performance in real time. By connecting to your web server logs stored in Amazon S3, you can visualize user traffic, page views, conversion rates, and more. The ability to refresh data at intervals as short as 1 minute means you're always looking at the most current information.

Hands-on Exercise: Building Your First QuickSight Dashboard

Theory is great, but nothing beats hands-on experience. Let's walk through creating a multi-visual dashboard using QuickSight. We'll assume that you have access to a sample e-commerce dataset stored in Amazon S3.

Prerequisites   You need to have an AWS account.

The first time you log in to Amazon QuickSight, you will need to create a new Quick-Sight account:

1. Open the Amazon QuickSight landing page (`https://quicksight.aws.amazon.com/sn/auth/signin?redirect_uri=https%3A%2F%2Fquicksight.aws`

`.amazon.com%2Fsn%2Fstart%3Fstate%3DhashArgs%2523%26isauthcode%3Dt` rue), and choose Sign Up for QuickSight (see Figure 7.8).

FIGURE 7.8   Signing up for QuickSight

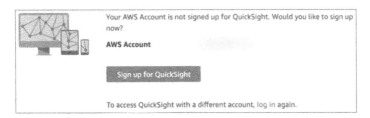

2. On the Create Your QuickSight Account screen, for Edition, choose Standard, and then choose Continue (see Figure 7.9).

FIGURE 7.9   Choosing the Standard edition

QuickSight

Create your QuickSight account

Edition	● Standard	⟋ Enterprise
First author with 1GB SPICE	FREE	FREE
Team trial for 60 days (4 authors)*	FREE	FREE
Additional author per month (yearly)**	$9	$18
Additional author per month (monthly)**	$12	$24
Additional readers (Pay-per-Session)	N/A	$0.30/session (max $5/reader/month) ****
Additional SPICE per month	$0.25 per GB	$0.38 per GB
Single Sign On with SAML or OpenID Connect	✓	✓
Connect to spreadsheets, databases & business apps	✓	✓
Access data in Private VPCs		✓
Row-level security for dashboards		✓

3. Enter a QuickSight account name and email address, and keep the remaining default selections (see Figure 7.10). Choose Finish.

4. Choose Go to Amazon QuickSight to open Amazon QuickSight in the AWS Management Console (see Figure 7.11).

Now that you have a QuickSight account, you're ready to continue with the exercise.

FIGURE 7.10   Entering your account name and email address

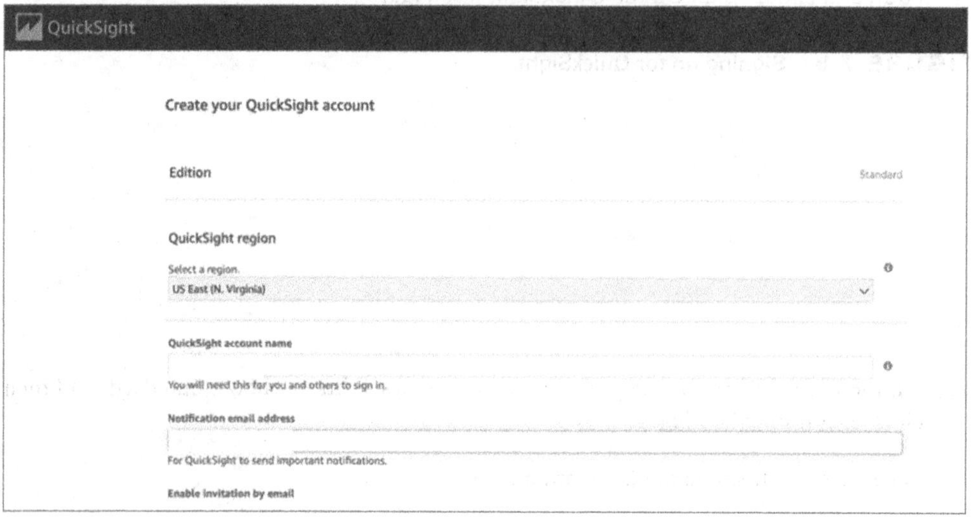

FIGURE 7.11   Opening Amazon QuickSight

Step 1: Create the Dataset

The first step in creating your multi-visual dashboard is to create a dataset:

1. Select the Data Sets tab on the left, and then select New Data Set.

2. Choose Upload a File as your data source (see Figure 7.12). The following files are supported: CSV, TSV, CLF, XLSX, and JSON.

3. In the Choose Your Sheet dialog box, select Orders, and then choose Edit/Preview Data (see Figure 7.13).

FIGURE 7.12   Uploading a file

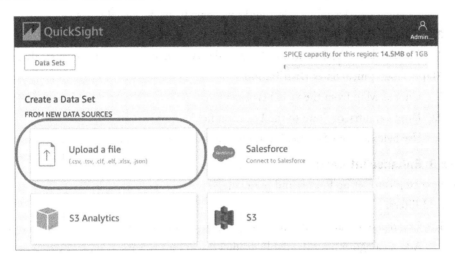

FIGURE 7.13   Editing and previewing data

4. Prepare your data. Now that you have uploaded your dataset, you need to prepare the data so that it is ready for reports. Preparing the data can include standardizing field names, removing fields, or adding calculations.

5. Once finalized, choose Save and Visualize.

Step 2: Create Your Visuals

Now that your data is imported, let's create three key visuals:

1. Bar Chart: Sales by Category

    1. Drag Category to the X-axis and Sales to the Y-axis.

    2. QuickSight will automatically create a bar chart. You can adjust the colors and sorting as needed.

2. Line Chart: Sales Trends Over Time

    1. Create a new visual by selecting Line Chart from the visual types.

    2. Place Date on the X-axis and Sales on the Y-axis.

    3. Use the date wheel to adjust the granularity (e.g., daily, weekly, or monthly).

3. Map: Geographical Sales Distribution

    1. Choose Map from the visual types.

    2. Drag Country or State to the Location field.

    3. Use Sales as your Size field to represent the sales volume.

Step 3: Enhance Interactivity

The next step is to set up fingers and parameters:

1. Add filters:

    1. Create a date range filter to allow users to adjust the time period of the analysis.

    2. Add a category filter to enable drilling down into specific product categories.

3. Create parameters:

    1. Set up a parameter for Sales Target.

    2. Use this to add a reference line on your bar chart, instantly showing which categories are meeting targets.

Step 4: Leverage ML Insights

Now you're ready to add machine learning insights:

1. Navigate to your line chart of sales over time.

2. Click Add Insight, and then choose Anomaly Detection.

3. QuickSight will automatically highlight unusual data points, potentially revealing unexpected sales spikes or dips.

Step 5: Publish and Share

Once you're satisfied with your dashboard, you're ready to share it with others:

1. Click Share in the upper-right corner.

2. Choose Publish Dashboard.

3. Set permissions for who can view or edit the dashboard.

AWS Glue DataBrew

AWS Glue DataBrew, as shown in Figure 7.14, is a powerful visual data preparation tool that empowers data analysts and data scientists to clean and normalize data without writing code. As a critical component in the AWS data visualization ecosystem, DataBrew simplifies the often complex and time-consuming task of data preparation, allowing professionals to focus more on analysis and less on data wrangling.

FIGURE 7.14   AWS Glue DataBrew

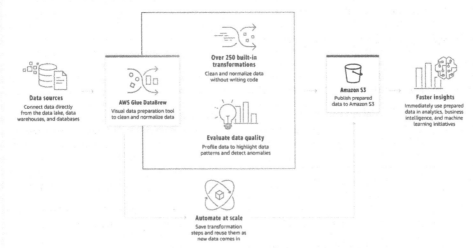

Key Features of AWS Glue DataBrew

AWS Glue DataBrew has several key features:

- **Visual interface for data transformation:** DataBrew provides an intuitive, point-and-click interface that allows users to easily explore and transform their data. This visual approach makes it accessible to team members who may not have extensive programming experience.

- **Over 250 built-in transformations:** With a vast library of built-in transformations, DataBrew covers a wide range of data preparation needs. These include:
  - Data cleansing operations (e.g., handling missing values, removing duplicates)
  - Format standardization (e.g., date/time formats, phone numbers)
  - Advanced transformations (e.g., pivot tables, joins, aggregations)

- **Data profiling and quality checks:** DataBrew automatically generates data profiles, providing insights into data distribution, patterns, and potential quality issues. This feature helps users quickly understand their data and identify areas that need attention.

- **Job scheduling and monitoring:** Users can schedule data preparation jobs to run automatically, ensuring that data is always up-to-date. Built-in monitoring tools allow teams to track job status and performance.

- **Integration with other AWS services:** DataBrew seamlessly integrates with other AWS services, including:
  - Amazon S3 for data storage

- AWS Glue Data Catalog for metadata management
- Amazon Redshift for data warehousing
- Amazon QuickSight for visualization

Use Cases for AWS Glue DataBrew

Common use cases for AWS Glue DataBrew include the following:

- **Cleaning and standardizing customer data:**
  - Scenario: A marketing team needs to prepare customer data for a targeted campaign.
  - Application: Use DataBrew to standardize addresses, remove duplicates, and format phone numbers consistently.
- **Preparing sales data for analysis:**
  - Scenario: A sales department wants to analyze quarterly performance across regions.
  - Application: Employ DataBrew to aggregate daily sales data, normalize product categories, and create calculated fields for year-over-year comparisons.
- **Transforming log data for security analysis:**
  - Scenario: A cybersecurity team needs to analyze server logs for potential threats.
  - Application: Utilize DataBrew to parse log entries, extract relevant fields (e.g., IP addresses, timestamps), and normalize data formats for easier analysis.

How Does It Work?

As previously mentioned, Amazon Glue DataBrew offers over 250 built-in transformations for data manipulation without coding, including automatic recommendations for tasks like filtering anomalies, correcting data issues, and normalizing formats. It supports advanced transformations using machine learning techniques like natural language processing (NLP). Users can combine and save transformations as reusable recipes. DataBrew handles common input formats such as CSV, JSON, Parquet, and Excel, and can output to various formats, including CSV, JSON, Parquet, Avro, ORC, and XML. This versatility makes DataBrew a powerful tool for efficient data preparation across different file types and complex transformation needs.

Figure 7.15 shows a high-level overview of the end-to-end process of using Amazon Glue Databrew.

Core Concepts

In Amazon Glue DataBrew, the following are the core concepts:

- **Dataset:** A read-only connection to your data, represented by metadata in DataBrew without altering the original data.
- **Project:** An interactive workspace in DataBrew for managing data, transformations, and scheduled processes.

- **Recipe:** A set of instructions or steps for DataBrew to transform raw data, which can be reused and versioned.

- **Job:** The process of executing a recipe's instructions to transform data, either on schedule or on demand.

- **Data lineage:** A visual representation of the data's origin and flow through different entities over time.

- **Data profile:** A summary report generated by DataBrew that provides insights into the shape, context, structure, and relationships of your data.

FIGURE 7.15   The Amazon Glue DataBrew process

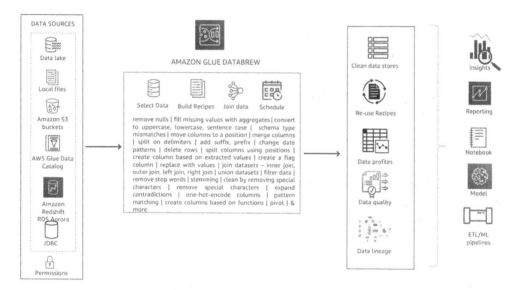

Hands-on Exercise: Getting Started with Amazon Glue DataBrew

In this exercise, we'll walk through the process of using AWS Glue DataBrew to prepare a sample dataset for analysis.

Prerequisites   An AWS account is needed for the following steps.

Step 1: Create a DataBrew Project

You begin by creating a DataBrew project:

1. Sign in to the AWS Management Console, and then navigate to AWS Glue DataBrew.

2. Click Create Project and provide a name for your project (e.g., SalesDataPrep).

3. For the dataset, select Upload from S3, and then choose a sample sales dataset. (You can use AWS-provided samples or upload your own.)

4. Review and confirm the settings, and then click Create Project.

Step 2: Apply Data Transformations

Next, you apply data transformations to your project:

1. In the DataBrew visual interface, explore your dataset by clicking on the column headers.

2. Handle missing values:

    1. Select the Revenue column.

    2. Choose Manage Missing Values from the Transforms menu.

    3. Select Fill Empty Cells with Average of Column, and then click Apply.

3. Standardize date formats:

    1. Select the Date column.

    2. Choose Change Data Type, and then select Date.

    3. Apply a standard date format (e.g., YYYY-MM-DD).

4. Create a new calculated column:

    1. Click Add Column, and then select Custom Formula.

    2. Name the column "Profit_Margin," and enter the following formula: (Revenue - Cost) / Revenue * 100

    3. Click Preview to check the results, and then click Apply.

Step 3: Create a Job to Run Transformations

Now you need a job to run your transformations:

1. In the DataBrew project view, click Create Job.

2. Name your job (e.g., DailySalesPrep), and select your recipe.

3. Choose an output location in S3 for the processed data.

4. Set a schedule (e.g., daily at 1:00 AM) for the job to run automatically.

5. Review and create the job.

Step 4: Analyze Data Profile and Quality Metrics

Now you need to check your quality:

1. In your DataBrew project, navigate to the Profile tab.

2. Explore the automatically generated data profile, noting the following:

    - Column statistics (min, max, mean, etc.)

    - Data type information

    - Value distributions

3. Check the Data Quality section for insights on the following:

    - Completeness (percentage of non-null values)

- Uniqueness
- Validity based on data type

4. Use these insights to identify any remaining data quality issues or areas for further transformation.

By completing this hands-on exercise, you'll gain practical experience with AWS Glue DataBrew and understand how it can streamline your data preparation processes. Remember that DataBrew's visual interface makes it easy to iterate on your data transformations, so don't hesitate to experiment with different approaches to achieve the best results for your specific use case.

Amazon Athena

Amazon Athena is a powerful, serverless, and interactive query service that allows you to easily analyze data stored in Amazon S3 using standard SQL. Athena is a completely managed service, meaning there is no infrastructure for you to provision or maintain. You simply point Athena to your data in S3, define the schema, and start querying using SQL. Athena uses the Presto query engine, providing ANSI SQL support and the ability to query a variety of data formats, including CSV, JSON, Parquet, and more. One of the key benefits of Athena is its pay-per-query pricing model—you only pay for the queries you run, based on the amount of data scanned. This makes Athena a cost-effective solution for ad hoc analytics and exploration of large datasets in S3. Additionally, Athena can provide fast, interactive query performance by executing queries in parallel across multiple servers. Overall, Athena is an excellent tool for analysts, data engineers, and business users who need to quickly gain insights from data in S3 without the overhead of managing any infrastructure.

Key Features of Amazon Athena

Amazon Athena has several key features:

- **Serverless architecture:** Athena is a fully managed, serverless service, meaning there is no infrastructure for you to provision or maintain. You simply point Athena to your data in Amazon S3 and start querying.

- **Interactive SQL queries:** Athena supports ANSI SQL and can execute complex queries, including joins, window functions, and array processing. This allows you to leverage your existing SQL skills.

- **Supports multiple data formats:** Athena can query a variety of data formats stored in Amazon S3, including CSV, JSON, Parquet, ORC, Avro, and more.

- **Pay-per-query pricing:** You only pay for the queries you run, based on the amount of data scanned. This allows for cost-effective analytics, especially on large datasets.

- **Fast, parallel execution:** Athena automatically executes queries in parallel, providing fast, interactive performance, even on large-scale data.

- **Integration with AWS Glue:** Athena integrates with the AWS Glue Data Catalog, allowing you to create a unified metadata repository across your data sources.

- **No ETL required:** With Athena, you can directly query data in Amazon S3 without the need to set up complex extract, transform, and load (ETL) pipelines.

- **Highly available and durable:** Athena utilizes the durability and availability of Amazon S3 as its underlying data store.

- **Scalable and secure:** Athena automatically scales to handle your query workloads, and integrates with AWS security services for data protection.

- **Ease of use:** Athena provides a simple, web-based query editor, making it accessible to analysts, data engineers, and business users alike.

Use Cases for Amazon Athena

Common use cases for Amazon Athena include the following:

- **Ad hoc data exploration:** Athena's serverless and pay-per-query model makes it an excellent choice for quickly exploring and analyzing data stored in Amazon S3, without the need for upfront infrastructure investments.

- **Business intelligence and reporting:** Athena's SQL support and integration with business intelligence tools like Amazon QuickSight allow users to generate reports and dashboards from data in S3.

- **Log and event analysis:** Athena can be used to efficiently analyze large volumes of log data and event data stored in Amazon S3, enabling use cases such as security analysis and operational monitoring.

- **Data lake analytics:** Athena is a natural fit for analyzing the data stored in an Amazon S3-based data lake, providing a flexible and cost-effective analytics solution.

- **Machine learning preprocessing:** Athena can be used to prepare and preprocess data stored in S3 for use in machine learning models, reducing the need for complex ETL pipelines.

- **IoT data analysis:** Athena can be used to query and analyze the large amounts of data generated by Internet of Things (IoT) devices and stored in Amazon S3.

Steps to Use Amazon Athena

To use Amazon Athena, follow these steps:

1. **Set up your data in Amazon S3:** Athena is designed to query data stored in Amazon S3, so you'll need to ensure that your data is properly organized and formatted in S3 buckets.

2. **Create a database and table:** In the Athena console, you'll need to create a database to hold your tables, and then define the tables that correspond to your data in S3. You can

either define the schema manually or use AWS Glue to crawl your data and automatically generate the table definitions.

3. **Write SQL queries:** With your database and tables set up, you can start writing SQL queries to analyze your data. Athena supports standard SQL syntax, including complex queries with joins, aggregations, and analytical functions.

4. **Execute queries:** You can execute your queries directly in the Athena web-based query editor. Athena will automatically scale to execute your queries in parallel, providing fast, interactive results.

5. **Optimize query performance:** To improve query performance and reduce costs, you can optimize your data by partitioning, compressing, and converting it to columnar formats like Parquet or ORC.

6. **Integrate with BI tools:** Athena seamlessly integrates with business intelligence tools like Amazon QuickSight, allowing you to build dashboards and reports directly on your data in S3.

7. **Monitor and manage:** Athena provides logging and monitoring capabilities through Amazon CloudWatch, allowing you to track query activity, costs, and performance. You can also set up alerts and notifications.

8. **Secure your data:** Athena integrates with AWS security services like AWS Identity and Access Management (IAM) and AWS Key Management Service (KMS) to help you control access and encrypt your data.

Hands-on Exercise: Running Amazon Athena

Ideally, it's recommended to do a hands-on exercise to get used to how Amazon Athena works. Here is the link to the Amazon Athena workshop, which has detailed steps to run Amazon Athena:

```
https://catalog.us-east-1.prod.workshops.aws/workshops/
9981f1a1-abdc-49b5-8387-cb01d238bb78/en-US/10-intro
```

Amazon SageMaker Data Wrangler

Amazon SageMaker Data Wrangler simplifies the process of data preparation and feature engineering for machine learning. We will discuss what Amazon SageMaker Data Wrangler is, but before that, let's touch on the machine learning development lifecycle.

Machine learning (ML) development is a complex and iterative process. However, you can categorize the machine learning lifecycle into several broad categories (see Figure 7.16):

1. Prepare
2. Build
3. Train and tune
4. Deploy and manage

FIGURE 7.16   The machine learning lifecycle

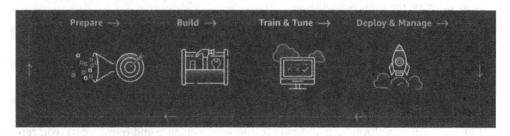

The Prepare Stage

The prepare stage consumes roughly 80% of an ML team's time, making it a critical yet often underappreciated phase of machine learning. Raw data typically requires extensive cleaning and transformation to address issues like missing values, outliers, and formatting inconsistencies. This preparation is essential because ML algorithms, such as logistic regression, need data in specific formats to function effectively. For example, binary classification models require numerical inputs and properly encoded target variables. The process involves data cleaning, visualization, analysis, and feature engineering—including techniques like one-hot encoding—to ensure the model can learn effectively and make accurate predictions.

The Build Stage

The build stage is where teams select and implement ML algorithms through systematic experimentation. Teams evaluate multiple algorithms based on factors like problem type, dataset characteristics, required accuracy, interpretability, and resource constraints. While existing algorithms may suffice, teams often develop custom solutions using frameworks like TensorFlow or PyTorch to address specific needs. This stage involves hyperparameter tuning, cross-validation, performance benchmarking, and comprehensive documentation. The process is inherently iterative, requiring teams to balance technical effectiveness with practical deployment considerations until they achieve satisfactory results.

The Train and Tune Stage

The train and tune stage is where the selected algorithm learns from the prepared data through two main components: training and hyperparameter tuning. During training, the model learns patterns by iteratively processing the data while being evaluated against a validation dataset. Hyperparameter tuning involves optimizing configuration settings such as learning rate, batch size, and model architecture parameters that control the learning process. This optimization can be achieved through various approaches, including grid search, random search, Bayesian optimization, or automated tools. The process is inherently iterative, requiring careful monitoring of metrics such as accuracy, precision, and learning curves, while balancing optimal performance with practical resource constraints.

The Deploy and Manage Stage

When you are satisfied with your model, you are ready to move into the deploy and manage phase. During this stage, you deploy your model to production, where it can serve real-time inference or produce predictions in batch. As your model serves predictions in the real world, you will need to carefully monitor its performance and scale the infrastructure to meet the increasing demands of your end users.

Now let's focus on Amazon Sagemaker Data Wrangler. Amazon SageMaker Data Wrangler is a feature within SageMaker Studio that streamlines data preparation for machine learning with minimal coding required. It offers comprehensive functionality, including data import from various sources (S3, Athena, Redshift, EMR), data flow creation for defining preparation steps, data transformation using standard tools, automated data quality insights, feature analysis through visualization tools, and flexible export options to locations like S3, SageMaker Pipelines, Feature Store, or Python scripts. Users can also customize workflows by adding their own Python scripts and transformations.

Key Features of Amazon SageMaker Data Wrangler

Amazon SageMaker Data Wrangler has several key features:

- Visual interface for data transformation
- Built-in data analysis capabilities
- Custom transformations using Python/PySpark
- Integration with SageMaker Studio
- Export to various formats and destinations

Use Cases for Amazon SageMaker Data Wrangler

Common use cases for Amazon SageMaker Data Wrangler include the following:

- Preparing data for machine learning models
- Feature engineering for predictive analytics
- Analyzing and visualizing data distributions

Figure 7.17 shows an example architecture of Amazon SageMaker Data Wrangler.

First, training data is loaded into Amazon S3, either through Data Wrangler's SQL interface for supported data sources or using other tools for additional sources. Here's the detailed workflow:

1. Training data is imported into Amazon S3 either via Data Wrangler's SQL (from supported sources) or using alternative tools (from any other sources).
2. A sample subset of records from the pre-staged S3 dataset is ingested into Data Wrangler's UI.
3. Exploratory data analysis is conducted, and a set of data transformations is defined. Optionally, sample data can be manually exported.

4. The transformations are saved as a recipe while a processing job orchestration code is generated and saved as a notebook.

5. The data processing job can either be triggered on-demand or as part of a training/inference pipeline.

6. The processing job applies the transformation recipe to the entire dataset. It runs a containerized Spark job, which allows for parallel processing.

7. The transformed data can be exported into either Feature Store or S3.

FIGURE 7.17   Amazon SageMaker Data Wrangler architecture

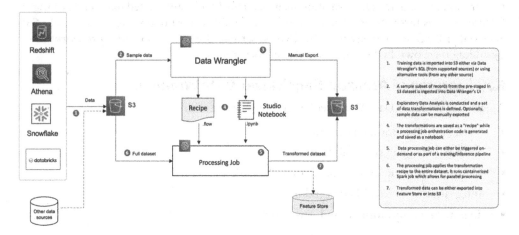

Hands-on Exercise: Testing It in Your Account

For hands-on experience with Amazon SageMaker Data Wrangler, we recommend testing it in your AWS account. You can follow our comprehensive workshop guide, which provides step-by-step instructions and practical exercises. This workshop will help you gain practical experience with Data Wrangler's features and capabilities. Access the workshop materials here: `https://catalog.us-east-1.prod.workshops.aws/workshops/327375b8-425b-49d4-b0da-241da0595ecf/en-US`.

Advanced SQL Techniques for Data Analysis

The mastery of SQL stands as a cornerstone in the modern data analyst's toolkit. While many practitioners encounter SQL early in their careers, often beginning with simple SELECT statements and basic joins, the language harbors depths that can transform how we

understand and manipulate data. This chapter delves into these advanced techniques, illumi-
nating the sophisticated ways SQL can be employed for complex data analysis.

The Evolution of SQL in Modern Data Platforms

The landscape of SQL has evolved far beyond its origins in traditional relational databases.
Today's data professionals work across a spectrum of platforms, from cloud data warehouses such as Amazon Redshift to serverless query engines such as Amazon Athena. While
our discussion will often reference Redshift's implementation, the concepts we explore tran-
scend any single platform. The true power of SQL lies in its fundamental principles, which
remain consistent even as syntax varies across different systems.

Modern SQL implementations have grown to accommodate the increasing complexity
of data analysis requirements. Where once SQL might have been viewed primarily as a data
retrieval language, it now serves as a sophisticated analytical tool, capable of performing
complex statistical calculations, window analyses, and hierarchical data processing. This
evolution reflects the growing demands of data-driven decision-making in contemporary
organizations.

Complex Join Operations: Beyond Simple Table Combinations

The art of joining tables represents perhaps the most fundamental yet nuanced aspect
of SQL mastery. While beginners often start with simple inner joins, the true complexity
emerges when we need to combine multiple tables in ways that preserve the integrity of our
analysis while handling the messy realities of real-world data.

Consider the common scenario of analyzing customer purchase patterns across multiple
retail channels. A simple approach might join customers directly to their orders, but a more
sophisticated analysis requires understanding the relationships between customers, their
orders, the products they purchase, and the various touchpoints along their journey. Here's
how we might approach this:

```
SELECT
    c.customer_name,
    o.order_date,
    p.product_name,
    s.shipping_status
FROM
    customers c
    INNER JOIN orders o ON c.customer_id = o.customer_id
    LEFT JOIN products p ON o.product_id = p.product_id
    LEFT JOIN shipping s ON o.order_id = s.order_id
WHERE
    o.order_date >= '2024-01-01';
```

This query tells a story: we begin with our customers, connect them to their orders, and then enrich this information with product details and shipping status. The choice of join types—INNER versus LEFT—reflects our business reality. We use an INNER JOIN between customers and orders because we're only interested in customers who have made purchases, but LEFT JOINs for products and shipping because we want to retain all orders even if some product details are missing or shipping information hasn't been recorded.

Window Functions: The Analytical Powerhouse

Window functions represent one of SQL's most powerful features for analytical work, yet they often remain underutilized by analysts who haven't fully explored their capabilities. These functions allow analysts to perform calculations across sets of rows while still returning detailed, row-level data—a capability that transforms how we can analyze trends and patterns in our data.

The true elegance of window functions lies in their ability to maintain the granularity of our data while simultaneously providing contextual information. Consider the challenge of analyzing employee salaries within departments. We might want to understand not just individual salaries, but how each employee's compensation compares to their peers:

```
SELECT
    department,
    employee_name,
    salary,
    AVG(salary) OVER (PARTITION BY department) as dept_avg_salary,
    salary - AVG(salary) OVER (PARTITION BY department) as diff_from_avg,
    PERCENT_RANK() OVER (PARTITION BY department ORDER BY salary) as
salary_percentile
FROM
    employees;
```

This query exemplifies the analytical power of window functions. For each employee, we can see their absolute salary, their department's average, their deviation from this average, and their percentile ranking—all in a single query. The PARTITION BY clause creates these window calculations within the context of each department, allowing for meaningful comparisons within relevant peer groups.

The Art of Subqueries and Common Table Expressions

As our analytical needs grow more complex, we often find ourselves needing to break down problems into manageable pieces. This is where subqueries and common table expressions (CTEs) become invaluable. While subqueries offer a way to nest queries within queries, CTEs provide a more readable and maintainable approach to complex query logic.

Consider the challenge of analyzing sales growth trends. We might need to calculate month-over-month growth rates, identify seasonal patterns, and highlight significant changes. A CTE-based approach allows us to build this analysis step by step:

```
WITH monthly_sales AS (
    SELECT
        DATE_TRUNC('month', sale_date) as month,
        SUM(amount) as total_sales
    FROM
        sales
    GROUP BY
        DATE_TRUNC('month', sale_date)
),
sales_growth AS (
    SELECT
        month,
        total_sales,
        LAG(total_sales) OVER (ORDER BY month) as prev_month_sales
    FROM
        monthly_sales
)
SELECT
    month,
    total_sales,
    ROUND(((total_sales - prev_month_sales) / prev_month_sales * 100), 2) as
growth_percentage
FROM
    sales_growth;
```

This structured approach to complex analysis demonstrates how CTEs can make our logic clearer and more maintainable. Each CTE serves as a building block, performing a specific part of our analysis, with the final query bringing everything together in a coherent result.

Pivot and Unpivot: Transforming Data Perspectives

Among SQL's more sophisticated features, pivot and unpivot operations stand as powerful tools for restructuring data. These operations fundamentally alter how we view and analyze our data, transforming between row-oriented and column-oriented formats. While seemingly straightforward in concept, their mastery opens up remarkable possibilities for data presentation and analysis.

Understanding the Need for Data Restructuring

Consider a common scenario in sales analysis: your database stores monthly sales figures as individual rows, with each record containing a date and amount. While this structure serves well for storage and basic querying, reporting often demands a different view—perhaps a matrix showing products across columns and quarters as rows, or vice versa. This transformation from rows to columns (or back again) lies at the heart of pivot and unpivot operations.

Let's explore a practical example. Imagine that we start with using the following to get a sales table structured like the one shown in Table 7.1:

```
SELECT * FROM sales_data;
```

TABLE 7.1   A simple sales table

product_category	quarter	sales_amount
Electronics	Q1	50000
Electronics	Q2	62000
Electronics	Q3	55000
Electronics	Q4	68000
Furniture	Q1	35000
Furniture	Q2	40000
Furniture	Q3	38000
Furniture	Q4	42000
Clothing	Q1	28000
Clothing	Q2	32000
Clothing	Q3	30000
Clothing	Q4	35000

The Art of Pivoting

Pivoting transforms this row-based data into a columnar format, creating a cross-tabulation that might be more suitable for reporting or analysis. The syntax varies across different SQL platforms, but the concept remains consistent. In most modern SQL implementations, we can write the following to produce a table more like the one shown in Table 7.2:

```
SELECT *
FROM (
    SELECT
        product_category,
        quarter,
        sales_amount
    FROM
        sales_data
)
PIVOT (
    SUM(sales_amount)
    FOR quarter IN ('Q1', 'Q2', 'Q3', 'Q4')
);
```

TABLE 7.2 A better sales table

product_category	Q1	Q2	Q3	Q4
Electronics	50000	62000	55000	68000
Furniture	35000	40000	38000	42000
Clothing	28000	32000	30000	35000

This transformed view offers immediate insights that might be less apparent in the original format. We can easily compare quarterly performance across product categories or spot seasonal trends. However, it's worth noting that pivoting isn't merely about presentation—it can fundamentally change how we analyze our data.

For platforms that don't support explicit PIVOT syntax, we can achieve the same result using conditional aggregation:

```
SELECT
    product_category,
    SUM(CASE WHEN quarter = 'Q1' THEN sales_amount END) as Q1,
    SUM(CASE WHEN quarter = 'Q2' THEN sales_amount END) as Q2,
    SUM(CASE WHEN quarter = 'Q3' THEN sales_amount END) as Q3,
    SUM(CASE WHEN quarter = 'Q4' THEN sales_amount END) as Q4
```

```
FROM
    sales_data
GROUP BY
    product_category;
```

The Complementary Power of Unpivoting

Unpivoting performs the inverse operation, converting columns back into rows. This transformation proves invaluable when we need to analyze data that arrives in a pivoted format or when we want to normalize data for specific types of analysis. Consider a scenario where we receive quarterly reports in a spreadsheet-like format and need to convert them for time-series analysis:

```
SELECT
    product_category,
    quarter,
    sales_amount
FROM
    quarterly_sales
UNPIVOT (
    sales_amount
    FOR quarter IN (Q1, Q2, Q3, Q4)
);
-- Results:
-- product_category | quarter | sales_amount
-- Electronics      | Q1      | 50000
-- Electronics      | Q2      | 62000
-- Electronics      | Q3      | 55000
-- [and so on...]
```

For databases without native UNPIVOT support, we can use UNION ALL to achieve the same result:

```
SELECT product_category, 'Q1' as quarter, Q1 as sales_amount
FROM quarterly_sales
UNION ALL
SELECT product_category, 'Q2' as quarter, Q2 as sales_amount
FROM quarterly_sales
UNION ALL
SELECT product_category, 'Q3' as quarter, Q3 as sales_amount
FROM quarterly_sales
UNION ALL
SELECT product_category, 'Q4' as quarter, Q4 as sales_amount
FROM quarterly_sales;
```

Strategic Applications and Considerations

The true power of pivot and unpivot operations emerges when we consider their analytical applications:

- **Time series analysis:** Unpivoting columnar time data enables the application of time-series functions and trending analysis.

- **Comparative analytics:** Pivoting can create side-by-side comparisons that illuminate patterns across categories or time periods.

- **Data quality assessment:** Transforming data between row and column formats can help identify anomalies and inconsistencies.

- **Report generation:** Pivot operations often create the exact format needed for management reporting and dashboards.

   However, these operations come with important considerations:

- **Performance impact:** Pivot and unpivot operations can be resource-intensive on large datasets. Consider materialized views or precalculated tables for frequently accessed pivoted data.

- **Data type consistency:** When pivoting, all values being aggregated must be compatible types.

- **NULL handling:** Define clear strategies for handling NULL values during these transformations.

- **Column limitations:** Some databases limit the number of columns that can be created through pivoting.

Beyond Basic Transformations

Advanced applications of pivot and unpivot operations often combine with other SQL features we've discussed. For instance, we might use window functions on unpivoted data to calculate moving averages across quarters, or embed pivoted results within CTEs for further analysis:

```
WITH unpivoted_sales AS (
    SELECT product_category, quarter, sales_amount
    FROM quarterly_sales
    UNPIVOT (
        sales_amount
        FOR quarter IN (Q1, Q2, Q3, Q4)
    )
)
SELECT
    product_category,
    quarter,
    sales_amount,
```

```
    AVG(sales_amount) OVER (
        PARTITION BY product_category
        ORDER BY quarter
        ROWS BETWEEN 3 PRECEDING AND CURRENT ROW
    ) as moving_avg
FROM
    unpivoted_sales
ORDER BY
    product_category, quarter;
```

This combination of techniques demonstrates the true flexibility of SQL as an analytical tool. By understanding when and how to reshape our data using pivot and unpivot operations, we can adapt our analysis to answer virtually any business question that arises.

The Future of SQL Analysis

As we look to the future, SQL continues to evolve and adapt to new analytical challenges. Modern implementations are incorporating features for handling semi-structured data, complex statistical calculations, and machine learning capabilities. Yet the fundamental principles we've explored—joins, window functions, structured query composition, and pivot/ unpivot operations—remain as relevant as ever.

The key to mastering advanced SQL lies not just in understanding individual techniques, but in knowing how to combine them effectively to solve real-world analytical challenges. As data volumes grow and business questions become more complex, the ability to write efficient, maintainable SQL becomes increasingly valuable.

Remember that while syntax may vary across platforms, the analytical thinking behind these techniques remains consistent. Focus on understanding the problems you're trying to solve and the logical steps needed to reach your answers. With practice, these advanced SQL techniques will become natural tools in your analytical toolkit, enabling you to tackle increasingly sophisticated data challenges with confidence and clarity.

Data Cleansing and Preparation

Data cleansing and preparation represent one of the most time-intensive aspects of data analytics, with industry surveys consistently showing that data professionals spend approximately 80% of their time on these crucial preliminary steps. In today's digital landscape, we encounter an ever-expanding array of data sources, which can be classified into three main categories: structured data (primarily comprising traditional databases), semi-structured data (including formats such as JSON, CSV, and XML files), and unstructured data (encompassing images, audio, video files, and various document formats).

While all data sources require thorough cleansing and preparation, the specific approach varies depending on the data type and its initial quality. Some datasets demand extensive cleansing before any preparation can begin, while others, already maintaining a reasonable level of quality, may proceed directly to the preparation phase. The distinction between these approaches lies in the inherent organization and standardization of the source data, with structured data typically requiring less initial cleansing than unstructured sources.

Data cleansing stands as a cornerstone of effective data analytics, serving as the foundation upon which all subsequent analysis is built. When executed properly, this meticulous process yields well-prepared datasets that generate more accurate insights and foster greater trust among data consumers. These consumers span a broad spectrum of professionals, from business intelligence analysts who transform data into meaningful visualizations to data scientists who rely on clean, well-prepared data to train and validate machine learning models. The quality of data preparation directly influences the accuracy of these models and, ultimately, the reliability of the decisions they inform.

Common Data Quality Issues in Modern Analytics

In today's data-driven environment, the quality of data directly impacts the reliability of analysis and decision-making processes. Organizations frequently encounter several critical data quality challenges that must be systematically addressed to ensure analytical integrity. This section explores the primary data quality issues that practitioners commonly face and their implications for data analysis.

Missing Values: The Silent Disruptor

Missing values pose a fundamental challenge in data analysis, manifesting as gaps in datasets that can significantly impact analytical outcomes. These gaps typically arise from various sources, including data entry errors, system malfunctions, and incomplete data collection processes. The implications of missing values extend beyond mere data incompleteness; they can introduce systematic bias, reduce statistical power, and compromise the validity of analytical models.

Donald Rubin classified missing data problems into three distinct categories of missing data: Missing Completely at Random (MCAR), where missingness is unrelated to any values; Missing at Random (MAR), where missingness depends on observed values; and Missing Not at Random (MNAR), where missingness depends on unobserved values.[1] Understanding these categories is crucial for selecting appropriate handling strategies.

Treatment approaches vary based on both the proportion and type of missing values. For numerical time series data, common strategies include interpolation, moving averages, or regression-based imputation. Categorical data may require different approaches, such as mode imputation or the creation of missing-value categories. The selection of an appropriate strategy depends on factors including the missingness mechanism, data structure, and analytical objectives.

---

[1] Rubin, Donald B. "Inference and Missing Data." *Biometrika* 63, no. 3 (1976): 581–90.

The key to effective missing data treatment lies in the careful evaluation of the missingness pattern and mechanism, followed by the implementation of suitable handling strategies that maintain analytical integrity while minimizing potential bias.

Duplicate Records: The Redundancy Challenge

Duplicate records, while seemingly straightforward to identify, often present subtle complexities that can significantly skew analytical outcomes. These duplications may emerge from multiple data entry points, system integration issues, or merge operations. Beyond exact duplicates, analysts must also contend with near-duplicates or partial matches that require sophisticated detection mechanisms. The presence of duplicate records can inflate sample sizes, bias statistical measures, and lead to overrepresentation of certain data points in analytical models.

Inconsistent Formats: The Standardization Imperative

Format inconsistencies manifest across various data elements, from datetime representations to measurement units and categorical variables. These inconsistencies often arise when data is collected from multiple sources or when data entry standards evolve over time. For example, date formats may vary between DD/MM/YYYY and MM/DD/YYYY, or measurement units might fluctuate between metric and imperial systems. Such inconsistencies can render comparative analyses invalid and necessitate careful standardization protocols.

Outliers and Anomalies: The Statistical Outliers

The identification and handling of outliers and anomalies require both statistical rigor and domain expertise. While outliers may represent genuine extreme values that merit investigation, they can also result from measurement errors or system malfunctions. Modern data analysis demands sophisticated approaches to anomaly detection that can distinguish between legitimate outliers that provide valuable insights and erroneous data points that require correction or removal. This distinction is particularly crucial in fields such as fraud detection and quality control.

Data Type Mismatches: The Structural Challenge

Data type mismatches occur when data elements are stored or processed in formats that don't align with their intended use. These issues often surface during data integration or migration processes, where different systems may interpret or store data types differently. For instance, numerical values stored as text strings can prevent mathematical operations, while improperly formatted categorical variables may disturb statistical analyses. Addressing these mismatches requires careful consideration of data type conversions and their implications for data integrity.

Integration and Mitigation Strategies

Successfully addressing these data quality issues requires a comprehensive approach that combines automated detection mechanisms with human oversight. Organizations should implement robust data quality frameworks that include the following:

- Regular data profiling and monitoring
- Standardized data cleaning protocols
- Clear documentation of data transformations
- Validation rules and constraints
- Regular audits and quality assessments

Understanding and addressing these common data quality issues is fundamental to maintaining analytical integrity and ensuring reliable insights. As datasets grow larger and more complex, the importance of systematic data quality management becomes increasingly critical for organizations seeking to leverage their data assets effectively.

Data Cleansing and Transformation Techniques

Data quality forms the foundation of reliable analytics. This section explores systematic approaches to data cleansing and transformation, which are essential skills for any data professional. We will examine proven methodologies for handling common data quality challenges and implementing robust transformation strategies. We can't list all the techniques here, as this requires a dedicated chapter; however, we will cover the most commonly used techniques. Data cleansing encompasses the identification, correction, and prevention of data quality issues. Before beginning any analysis, practitioners must address these fundamental aspects of data preparation.

Missing values are arguably the topmost data quality issue that we have encountered. The strategy to handle missing values varies based on the data. Most of the time, you would only drop the missing and null values if the data is missing at random. But be wary about its impact. You first need to understand what the impact would be to drop or delete the missing values. As discussed previously, the imputation technique is something that uses statistical methods like mean, average, or mode to impute missing values. There are other techniques, but they are outside the scope of this book, but you will definitely need the other techniques on the job.

Removing duplicates is another technique commonly used. This is to identify unique columns and also remove duplicate rows. If you are using SQL for this, it's: `SELECT DISTINCT * from your_table;` Other services, such as AWS Glue DataBrew, offer built-in transformations to remove duplicates.

Another area is to standardize the data for columns, such as phone numbers, emails, numbers, etc. Normally, this is handled at the application level to ensure the data quality. However, you cannot control everything; thus, as a data engineer, you will come across data joined from multiple sources, and you need to standardize such data.

Features like Data Profiling in Glue DataBrew and SageMaker Data Wrangler can help you understand your data. These features help you understand your data distribution and how your data is organized, as well as identify potential data quality issues, like missing data, data skew, duplicates, etc. They also help you understand any correlation between data fields.

Data Quality in Analytics

Data quality serves as the cornerstone of reliable analytics and informed decision-making. This section explores systematic approaches to data cleansing and transformation—essential competencies for modern data professionals. While comprehensive coverage of all techniques would require a dedicated chapter, we focus on fundamental methodologies for addressing common data quality challenges and implementing robust transformation strategies.

Core Data Quality Challenges

Data cleansing encompasses the systematic identification, correction, and prevention of data quality issues. Before conducting any analysis, practitioners must address these foundational aspects of data preparation to ensure the integrity of their results.

Missing values represent one of the most prevalent data quality challenges in analytics. The strategy for handling such gaps depends heavily on the data's context and distribution patterns. While dropping records with missing values may seem straightforward when data is missing at random (MAR), practitioners must carefully evaluate the impact of this approach on their dataset's representativeness and statistical validity. Statistical imputation methods—utilizing measures such as mean, median, or mode—offer alternative approaches, though advanced techniques may be necessary for complex scenarios encountered in professional settings.

Data Standardization and Deduplication

Duplicate record identification and removal constitute another critical aspect of data cleansing. Whether implementing this through SQL's `DISTINCT` clause or leveraging specialized tools like AWS Glue DataBrew's built-in transformations, establishing unique record sets remains fundamental to data integrity.

Data standardization presents particular challenges when dealing with semi-structured fields such as phone numbers, email addresses, and numerical formats. While optimal data quality controls should be implemented at the application level, data engineers frequently encounter scenarios requiring post hoc standardization, particularly when integrating data from multiple sources with varying formats and conventions.

Advanced Data Quality Tools

Modern data platforms offer sophisticated tools for data quality assessment and improvement. Features such as data profiling in AWS Glue DataBrew and Amazon SageMaker Data Wrangler enable comprehensive analysis of data distributions, organizational patterns, and potential quality issues. These tools facilitate the identification of data anomalies, including missing values, data skew, and duplicates, while also revealing correlations between fields—insights crucial for effective data preparation and analysis.

Data quality tools can be implemented at two critical stages: during data transit as part of ETL (extract, transform, and load) processes using AWS Glue, and on data at rest once it has been cataloged in the AWS Glue Data Catalog.

Data Aggregation and Transformation Techniques

Data transformation and aggregation form the cornerstone of modern data analysis, enabling practitioners to distill actionable insights from complex datasets. These techniques serve as the bridge between raw data and meaningful patterns, transforming seemingly chaotic information into structured, interpretable results.

Rolling averages provide crucial smoothing capabilities that reveal underlying trends while minimizing noise and outlier effects. For instance, in sales analysis, a 7-day rolling average smooths daily fluctuations while preserving weekly patterns, while a 30-day rolling average reveals longer-term trends. This technique proves particularly valuable when analyzing volatile metrics like stock prices or daily sales figures.

The following example computes a rolling average of quantities sold by date, ordering the results by date ID and sales ID[2]:

```
select salesid, dateid, sellerid, qty,
avg(qty) over
(order by dateid, salesid rows unbounded preceding) as avg
from winsales
order by 2,1;
```

```
salesid |   dateid   | sellerid | qty | avg
--------+------------+----------+-----+-----
30001 | 2003-08-02 |        3 |  10 |  10
10001 | 2003-12-24 |        1 |  10 |  10
10005 | 2003-12-24 |        1 |  30 |  16
40001 | 2004-01-09 |        4 |  40 |  22
10006 | 2004-01-18 |        1 |  10 |  20
20001 | 2004-02-12 |        2 |  20 |  20
40005 | 2004-02-12 |        4 |  10 |  18
20002 | 2004-02-16 |        2 |  20 |  18
30003 | 2004-04-18 |        3 |  15 |  18
```

---

[2] https://docs.aws.amazon.com/redshift/latest/dg/r_WF_AVG.html

```
30004 | 2004-04-18 |        3 |  20 |  18
30007 | 2004-09-07 |        3 |  30 |  19
(11 rows)
```

Data grouping allows analysts to aggregate information at various hierarchical levels. Consider a retail dataset: analysts can group sales by region, product category, or time period, calculating summaries like average sales, total revenue, or customer counts for each group. This flexibility enables both high-level strategic analysis and detailed operational insights. For example, consider the following simple query[3].

```
select listid, eventid, sum(pricepaid) as revenue,
count(qtysold) as numtix
from sales
group by listid, eventid
order by 3, 4, 2, 1
limit 5;
```

```
listid | eventid | revenue | numtix
-------+---------+---------+--------
89397  |      47 |   20.00 |       1
106590 |      76 |   20.00 |       1
124683 |     393 |   20.00 |       1
103037 |     403 |   20.00 |       1
147685 |     429 |   20.00 |       1
(5 rows)
```

In the preceding query, the select list consists of two aggregate expressions. The first uses the SUM function, and the second uses the COUNT function. The remaining two columns, listid and eventid, must be declared as grouping columns.

Pivoting operations transform row-level details into matrix-like formats, making complex relationships immediately apparent. We already discussed this in earlier sections, so we will not be adding more examples here. Just to summarize, a pivot table might display average sales with regions as rows and products as columns, instantly revealing regional product performance patterns. This restructuring facilitates cross-tabular analysis and helps identify correlations that might be hidden in the raw data.

Time-based transformations add temporal intelligence to datasets by extracting and analyzing time components. By decomposing dates into days, months, quarters, and seasons, analysts can identify day-of-week effects, seasonal patterns, and year-over-year trends. These transformations enable sophisticated analyses like month-over-month growth calculations and seasonal decomposition. The syntax varies from service to service, but the overall concept remains the same: aggregating data by time intervals.

Each of these transformation techniques serves a specific analytical purpose, and their effective combination enables sophisticated data analysis. When implementing these patterns, consider both the computational efficiency and the specific requirements of your analytical objectives.

---

[3] https://docs.aws.amazon.com/redshift/latest/dg/r_GROUP_BY_clause.html

Best Practices for Data Analysis

The foundation of effective data analysis lies in *maintaining simplicity and efficiency*. When approaching analytical problems, prioritize straightforward solutions over complex ones. For instance, if a simple database query can provide the desired outcome, implementing an elaborate ETL process would be counterproductive and resource-intensive.

Understanding your audience is crucial for delivering meaningful insights. Business users typically prefer clear visualizations and intuitive dashboards, while C-suite executives require concise executive summaries and high-level metrics. Technical users, such as data analysts, may need direct access to SQL queries or detailed analytical reports. This audience-centric approach ensures that the analysis meets specific user needs and delivers maximum value.

Selecting appropriate visualization methods is fundamental to effective data communication. Bar charts excel at comparing discrete categories, while line charts effectively demonstrate temporal trends. Scatter plots reveal relationships between variables; pie charts serve for proportional comparisons (though they should be used judiciously); and maps are essential for geographical data representation. Each visualization type serves a specific purpose in the data storytelling process.

Dashboard design requires careful attention to clarity and simplicity. Avoid visual clutter by eliminating unnecessary elements and using color strategically to emphasize key information. Limit the number of variables in each visualization to maintain focus and comprehension. Essential elements such as clear titles, precise labels, and comprehensive legends should always be included to provide necessary context.

Consistency in design elements, including color schemes and formatting, creates a professional and cohesive presentation. This uniformity helps users navigate and interpret the information more effectively while maintaining a polished appearance across all deliverables.

Data quality forms the bedrock of reliable analysis. Investing time in thorough data preparation is essential for producing trustworthy results. Begin by understanding the end users' requirements and work backward to design tailored solutions. This approach not only ensures the delivery of relevant insights but also builds lasting trust with stakeholders through accurate and reliable reporting.

Summary

In this chapter, we discussed the fundamental concepts and techniques of data visualization, starting with an introduction to its role in effectively communicating insights and supporting data-driven decision-making. We explored various types of visualizations, including bar charts, histograms, line charts, scatter plots, pie and donut charts, heatmaps, treemaps, and geospatial maps, detailing their unique strengths and applications.

We examined the principles of effective data visualization, emphasizing clarity, accuracy, and alignment with audience needs. Additionally, we evaluated the trade-offs between provisioned and serverless services, providing guidance on choosing the right approach for scalable and cost-effective data analysis.

The chapter provided an in-depth overview of AWS services for data analysis and visualization, focusing on practical use cases and workflows for Amazon QuickSight, AWS Glue DataBrew, Amazon Athena, and Amazon SageMaker Data Wrangler. Advanced SQL techniques, along with strategies for data cleansing, aggregation, and transformation, were discussed to ensure data readiness for visualization.

Finally, we outlined best practices for data analysis, offered exam tips for AWS certifications, and included practice questions to solidify the concepts covered. By the end of the chapter, readers should have a clear understanding of how to create meaningful visualizations and leverage AWS tools to analyze and present data effectively.

Exam Essentials

Understand data visualization principles.   Data visualization principles include understanding your audience, choosing the right chart type, and ensuring clarity and simplicity in presenting data. Use tools like Amazon QuickSight to create intuitive and interactive dashboards that convey insights effectively.

Know the AWS services for data analysis and visualization.   Key AWS services such as Amazon QuickSight, Redshift, and Glue are designed for data analysis and visualization. Familiarize yourself with their roles, such as Glue for data preparation, Redshift for analytics, and QuickSight for visualization.

Know the trade-offs between provisioned and serverless services.   Provisioned services offer predictable performance but require manual scaling, while serverless options, such as Redshift Serverless, scale automatically to match workloads. Consider the operational overhead and cost implications when choosing between these models.

Understand data preparation techniques.   Data preparation involves steps like cleaning, transforming, and normalizing data to make it analysis-ready. Tools like AWS Glue Data-Brew simplify these tasks with a user-friendly interface for creating repeatable workflows.

Understand how to choose the appropriate visualization technique for different data types and analysis goals.   Select visualization types based on data relationships and goals, such as bar charts for comparisons or heat maps for geospatial analysis. Ensure that the chosen technique highlights the most important insights effectively.

Use cost optimization strategies.   Optimize costs by using reserved instances for predictable workloads or serverless options for variable demand. Monitor resource usage with tools like AWS Cost Explorer to identify inefficiencies.

Understand geospatial and advanced visualizations.   AWS QuickSight supports geospatial visualizations with integrated map layers. Use advanced visualizations like heat maps or clustering techniques for comprehensive spatial data insights.

Practice writing and optimizing complex SQL queries.   Optimize SQL queries by avoiding unnecessary joins and using indexes effectively. Practice performance tuning with tools like Redshift's EXPLAIN command to analyze and refine query execution plans. Amazon Web Services (AWS) offers numerous workshops and hands-on exercises where you can develop your skills with real-world scenarios and performance optimization techniques.[4] These workshops cover everything from basic query construction to advanced optimization strategies.

Be prepared to explain the process of data cleansing and its importance in visualization.   Data cleansing ensures accuracy and relevance by removing duplicates, handling missing values, and standardizing formats. Clean data leads to more reliable visualizations and actionable insights.

Know how to use AWS services together to create an end-to-end data analysis and visualization pipeline.   Combine services like AWS Glue for ETL, Redshift for data warehousing, and QuickSight for visualization to build a seamless pipeline. Leverage integration capabilities for a unified approach to data analysis.

---

[4] https://workshops.aws

Review Questions

1. Which AWS service is best suited for creating interactive dashboards and embedding visualizations in applications?
   - A. Amazon Athena
   - B. AWS Glue DataBrew
   - C. Amazon QuickSight
   - D. Amazon SageMaker Data Wrangler

2. When using Amazon Athena to query data in S3, which of the following is *true*?
   - A. You need to load the data into a database before querying.
   - B. You can only query structured data.
   - C. You pay for the amount of data scanned in each query.
   - D. Athena requires provisioning of compute resources.

3. Which AWS service would you use for visual data preparation and transformation without writing code?
   - A. Amazon SageMaker
   - B. AWS Glue DataBrew
   - C. Amazon Redshift
   - D. AWS Lambda

4. In Amazon QuickSight, what does SPICE stand for?
   - A. Super-fast, Parallel, In-memory Calculation Engine
   - B. Structured, Processed, Integrated Calculation Environment
   - C. Simple, Powerful, Interactive Charting Engine
   - D. Serverless, Provisioned, In-memory Computing Engine

5. Which SQL clause is most appropriate for calculating running totals or moving averages in a query?
   - A. GROUP BY
   - B. HAVING
   - C. WINDOW
   - D. PARTITION BY

6. When using AWS Glue DataBrew, which of the following is *not* a built-in transformation?
   - A. Handling missing values
   - B. Standardizing date formats
   - C. Training machine learning models
   - D. Removing duplicate records

7. Which visualization type is best suited for showing the composition of a whole?
   A. Line chart
   B. Scatter plot
   C. Pie chart
   D. Bar chart

8. In Amazon Athena, what is the purpose of using partitions?
   A. To increase the maximum query complexity
   B. To reduce the amount of data scanned and lower query cost
   C. To enable real-time data analysis
   D. To create visualizations directly in Athena

9. Which AWS service would you use to create a flow chart or diagram to visualize a data pipeline?
   A. Amazon QuickSight
   B. AWS Glue
   C. Amazon Managed Workflows for Apache Airflow (MWAA)
   D. AWS Step Functions

10. Which of the following is *not* a best practice for effective data visualization?
    A. Using consistent color schemes across related visualizations
    B. Including as much data as possible in a single visualization
    C. Providing clear titles and labels for axes and data points
    D. Tailoring the complexity of the visualization to the audience

Chapter

8

Monitoring and Auditing Data

**THE AWS CERTIFIED DATA ENGINEER –
ASSOCIATE EXAM OBJECTIVES COVERED
IN THIS CHAPTER MAY INCLUDE, BUT ARE
NOT LIMITED TO, THE FOLLOWING:**

✓ **Domain 3: Data Operations and Support**

  ▪ 3.3: Maintain and monitor data pipelines

✓ **Domain 4: Data Security and Governance**

  ▪ 4.4: Prepare logs for audit

As a data engineer, one of your main responsibilities is to ensure that your application or environment is healthy, secure, and meets your service-level agreements (SLAs). With so many activities and responsibilities that require your time, understanding and implementing the best practices to run an environment that performs optimally is critical.

It is also critical that malicious players are detected before they can impact your environment or identified if they manage to get through, so that you can apply the appropriate preventative measures. In addition, you want visibility into the performance of your applications by monitoring certain metrics, such as CPU, RAM, and storage usage. It is important to create and maintain a detailed record of actions and events for your applications, where an application is defined as a type of workload. A workload is defined as a collection of resources and code that delivers value. Examples include a client-facing application, a back-end process, or users running daily reports to extract insights for their business.

There are four security processes that facilitate the preceding: logging, monitoring, alerting, and reporting. These processes work together to provide visibility into the health and performance of your applications. In this section, we will explore logging, monitoring, alerting, and reporting with AWS Cloud deployments in mind. However, these principles can also be applied to applications running in hybrid environments and other cloud providers.

We have all read stories of important business or government websites being taken down or environments not being available due to various events. This section aims to help you avoid or reduce the impact of such events when combined with other best practices around security and deployment, which are discussed in other chapters.

To start, let's define a few terms:

- **Application logging:** This is the process where the events generated by your application are collected and recorded in one or more log files. The log files can then be used to perform various analyses, such as security analysis (e.g., who accessed the application and who tried to access it but failed), performance analysis, troubleshooting application issues, and tracking resource changes.

- **Application monitoring:** This is the process where you assess the overall health and performance of your application. In this process, you monitor both the front end and the back end. In the cloud, there are logging and monitoring tools that can help with troubleshooting performance issues and assist with remediating security threats in real time.

- **Observability:** This introduces a way to measure the behavior of the application using different parameters and may include some complex correlations. An example is measuring how successful users are in accessing your application during a peak period, such as month-end or when you are running promotional events.

There are different levels available for logging and monitoring, and these vary depending on the application. Some of the factors that influence the monitoring and logging levels include the criticality of the application to business, the sensitivity of the data, the security risk of the application, and organizational policies and procedures. The general guidance is that public-facing applications require a higher level of monitoring and logging, while internal applications require a lower level.

For information beyond what is described in this chapter, visit `https://docs.aws .amazon.com/prescriptive-guidance/latest/logging-monitoring-for- application-owners/about-logging-monitoring.html`.

How to Log Application Data

It is important that organizations establish a well-thought-out and well-communicated logging strategy that defines which events and actions are to be logged. To create this strategy, you must understand internal policies around security and data governance, and consider these when developing your logging strategy. We recommend logging the following events, if applicable to your application.

- **Log validation failures:** These include both input and output validation failures. Examples of input validation failures, include violations of protocols and using incorrect parameter names and values. Examples of output validation failures include using incorrect data encoding and having a database record set mismatch.

- **Log all events that deal with access, such as authentication and authorization attempts:** You should log both successful and unsuccessful attempts to create a history that you can analyze periodically to identify patterns where needed. Take care not to log user names and passwords, as users can make mistakes and log passwords in the user name field, which is not a hidden field.

- **Log all changes to logging states:** Any changes to the logging state must be logged, whether it is starting, stopping, or pausing logging. Malicious actors will aim to disable logging to prevent being traced, and capturing changes to logging can help during audits or investigations.

- **Log changes to application states:** All changes to application states must be logged, together with the resource (user/application) that made the action.

- **Log application, session, and system errors or events:** These can include performance issues, connectivity failures, configuration changes, session cookie modifications, or file system errors.

- **Log changes related to administration tasks:** These include changes to network configurations, user management modifications, privilege modifications, and security (e.g., encryption changes). Data access and manipulation (import/export/modification) must also be logged. These tasks are normally performed by users with additional privileges who can abuse those privileges; hence, it is important that these tasks are logged for audit purposes.

As mentioned, the preceding is a recommended and non-exhaustive list. As someone with domain knowledge, you will be aware of any additional attributes that may be useful for monitoring, alerting, and reporting for your applications.

Table 8.1 provides an overview of event attributes and categories of their usage.

TABLE 8.1   Event Attributes

Attribute Category	Event Attribute	Description (What to Log)
When	Logging date and time	Capture the date and time when the specific event was added to the log file. It is important that you follow the agreed organizational guidance for capturing date-time format for consistency (e.g., yyyy-mm-dd hh:mm:ss)
	Event date and time	Capture the date and the time when the event occurred, which may not be the same as the preceding date and time event attribute.
	Event identifier	Each log entry must have a unique event identifier, such as a username or an account number, that is used to differentiate between events.
Where	Application identifier	Capture the name of the application, as well as the version. The version is also important, especially when doing retrospective troubleshooting after upgrades have occurred, and a rollback might be needed to go back to the known working version.
	Application address	Capture details about the physical devices, such as the server hostname, IP address, and access ports used. Details about the client, such as its name, also should be captured.
	Service	Capture the service name and the service protocol. Examples include file transfer services, web services, email services, network management services. Protocol examples include Domain Name Service (DNS), Transmission Control Protocol (TCP), and User Datagram Protocol (UDP).
	Geolocation	Capture the geolocation of the user. This can be important for various reasons, such as user safety, logistics, sales performance prediction, or fraud prevention.
	Window, form, or page	Capture the method of access, such as the URL, when a web application is used.
	Code location	Capture the script name or, if necessary, the name of the module being executed. This makes it easy to locate when required for troubleshooting purposes.

Attribute Category	Event Attribute	Description (What to Log)
Who (human or machine user)	Source address	Capture the user's device details, such as the device name, IP address, and any other information available. Other useful information, especially for criminal investigations, includes the mobile telephone number and cell phone tower identifier.
	User identity	Capture the unique user identifier, such as a username, employee number, or any other unique identifier.
	User type classification	Capture details about the type of user, which can be a public user, an authenticated user, test user, or a specific search engine.
	Request HTTP headers or HTTP user agent	When dealing with web applications, capture HTTP request header information, which impacts what information is sent to the server by the client.
What	Type of event	Capture the nature of the event, which helps with event classification and alerting. Event classification can be informational, warning, error, or escalation, which can be used to trigger specific actions, such as paging the on-call engineers.
	Severity of event	Capture the severity of the event (low, medium, high) as an additional classification mechanism.
	Security event flag	To help with identifying security events, if the log contains non-security data, consider adding a flag that will identify security events.
	Event description	You can include a brief description of the event, though this is not always necessary.
	Action or intent	Capture the aim of the request. This can either be a login or logout request, or session activities.
	User or application response	Capture the response that is received for that event. Possible responses can include a message, alerts to administrators, or the session being terminated. An example would be when you try to access resources from an expired session, which would terminate the request and provide a relevant message.
	Result status	Capture the result of the action, which can be success, fail, or deferred.
	Result reason	In addition to capturing the result of the request, capture additional details explaining the reason for the status. For example, a user request might fail due to the user entering an incorrect password.

TABLE 8.1   Event Attributes *(continued)*

Attribute Category	Event Attribute	Description (What to Log)
	Extended details	Where possible, capture additional information that can be used for debugging or troubleshooting.
	HTTP response status code	Capture the response code (e.g., 201, 504) that is returned for the request.
Which	Resources affected	Capture the details of resources that were acted upon in response to the request submitted.
	Object	Capture the details of the components affected by the request. These details include the user account and any resource affected, such as a file or session ID.
	Name of resource	Capture the details of the affected resources, such as its name or unique identifier.
	Resource tags	If tags are used, capture the tag information of the affected resources.
Other	Analytical confidence	If supported by the logging service, log the confidence level of detecting the event. Ideally, you want a high level to ensure that your service is able to capture all required events and their details.
	Internal classifications	If the organization has any additional classifications or compliance standards, these must be captured.
	External classifications	If there are external classification or compliance standards to adhere to, these must be captured too. Examples include the Security Content Automation Protocol (SCAP), which is a suite of specifications that standardize the format and naming of communicating security configuration and software flaw information between machines and humans.

Logging Best Practices

When it comes to logging, a range of best practices is important to know, especially those related to logging levels, cautions and exclusions, special data types, and access and change management.

Logging Levels

You should keep several considerations in mind regarding logging levels:

- Capture useful and actionable data. Excessive data logging can have a negative impact on performance and increase storage and processing costs.

- We recommend that you consider logging only 400-level (client-side errors) and 500-level (server-side errors) status codes. 200-level (success) and 300-level (redirection) status codes can generate a lot of data, so be cautious about logging these.

- Application development frameworks provide different levels of logging, such as info, debug, or error. In development environments, to help your developers with troubleshooting, it's advisable to use info and debug, while in production, we recommend disabling these.

Cautions and Exclusions

Please note the following cautions and exclusions related to logging:

- It is important to ensure that at all times the data that you are logging is permitted. Some jurisdictions have different login/data governance rules, and you are encouraged to understand what is allowed/not allowed in the specific jurisdiction. This can be particularly challenging for global organizations with customers and users in different jurisdictions. Knowledge of data protection acts, such as the General Data Protection Regulation (GDPR), is advised.

- It is important to keep in mind that log files can be used by different systems, which can be internal or external. As such, you must log all data and use a classification mechanism to differentiate the data.

- It is important not to collect information that you are not allowed to collect, or where the user hasn't granted explicit consent, or where the user's consent has expired.

- Some sensitive data should not be logged and should be masked, encrypted, sanitized, or hashed to prevent it from being visible in the log files. Examples of this data include:

  - Sensitive personal information, which can include personally identifiable information (PII) and health-related information.

  - Passwords, database connection strings, access tokens, encryption information, and keys.

  - Financial information, such as bank account details, data about payment card holders, and other commercially sensitive information.

  - Data classification levels mean that some data is more classified than other data. As such, it is important that data for which you don't have the right classification levels is not visible.

  - Your source code is your intellectual property, and if it lands in the hands of your competitors, it can result in a loss of competitive advantage and internal information being leaked. As such, this must not be visible in your logs.

Special Data Types

The following data, while useful for investigation and troubleshooting purposes, should be anonymized, hashed, or encrypted before the event is recorded:

- Internal network names and addresses
- File paths
- Non-sensitive personal data, such as personal names, telephone numbers, and email addresses

Access and Change Management

It is important to know the following access and change management concerns:

- Only administrative users should be able to carry out tasks that result in changes to logging status and configuration changes. Furthermore, these admistrative users' actions must be logged. It is best practice to have an approved change management process to handle configuration or logging change requests. Where possible, logging changes must be made automatically by the application using an approved mechanism. This will eliminate the need for manual user intervention, which can introduce the capability for malicous actions or, sometimes, honest mistakes where the user forgets to reenable logging.
- Some logging services have a log file integrity feature, which should be enabled if it is supported, as it helps with detection of modifications to log files. AWS CloudTrail provides this feature, which is used to determine whether a log file has been modified after CloudTrail delivered it, making it extremely complex and resource-intensive to modify log files without detection.

How to Log Access to AWS Services

Now that we've looked at how logging works, which events to log, and the best practices for logging to give you the best performance, we will look at the AWS services that you can use for your logging strategy. This section discusses AWS CloudTrail, Amazon CloudWatch, and Amazon Macie.

AWS CloudTrail

AWS CloudTrail records the actions taken by a user, role, or an AWS service, logging them as events in CloudTrail. These actions can be events taken in the AWS Management console, the AWS Command Line Interface (CLI), and the AWS SDKs and APIs. You can access CloudTrail by using the AWS Console, the AWS CLI, CloudTrail APIs, and AWS SDKs.

You don't have to enable anything to use CloudTrail; it is active in your account when you create it. CloudTrail provides three ways to record events:

- **Event History:** This provides an option to view, search, and download immutable records for the last 90 days. This view is enabled automatically when you create your account.

- **CloudTrail Lake:** This is a managed data lake where you capture, store, access, and analyze user activity for audit and security purposes. The key concept here is that events are aggregated into event data stores—immutable event collections based on specific criteria selected by you. Events in the data store can be kept for either 3,653 days (10 years) or 2,557 days (7 years).

- **Trails:** These capture a record of AWS activities, which are then sent and stored in an S3 bucket. You also have the option to send these logs to CloudWatch Logs and Amazon EventBridge. These logs can then be analyzed using solutions such as Amazon Athena or any third-party solution of your choosing.

To check who accesses your AWS services via the AWS Management Console, perform the following steps:

1. Log in to the AWS Management Console.
2. Go to the CloudTrail service.
3. Under Event history, note the recent API calls that have been made in your account.
4. The following options are available for filtering:
   - **Event Source** (e.g., S3, EC2)
   - **User Name** to see which IAM user made the request
   - **Event Time** for when the access happened

Each log entry will provide information about the following:

- **Who** made the request (IAM user or role)
- **What** actions were performed (e.g., launching an EC2 instance, accessing an S3 bucket)
- **When** the action was taken
- **Where** the request originated (IP address or region)

I advise you to complete this CloudTrail workshop, which will give you hands-on experience in creating a trail, configuring it to send events to CloudWatch Logs, using CloudWatch Logs to monitor your account for specific API calls and events, and querying CloudTrail logs using Athena: `https://mng.workshop.aws/cloudtrail.html`.

Amazon CloudWatch

You can use CloudWatch to monitor your AWS resources and the applications that you run in AWS in real time through the collection of metrics. Metrics are performance data about your systems, and by default, many services provide free metrics for resources (e.g., Amazon

RDS, Amazon EC2). CloudWatch then becomes a repository/storage area for the metrics about your services. You can then collect statistics about these metrics in the repository, which can either be from AWS services metrics or your own application metrics.

In addition to collecting the metrics and viewing the statistics, you can go a step further and configure alarms that automatically initiate actions on your behalf based on certain metric values. For example, you can configure an alarm to monitor CPU usage for your EC2 instance, and when it reaches 80% for a certain time period, a notification can be sent to an Amazon Simple Notification Service topic, which can send an email or SMS to your on-call engineer. Every AWS service that you use will have its metrics displayed automatically on the CloudWatch console, and you can also create custom display metrics and alarms for your applications.

CloudWatch works across AWS regions, too.

CloudWatch use cases include the following:

- **Application health monitoring:** You can enhance the observability of your services/applications by using CloudWatch ServiceLens to integrate traces, metrics, logs, and alarms in one place.

- **Synthetic monitoring:** You can create canaries to monitor your endpoints and APIs using CloudWatch Synthetics. The canaries, which are configurable scripts, mimic the same routes that are performed by customers, allowing you to continually verify the customer experience even when you don't have customer traffic. This is helpful to check the availability and latency of your endpoints and to monitor URLs and website content, and check for unauthorized changes from phishing, code injection, and cross-site scripting.

- **User monitoring:** You can perform real-time user monitoring using CloudWatch RUM to collect and view client-side data about your web application's performance. The data that you can collect includes page load times, user behavior, and client-side errors.

- **Anomalous behavior detection:** You can enable anomaly detection for a metric, where CloudWatch will apply statistical and machine learning algorithms that continually analyze system and application metrics to determine baselines and surface anomalies.

- **Feature validation and A/B experiments:** A useful feature of CloudWatch is CloudWatch Evidently, which can be used to safely validate new features by serving them to a specified percentage of your users while you roll out the feature. This helps you reduce risk and identify unintended consequences before a full launch. You can also perform A/B experiments, which allow you to compare different variations to identify which variation of the feature performs better based on collected data and statistical methods.

CloudWatch Logs

Amazon CloudWatch Logs is a highly scalable service that enables you to centralize all the logs from your systems, applications, and AWS services. From here, you can view, search, and filter them based on specific patterns or error codes. You also have the option to securely archive them for future usage. In CloudWatch Logs, you can view all the events, sort and query them, and also create custom computations, and then visualize the log data in dashboards.

Events in CloudWatch Logs are arranged into log streams or log groups:

- Log streams are a sequence of log events that share the same source.
- Log groups define one or more streams that share similar settings, such as retention, monitoring, and access control.

Each log stream must belong to at least one log group.

To analyze log data in Amazon CloudWatch Logs, you can use CloudWatch Logs Insights, which allows you to perform queries that help you respond quickly to operational issues. When an issue occurs, you can also use CloudWatch Logs Insights to identify potential causes and validate deployed fixes. An additional feature of CloudWatch Logs is the ability to search and filter log data coming into CloudWatch Logs by creating one or more metrics filters. These filters define terms and patterns to search for in the log data as it is sent to CloudWatch Logs, which then uses these filters to turn log data into numerical CloudWatch metrics that you can graph or use to set alarms.

CloudWatch Logs use cases include the following:

- **Monitoring CloudTrail logs**: Using CloudWatch, you can create alarms and then receive notifications of API activity captured by CloudWatch logs. You can then perform troubleshooting using the notification.
- **Logging AWS API calls**: You can use CloudWatch Logs to log API calls if you have a third-party solution and use the third-party solution to analyze the log.
- **Configuring log retention**: You can adjust the retention level of CloudWatch logs to between one day and 10 years, as opposed to them being kept indefinitely, which is the default configuration.
- **Archiving and storing logs**: CloudWatch Logs can be used to store log data in highly durable storage. You can then access the raw data when you need it.

VPC Flow Logs

This is a feature of Amazon Virtual Private Cloud (Amazon VPC) that captures information about the IP traffic going to and from network interfaces in a VPC. Flow logs can be created for a VPC, a network interface, or a subnet. When you create a flow log for a subnet or a VPC, each network interface in that subnet or VPC is monitored.

Here are some things to note about flow logs:

- Flow log data for a monitored interface is recorded as flow log records.
- A flow log record represents a network flow in your VPC.
- A record includes values for the different components of the IP flow—for example, the source, destination, and protocol.
- Flow log data can be published to several AWS services, including CloudWatch Logs.
- Flow log data does not affect network throughput, as it is corrected separately from the path of your network traffic and doesn't impact network performance.
- You can use VPC flow logs to aid troubleshooting, such as when you want to identify which security groups are not allowing traffic, check the direction traffic is taking, and monitor which traffic is reaching your application instance.

AWS X-Ray

AWS X-Ray is a service that enables you to collect data about requests served by your application. With this data, you can analyze and debug issues with your application to identify opportunities for better performance. With X-Ray, you can create service maps by tracking the requests made to your application, giving you a view of the connections that are made among the services in your applications. You can also use X-Ray to automatically identify errors and bugs by analyzing the response codes of each request made to your application, which enables easy debugging of application code. Lastly, with X-Ray, you can build your own analysis apps that use data X-Ray records through the set of APIs provided by X-Ray.

Review the following FAQ for an additional overview of X-Ray concepts: `https://aws .amazon.com/xray/faqs`.

Amazon Macie

The final service that we are reviewing is Amazon Macie, which uses machine learning and pattern matching to automatically detect sensitive data and provide automatic protections against the risks posed by that sensitive data. It detects a large number of sensitive data types, including personally identifiable information (names, addresses, and credit card numbers). With Macie, you get constant visibility into your data stored in your AWS object store, S3, by configuring Macie to perform automated sensitive data discovery and by creating and running sensitive data discovery jobs. Setting up Macie is very easy and can be done by a single selection on the AWS Management Console or via a single API call.

Sensitive data discovery is when Macie evaluates your S3 bucket inventory daily and then uses statistical sampling to identify representative objects from your buckets. These selected objects will then be analyzed and inspected for sensitive data.

If you are looking for a deeper and more targeted analysis, then sensitive data discovery jobs will do the trick. With this option, you specify the buckets to be analyzed, and then you can define a one-time job to run, or you can define a recurring job that does the assessment and monitoring.

I encourage you to review the following FAQ for an additional overview of Macie concepts: `https://aws.amazon.com/macie/faq`.

Analyzing Logs Using AWS Services

AWS provides several services that can be used to analyze log files. Let's look at some common ones:

- **Amazon Athena:** Amazon Athena is an interactive serverless service that allows you to analyze data stored in S3 using Structured Query Language (SQL). Because it is serverless, you can immediately start analyzing the log data without the need to set up infrastructure, and the data is queried directly from S3. For more practical experience, visit the Analyze Data in S3 Using Amazon Athena page: `https://aws.amazon.com/ blogs/big-data/analyzing-data-in-s3-using-amazon-athena`.

- **Amazon EMR:** Amazon EMR (Elastic MapReduce) is a cloud data platform used for processing large amounts of data. EMR allows you to run petabyte-scale analysis for workloads on Amazon EC2 instances, Amazon EKS clusters, or on-premises using EMR on AWS Outposts. For more practical experience, visit the Monitor and Optimise Analytic Workloads on Amazon EMR with Prometheus and Grafana page: `https://aws.amazon.com/blogs/big-data/analyzing-data-in-s3-using-amazon-athena`.

- **Amazon OpenSearch:** Amazon OpenSearch is a fully managed service that allows you to go from raw data to insights very quickly through its built-in integrations with other AWS Services, such as Amazon Data Firehose, AWS Lambda, and Amazon CloudWatch. OpenSearch enables you to analyze activity logs for customer-facing applications and websites, as well as analyze CloudWatch Logs and other use cases. For more practical experience, visit `https://aws.amazon.com/blogs/big-data/analyzing-amazon-s3-server-access-logs-using-amazon-opensearch-service`.

- **Amazon Redshift:** Amazon Redshift is a fully managed peta-scale cloud data warehouse service that allows you to access and analyze your data. For more information, visit the Analyze Database Audit Logs for Security and Compliance Using Amazon Redshift Spectrum page: `https://aws.amazon.com/blogs/big-data/analyze-database-audit-logs-for-security-and-compliance-using-amazon-redshift-spectrum`

Summary

This chapter looked at how one of the main responsibilities of a data engineer is to keep your environment secure, healthy, and meeting SLAs. We then discussed four important processes—logging, monitoring, alerting, and reporting—that help data engineers keep their environments secure.

We then looked at logging best practices, including logging levels, what to log and monitor, and where monitoring should happen.

We proceeded to look at five AWS services that are useful for logging and monitoring. To close off the chapter, we then looked at how you can use AWS services to perform log analysis.

Exam Essentials

Understand the importance of maintaining and monitoring data pipelines. This includes the use of logging to capture data that can be used to detect malicious actors, gain visibility into application performance, and receive alerts in response to specific events.

Understand logging best practices. These include the different logging levels, what to include and exclude, and more.

Know the different AWS services that you can use for logging.   These include Amazon CloudTrail, CloudWatch Logs, Amazon Macie, VPC Flow Logs, and AWS X-Ray. You must know the different use cases that are applicable to the different services you can use for your logging strategy.

Be able to determine which AWS service is suitable for the different logging use cases or requirements.   You must be able to configure the different AWS services used for logging purposes to capture useful data.

Review Questions

1. A highly regulated financial services company wants to track API calls and user activities across its AWS account for compliance purposes. Which AWS service should it primarily use?

    A. Use Amazon CloudWatch for metric collection and set up custom dashboards for visualization of API activities.

    B. Implement AWS CloudTrail to record API activities and store logs in an S3 bucket for auditing purposes.

    C. Deploy Amazon Inspector to automatically assess API calls and user activities for security vulnerabilities.

    D. Utilize AWS Config to track resource changes and API calls made to various AWS services.

2. An e-commerce company needs to monitor its AWS resources and applications in real time. Which service should it use to collect metrics, set up alarms, and create dashboards?

    A. Use AWS X-Ray for application performance monitoring and distributed tracing.

    B. Use Amazon CloudWatch for collecting metrics, setting alarms, and creating custom dashboards.

    C. Use AWS CloudTrail for tracking resource usage and creating visualizations of API activity.

    D. Use Amazon Elasticsearch Service for real-time monitoring and log analysis.

3. A security team needs to analyze IP traffic going to and from network interfaces in their VPC for troubleshooting and security analysis. Which AWS feature should they enable?

    A. Enable AWS CloudTrail and configure it to log VPC-related events. Use Amazon Athena to query the logs stored in S3 for traffic analysis.

    B. Implement VPC flow logs to capture information about IP traffic. Store the logs in CloudWatch Logs or S3, and use CloudWatch Logs Insights for analysis.

    C. Deploy Amazon GuardDuty to continuously monitor VPC traffic. Use the findings to analyze suspicious IP traffic patterns and potential security threats.

    D. Set up AWS Config rules to track changes in VPC configurations. Use AWS Config advanced queries to analyze historical changes in network interfaces and security groups.

4. A development team wants to trace and analyze requests made to their distributed application to identify performance bottlenecks and troubleshoot issues. Which AWS service should they use?

    A. Implement Amazon CloudWatch and use CloudWatch ServiceLens to correlate metrics, logs, and traces. Set up CloudWatch alarms to alert on performance issues.

    B. Deploy AWS X-Ray to trace requests across microservices. Use X-Ray analytics to identify bottlenecks and create service maps to visualize application architecture.

    C. Utilize AWS CloudTrail to log API calls made by the application. Analyze the logs using Amazon Athena to identify slow-performing API requests and potential bottlenecks.

    D. Set up Amazon Elasticsearch Service and use the ELK (Elasticsearch, Logstash, Kibana) stack to ingest, process, and visualize application logs for performance analysis.

5. A company wants to automatically detect and protect sensitive data stored in its S3 buckets. Which AWS service should it implement?

   A. Use AWS Identity and Access Management (IAM) to set up fine-grained access controls on S3 buckets. Implement S3 bucket policies to restrict access to sensitive data.

   B. Deploy Amazon Macie to automatically discover and protect sensitive data. Configure Macie to perform automated sensitive data discovery jobs on S3 buckets.

   C. Implement AWS Key Management Service (KMS) to encrypt all data in S3 buckets. Use AWS CloudHSM for additional hardware-based key management.

   D. Set up AWS Config rules to monitor S3 bucket configurations. Use AWS Lambda to automatically remediate any misconfigurations that could expose sensitive data.

6. An organization wants to implement a comprehensive logging strategy for its AWS-based applications. Which of the following events should it prioritize logging according to the best practices?

   A. Log all successful API calls, user logins, and data access events to create a complete audit trail of all system activities.

   B. Focus on logging input validation failures, authentication failures, and use of higher-risk functionality to identify potential security threats.

   C. Implement detailed logging of all network traffic, including successful connections, to monitor for unusual patterns or potential data exfiltration.

   D. Log all application errors and system events, including non-critical warnings, to ensure complete visibility into system behavior.

7. A data engineering team wants to analyze their CloudTrail logs to identify potential security issues. Which AWS service should they use for efficient querying of these logs?

   A. Use Amazon RDS to store CloudTrail logs in a relational database. Create SQL queries to analyze the log data for security patterns.

   B. Implement Amazon Elasticsearch Service to index CloudTrail logs. Use Kibana for visualization and to create security dashboards.

   C. Store CloudTrail logs in Amazon S3 and use Amazon Athena for SQL-based querying of the log data. Create custom queries to identify security issues.

   D. Deploy Amazon Redshift to store and analyze CloudTrail logs. Use Redshift Spectrum to query logs directly from S3 for long-term analysis.

8. A company wants to implement real-time monitoring of its application's performance and set up automated alerts. Which CloudWatch feature should it use?

   A. Use CloudWatch Logs Insights to analyze application logs in real-time. Set up metric filters to create custom metrics from log data.

   B. Implement CloudWatch Synthetics to create canaries that monitor application endpoints and APIs. Set up alarms based on the canary results.

   C. Deploy CloudWatch Service Lens to gain insights into application health. Use built-in service maps to visualize the application architecture.

   D. Configure CloudWatch Alarms based on key performance metrics. Set up actions to send notifications via Amazon SNS when thresholds are breached.

9. An e-commerce company wants to implement logging for its web application while optimizing storage costs and maintaining performance. Which logging approach should it take?

   A. Enable detailed logging for all HTTP requests, including 200-level and 300-level status codes. Store all logs indefinitely in Amazon S3 for comprehensive analysis.

   B. Implement application-level logging to capture all user interactions. Use Amazon Kinesis Data Firehose to stream logs to Elasticsearch for real-time analysis.

   C. Log only 400-level and 500-level errors. Use CloudWatch Logs for storage and set up log retention policies to archive older logs to Amazon S3 for cost optimization.

   D. Deploy AWS X-Ray to trace all requests and store detailed logs in DynamoDB. Use DynamoDB Streams to process logs in real-time for performance monitoring.

10. A company wants to implement logging for their AWS resources but is concerned about the potential impact on performance. Which AWS logging service should they choose to minimize the impact on network throughput?

   A. Enable detailed VPC flow logs with maximum verbosity to capture all network traffic for comprehensive analysis. Send the logs to Redshift for analysis.

   B. Implement a CloudWatch Logs agent on all EC2 instances to stream logs in real time to CloudWatch. Use Athena to analyze the logs.

   C. Use VPC flow logs, which capture information about IP traffic without affecting network throughput.

   D. Deploy AWS X-Ray to trace all network requests and responses for detailed performance analysis. Send the trace logs to S3 for storage.

Chapter

9

Maintaining and Troubleshooting Data Operations

THE AWS CERTIFIED DATA ENGINEER –
ASSOCIATE EXAM OBJECTIVES COVERED
IN THIS CHAPTER MAY INCLUDE, BUT ARE
NOT LIMITED, TO THE FOLLOWING:

✓ **Domain 3: Data Operations and Support**

    ▪ 3.1 Automate data processing by using AWS services

Introduction to Automating Data Processing Using AWS Services

In this chapter, we will look at the tasks data engineers perform to automate data processing. Some of the services that we will refer to were covered in previous chapters, and in this chapter, we will focus on bringing it all together to automate your data processing by discussing key concepts and best practices.

In the following sections, we will dive deeper into the different activities and services that you can use as a data engineer to manage your data pipelines and help you achieve your business outcomes.

Maintaining and Troubleshooting Data Processing

Maintaining and troubleshooting your data processing pipeline is important because it helps you identify and fix issues before they result in loss of service and loss of revenue for your organization. Think of the maintenance and troubleshooting of a data pipeline as being as important as that of critical assets, such as movable assets like a motor vehicle or an airplane or immovable assets like a house or office building. For example, a motor vehicle typically has a maintenance plan that, if followed well, ensures your car is safe to drive, reduces the risk of mechanical problems, and prevents excessive repair issues by catching potential issues early.

Here are some of the key concepts:

- Set up logging and monitoring using AWS CloudWatch. CloudWatch can be used for application health monitoring, synthetic monitoring, user monitoring, anomalous behavior detection, and feature validation.

  - Use log groups to organize logs by application or process. This will make it easier for you to manage and analyze logs based on the application or process that creates them.

- Use CloudWatch Insights for log analysis and querying to help you respond to operational issues efficiently.

- Set up custom metrics to track business-specific KPIs, including error rates, data quality scores, or time to insight for your organization's critical reports.

- Set up alarms for critical metrics and errors.

  - Define thresholds for key indicators and then set up CloudWatch Alarms to alert when there is a breach. Using SNS, notifications can be set up to create immediate awareness.

  - Set up your alarms for different severity levels—for example, an initial threshold can trigger a warning, followed by a critical alert.

- Use AWS X-Ray to trace and debug.

  - X-Ray enables you to visualize and analyze the behavior of your applications, identify performance bottlenecks, and troubleshoot request failures.

  - X-ray also allows you to gain insights into your application's behavior over time, allowing you to observe patterns.

- Implement error handling and retry mechanisms.

  - You must design a strategy that implements error handling for all your pipeline components.

  - Implement exponential backoff for retrying failed operations. Please review this guide about exponential backoff on AWS: `https://docs.aws.amazon.com/prescriptive-guidance/latest/cloud-design-patterns/retry-backoff.html`.

  - Your error handling strategy must differentiate between transient and permanent errors.

- Schedule regular reviews and optimizations of your pipelines.

  - This must be part of your operational cadence (daily, weekly, monthly, quarterly, yearly).

  - Analyze performance metrics and identify areas of improvement.

  - Keep up with service updates and new features that could enhance your workflows.

- Follow best practices and use version control and change management.

  - Use version control systems for all code and configurations.

  - Implement CI/CD pipelines for automated testing and deployment.

  - Maintain thorough documentation of your workflows.

  - Utilize AWS CloudFormation or Terraform for infrastructure as code.

- Identify performance and cost optimizations.

  - Review your queries to find opportunities for optimizations.

- Review your resources to identify underutilization and opportunities to use smaller resources or shut down or clean up unused resources.
- Use AWS Cost Explorer to analyze your spending and utilize Spot or Reserved Instances where possible.

- Adopt security and compliance best practices.
  - Implement encryption in transit and at rest. This is covered in detail in Chapter 11.
  - Use IAM roles and policies.
  - Periodically audit and rotate your access keys.
  - Understand applicable data protection regulations (e.g., GDPR) and ensure that your systems and applications are compliant. Please review the following on Compliance on AWS: `https://aws.amazon.com/compliance`.
- Implement disaster recovery and backup best practices.
  - Schedule regular backups for your critical data and configurations.
  - Design for high availability using features such as Multi-AZ or Multi-Region.
  - Test your backup and recovery procedures by scheduling game days.
  - Centralize your backup management by using AWS Backup.

I also recommend reviewing the AWS Well-Architected Framework, which helps you to build secure, high-performing, and resilient infrastructure for applications and workloads such as data pipelines. It can be found here: `https://aws.amazon.com/architecture/well-architected/?wa-lens-whitepapers.sort-by=item.additionalFields.sortDate&wa-lens-whitepapers.sort-order=desc&wa-guidance-whitepapers.sort-by=item.additionalFields.sortDate&wa-guidance-whitepapers.sort-order=desc`.

API Calls for Data Processing

Imagine a simple pipeline of loading data to S3 from an EC2 instance. The data must then be batch-loaded to a Redshift cluster at midnight, execute some analytics jobs at 4 a.m., and run reports for users to find ready when they start work at 8 a.m. These individual pipeline actions can be executed manually by a person at these challenging hours, of course, but the ideal scenario is to automate them so they can run on their own without manual intervention. Imagine a situation where the engineer oversleeps and doesn't wake up to run the batch load job at midnight or the reports at 4 a.m. Or they run the wrong batch load job? Furthermore, how do you ensure that the engineer runs the jobs on time every day? How do you factor in weekends and holidays?

The preceding example illustrates the challenges that can arise due to manual management of your data pipeline and how automation provides numerous benefits, such as increased efficiency, reduction of human error, scalability, cost reduction, improved quality and control, enhanced disaster recovery, and business continuity.

To implement automation programmatically, AWS provides Application Programming Interfaces (APIs) to interact programmatically with your AWS services. AWS also provides Software Development Kits (SDKs), which are collections of platform-specific tools you can use to create and manage applications on AWS. To summarize the relationship between APIs and SDKs: APIs define the interface for interacting with a service. while SDKs provide tools and libraries that implement APIs, making it easier for developers to integrate the service into their applications.

Some key points to consider include:

- Familiarize yourself with the AWS SDK for your preferred languages. See this guide for more information: `https://aws.amazon.com/developer/tools`.

- Use the AWS Command Line Interface (CLI), a unified tool to manage your AWS services. With the CLI, you can run ad-hoc command-line operations, script tasks, and get information about AWS service capabilities. For more information on the CLI tool, please refer to this guide: `https://aws.amazon.com/cli`.

To get started on the CLI, you need to install it and then configure your credentials. You can then run the following commands to interrogate your AWS environment/resources:

```
aws s3 ls
aws ec2 describe-instances
aws dynamodb list-tables
```

Services That Accept Scripting

Services such as Amazon EMR, Amazon Redshift, and AWS Glue, which have been covered in previous chapters, are critical for your engineering pipelines and tasks. These services can be integrated with each other, such as using Glue to catalog your data, EMR to process it, and then loading the results to Redshift for analysis. Automations for these services can be done via scripts using AWS Step Functions, Lambda, or EventBridge.

In summary, the following are important to know:

- **Amazon EMR:** Use Spark, Hive, or other frameworks for big data processing.

- **Amazon Redshift:** Leverage SQL and stored procedures for data warehousing tasks.

- **AWS Glue:** Write ETL jobs using Python or Scala.

Orchestrating Data Pipelines

As discussed in Chapter 2, Amazon MWAA, AWS Step Functions, and AWS Glue serve as orchestration tools. They help you define and schedule data processing tasks, manage their dependencies, and perform error handling on your behalf. They are key tools for automating your data pipeline and understanding how they work and their use cases is important. Table 9.1 provides a comparison of the three orchestration services.

TABLE 9.1   Orchestration services

Service	Strengths	Use Cases
AWS Step Functions	Orchestration, visual work-flows, branching logic, parallel processing	Complex multiservice pipelines Event-driven workflows Long-running workflows
Amazon MWAA	Managed Apache Airflow, scheduling, dependency management, scalability	Preference over managed service for widely used open-source technologies, ETL pipelines, data lake ingestion, machine learning pipelines, and complex scheduling
AWS Glue	ETL operations, Apache Spark integration, Data Catalog, serverless	Data transformation, data loading, working with diverse data formats

Troubleshooting Amazon Managed Workflows

Like all services, there will be instances where you need to troubleshoot issues and errors you encounter. To achieve this, MWAA integrates with Amazon CloudWatch to provide comprehensive monitoring and logging capabilities for Apache Airflow environments.

Airflow Logs

There are several things to understand about Apache Airflow logs:

- You can enable Apache Airflow Logs at INFO, WARNING, ERROR, or CRITICAL levels, and these logs will be sent to CloudWatch Logs.

- To identify issues such as delays or workflow errors, CloudWatch allows you to view multiple environments from a single location.

- To view Apache Airflow DAG processing, tasks, web server, and worker logs in Cloud-Watch, you need to enable Apache Airflow logs in the Amazon Managed Workflows for Apache Airflow console.

- To troubleshoot common errors you may encounter, please review this guide: `https://docs.aws.amazon.com/mwaa/latest/userguide/troubleshooting.html`.

Audit Logs

Key things to know about audit logs include the following:

- Audit logs are captured in CloudTrail, which is enabled in your account when you create it.
- CloudTrail captures all events from the MWAA console and all calls to MWAA APIs, which can then be viewed and downloaded from the CloudTrail console. You can download the past 90 days' worth of events.
- CloudTrail doesn't capture read-only actions, such as GetEnvironment or PublishMetrics.
- For more on creating a CloudTrail, please see this guide: `https://docs.aws.amazon.com/mwaa/latest/userguide/monitoring-cloudtrail.html`.

Monitoring and Alarms

Amazon CloudWatch allows you to create dashboards and alarms for any of the metrics that are available to your Apache Airflow version. These dashboards and alarms can then be used to monitor your MWAA environment's health status.

To get hands-on experience with automating Amazon CloudWatch dashboards and alarms for MWAA, I recommend the tutorial at `https://aws.amazon.com/blogs/compute/automating-amazon-cloudwatch-dashboards-and-alarms-for-amazon-managed-workflows-for-apache-airflow`.

Using AWS Services for Data Processing

As described in depth in Chapter 3, Amazon EMR, Amazon Redshift, and AWS Glue are three services used for data processing. Table 9.2 provides a summary and comparison of the services.

TABLE 9.2   Comparison of Amazon EMR, Amazon Redshift, and AWS Glue

Feature	Amazon EMR	Amazon Redshift	AWS Glue
Primary purpose	Big data processing and analysis	Data warehousing and analytics	ETL (extract, transform, load) and data integration
Data processing model	Distributed computing	MPP (Massively Parallel Processing)	Serverless ETL
Scalability	Highly scalable, can add/remove nodes	Scalable, can resize clusters	Automatically scales based on workload

Continued

TABLE 9.2   Comparison of Amazon EMR, Amazon Redshift, and AWS Glue *(continued)*

Feature	Amazon EMR	Amazon Redshift	AWS Glue
Data volume handling	Petabyte-scale	Petabyte-scale	Works with various data volumes
Query language	Supports multiple languages (e.g., Spark SQL, Hive QL)	SQL	Supports Python and Scala
Real-time processing	Yes, with Spark Streaming	Yes, streaming ingestion	Yes, with AWS Glue streaming
Pricing model	Pay for EC2 instances and EBS volumes	For provisioned, pay for DB by the hour, while for serverless pay for capacity consumed while processing the workload	Pay for ETL jobs runtime
Managed service	Semi-managed (cluster management)	Fully managed	Fully managed
Use cases	Big data processing, machine learning, streaming analytics	Business intelligence, data warehousing	Data preparation, ETL workflows
Integration with other AWS services	Extensive	Good	Extensive
Setup complexity	Moderate	Low	Low
Flexibility	High (supports multiple frameworks)	Moderate (SQL-based)	High (custom ETL jobs)

You should explore the following hands-on tutorials for working with these services:

- Amazon EMR: `https://docs.aws.amazon.com/emr/latest/ManagementGuide/emr-gs.html`
- Amazon Redshift: `https://docs.aws.amazon.com/redshift/latest/dg/tutorials-redshift.html`
- AWS Glue: `https://docs.aws.amazon.com/glue/latest/dg/streaming-tutorial-studio.html`

Consuming and Maintaining Data APIs

Traditionally, connecting to relational databases was through the use of drivers, which provided a persistent connection between the application and the database. However, with the introduction of serverless applications, such as AWS Lambda—which are by nature stateless—persistent connections are no longer practical. AWS introduced the Data API, a secure HTTPS API used for running SQL queries against relational databases, allowing you to accelerate modern application development.

AWS makes available the Data APIs, which allow you to programmatically access database data without the need to manage database drivers, credentials, connections, network configurations, and more. With the AWS SDK, you can run SQL statements using the Data API operations as part of the automation integrated into your data pipelines. Some of the features of the Data API include the following:

- The Data API doesn't require a persistent connection to your database but provides a secure HTTP endpoint and integration with AWS SDKs.

- The Data API eliminates the use of drivers and improves scalability by automatically pooling and sharing database connections.

- You can use your endpoint to run SQL statements without managing connections.

- Calls made to the Data API are asynchronous, meaning that the API does not return data immediately and can continue executing. The data can be delivered later.

- To access your database, the Data API uses either temporary database credentials or credentials stored in AWS Secrets Manager.

- As of November 2024, the Data API is available for the following:

    - Amazon RDS Data API for the following Aurora databases:

        - Aurora PostgreSQL - Serverless v2, provisioned, and Serverless v1

        - Aurora MySQL - Serverless v2, provisioned, and Serverless v1

    - Amazon Redshift Data API

- For RDS, the Data API must be enabled on the DB instance, while for Redshift, it is immediately available to use using SDK/CLI for any launched cluster.

    Next, we will dive deeper into the Amazon Redshift Data API.

Amazon Redshift Data API

As a data engineer, there may be use cases where you want to interact with Amazon Redshift to query or load data with an API endpoint without having to manage connections. The Amazon Redshift Data API allows you to access your Redshift databases without having to configure a JDBC or ODBC connection, making it secure and easier to interact with Amazon Redshift (see Figure 9.1). The API simplifies Redshift access from a variety of applications, which can be traditional, cloud native, serverless web service-based, or event-driven applications. The Redshift Data API also enables access from programming languages supported by the AWS SDK, such as Python, Java, Node.js, PHP, C++, Ruby, and Go. The Amazon Redshift Data API can be used to access databases for both provisioned and serverless workgroups.

FIGURE 9.1   Applications can connect to Redshift using the Redshift Data API

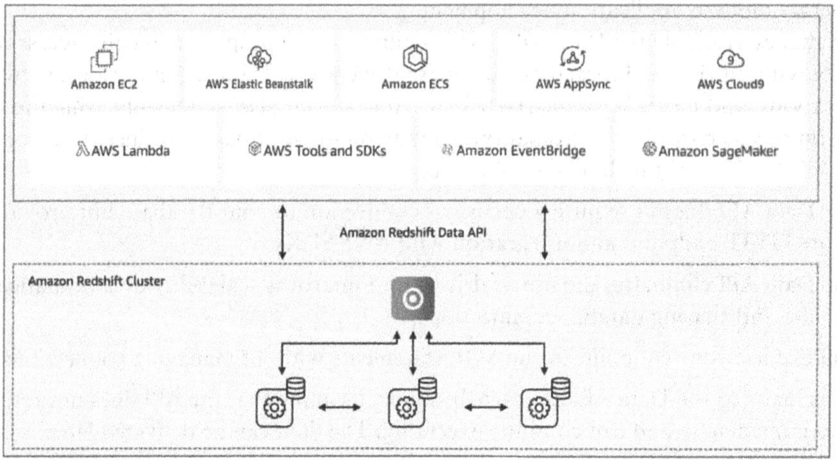

Calling the Data API and Available Commands

The Data API can be called from the AWS CLI, your own code, or the query editor in the Amazon Redshift console. The primary operations to run SQL statements are Execute Statement and BatchExecuteStatement, as found in the Amazon Data API Reference. Table 9.3 provides the complete list of available actions.

TABLE 9.3   Overview of the actions

Action	Description
BatchExecuteStatement	Runs one or more SQL statements, which can either be Data Manipulation Language or Data Definition Language (DDL).
CancelStatement	Cancels a running query.
DescribeStatement	Describes an instance of a specific query execution and provides details such as query start time, end time, status, rows returned, and the statement itself.
DescribeTable	Describes detailed information about a table from the cluster metadata.

Action	Description
ExecuteStatement	Runs an SQL statement, which can be either DML or DDL and must be a single SQL statement.
GetStatementResult	Fetches the temporarily cached result of an SQL statement in JSON format. The ExecuteStatement or BatchExecute Statement operation that ran the statement must have specified ResultFormat as JSON.
GetStatementResultV2	Fetches the temporarily cached result of an SQL statement in CSV format. The ExecuteStatement or BatchExecute Statement operation that ran the statement must have specified ResultFormat as CSV.
ListDatabases	Provides a list of databases in a cluster.
ListSchemas	Provides a list of the schemas in a database.
ListStatements	Provides a list of SQL statements that have finished as the default behavior.
ListTables	Provides the list of tables in a database.

In addition to the statements in Table 9.3, the Redshift Data API contains several data types that can be used by the actions. These are found in this guide: https://docs.aws.amazon.com/redshift-data/latest/APIReference/API_Types.html.

Example Statements and Their Output

Now let's look at a couple of example statements and their output.

Example 1: Statement from the CLI

```
aws redshift-data execute statement
--cluster-identifier my-redshift-cluster
--database dev
--db-user awsuser
--sql 'select data from redshift_table';
```

Example 2:   Code using Python

```
boto3.client("redshift-data").execute_statement(
    ClusterIdentifier = 'my-redshift-cluster',
    Database = 'dev',
    DbUser = 'awsuser',
    Sql = 'select data from redshift_table')
```

Considerations When Using the Redshift Data API

The following list shows considerations to keep in mind when calling the Redshift Data API (as of November 2024). Please refer to the AWS guide (https://docs.aws.amazon.com/redshift/latest/mgmt/data-api.html#data-api-calling-considerations) to see if there have been any updates since.

- The Amazon Redshift Data API can access databases in Amazon Redshift provisioned clusters and Redshift Serverless workgroups. For a list of AWS Regions where the Redshift Data API is available, see the endpoints listed for Redshift Data API in the Amazon Web Services General Reference.

- The maximum duration of a query is 24 hours.

- The maximum number of active queries (STARTED and SUBMITTED) per Amazon Redshift cluster is 500.

- The maximum query result size is 100 MB (after gzip compression). If a call returns more than 100 MB of response data, the call is ended.

- The maximum retention time for query results is 24 hours.

- The maximum query statement size is 100 KB.

- The Data API is available to query single-node and multiple-node clusters of the following node types: dc2.large, dc2.8xlarge, ra3.large, ra3.xlplus, ra3.4xlarge, and ra3.16xlarge.

- The cluster must be in a virtual private cloud (VPC) based on the Amazon VPC service.

- By default, users with the same IAM role or IAM permissions as the runner of an ExecuteStatement or BatchExecuteStatement API operation can act on the same statement with CancelStatement, DescribeStatement, GetStatementResult, GetStatementResultV2, and ListStatements API operations. To act on the same SQL statement from another user, the user must be able to assume the IAM role of the user who ran the SQL statement. For more information about how to assume a role, see Authorizing Access to the Amazon Redshift Data API (https://docs.aws.amazon.com/redshift/latest/mgmt/data-api-access.html).

- The SQL statements in the `Sqls` parameter of `BatchExecuteStatement` API operation are run as a single transaction. They run serially in the order of the array. Subsequent SQL statements don't start until the previous statement in the array completes. If any SQL statement fails, then because they are run as one transaction, all work is rolled back.

- The maximum retention time for a client token used in `ExecuteStatement` or `BatchExecuteStatement` API operations is 8 hours.

- Each API in the Redshift Data API has a transactions per second quota before throttling requests. For the quota, see Quotas for Amazon Redshift Data API (`https://docs.aws.amazon.com/redshift/latest/mgmt/amazon-redshift-limits.html#data-api-quotas-account`). If the rate of request exceeds the quota, a `ThrottlingException` with HTTP Status Code: 400 is returned. To respond to throttling, use a retry strategy, as described in Retry Behavior in the *AWS SDKs and Tools Reference Guide* (`https://docs.aws.amazon.com/sdkref/latest/guide/feature-retry-behavior.html`). This strategy is implemented automatically for throttling errors in some AWS SDKs.

Amazon Redshift Data API Use Case

Imagine a large e-commerce company, AnyCompany, that uses Amazon Redshift as its data warehouse. AnyCompany wants to create a real-time analytics dashboard for executives and managers to monitor key business metrics throughout the day. The dashboard needs to display up-to-date information on sales, inventory, customer behavior, and marketing campaign performance.

In this scenario, the Redshift Data API could be used as follows:

1. Dashboard backend:
   - A Node.js application serves as the backend for the dashboard.
   - It uses the Redshift Data API to execute queries and fetch data in real time.

2. Periodic data refresh:
   - The application runs a series of predefined queries every 3 minutes to update the dashboard.
   - These queries aggregate data on recent sales, top-selling products, inventory levels, and active user counts.

3. On-demand drill-down:
   - When an executive wants to explore a specific metric in more detail, the dashboard allows for interactive drill-downs.
   - These drill-downs trigger new queries via the Redshift Data API to fetch more granular data.

4. Automated alerting:
   - The application also runs hourly checks for anomalies or important thresholds.
   - If a metric falls outside expected ranges, it uses the Redshift Data API to gather relevant details and triggers an alert.

5. Ad-hoc analysis:
   - The dashboard includes a feature for executives to run custom queries for quick ad-hoc analysis.
   - These custom queries are executed using the Redshift Data API, with results displayed directly in the dashboard.

6. Performance optimization:
   - The application uses the asynchronous nature of the Redshift Data API to run multiple queries in parallel, improving dashboard responsiveness.

7. Security:
   - The application uses IAM roles and temporary credentials to securely access the Redshift cluster without storing long-term credentials.

This scenario leverages key advantages of the Redshift Data API:

- It gives real-time data access without maintaining persistent database connections.
- It provides the ability to run queries asynchronously and in parallel.
- It simplifies security management through IAM integration.
- It provides scalability to handle varying loads from multiple users and automated processes.

By using the Redshift Data API in this way, AnyCompany can provide its leadership with a responsive, secure, and up-to-date analytics dashboard, enabling data-driven decision-making without the need for complex ETL processes or maintaining a separate analytics database.

Monitoring the Redshift Data API

To monitor the Data API, you can use Amazon EventBridge and AWS CloudTrail. On the one hand, Amazon EventBridge can be used to respond automatically to system events, such as application availability or resource changes. You can then write rules to trigger automated actions based whenever an event matches a rule. On the other hand, AWS CloudTrail captures API calls and delivers the log files to an Amazon S3 bucket, which you can then analyze to identify information such as which users/accounts made API calls, when the calls were made, and the source IP addresses from which the calls were made.

Troubleshooting Common Issues for the Redshift Data API

Table 9.4 describes how to deal with some common error messages with the Redshift Data API.

TABLE 9.4 Troubleshooting error messages

Error Message	Solution
Packet for query is too large.	The Data API size limit 64 KB per row in the result set returned by the database. Make sure each row in the result set is at or below this threshold.
Database response exceeded size limit.	The size of the result set limit is 100 MB. Make sure calls to the Data API return 100 MB of data or less. If you require more than 100 MB, you can run multiple statements and use the LIMIT clause in your query.

For hands-on experience with the Redshift Data API, please see these guides:

https://aws.amazon.com/blogs/big-data/using-the-amazon-redshift-data-api-to-interact-with-amazon-redshift-clusters

https://aws.amazon.com/blogs/big-data/get-started-with-the-amazon-redshift-data-api

Using Lambda for Data Processing

Chapters 2 and 3 described Lambda in detail, including various use cases. In this section we reiterate the following about Lambda, which you must consider to simplify and modernize your data operations:

- Lambda removes the task of managing servers.
- It runs your code on highly available infrastructure that is fault tolerant.
- You do not have to worry about administration, maintenance, or patching of your infrastructure.
- Lambda has built-in logging and monitoring, which integrates with AWS CloudTrail, CloudWatch Logs, and Amazon CloudWatch.
- Lambda enables you to modernize your applications by using pre-trained machine learning (ML) models to easily incorporate artificial intelligence.

Summary

This chapter discussed how to manage data operations in your environment, including the tools and services that make it possible. The overarching theme of the chapter is to use automation as much as possible for your data pipeline to simplify its setup, management, and troubleshooting. We started by looking at some best practices for maintaining the data processing pipeline, such as setting up logging and monitoring using CloudWatch, setting up alarms for critical events and errors, using AWS X-Ray to trace and debug, and implementing error handling and retry mechanisms for when things go wrong.

We then looked at the importance of scheduling regular reviews for your pipelines to identify optimization opportunities. We looked at the importance of version control and change management best practices, security and compliance, disaster recovery and tuning, performance and cost optimizations, and using the AWS Cost Explorer to analyze your spend.

Next, we explored how using the AWS APIs and SDKs enables programmatic interaction of applications with AWS services to modernize application development and management.

We then compared the three data orchestration services: MWAA, AWS Glue, and AWS Step Functions. This was followed by an exploration of how to troubleshoot MWAA. We then compared three services used for data processing: Amazon EMR, Amazon Redshift, and AWS Glue.

We then looked at consuming and maintaining the Data API, with a focus on the Redshift Data API. The chapter finished with an overview of the benefits of using Lambda in your data operations.

Exam Essentials

Understand the importance of using automation to simplify the setup, management, and troubleshooting of your data pipeline.   This includes knowing the different activities and services you can use as a data engineer to manage your data pipelines to help you achieve business outcomes. You must also know how to use API calls for programmatic and automated interactions with AWS services.

Understand the Data API.   You need to know why the Data API is useful and what services support it. You also must know the basic Data API commands and when to use them.

Understand the different AWS services.   These include the services that are used for data processing, orchestration, and those that support scripting.

Be able to maintain and troubleshoot a data processing pipeline.   You must be able to determine which services to use to troubleshoot issues and errors that you may encounter. You also must be able to determine the differences and use cases of the different orchestration services, such as AWS Step Functions, Amazon MWAA, and AWS Glue.

Understand the different data processing services.   You need to know the differences between Amazon EMR, Amazon Redshift, and AWS Glue. You must be able to determine which of the data processing services can be used depending on the use case.

Review Questions

1. Which AWS service is used to respond automatically to system events, such as application availability issues when monitoring the Redshift Data API?

   A. Amazon CloudWatch

   B. AWS CloudTrail

   C. Amazon EventBridge

   D. AWS Systems Manager

2. Which AWS service is best suited for visualizing and analyzing the behavior of applications, identifying performance bottlenecks, and troubleshooting request failures?

   A. Amazon CloudWatch

   B. AWS CloudTrail

   C. AWS X-Ray

   D. Amazon EventBridge

3. What is the primary advantage of using AWS Lambda for data processing?

   A. It provides persistent connections to databases.

   B. It removes the task of managing servers or provisioning servers.

   C. It allows for real-time querying of large datasets.

   D. It offers unlimited processing time for long-running jobs.

4. What is the primary advantage of using the Amazon Redshift Data API over traditional database drivers?

   A. It improves query performance.

   B. It allows for larger result sets.

   C. It eliminates the need for persistent connections.

   D. It supports more complex SQL operations.

5. Which AWS service is used for infrastructure as code and can be utilized for maintaining data processing pipelines?

   A. AWS Lambda

   B. AWS CloudFormation

   C. Amazon EMR

   D. AWS Glue

6. Which of the following is *not* a primary purpose of the listed AWS services?

   A. Amazon EMR: Big data processing and analysis

   B. Amazon Redshift: Data warehousing and analytics

   C. AWS Glue: ETL and data integration

   D. Amazon MWAA: Real-time data processing

7. What is the purpose of implementing exponential backoff in AWS data processing pipelines?

 A. To increase the speed of data processing in your pipelines

 B. To reduce costs by minimizing usage of your resources

 C. To handle transient errors by retrying failed operations

 D. To compress data before transmission to other services

8. What is the maximum retention time for query results when using the Amazon Redshift Data API?

 A. 6 hours

 B. 12 hours

 C. 24 hours

 D. 48 hours

9. Which of the following services supports real-time processing through streaming capabilities?

 A. Amazon EMR

 B. AWS Glue

 C. Amazon Redshift

 D. All of the above

10. Which AWS orchestration service is most suitable for complex, multiservice data pipelines that require visual workflows and branching logic?

 A. Amazon EMR

 B. AWS Glue

 C. AWS Step Functions

 D. Amazon Redshift

Chapter

10

Authentication and Authorization

**THE AWS CERTIFIED DATA ENGINEER –
ASSOCIATE EXAM OBJECTIVES COVERED
IN THIS CHAPTER MAY INCLUDE, BUT ARE
NOT LIMITED TO, THE FOLLOWING:**

✓ **Domain 4: Data Security and Governance**

   ▪ 4.1: Apply authentication mechanisms

   ▪ 4.2: Apply authorization mechanisms

Introduction to Authentication

Authentication is simply the process of verifying who someone is. It's like checking an ID to make sure the person is who they say they are. Authentication in AWS is the process of verifying the identity of users, services, or applications that attempt to interact with AWS resources. Before we talk about authentication, let's look at the different ways and means by which you would need to interact with an AWS service.

Before exploring access and authorization, which are discussed in the latter half of this chapter, let's take a moment to review the ways that you can interact with AWS. AWS has placed a limited number of access points to the cloud for a more comprehensive monitoring of inbound and outbound communications and network traffic. These user access points are called *API endpoints*.

Figure 10.1 summarizes the mechanisms by which you can interact with an AWS service, which include the following:

- The AWS Management Console is a web interface that can be used from standard browsers and provides functionality for the majority of the features.

- The AWS Command Line Interface (AWS CLI) is a tool that promotes automation by offering commands for a broad set of AWS products.

- AWS SDKs abstract APIs into easily consumable functions that are specific to a programming language or platform.

- AWS also supports a variety of open-source and third-party tools that generate RESTful HTTP(S) API requests. Other AWS services can also create API calls to a specific AWS service API endpoint.

API Endpoints

API endpoints are essentially a gateway to interact with AWS services and resources. Properly securing these endpoints through authentication ensures that only legitimate users or systems can initiate communication with them, preventing unauthorized access.

FIGURE 10.1   Different ways of interacting with AWS service endpoints

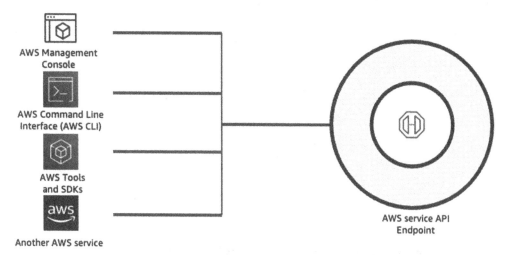

Before diving into IAM (and the AWS Identity and Access Management service) and permissions, it is important to review how API endpoints are used to access AWS services and some key concepts that affect how you create and maintain permissions. At a high level, there are two basic types of endpoints:

- Regional endpoints
- Global endpoints

Most AWS services offer a regional API endpoint to make your requests. An endpoint is made up of a URL. For example, the entry point for the AWS CloudTrail service in Sao Paulo, Brazil is https://cloudtrail.sa-east-1.amazonaws.com. Using regional endpoints is extremely helpful when making direct API calls for individual AWS services within the same AWS Region as your company or customer. Figure 10.2 shows an example of all CloudTrail regional endpoint locations.

Some services—for example, AWS IAM and Amazon CloudFront—have a single-entry point and do not support Regions. Therefore, their endpoints do not include a Region in the URL. These endpoints are known as *global endpoints*.

However, if you look at some other services, such as Amazon Elastic Cloud Compute (Amazon EC2), they will let you specify an endpoint that does not include a specific Region—for example, https://ec2.amazonaws.com. In this case, AWS routes the endpoint to us-east-1. If a service supports Regions, that service is deploying resources within a Region, as opposed to services that deploy resources outside a Region and have a single-entry point to the API layer.

Since this is a book about data engineering, you might be wondering how this is relevant at all to the data engineering exam. Many AWS analytics services have regional endpoints, while a few have global endpoints, and knowing when to use which is critical for the exam. While endpoints are not explicitly addressed on the exam, they may come up in a few questions, so it's important to know what they are.

FIGURE 10.2   CloudTrail regional endpoint locations

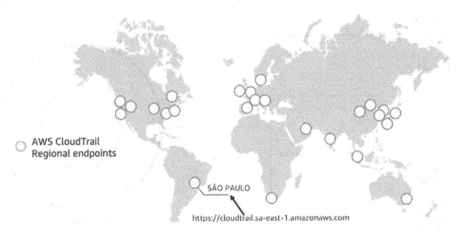

Here's a list that's split between regional and global endpoints:

- Regional endpoints:
    - Amazon Athena
    - Amazon Elastic MapReduce (Amazon EMR)
    - Amazon Kinesis
    - Amazon Redshift
    - Amazon QuickSight
    - AWS Glue
- Global endpoints:
    - AWS Lake Formation (uses IAM's global endpoint)

Amazon S3, one of the key services covered on the exam, uses regional endpoints. A regional endpoint for Amazon S3 uses the following format:

`s3.{region}.amazonaws.com`

For example, the regional endpoint for Amazon S3 in the US East (N. Virginia) Region would be

`s3.us-east-1.amazonaws.com`

It's important to note that while S3 uses regional endpoints, it's designed to automatically recover from the failure of an Availability Zone within a Region. S3 spreads requests and data across multiple Availability Zones to enhance durability and availability.

Additionally, Amazon S3 offers a feature called *Multi-Region Access Points*, which provides a global endpoint for routing S3 request traffic between AWS Regions. This feature can be useful for scenarios requiring improved performance, failover capabilities, or multi-region applications.

Amazon Redshift is another service that appears quite frequently in various exam questions. It uses regional endpoints, which means you connect to a specific endpoint based on the AWS Region where your Redshift cluster is located.

The general format for a Redshift endpoint is as follows:

`redshift.{region}.amazonaws.com`

An example of a Redshift endpoint across various Regions may look like this:

- US East (N. Virginia): `redshift.us-east-1.amazonaws.com`
- US West (Oregon): `redshift.us-west-2.amazonaws.com`
- Europe (Ireland): `redshift.eu-west-1.amazonaws.com`

Amazon Redshift also offers a unique cluster-specific endpoint. This endpoint includes the cluster name and is used for connecting to your specific cluster. The format is

`{cluster-name}.{unique-id}.{region}.redshift.amazonaws.com`

Please note that VPC endpoints are different. A VPC endpoint is a way for resources in your virtual private cloud (VPC) to privately connect to AWS services without going through the public Internet. If you're using Redshift within a VPC, you can create a VPC endpoint to connect to your cluster privately without going over the public Internet. Again, this may come up as a scenario where you may be asked about the possible ways to avoid your traffic being routed to the Internet.

For the most up-to-date and detailed information on AWS service endpoints, including S3, we recommend checking the official AWS documentation.

AWS Identity and Acess Management

AWS Identity and Access Management (IAM) is a service that helps organizations control access to AWS resources. IAM is used to control who can use AWS resources (authentication), what resources they can use, and in what ways (authorization). With IAM, you can grant permissions to principals (actors that perform actions)—such as IAM users, federated users, IAM roles, or identity providers—so that they can administer and use resources (S3 buckets, Redshift clusters, EMR clusters) in your AWS account without having to share your password or access key.

There are two types of IAM permissions:

- Identity-based
- Resource-based

They are nearly identical in appearance and function but have some slight syntax differences. The difference between the two types of permissions is in where they are applied. *Identity-based permissions* are attached to an IAM entity and indicate what the user or group is permitted to do. *Resource-based permissions* are attached to a resource and indicate what a specified user is permitted to do with it. For example, Amazon Simple Storage Service (Amazon S3) bucket policies and AWS Key Management Service (AWS KMS) key policies are resource-based policies. You cannot identify a user group as a principal in a policy (such as a resource-based policy) because groups relate to permissions, not authentication, and principals are authenticated IAM entities.

With IAM, you define policies that control which AWS services your users and resources can access and what they can do with them. Permissions in the policies determine whether the request is allowed or denied. Besides IAM user policies, there are other authentication and authorization options available outside of IAM. Certain services provide additional security access controls that can be used also. For example, Amazon S3 has object access control lists (ACLs) and object locks as additional security controls that are not part of the IAM policy evaluation logic.

Figure 10.3 shows the key IAM components and the IAM process flow.

FIGURE 10.3   IAM components and process flow

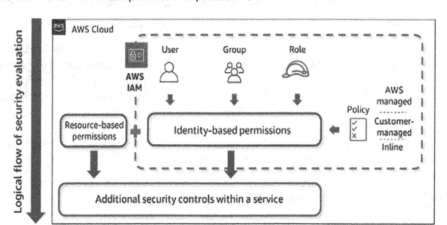

IAM Users and Groups

In AWS Identity and Access Management (IAM), users represent individual entities (such as people, applications, or services) that need to interact with AWS resources. These users are granted specific credentials, such as access keys or passwords, to authenticate and perform actions based on the permissions they have been given.

Managing permissions for individual users can become complex as the number of users grows. To streamline this, AWS allows you to organize users into groups. An IAM group is a collection of IAM users that share similar access requirements. By placing users in groups, you can define permissions at the group level using IAM policies. These policies specify what actions are allowed or denied on specific AWS resources.

For example, you might have a Developers group that needs access to EC2 instances and S3 buckets. Instead of assigning these permissions to each developer individually, you can attach a policy to the Developers group, and every user in that group will automatically inherit those permissions. This simplifies management by enabling you to modify the group's permissions once, and the changes will apply to all users in the group. Similarly, if a new developer joins the team, they can be added to the Developer" group to automatically gain the required permissions.

Figure 10.4 shows IAM organizing users into groups of Admins, Analysts, and Billing.

FIGURE 10.4   Users and groups in IAM

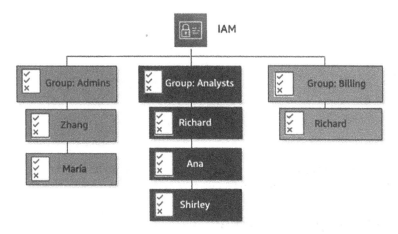

In summary, using IAM users and groups helps to:

- Maintain better organization by grouping users based on roles or responsibilities
- Simplify permission management by handling policies at the group level rather than on a per-user basis
- Enhance security by ensuring consistent access control and reducing the chance of granting excessive permissions to individual users

IAM Roles

You create a role in the AWS account that contains the resources you want to allow access to. When you create the role, you specify two policies. The *trust policy* specifies who is allowed to assume the role (the *trusted entity* or *principal*). The principal can be an AWS account, an AWS service such as Amazon EC2, a SAML provider, or an identity provider (IdP) such as a login with Amazon, Facebook, or Google. The principal can also be an IAM user or role from other AWS accounts, including those not owned by you. The *access policy* (permissions) defines which actions and resources the principal is allowed access to.

For example, in Figure 10.5, the IAM users Richard, Ana, and Shirley are members of the Analysts user group. As members of the Analysts group, these users inherit the permissions assigned to the group. Another IAM role, which is called DevApp1, is being used for testing purposes. DevApp1 has its own set of permissions. Ana and Shirley can assume the role and temporarily use the permissions specific to the DevApp1 role.

FIGURE 10.5   Roles in IAM

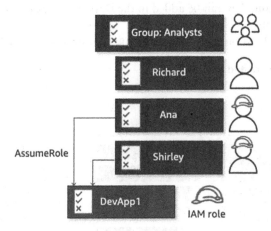

While they assume this role, Ana and Shirley only have the permissions that are granted to the role and do not follow their group's inherited permissions.

Access Keys and Credentials

Access keys are a type of security credential used to grant programmatic access to AWS services through the AWS Command Line Interface (CLI), software development kits (SDKs), or application programming interfaces (APIs). These keys are generated for IAM users who need to interact with AWS resources programmatically, as opposed to using the AWS Management Console.

An access key consists of two parts:

- **Access key ID:** This functions similarly to a username, uniquely identifying the key.

- **Secret access key:** This functions like a password and is used to authenticate the associated access key ID.

Together, these credentials allow IAM users to make API requests and interact with AWS services securely. For example, when automating interactions with Amazon Redshift, such as querying data using the Redshift Data API via scripts, the IAM user or service running the script would need access keys. The keys authenticate programmatic requests, allowing secure access to execute SQL queries and retrieve the results from the Redshift cluster. However, because access keys provide direct access to your AWS resources, it is critical to handle them with care. Some best practices include:

- **Store access key securely:** Access keys should never be hardcoded in application code or shared publicly (e.g., in code repositories like GitHub). Instead, use secure storage mechanisms such as AWS Secrets Manager (discussed later in the chapter) or environment variables.

- **Rotate access keys regularly**: To reduce the risk of compromised credentials, access keys should be rotated periodically. AWS provides mechanisms for creating new access keys while deactivating and eventually deleting old ones.

- **Apply the least privilege principle**: When assigning access keys, apply the least privilege principle, meaning users should only have permissions necessary to perform their tasks.

You can help mitigate security risks while allowing programmatic access to AWS services by securely managing and rotating access keys.

Multi-Factor Authentication

To enhance the security of your AWS account, you can also enable multi-factor authentication (MFA) for IAM users. MFA adds an extra layer of protection by requiring users to provide not only their password but also a second authentication factor. This additional factor is usually a one-time code generated by an authenticator app (like Google Authenticator) or a hardware token.

By enabling MFA, even if an unauthorized person gains access to an IAM user's password, they still cannot sign in without also having access to the second factor, making unauthorized access significantly more difficult.

Some best practices for using MFA include:

- **Enforce MFA**: You can require MFA for specific high-privilege users or roles (e.g., administrators managing Redshift clusters or critical services like EC2 or S3) to ensure access is as secure as possible.

- **Use MFA for API access**: In addition to console login, MFA can be enforced for programmatic access (e.g., through CLI or SDK) using specific policies.

By requiring MFA for IAM users, you significantly reduce the likelihood of unauthorized access to your AWS resources, providing an important security control for safeguarding sensitive environments.

AWS Security Token Service

AWS Security Token Service (STS) allows you to generate temporary security credentials for IAM users, roles, or federated users. These temporary credentials are time-bound and provide limited access to AWS resources, helping to reduce the risks associated with long-term credentials. When requesting these credentials, you can define the specific permissions granted and the duration for which they are valid, allowing for fine-grained control over access.

Temporary credentials generated by STS are useful in scenarios where short-term, controlled access is needed. For example, consider a data processing pipeline using AWS Glue. Suppose an external data science team needs to run ETL jobs in AWS Glue for a limited period to process sensitive data. Instead of granting them permanent access via IAM user credentials, you can use AWS STS to issue temporary security credentials. These credentials will allow the team to interact with Glue services, such as launching jobs or accessing the Glue Data Catalog, for the duration of their work.

By using STS:

■   You control the scope of permissions, ensuring the team can only access the necessary resources (like Glue jobs and data catalogs) without broader access to other AWS services.

■   The credentials expire after a defined period, reducing the risk of credential misuse after the task is completed.

Some benefits of using AWS STS include:

■   **Security**: Since the credentials are temporary, there is less risk of long-term credential compromise.

■   **Flexibility**: You can grant granular permissions and dynamically adjust the session duration based on the use case.

It is important to note that AWS STS helps enhance security by limiting access duration and scope (one of the most critical security aspects), ensuring that users and applications have only the temporary access they need to perform specific tasks.

Assuming Roles

In AWS Identity and Access Management (IAM), roles are a secure way to grant permissions to entities you trust, allowing them to access AWS resources without needing to share long-term security credentials like access keys. An IAM role is an identity with a set of permissions that are not associated with a specific user or group. Instead, trusted entities can *assume* a role to temporarily acquire its permissions. These entities can be IAM users, applications, AWS services, or even users from another AWS account. Figure 10.6 shows how assuming a role works.

FIGURE 10.6   Assuming a role

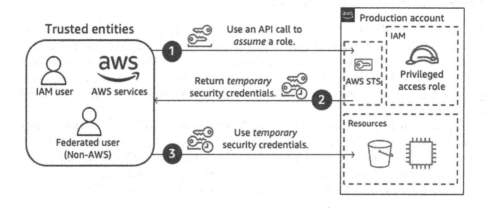

When an entity assumes a role, it receives temporary security credentials from AWS STS, which include an access key ID, a secret access key, and a session token. These credentials grant the permissions defined in the role's policies for the duration of the session.

During the exam, you should consider assuming roles as a viable choice, especially when you come across the following scenarios:

- **Cross-account access:** Allowing users or services in one AWS account to access resources in another account securely.

- **AWS services accessing other services:** Enabling applications running on AWS services like EC2, Lambda, or EMR to interact with other AWS resources without embedding credentials.

Sample Exam Scenario with Amazon Elastic MapReduce

Consider a scenario where you have an Amazon Elastic MapReduce (Amazon EMR) cluster that processes large amounts of data stored in Amazon S3. To securely allow the EMR cluster to access the data in S3 and write the processed results back to S3, you can configure an IAM role that the EMR cluster will assume.

Here's how it works:

1. Create an IAM role for EMR:
   - Define an IAM role (e.g., `EMR_DefaultRole`) with the necessary permissions to access S3 buckets and any other AWS services required for data processing tasks.
   - Attach an IAM policy to this role that grants permissions like `s3:GetObject`, `s3:PutObject`, and `s3:ListBucket` for the specific S3 buckets your EMR jobs will interact with.

2. Configure the EMR cluster to assume the role:
   - When launching the EMR cluster, specify the `EMR_DefaultRole` as the service role for the cluster.
   - The EMR service will then assume this role on behalf of the cluster nodes.

3. EMR cluster nodes assume the role:
   - Each node in the EMR cluster obtains the temporary security credentials associated with `EMR_DefaultRole`.
   - The nodes use these credentials to access S3 and other AWS services securely during data processing tasks.

Benefits of This Approach

Here are some of the benefits:

- **Improved security:** You don't have to embed long-term access keys in the applications or configure them on the instances. If the cluster is terminated, the temporary credentials expire automatically.

- **Fine-grained access control:** You can define precisely which resources the EMR cluster can access by adjusting the permissions in the IAM role's policy.

- **Ease of management:** If you need to update permissions, you can modify the IAM role's policies without changing the application or redeploying the cluster.

Additional Use Cases

Here are some use cases to consider:

- **Cross-account access:** If your data is stored in an S3 bucket in a different AWS account, you can set up a trust relationship that allows your EMR cluster to assume a role in that account, granting it access to the bucket.

- **Access to other AWS services:** The EMR cluster can assume roles that grant access to services like DynamoDB, Redshift, or Kinesis for more complex data processing workflows.

Key Points to Note for the Exam

Here are some key points to keep in mind:

- **Trusted entities:** The entities that can assume a role are defined in the role's trust policy. In the EMR example, the trusted entity is the EMR service itself (`elasticmapreduce.amazonaws.com`).

- **Temporary credentials:** Roles provide temporary credentials that expire after a certain period, enhancing security by reducing the window of opportunity for compromise.

- **Secure interaction between services:** By using roles, AWS services can interact securely without the need for manual credential management.

Federation

Identity federation in AWS allows you to leverage existing authentication systems to grant users access to AWS resources without the need to create separate IAM users for each individual. By setting up identity federation, you enable users to authenticate using credentials from an external identity provider (IdP), such as Microsoft Active Directory, LDAP directories, or any SAML (Security Assertion Markup Language)-based IdP. This approach facilitates single sign-on (SSO), allowing users to access AWS resources seamlessly with their existing corporate credentials.

How Federation Works

Here's how federation works:

1. User authentication with external IdP:
   - A user attempts to access AWS resources and is redirected to authenticate with the external IdP.
   - The IdP verifies the user's credentials (i.e., username and password).

2. Issuance of SAML assertion:
   - Upon successful authentication, the IdP issues a SAML assertion that contains information about the user and their group memberships or roles.
3. Assuming an IAM role in AWS:
   - AWS uses the SAML assertion to map the user to an IAM role.
   - The user assumes this role and receives temporary security credentials via AWS Security Token Service (STS).
4. Access granted to AWS resources:
   - With these temporary credentials, the user can access AWS resources according to the permissions defined in the IAM role.

Example Scenario with Amazon EMR

Imagine a scenario where a company has a team of data scientist who need to run big data analytics jobs on Amazon EMR (Elastic MapReduce) clusters. The company uses Microsoft Active Directory (AD) as its central identity store and wants to allow data scientists to access EMR resources using their existing AD credentials.

Here's how identity federation can be implemented in this scenario:

1. Set up an identity provider (IdP):
   - Configure Active Directory Federation Services (AD FS) to act as a SAML-based IdP.
   - Establish trust between AD FS and AWS by uploading AWS's metadata to AD FS and vice versa.
2. Create IAM roles for federated access:
   - In AWS IAM, create a role (e.g., `DataScientistRole`) that trusts the SAML provider (AD FS).
   - Attach policies to this role that grant necessary permissions to manage and interact with EMR clusters, such as:
     - Launching and terminating EMR clusters
     - Submitting jobs and accessing cluster logs
     - Reading and writing data to Amazon S3 buckets associated with EMR
3. Configure role mappings in the IdP:
   - Map AD groups to IAM roles in AWS. For example, members of the `DataScientists` group in AD are allowed to assume the `DataScientist Role` in AWS.
   - This mapping is defined in the SAML assertions sent by AD FS to AWS during authentication.
4. User authentication and access flow:
   - A data scientist attempts to access the AWS Management Console or uses the AWS CLI to interact with EMR.

- The user is redirected to authenticate with AD FS using their AD credentials.
- After successful authentication, AD FS issues a SAML assertion with the user's group membership.
- AWS STS processes the SAML assertion, and the user assumes the DataScientistRole, receiving temporary security credentials.
- The user can now access EMR resources as permitted by the role's policies.

Benefits of Using Federation

Here are some of the benefits of using federation:

- Single sign-on (SSO):
  - Users enjoy a seamless login experience using their existing credentials.
  - Reduces the need to remember multiple usernames and passwords.
- Centralized identity management:
  - User accounts, permissions, and password policies are managed centrally in Active Directory.
  - Simplifies onboarding and offboarding processes.
- Enhanced security:
  - Eliminates the need to create long-term IAM user credentials.
  - Temporary credentials obtained via STS have a limited lifespan, reducing the risk window.
- Scalability:
  - Easily scales to large numbers of users without additional IAM user management overhead.
  - Changes in user roles or permissions are managed in the IdP and automatically reflected in AWS access.

Additional Use Cases

Here are some use cases to consider:

- **Cross-account access:** Federation can be used to grant users in one AWS account access to resources in another account without creating IAM users in each account.
- **Mobile and web applications:** Use Amazon Cognito or other OIDC-compliant IdPs to federate user access for customer-facing applications.

Key Considerations

Here are some key considerations:

- **Role permissions:** Carefully design IAM role policies to grant only the necessary permissions following the principle of least privilege.

- **Session duration:** Configure appropriate session durations for the temporary credentials to balance security and usability.
- **Audit and monitoring:** Use AWS CloudTrail and AWS CloudWatch to monitor and log federated user activities for compliance and security auditing.

Amazon Cognito

Amazon Cognito is a managed service that enables you to add user sign-up, sign-in, and access control to your web and mobile applications quickly and securely. It simplifies authentication by providing built-in user management and authentication flows, reducing the amount of custom code you need to write. Cognito also supports authentication with social identity providers like Facebook, Google, and Amazon, as well as enterprise identity providers via SAML 2.0 and OpenID Connect.

Key Components of Amazon Cognito

Here are some of the key components of Amazon Cognito:

1. User pools:
    - A *user pool* is a user directory in Amazon Cognito that manages user registration and authentication.
    - It provides features such as sign-up and sign-in services, password recovery, multi-factor authentication (MFA), and user profile management.
    - You can customize the user experience with branding and localization, and integrate with OAuth 2.0 flows for web and mobile apps.
2. Identity pools (federated identities):
    - An *identity pool* enables you to grant users temporary AWS credentials to access AWS services directly.
    - It supports authenticated identities (users who have signed in) and unauthenticated identities (guest users).
    - Identity pools can federate identities from user pools and external identity providers, consolidating them into a single AWS identity.

How Amazon Cognito Works

When a user authenticates through a user pool, they receive a JSON Web Token (JWT) that contains their identity information. This token can be used to access resources that require authentication. To access AWS services directly from your application, the user can exchange the token with an identity pool to obtain temporary AWS credentials via AWS Security Token Service (STS). These credentials have the permissions defined by IAM roles associated with the identity pool.

Example Exam Scenario

Imagine you are developing a mobile gaming application that allows users to:

- Sign up and sign in to save their game progress
- Share achievements with friends
- Access personalized game content
- Upload and download game assets from Amazon S3

Here's how you can use Amazon Cognito in this scenario:

1. Set up a user pool:
   - Create a user pool in Amazon Cognito to handle user registration and authentication.
   - Configure sign-up options to collect necessary information, such as email and password.
   - Enable MFA for enhanced security, if desired.
   - Customize the sign-in and sign-up UI to match your game's branding.

2. Integrate user authentication:
   - Use the AWS Mobile SDKs to integrate the user pool into your mobile app.
   - Implement features like sign-up, sign-in, password recovery, and user profile updates.
   - Handle authentication flows securely without managing backend infrastructure.

3. Set up an identity pool:
   - Create an identity pool in Amazon Cognito to grant users temporary AWS credentials.
   - Configure the identity pool to accept authenticated identities from your user pool.
   - Define IAM roles for authenticated and unauthenticated users, specifying the AWS resources they can access.

4. Grant temporary AWS credentials:
   - When a user signs in, your app exchanges the user pool token for temporary AWS credentials through the identity pool.
   - These credentials allow the user to interact with AWS services directly from the app.

5. Access AWS services:
   - Amazon S3: Users can upload and download game assets, like custom avatars or saved game states, to an S3 bucket.
     - Assign permissions such as `s3:PutObject` and `s3:GetObject` to the IAM role associated with authenticated users.
   - Amazon DynamoDB: Store user preferences or high scores in a DynamoDB table.

- Grant `dynamodb:PutItem` and `dynamodb:GetItem` permissions as needed.
- Amazon API Gateway and AWS Lambda: Access serverless APIs for game logic or social features.
  - Provide the necessary invoke permissions in the IAM role.

Benefits of Using Amazon Cognito

Here are some of the benefits of using Amazon Cognito:

- Scalability and performance:
  - Cognito can handle millions of users and scales automatically with your application's usage.
- Security:
  - User credentials are securely managed, and AWS ensures compliance with security standards.
  - Amazon Cognito supports MFA, encryption at rest and in transit, and advanced security features like adaptive authentication.
- Integration with external identity providers:
  - Users can sign in using existing credentials from social providers (Facebook, Google) or enterprise identities (SAML).
- Cost-effective:
  - The pay-as-you-go pricing model offers a generous free tier, reducing costs for user management.
- Simplified development:
  - Amazon Cognito reduces the need to build and maintain custom authentication backend services.
  - It provides SDKs and libraries for popular platforms (iOS, Android, and JavaScript).

Additional Features

Here are some of the additional features:

- **Custom authentication flows:** Amazon Cognito enables you to implement custom challenges or validations during authentication.
- **User migration:** You can migrate users from existing directories into Cognito user pools with minimal disruption.
- **Event logging and monitoring:** Amazon Cognito integrates with Amazon CloudWatch for monitoring and AWS CloudTrail for auditing user actions.

During the exam, you will often come across Amazon Cognito in questions. You need to remember that by using Amazon Cognito, you can:

- **Enhance overall security:** Provide secure authentication and authorization mechanisms without the overhead of managing user directories.

- **Improve user experience:** Offer seamless sign-up and sign-in experiences, including social logins.

- **Simplify access to AWS services:** Grant temporary, limited-privilege AWS credentials to users, allowing your application to access AWS resources securely.

- **Accelerate development:** Focus on your application's core functionality rather than building and maintaining authentication systems.

Kerberos-Based Authentication

Kerberos, originally developed as part of Project Athena at MIT in the 1980s, is a network authentication protocol designed to provide strong security for client-server applications using secret-key cryptography. The protocol is named after the mythical three-headed dog Cerberus (often spelled Kerberos), who guards the gates of the underworld in Greek mythology. This symbolism is reflected in the protocol's architecture, where the three heads of Kerberos represent the *client*, the *server*, and the *key distribution center (KDC)*. These components work together to enable secure, mutual authentication over potentially insecure networks, ensuring that both users and services verify each other's identities without transmitting passwords over the network.

In AWS, Kerberos-based authentication enhances the security of services by requiring both users and services to confirm each other's identities before establishing a connection. By using Kerberos, sensitive information, such as passwords, is never directly transmitted, further protecting communication against eavesdropping or replay attacks. Its implementation in AWS services, such as Amazon EMR or Relational Database Service (Amazon RDS), ensures secure interactions in large, distributed environments.

How Kerberos Works

Here's how Kerberos works:

1. Key distribution center (KDC):
   - The core component of Kerberos is the KDC, which consists of two services:
     - Authentication service (AS): Validates user identities and issues ticket-granting tickets (TGTs).
     - Ticket-granting service (TGS): Issues service tickets based on the TGT, allowing access to specific services.

2. Authentication flow (see Figure 10.7):
   - User authentication:
     - A user logs in and sends a request to the AS.
     - The AS verifies the user's credentials and issues a TGT encrypted with the user's secret key.

- Service request:
  - The user presents the TGT to the TGS when requesting access to a service.
  - The TGS issues a service ticket encrypted with the service's secret key.
- Accessing the service:
  - The user presents the service ticket to the desired service.
  - The service decrypts the ticket and, if valid, grants access.

FIGURE 10.7   Kerberos authentication flow

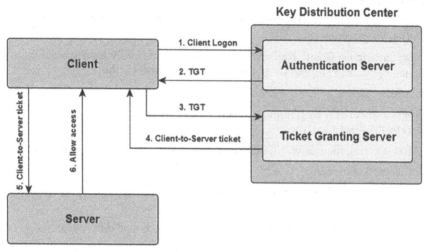

Source: DataSunrise, Inc. / https://www.datasunrise.com/blog/professional-info/configuring-firewall-to-work-with-kerberos, last accessed on 19 December 2024.

Example Scenario with Amazon EMR

Consider a scenario where an organization uses Amazon EMR (Elastic MapReduce) to process sensitive data with applications like Apache Hadoop, Spark, or Hive. To secure the cluster and ensure that only authenticated users and services can access data and resources, the organization implements Kerberos-based authentication.

Steps to Implement Kerberos Authentication in Amazon EMR

Follow these steps to implement Kerberos authentication in Amazon EMR:

1. Set up a key distribution center (KDC):
   - Option 1: Use an external KDC, such as one provided by your organization's Active Directory.
   - Option 2: Let EMR create and manage an EMR-managed KDC within the cluster.

2. Configure the EMR cluster:
   - When launching the EMR cluster via the AWS Management Console, CLI, or SDK, enable Kerberos authentication by specifying:
     - Kerberos realm: Defines the authentication domain (e.g., `EXAMPLE.COM`).
     - KDC server details: If you are using an external KDC, provide the hostname and port.
     - Cross-realm trusts: Set up cross-realm trusts if you are integrating with other Kerberos realms or Active Directory domains.

3. Create service and user principals:
   - Service principals: EMR automatically creates principals for Hadoop services (e.g., `hdfs`, `yarn`, `hive`).
   - User principals: Create Kerberos principals for each user who needs access to the cluster (e.g., `alice@EXAMPLE.COM` and `bob@EXAMPLE.COM`).

4. Authenticate users:
   - Users authenticate by obtaining a TGT from the KDC (e.g., `kinit alice@EXAMPLE.COM`).
   - After entering the password, the user receives a TGT to access cluster services.

5. Secure access to services:
   - With a valid TGT, users can securely interact with services like HDFS, YARN, Hive, and Spark.
   - Service tickets are obtained transparently when accessing different services.

Benefits of Using Kerberos with Amazon EMR

The benefits of using Kerberos include the following:

- Enhanced security:
  - Kerberos ensures that only authenticated users and services can access data and resources.
  - Kerberos protects sensitive data by encrypting authentication exchanges.
- Mutual authentication:
  - Both clients (users) and servers (services) verify each other's identities.
- Centralized authentication management:
  - Kerberos integrates with existing identity systems, such as Active Directory, for user management.
  - Kerberos simplifies user provisioning and deprovisioning.

- Compliance:
  - Kerberos helps meet regulatory requirements for data security and access control.

Additional Considerations

Here are some other considerations:

- Complexity:
  - Implementing Kerberos adds complexity to cluster configuration and management.
  - Implementing Kerberos requires careful planning, especially when integrating with external KDCs or Active Directory.
- Performance:
  - Kerberos adds slight overhead due to authentication processes, but it is generally minimal compared to overall cluster performance.
- Credential management:
  - Secure handling of keytabs and credentials is essential.
  - Regularly update and rotate keys according to security best practices.

Other AWS Services Supporting Kerberos Authentication

Other services that support Kerberos include:

- Amazon RDS for Oracle and Microsoft SQL Server:
  - Supports Kerberos and Active Directory authentication.
  - Allows seamless integration with corporate authentication systems.
- Amazon EC2 instances:
  - Can be joined to a Microsoft Active Directory domain.
  - Applications running on EC2 can use Kerberos for authenticating users.

By implementing Kerberos-based authentication, you enhance the security of your AWS resources by ensuring that only authenticated users and services can access sensitive data and operations. For the purposes of the data engineering exam, you need to know that Kerberos secures both user access and inter-service communication within the EMR cluster. While it adds complexity, the benefits in terms of security and compliance often outweigh the additional effort, especially for organizations processing sensitive or regulated data.

Data Services Authentication Mechanisms

We've looked at the various authentication mechanisms available with AWS. Table 10.1 summarizes the list of different authentication mechanisms across different AWS services.

TABLE 10.1   Authentication mechanisms for AWS services

Service	Supported Authentication Mechanisms
Amazon RDS	**Database credentials (username/password):** Traditional authentication using database-specific usernames and passwords. **IAM database authentication:** Use IAM credentials to authenticate to RDS MySQL and PostgreSQL instances. **SSL/TLS encryption:** Secure connections between the client and the database instance. **Kerberos authentication:** For RDS Oracle databases, integrate with external Kerberos authentication.
AWS Database Migration Service (DMS)	**IAM roles and policies:** Grant DMS permissions to access AWS resources like S3 and KMS. **Database credentials:** Use source and target database usernames and passwords for migration tasks. **SSL/TLS encryption:** Secure connections to databases during migration.
AWS Glue	**IAM roles and policies:** Assign IAM roles to Glue jobs and crawlers for accessing AWS resources. **Database credentials:** When connecting to data stores like RDS, Redshift, or on-premises databases. **Kerberos authentication:** For secure authentication with data sources like Hive metastore or Hadoop clusters.
Amazon Kinesis Data Streams	**IAM roles and policies:** Control access to Kinesis streams via IAM. **Access keys:** For programmatic access using AWS CLI or SDKs. **Amazon Cognito:** Authenticate users in mobile or web applications to access streams securely.
Amazon Kinesis Data Firehose	**IAM roles and policies:** Grant Firehose delivery streams permissions to read from sources and write to destinations like S3, Redshift, or Elasticsearch/OpenSearch. **Access keys:** For programmatic configuration and management. **Amazon Cognito:** For authenticated access in applications.
Amazon Kinesis Data Analytics for Apache Flink	**IAM roles and policies:** Assign roles to analytics applications for accessing AWS resources like Kinesis Data Streams, S3, and DynamoDB. **Access keys:** For programmatic interactions using AWS SDKs. **VPC connectivity:** Secure access to data sources within a VPC.

Service	Supported Authentication Mechanisms
Amazon Managed Streaming for Apache Kafka (MSK)	**IAM roles and policies**: Manage cluster permissions and broker configurations via IAM. **TLS encryption**: Secure client-broker communications with TLS. **Mutual TLS authentication**: Both client and broker authenticate each other using certificates. **SASL/SCRAM authentication**: Use username and password for client authentication. **SASL/IAM authentication**: Leverage IAM for authentication using AWS access keys and secrets.
Amazon Redshift	**Database credentials (username/password)**: Standard authentication to Redshift clusters. **IAM authentication**: Use IAM credentials to generate temporary database credentials. **Federated authentication (SAML 2.0)**: Single sign-on using corporate directories like Active Directory. **SSL/TLS encryption**: Encrypt connections to clusters. **Amazon Cognito authentication**: For web and mobile apps connecting to Redshift.
Amazon EMR	**IAM roles and policies**: Assign service roles to EMR clusters and instance profiles for EC2 instances to access AWS resources. **Kerberos authentication**: Secure Hadoop ecosystem components within the cluster. **SSH key pairs**: For secure shell access to cluster nodes. **EMR Notebook authentication**: Use IAM or LDAP credentials for accessing EMR notebooks.
Amazon QuickSight	**QuickSight user credentials**: Manage users and groups within QuickSight itself. **Federated SSO (SAML 2.0)**: Single sign-on with corporate identity providers like Okta or ADFS. **Active Directory integration**: Authenticate using AWS Managed Microsoft AD or self-managed AD. **IAM roles and policies**: Access AWS data sources securely, such as S3 or Athena.
Amazon Open-Search Service	**IAM roles and policies**: Control access to OpenSearch domains via IAM policies. **Fine-grained access control**: Implement user- and role-based permissions within OpenSearch for indexes and documents. **Amazon Cognito authentication**: For Kibana/OpenSearch Dashboards access using user pools and identity pools. **SAML-based federation**: Single sign-on with enterprise IdPs for dashboard access. **HTTP basic authentication**: Using a username and password (not recommended without SSL/TLS).

TABLE 10.1   Authentication mechanisms for AWS services *(continued)*

Service	Supported Authentication Mechanisms
AWS Managed Workflows for Apache Airflow (MWAA)	**IAM roles and policies**: Assign execution roles to MWAA environments for accessing AWS resources. **IAM authentication**: Access Airflow UI and APIs using IAM credentials when enabled. **Airflow native authentication**: Use Airflow's built-in username and password authentication (if configured). **AWS SSO integration**: For federated access to the Airflow UI.
Amazon DocumentDB	**Database credentials (username/password)**: Authenticate to the DocumentDB cluster using MongoDB-compatible credentials. **TLS/SSL encryption**: Secure connections to the cluster. **IAM authentication**: As of 2023, DocumentDB supports IAM authentication, allowing users to connect using IAM credentials for enhanced security. **VPC security groups**: Control network-level access to the cluster.
Amazon DynamoDB	**IAM roles and policies**: Fine-grained access control via IAM for tables and items. **Access keys**: For programmatic access using AWS CLI or SDKs. **Amazon Cognito**: Authenticate users in mobile and web apps to access DynamoDB directly. **VPC endpoints**: Secure access within a VPC without traversing the public internet.
Amazon S3	**IAM roles and policies**: Control access to buckets and objects via IAM users, groups, and roles. **Access keys**: For CLI and SDK access to S3. **Pre-signed URLs**: Temporary access to objects without requiring AWS credentials. **Amazon Cognito**: For authenticated access in mobile and web applications. **Bucket policies**: Define resource-based permissions for buckets and objects. **VPC endpoints**: Secure access to S3 within a VPC.

Authentication in the Data Engineering Exam

From an exam perspective, you need to understand the following features of authentication and how they are relevant across different use cases and workloads:

- Temporary user permissions
- Federated user access

- Cross-account access
- AWS service access
- Multi-factor authentication

We've covered all of these topics in the "Introduction to Authentication" section. However, the topic is so comprehensive that it is hard for a single chapter to cover it. We recommend the following resources to help you build a solid understanding of the different services:

- Security Best Practices in IAM: `https://docs.aws.amazon.com/IAM/latest/UserGuide/best-practices.html`
- IAM Policy Types: How and When to Use Them: `https://aws.amazon.com/blogs/security/iam-policy-types-how-and-when-to-use-them`
- Security Pillar – AWS Well-Architected Framework: `https://docs.aws.amazon.com/wellarchitected/latest/security-pillar/welcome.html`

Next, let's have a close look at authorization, the second major topic for this chapter.

Introduction to Authorization

Authorization is a cornerstone of securing data and ensuring that only permitted individuals or services have access to sensitive information. It is essential to distinguish authorization from authentication, discussed earlier in this chapter, which is basically a process of verifying the identity of a user or service. While authentication answers the question *Who are you?*, authorization determines *What are you allowed to do?* Together, these processes form the foundation of a secure data architecture. A comprehensive understanding of AWS authorization mechanisms is crucial for building robust, compliant, and efficient data systems. Key components to master include identity policies, resource policies, IP-based policies, fine-grained access control, item-level authorization, and advanced services like AWS Lake Formation, Redshift database-level security, and tools such as Apache Ranger when applicable.

Let's look at each of these and discuss how you can define authorization across various AWS services and different workloads.

IAM Policies

In AWS, permissions are defined and enforced through IAM policies, which are structured as JSON (JavaScript Object Notation) documents. These policies contain a set of rules that specify what actions are allowed or denied on specific AWS resources. By using policies, you can precisely control access to AWS services, ensuring that each identity (whether a user, group, or role) has the appropriate level of access needed to perform their tasks.

An IAM policy typically includes several components, such as:

- **Actions:** These are the specific operations that can be performed on AWS resources, such as `redshift:createCluster` to create a Redshift cluster or `ec2:StartInstances` to start EC2 instances.

- **Resources:** Policies specify the resources on which actions can be performed. For example, you might restrict actions to a particular S3 bucket, EC2 instance, or DynamoDB table.

- **Effect:** This defines whether the specified actions are allowed (Allow) or denied (Deny).

- **Conditions:** Policies can also include conditions to further refine when the policy applies. For instance, you could allow access to a resource only from a specific IP address or during a certain time window.

IAM policies can be attached to individual IAM users, groups, or roles. When you attach a policy to a user, that user gains the permissions defined in the policy. Similarly, attaching a policy to a group means that all users in the group inherit the permissions defined by the policy. This helps simplify access management, as permissions can be centrally managed for multiple users.

There are three types of policies:

- **Identity policies:** These policies are attached to AWS Identity and Access Management (IAM) identities—users, groups, and roles. They define what actions an identity can perform on which resources. Understanding identity policies is fundamental because they are the primary means of granting permissions to entities within AWS. Figure 10.8 shows the different types of identity-based policies.

FIGURE 10.8 Types of identity policies

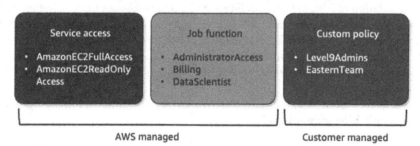

Figure 10.9 shows an example of an identity-based policy and some of the key sections of this policy.

- **Resource policies:** Attached directly to AWS resources like S3 buckets or DynamoDB tables, resource policies specify who has access to the resource and under what conditions. They are crucial for controlling access at the resource level and are essential for enabling cross-account access securely. Figure 10.10 shows an example of a resource-based policy.

FIGURE 10.9   Example of an identity policy

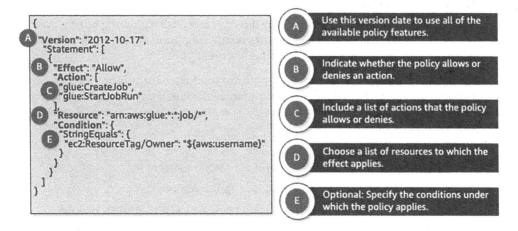

FIGURE 10.10   Example of a resourced-based policy

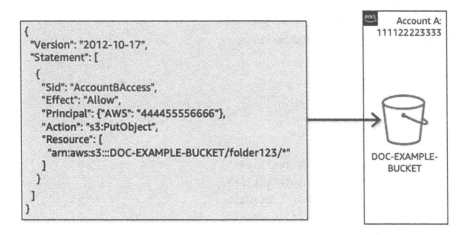

- **IP-based policies:** These policies restrict access based on the originating IP address of a request. They are vital for enhancing security by ensuring that only requests from trusted IP addresses or networks can access sensitive resources, thus mitigating unauthorized access risks.

There are two major ways to manage IAM policies:

- **Managed policies:** These are reusable policies that can be created by either AWS (AWS Managed Policies) or the customer (Customer Managed Policies). They can be attached to multiple identities, allowing you to reuse them across your environment. Example of managed policies include AmazonRedshiftFullAccess, AWSGlueServiceRole, and AmazonElasticMapReduceRole.

- **Inline policies:** These are policies that are directly embedded within a specific IAM user, group, or role. Inline policies are more tightly coupled with the identity they are attached to and aren't reusable across other identities.

By carefully designing and applying IAM policies, you follow the principle of least privilege, meaning users, groups, and roles are only granted the minimum permissions necessary to perform their tasks. This enhances security by preventing accidental or unauthorized access to AWS resources.

In summary, IAM policies allow you to:

- Precisely define and manage access control for AWS resources
- Ensure security through granular permissions and conditions
- Simplify permission management by attaching policies to users, groups, or roles

The following code is an example of a Redshift policy that allows users or roles to perform any of the following actions:

- Create, describe, modify, and delete Redshift clusters
- Access Redshift databases for querying data
- Describe cluster snapshots and backups

```
{
    "Version": "2012-10-17",
    "Statement": [
        {
            "Effect": "Allow",
            "Action": [
                "redshift:CreateCluster",
                "redshift:DeleteCluster",
                "redshift:DescribeClusters",
                "redshift:ModifyCluster",
                "redshift:RebootCluster"
            ],
            "Resource": "*"
        },
        {
            "Effect": "Allow",
            "Action": [
                "redshift:AuthorizeSnapshotAccess",
```

```
                "redshift:CopyClusterSnapshot",
                "redshift:CreateClusterSnapshot",
                "redshift:DeleteClusterSnapshot",
                "redshift:DescribeClusterSnapshots",
                "redshift:RestoreFromClusterSnapshot"
            ],
            "Resource": "*"
        },
        {
            "Effect": "Allow",
            "Action": [
                "redshift-data:ExecuteStatement",
                "redshift-data:DescribeStatement",
                "redshift-data:CancelStatement",
                "redshift-data:ListTables",
                "redshift-data:DescribeTable",
                "redshift-data:GetStatementResult"
            ],
            "Resource": "*"
        }
    ]
}
```

IAM Permissions Boundaries

In AWS, IAM (Identity and Access Management) permissions boundaries provide an additional layer of security by defining the *maximum* permissions that an IAM user or role can have, regardless of the permissions granted by their attached IAM policies. Permissions boundaries are essential for enforcing strict access controls, especially in environments where multiple administrators manage IAM policies, ensuring that no single policy can inadvertently or maliciously grant excessive permissions.

Permissions boundaries act as a boundary or ceiling for the permissions that an IAM entity (user or role) can possess. While IAM policies (both identity and resource policies) define the permissions granted to an entity, permissions boundaries limit these permissions to a predefined scope. This dual-layered approach ensures that even if an IAM policy attempts to grant broader access, the permissions boundary will restrict the actual permissions to the defined maximum.

Details of permissions boundaries are beyond the scope of this book. If you would like to learn more, please visit https://docs.aws.amazon.com/IAM/latest/UserGuide/access_policies_boundaries.html.

Permissions Boundaries vs. IAM Policies

While both permissions boundaries and IAM policies are essential for access control in AWS, they serve distinct purposes:

- Permissions boundaries:
  - Purpose: Define the maximum permissions an IAM entity can have, acting as a cap.
  - Attachment: Can be attached only to users and roles, not to groups.
  - Control: Limit the effective permissions granted by IAM policies, ensuring that even if a policy tries to grant broader access, the boundary restricts it.
- IAM policies:
  - Purpose: Define what actions an IAM entity can perform on specific resources.
  - Attachment: Can be attached to users, groups, or roles.
  - Flexibility: Directly grant permissions based on policy statements.

Figure 10.11 shows two policy categories: set maximum permissions and grant permissions.

FIGURE 10.11   IAM permissions boundaries

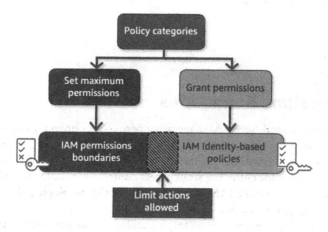

Data Engineering Sample Exam Scenario

Imagine an IAM role with an attached policy that allows full access to Amazon S3 (s3:*). If a permissions boundary is applied to this role that only allows s3:GetObject and s3:ListBucket, the role will be restricted to only these two actions, despite the broader permissions defined in its policy.

Exam Use Cases for Permissions Boundaries

During the AWS Certified Data Engineering – Associate exam, the following use cases may come up as exam scenarios, and they will be a good fit for permissions boundaries.

- **Delegated administration:** When delegating IAM management to different teams or administrators, permissions boundaries ensure that these teams cannot grant excessive permissions beyond what is defined.

- **Third-party applications:** When integrating third-party applications that require specific AWS permissions, permissions boundaries can restrict the permissions these applications can utilize, enhancing security.

- **Multi-tenancy environments:** In environments where multiple tenants or departments share the same AWS account, permissions boundaries can enforce strict access controls to prevent cross-tenant access.

- **Automated provisioning:** When using automation tools or scripts to create IAM roles and users, permissions boundaries ensure that the automated processes cannot inadvertently grant excessive permissions.

Access Control Lists

Access control lists (ACLs) provide a mechanism to manage access to specific resources by defining which AWS accounts or predefined groups are granted access and the level of access they receive. ACLs are particularly useful for setting permissions on resources such as Amazon S3 buckets and objects, enabling fine-grained control over who can read, write, or modify these resources. Understanding ACLs is crucial for ensuring that your data remains secure and is only accessible to authorized users.

While the details of ACLs are beyond the scope of this chapter, you may want to visit AWS ACL documentation to learn more about them.

Sample Exam Scenario

Imagine you have an Amazon S3 bucket that stores public data. You can use an ACL to grant read access to everyone by setting the bucket's ACL to include the `AllUsers` group with `READ` permissions. This configuration allows anyone to access the objects in the bucket without needing specific IAM policies.

Example: Granting Public Read Access to an S3 Bucket

Here is an example:

1. Navigate to the S3 Console (`https://us-east-2.signin.aws.amazon.com/oauth?client_id=arn%3Aaws%3Asignin%3A%3A%3Aconsole%2Fs3tb&code_challenge=Syl6i1G6wjGLlvRLBDWjHq-KycMnk2yD2dJNg2qu2uI&code_challenge_method=SHA-256&response_type=code&redirect_uri=https%3A%2F%2Fconsole.aws.amazon.com%2Fs3%2F%3FhashArgs%3D%2523%26isau`

thcode%3Dtrue%26oauthStart%3D1731879213674%26state%3DhashArgsFro
mTB_us-east-2_9e56ba58564ac170).

2. Click the bucket you want to modify.

3. Navigate to the Permissions tab.

4. Under Access Control List (ACL), click Edit.

5. In the Public Access section, check the box for Read Objects for the Everyone group.

6. Click Save changes to apply the ACL.

```
{
    "Owner": {
        "DisplayName": "owner-name",
        "ID": "owner-id"
    },
    "Grants": [
        {
            "Grantee": {
                "Type": "Group",
                "URI": "http://acs.amazonaws.com/groups/global/AllUsers"
            },
            "Permission": "READ"
        }
    ]
}
```

In this example:

- `Grantee`: Specifies the `AllUsers` group, which represents anyone on the Internet.

- `Permission`: Grants `READ` access, allowing public users to view objects within the bucket.

Sample Exam Use Cases for Access Control Lists

Here are some use cases to consider:

- Public read access for S3 buckets:
  - Description: When you want to make certain S3 buckets or objects publicly readable, ACLs can be used to grant read permissions to the `AllUsers` group.
  - Implementation: Set the ACL of the bucket or specific objects to include `AllUsers` with `READ` permissions.
- Cross-account access:
  - Description: When sharing specific resources like S3 buckets or objects with users from another AWS account, ACLs can specify permissions for those external accounts without needing to modify IAM policies.
  - Implementation: Add the external AWS account's canonical user ID to the ACL with the desired permissions (e.g., `READ`, `WRITE`).

- Resource-specific permissions:
  - Description: When you need to set different permissions for individual resources (e.g., different objects in an S3 bucket), ACLs provide a way to manage access at the resource level.
  - Implementation: Apply unique ACLs to each object within a bucket to control access independently.
- Legacy applications:
  - Description: For applications that rely on ACL-based access control, using ACLs ensures compatibility and proper access management without altering the application's permission model.
  - Implementation: Maintain ACLs as the primary access control method for these applications while managing other resources with IAM policies.

Access control lists (ACLs) are a vital tool in AWS for managing access to specific resources at a granular level. By specifying which AWS accounts or groups have access and defining the type of access they possess, ACLs enable precise control over your resources. Implementing ACLs alongside other access control mechanisms ensures that your Amazon S3 buckets and objects are securely accessible only to authorized users and applications, thereby maintaining the integrity and confidentiality of your data engineering workflows.

Role-Based Access Control

Role-based access control (RBAC) is a strategic method for managing permissions by assigning users to roles based on their job functions. RBAC streamlines access management by grouping permissions into roles that reflect organizational roles, such as administrators, developers, or data analysts. This approach ensures that users receive the appropriate level of access needed to perform their tasks, enhancing both security and operational efficiency within your AWS environment.

While we will touch upon RBAC at a high-level, please visit `https://docs.aws .amazon.com/IAM/latest/UserGuide/introduction.html`to learn more about RBAC.

Exam Use Cases for Role-Based Access Control

Imagine you have a team of data engineers responsible for managing Amazon Redshift clusters, running extract, transform, and load (ETL) jobs, and accessing data stored in Amazon S3. Instead of assigning individual permissions to each engineer, you can create specific roles that encapsulate the required permissions.

Example: Creating a Role for Data Engineers

Here is an example:

1. Define the role:
   - Role Name: `DataEngineerRole`
   - Permissions: Allow actions such as `redshift:*`, `s3:GetObject`, `s3:PutObject`, and `glue:*` to enable managing Redshift clusters, accessing S3 data, and running Glue ETL jobs.

2. Create the role in IAM:

    - Navigate to the IAM console.

    - Select Roles and click Create Role.

    - Choose the appropriate service that will use the role (e.g., EC2 if data engineers access Redshift from EC2 instances).

    - Attach the policy that defines the permissions for the `DataEngineerRole`.

3. Assign users to the role:

    - Add data engineers to the role by assigning them to assume the `DataEngineerRole`, either directly or through group membership.

By assigning the `DataEngineerRole` to users, all data engineers inherit the permissions defined in the role, ensuring consistent and secure access management across the team.

Here are some additional use cases to consider for the exam:

- Simplified permission management:
    - Description: Manage permissions by assigning users to roles instead of handling individual permissions.
    - Implementation: Create roles that correspond to different job functions and assign users to these roles based on their responsibilities.

- Scalability:
    - Description: Easily scale access control as the organization grows by adding new users to existing roles without modifying policies.
    - Implementation: When new team members join, simply assign them to the appropriate role to grant the necessary permissions.

- Enhanced security:
    - Description: Reduce the risk of over-permissioning by strictly defining roles based on the principle of least privilege.
    - Implementation: Define roles with only the permissions necessary for specific tasks, ensuring users do not have more access than required.

- Compliance and auditing:
    - Description: Facilitate compliance with regulatory requirements by maintaining clear and consistent access controls.
    - Implementation: Use roles to ensure that access permissions are consistently applied and easily auditable across the organization.

- Temporary access:
    - Description: Grant temporary access to resources by assigning roles for limited periods—useful for contractors or specific projects.
    - Implementation: Use IAM roles with time-bound permissions that automatically expire after the defined period.

RBAC offers a structured and efficient approach to managing permissions in AWS by aligning access controls with organizational roles. By grouping permissions into roles and assigning users to these roles based on their job functions, RBAC simplifies access management, enhances security, and supports scalability and compliance requirements. Implementing RBAC ensures that users have the appropriate level of access to perform their tasks while maintaining the integrity and security of your AWS environment. Please note that in most exam questions, whenever you have to choose between giving a user a permission to access a resource vs. setting up a role to do the same task, the role-setup is often the correct answer.

Attribute-Based Access Control

Attribute-based access control (ABAC) is a flexible and scalable method for managing permissions based on attributes associated with users, resources, and the environment. Unlike traditional role-based access control (RBAC), which relies on predefined roles, ABAC allows for fine-grained access management by evaluating policies against dynamic attributes. This approach enables organizations to implement more granular and context-aware access controls, simplifying permission management as the number of users and resources grows.

Exam Use Cases for Attribute-Based Access Control

Imagine you have an Amazon S3 data lake where data is categorized by department and sensitivity level. Using ABAC, you can create policies that grant access to S3 buckets and objects based on attributes such as the user's department and the data's sensitivity.

Example: Granting Department-Based Access to an S3 Bucket

Here is an example:

1. Define user attributes:

   - Assign attributes to IAM users, such as Department=Finance or Department=Marketing.

2. Tag S3 resources:

   - Tag your S3 buckets and objects with corresponding attributes—for example, Department=Finance and Sensitivity=Confidential.

3. Create an ABAC policy:

```
{
    "Version": "2012-10-17",
    "Statement": [
        {
            "Effect": "Allow",
            "Action": "s3:*",
            "Resource": [
                "arn:aws:s3:::data-lake/finance/*"
            ],
```

```
                "Condition": {
                    "StringEquals": {
                        "aws:PrincipalTag/Department": "Finance"
                    }
                }
        },
        {
            "Effect": "Allow",
            "Action": "s3:GetObject",
            "Resource": "arn:aws:s3:::data-lake/*",
            "Condition": {
                "StringEquals": {
                    "s3:ExistingObjectTag/Sensitivity": "Public"
                }
            }
        }
    ]
}
```

- **First statement:** Grants full S3 access to objects within the data-lake/finance/ prefix for users tagged with Department=Finance.

- **Second statement:** Allows all users to read objects tagged with Sensitivity=Public regardless of their department.

4. Attach the policy:

   - Attach this policy to IAM roles or users as needed, ensuring that access is dynamically granted based on the defined attributes.

Here are some additional use cases to consider for the exam:

- Dynamic access management:

  - Description: Automatically adjust permissions as user attributes or resource tags change without the need to update IAM policies manually.

  - Implementation: Use ABAC policies that reference user and resource attributes to grant or restrict access dynamically.

- Scalable permission management:

  - Description: Simplify access control in large organizations with numerous users and resources by reducing the need for extensive role definitions.

  - Implementation: Implement ABAC to manage permissions based on attributes like department, project, or data sensitivity, allowing for scalable and maintainable access control.

- Compliance and data governance:
  - Description: Enforce compliance requirements by ensuring that only authorized users can access sensitive data based on predefined attributes.
  - Implementation: Tag resources with compliance-related attributes and create ABAC policies that restrict access accordingly, ensuring adherence to regulations like GDPR or HIPAA.
- Environment-based access control:
  - Description: Control access based on the environment in which resources are accessed, such as restricting production data access to specific users.
  - Implementation: Use environment attributes (e.g., Environment=Production) in ABAC policies to grant or deny access based on the context of the request.
- Project-based access control:
  - Description: Grant team members access to resources based on the projects they are assigned to.
  - Implementation: Tag both users and resources with project identifiers and create ABAC policies that allow access when user and resource project tags match.

Attribute-based access control (ABAC) offers a powerful and adaptable approach to managing permissions in AWS by leveraging attributes associated with users, resources, and the environment. This helps organizations implement precise and dynamic access controls that can scale with their evolving needs. By defining policies that evaluate these attributes, ABAC simplifies permission management, enhances security, and supports compliance requirements.

AWS Resource Access Manager and IAM Access Analyzer

In AWS, Resource Access Manager (RAM) and IAM Access Analyzer are essential tools for managing and securing access to your AWS resources. AWS RAM facilitates the sharing of AWS resources across different accounts within your organization or with specific external accounts, enabling efficient resource utilization and collaboration. IAM Access Analyzer helps you identify and monitor the resources in your environment that are accessible to external entities, ensuring that your access configurations adhere to your security and compliance requirements. Together, these services provide a comprehensive approach to resource sharing and access auditing, enhancing both operational efficiency and security within your AWS infrastructure.

Exam Use Cases for AWS Resource Access Manager and IAM Access Analyzer

Consider an example where you have multiple AWS accounts within your organization, each designated for different departments, such as Finance, Marketing, and Development. As a business, you want to share an Amazon RDS database from the Finance account with the

Marketing and Development accounts without duplicating the database. Here's how AWS RAM and IAM Access Analyzer work together to achieve this:

1. Sharing with AWS RAM:

   ■ Step 1: In the Finance account, navigate to the AWS RAM console.

   ■ Step 2: Create a resource share and select the Amazon RDS database you want to share.

   ■ Step 3: Specify the AWS accounts (Marketing and Development) with which you want to share the database.

   ■ Step 4: Define the permissions, such as read-only or read-write access, for each shared account.

   ■ Step 5: Complete the resource share setup, enabling the Marketing and Development accounts to access the shared RDS database.

2. Analyzing access with IAM Access Analyzer:

   ■ Step 1: In the Finance account, navigate to the IAM Access Analyzer console.

   ■ Step 2: Create an analyzer to review the shared Amazon RDS database.

   ■ Step 3: The analyzer inspects the resource share configurations and identifies which external entities (Marketing and Development accounts) have access to the database.

   ■ Step 4: Review the findings to ensure that only authorized accounts have the intended level of access, and make adjustments if necessary.

This example demonstrates how AWS RAM enables seamless resource sharing across accounts, while IAM Access Analyzer provides visibility and assurance that the shared access aligns with your security policies.

Here are some additional use cases to consider for the exam:

■ Cross-account resource sharing:

   ■ Description: Share resources such as Amazon RDS databases, Amazon EC2 instances, or Amazon S3 buckets across multiple AWS accounts within your organization.

   ■ Implementation: Use AWS RAM to create resource shares and specify the target accounts and permissions.

■ Centralized resource management:

   ■ Description: Manage shared resources from a central account, reducing redundancy and optimizing resource utilization.

   ■ Implementation: Designate a central account to host shared resources and use AWS RAM to distribute access to other accounts as needed.

■ Enhanced security and compliance:

   ■ Description: Ensure that shared resources are not inadvertently exposed to unauthorized external entities.

   ■ Implementation: Utilize IAM Access Analyzer to continuously monitor and audit resource access, identifying and mitigating potential security risks.

- Collaboration with external partners:
  - Description: Share specific AWS resources with external partners or vendors securely without granting full account access.
  - Implementation: Use AWS RAM to share only the necessary resources and IAM Access Analyzer to verify and monitor the shared access.
- Automated access reviews:
  - Description: Regularly review and validate the access permissions of shared resources to maintain security standards.
  - Implementation: Schedule periodic analyses with IAM Access Analyzer to generate reports on resource access and take corrective actions if discrepancies are found.

AWS Resource Access Manager (RAM) and IAM Access Analyzer work in tandem to provide a comprehensive framework for resource sharing and access auditing in your AWS environment. AWS RAM simplifies the process of sharing resources across multiple accounts, promoting efficient collaboration and resource utilization. Concurrently, IAM Access Analyzer offers critical insights into who has access to your resources, enabling you to enforce security best practices and maintain compliance. By leveraging both services, organizations can achieve a balanced approach to resource management and security, ensuring that their AWS infrastructure remains both agile and secure.

AWS Lake Formation

AWS Lake Formation simplifies the process of building, managing, securing, and sharing data lakes by introducing database-style fine-grained permissions across the entire data lake stack. By providing centralized governance and security management, AWS Lake Formation makes it easier for organizations to ensure that data is secure, accessible, and compliant across various analytics and machine learning tools.

Key Features of AWS Lake Formation

Here are some of the key features of AWS Lake Formation:

- Fine-grained permissions:
  - AWS Lake Formation introduces database-like, fine-grained permissions that manage access to both Amazon S3 buckets and their associated objects. These permissions extend across the entire data lake stack, including a wide variety of analytics and machine learning engines, such as Amazon Athena, Amazon EMR, and Amazon SageMaker.
  - AWS Lake Formation allows for row-level and column-level security, ensuring users can only access the portions of the data they are authorized to, making governance and compliance easier to enforce.
- Lake Formation tag-based access control (LF-TBAC):
  - To simplify the scaling of permission management across an organization, AWS Lake Formation offers Lake Formation tag-based access control (LF-TBAC). With LF-TBAC, administrators can assign permissions based on tags (e.g., data sensitivity,

department), which can be applied across users, groups, and roles. This approach allows for scalable and flexible permission management as data grows and becomes more diverse.

- Centralized data catalog:
  - AWS Lake Formation integrates deeply with AWS Glue Data Catalog, a centralized metadata store that makes data discoverable and easily accessible across the organization. Users can browse the data catalog, quickly find the right datasets, and access them securely using the permissions enforced by AWS Lake Formation.
- Audit and monitoring:
  - Because all data access—whether to metadata or S3 objects—happens through AWS Lake Formation, it becomes easier to audit and monitor data access. This capability ensures that data lake usage can be monitored centrally to verify compliance with organizational policies and regulatory standards.
- Simplified data sharing:
  - AWS Lake Formation supports secure and efficient cross-account sharing of data without requiring data duplication. Organizations can use AWS Lake Formation to implement a data mesh architecture, enabling teams across different accounts or regions to collaborate on shared datasets, while maintaining strict security and compliance.
  - Integration with AWS Data Exchange allows customers to purchase and subscribe to third-party datasets, further enhancing the ability to securely share and consume external data.
- Transactional data lakes (AWS managed tables):
  - AWS Lake Formation supports the creation and management of transactional data lakes using open table formats like Apache Iceberg, Hudi, and Delta. This capability helps organizations maintain consistency and performance while performing real-time updates and modifications to data in the lake.

Sample Exam Use Case

Suppose your organization is operating multiple AWS accounts for different departments, such as Finance, Marketing, and Data Science. Using AWS Lake Formation, you can:

1. Set up and secure the data lake:
   - Import datasets from various sources, including transactional data, and store them in Amazon S3.
   - Use the Glue Data Catalog to organize these datasets and assign fine-grained permissions using LF-TBAC, ensuring that only authorized users from each department have access to the relevant data.

2. Define permissions:
   - Grant the Finance team full access to specific databases (e.g., `FinanceDB`) while restricting Marketing and Data Science teams to read-only access on relevant datasets.
3. Cross-account sharing:
   - Share datasets across accounts for collaboration, ensuring secure access without moving or duplicating data.
4. Audit access:
   - Use AWS Lake Formation's built-in auditing capabilities to track who accesses the data and when, ensuring that all actions are compliant with internal and external regulations.

AWS Lake Formation simplifies the creation and management of secure data lakes with centralized governance and fine-grained access control. By offering database-style permissions, tag-based access control, seamless integration with analytics and ML tools, and centralized auditing, AWS Lake Formation helps organizations unlock the full potential of their data while ensuring strict security and compliance.

Its powerful features, such as cross-account sharing, support for transactional data lakes, and integration with external services like AWS Data Exchange, make it an essential tool for any organization looking to implement modern, scalable, and secure data lake architectures.

Database-Level Authorization in AWS Services (Redshift, RDS, and Analytic Services)

In AWS, database-level security is critical for protecting sensitive data, ensuring that only authorized users can access and perform actions on specific data sets. AWS services like Amazon Redshift, Amazon RDS, and various other analytics services offer built-in security mechanisms that enable fine-grained authorization and access control. These services provide comprehensive tools for managing data access, enforcing compliance, and enhancing security, all integrated within the database and analytic platforms themselves.

Amazon Redshift Database-Level Security

Amazon Redshift offers robust in-service authorization capabilities that allow administrators to control access at the database, schema, table, and even column level. This flexibility enables organizations to apply granular security policies based on the role or privilege of each user or group.

- **Role-based access control (RBAC):** Redshift allows you to define roles and grant specific permissions for database operations, ensuring that only authorized users can read, write, or modify data.

- **Column-level security:** With Redshift, you can apply access control at the column level, restricting sensitive data such as personally identifiable information (PII) to authorized personnel only.

- **Data sharing with security:** Redshift also supports data sharing, enabling users to securely share data between different Redshift clusters, even across AWS accounts, without moving or duplicating data. Fine-grained controls ensure that only approved users can access the shared data.

Amazon RDS Database-Level Security

Amazon RDS (Relational Database Service) provides robust security mechanisms that ensure fine-grained access control to your databases, supporting multiple database engines, including MySQL, PostgreSQL, SQL Server, MariaDB, and Oracle.

- **IAM database authentication:** Amazon RDS supports IAM-based authentication, allowing users to connect to RDS instances using their AWS credentials without needing to manage database-specific passwords. This simplifies access management and enhances security by centralizing user identity.

- **Database-level privileges:** Amazon RDS lets you define database-level privileges by managing user roles and permissions directly within the database engine, enabling granular control over who can perform actions like SELECT, INSERT, UPDATE, and DELETE on different databases, tables, or views.

- **Network isolation:** Through Amazon VPC integration, Amazon RDS provides network-level security by allowing you to place your databases inside isolated VPCs, ensuring access is only allowed from trusted networks or IP addresses.

Amazon Athena and Amazon EMR Security

AWS analytics services such as Amazon Athena and Amazon EMR offer built-in security mechanisms for managing access to data and ensuring compliance with organizational security policies.

- Amazon Athena:
  - Fine-grained access control: Athena integrates with AWS Lake Formation, allowing you to enforce fine-grained permissions at the table, row, and column levels. This integration ensures that users can only query the data they are authorized to access, based on the policies defined in Lake Formation.
  - S3-level permissions: Since Athena queries data stored in S3, you can control access by applying S3 bucket policies and IAM roles, ensuring only approved users and applications can run queries on specific datasets.
- Amazon EMR (Elastic MapReduce):
  - Cluster-level authorization: EMR supports Kerberos Authentication and integration with Apache Ranger for centralized security policy management. Using Apache

Ranger, you can apply fine-grained security policies to manage access control across different data processing tools like Apache Hive, HBase, and Spark.

- IAM role-based access: You can define IAM roles for your EMR clusters to control what actions users can perform, ensuring that sensitive operations like modifying or terminating clusters are restricted to authorized personnel.

Amazon OpenSearch Service

Amazon OpenSearch Service (formerly Amazon Elasticsearch Service) offers several built-in security features for managing data access within search and analytics workloads.

- **Fine-grained access control:** OpenSearch Service provides fine-grained access control, enabling you to define permissions at the index, document, and field levels. You can control who can search, view, and modify specific pieces of data, ensuring secure access.
- **OpenSearch Dashboards authorization:** Integration with OpenSearch Dashboards allows you to manage user access to dashboards and reports. You can restrict users to specific visualizations and data based on their roles and access levels.

AWS Secrets Manager

AWS Secrets Manager is a fully managed service designed to help securely manage, rotate, and retrieve secrets such as database credentials, API keys, tokens, and other sensitive information used in applications. Secrets Manager enables organizations to enhance their security posture by eliminating hard-coded secrets in application code, configuration files, or environments, thus preventing unauthorized access to sensitive data and services.

Data engineers and administrators can securely store and retrieve secrets for various AWS services and third-party applications using AWS Secrets Manager. The service supports automatic rotation of secrets, helping maintain security compliance and reducing the risks associated with long-term static credentials.

Key Features and Benefits of AWS Secrets Manager

Here are some of the key features and benefits:

- Secret storage and management:
  - AWS Secrets Manager allows you to store credentials, passwords, API keys, and other sensitive data in encrypted form. The encryption is managed using AWS Key Management Service (KMS), which ensures that the secrets are securely stored and accessible only to authorized users or services.
  - Secrets Manager automatically handles secret versioning, making it easy to track and manage multiple versions of a secret.
- Automatic secret rotation:
  - A key feature of AWS Secrets Manager is its ability to automatically rotate secrets at scheduled intervals without downtime for your applications. The service integrates

seamlessly with services like Amazon RDS, Redshift, and Document-DB to rotate database credentials. You can also set up custom Lambda functions to rotate secrets for non-native services, like third-party APIs or in-house applications.

- Automatic rotation ensures that secrets are periodically refreshed, reducing the risk of unauthorized access due to compromised or outdated credentials.

- Fine-grained access control with IAM:

  - Access to secrets is tightly controlled through AWS Identity and Access Management (IAM) policies. By defining granular policies, you can specify which IAM users, roles, or services are authorized to retrieve, modify, or rotate secrets.

  - For example, you can allow an application running on an Amazon EC2 instance or Lambda function to access specific secrets via IAM roles, ensuring that secrets are not exposed to unauthorized entities.

- Auditing and compliance:

  - AWS Secrets Manager integrates with AWS CloudTrail to provide a comprehensive audit trail of all actions taken on your secrets. This includes retrieving, modifying, rotating, or deleting secrets. CloudTrail logs help organizations meet regulatory compliance requirements by providing visibility into who accessed or modified sensitive information.

  - Compliance frameworks such as GDPR, HIPAA, and PCI DSS often require strict control and monitoring of sensitive data access. AWS Secrets Manager helps meet these requirements by securing sensitive credentials and providing the necessary audit capabilities.

- Seamless integration with AWS services:

  - Secrets Manager integrates natively with several AWS services, including Amazon RDS, Amazon Redshift, AWS Lambda, and more. This allows applications to securely retrieve secrets without exposing them to unauthorized users or systems.

  - Secrets can be fetched dynamically using API calls, which eliminates the need to hard-code sensitive data in applications. For example, an application can retrieve database credentials from Secrets Manager just before connecting to the database, thereby reducing the risk of compromised secrets.

When to Use AWS Secrets Manager

Imagine your organization is running several microservices in a serverless architecture that require access to multiple databases and third-party APIs. Instead of hard-coding API keys or database credentials into your Lambda functions or EC2 instances, you can store these secrets securely in AWS Secrets Manager.

For example, the following setup can be employed to ensure secure authorization:

1. Store API keys and database credentials:

   - Store secrets such as database credentials (e.g., for Amazon RDS or Redshift) and third-party API keys in Secrets Manager.

2. Configure IAM Policies for access:

   ▪ Create IAM roles for each Lambda function or EC2 instance that defines the permissions to retrieve specific secrets. For instance, the `OrderService` Lambda function will be granted access to retrieve only the database credentials necessary to interact with the orders database.

3. Enable automatic secret rotation:

   ▪ Set up automatic secret rotation for the database credentials, ensuring that the credentials are changed periodically and automatically updated in your applications without requiring downtime or manual intervention.

Example: Using AWS Secrets Manager for Authorization in an Application

Here is an example:

1. **Store secrets:** Store the credentials for your database (e.g., Amazon RDS) in AWS Secrets Manager, including the database username and password.

2. **Configure IAM policies:** Create an IAM policy that grants the application's EC2 instance or Lambda function permission to retrieve the secret:

```
{
  "Version": "2012-10-17",
  "Statement": [
    {
      "Effect": "Allow",
      "Action": [
        "secretsmanager:GetSecretValue"
      ],
      "Resource": "arn:aws:secretsmanager:region:account-id:secret:secret-name"
    }
  ]
}
```

3. **Retrieve secrets dynamically:** Use the AWS SDK or CLI to retrieve the secret from Secrets Manager within your application code:

```
import boto3
from botocore.exceptions import NoCredentialsError, PartialCredentialsError

def get_secret():
    client = boto3.client('secretsmanager')
    secret_name = "my-database-secret"

    try:
        response = client.get_secret_value(SecretId=secret_name)
```

```
        secret = response['SecretString']
        return secret
    except NoCredentialsError as e:
        print("No credentials error: ", e)
    except PartialCredentialsError as e:
        print("Partial credentials error: ", e)
```

Exam Use Cases for AWS Secrets Manager

Here are some use cases to consider:

- Centralized secret management:
    - Description: Manage all secrets (database credentials, API keys, OAuth tokens, etc.) in a centralized location.
    - Implementation: Use Secrets Manager to store and rotate credentials for various AWS services (e.g., Amazon RDS, Redshift) and third-party APIs. Applications can retrieve these secrets securely through API calls.

- Rotating database credentials:
    - Description: Automatically rotate database credentials without requiring application downtime or manual intervention.
    - Implementation: Enable automatic secret rotation for RDS or Redshift databases, ensuring credentials are changed regularly and updated securely in your applications.

- Managing multi-region secrets:
    - Description: Ensure your secrets are replicated across multiple regions for high availability.
    - Implementation: Use Secrets Manager's multi-region secret replication to store copies of your secrets in multiple AWS regions, ensuring disaster recovery capabilities.

- Dynamic authorization with IAM:
    - Description: Enhance security by granting dynamic access to secrets based on IAM roles.
    - Implementation: Use IAM policies to control access to specific secrets for different applications or services, ensuring only authorized entities can retrieve them.

- Secure microservices communication:
    - Description: Protect sensitive API keys and tokens used in microservice architectures.
    - Implementation: Store API keys and tokens in Secrets Manager, allowing services to retrieve them securely at runtime instead of hard-coding them in the application.

AWS Secrets Manager is quite a critical service for securing and managing sensitive information like credentials, API keys, and other secrets. Its integration with IAM provides fine-grained access control, ensuring that only authorized users and services can retrieve secrets. Automatic secret rotation enhances security by ensuring that secrets are regularly updated without manual intervention. By adopting AWS Secrets Manager in your architecture, you can reduce security risks, improve compliance, and maintain robust authorization strategies across your AWS environment. Secrets Manager works seamlessly with other AWS services, making it an essential tool for securing sensitive data in modern cloud-based applications. During the example, Secrets Manager may appear as an option for securing and managing database credentials vs. storing them in your *git repositories.* Having the secrets separated from your code is a good practice.

Apache Ranger in Amazon EMR

Apache Ranger is a robust open-source framework integrated with Amazon EMR (Elastic MapReduce) that provides centralized security administration and fine-grained access control for big data environments. Apache Ranger enables data engineers to define, manage, and enforce security policies consistently across various data processing tools such as Apache Hive, Apache HBase, Apache Spark, and more within EMR clusters. By leveraging Ranger, organizations can ensure that sensitive data is protected, access is appropriately restricted, and compliance requirements are met, all while simplifying permission management in complex data engineering workflows.

When to Use Ranger

Consider a scenario where your organization operates multiple EMR clusters handling diverse datasets, including sensitive financial records and public marketing data. Using Apache Ranger, you can create and enforce policies that grant the Finance team full access to the FinanceDB database while restricting the Marketing team to read-only access to the MarketingAnalytics database. This ensures that each team can perform their tasks without accessing data beyond their authorization, thereby maintaining data integrity and security.

Example: Defining a Ranger Policy for EMR

Here is an example:

1. Install and configure Apache Ranger on EMR:
   - Launch an EMR cluster with Apache Ranger enabled.
   - Integrate Ranger with your authentication system (e.g., LDAP, Active Directory) to manage user identities.

2. Create security policies:
   - Finance Team Policy:
     - Database: FinanceDB
     - Permissions: SELECT, INSERT, UPDATE, DELETE
     - Groups: FinanceGroup

- Marketing Team Policy:
    - Database: MarketingAnalytics
    - Permissions: SELECT
    - Groups: MarketingGroup

3. Apply policies:

- Assign the defined policies to the respective user groups through the Ranger Admin Console.
- Apache Ranger enforces these policies across all connected data processing tools on the EMR cluster.

This setup ensures that Finance team members can fully manage financial data, while Marketing team members can only view marketing analytics, preventing unauthorized data manipulation.

Exam Use Cases for Apache Ranger in Amazon EMR

Here are some use cases to consider:

- Centralized policy management:
    - Description: Manage access policies for multiple data processing tools from a single interface.
    - Implementation: Use Ranger's admin console to create and update policies that apply uniformly across Hive, HBase, Spark, and other EMR-integrated services.
- Fine-grained access control:
    - Description: Define detailed permissions at the database, table, and column levels.
    - Implementation: Specify which users or groups can perform specific actions (e.g., SELECT, INSERT) on particular data assets, ensuring precise control over data access.
- Auditing and compliance:
    - Description: Track and log data access for auditing and regulatory compliance.
    - Implementation: Utilize Ranger's auditing capabilities to monitor who accessed what data and when, helping meet compliance standards like GDPR or HIPAA.
- Dynamic authorization:
    - Description: Adjust access permissions in real-time based on organizational changes.
    - Implementation: Update Ranger policies as team structures evolve or as new data sensitivity requirements emerge, without needing to restart EMR clusters.
- Integration with IAM:
    - Description: Enhance security by combining AWS IAM roles with Ranger policies.
    - Implementation: Map IAM roles to Ranger policies to provide seamless and secure access control across AWS services and EMR clusters, ensuring that IAM-defined identities adhere to Ranger-enforced data access rules.

Apache Ranger in Amazon EMR offers a comprehensive solution for managing and securing access to big data resources. By providing centralized security administration and fine-grained access control, Ranger ensures that only authorized users can access specific data and perform permitted actions within your EMR clusters. This not only enhances data security and compliance but also simplifies permission management across complex data engineering environments. Implementing Apache Ranger alongside other AWS security tools enables organizations to maintain robust authorization strategies, safeguarding their data assets while supporting efficient and secure data processing workflows.

Understanding these components is critical for implementing effective authorization strategies in AWS data engineering. They collectively ensure that data is accessed securely, compliantly, and efficiently, safeguarding sensitive information while enabling legitimate data processing and analytical activities.

Authorization Methods Summary

Table 10.2 provides a summary of the various authorization methods covered as part of the exam.

TABLE 10.2   Summary of authorization methods covered in the exam

AWS Service	Authorization Mechanisms
AWS DMS (Database Migration Service)	**IAM roles and policies**: Service role for DMS to access AWS resources **Database authentication**: Username/password, SSL/TLS for source and target databases **AWS KMS**: For encryption keys management **Network configurations**: VPC, security groups for controlling network access
Amazon S3	**IAM roles and policies**: Control access to buckets and objects **Bucket policies**: Resource-based policies attached to buckets **Access control lists (ACLs)**: Object and bucket-level permissions **Pre-signed URLs**: Temporary access with embedded credentials **AWS KMS**: Encryption keys **VPC endpoints**: Private access within a VPC
Amazon Redshift	**IAM roles and policies**: Access to cluster operations and data loading **Database authentication**: Username/password for database users **IAM authentication**: Use IAM credentials for authentication **AWS KMS**: Encryption at rest **SSL/TLS**: Encryption in transit **Security groups**: Network access control

TABLE 10.2   Summary of authorization methods covered in the exam *(continued)*

AWS Service	Authorization Mechanisms
AWS Glue	**IAM roles and policies**: Cluster operations and EC2 instance profiles **Kerberos authentication**: Secure Hadoop clusters **Security groups**: Network traffic control **SSH key pairs**: Access to EC2 instances **AWS KMS**: Encryption at rest **SSL/TLS**: Encryption in transit
Amazon Athena	**IAM roles and policies**: Access to Athena APIs and S3 data **S3 bucket policies**: Control access to data **AWS KMS**: Encrypt query results **SSL/TLS**: Encryption in transit
Amazon Open-Search Service	**IAM roles and policies**: Access control to clusters **Resource-based policies**: Attached to domains **Fine-grained access control**: User-based permissions **Amazon Cognito Authentication**: For dashboard access **AWS KMS**: Encryption at rest **VPC access**: Deploy within a VPC **SSL/TLS**: Encryption in transit
Amazon RDS	**Database authentication**: Username/password for users **IAM database authentication**: For MySQL and PostgreSQL **IAM roles and policies**: Control API actions **AWS KMS**: Encryption at rest **Security groups**: Network access control **SSL/TLS**: Encryption in transit
Amazon QuickSight	**IAM roles and policies**: Control API actions **SASL/SCRAM authentication**: Secure client access **TLS encryption**: Encryption in transit **AWS KMS**: Encryption at rest **Security groups**: Network access control
Amazon Kinesis Family	**IAM roles and policies**: Access to Kinesis APIs **AWS KMS**: Encryption at rest **SSL/TLS**: Encryption in transit **VPC endpoints**: Private access within a VPC

AWS Service	Authorization Mechanisms
Amazon Managed Workflows for Apache Airflow (MWAA)	**IAM roles and policies**: Access control to MWAA APIs **Airflow UI authentication**: Secure web interface **AWS KMS**: Encryption at rest **VPC access**: Deploy within a VPC **Security groups**: Network access control

Summary

This chapter provided a comprehensive overview of authentication and authorization methods in AWS, essential for verifying identities and controlling access to resources. It covered authentication mechanisms like IAM users, groups, roles, access keys, MFA, STS, role assumption, federation with external identity providers, Amazon Cognito, and Kerberos-based authentication. On the authorization front, we discussed IAM policies, permissions boundaries, ACLs, RBAC, ABAC, AWS Resource Access Manager, IAM Access Analyzer, AWS Lake Formation, and database-level security in services like Amazon Redshift and RDS, including the use of Apache Ranger in Amazon EMR for fine-grained access control.

Understanding these mechanisms is crucial for building secure and efficient data systems in AWS and for passing the AWS Certified Data Engineering exam. These topics, however, cover one element of the security, and we still need to cover data encryption, logging, data privacy, and overall governance. The next chapter will dive deeper into security elements, focusing on encryption and logging to further enhance data protection and compliance.

Exam Essentials

Understand the various security and access management concepts within AWS. This includes the ability to create and update VPC security groups, ensuring proper management of inbound and outbound traffic rules for resources within your VPC.

Be proficient in creating and updating IAM groups, roles, and service endpoints to manage access control effectively. This includes setting up IAM roles for services such as AWS Lambda, Amazon API Gateway, AWS CLI, and CloudFormation. Furthermore, applying IAM policies to roles, service endpoints, and resources such as S3 Access Points and AWS PrivateLink is necessary to fine-tune access control and ensure that resources are protected from unauthorized access.

Be able to create and rotate credentials for password management.   Particularly, know how to use tools like AWS Secrets Manager, which are essential for maintaining secure operations.

Know how to work with the available authentication methods.   These include password-based, certificate-based, and role-based authentication.

Have a solid understanding of role-based access control and common access patterns, and know how to safeguard data from unauthorized access across various AWS services.   This involves creating custom IAM policies when managed policies don't meet your specific requirements, storing sensitive credentials such as application and database passwords securely using tools like AWS Secrets Manager and AWS Systems Manager Parameter Store, and granting proper access and authority to database users, groups, and roles in services like Amazon Redshift.

Understand the range of methods that are essential for authorization.   These include role-based, policy-based, tag-based, and attribute-based authorization.

Understand the principle of least privilege.   The principle of least privilege ensures that users and services only have the minimum permissions required for their tasks.

Know how to manage permissions through a range of services to ensure data is securely accessed and controlled within their environments.   These include AWS Lake Formation for data services such as Amazon Redshift, Amazon EMR, Amazon Athena, and Amazon S3.

Review Questions

1. During a routine security assessment, a Cloud Data Engineering Team finds that their AWS environment, which includes services like Amazon S3, RDS, Redshift, and DynamoDB, might be susceptible to unauthorized data access. They need to devise a strategy that not only secures the data but also adheres to their organization's strict data governance and compliance requirements. The team needs to ensure that only specific personnel and services have access to sensitive data, and they must track who accessed the data and when. Which combination of AWS features and best practices should the team implement to meet these requirements effectively?

   A. Use AWS Identity and Access Management (IAM) to restrict access, enable server-side encryption (SSE) with AWS KMS for data at rest, and utilize AWS CloudTrail for auditing data access.

   B. Implement a virtual private cloud (VPC) to isolate resources, apply resource-based IAM policies, and enable Amazon Macie for automatic data classification and anomaly detection.

   C. Apply AWS Lambda-based triggers to monitor and log all data access attempts, use Amazon Inspector for security assessments, and enable SSE with Amazon S3-managed keys (SSE-S3).

   D. Set up a dedicated security account within AWS Organizations to manage permissions, encrypt data using client-side encryption before storing in AWS, and utilize AWS Config for continuous monitoring and change management.

2. A company's security team mandates that their Amazon RDS databases should only accept connections from specific, known IP addresses to ensure security. As a data engineer, you are tasked with implementing this requirement for an RDS instance that will be accessed by multiple clients located in different geographical locations, each with a fixed set of IP addresses. Which of the following would be the most effective and secure way to comply with this security requirement?

   A. Modify the inbound rules of the RDS instance's security group to allow traffic from the known IP addresses and deny all other traffic.

   B. Implement a network access control list (ACL) with rules to allow the known IP addresses and deny all others, applying these to the subnet associated with the RDS instance.

   C. Utilize AWS Identity and Access Management (IAM) policies to restrict database access to the specific IP addresses.

   D. Configure AWS WAF with a set of rules to allow the specific IP addresses, and associate these rules with the RDS instance.

3. A Cloud Data Engineering Consultant has been tasked with organizing access control for a team of analysts using an Amazon Redshift data warehouse. The team requires varying levels of access to sensitive financial data for reporting and analysis. The consultant needs to define a strategy that provides the necessary access for the analysts to perform their duties while ensuring that principles of least privilege and data governance are upheld. Which of the following actions should the consultant take to appropriately manage user access and permissions within the Amazon Redshift database? (Choose two.)

   A. Grant superuser privileges to all analysts to ensure they have the ability to query all necessary tables within the Redshift cluster, and then audit queries periodically for compliance.

   B. Implement row-level security within Redshift tables to control access to rows of data based on user roles, ensuring analysts only see data relevant to their analysis.

   C. Set up database groups within Redshift and assign users to groups based on their access requirements, and then grant group-specific permissions to the relevant schemas and tables.

   D. Enable Amazon Redshift Spectrum to manage external tables and use IAM policies to grant access to these tables.

   E. Create individual IAM users for each analyst with attached policies that define the level of access to Redshift resources, and use those IAM users for database authentication.

4. A data engineering team wants to implement a secure authentication mechanism for their AWS environment that supports single sign-on and reduces the need for multiple credentials. Which AWS service would be most appropriate for achieving this goal?

   A. AWS IAM Users

   B. Amazon Cognito

   C. AWS Security Token Service (STS)

   D. AWS Key Management Service (KMS)

5. A company wants to grant temporary access to AWS resources for a third-party data analytics vendor. What would be the most secure method to provide this access?

   A. Share the root AWS account credentials.

   B. Create permanent IAM users for the vendor.

   C. Use IAM roles with time-limited permissions.

   D. Disable all security groups for the duration of their work.

6. A data engineering team is setting up an AWS Glue ETL job that needs to access data from multiple sources, including an Amazon RDS database and an Amazon S3 bucket. What is the most secure method to provide the necessary authentication and authorization for the Glue job?

   A. Store database credentials directly in the Glue job script.

   B. Create an IAM role with specific permissions for the Glue job.

   C. Use shared access keys for all team members.

   D. Disable security settings to ensure job compatibility.

7. A data engineering team is deploying a sensitive financial data processing cluster using Amazon EMR running Apache Hadoop. Which authentication mechanism would provide the most robust security for protecting cluster resources and data access?

    A. Use default EMR security group settings.

    B. Implement Kerberos authentication for the Hadoop ecosystem.

    C. Share a single administrator account for all cluster users.

    D. Disable authentication to improve job performance.

8. A data engineering team needs to implement fine-grained access control for a multi-team Amazon EMR cluster running various Hadoop ecosystem tools like Hive and Spark. What would be the most effective approach to manage authorization and ensure each team can only access their designated data resources?

    A. Use default IAM roles for the entire EMR cluster.

    B. Implement Apache Ranger for centralized policy management.

    C. Manually configure individual file permissions for each team.

    D. Disable all security controls to simplify cluster management.

9. A financial services company wants to implement a secure authentication mechanism for their Amazon Redshift data warehouse that integrates with their existing corporate identity management. Which authentication method would provide the most comprehensive and secure approach?

    A. Use standard database username and password authentication.

    B. Implement IAM database authentication.

    C. Share a single admin account across the data team.

    D. Disable authentication to improve query performance.

10. A data engineering team wants to implement a secure authentication mechanism for their Amazon OpenSearch Service domain that supports single sign-on, granular access control, and the ability to manage user permissions. Which authentication method would provide the most comprehensive solution?

    A. Use standard HTTP basic authentication.

    B. Configure SAML authentication with fine-grained access control.

    C. Use only IAM roles for authentication.

    D. Disable authentication to improve performance.

11. A data engineering team needs to implement granular access control for their OpenSearch cluster, ensuring that different teams have varying levels of access to indices and data. They want to implement a solution that allows:

    - Restricting access to specific indices

    - Controlling document-level visibility

    - Limiting field-level access

    - Implementing role-based permissions

Which approach would provide the most comprehensive fine-grained access control?

A. Use standard IAM policies to manage access.

B. Implement fine-grained access control with role mapping and custom roles.

C. Rely on network-level security groups.

D. Disable security features to improve cluster performance.

Chapter

11

Data Encryption and Masking

**THE AWS CERTIFIED DATA ENGINEER -
ASSOCIATE EXAM OBJECTIVES COVERED
IN THIS CHAPTER MAY INCLUDE, BUT ARE
NOT LIMITED TO, THE FOLLOWING:**

✓ **Domain 4: Data Security and Governance**

 ▪ 4.3: Ensure data encryption and masking

Introduction

This chapter focuses on two essential topics for building secure data systems on AWS: data encryption and data masking. At AWS, security is considered "job zero," meaning it is even more important than any other priority. Encryption and masking are vital aspects of data security. In this chapter, we will discuss what encryption and masking are, why they are necessary, and how they are implemented on AWS.

This chapter covers security within the data engineering lifecycle, as shown in Figure 11.1.

FIGURE 11.1 The data engineering lifecycle

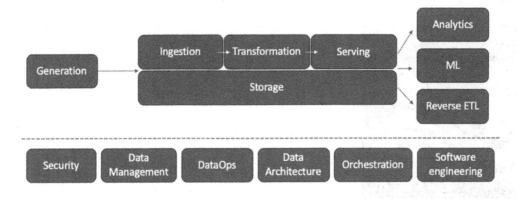

What Is Encryption and Why Is It Needed?

In basic terms, encryption is a process that transforms data into an unreadable format, providing an additional layer of security on top of authentication controls. This ensures that even if a malicious actor gains access to the data, whether stored on a disk or transmitted over a network, the data has no meaning or value. As a simple example of encryption, an email address like `tim.jones@somewhere.com` could be converted into an indecipherable string, such as `c0ee91b4c4203030`.

Encryption uses algorithms and keys to generate a scrambled version of data, known as *ciphertext*. The only way to revert this ciphertext back to its original readable form is by using the corresponding decryption key. The key acts as a safeguard, ensuring that only users authorized to access it can access the raw data. It works like a key in the physical world by locking (encrypting) and unlocking (decrypting) data.

An encryption key is a string of characters an encryption algorithm uses to transform data into a scrambled format and back again. With robust encryption algorithms, breaking the encryption without the key is virtually impossible with any standard computing power. The industry standard for encryption—and the method used to encrypt data in AWS—is the Advanced Encryption Standard (AES) with 256-bit keys (AES-256). AES-256 is currently regarded as the most secure encryption algorithm available and is considered virtually unbreakable. It would take millions of years to crack using conventionally available computing power.

Encryption Concepts

The following are essential encryption concepts to understand:

Encryption at Rest   Encryption at rest refers to encrypting any data that is persisted to disk or "resting." This includes data in S3 object storage, databases like RDS, and streaming storage layers in Kinesis. AWS uses AES-256 for all encryption at rest, with the AWS Key Management Service (KMS) to create and manage keys.

Encryption in Transit   Encryption in transit is the encryption of data moving through a network from one system or device to another. This could be Redshift returning data to an SQL client tool or a user uploading files to S3 from their laptop. AWS uses the Transport Layer Security (TLS) protocol for encryption in transit.

Server-side Encryption   With server-side encryption (SSE), data is encrypted at the destination (the server). Encryption processing is performed on the server, and the encryption keys are also stored on the server. For example, Amazon S3 encrypts objects as it writes them to disk and decrypts them when they are downloaded, using keys managed by S3 or KMS.

Client-side Encryption   With client-side encryption (CSE), data is encrypted at the source (the client) before sending it to the destination (the server). The client manages the encryption keys and processing. AWS provides libraries like the Amazon S3 Encryption Client to perform client-side encryption.

Symmetric Encryption   Symmetric encryption algorithms use the same key to both encrypt and decrypt.

Asymmetric Encryption   Asymmetric encryption algorithms use two different but mathematically linked keys: a public key for encrypting data, which can be distributed, and a private key for decrypting data, which is kept private.

Encryption on AWS

On AWS, the primary way to control access to data is through AWS Identity and Access Management (IAM), such as limiting access to an S3 bucket to particular users and roles. By also encrypting the data, you add an additional layer of security to it. Users may have the correct IAM permissions to access an S3 bucket, but they won't be able to view the raw data if they don't have access to the decryption key. This is known as a *defense in depth* strategy, with multiple security layers protecting an asset so that if one layer fails, additional layers provide protection. This section will focus on the encryption layer of data security and how it works on AWS, starting with the primary service for managing encryption keys and encryption at rest on AWS, the AWS Key Management Service (KMS).

AWS Key Management Service

AWS KMS simplifies the creation, management, and security of encryption keys in the cloud. It stores keys securely and durably in hardware security modules (HSMs) validated to industry standards (FIPS 140-2) and integrates with many AWS services, including Amazon S3, Amazon RDS, and Amazon Redshift, allowing you to centralize key management across your entire AWS cloud environment. KMS works with AWS CloudTrail to log any interactions with the KMS API for detailed audit logging and is certified by third-party auditors for multiple industry compliance programs, including HIPAA, SOC, PCI, and FedRAMP.

Key Types

KMS supports AES-256 symmetric keys for encryption/decryption and asymmetric key pairs for encryption/decryption or signing and verification. KMS stores the following three types of keys:

Customer Managed   Customer-managed KMS keys are keys that you create, own, and manage in your account. You can enable or disable them, rotate them, add tags, create aliases, manage key and IAM policies, and schedule them for deletion.

AWS Managed   AWS-managed KMS keys are stored in your account and used on your behalf by other AWS services that integrate with KMS.

AWS Owned   AWS-owned KMS keys are used by other AWS services that integrate with KMS but are not stored in your account and are used across multiple accounts. Other AWS services can use AWS-owned keys to protect assets in your account.

Customer-managed keys give you the most control over your encryption solution, whereas AWS-managed and AWS-owned keys are more convenient and require less administration.

Key Policies

Access to KMS keys can be controlled with KMS *key policies*. KMS key policies resemble IAM policies but are specific to KMS keys. With KMS customer-managed keys, you can define Key Administrators (IAM users and roles who can manage a key through KMS) and Key Users (IAM users and roles who can use a specific key for encryption and decryption). You can also grant access to other accounts to use a key.

Envelope Encryption

While you can send data directly to AWS KMS for encryption or decryption, this method is not typically used for cryptographic processing on AWS. This is because KMS can only process data up to 4 KB in size, and sending large amounts of data over a network to and from KMS is inefficient. Instead, the encryption processing of large amounts of data is usually done locally with a key called a *data key*. A data key is created by KMS but not stored or managed by KMS; it is stored alongside the data, allowing you to encrypt and decrypt large amounts of data faster.

Of course, it's essential that only authorized users can use the data key; therefore, to secure it, the data key is also encrypted with another key called a *master key*. A master key, also known as a KMS key, is created and stored in KMS. This method of encrypting a key with another key is called *envelope encryption*. When you need to decrypt your data, you call KMS to decrypt the data key with the master (KMS) key. Then, you use the plaintext data key locally for your processing.

The following steps are an example of using envelope encryption to encrypt data:

1. Use KMS to create a master key.

2. Use KMS to create a data key encrypted by the master key.

3. Make a call to KMS to decrypt the data key with the master key.

4. Encrypt your data locally with the plaintext data key.

   Then, do the following to decrypt the data:

1. Make a call to KMS to decrypt the data key with the master key.

2. Decrypt your data locally with the plaintext data key.

Envelope encryption is used by AWS services that integrate with KMS. Services like Redshift and RDS encrypt data and store the encrypted data key along with the encrypted data. When the service needs to decrypt the data, it calls KMS to decrypt the data key using the KMS master key. The AWS service then uses the decrypted data key to decrypt the data before returning it to the user.

Envelope encryption can involve more than two keys (master and data). For additional security, you can have multiple encrypted data keys in a hierarchy. Figure 11.2 shows envelope encryption used on Redshift with a four-tier hierarchy of encryption keys: KMS master key, cluster encryption key, database encryption key, and data encryption keys.

FIGURE 11.2   Envelope encryption on Amazon Redshift

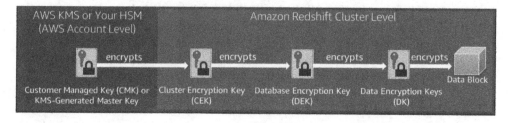

Run the following lab for a simple example of envelope encryption with KMS:

```
https://catalog.us-east-1.prod.workshops.aws/workshops/
aad9ff1e-b607-45bc-893f-121ea5224f24/en-US/keymanagement-kms/
envelope-encryption
```

Cross Account Key Access

You may have a requirement to encrypt data using a KMS key that is stored in a different account. This is possible with a customer-managed key, and there is a two-stage process to enable it:

Stage 1   In the account that owns the KMS key, grant the external account access to the key using the key's key policy. Access to the key can be granted at the account, user, or role level. You can see this in step 1 of Figure 11.3.

For example, to allow access to a key in account A from account B, you would add account B as a principal on the key's policy in account A, along with the required actions, such as kms:Encrypt, kms:Decrypt, etc.

Stage 2   In the external account, create an IAM policy with the required permissions on the key and attach the policy to users or roles who need access to the key. You can see this in steps 2 and 3 of Figure 11.3.

FIGURE 11.3   Enabling cross-account key access

1. Add account B as principal on key policy in account A.

2. Create IAM policy in account B to allow access to key in account A.

3. Attach IAM policy to users and roles.

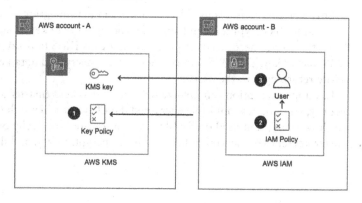

For example, to allow access to a key in account A from account B, you would create an IAM policy in account B that allows access to the key in account A, with the required actions listing the key's Amazon Resource Name (ARN) as the resource. Then, you would attach the policy to users and roles.

Calls to the KMS API for cross-account key access are logged in AWS CloudTrial in both the account using the key and the account owning the key.

Encryption on AWS Data Services

This section covers the encryption options for various AWS analytics and database services.

Amazon S3

Let's look at the encryption at rest and the encryption in transit considerations for Amazon S3.

Encryption at Rest

Amazon S3 supports client-side encryption (CSE) and server-side encryption (SSE) for data at rest, offering multiple options to suit different security requirements:

Server-Side Encryption with Amazon S3-Managed Keys (SSE-S3)   Amazon S3 manages the entire encryption process, including the keys, using AES-256. This option is ideal for users who prefer simplicity and do not require control over the encryption keys and auditing. SSE-S3 is the default encryption for S3 buckets.

Server-Side Encryption with AWS Key Management Service Keys (SSE-KMS)   AWS KMS is used with customer-managed encryption keys, providing more granular control and auditing through AWS CloudTrail. SSE-KMS also enables features such as key rotation and access control with key policies.

Dual-Layer Server-Side Encryption with AWS Key Management Service Keys (DSSE-KMS)   DSSE-KMS encrypts the S3 object twice using different applications of the Advanced Encryption Standard with Galois Counter Mode (AES-GCM) algorithm and different keys managed by KMS. DSSE-KMS provides a more robust level of encryption to meet very strict security regulations.

Server-Side Encryption with Customer-Provided Keys (SSE-C)   SSE-C allows users who want full control over their encryption keys to manage and provide their own keys, while S3 manages the encryption process without any code needing to be maintained by the user. To use SSE-C, you provide the key with your request when you upload or download files from S3.

Client-Side Encryption   The client encrypts the object before it is uploaded to S3 and decrypts it after it is downloaded from S3. Encryption libraries and processing are handled on the client-side. Keys can be created and managed either by the client or by KMS.

Figure 11.4 shows an example of S3 server-side encryption options.

FIGURE 11.4   S3 server-side encryption options when uploading a file

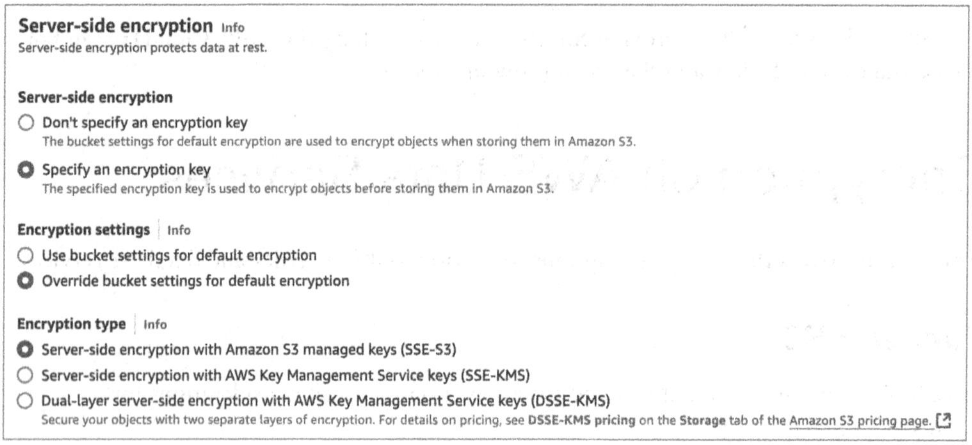

Run the following lab to learn about server-side and client-side encryption at rest on S3:

```
https://catalog.us-east-1.prod.workshops.aws/workshops/aad9ff1e-
b607-45bc-893f-121ea5224f24/en-US/s3
```

Encryption in Transit

Amazon S3 secures data in transit using the TLS encryption protocol through HTTPS, which can be mandated with a bucket policy. The IAM condition `aws:SecureTransport` can be included in a policy to permit only encrypted connections to your S3 bucket.

Amazon Redshift

Let's look at the encryption at rest and encryption in transit considerations for Amazon Redshift.

Encryption at Rest

To protect data at rest, a Redshift cluster's data and backups can be encrypted with AES-256. There is no difference in how an encrypted cluster is queried compared to an unencrypted cluster. Serverless namespaces are encrypted by default, while provisioned clusters can be optionally encrypted, which is highly recommended. Key management is handled by the AWS Key Management Service (AWS KMS) using either a customer-managed or AWS-managed key.

Encryption in Transit

Connections to a Redshift cluster from an SQL client tool over JDBC/ODBC can be encrypted via Secure Sockets Layer (SSL). Set the `require_SSL` parameter to `true` in the cluster's parameter group to accept only SSL connections to your cluster.

Redshift uses hardware-accelerated SSL within the AWS cloud for data movement between S3 for `COPY`, `UNLOAD`, and snapshot creation and restore operations. Files on S3 encrypted with client-side encryption can be loaded into Redshift by specifying the symmetric key in the `COPY` command. Files created on S3 from Redshift using the `UNLOAD` command are automatically encrypted with S3 server-side encryption (SSE-S3). Client-side encrypted files can be created in S3 using the `UNLOAD` command with the `ENCRYPTED` option.

Amazon DynamoDB

Let's look at the encryption at rest and encryption in transit considerations for Amazon DynamoDB.

Encryption at Rest

By default, DynamoDB tables are encrypted at rest using server-side encryption with AWS-owned KMS keys. Users can change the encryption method to use KMS AWS-managed or customer-managed keys, but encryption cannot be disabled on a new or existing table.

Encryption in Transit

DynamoDB encrypts all of your data during transit. Communications to and from DynamoDB use HTTPS by default with SSL/TLS encryption protocols. AWS also provides the Amazon DynamoDB Encryption Client, a client-side encryption library that allows you to encrypt data before sending it to DynamoDB.

Amazon RDS

Let's look at the encryption at rest and encryption in transit considerations for Amazon RDS.

Encryption at Rest

Amazon RDS provides data security at rest by allowing you to encrypt data stored on your database server using the AES-256 advanced encryption standard. This includes data for DB instances, read replicas, and automatic and manual snapshots. Data decryption is handled automatically and seamlessly; clients don't require additional processing. Amazon Key Management Service (KMS) manages the encryption keys, and you can use an AWS-managed key or create a customer-managed key.

DB instances are not encrypted by default. When creating a new DB instance, you can enable encryption. To encrypt an existing cluster, you must perform a multistep process:

1. Create a snapshot of the unencrypted instance.

2. Copy the snapshot to an encrypted snapshot.

3. Restore an instance from the encrypted snapshot.

The new instance will use the same KMS key as the source snapshot.

Encryption in Transit

RDS provides encryption in transit using Secure Sockets Layer (SSL) or Transport Layer Security (TLS) to protect data moving between your client and a DB instance. Each DB engine has its own process for using SSL/TLS. For further details on a specific DB engine, see the Amazon Relational Database Service User Guide documentation.

Amazon EMR

Let's look at the encryption at rest and encryption in transit considerations for Amazon EMR.

Encryption at Rest

Amazon EMR has different storage layers that utilize different options for data encryption rest. Encryption options can be saved in a security configuration and used across multiple EMR clusters.

S3 Encryption

Amazon S3 encryption uses EMRFS:

EMRFS Data on Amazon S3 Encryption Amazon EMR File System (EMRFS) works with Amazon S3 as a data source or destination. You can enable server-side encryption with SSE-S3 or SSE-KMS keys, or client-side encryption with keys managed by KMS (CSE-KMS) or the client (CSE-C). The type of encryption can be set differently on specific buckets with an EMR security configuration.

Local Disk Encryption

Data stored on EMR local disk volumes (instance stores and EBS) is encrypted at rest with a combination of methods:

HDFS Encryption HDFS is used for data reads and writes from instance store volumes and local EBS volumes. When you enable local disk encryption, EMR activates open-source HDFS encryption options, including Secure Hadoop RPC and data encryption on HDFS block data transfers.

Instance Store Encryption Encryption on instance stores depends on the EC2 instance type. NVMe-based SSDs use NVMe (non-volatile memory express) encryption, while other instance store volumes use Linux Unified Key Setup (LUKS) encryption.

EBS Volume Encryption   Some AWS regions encrypt EBS volumes by default. If your account is in one of these regions, your EBS volumes will be encrypted even if you haven't explicitly enabled encryption. Otherwise, you can enable EBS encryption or use LUKS encryption. EBS encryption is recommended.

Encryption in Transit

Encryption is automatically enabled for all network traffic in EMR, which consists of the following:

S3 to Cluster Encryption   EMRFS data transferred between S3 and EMR clusters is encrypted using Transport Layer Security (TLS).

In-cluster Encryption   EMR supports encryption for communication between nodes within the cluster using TLS and open-source encryption for distributed applications.

Figure 11.5 shows the encryption options.

FIGURE 11.5   EMR security configuration encryption options

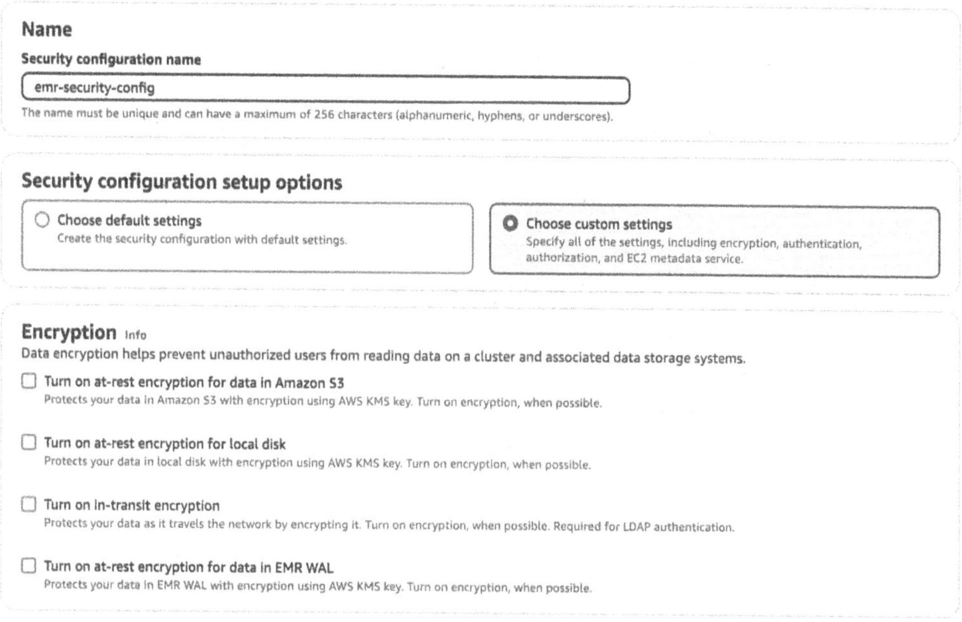

Name

Security configuration name

emr-security-config

The name must be unique and can have a maximum of 256 characters (alphanumeric, hyphens, or underscores).

Security configuration setup options

○ Choose default settings
Create the security configuration with default settings.

● Choose custom settings
Specify all of the settings, including encryption, authentication, authorization, and EC2 metadata service.

Encryption Info
Data encryption helps prevent unauthorized users from reading data on a cluster and associated data storage systems.

☐ Turn on at-rest encryption for data in Amazon S3
Protects your data in Amazon S3 with encryption using AWS KMS key. Turn on encryption, when possible.

☐ Turn on at-rest encryption for local disk
Protects your data in local disk with encryption using AWS KMS key. Turn on encryption, when possible.

☐ Turn on in-transit encryption
Protects your data as it travels the network by encrypting it. Turn on encryption, when possible. Required for LDAP authentication.

☐ Turn on at-rest encryption for data in EMR WAL
Protects your data in EMR WAL with encryption using AWS KMS key. Turn on encryption, when possible.

AWS Glue

Let's look at the encryption at rest and encryption in transit considerations for AWS Glue.

Encryption at Rest

AWS Glue has the following options for encrypting data at rest:

Glue Data Catalog Encryption   Metadata stored in the Glue Data Catalog can be encrypted with KMS AWS-managed or customer-managed keys.

Job Output to S3 Encryption   Data written to S3 from Glue ETL jobs to a data target or a temporary directory can be encrypted with S3-managed keys (SSE-S3) or KMS customer-managed keys (SSE-KMS). A security configuration can be created to specify encryption settings, which can be used across multiple ETL jobs.

Job Bookmark Encryption   Job bookmarks used in Glue ETL jobs can be encrypted with client-side KMS keys (CSE-KMS) before being written to S3.

Amazon CloudWatch Log Encryption   Logs in CloudWatch created from Glue ETL jobs and crawlers can be encrypted in S3 with server-side KMS keys (SSE-KMS).

Figure 11.6 shows the encryption at rest options.

FIGURE 11.6   AWS Glue security configuration encryption at rest options

Security configuration properties

Name

glue-job-security-config

Name can be up to 255 characters long. Some character set including control characters are prohibited.

Encryption settings   Info

Enable and choose options for at-rest encryption.

☐ **Enable S3 encryption**
   Enable at-rest encryption for data stored on S3.

☐ **Enable CloudWatch logs encryption**
   Enable at-rest encryption when writing logs to Amazon CloudWatch.

▼ **Advanced settings**

☐ **Enable job bookmark encryption**
   Enable at-rest encryption of job bookmark.

☐ **Enable data quality encryption**
   Enable at-rest encryption of data quality.

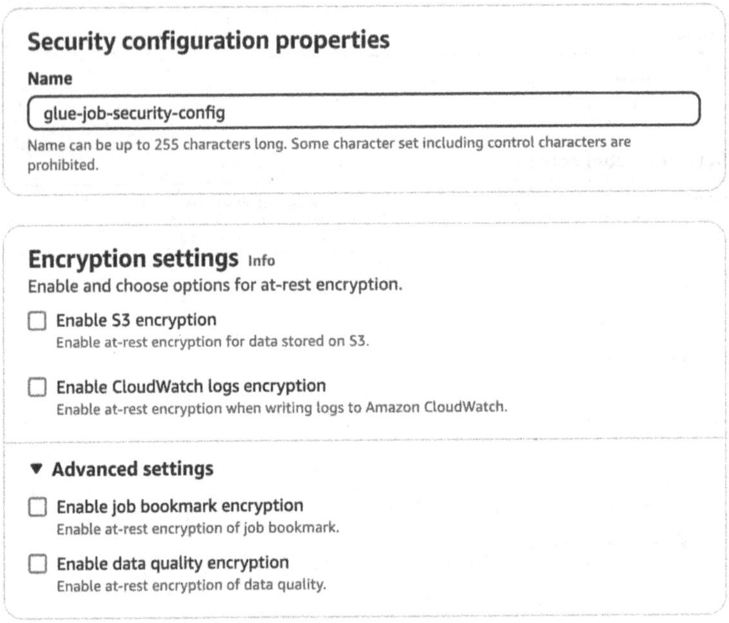

Encryption in Transit

AWS Glue encrypts data in transit between Glue and S3 using Transport Layer Security (TLS). Glue Data Catalog connectors can enforce Secure Sockets Layer (SSL) for JDBC database connections.

Amazon Kinesis

Let's look at the encryption at rest and encryption in transit considerations for Amazon Kinesis.

Encryption at Rest

Kinesis Data Streams supports server-side encryption using KMS keys to protect data at rest in the Kinesis stream storage layer. You can choose to use either an AWS-managed key or a customer-managed key.

Encryption in Transit

Kinesis uses TLS via HTTPS by default to encrypt all data transferred between producers, consumers, and the Kinesis stream.

Amazon Managed Streaming for Apache Kafka

Let's look at the encryption at rest and encryption in transit considerations for Amazon Managed Streaming for Apache Kafka (Amazon MSK).

Encryption at Rest

Amazon MSK encrypts all data stored in Kafka clusters with server-side encryption using KMS-managed keys. Data is always encrypted in MSK with an AWS-managed key, or you can create a cluster using a customer-managed key.

Encryption in Transit

TLS encryption is enforced by default for data transferred between Kafka brokers and between clients and the Kafka cluster. Encryption in transit on MSK may introduce a few milliseconds of latency. Although it's possible to disable it, it is strongly advised not to do so.

Amazon OpenSearch Service

Let's look at the encryption at rest and encryption in transit considerations for Amazon OpenSearch.

Encryption at Rest

OpenSearch allows you to encrypt all data stored at rest using KMS with AWS-owned or customer-managed keys. This includes index data, automated snapshots, swap files, and logs.

Encryption in Transit

OpenSearch enforces encryption for data transferred between the OpenSearch nodes with TLS and between the cluster and clients using HTTPS.

Amazon QuickSight

Let's look at the encryption at rest and encryption in transit considerations for Amazon QuickSight.

Encryption at Rest

QuickSight encrypts all metadata and analysis results at rest using KMS-managed keys. Metadata includes user data like email addresses and passwords as well as data source connection information. Analysis results include SPICE datasets and other data at rest, such as email reports. SPICE datasets can be encrypted with KMS AWS-managed or customer-managed keys.

Encryption in Transit

QuickSight supports SSL to encrypt all data transmissions between users and the service, data sources to SPICE, and live connections from data sources to QuickSight.

Data Masking

Data masking is similar to data encryption in that it obfuscates data, making it worthless to a bad actor who has gained unauthorized access. However, there are fundamental differences in how encryption and masking work and the use cases for which they are applied. Encryption scrambles data into an unreadable format and requires a cryptographic key to convert it back to a readable one. Masking differs from encryption in two main ways:

- Masking modifies data by redacting or replacing sensitive information, making it of no value to an unauthorized person while still remaining readable.

- Masked data cannot be converted back to its original form, while encrypted data can.

The purpose of encrypting data is to make it completely unusable and worthless to unauthorized individuals. In contrast, masked data retains value for certain use cases while not revealing sensitive information. For example, a typical use case for masked data is populating data lakes and databases in dev and test environments with data from production environments. Production environments contain all of a company's live data, including highly sensitive information like customer names, email addresses, and credit card numbers—known as *Personally Identifiable Information (PII)*. Developers and testers need to have representative data to do their jobs; however, there's no need for them to see sensitive customer information like PII fields, and exposing these fields in lower environments is a security risk. By masking specific sensitive fields, the data can be used to develop and test new applications and features without the risk of exposing sensitive information.

Data masking can be as simple as substituting character values with a replacement value (e.g., credit card numbers could be masked to a string like XXXX-XXXX-XXXX-XXXX), or it can be more complex and use deterministic algorithms to ensure the value being masked is consistently masked with the same value (e.g., the name "Scott" is converted to the name "John" throughout the whole data set). This could be needed to test a name and address matching engine, for example. Another type of complex masking applies mathematical algorithms to keep the distribution and relationships of masked data the same as the original data, allowing statistical analysis to be run on the masked data with the same or similar results as the original data.

There are two main ways to implement data masking:

Static Data Masking   With static data masking, data such as PII fields in a database or data lake are updated and persisted, permanently masking them for all users. Static masking is commonly processed in batches, such as an Amazon EMR job that performs masking while copying data from one layer of a data lake to another. AWS Glue Data-Brew has built-in data masking transformations that allow users to mask data statically without writing any code.

Dynamic Data Masking   Dynamic data masking alters how data is masked depending on the identity viewing the data, and, in contrast to static masking, it changes the data in real-time as it's being viewed. For example, a call center representative may only need to see the last four characters of a credit card number with the rest masked (e.g., XXXX-XXXX-XXXX-1234), while a member of the fraud investigation team may need to see the entire number. The dynamic data masking logic in the application will determine who is logged in and viewing the data, showing the call center representative a partly masked version of the credit card number and the fraud team member an unmasked version.

Amazon Redshift has native dynamic data masking. Refer to Chapter 5 for an explanation of how it works on Redshift. Third-party vendors like Protegrity also provide comprehensive solutions for dynamic data masking on AWS services.

Amazon Macie

Protecting sensitive data with masking is essential, but first, you need to know what sensitive data you have before you can mask it. Traditionally, this task was handled by data analysts who would manually review data models. However, in today's cloud environment, companies often have massive data lakes with thousands of objects and new objects being constantly added. Manually identifying sensitive data at this scale is not practicable, which is where *Amazon Macie* helps.

Amazon Macie uses machine learning and pattern matching to automatically discover and report sensitive data on Amazon S3. It also detects security issues with S3 buckets, such as a bucket being publicly accessible. It has built-in checks, called *managed data identifiers*, to detect common types of sensitive data, such as Personally Identifiable Information (PII), medical information, and credential information like passwords. You can also create your own *custom data identifiers* with regular expressions and character sequences to handle specialized types of sensitive data specific to your organization.

When Macie detects sensitive data or security issues with your S3 buckets, it generates a *finding*—a report that includes details about the issue and a severity rating. You can view findings from the Macie console, Macie API, and Amazon EventBridge. You can also publish findings to AWS Security Hub.

Summary

In this chapter, we first discussed what encryption is and why it is needed. We then explained the fundamental encryption concepts to be aware of, including encryption at rest, encryption in transit, server-side encryption (SSE), and client-side encryption (CSE). We then covered how encryption is implemented and managed on AWS, along with the primary service for creating and managing encryption keys, the AWS Key Management Service (KMS), and how it uses envelope encryption to protect keys.

Next, we discussed the encryption options for AWS analytics and database services, such as Amazon S3, Amazon RDS, and Amazon Redshift. Finally, we covered data masking, how it differs from encryption, and how it protects sensitive data like Personally Identifiable Information (PII).

Exam Essentials

Understand what encryption is and why it's needed.   Encryption transforms data into an unreadable format, adding another layer of security. It ensures that if a malicious actor can bypass existing security and access data, whether stored or transmitted, it remains meaningless and valueless.

Know the difference between client-side encryption and server-side encryption.   Client-side encryption (CSE) encrypts data at the source before sending it to the server, with the client handling encryption keys and processing. In contrast, server-side encryption (SSE) encrypts data once it reaches the server, where processing and key management occur. For example, with server-side encryption on Amazon S3, S3 encrypts objects upon writing to disk and decrypts them during download with S3 or KMS-managed keys.

Understand encryption at rest and encryption in transit.   Encryption at rest involves encrypting data stored on disk, including S3, RDS databases, and Redshift. AWS uses AES-256 for encryption at rest and KMS for key management. Encryption in transit protects data moving across networks, such as Redshift returning data to SQL clients or file uploads to S3. AWS uses Transport Layer Security (TLS) for this purpose.

Understand AWS Key Management Service and how it works.   AWS KMS simplifies creating, managing, and securing encryption keys in the cloud. It stores keys securely and integrates with many AWS services, enabling you to centralize your key management. Know the different types of keys (customer-managed, AWS-managed, and AWS-owned), how to create keys in KMS, and how to use them to encrypt and decrypt data.

Know how to configure encryption across AWS accounts.   In the account that owns the KMS key, grant the external account access to the key on the key's policy. Next, in the external account, create an IAM policy with the required permissions on the key and attach the policy to users or roles who need access to the key.

Know the options for encrypting data at rest in S3.   S3 has five ways to encrypt data at rest: Server-Side Encryption with Amazon S3-Managed Keys (SSE-S3), Server-Side Encryption with AWS Key Management Service Keys (SSE-KMS), Dual-Layer Server-Side Encryption with AWS Key Management Service Keys (DSSE-KMS), Server-Side Encryption with Customer-Provided Keys (SSE-C), and Client-Side Encryption.

Know the encryption options available in AWS analytics services.   Learn the options for encryption at rest and encryption in transit for AWS services, including Amazon S3, Amazon Redshift, Amazon EMR, AWS Glue, Amazon RDS, Amazon Kinesis, etc.

Understand what sensitive data is and how to protect it.   Sensitive data includes Personally Identifiable Information (PII), financial information, medical information, credential information, or any data that could cause a severe security issue if exposed to an unauthorized user. Amazon Macie can automatically detect and report sensitive data in Amazon S3.

Understand the basics of data masking.   Data masking modifies data by redacting or replacing sensitive information, making it still readable but of no value to an unauthorized person. Masked data cannot be converted back to its original form. Data masking can be static (sensitive fields are updated and persisted) or dynamic (data is masked in real time depending on the identity viewing the data).

Review Questions

1. You're working for the Cloud Security department of a company that uses Amazon RDS and Amazon DynamoDB for its operational systems, Amazon S3 for its data lake, and Redshift for data warehousing. The company wants to encrypt all of its data in these services at rest and needs a way to manage encryption keys centrally. What service would you recommend for this task?

    A. AWS CloudHSM

    B. AWS Key Management Services (KMS)

    C. AWS Certificate Manager

    D. Amazon SQS

2. You are working for a global company with multiple AWS accounts. There is a requirement to perform cross-account encryption where one account uses a KMS key from a different account to access an S3 bucket. What two steps are required to configure encryption across these AWS account boundaries securely? (Choose two.)

    A. In the account that owns the key, enable S3 Server-Side Encryption with AWS Key Management Service Keys (SSE-KMS) and assign the KMS customer-managed key to the S3 bucket.

    B. In the account that owns the key, enable S3 Server-Side Encryption with AWS Key Management Service Keys (SSE-KMS) and assign the KMS customer-managed key to the S3 bucket. Grant access to the external account on the key's key policy in AWS KMS.

    C. In the external account, create an IAM policy with the required permissions on the key and attach the policy to users or roles who need access to the key.

    D. In the external account, enforce TLS for S3 access by specifying `aws:SecureTransport` on bucket policies.

3. Which features can encrypt data at rest on Amazon S3? (Choose all that apply.)

    A. SSE with Amazon S3-Managed Keys (SSE-S3)

    B. SSE with Customer Master Keys (CMKs) in AWS KMS (SSE-KMS)

    C. SSE with Customer-Provided Keys (SSE-C)

    D. SSL

    E. TLS

4. A large digital newspaper business is running a data warehouse on a provisioned Amazon Redshift cluster that is not encrypted. Its security department has mandated that the cluster be encrypted to meet regulation requirements with keys that can be rotated and have comprehensive logging. What is the easiest and fastest way to do this?

    A. UNLOAD the data into S3, apply SSE-S3 encryption, and load the data back into Redshift via the COPY command.

    B. UNLOAD the data into S3, apply SSE-KMS encryption, and load the data back into Redshift via the COPY command.

    C. Take a manual snapshot of the cluster and create a new cluster from the snapshot with encryption enabled.

    D. Enable encryption on the cluster with a KMS customer-managed key.

5. What options does AWS Glue have for encrypting data at rest? (Choose all that apply.)

   A. Glue Data Catalog encryption

   B. Job bookmark encryption

   C. EMRFS data on S3 encryption

   D. Job output to S3 encryption

6. You are working for a financial services company and have been given a requirement to encrypt the contents of an S3 bucket at rest. The key must be customer-managed and meet strict regulatory requirements, including being rotated once per year and fully audited. What would be the best solution for these requirements with the least management overhead?

   A. Use Server-Side Encryption with Amazon S3-Managed keys (SSE-S3) and AWS Cloud-Trail for auditing.

   B. Use client-side encryption (CSE) with customer-managed keys, processing, and logging.

   C. Use Server-Side Encryption with AWS KMS-Managed keys (SSE-KMS), utilizing an AWS-managed key, and AWS CloudTrail for auditing.

   D. Use Server-Side Encryption with AWS KMS-Managed keys (SSE-KMS), utilizing a customer-managed key, and AWS CloudTrail for auditing.

7. To fulfill regulatory compliance, an organization must automatically rotate encryption keys used in its applications. Which service should it use to manage this securely?

   A. AWS Secrets Manager

   B. AWS CloudHSM

   C. AWS Key Management Services (KMS)

   D. AWS Config

8. Which AWS service automatically detects and reports sensitive data stored in Amazon S3 and security issues with S3 buckets?

   A. AWS Security Hub

   B. Amazon Macie

   C. Amazon EventBridge

   D. Amazon Key Management Service (AWS KMS)

9. You are working for a health services provider with strict security policies on Personally Identifiable Information (PII) like names and addresses and medical records. You need to build a batch process to mask a large amount of sensitive data stored in Amazon S3. How would you best do this?

   A. Push the data into Amazon Kinesis Data Firehose and mask the data with SQL using Kinesis Data Analytics.

   B. Use the COPY command to load the data into Amazon Redshift. Mask the sensitive fields with SQL and UNLOAD the data back to S3.

   C. Use AWS Lambda to mask the sensitive fields with a Python anonymization library.

   D. Use Amazon EMR to transform the data and mask the sensitive fields.

10. Which AWS service has native dynamic data masking?

    A. Amazon Key Management Service (AWS KMS)

    B. AWS Security Hub

    C. Amazon Redshift

    D. Amazon EMR

Chapter

12

Data Privacy and Governance

**THE AWS CERTIFIED DATA ENGINEER –
ASSOCIATE EXAM OBJECTIVES COVERED
IN THIS CHAPTER MAY INCLUDE, BUT ARE
NOT LIMITED, TO THE FOLLOWING:**

✓ **Domain 4: Data Security and Governance**

   ▪ 4.5 Understand data privacy and governance

Introduction

In today's data-driven world, the exponential growth of data volumes, diversity of data types, and proliferation of data sources has made data privacy and governance fundamental to any successful data strategy. This chapter aligns with Domain 4 of the AWS Certified Data Engineer Associate Exam Guide, specifically focusing on Task Statement 4.5: Understanding data privacy and governance.

Protecting sensitive information and ensuring proper data governance are critical responsibilities for data engineers. This chapter explores the essential concepts and practices of data privacy and governance in AWS, focusing on personally identifiable information (PII) protection and data sovereignty requirements.

Chapter Scope and Objectives

This chapter equips you with the essential knowledge and practical skills for implementing data privacy and governance within AWS environments. You'll learn to design and maintain secure data architectures that comply with regulatory requirements while enabling efficient data operations. AWS's comprehensive coverage includes protecting personally identifiable information (PII), understanding data sovereignty concepts, and implementing robust governance frameworks.

Key Learning Areas

The chapter focuses on the following four critical competency areas:

1. Data sharing and permissions management
   - Implementing secure data sharing mechanisms (e.g., Amazon Redshift data sharing)
   - Establishing appropriate access controls and permission boundaries
2. PII protection and identification
   - Implementing PII detection (e.g., by AWS Macie with Lake Formation)
   - Implementing automated PII protection mechanisms

3. Data privacy strategies
   - Preventing unauthorized data replication across AWS regions
   - Implementing regional data sovereignty controls
   - Managing cross-region backup strategies
4. Configuration management
   - Tracking configuration changes in an AWS account (e.g., using AWS Config)
   - Maintaining audit trails of governance-related modifications

Practical Application

Throughout this chapter, you'll encounter real-world scenarios that demonstrate how to implement these concepts in production environments. This practical approach ensures that you'll be well prepared for both the certification exam and real-world implementation challenges.

Service Coverage Note

While Amazon DataZone represents AWS's latest offering in data governance, it falls outside the current exam scope and won't be covered in detail. However, we recommend familiarizing yourself with this service if you're actively implementing data governance solutions in your organization.

This chapter serves as both an exam preparation resource and a practical guide for implementing robust data privacy and governance frameworks in AWS environments. The concepts and skills covered here form the cornerstone of secure and compliant data architectures in modern cloud environments.

AWS Shared Responsibility Model

Data security is a critical concern for every organization's data infrastructure. When designing data architectures in AWS, it's essential to understand the shared responsibility model, which clearly delineates security obligations between AWS and its customers. The model establishes that AWS maintains responsibility for "security *of* the cloud" while customers are accountable for "security *in* the cloud" (see Figure 12.1).

"Security *of* the cloud" encompasses AWS's responsibility to protect the underlying infrastructure powering all AWS services. This includes safeguarding the physical hardware, virtualization software, global networking infrastructure, and data center facilities that constitute the AWS Cloud environment.

"Security *in* the cloud" defines the customer's security obligations, which vary depending on the chosen AWS data services. This determines the scope of security configurations customers must implement. For instance, when using provisioned Amazon EMR (Elastic MapReduce), customers must handle all aspects of cluster security, including network configuration, data encryption, and access controls. In contrast, with serverless services like Amazon QuickSight or AWS Glue, AWS handles the underlying infrastructure security, while customers focus on data-specific security measures such as configuring Identity and Access Management (IAM), encryption, implementing data governance policies, and managing user permissions. Customers retain responsibility for protecting their data assets, implementing appropriate classification schemes, and ensuring proper access controls regardless of the service used.

FIGURE 12.1   AWS and customer security responsibilities

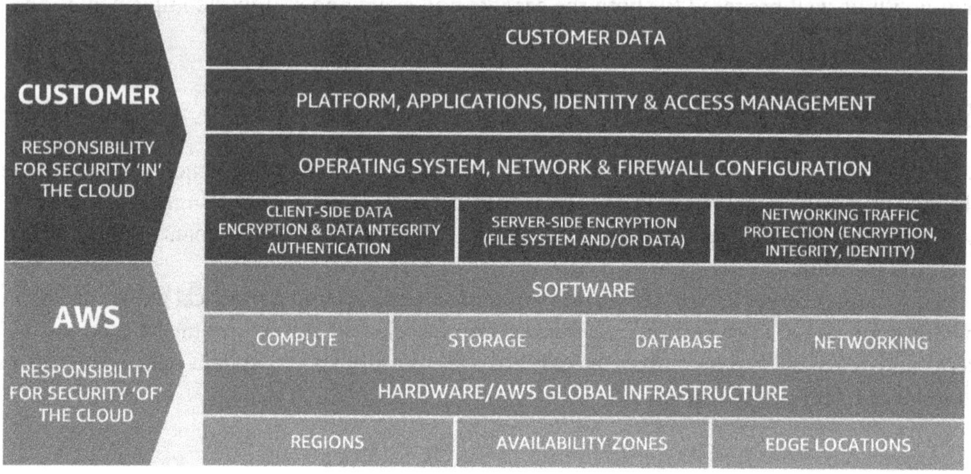

Understanding Data Privacy Fundamentals

Data privacy represents a critical cornerstone of modern data engineering, encompassing the systematic protection and handling of sensitive information throughout its lifecycle. While data security provides the broader framework for protecting information assets, data privacy focuses specifically on the proper handling, processing, storage, and usage of personal information in accordance with regulatory requirements and ethical considerations.

As data engineers working with AWS services, implementing privacy controls must be considered a "Day 0" priority—meaning it should be architected into solutions from the very beginning rather than added as an afterthought. This approach aligns with AWS's shared responsibility model and helps ensure compliance with global privacy regulations, such as the GDPR, the CCPA, and other regional requirements.

The following two fundamental concepts form the foundation of data privacy implementation in AWS:

- Data classification and identification
- Privacy by design

Data Classification and Identification

Data classification forms the cornerstone of effective data security and governance in cloud environments. As a data engineer preparing for the AWS Certified Data Engineer Associate examination, understanding how to properly classify and protect sensitive information is essential for implementing robust security measures.

Modern enterprises handle various categories of sensitive information that require specific protection measures. The primary classification types include:

- **Personally identifiable information (PII)**: Information that can identify individuals, such as names, Social Security numbers, and email addresses
- **Protected health information (PHI)**: Medical records, treatment information, and other health-related data subject to regulatory compliance
- **Financial data**: Banking information, transaction records, and other monetary data requiring strict security controls
- **Confidential business information**: Trade secrets, strategic plans, and proprietary information
- **Customer-specific data elements**: Unique identifiers and preferences associated with specific customers

These classifications directly influence crucial decisions in your AWS infrastructure. Your choice of encryption methods must align with the sensitivity of the data being protected across different AWS services.

Access control mechanisms and policies should reflect the principle of least privilege, ensuring that only authorized personnel can access specific data categories. Data handling procedures within services like Amazon S3, Amazon Redshift, and Amazon RDS must be designed to maintain data security throughout its lifecycle. Additionally, compliance monitoring and reporting requirements must be implemented to track and verify that all security measures remain effective.

When approaching exam questions about data protection, focus on implementation strategies rather than memorizing classification definitions. The exam typically presents scenarios requiring you to identify appropriate protection mechanisms based on data type. You need to demonstrate an understanding of how to select suitable AWS services for data security and implement proper access controls and encryption methods. The questions often require you to evaluate trade-offs between different security approaches and choose the most appropriate solution for specific business requirements.

For scenarios requiring data masking during analytics processing, a comprehensive approach is necessary. The process typically begins with storing raw data in Amazon S3 with appropriate encryption and access controls. The data transformation phase utilizes Amazon EMR or AWS Glue with Spark ETL jobs for anonymization, ensuring sensitive information is properly masked before analysis. The anonymized data is then maintained in a separate secure location, allowing for safe analytical processing while preserving the confidentiality of the original data.

When automatic anonymization at access time is needed, AWS Lake Formation provides an ideal solution. This service enables granular security control over your data lake, allowing you to implement column-level and row-level security precisely. You can configure appropriate access policies for different user groups, ensuring that sensitive data is automatically masked or filtered based on user permissions. This approach provides a dynamic and maintainable solution for protecting sensitive data while still enabling necessary business operations.

Understanding these implementation patterns and their appropriate use cases is crucial for both the examination and real-world applications in AWS environments. The key to success lies not just in knowing the technical capabilities of each service, but in understanding how to apply them effectively to meet specific security and compliance requirements.

Privacy by Design

Privacy by design is an approach to system engineering initially developed by Ann Cavoukian (former Information and Privacy Commissioner for the Canadian province of Ontario). Privacy by design takes privacy into account throughout the whole engineering process. It especially focuses on systems or applications that capture and process personal data.

There is an increased focus on ensuring that personal data is processed lawfully, fairly, and transparently in relation to the data subject. Another concern is that the data processing is adequate, relevant, and limited in relation to the purpose for which the information is used. To embed this into data engineering practices, you need to do the following:

- **Data minimization:** Collecting and retaining only necessary data that is relevant for the task rather than processing all information. This can be applied at the point of access using role-based access controls (RBACs) or you can preprocess the data containing only the necessary data.

- **Data anonymization:** This is a broader subject that includes anonymization, pseudonymization, or tokenization. It refers to either rendering data anonymous or encoding data in such a manner that the data is no longer identifiable.

- **Purpose limitation:** Using data only for specified, legitimate purposes. As we discussed previously, identifying the purpose of the data is key in classifying the data accordingly.

- **Storage limitation:** Implementing appropriate retention policies. This could align with your compliance requirements as well as your business requirements. This provides three benefits. The first benefit is obvious: aligning with your organization's goals (e.g., cost optimization, data retention). The second benefit is aligning with your compliance requirements (e.g., data retention). The third benefit is aligning with your business goals (e.g., gaining insights from historic data).

- **Data subject rights:** Building systems that can accommodate privacy requests. This particular right is for an individual to request information from the data controller— that is, how their personal data is being processed. The idea is to have an automated process to be able to answer subject access requests (SARs).

- **Privacy impact assessments:** Evaluating privacy risks before implementing new processes. Before implementing any new process, you should run a privacy impact assessment.

For further information on this concept, please visit the AWS documentation at `https://docs.aws.amazon.com/wellarchitected/latest/analytics-lens/best-practice-3.1-privacy-by-design.html`.

AWS Services for Privacy Implementation

Data privacy and governance represent critical considerations for AWS data engineers, particularly as organizations face increasing regulatory requirements and security challenges. Understanding how to implement and maintain privacy controls using AWS services is essential for the AWS Certified Data Engineer Associate exam.

Understanding AWS Privacy Services

At the heart of AWS's privacy capabilities is Amazon Macie, a fully managed data security and privacy service that leverages machine learning and pattern matching to discover and protect sensitive data. Macie automatically scans your S3 buckets to identify personally identifiable information (PII) and other sensitive data types, making it invaluable for maintaining data privacy compliance. For example, when processing customer data, Macie can automatically detect and alert you to the presence of credit card numbers, Social Security numbers, or other sensitive information that might require special handling.

Working alongside Macie, AWS Key Management Service (KMS) provides the encryption infrastructure necessary for protecting sensitive data. KMS manages the lifecycle of encryption keys and integrates seamlessly with other AWS services. Data engineers should understand how KMS enables both server-side and client-side encryption options, as well as how it supports key rotation and cross-account access patterns. When implementing encryption strategies, it's crucial to consider both data at rest and data in transit, ensuring comprehensive protection throughout your data pipeline.

AWS Lake Formation adds another layer to privacy controls by providing centralized governance for data lakes. It enables fine-grained access control at both the column and row level, which is particularly important when different teams or applications need varying levels of access to sensitive data. For instance, you might use Lake Formation to ensure that analysts can see aggregated customer data while restricting access to individual customer details.

Implementing Privacy Controls

The implementation of privacy controls requires a thoughtful approach to data classification and access management. Data engineers should start by identifying and classifying sensitive data, often using Macie's automated discovery capabilities. This classification informs the appropriate levels of encryption and access controls needed for different data types.

Consider a scenario where your organization processes customer information across multiple departments. You might use Macie to identify sensitive fields, KMS to manage the encryption of this data, and Lake Formation to ensure that different departments only access the specific data fields they need. CloudWatch and CloudTrail would then provide the necessary audit trail of how this data is accessed and used.

Access control implementation should follow the principle of least privilege, using a combination of IAM roles and Lake Formation permissions. For example, data scientists might need access to anonymized customer data for analysis, while customer service representatives might need access to individual customer records but not aggregate data. Lake Formation's fine-grained permissions make this type of access control possible while maintaining data security.

Monitoring and Compliance

Effective privacy governance requires continuous monitoring and regular audits. CloudTrail plays a crucial role by logging all API activity, which helps track who accessed what data and when. CloudWatch complements this by enabling alerts on suspicious activity patterns. Together, these services provide the visibility needed to maintain compliance with privacy requirements.

Regular privacy audits should review the following:

- Macie findings for newly discovered sensitive data
- KMS key usage and rotation schedules
- Lake Formation access patterns and permissions
- CloudTrail logs for unusual access patterns

Cross-Region Privacy Considerations

Data sovereignty and cross-region privacy requirements present unique challenges for data engineers. AWS provides tools to prevent unauthorized data replication across regions, such as bucket policies and KMS key restrictions. Understanding how to implement these controls is crucial, as many organizations must comply with regulations requiring data to remain within specific geographical boundaries.

Privacy in Data Pipelines

When designing data pipelines, privacy considerations must be built in from the start. This means implementing encryption for data in transit between services, ensuring appropriate access controls at each stage of the pipeline, and maintaining audit logs throughout the process. For example, when moving data from an S3 data lake to Redshift for analysis, you need to ensure that encryption and access controls are maintained consistently across both services.

Exam Considerations

For the AWS Certified Data Engineer Associate exam, focus on understanding how these privacy services work together rather than memorizing individual features. Key areas to understand include:

- How to use Macie for automated sensitive data discovery
- When and how to implement KMS encryption
- How Lake Formation permissions interact with underlying data sources
- The role of CloudTrail and CloudWatch in privacy monitoring
- Common privacy-related architectural patterns

Remember that exam questions often present scenarios requiring you to choose the most appropriate combination of services to meet specific privacy requirements. Understanding the strengths and integration points of each service will help you select the optimal solution for each scenario.

The exam may also test your understanding of privacy best practices in the context of cost optimization. For instance, you might need to balance the cost of continuous Macie scans against privacy requirements, or consider the performance implications of different encryption options.

Privacy and governance in AWS continue to evolve as new services and features are released. While this section covers the core concepts needed for the exam, staying current with AWS privacy capabilities will serve you well in both the exam and real-world implementations.

Data Governance

Building on our previous discussion of data privacy and classification, we now turn our attention to implementing effective data governance through AWS's comprehensive toolset. Data governance, a vast domain that could warrant its own book, demands focused attention within the scope of the AWS Data Engineer Associate certification.

At its core, data governance encompasses the methodologies and practices that ensure data maintains its integrity, security, and utility in supporting business operations. AWS has structured its data governance framework around three fundamental pillars: understanding, protection, and curation (see Figure 12.2).

The *understanding* pillar forms the foundation of data governance through three critical components. Data profiling provides insights into data patterns and characteristics, while data lineage tracks the data's journey and transformations throughout its lifecycle. The data catalog serves as a centralized repository of metadata, making data assets discoverable and manageable across the organization.

Protection, the second pillar, addresses the security and compliance aspects of data management. This encompasses data security measures, compliance with regulatory requirements, and lifecycle management—ensuring data is retained, archived, or deleted according to business and regulatory needs. In heavily regulated industries like healthcare and financial services, data sovereignty is a key requirement; it refers to the concept that information is subject to the laws and governance structures of the country in which it is located. When designing your system, you should carefully consider and review data storage location, cross-border data transfers, regional compliance requirements, and backup and disaster recovery strategies.

The final pillar, *curation*, focuses on maintaining data quality and accessibility. It includes master data management for consistent representation of core business entities, data integration to ensure seamless data flow between systems, and data quality management to maintain accuracy and reliability.

This framework, documented in AWS's technical resources, applies equally well to both analytics and machine learning governance scenarios. While each organization may implement these pillars differently, understanding this structure is crucial for AWS Data Engineers, as it influences architectural decisions and service selection within the AWS ecosystem.

Data Sharing in AWS

Modern data architectures require sophisticated methods for sharing data across organizational boundaries while maintaining strict security and governance controls. As organizations grow, the need to share data securely between different departments, regions, and even external partners becomes increasingly critical. AWS has developed robust solutions to address these challenges, with Amazon Redshift data sharing and AWS Lake Formation being the primary services you need to understand for the AWS Certified Data Engineer Associate exam.

FIGURE 12.2   The three pillars of data governance

Amazon Redshift Data Sharing

Amazon Redshift data sharing represents a significant advancement in how organizations can share and access data. Unlike traditional data sharing methods that often involve creating copies or moving data between systems, Redshift data sharing enables secure data access across different AWS accounts and regions without physically relocating the data. This approach brings several compelling advantages to organizations managing large-scale data operations.

The most significant benefit of Redshift data sharing is its ability to completely decouple compute resources from data access. When consumers access shared data, they use their own compute cluster rather than drawing resources from the producer's cluster. This separation provides clear workload management benefits and enables precise cost allocation between data producers and consumers. Furthermore, since data only moves in response to specific queries, organizations can maintain efficient resource utilization while ensuring data freshness.

To implement Redshift data sharing effectively, organizations must follow several key best practices. First and foremost is the implementation of least-privilege access, ensuring that consumers have access only to the specific data they need. Regular auditing of sharing permissions is equally crucial, as it helps maintain security and compliance over time. Organizations should also maintain detailed documentation of sharing relationships and monitor shared data usage patterns to optimize performance and cost.

AWS Lake Formation and Centralized Governance

While Redshift data sharing provides powerful capabilities for specific use cases, AWS Lake Formation serves as a comprehensive solution for data governance and security across your entire data lake (see Figure 12.3). Lake Formation introduces a permissions model that complements existing IAM permissions, offering fine-grained access control at the column, row, and cell levels. This granularity allows organizations to implement precise data access policies that meet even the most stringent compliance requirements.

FIGURE 12.3   AWS Lake Formation

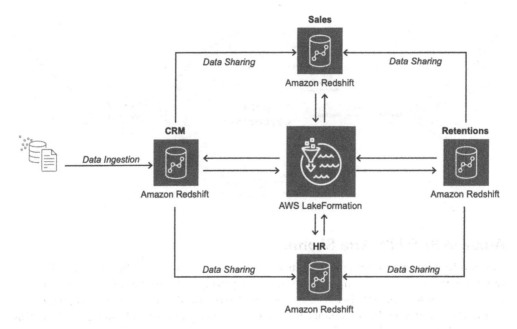

Lake Formation's hybrid access mode is particularly noteworthy for organizations transitioning to more sophisticated data governance models. This mode allows organizations to use both Lake Formation permissions and traditional IAM policies simultaneously, enabling a gradual and controlled migration to the new permissions model. Data administrators can selectively implement Lake Formation permissions, focusing on specific use cases or departments while maintaining existing access patterns elsewhere in the organization.

The service's integration capabilities extend its utility significantly. Lake Formation works seamlessly with key AWS analytics services, including Amazon Athena, Amazon QuickSight, Amazon Redshift Spectrum, Amazon EMR, and AWS Glue. This broad integration ensures consistent access control across your entire analytics ecosystem, regardless of which tools your teams use to analyze data.

Data Sharing Beyond Traditional Boundaries

Lake Formation's data sharing capabilities extend beyond simple access control. The service enables sharing across AWS accounts, organizations, and even directly with specific IAM principals in other accounts. This flexibility is crucial for organizations that need to share data with external partners or maintain separate environments for different business units.

When it comes to external data sharing, Lake Formation provides sophisticated options for connecting to external metastores and managing permissions on datasets stored outside of Amazon S3. Organizations can set up and manage permissions on datasets in Amazon Redshift without migrating the data to S3, and can use the Data Catalog federation feature to connect to external metastores. This capability is particularly valuable for organizations with existing data infrastructure that they need to integrate with their AWS environment.

Advanced Integration Scenarios

Lake Formation's integration with Amazon Redshift data sharing deserves special attention. This integration allows organizations to centrally manage database-, table-, column-, and row-level access permissions for Redshift datashares, providing fine-grained control over who can access specific objects within a datashare. Similarly, the service's support for AWS Data Exchange enables organizations to license their data through established channels, opening up new possibilities for data monetization.

Looking to the Future

While Amazon DataZone represents AWS's newest offering in the data governance space, providing end-to-end data governance capabilities, it's important to note that this service is currently out of scope for the AWS Certified Data Engineer Associate exam. Instead, focus your exam preparation on understanding the core concepts and capabilities of Redshift data sharing and Lake Formation, as these services form the foundation of AWS's data sharing and governance strategy.

As data sharing and governance requirements continue to evolve, AWS's solutions in this space will undoubtedly continue to expand and improve. However, the fundamental principles of secure data sharing, fine-grained access control, and centralized governance will remain crucial for data engineers working with AWS services. Understanding these principles and how to implement them using AWS's current toolset is essential for success in both the certification exam and real-world data engineering scenarios.

Regional Data Privacy Strategies

This section explores regional data movement controls and cross-region considerations.

Regional Data Movement Controls

Data governance in AWS requires implementing robust policies to prevent unauthorized data movement across regions while ensuring compliance with organizational requirements. The principle of least privilege forms the foundation of this approach, ensuring that permissions are granted at the minimum necessary level for business operations.

Service control policies (SCPs) at the organization level provide the first line of defense for enforcing cross-region data movement restrictions. These policies can effectively control data transfers by denying specific actions outside allowed regions. Here's a practical example that limits S3 cross-region replication to your allowed region:

```
{
  "Version": "2012-10-17",
  "Statement": [
    {
      "Sid": "DenyS3CrossRegionReplication",
```

```
    "Effect": "Deny",
    "Action": [
      "s3:PutBucketReplication",
      "s3:ReplicateObject",
      "s3:ReplicateDelete",
      "s3:ReplicateTags"
    ],
    "Resource": "*",
    "Condition": {
      "StringNotEquals": {
        "aws:RequestedRegion": "<YourAllowedRegion>"
      }
    }
    }
  ]
}
```

You can also configure AWS backup policies to respect regional boundaries, as illustrated by the following policy:

```
{
  "Version": "2012-10-17",
  "Statement": [
    {
      "Sid": "DenyCrossRegionBackup",
      "Effect": "Deny",
      "Action": [
        "backup:CopyFromBackupVault",
        "backup:CopyIntoBackupVault"
      ],
      "Resource": "*",
      "Condition": {
        "StringNotEquals": {
          "aws:RequestedRegion": "<YourAllowedRegion>"
        }
      }
    }
  ]
}
```

This SCP denies actions related to copying backups into and from backup vaults in regions other than <YourAllowedRegion>.

For effective monitoring of regional compliance, AWS Config provides two types of rules: managed and custom.

Managed rules, such as `required-tags`, `s3-bucket-public-read-prohibited`, and `encrypted-volumes`, handle common compliance scenarios, while custom rules, implemented through Lambda functions, address organization-specific requirements.

To maintain effective regional data governance:

1. Enable AWS Config in each region requiring compliance monitoring.

2. Implement appropriate SCPs to restrict cross-region data movement.

3. Use AWS Config rules to continuously monitor compliance.

4. Regularly review and update policies to reflect changing business needs.

This approach ensures comprehensive control over regional data movement while maintaining compliance with organizational and regulatory requirements.

Cross-Region Considerations

Data engineers preparing for the AWS Data Engineer Associate certification must master the complexities of multi-region architectures, as this topic frequently appears in exam scenarios. The ability to design and implement cross-region solutions while balancing security, compliance, and performance requirements is a crucial skill tested throughout the certification.

When approaching multi-region architectures, your first consideration should be thorough documentation of regional data requirements. The exam often presents scenarios where you need to determine which datasets require cross-region replication and which should remain local. You might encounter questions about using Amazon S3 Cross-Region Replication (CRR) for data lakes, or implementing Amazon RDS Read Replicas for global database access. Understanding the trade-offs between these options and their impact on cost and performance is essential for success on the exam.

Access control across regions presents unique challenges that are commonly tested. The exam frequently includes questions about implementing region-specific IAM policies while maintaining consistent security standards. You need to demonstrate an understanding of how AWS Organizations provides centralized policy management and how AWS Control Tower ensures consistent governance across regions. Questions often focus on the practical application of these tools in real-world scenarios, such as managing data access for global teams while maintaining regional compliance requirements.

Monitoring and cost optimization of cross-region data transfers is another critical area tested in the exam. You should be prepared to identify appropriate CloudWatch metrics for tracking transfer patterns and implementing cost-effective solutions. The exam may ask you to evaluate scenarios where you need to choose between different data transfer methods, such as S3 Transfer Acceleration versus direct transfer, based on specific performance and cost requirements.

Compliance and data sovereignty form a significant portion of cross-region architecture questions. The exam tests your ability to implement solutions that meet regional data privacy laws while maintaining operational efficiency. You need to understand how to use AWS

KMS for region-specific encryption, manage data lifecycle policies across regions, and ensure data residency requirements are met. Questions often present scenarios where you must balance these compliance requirements with performance and cost considerations.

Performance optimization in cross-region architectures requires a deep understanding of AWS's global infrastructure and services. The exam tests your ability to evaluate and implement appropriate replication strategies, whether using database read replicas, S3 CRR, or DynamoDB global tables. You should be prepared to analyze scenarios and recommend solutions that balance data consistency requirements, acceptable latency, and cost constraints while meeting business requirements.

Summary

Data privacy and governance in AWS encompass a comprehensive framework designed to protect sensitive information while ensuring regulatory compliance across cloud operations. At its foundation, AWS provides sophisticated tools for protecting personally identifiable information (PII) through services such as Amazon Macie and AWS Lake Formation, which work in tandem to automatically discover, classify, and secure sensitive data throughout the organization's data landscape.

The platform's governance capabilities extend through Amazon Redshift's data sharing features, enabling secure cross-account collaboration while maintaining strict access controls. This proves particularly valuable in enterprise environments where different business units or partner organizations require carefully managed access to specific datasets. AWS Config further strengthens this framework by providing continuous monitoring and compliance assessment of resource configurations, maintaining detailed audit trails, and enabling automated remediation actions when needed.

Data sovereignty considerations are addressed through AWS's region-specific data storage and processing capabilities. Organizations can implement strict controls to prevent unauthorized data replication or backup across geographical boundaries, ensuring compliance with regulations like GDPR and industry-specific requirements. This regional approach, combined with comprehensive access controls and monitoring capabilities, creates a robust foundation for maintaining data privacy while enabling efficient data operations.

Successful implementation requires data engineers to focus on automated PII detection, clear access patterns, comprehensive audit trails, and regular policy reviews. The integration of these elements, supported by continuous monitoring and validation, ensures organizations can maintain effective data privacy and governance while meeting their operational objectives and compliance requirements.

Exam Essentials

Understand data privacy and governance implementations.   You should thoroughly comprehend the integration capabilities between AWS Macie and Lake Formation. This powerful combination enables automated sensitive data discovery, classification, and protection across data lake environments—a crucial concept frequently tested in the exam.

Master the nuanced distinctions between cross-region replication restrictions and data sovereignty requirements.   While these concepts are related, they serve different purposes in AWS's privacy framework. Understanding how to implement proper controls for each scenario, particularly in multi-region deployments, is essential for demonstrating proficiency in cloud data engineering.

Know Amazon Redshift's data sharing functionalities.   You should be well-versed in configuring cross-account access, managing permissions, and implementing security controls within shared data environments. This includes understanding the underlying mechanisms for producer and consumer cluster configurations, as well as the associated security implications.

Understand AWS Config and configuration rule implementation, compliance monitoring, and automated remediation actions.   The exam frequently tests scenarios involving resource configuration tracking and compliance validation, making this knowledge particularly valuable.

Understand the region-specific constraints in data privacy implementations.   This includes understanding how to design and implement solutions that comply with geographical data restrictions, manage cross-region data transfers, and ensure that proper data residency requirements are met. Success on the exam requires not just knowing these constraints but also understanding how to apply them in various real-world scenarios.

Review Questions

1. A healthcare company needs to implement a solution to automatically detect and protect patient records containing sensitive information across its data lake, which processes over 1 million records daily. Which combination of AWS services would be most effective for this requirement?

   A. Amazon Inspector and AWS Lake Formation

   B. AWS Macie and AWS Lake Formation

   C. Amazon GuardDuty and AWS Glue

   D. AWS Shield and AWS Lake Formation

2. A multinational bank processes customer data from European and Asian markets, with strict requirements to keep regional customer data within its respective geographic boundaries. The bank needs to implement a solution that prevents accidental replication of EU customer data to Asia-Pacific regions. The solution should be automated and provide compliance reporting. Which approach would be most suitable?

   A. Use Amazon S3 bucket policies with manual region restriction checks.

   B. Implement AWS Config rules with AWS Organizations' service control policies (SCPs).

   C. Configure AWS CloudWatch with custom metrics for data movement.

   D. Deploy AWS Backup with cross-region replication enabled.

3. An e-commerce giant needs to share daily transaction data with its analytics team in a separate AWS account while ensuring that customer payment information is masked and access is strictly controlled. What is the most efficient solution?

   A. Export data to S3 and use bucket policies with custom encryption.

   B. Use Amazon Redshift cross-account data sharing with column-level access controls.

   C. Implement AWS Glue jobs to copy and transform data between accounts.

   D. Use Amazon RDS read replicas with encryption.

4. A pharmaceutical research company needs to automatically identify and classify research documents containing DNA sequencing data across their AWS data lake. They process approximately 50,000 new documents daily. Which solution would best meet their requirements?

   A. Use Amazon Comprehend with custom classification rules.

   B. Implement AWS Macie with custom data identifiers.

   C. Deploy Amazon Rekognition with document analysis.

   D. Use AWS Glue classifiers with custom patterns.

5. An insurance company needs to implement a solution to track and audit all configuration changes made to its data lake resources, ensuring compliance with industry regulations. Which AWS service combination would be most appropriate?

   A. AWS CloudTrail with Amazon S3 logging

   B. AWS Config with AWS CloudTrail Lake

   C. Amazon CloudWatch with custom metrics

   D. AWS Lake Formation with basic logging

6. A government agency processes sensitive citizen data and needs to implement a solution that automatically detects and blocks any attempts to share its Amazon Redshift data with external AWS accounts. The solution must provide immediate alerts and detailed audit logs. Which combination would be most effective?

   A. Amazon CloudWatch Logs with custom Lambda functions

   B. AWS Organizations' SCPs with AWS Config and Amazon SNS

   C. Amazon GuardDuty with AWS CloudTrail

   D. AWS Lake Formation with basic access controls

7. A financial services company needs to implement automated data lifecycle policies that ensure customer transaction data is retained for exactly 7 years and then permanently deleted, as required by regulations. Which solution would be most appropriate?

   A. Amazon S3 Lifecycle rules with AWS Backup

   B. AWS Config rules with custom Lambda functions

   C. Amazon S3 Glacier with manual deletion processes

   D. AWS Storage Gateway with custom retention policies

8. A healthcare analytics company needs to implement data governance controls that ensure all PII data is automatically encrypted and access-logged before being processed in its data lake. It processes over 100 GB of new data daily. Which solution best meets these requirements?

   A. AWS Lake Formation with AWS KMS and CloudTrail

   B. Amazon S3 with server-side encryption

   C. AWS Glue with basic encryption

   D. Amazon EFS with encryption at rest

9. A retail company needs to implement a solution that automatically identifies and categorizes sensitive customer data across multiple AWS accounts and regions, while ensuring compliance with GDPR requirements. Which approach would be most effective?

   A. Use AWS Macie with Organizations and Lake Formation.

   B. Deploy custom Lambda functions with S3 event triggers.

   C. Implement Amazon Inspector across accounts.

   D. Use AWS Shield with WAF rules.

10. A telecommunications company needs to implement a solution that prevents the accidental sharing of customer call records containing PII across AWS accounts while maintaining an audit trail of all access attempts. Which combination of services would best meet this requirement?

   A. AWS IAM policies with CloudWatch Logs

   B. Lake Formation with AWS CloudTrail and Macie

   C. S3 bucket policies with access logging

   D. AWS Backup with cross-account controls

Chapter

13

How to Take
the Exam

Chapter Overview

Over the past 12 chapters, you have explored a wide range of topics spanning the four key domains of the exam:

- **Domain 1:** Data Ingestion and Transformation (34% of the exam content)
- **Domain 2:** Data Store Management (26% of the exam content)
- **Domain 3:** Data Operations and Support (22% of the exam content)
- **Domain 4:** Data Security and Governance (18% of the exam content)

This final chapter is dedicated to helping you navigate the process of booking your exam, conducting your final review, and preparing for exam day itself. Following the best practices outlined in this chapter could be the key to achieving a high pass score versus just making it through. We'll guide you through strategies for managing your time, staying calm, and making the most of your preparation on the big day.

Register for the Exam

The AWS Training and Certification page provides comprehensive information on the various methods for registering for your exam. If this is your first time registering for an AWS certification, this section will guide you step-by-step through the process, ensuring that you're fully prepared to secure your exam slot with ease.

1. Go to https://aws.amazon.com/certification/certified-data-engineer-associate and select Schedule Your Exam. This will take you to the AWS Training and Certification sign-in page, which should look something like Figure 13.1.

2. Click the Sign In button. This will open a page for you to select a Sign In option (see Figure 13.2). Choose the preferred option. For individuals, the recommended option is to Create Your Builder ID or Sign In with an Existing ID if you have already taken certification exams in the past.

FIGURE 13.1   The AWS Certification sign-in page

3. Enter your email address if you are creating a new AWS Builder ID, and then press Next or select Already Have AWS Builder ID? Sign In if you are using your existing credentials. We are going to go with the creation of a new AWS Builder ID process, as shown in Figure 13.3.

4. Once you enter your email, the system checks if a builder with a similar email already exists and performs other checks before prompting you for your name (see Figure 13.4). You should enter your correct name, as this will be visible to other people using AWS. Press Next. This will send a verification code to your email address.

5. Enter the verification code. Upon verification, you will be taken to a screen where you choose your password. The password must meet the following criteria:

   ▪ Be between 8 and 64 characters

   ▪ Include uppercase and lowercase letters

   ▪ Contain numbers

   ▪ Include nonalphanumeric characters

FIGURE 13.2 Sign-in options

6. You now have an AWS Builder ID. You can use it to register for exams. Now, log in to your profile. Go to `https://www.aws.training/SignIn?returnUrl=%2F Certification` and enter your Builder ID.

   ▪ You will be prompted to Accept Terms and Conditions if this is your first time logging in with your credentials. Select Accept Terms to be taken to the Certification Registration page.

FIGURE 13.3   Creating an AWS Builder ID

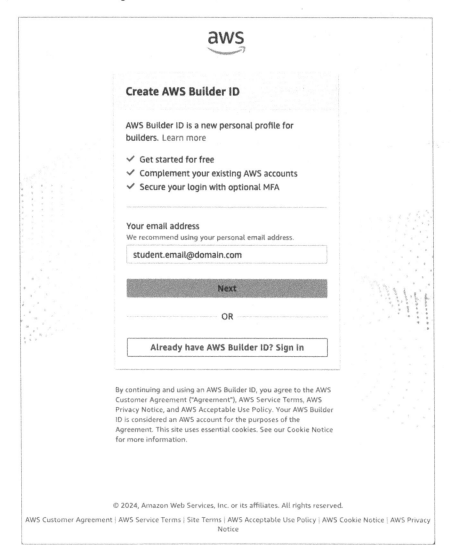

- Enter your profile details, and you will be taken to the Create a New AWS Certification Account page (see Figure 13.5).

7. This will create your certification account and take you to the AWS Certification Program Agreement. On the top right of the page will be your candidate ID and

your name. This is the ID you will use to register your exams with the certification providers. On this page:

- Accept the certification agreement.
- Provide your name, which should match your ID that will be required at the certification center.
- Provide your mailing address.
- Provide other details, and then select Next.

FIGURE 13.4 Create AWS Builder ID - Profile

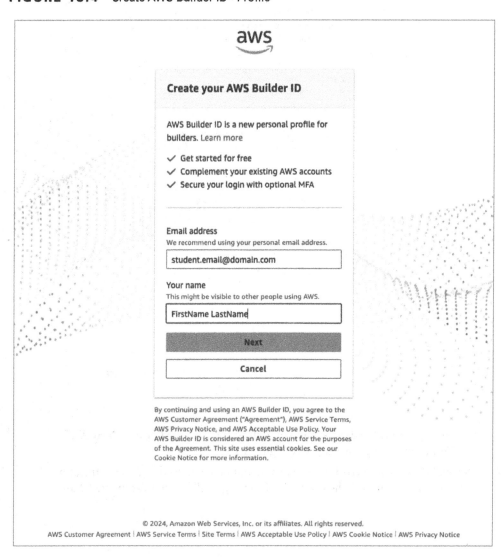

FIGURE 13.5   Create New AWS Certification Account

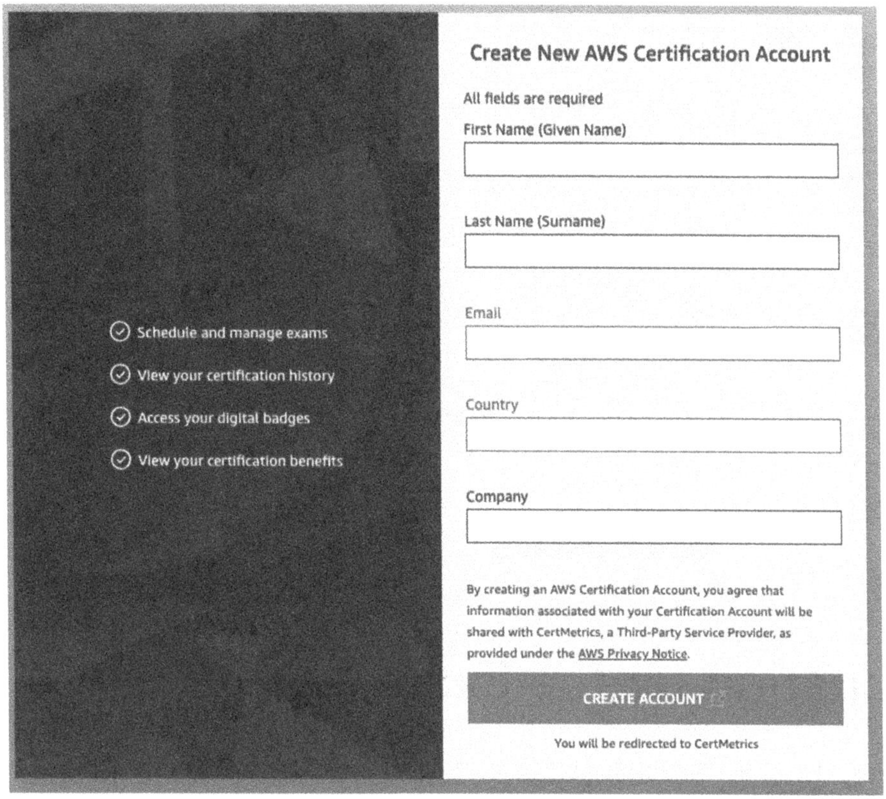

You will now be taken to your Exam dashboard (see Figure 13.6).

8. Select the Exam Registration drop-down on the left-hand side of the screen, and then select Schedule an Exam. The rest of the steps are self-explanatory:

    - Authorize the exam.

    - Press Schedule.

    - On the Pearson VUE website, you can select Exam Taking Options from In-person Exam at a Test Center, or you can select Online with OnVUE.

    - Select your preferred language (Chinese, English, Japanese, Korean).

    - Accept the terms and conditions.

    - Select your nearest test center (if you have chosen physical) or choose a preferred slot (if virtual).

    - Pay the fee (Selected Credit cards. Or exam voucher).

9. Get ready for the big day!

FIGURE 13.6 Exam registration

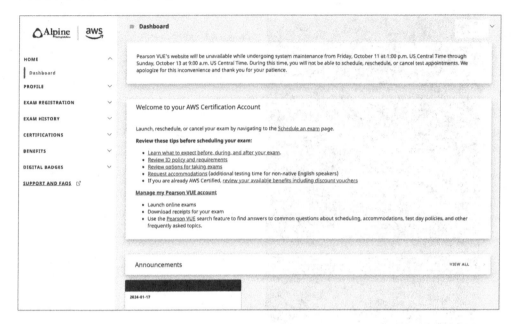

Preparing for the Exam

Here are a few important tips to keep in mind before you take the exam.

Practical Experience Is Irreplaceable

You've likely amassed a substantial amount of knowledge about data engineering on AWS through studying various chapters. The authors, who are experts in their respective domains, have dedicated significant effort to ensure that all essential topics are thoroughly covered. However, data engineering is an expansive field, and the AWS Data Engineering exam stands out as one of AWS's most challenging certifications due to its extensive range of services. Consequently, merely reviewing the certification materials may not suffice to secure a passing score.

To enhance your chances of success, it's highly advisable to gain hands-on experience with these services. Additionally, engage with the workshops available on the AWS Workshops website (`workshops.aws.com`).

Here are 10 key workshops that I recommend you begin with:

- AWS Serverless Data Lake Jumpstart: `https://catalog.us-east-1.prod .workshops.aws/workshops/276faf92-bffc-4843-8a8e-8078add48194`

- AWS Glue Hands-On Labs: `https://aws-glue-hands-on-labs.workshop.aws`

- AWS Database Migration Workshop: `https://catalog.workshops.aws/databasemigration`
- Real Time Streaming with Kinesis: `https://real-time-streaming-with-kinesis.workshop.aws`
- Redshift Immersion Labs: `https://redshift-immersion.workshop.aws`
- Amazon Redshift Deep Dive: `https://redshift-deepdive.workshop.aws`
- Amazon OpenSearch workshop: `https://catalog.workshops.aws/workshops/c87214bf-11ea-46b7-82d9-4d934c2a7f53`
- Amazon EMR Workshop: `https://emr-etl.workshop.aws`
- QuickSight Workshops: `https://catalog.workshops.aws/quicksight`
- AWS Lake Formation Workshop: `https://lakeformation.workshop.aws`

Practice Tests, Practice Tests, and More Practice Tests

After thoroughly reviewing the study materials, taking practice tests is an excellent strategy to prepare for the actual exam. The AWS Data Engineering exam lasts approximately 130 minutes and consists of 65 questions, giving you about 2 minutes per question. While some questions are brief and require minimal reading, many are scenario-based, necessitating careful analysis and understanding of complex situations. To excel, you need to practice handling these types of questions efficiently.

We offer a variety of practice questions designed to assess your knowledge and simulate the exam environment. These questions closely resemble those you'll encounter during the actual test, providing valuable insight into the exam format and question types. Additionally, Wiley provides a test simulator, which can be an invaluable tool in your preparation. Utilizing these resources will help you become more comfortable with the exam structure and improve your time management skills, ultimately increasing your chances of passing the exam successfully.

Attempting Tough Questions

While we hope the material in this book fully prepares you for the exam, there will be times when you encounter particularly difficult questions. One of the most challenging aspects of AWS exams is that every option seems valid and plausible. This means that while the answers represent valid implementations, they may not apply to the specific scenario asked. So, how should you approach these tricky questions?

Let's consider an example:

Question:

You need a cost-effective solution to store a large collection of video files as well as a fully managed data warehouse service to track and analyze all your metadata efficiently using your existing business intelligence tools. Which of the following would fulfill the requirements? (Choose one.)

Options:

A. Store the data in Amazon DynamoDB and reference its location in Amazon Redshift.

B. Store the data in Amazon S3 and reference its location in Amazon EMR.

C. Store the data in Amazon S3 and reference its location in Amazon DynamoDB.

D. Store the data in Amazon S3 and reference its location in Amazon Redshift.

How should you approach this question?

First, focus on the core requirements:

- **Cost-effective storage** for a large collection of video files
- **Fully managed data warehouse** to analyze metadata
- Compatibility with **existing BI tools**

Now, break down the answer choices, as shown in Table 13.1.

TABLE 13.1 Breaking down the answer choices

Option	Data Storage	Metadata Storage
A	Amazon DynamoDB	Amazon Redshift
B	Amazon S3	Amazon EMR
C	Amazon S3	Amazon DynamoDB
D	Amazon S3	Amazon Redshift

Let's quickly eliminate one option.

Option A proposes storing video files in Amazon DynamoDB, which is a key-value store with size limitations—not suitable for large video files. Therefore, Option A is out.

Now, focus on the remaining options, which all use Amazon S3 for storing the video files (a suitable choice). The key difference is in the metadata storage:

- **Amazon EMR** is more suited for big data processing.
- **Amazon DynamoDB** is a NoSQL database, less ideal for complex queries and analysis.
- **Amazon Redshift** is a fully managed data warehouse, perfect for analyzing metadata with BI tools.

Given that the question specifically asks for a fully managed data warehouse and BI tool compatibility, the best answer is Option D: Amazon S3 with Amazon Redshift.

Breaking down the question and identifying core requirements helps in eliminating distractors and choosing the right solution. Always focus on what the question is really asking, and match your answer to the specific scenario.

Handling Long Question Text / Skimming for Keywords

A significant number of questions in the exam are framed using lengthy texts, which can be challenging, especially for those who struggle to grasp the core requirement on the first read. This often leads to candidates rereading the question multiple times. However, a simple strategy can help you improve your reading speed and identify the key elements more effectively.

We suggest starting with the last two lines of the question before reading it from the top. This approach works well because, in Amazon's writing style, the most critical point is often conveyed in the final sentence. For instance, it may reveal whether the question focuses on security, performance, cost, reliability, or another key factor. With this context in mind, as you read the rest of the question, your subconscious will automatically begin identifying relevant information.

Additionally, it may be helpful to glance at the possible answers before reading the full question. This will give you an idea of what to look for, enabling you to focus on the relevant details from the start.

Use Diagrams or Notes

When faced with complex scenarios in a question, it can be extremely helpful to draw a quick diagram or outline the key components in a note form. Visualizing the problem allows you to see relationships between different parts of the question more clearly, making it easier to identify patterns or key dependencies. For example, in AWS-related questions, you might be asked to evaluate storage options, networking configurations, or security architectures. By sketching a rough diagram, you can better map out how different services interact and highlight areas that match the question's requirements. This approach can also be useful in organizing your thoughts, helping you to reduce confusion and focus on the relevant aspects of the problem.

Flag Questions to Return to Later

Flagging questions is a useful strategy for several reasons:

- **Time management:** AWS exams are often time-constrained, and it's easy to get bogged down on one difficult question. Flagging allows you to skip tough questions initially and return to them later, ensuring you answer as many questions as possible within the time limit. This prevents you from wasting too much time on a single question while other, possibly easier questions remain unanswered.

- **Reduced stress:** Spending too much time on a tricky question can increase stress and hurt your confidence. Flagging it and moving on allows you to maintain your momentum and avoid unnecessary anxiety. When you come back to the flagged questions later, you'll have a fresh perspective, and the pressure will be reduced since you've already answered other questions.

- **Fresh perspective:** Sometimes, questions become clearer after taking a break and returning with a fresh mindset. As you work through other parts of the exam, you may also come across clues or concepts that help you answer the previously flagged question more easily. Flagging allows you to revisit questions with new insights or ideas.

- **Maximizing score potential:** By flagging questions you're unsure about and focusing on the ones you're more confident in first, you maximize your score potential. It's a more efficient approach, ensuring that you accumulate as many points as possible by answering the questions you know well, rather than potentially missing out because you spent too long on one difficult question.

Pace Yourself

If a question feels particularly difficult, flag it and move on to the next question. Answering easier questions first can build confidence and give you more time to think about the harder ones later.

The Day Before the Exam

The day before the exam, as well as the day of the exam, needs to be planned carefully.

Review Key Concepts, Not Everything

Avoid trying to cram or learn new topics the day before the exam. Instead, focus on reviewing high-impact concepts, key terms, and areas where you feel less confident. Go through any condensed study materials or flashcards you've created over your preparation period. Revisit the critical services, definitions, and concepts that are likely to be tested.

Familiarize Yourself with the Exam Format

If you haven't already, ensure that you're familiar with the exam structure and the type of questions (multiple-choice, multiple-response, scenario-based, etc.). Practice with mock exams, but don't overdo it. Simply get comfortable with how the questions are presented and how the time will be managed.

Get Your Documents Ready

Ensure that you have all the necessary documents for the exam day, such as your identification (passport, driver's license, etc.), any exam registration details, and, if applicable, a printout of your confirmation email. If you're taking the exam online, make sure you have everything ready—this includes a stable Internet connection, a functioning webcam, and a quiet environment.

Plan Your Logistics

If you're going to a physical exam center, double-check the location and ensure you know how to get there. Plan your commute to avoid stress and make sure you arrive early. If you're taking the exam online, check your system, Internet, and workspace setup to avoid last-minute issues.

Light Revision Only

The day before an exam, it's important to keep the revision light. Go over summary sheets, diagrams, or mind maps you may have created. Consider revising the concepts you find tricky, but don't overwhelm yourself with too much material. The focus should be on consolidation, not cramming.

Relax and Unwind

It's vital to take some time to relax. Your brain needs to rest to process and retain information, so take breaks to unwind. Engage in a relaxing activity, whether it's going for a walk, listening to music, or doing some light reading. Avoid anything that causes stress or anxiety.

Get a Good Night's Sleep

Aim for 7–8 hours of sleep the night before the exam. Studies show that adequate sleep significantly improves memory retention and cognitive function. Trying to pull an all-nighter could leave you tired and less sharp during the exam.

Eat Healthy and Stay Hydrated

Your brain needs energy to function at its best. Eat a balanced meal the night before, and drink plenty of water throughout the day. Avoid heavy, greasy, or overly sugary foods that could affect your energy levels or disrupt your sleep.

Set Your Alarm and Prepare in Advance

Set an alarm for exam day, and if you have to be at a specific location, leave plenty of time for delays. If you're taking the exam online, make sure your environment is prepped—clear your workspace, have your materials ready, and ensure all electronics are charged.

Visualize Success

Spend a few minutes visualizing yourself completing the exam successfully. Positive visualization can help boost confidence and reduce anxiety. Remind yourself that you've prepared and are capable of doing well.

The Day of the Exam

The day of the exam will likely go better if you plan appropriately.

Wake Up Early

Ensure you wake up with plenty of time before the exam to avoid rushing. Rushing can cause anxiety and stress, which may negatively affect your performance.

Eat a Healthy Breakfast

Have a light, balanced meal that provides energy and keeps you full. Choose foods that release energy slowly, such as oatmeal, whole grains, fruit, and protein. Avoid heavy, greasy, or sugary foods that might cause a crash in energy levels later.

Stay Hydrated

Drink water before the exam, but not so much that you'll need frequent bathroom breaks during the test. Staying hydrated keeps your brain functioning at its best.

Arrive Early

If your exam is at a physical test center, plan to arrive at least 30 minutes early. This will give you time to check in, settle down, and relax before the exam starts. I typically try to arrive at least 30 minutes before the exam. Some of the test centers are quite helpful, letting you begin the test early if you arrive. If it's an online exam, log in at least 15–20 minutes early to ensure your system is working properly and that you have time to deal with any potential technical issues.

Do a Final Check of Documents

Make sure you have all the necessary documents with you (ID, exam confirmation, etc.). If you're taking an online exam, ensure that your computer, camera, and microphone are functioning properly.

Stay Calm and Breathe

Being nervous before an exam is normal, but try not to let anxiety overwhelm you. Take deep breaths and remind yourself that you've prepared for this moment. Positive thinking can have a huge impact on your performance.

Read the Questions Carefully

Once the exam starts, don't rush. Take a moment to read each question carefully. Typically, the last sentence of the question statement indicates what the question is really about. While looking at the answers before the questions statement can help you focus on the key ask of the question, it is important that you fully understand what is being asked before selecting the right answer choice. As mentioned earlier, all AWS exams have lengthy or complex questions, so carefully reading them can prevent you from missing important details.

Answer Easy Questions First

Start by answering questions you know well. This boosts your confidence and ensures you secure easy points early on. If you come across a question that's tough or unclear, flag it and move on. You can return to it later with a clearer mind.

Manage Your Time Wisely

Keep track of your time throughout the exam. Allocate your time based on the number of questions, and ensure you leave enough time to review any flagged or difficult questions at the end. Don't spend too much time on one question; move on and come back later if necessary.

Eliminate Wrong Answers

For multiple-choice questions, try to eliminate clearly wrong options first. This improves your chances of selecting the correct answer, even if you're unsure. AWS exams often have multiple plausible options, so focus on matching the answer to the specific scenario provided.

Trust Your Preparation

Avoid second-guessing yourself or changing your answers unless you have a solid reason to do so. Often, your first instinct is correct. Trust the preparation you've done and approach each question confidently.

Take Short Mental Breaks

If you feel overwhelmed or stuck, take a quick mental break. Close your eyes, breathe deeply, and clear your mind for a few seconds. This will help reset your focus and prevent burnout mid-exam.

Review Your Answers If Time Permits

Once you've completed the exam, use any remaining time to review your answers. Pay close attention to flagged questions or areas where you were unsure. Make sure you've answered all questions before submitting the exam.

Stay Positive Post-Exam

After the exam, avoid overanalyzing your performance. Focus on the effort you put in, and trust that you've done your best. Reflecting on difficult questions right after the exam might only add unnecessary stress.

After the Exam

You'll get the test result immediately after the exam. Don't forget to tag us on LinkedIn when you pass the exam. Good luck!

Appendix A

Answers to Review Questions

Chapter 1: Streaming and Batch Data Ingestion

1. A, D. Amazon Kinesis Data Streams can handle high-volume, real-time data ingestion from multiple sources simultaneously and can automatically scale to handle varying data volumes. Amazon Kinesis Data Analytics is designed for real-time processing of streaming data and can analyze the ingested data as it arrives, making it perfect for generating real-time insights. It can output the processed data to various destinations, including real-time dashboards. While not explicitly chosen, the processed data from Kinesis Data Analytics can be easily stored in services like Amazon S3 or Amazon Redshift for future analysis. By combining Kinesis Data Streams (A) for ingestion and Kinesis Data Analytics (D) for processing, the team can create a robust, scalable, real-time data processing pipeline that meets all the stated requirements.

2. A. Kinesis Data Streams is designed to handle high-volume, real-time data ingestion from multiple sources, making it suitable for IoT sensor data, and enhanced fan-out consumers allow multiple consumers to read from the stream simultaneously, each with their own dedicated throughput, which enables real-time processing of data as it arrives. While not explicitly mentioned in the answer, processed data from Kinesis Data Streams can be easily stored in services like Amazon S3 or Amazon Redshift for long-term analysis. Using Kinesis Data Streams with enhanced fan-out reduces the need for manual scaling and management of consumer applications. Provisioned Throughput mode allows the team to specify the exact capacity needed, ensuring that the stream can handle the incoming data volume without data loss. By using Kinesis Data Streams with enhanced fan-out consumers and Provisioned Throughput mode, the team can create a system that meets all the requirements with minimal operational overhead and maximum data processing reliability.

3. C. MSK Auto Scaling automatically adjusts the number of broker nodes in response to changes in workload and monitors the broker storage utilization and adds or removes brokers as needed, ensuring that the cluster can handle sudden spikes in traffic by automatically scaling out and scaling back in when the additional capacity is no longer needed. It eliminates the need for manual capacity planning and management and ensures high availability and durability of the Kafka cluster. The other answers are incorrect because: MSK Connect (A) is a feature for connecting MSK clusters to other AWS services, not for handling traffic increases; MSK Serverless (B) removes the need to manage Kafka clusters but is a separate offering and not a feature to enable on existing MSK clusters; and MSK Cruise Control (D) is an open-source tool for balancing Kafka clusters but is not a native AWS feature for auto-scaling.

4. C. Enabling IAM access control for the MSK cluster and using IAM roles or users for client authentication provides for seamless integration with existing AWS IAM infrastructure, fine-grained access control at the Kafka operation level, and centralized management of permissions across AWS services. Option A is incorrect because while SASL/SCRAM is a valid authentication method for MSK, it doesn't integrate directly with IAM for authentication. Option B is incorrect because SSL uses certificates for authentication and IAM roles for

authorization. SSL certificates can be used for encryption, but this method doesn't integrate with IAM for authentication. Option D is incorrect because Kerberos is a supported authentication method for MSK, but it doesn't provide direct integration with IAM.

5. B. Using AWS Key Management Service (KMS) customer managed keys provides full control over encryption keys, native integration with Kinesis Data Firehose, comprehensive auditing through AWS CloudTrail, fine-grained access control using IAM policies, and compliance with requirements mandating control over encryption keys. Enabling encryption in transit for Amazon Data Firehose (A) ensures data is encrypted while in transit but doesn't address encryption at rest in S3. Using client-side encryption before sending data to Amazon Data Firehose (C) would prevent Firehose from performing any data transformation and could complicate the overall architecture. Using S3-managed encryption keys (D) provides encryption at rest, but it doesn't offer the same level of control over the keys as customer managed KMS keys.

6. B. AWS Glue is a fully managed ETL service designed to handle semi-structured data like JSON. It offers a visual interface (Glue Studio) for creating ETL jobs with minimal coding and automatically generates Scala or Python code for the ETL jobs. Glue also provides seamless integration and built-in support for processing data in Amazon S3 and loading it into Amazon Redshift. While EMR (A) can handle this task, it requires more setup and management compared to Glue and is better suited for more complex, distributed data processing tasks that require fine-grained control. Lambda (C) is suitable for small-scale data processing tasks but may not be efficient for large volumes of data, and it also requires writing and maintaining custom code, which goes against the team's requirement. Redshift Spectrum (D) allows querying data in S3 directly but doesn't provide ETL capabilities, and it's more suitable for analyzing data that's already in a query-friendly format.

7. C. AWS Glue provides automated data discovery and cataloging capabilities through Glue crawlers, and it supports both cloud and on-premises data sources through JDBC connections. It also offers ETL capabilities to transform and prepare data for analysis and can automatically detect and adapt to schema changes in the source data. The AWS Glue Data Catalog offers a centralized metadata repository that's searchable and integrates with other AWS services. Athena (A) is a query service that can work with data in a data lake, but it doesn't provide data discovery, cataloging, or ETL capabilities required in this scenario. Data Pipeline (B) is used for moving and processing data between different AWS services and on-premises data sources and can be part of a data lake solution, but it doesn't offer the automated cataloging and schema evolution features needed here. Lake Formation (D) builds on top of AWS Glue and provides additional security and governance features for data lakes. While it could be used in this scenario, Glue alone provides the core functionality required and is a more direct answer to the question.

8. D. AWS DMS offers minimal downtime, heterogeneous migration, change data capture (CDC), custom data transformations, large dataset handling, and BLOB data support. While AWS Glue (A) is excellent for ETL jobs, it isn't designed for the continuous, low-latency data replication required in this scenario and would struggle to capture real-time changes during the migration process. AWS DataSync (B) is primarily designed for transferring large amounts of data between on-premises storage and AWS storage services, and it isn't suitable for database migration, especially when continuous replication and schema conversion are required.

Amazon EMR (C) is a big data processing platform. While it could potentially be used for this task with custom scripts, it would require significant development effort and wouldn't provide the out-of-the-box features for continuous replication and schema conversion that DMS offers.

9. C. Snowball can handle large-scale data transfers (up to 80 TB per device) and allows for offline data transfer, bypassing the need for high-bandwidth Internet connections and completing the transfer much faster than online transfer methods. It also provides for minimal impact on daily operations because offline transfer doesn't consume the institute's Internet bandwidth. Snowball devices also offer end-to-end security with encryption and tamper-resistant features. Direct Connect (A) provides a dedicated network connection to AWS, but it's not suitable for this scenario due to the institute's remote location, the time required to set up a Direct Connect connection, and the limited bandwidth issue. DataSync (B) is designed for online data transfer and would be constrained by the limited internet bandwidth. Transferring 80 TB over a 100Mbps connection would take significantly longer than the two-week requirement. S3 Transfer Acceleration (D) can improve transfer speeds, but it still relies on Internet connectivity. Given the large data volume and limited bandwidth, this option would not meet the two-week transfer requirement and would significantly impact the institute's daily Internet usage.

10. D. The Amazon Redshift COPY command can efficiently load large amounts of data directly from S3 into Redshift tables without intermediate steps, suitable for the 500GB daily ingestion. It supports basic transformations like data type conversions during the load process and can handle occasional schema changes by allowing column mapping and ignoring extra columns. It provides high performance because it's optimized for parallel loading, and as a native Redshift feature, it doesn't require additional services or compute resources, making it cost-efficient. AWS Glue (A) is a powerful ETL service, but it introduces unnecessary complexity and potential cost for this scenario, where data is already in S3 and only basic transformations are needed. DistCp (B) is a tool for copying large amounts of data, but it's typically used for copying between Hadoop-compatible file systems, and it isn't designed for loading data into Redshift, so it would require additional steps and complexity. Sqoop (C) is primarily designed for transferring data between Hadoop and relational databases. While it can be used with S3 and Redshift, it's not the most efficient choice for this scenario, especially when the data is already in S3 and Redshift has native tools for data ingestion.

Chapter 2: Building Automated Data Pipelines

1. B. AWS Step Functions allows you to create and manage visual workflows to orchestrate AWS services and custom code. Step Functions provides a user-friendly interface to define workflows as state machines, enabling coordination of tasks and services. It integrates seamlessly with other AWS services like Lambda, S3, and DynamoDB, offering a powerful tool for building scalable, distributed applications. The other options are incorrect because

AWS Lambda focuses on running individual functions; AWS Glue is specialized for data integration and ETL; and Amazon MWAA is tailored for managing Apache Airflow workflows rather than AWS-native orchestration. Step Functions stands out as the most suitable solution for this use case.

2. A. Amazon MWAA is specifically designed to manage Apache Airflow workflows in a fully managed environment. It enables users to build, schedule, and monitor workflows, often used for automating complex data pipelines. Unlike AWS Step Functions, which focuses on AWS-native workflows, MWAA supports open-source Apache Airflow, making it ideal for integrating with hybrid or multi-cloud environments. The other options are incorrect because Amazon MWAA does not directly orchestrate Lambda functions, perform data transformations, or manage data lakes—those are tasks suited to other AWS services like Step Functions, Glue, or Lake Formation, respectively.

3. C. AWS Glue provides a serverless Apache Spark environment and a Data Catalog specifically designed for building and automating ETL pipelines. AWS Glue includes features like an integrated Data Catalog for metadata management and serverless Apache Spark for scalable ETL processing without infrastructure management. It simplifies data preparation workflows for analytics and machine learning. The other options are incorrect: AWS Step Functions focuses on workflow orchestration; Amazon MWAA manages Apache Airflow workflows; and AWS Lambda executes serverless functions but is not built for ETL or Spark-based pipelines. AWS Glue is the purpose-built service for this use case.

4. A. Amazon EventBridge is an event-driven service that enables the integration and orchestration of data pipelines by triggering actions in response to events from AWS services, custom applications, or third-party SaaS providers. It is designed to seamlessly connect event sources to targets like Lambda, Step Functions, or other AWS services to automate workflows. The other options are incorrect: EventBridge does not perform data transformations, manage data lakes, or provide an Apache Airflow environment, as those tasks are handled by AWS Glue, Lake Formation, and Amazon MWAA, respectively. EventBridge is ideal for event-based pipeline orchestration.

5. A. Amazon SNS is designed to send notifications and alerts for various events, including data pipeline failures or completions. Amazon Simple Notification Service (SNS) is a fully managed messaging service that enables the publishing of messages to subscribers via email, SMS, or other endpoints, making it ideal for alerting. While AWS CloudTrail provides logging and auditing of API calls, and Amazon CloudWatch offers monitoring and metrics, they don't directly handle notifications. AWS Glue is a data integration service and doesn't manage notifications either. For sending alerts related to pipeline events, Amazon SNS is the most appropriate service.

6. A. Infrastructure as code (IaC) allows you to define and provision your infrastructure (e.g., data pipelines, servers, databases) using code templates. This approach ensures that deployments are automated, version-controlled, and consistent across environments such as development, testing, and production. The other options are incorrect: IaC does not perform data transformations, orchestrate pipelines, or handle notifications—these tasks are managed by services like AWS Glue, Step Functions, and SNS, respectively. IaC focuses on automating infrastructure deployment for reliability and efficiency.

7. B. AWS Lambda is designed to execute custom code for data processing or transformation within data pipelines. AWS Lambda is a serverless compute service that runs your code in response to events from various sources, such as Amazon S3, DynamoDB, or EventBridge. It is well-suited for implementing custom logic because it supports multiple programming languages and integrates seamlessly with other AWS services. The other options are incorrect: AWS Step Functions is used for orchestration; Amazon MWAA manages Apache Airflow workflows; and Amazon EventBridge triggers workflows based on events but does not perform data processing. Lambda is the ideal choice for custom transformations.

8. C. Git is a distributed version control system that is widely used in software development, including data pipeline development. It enables teams to track changes, manage code repositories, and collaborate effectively. By using Git, developers can maintain version control, revert to previous versions, and resolve conflicts in a collaborative environment. The other options are incorrect: Git does not perform data transformations, orchestrate pipelines, or send notifications. Its primary purpose is to streamline development and collaboration through robust version control.

9. B. Data quality testing is specifically focused on validating the quality and integrity of data processed by a data pipeline. Data quality testing involves checking data against predefined rules, such as verifying data completeness, consistency, accuracy, and format validity, to ensure that the output meets the required standards. While unit testing is used to validate individual components of the pipeline, and logging and monitoring help track pipeline performance and issues, they do not directly assess data quality. Debugging tools assist in identifying and fixing code issues but are not designed for data validation. Data quality testing is the appropriate technique for ensuring data integrity.

10. C. Amazon CloudWatch is designed to collect and track metrics, monitor logs, and set alarms for AWS resources and applications, including data pipelines. In the context of data pipeline orchestration, it helps identify performance bottlenecks, troubleshoot failures, and ensure the smooth operation of pipelines. The other options are incorrect: CloudWatch does not perform data transformations, orchestrate pipelines, or manage code changes and version control—those functions are handled by services like AWS Glue, Step Functions, and Git, respectively. CloudWatch is the ideal service for monitoring and logging.

Chapter 3: Data Transformation

1. A. The `groupSize` parameter is used to group files that are being read from Amazon S3. The parameter also enables you to specify the target size of the group in bytes. This property enables each ETL task to read a group of input files into a single in-memory partition, especially when there is large number of small files in your S3 data store. The `boundedSize` parameter is used to prevent a Glue job from processing too much data. This allows you to solve OOM errors. The `repartition` partition is used to reduce the number of partitions and shuffle all the data. Changing to a different worker type with higher DPUs will not solve the stated problem. Hence, setting the `groupSize` is the recommended approach.

2. B. AWS Step Functions is an orchestration service. You can perform ETL operations and incremental data processing with the rest of the options mentioned. However, considering the least operational overhead criteria, AWS Glue is the recommended option. AWS Glue uses job bookmarks to track the data that has already been processed. Once enabled, for Amazon S3, Glue job bookmarks check the last modified time of the objects to verify which objects need to be processed.

3. D. Predicate pushdown is an optimization technique that helps to retrieve selective data, thereby reducing the time and amount of the data being processed. Th other options will not help solve the OOM errors.

4. A. Storing the data in Amazon S3 is the most cost-effective and durable solution. Additionally, using transient clusters for batch jobs is recommended, as the cluster automatically terminates once the last step runs. Amazon EMR also allows you to reuse the existing jobs developed with Hadoop frameworks on-premises. Hence, the recommended option here is to migrate to Amazon EMR, and then launch transient clusters with data stored in Amazon S3.

5. D. To optimize the cost of data quality scans, leveraging Glue job bookmarks is the recommended approach for an ETL data pipeline. Glue job bookmarks avoid reprocessing the entire dataset and efficiently process new or changed data since the last successful job run. The data quality checks can then be applied on the incremental dataset.

6. B. Random Cut Forest (RCF) is an algorithm widely used for anomaly detection use cases. Amazon Managed Service for Apache Flink can be configured to run RCF on input streams with large throughput.

7. D. The requirement mentions an optimal and cost-effective solution. Using Amazon Redshift Spectrum, customers can easily query the data in Amazon S3. The older and historical data (cold layer) can be accessed by the users and can be joined with the latest data in the Amazon Redshift cluster. With Amazon Redshift Spectrum, you only pay for the resources you consume for the duration of your query. Only the frequently accessed current data (hot layer) will be stored in the Amazon Redshift table.

8. A, C, F. AWS Glue crawlers can scan your data lake and keep the catalog in sync with the underlying data. Although AWS Glue can do both the data transformations, considering the requirement to provide a cost-effective solution, Amazon EMR is the recommended option to process the archived data. Amazon EMR is more suitable for handling one-time data transformations against terabytes of data, and incremental data can be processed using Glue job bookmarks using AWS Glue. The use case is not for building, training, and deploying machine learning models; hence, Amazon SageMaker is not suitable for this use case. Considering the condition of mixed-format data and a cost-effective solution, performing data transformations within Amazon Redshift is also not recommended for this use case.

9. C. Amazon Data Firehose is the easiest way to load the streaming data into S3. When you enable the record transformation, JSON data automatically gets converted to the Parquet format. Amazon Data Firehose references table definitions stored in AWS Glue. You can choose to select the Glue Catalog table and specify the schema for your source records.

10. B. Using the COPY and UNLOAD commands is the most effective way to move the data back and forth from S3 to Redshift. With Redshift Spectrum, the data becomes available immediately. However, you need a Redshift cluster along with a SQL client to run these SQL commands. DMS does not support Redshift as the source and internally uses COPY commands to load the data from S3 to Redshift. S3 Transfer Acceleration is used to speed up the data transfers over long distances between your S3 bucket and client applications. So, with the given options, the recommended approach is to use the COPY and UNLOAD commands.

11. D. Open table formats like Apache Hudi, Apache Iceberg, and Delta Lake tables are recommended to implement upserts and deletes on Amazon S3 data lakes. Redshift Spectrum with Apache Iceberg and Amazon Athena with Apache Hudi support only read-only formats. To cater to the least operational overhead, configuring the tables using Apache Iceberg and deleting the records using Amazon Athena is the recommended approach for this use case.

12. A. AWS Lambda supports Parallelization Factor, which allows you to process a shard of Kinesis or DynamoDB data streams with more than one Lambda invocation simultaneously. By default, Lambda invokes a function with one batch of data records from one shard at a time. This allows faster stream processing without the need to over-scale the number of shards while still guaranteeing the order of records processed.

13. D, E. There is no need to add a task node, as the current job takes less time than required by the SLA. Considering the cost reduction, the recommended approach is to use an instance fleets configuration. You can specify target capacities for on-demand and Spot instances within each fleet. When the cluster launches, Amazon EMR provisions instances until the targets are fulfilled. When Amazon EC2 reclaims the Spot instance in a running cluster, EMR tries to replace the instance with the instance type that you specify.

14. D. AWS Glue DataBrew is a visual data preparation tools that enables data analysts to clean and normalize data. It is a low-code/no-code data processing service recommended for data preparation and data quality use cases.

15. A. AWS Lambda layers (.zip file) allow you to package libraries, custom runtimes, and other dependencies that can be reused across multiple Lambda functions.

16. C. AWS Glue Data Quality allows you to measure and monitor the quality of data. You can implement data quality rules in AWS Glue DataBrew to define constraints on data values and to validate the consistency and integrity of the data.

17. D. Using Amazon Redshift Data API, customers can run individual queries from within your application or submit a batch of SQL queries within a transaction. There is no need to manage WebSocket or JDBC connections.

18. C. The FLEX execution class in an AWS Glue job allows the jobs to run on spare compute capacity instead of dedicated hardware. This significantly reduces the costs compared to the STANDARD execution class.

19. A, B. Glue data quality checks can be applied at rest as well as in transit. Data quality checks at rest can be applied on Glue Catalog tables, while in-transit checks can be applied during ETL processing using AWS Glue DataBrew, AWS Glue Studio UI, or AWS Glue Notebooks.

20. D. A custom JAR runs a compiled Java program that you can upload to S3. You can compile the program against the version of Hadoop you want to launch, and then submit the `CUSTOM_JAR` step to your EMR cluster.

Chapter 4: Storage Services

1. D. Implement a lifecycle policy to store data in S3 Standard for 30 days, then transition to S3 Standard-IA for long-term storage. Use S3 Inventory to regularly audit object storage classes and ensure the lifecycle policy is working correctly. Enable S3 Storage Lens to monitor usage patterns and costs across storage classes.

2. B. Implement Amazon FSx for Lustre, which is designed for high-performance computing (HPC), configuring it for the highest available performance. Use data compression to optimize storage efficiency and costs. Set up FSx for Lustre linked to an S3 bucket for long-term data storage and easy data import/export.

3. C. Implement Amazon S3 as the foundation for the data lake. Use S3 Storage Classes to optimize costs based on data access patterns. Implement S3 Select and Glacier Select for efficient querying of specific data. Use AWS Glue for data catalog and ETL processes.

4. D. Use Parquet files for efficient compression and query performance. Use AWS Glue to convert incoming data to Parquet format. Leverage Athena or Redshift Spectrum for high-performance queries. Implement S3 lifecycle policies to transition older data to Glacier.

5. A. Use Amazon Redshift Spectrum to query data directly in S3 without loading it into Redshift. Create external tables in Redshift to map to S3 data. Implement a columnar format like Parquet for improved query performance. Use Redshift Workload Management (WLM) to optimize query execution.

6. C. Configure S3 Object Lock in Compliance mode to enforce retention periods. Set up AWS CloudWatch alarms to monitor any attempts to modify or delete locked objects. Implement regular audits using AWS Macie to detect any sensitive data that may not be properly protected.

7. B. Configure S3 Cross-Region Replication (CRR) to automatically replicate data to specified regions. Set up IAM roles for S3 replication. Use replication metrics and S3 event notifications to monitor the replication process and ensure data consistency across regions.

8. B. Implement Amazon S3 with Transfer Acceleration for fast uploads. Use S3 event notifications to trigger Lambda functions for image processing. Set up Amazon CloudFront distributions with S3 as the origin for low-latency global content delivery.

9. D. Use S3 Standard storage class for high durability and availability. Implement Amazon CloudFront for content delivery, creating a CloudFront distribution with S3 as the origin. Use CloudFront field-level encryption to protect sensitive data. Implement Lambda@Edge for personalized content delivery and dynamic content at the edge.

10. C. Implement S3 Object Lock in Compliance mode with a specified retention period. Enable S3 Versioning to maintain object history. Use S3 Inventory and S3 Storage Lens to monitor object retention and compliance. Implement AWS CloudTrail and AWS Config for comprehensive auditing and compliance monitoring.

Chapter 5: Databases and Data Warehouses on AWS

1. C. Using the Redshift COPY command to bulk-load data is the most efficient method because Redshift can parallelize the load across its multiple compute nodes. It is also cost-effective because, unlike Redshift Spectrum, there is no extra charge.

2. B. The Redshift UNLOAD command is the most efficient way to export data from Redshift into S3. Like the COPY command, it runs the process in parallel across multiple compute nodes.

3. D. The Redshift Data API is the best option for the requirements. It allows you to connect asynchronously to Redshift, can paginate results back to the client, and greatly simplifies application connection management.

4. C. The KEY distribution style will co-locate rows related by the join column on the same compute nodes. This allows Redshift to join rows on each compute node without having to move data around the nodes, which can be expensive.

5. C. Redshift federated queries allow you to query external databases, such as RDS MySQL, directly in real time. The results can be combined in a single query or database view with historical data stored locally in Redshift.

6. B. DynamoDB auto scaling will adjust capacity dynamically to match the current load. You can define an upper and lower range for read and write capacity units and a target utilization percentage within that range. DynamoDB will scale to maintain the target utilization.

7. A. The DynamoDB Streams feature simplifies tracking and auditing data changes. Streams can be combined with Lambda functions to build near-real-time applications triggered by changes to items in a table.

8. C. Amazon RDS is the correct service to use for relational data. RDS Multi-AZ DB instances ensure durability, high availability, and disaster recovery, with a standby instance created in a different AZ and synchronous replication from the primary instance to the standby.

9. A. Amazon DynamoDB is a NoSQL database designed for handling data in the JSON format with high performance at scale and low latency.

10. C. Amazon Neptune is a high-performance graph database that is purpose-built for highly connected datasets. It can efficiently and quickly traverse data with large numbers of complex relationships.

Chapter 6: Data Catalogs

1. D. AWS Glue Data Catalog is a centralized repository that stores metadata of your organization's datasets. This metadata is populated using an AWS Glue crawler. The crawler automatically scans diverse data sources and extracts the metadata information.

2. C. You can configure Hive to use the AWS Glue Data Catalog as its metastore. While using an Amazon Aurora database as your external metastore for Hive is a valid option, it is not as simple to implement as Glue Data Catalog.

3. B. Although all the options are valid, AWS Glue requires the least amount of setup and maintenance since it is serverless and doesn't require management of infrastructure.

4. B. AWS Glue Data Catalog supports column-level statistics that integrate with the cost-based optimizer from Amazon Athena and Amazon Redshift Spectrum. This results in improved query performance and potential cost savings.

5. C. AWS Glue Data Catalog is a centralized repository that stores metadata of your organization's datasets. This metadata is populated using an AWS Glue crawler. The crawler automatically scans diverse data sources and extracts the metadata information.

6. A. AWS Glue allows you to define data quality checks at rest (Glue Data Catalog tables) and in transit (AWS Glue ETL jobs). You can schedule periodic runs to analyze the data against the defined rules and identify quality issues. Although Amazon EMR can run custom data quality checks using Spark jobs, it requires setting up and managing clusters, leading to potentially higher costs compared to serverless options.

7. B. AWS Glue Data Catalog can be used as a centralized repository to store the metadata about your organization's datasets. The data catalog supports wide range of data sources, including Amazon S3, Amazon Redshift, Amazon RDS, Apache Hive, and so on. This approach not only minimizes the development effort to connect to the data in the data lakes with analytics tools but also reduces the costs by avoiding the need to store duplicate copies of data to each tool.

8. C. Amazon Redshift automatically mounts the AWS Glue Data Catalog as a database and allows you to query the data stored in Amazon S3 with three-part-notation.

9. A. AWS Glue enables you to define data quality checks at rest (Glue Data Catalog tables) and in transit (AWS Glue ETL jobs). You can schedule periodic runs to analyze the data against the defined rules and identify quality issues.

10. D. AWS Glue Data Catalog supports column-level statistics to improve query planning and execution. Query engines like Amazon Athena and Amazon Redshift Spectrum can use these statistics to optimize the query plans by applying the most restrictive filters as early as possible during the query processing, thereby limiting the amount of data processed and memory usage. This also leads to cost savings in pay-per-query services.

11. D. AWS Glue Data Catalog natively supports Apache Iceberg, Apache Hudi, and Delta Lake table formats. These table formats allow for more efficient data access patterns, leading to faster query execution, and adapt to changing data structures over time without breaking the existing queries.

12. C. An AWS Glue crawler can infer the schema and create metadata in the data catalog. Using EventBridge, you can trigger the Glue crawler on the arrival of any new files on the data lake to detect any changes in the schema. The crawler also compares the previously generated metadata with the new data. As these are native capabilities with an AWS Glue crawler, it is the recommended option to achieve the requirement with least operational overhead.

13. B. Within your ETL script, AWS Glue ETL jobs provides features that you can use to update your schema, partitions in the AWS Glue Data Catalog. You can enable this feature by adding few lines of code to your ETL script by using `enableUpdateCatalog` and `partition Keys` argument. These arguments indicate that the Data Catalog is to be updated during the job run as the new partitions are created. Please refer to this URL for more information: `https://docs.aws.amazon.com/glue/latest/dg/update-from-job.html# update-from-job-updating-table-schema`

14. A. In Amazon Athena, after a partitioned table is created, any new data partitions added to S3 remain unrecognized by Athena. The `MSCK REPAIR TABLE` command synchronizes the table's metadata with the actual data layout in S3.

Chapter 7: Visualizing Your Data

1. C. Amazon QuickSight is a fully managed business intelligence service that allows you to create and publish interactive dashboards. It also provides embedding capabilities, making it the best choice for creating interactive dashboards and embedding visualizations in applications.

2. C. Amazon Athena is a serverless query service that allows you to analyze data directly in S3 without loading it into a database. It supports structured, semi-structured, and unstructured data. Athena uses a pay-per-query pricing model, where you're charged based on the amount of data scanned by each query.

3. B. AWS Glue DataBrew is a visual data preparation tool that allows you to clean and normalize data without writing code. It provides a visual interface for data transformation and over 250 built-in transformations.

4. A. SPICE stands for Super-fast, Parallel, In-memory Calculation Engine. It's QuickSight's in-memory engine designed for fast performance on large datasets.

5. C. The `WINDOW` clause, often used with `OVER()`, is the most appropriate for calculating running totals or moving averages. It allows you to perform calculations across a set of rows that are related to the current row.

6. C. AWS Glue DataBrew provides many built-in transformations for data cleaning and preparation, including handling missing values, standardizing formats, and removing duplicates. However, training machine learning models is not a built-in transformation in DataBrew.

7. C. Pie charts are best suited for showing the composition of a whole, where each slice represents a category's proportion of the total. However, they should be used sparingly and typically with a small number of categories for clarity.

8. B. Partitioning in Athena divides tables into parts based on column values, such as date, country, or category. This allows Athena to scan only the relevant partitions instead of the entire table, reducing the amount of data scanned and lowering query costs.

9. D. While AWS Glue can be used for ETL workflows, AWS Step Functions provides a visual workflow service that enables you to create and run a series of checkpointed and event-driven workflows that maintain the application state. It offers a visual interface to create flow charts representing your data pipelines or other workflows.

10. B. While it's important to provide comprehensive information, including too much data in a single visualization can lead to clutter and confusion. Best practices for data visualization include keeping visualizations simple and focused, using consistent design elements, providing clear labels and context, and adjusting the complexity based on the audience's needs and expertise.

Chapter 8: Monitoring and Auditing Data

1. B. Implement AWS CloudTrail to record API activities and store logs in an S3 bucket for auditing purposes.

2. B. Use Amazon CloudWatch for collecting metrics, setting alarms, and creating custom dashboards.

3. B. Implement VPC flow logs to capture information about IP traffic. Store the logs in CloudWatch Logs or S3, and use CloudWatch Logs Insights for analysis.

4. B. Deploy AWS X-Ray to trace requests across microservices. Use X-Ray analytics to identify bottlenecks and create service maps to visualize application architecture.

5. B. Deploy Amazon Macie to automatically discover and protect sensitive data. Configure Macie to perform automated sensitive data discovery jobs on S3 buckets.

6. B. Focus on logging input validation failures, authentication failures, and use of higher-risk functionality to identify potential security threats.

7. C. Store CloudTrail logs in Amazon S3 and use Amazon Athena for SQL-based querying of the log data. Create custom queries to identify security issues.

8. D. Configure CloudWatch Alarms based on key performance metrics. Set up actions to send notifications via Amazon SNS when thresholds are breached.

9. C. Log only 400-level and 500-level errors. Use CloudWatch Logs for storage and set up log retention policies to archive older logs to Amazon S3 for cost optimization.

10. C. Use VPC flow logs, which capture information about IP traffic without affecting network throughput.

Chapter 9: Maintaining and Troubleshooting Data Operations

1. C. Amazon EventBridge is used to respond automatically to system events such as application availability issues or resource changes when monitoring the Redshift Data API.

2. C. AWS X-Ray allows you to visualize and analyze the behavior of your applications, identify any performance bottlenecks, and troubleshoot request failures. It provides insights into your application's behavior over time, allowing you to observe patterns, which you can use to improve the performance of your applications.

3. B. AWS Lambda removes the task of managing or provisioning servers, allowing you to focus on your code while AWS handles the infrastructure management, including administration, maintenance, and patching.

4. C. The Amazon Redshift Data API eliminates the need for persistent connections, providing a secure HTTP endpoint and integration with AWS SDKs, which is particularly useful for serverless applications.

5. B. AWS CloudFormation is a tool for implementing infrastructure as code, which can be used for maintaining and version controlling data processing pipelines.

6. D. While Amazon MWAA (Managed Workflows for Apache Airflow) is used for orchestrating data pipelines, it's not primarily designed for real-time data processing. Its main purpose is workflow management and scheduling.

7. C. Implementing exponential backoff is a strategy for retrying failed operations, which is particularly useful for handling transient errors in data processing pipelines.

8. C. When using the Amazon Redshift Data API, the maximum retention time for query results is 24 hours.

9. D. All of the options are correct, as they all have the following real-time streaming capabilities: Amazon EMR (Spark streaming), AWS Glue (Glue streaming), and Amazon Redshift (streaming ingestion).

10. C. AWS Step Functions enable you to implement a business process as a series of steps that make up a workflow. As such, they are suitable for complex multiservice pipelines with visual workflows and branching logic.

Chapter 10: Authentication and Authorization

1. A. IAM restricts data access to authorized users and roles, ensuring that only specific personnel and services can access sensitive data. SSE with AWS KMS provides robust encryption for data at rest, with the added benefit of managing keys and defining key usage policies. AWS CloudTrail enables logging and tracking of all API calls made within the AWS environment, including who accessed what data and when, which is crucial for compliance and security auditing. While helpful, option B lacks a direct means of tracking and auditing specific data access and does not necessarily guarantee encryption for data at rest. Option C is incorrect because the use of Lambda for monitoring and logging is not a standard or scalable approach for auditing data access across multiple AWS services, and Amazon Inspector is useful for security assessments but doesn't directly address the requirement for data access monitoring and encryption. Option D is incorrect because a dedicated security account and client-side encryption provide a high level of security but may not be practical or necessary for most scenarios. Moreover, AWS Config is more suited for monitoring configurations and compliance of AWS resources than for auditing data access.

2. A. Security groups in AWS act as a virtual firewall for controlling traffic to and from an RDS instance. Modifying the inbound rules to specifically allow the set of known IP addresses and denying all others is a straightforward and effective way to ensure that only traffic from those IPs can reach the RDS instance. This is the standard method for controlling access at the instance level in AWS. Option B is incorrect because AWS WAF (Web Application Firewall) is primarily used to protect web applications by controlling HTTP and HTTPS requests that are allowed to reach the application, and it isn't typically used for database instances like Amazon RDS, which don't communicate over these protocols for standard database operations. Option C is incorrect because network ACLs operate at the subnet level and provide a layer of security that controls traffic entering and leaving a subnet. While ACLs can be configured to allow and deny traffic from specific IP ranges, using them solely for RDS IP filtering is less granular and can be overly complex compared to using security groups. Option D is incorrect because AWS IAM policies are used for controlling access to AWS services and resources and defining what actions and resources users and services can or cannot use, but they do not directly manage network traffic or IP address filtering for RDS instances.

3. B, C. Implementing row-level security allows the data engineering consultant to control access to data at a fine-grained level so that analysts can be given access to the entire table but restricted to specific rows based on their roles or other criteria, ensuring they only access data necessary for their work. Setting up database groups within Amazon Redshift and assigning users to these groups is a robust way to manage access, granting users specific privileges based on their group's function, and managing permissions at the group level rather than for individual users. Option A is incorrect because granting superuser privileges to all analysts is not a best practice and violates the principle of least privilege, which could lead to unauthorized access to sensitive data and potential security breaches. Option D is incorrect because creating individual IAM users for each analyst and using IAM for database authentication is not typically how access is managed within Redshift, which has its own user and group management system for database access, and IAM users are used for managing access to AWS resources at the service level, not the data level within those services. Option E is incorrect because Amazon Redshift Spectrum is useful for querying data across Redshift and S3, but it does not replace the need for managing permissions within Redshift itself. Moreover, relying solely on IAM for data access within Spectrum can neglect the nuances of database-level permissions management.

4. B. Amazon Cognito specifically addresses the data engineering team's needs by:

- Supporting multiple authentication methods (social identity providers, enterprise directories)
- Providing user pools for managing user directories
- Enabling single sign-on across web and mobile applications
- Offering secure, scalable user authentication and authorization
- Integrating with AWS services for seamless access management
- Reducing complexity of credential management
- Supporting multi-factor authentication
- Allowing custom authentication workflows

The comprehensive nature of Amazon Cognito makes it the most appropriate choice for implementing a secure, flexible authentication mechanism that supports single sign-on and reduces credential management complexity.

Option A is incorrect because although AWS IAM users are fundamental to AWS access management, they do not inherently support single sign-on or simplified credential management across multiple identity providers.

Option C is incorrect because AWS STS is primarily a service for generating temporary, limited-privilege credentials, not a comprehensive authentication mechanism.

Option D is incorrect because AWS KMS is a key management service focused on encryption key creation, control, and audit. It is not an authentication service and has significant differences from authentication requirements.

5. C. Option C is correct because using IAM roles with time-limited permissions:

- Provides granular, time-bound access to specific AWS resources
- Follows the principle of least privilege
- Allows for precise control over permissions and access duration
- Automatically expires access after a set time
- Eliminates the need for manual credential revocation
- Enables fine-grained resource access without permanent account modifications
- Supports secure, temporary collaboration with external vendors
- Minimizes security risks associated with long-term access credentials

Option A is incorrect because sharing the root AWS account credentials is an extremely dangerous and insecure approach that:

- Exposes the entire AWS account to potential misuse
- Violates fundamental security best practices
- Provides unrestricted access to all account resources
- Cannot be easily limited or tracked
- Risks complete account compromise
- Breaks AWS security recommendations
- Potentially violates compliance requirements

Option B is incorrect because creating permanent IAM users for the vendor is a problematic approach that:

- Creates ongoing security risks
- Provides continuous access beyond the required timeframe
- Requires manual management of user credentials
- Complicates access revocation process
- Increases potential attack surface
- Does not align with temporary access requirements
- Requires ongoing credential management

Option D is incorrect because disabling all security groups for the duration of their work is an inappropriate and dangerous method that:

- Compromises overall account security
- Removes critical network-level protection
- Exposes all resources to potential unauthorized access
- Creates a massive security vulnerability
- Fails to provide granular access control

- Represents an extreme and unacceptable security approach
- Potentially violates security compliance standards

6. B. Creating an IAM role with specific permissions for the Glue job is correct because it:
   - Follows the principle of least privilege
   - Provides granular, precise access to required resources
   - Allows specification of exact permissions needed for the ETL job
   - Enables secure, temporary access to multiple AWS services
   - Supports comprehensive audit and tracking of job access
   - Eliminates the need for hard-coded credentials
   - Allows easy management and rotation of access permissions
   - Integrates seamlessly with AWS security best practices

   Option A is incorrect because storing database credentials directly in the Glue job script is a highly insecure approach that:
   - Exposes sensitive credentials within the code
   - Violates security best practices
   - Makes credential rotation difficult
   - Risks potential credential exposure if script is shared or compromised
   - Creates challenges in managing access across different environments
   - Lacks centralized credential management
   - Increases security vulnerabilities

   Option C is incorrect because using shared access keys for all team members is a problematic method that:
   - Creates shared security risks
   - Makes it difficult to track individual access
   - Complicates access revocation and management
   - Violates the principle of individual accountability
   - Increases potential for unauthorized access
   - Makes it challenging to implement fine-grained permissions
   - Creates compliance and auditing challenges

   Option D is incorrect because disabling security settings to ensure job compatibility is an inappropriate approach that:
   - Completely compromises system security
   - Removes critical access controls

- Exposes resources to potential unauthorized access
- Fails to provide any meaningful access management
- Represents a severe security risk
- Potentially violates organizational security policies
- Creates significant compliance challenges

7. B. Option B, implementing Kerberos authentication for the Hadoop ecosystem, is correct because it:

- Provides mutual authentication for Hadoop ecosystem components
- Ensures secure communication between cluster nodes and services
- Supports fine-grained access control across Hadoop services
- Enables centralized authentication management
- Prevents unauthorized access to cluster resources
- Supports integration with enterprise identity providers
- Provides strong encryption for authentication exchanges
- Meets compliance requirements for secure data processing

Option A is incorrect because using default EMR security group settings is a weak authentication approach that:

- Relies on minimal default security configurations
- Provides limited access control
- Does not offer comprehensive authentication
- Leaves the cluster potentially vulnerable to unauthorized access
- Lacks granular security mechanisms
- Does not protect against internal threats
- Fails to provide robust authentication across Hadoop services

Option C is incorrect because sharing a single administrator account for all cluster users is a dangerous method that:

- Eliminates individual accountability
- Creates significant security risks
- Makes it impossible to track individual user actions
- Violates the principle of least privilege
- Prevents granular access control
- Increases potential for unauthorized data access
- Complicates audit and compliance efforts

Option D is incorrect because disabling authentication to improve job performance is an extremely risky approach that:

- Completely removes security protections
- Exposes all cluster resources to potential unauthorized access
- Sacrifices security for marginal performance gains
- Creates massive security vulnerabilities
- Violates basic security best practices
- Risks the complete compromise of sensitive data
- Makes the cluster an easy target for malicious actors

8. B. Option B is correct because implementing Apache Ranger for centralized policy management:

- Provides centralized, fine-grained access control across the Hadoop ecosystem
- Enables policy management for multiple services (e.g., Hive, Spark, and HDFS)
- Supports row-level and column-level security
- Allows dynamic policy creation and modification
- Integrates seamlessly with existing authentication mechanisms
- Provides comprehensive auditing and compliance tracking
- Supports complex authorization rules across different data services
- Ensures that the principle of least privilege is maintained

Option A is incorrect because using default IAM roles for the entire EMR cluster is a limited authorization approach that:

- Provides only coarse-grained access control
- Lacks granular permissions within Hadoop services
- Cannot differentiate access between different team members
- Fails to provide service-level authorization
- Does not support complex data access rules
- Increases risk of unauthorized data access
- Limits the ability to implement precise access controls

Option C is incorrect because manually configuring individual file permissions for each team is an impractical and error-prone method that:

- Requires extensive manual configuration
- Becomes unmanageable as cluster complexity grows
- Is prone to human error and inconsistent implementation
- Lacks centralized policy management

- Makes audit and compliance difficult
- Does not scale with growing team and data needs
- Creates significant administrative overhead

Option D is incorrect because disabling all security controls to simplify cluster management is an extremely dangerous approach that:

- Completely removes authorization protections
- Exposes all cluster data to unrestricted access
- Violates fundamental security principles
- Creates massive security vulnerabilities
- Eliminates any form of access control
- Risks the complete compromise of sensitive data
- Makes compliance impossible

9. B. Option B is correct because implementing IAM database authentication:

- Provides centralized identity management through AWS IAM
- Supports temporary, time-limited credential generation
- Enables seamless integration with existing IAM roles and policies
- Supports multi-factor authentication
- Allows for easy credential rotation
- Provides comprehensive auditing of database access
- Aligns with enterprise security best practices

Option A is incorrect because using standard database username and password authentication:

- Is a limited approach that requires manual credential management
- Creates challenges in credential rotation
- Lacks integration with enterprise identity systems
- Increases risk of credential compromise

Option C is incorrect because sharing a single admin account across the data team:

- Eliminates individual accountability
- Prevents tracking of individual user actions
- Violates the principle of least privilege
- Creates significant security vulnerabilities
- Makes comprehensive auditing impossible

Option D is incorrect because disabling authentication to improve query performance:

- Completely removes all access controls
- Exposes the entire database to unrestricted access
- Sacrifices security for negligible performance gains
- Creates massive security risks
- Violates fundamental security principles

10. **B.** Option B is correct because configuring SAML authentication with fine-grained access control:

- Provides single sign-on capabilities through third-party identity providers
- Supports fine-grained access control for precise permission management
- Enables integration with enterprise identity providers like Okta, Active Directory, and AWS IAM Identity Center
- Allows mapping users to specific roles and permissions
- Supports both SP-initiated and IdP-initiated authentication flows
- Provides comprehensive security and flexible authentication options

Option A is incorrect because using standard HTTP basic authentication is a limited approach that:

- Lacks enterprise-grade single sign-on capabilities
- Provides minimal security and authentication options
- Does not support granular access control
- Requires manual user management
- Difficult to scale and integrate with existing identity systems

Option C is incorrect because using only IAM roles for authentication is an insufficient method that:

- Limits authentication to AWS-specific identities
- Does not support single sign-on with external identity providers
- Requires complex IAM role management
- Lacks flexibility for non-AWS users
- Does not provide comprehensive access control mechanisms

Option D is incorrect because disabling authentication to improve performance is an extremely risky approach that:

- Completely removes all authentication protections
- Exposes the OpenSearch domain to unauthorized access
- Violates security best practices

- Creates significant security vulnerabilities
- Makes compliance impossible

11. B. Option B is correct because implementing fine-grained access control with role mapping and custom roles:

- Provides multi-layered security with role-based access control
- Enables document-level security to restrict visible documents
- Supports field-level security to control which fields users can access
- Allows precise role mapping to specific user groups
- Supports creating custom roles with granular permissions
- Provides comprehensive control over cluster and index access

Option A is incorrect because using standard IAM policies to manage access is a limited approach that:

- Lacks granular control within the OpenSearch cluster
- Cannot implement document- or field-level security
- Provides only service-level access management
- Does not support fine-grained index or data-level permissions
- Limits authorization to AWS service-level controls

Option C is incorrect because relying on network-level security groups is an insufficient method that:

- Only provides network-level access control
- Cannot implement granular data access restrictions
- Lacks the ability to control index- or document-level permissions
- Does not support role-based access within the cluster
- Provides minimal security granularity

Option D is incorrect because disabling security features to improve cluster performance is an extremely risky approach that:

- Completely removes all access control mechanisms
- Exposes the entire cluster to unrestricted access
- Violates fundamental security principles
- Creates massive security vulnerabilities
- Makes compliance impossible

Chapter 11: Data Encryption and Masking

1. B. AWS KMS centrally manages the creation, storage, and management of encryption keys. It integrates with AWS services to encrypt data at rest using AES-256.

2. B, C. To enable cross-account encryption, you need to grant access to the KMS key to the second account on the key's key policy, and then create an IAM policy in the second account with permissions on the key and assign it to users and roles.

3. A, B, C. SSE-S3, SSE-KMS, and SSE-C are methods to encrypt data at rest on S3. SSL and TLS are protocols for encrypting data in transit.

4. D. The easiest and fastest way is to enable encryption on the cluster. Redshift will encrypt the data files without requiring you to create a snapshot or unload the data. A KMS customer-managed key provides in-depth logging and allows you to rotate keys.

5. A, B, D. AWS Glue supports encryption for the data catalog, job bookmarks, and job output to S3. EMRFS is the Amazon EMR File System.

6. D. SSE-KMS with a customer-managed key satisfies the requirement of encrypting an S3 bucket at rest with rotatable keys and in-depth logging with CloudTrail. CSE requires management overhead. SSE-S3 does not give you control over the key and auditing. SSE-KMS with an AWS-managed key does not meet the requirement for a customer-managed key.

7. C. AWS KMS supports automatic key rotation for managed keys, allowing for secure key management that can meet regulatory compliance requirements.

8. B. Amazon Macie provides automatic detection and visibility of sensitive data in Amazon S3, like Personally Identifiable Information (PII), and security issues with S3 buckets, such as public accessibility.

9. D. Amazon EMR is ideal for batch processing of large datasets and can utilize Apache Spark to implement custom data masking transformations on sensitive information.

10. C. Amazon Redshift has native dynamic data masking that modifies the masking depending on the user running the query.

Chapter 12: Data Privacy and Governance

1. B. AWS Macie specifically focuses on discovering sensitive data using machine learning and pattern matching, and Lake Formation provides fine-grained access controls for data lake security. The combination provides automated discovery and protection of sensitive data,

scales well for large volumes of data, and integrates seamlessly with existing AWS data lake infrastructure. Option A is incorrect because Amazon Inspector focuses on EC2 instance security assessment. Option C is incorrect because GuardDuty is for threat detection, not sensitive data discovery. Option D is incorrect because AWS Shield is for DDoS protection, not data privacy.

2.   B. SCPs provide preventive controls at the organization level, and AWS Config rules enable automated compliance monitoring. Option B provides automated enforcement and reporting, scales across multiple accounts and regions, and provides an audit trail for compliance purposes. Option A is incorrect because manual checks are not scalable and are prone to human error. Option C is incorrect because CloudWatch alone doesn't prevent unauthorized data movement. Option D is incorrect because this would enable cross-region replication, contradicting the requirement.

3.   B. Option B is correct because it provides native column-level access controls, maintains a single source of truth, requires no data movement or copying, allows for real-time access to updated data, and offers built-in security and governance controls. Option A is incorrect because it requires additional data movement and management overhead. Option C is incorrect because it introduces unnecessary data duplication and latency. Option D is incorrect because read replicas don't provide column-level security controls.

4.   B. Macie supports custom data identifiers for specific patterns, provides automated, continuous monitoring, scales automatically with data volumes, integrates with data lake services, and offers detailed classification reporting. Option A is incorrect because Amazon Comprehend focuses on natural language processing, not pattern matching. Option C is incorrect because Rekognition is for image and video analysis. Option D is incorrect because Glue classifiers are for schema discovery, not sensitive data identification.

5.   B. AWS Config provides detailed resource configuration tracking, and CloudTrail Lake enables advanced query capabilities. The combination offers automated compliance reporting, provides historical configuration data, and enables automated remediation actions. Option A is incorrect because it lacks comprehensive configuration tracking capabilities. Option C is incorrect because it is focused on performance monitoring rather than configuration tracking. Option D is incorrect because basic logging doesn't provide detailed configuration change tracking.

6.   B. SCPs provide preventive controls at organization level; AWS Config enables real-time monitoring of sharing configurations; and SNS provides immediate alerting capabilities. The combination offers a comprehensive audit trail and enables automated remediation actions. Option A is incorrect because it provides a reactive solution without preventive controls. Option C is incorrect because GuardDuty focuses on threat detection, not data sharing controls. Option D is incorrect because basic access controls lack comprehensive monitoring and alerting.

7.   A. S3 Lifecycle rules provide automated retention management, and AWS Backup ensures comprehensive backup compliance. The combination enables precise control over retention periods, provides automated deletion after retention period, and maintains detailed audit trails. Option B is incorrect because Amazon Config rules monitor but don't manage the object lifecycle. Option C is incorrect because manual processes are error-prone and not scalable. Option D is incorrect because Storage Gateway doesn't provide automated lifecycle management.

8. A. Answer A provides comprehensive data lake governance, integrates natively with AWS KMS for encryption, offers detailed access logging through CloudTrail, enables fine-grained access controls, and scales automatically with data volumes. Answer B is incorrect because it lacks comprehensive governance features. Answer C is incorrect because basic encryption doesn't provide a complete governance solution. Answer D is incorrect because EFS is not designed for data lake implementations.

9. A. Macie provides automated sensitive data discovery; Organizations enables central management; and Lake Formation adds governance controls. This solution supports cross-region compliance and provides GDPR-specific detection capabilities. Answer B is incorrect because custom solutions lack built-in compliance capabilities. Answer C is incorrect because Inspector focuses on EC2 security assessment. Answer D is incorrect because Shield and WAF focus on network security.

10. B. Lake Formation provides fine-grained access controls; CloudTrail maintains comprehensive audit logs; and Macie automatically identifies PII data. This solution enables preventive access controls and provides detailed access reporting. Answer A is incorrect because it lacks automated PII detection capabilities. Answer C is incorrect because basic bucket policies don't provide comprehensive protection. Answer D is incorrect because AWS Backup doesn't address data sharing controls.

Appendix B

References

Chapter 1: Streaming and Batch Data Ingestion

1. AWS Certified Data Engineer – Associate (DEA-C01) Exam Guide: `https://d1.awsstatic.com/training-and-certification/docs-data-engineer-associate/AWS-Certified-Data-Engineer-Associate_Exam-Guide.pdf`

2. Real Time Streaming with Amazon Kinesis: `https://catalog.us-east-1.prod.workshops.aws/workshops/2300137e-f2ac-4eb9-a4ac-3d25026b235f`

3. Amazon MSK Labs: `https://catalog.us-east-1.prod.workshops.aws/workshops/c2b72b6f-666b-4596-b8bc-bafa5dcca741`

4. AWS Glue Immersion Day: `https://catalog.us-east-1.prod.workshops.aws/workshops/ee59d21b-4cb8-4b3d-a629-24537cf37bb5`

5. AWS Glue DataBrew Immersion Day: `https://catalog.us-east-1.prod.workshops.aws/workshops/6532bf37-3ad2-4844-bd26-d775a31ce1fa`

6. AWS Database Migration Workshop: `https://catalog.workshops.aws/databasemigration`

7. IDC prediction on datasizes by 2025 - `https://www.networkworld.com/article/966746/idc-expect-175-zettabytes-of-data-worldwide-by-2025.html`

Index

D

E

L

M

Online Test Bank

To help you study for your AWS Certified Data Engineer Associate certification exam, register to gain one year of FREE access after activation to the online interactive test bank—included with your purchase of this book!

To access our learning environment, simply visit www.wiley.com/go/sybextestprep, follow the instructions to register your book, and instantly gain one year of FREE access after activation to:

- Hundreds of practice test questions, so you can practice in a timed and graded setting.
- Flashcards
- A searchable glossary

SYBEX
A Wiley Brand